THE BOAT

The tense, shadowy world of a German submarine at war is here recreated by someone who served in the battle for the Atlantic.

Of the 41,000 eighteen-to-thirty-year-olds who sailed with the German U-Boat packs, 26,000 never returned. Lothar-Günther Buchheim was one of those who did and in this novel, written almost thirty years later, he tells his extraordinary story.

Vividly he describes the claustrophobic world at the bottom of the sea – the weeks of boredom, frustration and fruitless patrols, interspersed with hours of terrifying attacks; the sense of helplessness at being a sitting target for any marauding enemy destroyer; the sheer discomfort of the cramped, stinking living quarters in the bowels of the ship.

Here is the war from 'the other side' – and the men who fought it are no less brave, no less tough and no less human.

LOTHAR-GÜNTHER BUCHHEIM

The Boat

Translated by J. Maxwell Brownjohn
Abridged Edition

Fontana/Collins

First published in Germany under the title *Das Boot*
First published in the UK by William Collins Sons & Co. Ltd
as *U-Boat* 1974
This abridged edition first issued in Fontana Paperbacks 1976
Second impression under the title *The Boat* May 1982
Eighth impression June 1988

Printed and bound in Great Britain by
William Collins Sons & Co. Ltd, Glasgow

CONTENTS

U-BOAT CLASS VIIC

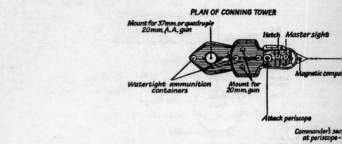

PLAN OF CONNING TOWER

Mount for 37mm. or quadruple 20mm. A.A. gun

Hatch   Master sight

Watertight ammunition containers

Mount for 20mm. gun

Magnetic compa

Attack periscope

Commander's sea at periscope

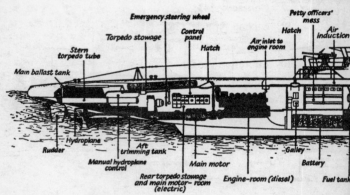

Emergency steering wheel

Torpedo stowage

Control panel

Hatch

Air inlet to engine room

Petty officers' mess

Hatch   Air induction

Stern torpedo tube

Main ballast tank

Hydroplane

Rudder

Aft trimming tank

Manual hydroplane control

Rear torpedo stowage and main motor-room (electric)

Main motor

Engine-room (diesel)

Galley

Battery

Fuel tank

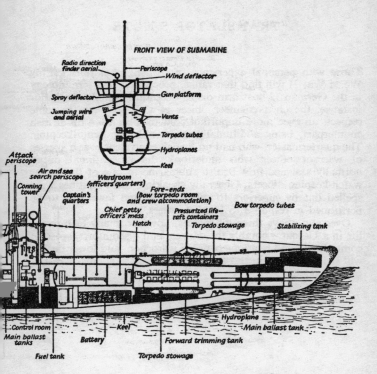

FRONT VIEW OF SUBMARINE

Radio direction
finder aerial — Periscope
— Wind deflector
Spray deflector — Gun platform
Jumping wire
and aerial — Vents
— Torpedo tubes
— Hydroplanes
— Keel

Attack
periscope
Air and sea
search periscope
Conning tower
Captain's
quarters
Chief petty
officers' mess
Wardroom
(officers' quarters)
Fore-ends
(Bow torpedo room
and crew accommodation)
Bow torpedo tubes
Pressurized life-
raft containers
Torpedo stowage
Stabilizing tank
Hatch

Control room
Main ballast
tanks
Keel
Battery
Hydroplane
Forward trimming tank
Main ballast tank
Fuel tank
Torpedo stowage

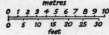

metres
0 1 2 3 4 5 6 7 8 9 10
0   5   10 15 20 25 30
feet

TRANSLATOR'S NOTE

Those with personal experience of British submarines during World War II will find that ranks, procedures and terminology in the German U-boat arm display certain unfamiliarities. For instance, the chief engineer officer of a U-boat was in some respects an even more important crew-member than his British counterpart, being additionally responsible for depth-keeping. The quartermaster, who had no British equivalent, was a species of warrant officer who undertook the navigational duties normally assigned in a British submarine to one of the junior watch-keeping officers. Generally speaking, more routines were spelled out by superiors to subordinates and fewer left to be performed in response to blanket orders.

Over and above these differences, however, many features of life in a U-boat – notably the dangers and discomforts, sense of comradeship and relations between wardroom and lower deck – will strike a chord in those who also served in submarines, but on 'our side'.

December 1973   J. MAXWELL BROWNJOHN

THE CREW OF THE *U-A*

Officers:

Captain	
First Lieutenant	Second Engineer (supernumerary)
Second Lieutenant	Narrator—a naval war correspondent
Chief Engineer	Midshipman Ullmann

Ratings:

Ario	stoker
Bachmann ('Gigolo')	stoker
Behrmann	coxswain
Benjamin ('Manchu')	seaman
Böckstiegel	seaman
Dorian	seaman petty officer
Dufte	seaman
Dunlop	torpedo-man
Fackler	stoker
Franz	engine-room artificer (ERA)
Frenssen	stoker petty officer
Hacker	torpedo gunner's mate (TGM)
Hagen	electrician
Herrmann	petty officer telegraphist
Hinrich	petty officer telegraphist
Isenberg	control-room petty officer
Jakob	seaman
Jens	seaman
Johann	engine-room artificer (ERA)
Katter	cook (chef')
Kleinschmidt	seaman petty officer
Kriechbaum	quartermaster
Markus	stoker
Merker	seaman
Pilgrim	petty officer electrician
Rademacher	petty officer electrician
Sablonski	stoker
Schwalle	seaman
Steward, the Turbo	control-room hand
'Vicar', the	control-room hand
Wichmann	seaman petty officer
Zeitler	seaman petty officer
Zörner	electrician

and ten others unnamed

This book is a novel, but not a work of fiction. The events recounted here were witnessed by the author. They form the sum of his wartime experiences in German submarines, though the leading characters are not portrayals of persons alive or dead.

Of the 41,000 German submariners who served in World War II, 26,000 never returned.

THE BAR ROYAL

The road from the Majestic to the Bar Royal hugged the shore in a single sweeping curve three miles long. There was no moon yet, but the asphalt threaded the gloom like a pallid ribbon.

The Captain's foot was kneading the accelerator Le Mans fashion. Suddenly it switched to the brake pedal. Tyres screamed as he braked, released and braked again. The heavy car came to a stop without slewing, inches short of a wildly gesticulating figure in a blue uniform. His CPO's cap was askew. The badge on his sleeve said coxswain.

He stood there waving his arms outside the cone of light projected by our headlamps. I couldn't see his face. The Captain was just edging forwards again when he slammed our bonnet with the flat of his hand and bellowed: 'You cheeky sod, you! I'll have your guts for garters!'

I thought the Captain was going to explode. Instead, he flung the car into reverse with a jolt that nearly sent my head through the windscreen.

Into first. A slalom turn, tyres howling, then second.

'Our coxswain,' the Captain informed me. 'Pissed as a fiddler's bitch.'

The chief engineer, who was sitting behind us, muttered something unintelligible.

The Captain had scarcely wound up the car when he was forced to brake again. More leisurely this time, because we spotted the wavering line of figures in our headlights a long way off. There were at least ten men strung out across the road, all of them ratings in going-ashore rig.

As we drew nearer I saw that they had their trouser-flaps down. From each fly dangled a resplendent penis.

The Captain flashed his lights, the ranks parted, and we ceremoniously drove through a lattice-work of urine.

'Fire-boat display, they call it. Members of our crew, the whole bunch.'

Behind us, the Chief gave a snort of disapproval.

'The rest are in the ratings' brothel,' the Captain explained. 'Business must be brisk tonight. Merkel sails tomorrow morning too.'

Not another soul in sight for the next mile. Then a shore

patrol swam into the glare of our headlights.

'Let's hope we aren't half a dozen men short when we sail,' the Chief grumbled from the back seat. 'They love mixing it with the law when they've had a drop.'

'Didn't even recognize their Old Man,' mused the Captain. 'A bit much, I call it.'

He was driving more slowly now.

'Can't say I feel too fresh myself,' he went on, half over his shoulder. 'Too much excitement for one day. First the funeral at St Nazaire this morning – the coxswain who bought it in the raid on Châteauneuf. There was another air raid while we were at it. Hardly respectful, during a military burial. The flak boys brought down three big ones.'

'What else?' I asked.

'Nothing today, but that firing squad business yesterday turned my stomach. Stoker, nineteen years old, clear case of desertion. On top of that, they slaughtered a pig at the Majestic. Fresh broth for lunch. It was meant to be a treat, I suppose. Nobody fancied it.'

The Captain drew up outside an establishment inscribed BAR ROYAL in letters half the height of a man. A concrete monstrosity designed to resemble a ship, it lay between the coast road and a minor road which emerged at an acute angle from the pinewoods. Running across the whole building was a glass façade like a bridge superstructure.

Inside Monique greeted us, a dark-haired, dark-eyed bundle of temperament with big breasts. She was an Alsatian whose fragmentary German consisted of lower-deck slang.

The only other attractions were three waitresses in open-work blouses and a three-man band – cowed and colourless-looking apart from the half-caste drummer, who seemed happy in his work.

The Todt Organization had commandeered the place and redecorated it in a blend of *fin de siècle* and House of German Art. Flotilla had re-commandeered it on the grounds that submarine ratings needed relaxation, submarine officers couldn't spend their whole time in brothels, and 'our lads' would benefit from a more refined atmosphere.

The refined atmosphere consisted of expanses of glossy white paint with artificial vine-leaves *à la* Rüdesheim, red shades over the wall-lights, and red plush curtains over the windows.

The Captain surveyed the room with a grin, then scrutinized each table in turn, chin retracted and brow furrowed. At last he laboriously drew up an armchair, slumped into it and stretched his legs. Clémentine, one of the waitresses, tittupped across with bobbing breasts. Beers all round.

We were still waiting for them when the swing doors burst open. A knot of five men barged in – all lieutenant-commanders – followed by three lieutenants and a sub-lieutenant. Three of the lieutenant-commanders wore the white cap of a U-boat captain.

Among them I recognized Flossmann, an unpleasant, quick-tempered young man with broad shoulders and sandy hair. His most recent boast was that he had opened an attack on an unescorted freighter by riddling her lifeboats with machine-gun bullets – 'just to get things straight from the start.'

The other two white-caps were the inseparables, Kupsch and Stackmann, who never got farther than Paris during their last home leave and had bubbled over with brothel anecdotes ever since.

The Captain grimaced. 'Another hour and the whole flotilla will be here. I've often wondered why the British don't mount a commando raid on this place – not to mention the C-in-C's château at Kernével. Can't understand why they've never tried it, what with the sea a stone's throw away and Port Louis bang next door. They could lasso us if they wanted to. Tonight would be a perfect time.'

The Captain had neither the lean thoroughbred features of the picture-book U-boat hero nor the wiry physique. He looked more like a bluff Hamburg-America Line skipper, and his movements were ponderous.

The bridge of his nose narrowed, kinked to the left and widened again. His pale blue eyes were half hidden beneath brows permanently puckered with concentration. He usually screwed up his eyes so tight that only two thin slits could be seen in the shadow of his eyebrows. There were fan-shaped accumulations of crow's-feet at their outer extremities. His lower lip was full, his pronounced chin flecked with reddish stubble by early afternoon. The strong, rough-hewn planes of his face lent it a certain earnestness. Anyone ignorant of his age would have put him at forty. He was ten years younger, but a thirty-year-old was elderly in comparison with most submarine commanders.

The Captain was no lover of long words. His patrol reports read like an account of some children's game. It was hard to get anything out of him. He carefully avoided calling a spade a spade. A faint note of irony, a twist of the lip, and I immediately knew what the Old Man was driving at. If he said something complimentary about C-in-C U-boats and looked obliquely past me, his true meaning was plain.

Our last night ashore. Stitched like an invisible thread into all the repartee, all the banter, a nagging fear: was our number up, or would we make it?

To soothe my nerves I conducted an interior monologue. The Captain . . . One of the best. Nothing ever shook him. No slave-driver, no raving fanatic. He'd even done a spell under sail. Fists that might have been designed to subdue billowing canvas and handle heavy tackle. He'd always pulled it off before, so why not now? 200,000 tons – a whole harbourful of enemy shipping. However hot the opposition, he invariably sneaked out from under . . .

My new roll-neck would come in handy if we went north. Simone mustn't come to the harbour with me – there'd only be trouble. Those sods in the Security Service were hot on fraternization with the French – envious bastards. Doenitz's private navy, they called us, but they couldn't lay a finger on us.

Not a clue where we were bound for. Central Atlantic, probably. Not many boats out. A pretty bad month, thanks to heavier convoy protection. The Brits had learnt enough lessons to turn the tide. Prien, Schepke, Kretschmer – all killed in action against convoys, all sunk except Kretschmer. They had all bought it at almost the same time – February, March. Schepke went the hard way, pinned between periscope standards and bridge casing when a destroyer rammed his bomb-blasted hulk. The U-boat aces . . . A dying race. Endrass's nerves were shot, but not the Captain's. Cool as a cucumber still. He wasn't drinking himself into a stupor. He looked genuinely relaxed as he sat there.

I needed a leak. In the wash-room I listened to two lieutenants standing alongside me.

'. . . must have one last poke.'

'Mind you dip your wick in the right hole – you're pissed.'

The first speaker was halfway out of the door when the second yelled after him: 'And give her one from me while you're at it!'

Officers from Merkel's boat. Drunk, or they might have been fractionally less coarse.

I went back to our table. The Chief extended his hand and hooked a glass towards him. Twenty-seven years old and the Captain's right-hand man. Quite unlike the Captain. His dark eyes and pointed black beard made him look as Spanish as an El Greco painting. Nervy rather than nervous, and he knew his job inside out. The two of them had sailed together from the first. They communicated with a minimum of words.

'Where's the second lieutenant?' asked the Captain.

'On board. It's still his watch – he'll probably turn up later.'

'Ah well, someone has to do the work.' The Captain shrugged. 'What about our worthy Number One?'

'Brothel-creeping.'

'Him in a brothel? Don't make me laugh.'

'He's probably making his will – you know how tidy-minded he is.'

The Captain hadn't even mentioned the junior engineer officer who was coming with us as the Chief's designated replacement after this patrol. It meant we'd be six officers in the wardroom – a tight squeeze round the diminutive table.

'Where's Thomsen got to?' asked the Chief. 'He wouldn't stand us up, would he?'

Thomsen, commander of U-F and a brand-new recipient of the Knight's Cross, had given us a personal account of his latest patrol that afternoon, from the depths of a leather armchair in the Hotel Majestic. He reminisced with his elbows propped and his hands folded as in prayer, staring at the opposite wall.

'. . . they clobbered us for about forty-five minutes. Immediately after diving we took seven or eight depth-charges at about 60 metres, pretty near the boat. One of them exploded above us, roughly abreast the gun and 60 or 70 metres away on the port beam. The others were all 800 to 1000 metres off. Then, around midnight, they dropped another pattern. We stayed deep for a while and edged up at Slow One. Finally we surfaced and set off after the convoy. Next morning a destroyer made a pass in our direction. Sea 3, some wind, squalls, partly overcast – good conditions for an attack from periscope depth. We dived and fired twice – missed both times. Then we fired the stern tube. That did the trick. We followed the convoy till we were ordered to turn back. Zetschke sighted the second convoy. We came up with it just before 1800. Weather good, sea 2 to 3, partly overcast.'

Thomsen paused. 'Funny thing is, whenever we struck lucky it happened to be someone's birthday. The first time it was a stoker, the second time a telegraphist. The lone ship went down on the chef's birthday and the destroyer on the TGM's. Odd, isn't it?'

Thomsen's boat had been wearing four pennants on her half-raised periscope when she came in on the early morning tide, three white ones for sunk merchantmen and a red one for the destroyer.

Thomsen's voice rang out across the oily, brackish water of the harbour, hoarse as a dog's bark : 'Stop both engines!'

The submarine was making enough way to glide noiselessly alongside. Seen bow-on, she protruded from the viscous gravy of the stinking basin like an over-stuffed vase of dried flowers. The flower-heads were faded spots of colour set in dark moss. As they came nearer, they turned into pale and emaciated faces fringed with beard. Black-vignetted eyes sunk deep in their sockets, some of them shining feverishly. Chalky skin, salt-encrusted leathers bleached to a dirty grey, caps precariously perched on thick tufts of hair. Thomsen, who was hollow-cheeked and thin as a beanpole, looked genuinely ill. There was something skeletal about his friendly grin.

'I have the honour to report U-F returned from patrol!'

Three full-throated cheers greeted his half-facetious announcement. They re-echoed harshly from No. 1 Warehouse, then, more faintly, from the Penhoët dockyard . . .

Tonight, the Captain had demonstrated his contempt for spit-and-polish by wearing his oldest jacket. The front of his running rig, which had long faded from blue to grey, was spotted and discoloured. Verdigris adorned the once-gold buttons and his shirt had gone an indeterminate colour – bluish grey verging on lilac. The red-white-and-black ribbon from which his Knight's Cross dangled might have been a twisted bootlace.

'Times have changed,' he lamented, critically surveying a party of young watch-keeping officers at the centre table. 'The line-shooters have taken over.'

For a while now, patrons of the Bar Royal had fallen into two categories : the 'old salts', as the Captain's contemporaries called themselves, and the 'young Turks' or ideologically processed youngsters with faith in the Führer and an eagle gaze focused on final victory – the teeth-gritters, as the Captain styled them – who practised martial expressions in the mirror and tensed their gluteal muscles for no good reason except that it was fashionable to cultivate a springy, tight-buttocked walk which threw the weight slightly forwards on the ball of the foot.

I stared at this assortment of budding heroes as if I were seeing them for the first time. Mouths like operation scars, rasping voices, faces bloated with a sense of élitism, heads filled with phrases like 'The Führer's eyes are on you' and 'Our flag means more than death.' One of them had shot himself in the Majestic a fortnight back because he had contracted syphilis. 'He fell for Führer and Fatherland' was how they put it to his fiancée.

Apart from the old salts and the young Turks, there was one notable outsider in the shape of Kügler, who shared a small table with his first lieutenant close to the wash-room door. Kügler, the Parsifal of the deep, stern believer in Germany's unique destiny. Steel-blue eyes, back like a ramrod, not an ounce of superfluous fat. A flawless specimen of the master race, Kügler was reputed to plug each ear with an outraged fingertip when smutty stories or subversive remarks flowed from those whose faith in victory was less unqualified than his own.

The table next to Kügler's was occupied by the flotilla surgeon-commander, another exception to the general rule. He had an infinite capacity for remembering obscene anecdotes, hence his nickname, Dirty Doc. Dirty Doc felt confident that Hitler's Thousand-Year Reich had already used up most of its millennium and said so whenever he was drunk or deemed it appropriate.

Nevertheless at thirty, he enjoyed universal respect. During this third patrol he had assumed command and brought the vessel back to base after enemy aircraft had killed the captain and confined the two watch-keeping officers to their bunks with severe wounds.

Now his voice soared above the general buzz of conversation. 'Whassa matter, somebody died?' he yelled. 'Anyone'd think this was a wake.'

'There's enough noise as it is,' grumbled the Captain, taking a modest pull at his beer.

Monique seemed to have got the surgeon-commander's message. She clamped the microphone to her garish red mouth like a lollipop, dramatizing the song with twists of her body, strenuous hip-work and undulations of her opulent blue-white breasts. She held a bunch of ostrich feathers which she drew caressingly between her thighs. Then she rolled her eyes heavenwards, stroked the feathers tenderly, jerked her pelvis at them, drew them up her body, swung her hips, blew at the plumage with pouting lips . . . Suddenly, across the tables, she glanced towards the door. The flotilla captain and his aide had just come in. Monique didn't waste more than a flick of the eye on his gangling figure with its undersized schoolboy's head.

'Look who's slumming it tonight!' Monique's throaty sobs were drowned by Trumann, one of the more refractory members of the old guard. He rose unsteadily from his seat and tottered over to the flotilla captain. 'Hallo, old cock. Felt like a spot of active service, did you? Tell you what, why not swop places with me? Ringside seat – worm's-eye view of the whole lovely landscape . . . No? Fair enough, suit yourself – I always do.'

Trumann was, as usual, three sheets in the wind. He was even wearing his Knight's Cross back to front.

Trumann's U-boat enjoyed a legendary reputation. He had been dogged by bad luck ever since his third patrol, seldom spending more than a week at sea. Limping back to base had become routine. He was always caught on his way to the patrol area and plastered with bombs or depth-charges. Malfunctioning equipment, fractured exhaust pipes and burst compressors took over where the enemy left off. Everyone in the flotilla secretly marvelled that Trumann and his crew could endure such an unbroken run of disaster.

The party at the next table began to sing under the direction of the surgeon-commander, who conducted their limping chorus with a wine bottle. The big round table next to the platform was reserved by tacit consent for the old salts. At it, seated or sprawled according to their degree of intoxication, were the Captain's classmates: the 'Siamese twins' Kupsch and Stackmann, 'Baldy' Keller, and 'Big Chief' Kortmann, so called because of his leathery red skin and beaky nose. Young men all but old in experience, sea-borne gladiators whose cool manner belied their full awareness of the odds against them. They could sit in an armchair for hours, faces impassive and bodies almost motionless, but they were incapable of holding a glass rock-steady.

Each of them could look on at least half a dozen tough patrols, extremes of nervous tension, emotional torment, desperate situations which turned to their advantage by the merest quirk of fate. Each of them knew what it was to return with a crippled boat, its casing devastated by bombs or the conning-tower rammed, bows stove in or pressure hull strained in every gland, but each time they stood bolt upright on the bridge and acted as if the whole business were routine.

It was part of the code to pretend complete sang-froid. The code forbade weeping and gnashing of teeth, and C-in-C U-boats kept the charade going. To C-in-C U-boats, any officer with a head and four limbs was fit for service. To C-in-C U-boats, anyone was sane who didn't actually froth at the mouth. He had long been compelled to put unblooded replacements in command of operational boats. Unfortunately, replacements with intact nerves were nowhere near as competent as older commanders, and older commanders used every trick in the book to avoid parting with experienced watch-keeping officers who should have been given commands of their own.

Endrass should never have been allowed to sail, not in his condition. His nerves were shattered, but that was the way of it. C-in-C U-boats couldn't see when a man was finished – or wouldn't. After all, it was the battle-seasoned aces who reaped the bulk of his successes and filled his special communiqué tray.

The band took a breather. I could hear snippets of conversation again.

'Where's Kallmann?'

'He won't be coming, not tonight.'

'Can't blame the poor bugger.'

Kallmann had returned forty-eight hours earlier with three white victory pennants on his periscope. He sank the last merchantman by gunfire in shallow coastal waters. 'She took more than a hundred rounds, that one. Heavy sea running. We had to fire from stopped with the sea on the starboard bow. At dusk, just before 1900, we fired from dived. Two hits on a 12,000-tonner, one miss. Then they had us. Eight hours of it. I reckon they only stopped when they ran out of depth-charges.'

Kallmann looked like Christ crucified with his hollow cheeks and stringy beard. He kneaded his hands together as if trying to squeeze the words out.

We listened tensely, masking our uneasiness with an exaggerated air of interest, wondering when he would come out with the question we dreaded.

Kallmann stopped kneading his hands and sat there without moving, elbows resting on the arms of his chair and palms pressed together. Staring past us over his fingertips, he asked with studied indifference: 'Any news of Bartel?'

No one answered. The flotilla captain merely inclined his head a little.

'I see. I guessed as much when he stopped transmitting.' There was a minute's silence. Then he asked, with a note of urgency: 'No news at all?'

'Not a word.'

'Any hope?'

'No.'

Cigarette smoke hung motionless in the air.

'We spent the whole of our refit together – I even led him out,' Kallmann said eventually. He looked helpless, downcast.

We all knew how close he had been to Bartel. They always managed to go out together. They attacked the same convoys. I remembered hearing Kallmann say, not long ago: 'It puts backbone into you, somehow, knowing you aren't on your own.'

Bechtel came through the swing doors. His white-blond hair, lashes and eyebrows gave him a bleached look. His freckles stood out vividly against his exceptional pallor.

A big hello greeted the new arrival and Bechtel was quickly surrounded by a group of young officers. Bechtel had just undergone an experience which even the Captain termed 'quite something'. Surfacing in the half-light of dawn after a fierce counter-attack which had inflicted a variety of damage on his boat, Bechtel found a depth-charge lodged on his casing, just forward of the gun. A British corvette in the offing and a live depth-charge hissing away merrily in front of the con-ning-tower . . . The charge was set to explode below the depth at which Bechtel had scooped it up on his casing, so there was time in hand.

Bechtel promptly ordered both engines full ahead and the coxswain rolled it overboard like a tar-barrel. 'It went up after twenty-five seconds.' They were then forced to dive again and treated to another twenty depth-charges.

'Why didn't you bring it home as a souvenir?' bellowed Merkel.

'Would have done, except we couldn't stop the nasty noise. Couldn't find the button anywhere. Laugh? We nearly bust a gut!'

The Bar Royal was rapidly filling up, but still no sign of Thomsen.

'Where the hell's he got to?'

'Maybe he's having a crafty poke.'[1]

'In his condition? I doubt it.'

'Must be a brand-new sensation for him, doing it with a Knight's Cross round his neck.'

Thomsen had stood like a stone statue that afternoon while the flotilla captain decorated him, muscles so taut that his face was almost drained of blood. He couldn't have absorbed a word of the flotilla captain's forceful address.

'Stuffed shirt!' Trumann hissed, as the flotilla captain de-parted with a virile handshake and man-to-man flash of the eye. He jerked his thumb at the obituary photographs that covered three walls of the dining-room in the nearby Majestic. 'Room for a few more by the door.'

I could already visualize the next photo in its little black surround: Beckmann's.

Beckmann should have been back days ago. It wouldn't be
long before he was posted officially missing. He was dead
drunk when they fetched him from the Paris train. It took
four men to haul him out while the train stood waiting. Fucked
to a standstill, eyes like an albino, and only twenty-four hours
to sailing time. Dirty Doc must have worked a medical miracle
to get him back on his legs. Probably sunk by enemy aircraft
– he had failed to report his position soon after leaving base.
The Brits were getting cheeky these days. You couldn't feel
safe anywhere, not even inside our own approach buoys.

Flechsig, an uncouth, heavily-built man who belonged to
the Captain's class, flung himself into the last vacant chair at
our table. Hardly a word had escaped him since he returned
from Berlin last week, but now he waxed eloquent.

'Waltzed up to me in the street, he did, this fairy of a
staff officer. "Lieutenant-Commander," he said, "there's nothing
in dress regulations to permit the wearing of white caps by
submarine captains." "In that case," I said, "I respectfully
suggest you issue an amendment." '

Flechsig took a few hefty swallows of Martell and laboriously
wiped the surplus from his lips with the back of his hand.

'I ask you, all that fuss about a white cap!'

The swing doors crashed back on their hinges to reveal Erler,
a young lieutenant fresh from his first patrol in command.
A pair of pink panties frothed from his breast pocket. Back
from leave that morning, he had spent the afternoon in the
Majestic, sounding off about his hero's welcome. According
to Erler, this had included a torchlight procession and the
bestowal of half a pig by the mayor. He had newspaper
cuttings to prove it. There he stood on the town hall balcony,
right arm raised in the Hitler salute – a German naval hero
fêted by the proud inhabitants of his home town.

'Give him time,' murmured the Captain. 'He'll simmer
down.'

Erler's entourage included Eugen Kress, an unctuous radio
correspondent, and Willi Marks, a former Party official who
now wrote morale-boosting articles for the press. They looked
like Laurel and Hardy in naval uniform, the journalist thin
and wizened, the radio correspondent plump and oily. The
Captain snorted explosively at the sight of them.

Kress's favourite adjective was 'unparalleled'. 'Unparrralleled
losses inflicted', 'unparrralleled will to win', 'unparrralleled
increase in production'.

Erler stationed himself in front of the Captain and briskly

invited him to have a drink. The Old Man, sprawled in his chair like a barber's best customer, didn't react for quite a while. Eventually he said: 'If you're paying, why not?'

I knew what was coming. Erler loved to demonstrate his method of opening champagne bottles with one upward sweep of a knife-blade against the ridge of glass round the neck. The cork flew off complete with glass rim. No splinters, just a geyser of bubbly like the jet from a foam extinguisher. I couldn't help recalling a display I'd seen by the Dresden fire brigade, outside the opera house. They'd put up a steel mast topped by a swastika made of piping. A herd of red fire-engines stood clustered round the foot of the mast and the whole huge square was thronged with expectant onlookers. A raucous word of command from the loudspeakers, and the four extremities of the swastika spewed foam. The emblem started to rotate, faster and faster, until it turned into a frothing Catherine-wheel. There was a concerted 'Aaah!' from the crowd. The foam gradually turned pink, then red, then violet, then blue, then green, then yellow. The spectators clapped as an ankle-deep lake of aniline-tinged foam spread across the square . . .

The swing doors gave another crash. Thomsen had made it at last. Half supported, half propelled by his officers, he tottered in with glazed eyes. I hurriedly pulled up some chairs so that he and his party could join our table.

'Where's the flotilla captain?' demanded the Old Man.

We noticed for the first time that the flotilla captain had vanished – before the festivities proper, so to speak. Kügler had gone too.

'No stamina,' sneered Trumann. He rose with an effort and threaded his way unsteadily between the tables. A minute later he reappeared holding a lavatory brush.

'Ugh!' ejaculated the Captain, but Trumann tottered closer. With one hand clamped to the edge of our table for support, he drew a couple of deep breaths and yelled 'Quiet!' at the top of his voice.

Promptly, the music died away. Trumann's dripping lavatory brush winnowed the air only inches from Thomsen's face.

'Our revered and unbedded, illustrious and abstemious Führer,' he declaimed in a voice charged with false emotion, 'the house-painter's apprentice who has so gloriously risen to become the greatest military commander of all time . . .'

He drunkenly savoured his own eloquence for a few moments before continuing: 'The supreme naval expert and unrivalled naval strategist whom it has pleased in his infinite wisdom . . . How does it go on?'

He surveyed the room enquiringly and gave a resounding belch before he went on: 'Anyway, the great German Sea Lord has finally shown that British bed-wetter and cigar-puffing syphilitic, to quote his own immortal description of that arse-hole Winston Churchill, what it means to tangle with the German navy.'

Trumann slumped exhaustedly into his chair, blasting me with a cognac-laden gust of breath as he did so. His face looked green in the subdued lighting.

Laurel and Hardy wormed their chairs into our circle and tried to ingratiate themselves with Thomsen, the new holder of the Knight's Cross, in the hope of eliciting some colourful details of his last patrol. Nobody knew why they ever bothered to interview anyone – their reports were a morass of patriotic clichés which contained little in the way of hard facts. Besides, Thomsen was long past pumping. He just stared stupidly at them and agreed with everything they said. 'Sure, thassit. Went down like a stone. Hit her just abaft the bridge. Blue Funnel Line. Got it? No, not funny, funnel!'

Kress, who sensed that Thomsen was leading him nowhere, gulped drily. His Adam's apple jerked up and down comically. The Captain relished his difficulties and did nothing to help.

Thomsen's powers of comprehension finally deserted him. 'Balls to the whole thing!' he roared. 'Bloody useless fish!'

I knew what he meant. There had been one torpedo failure after another in recent weeks – too many malfunctions to be coincidental. Rumours of sabotage were rife.

Suddenly Thomsen leapt to his feet with a look of horror. Our glasses went flying. The telephone had rung behind the bar – he must have taken it for an alarm bell.

I listened with half an ear to Merkel addressing his party from the chair behind me.

'The control-room PO was good – first-class chap. Had to get rid of the ERA – useless . . . The corvette was right on top of us. The Chief didn't take her down quick enough . . . One of them was floating in the drink. Looked like a seal. We ran in close because we wanted to get the ship's name. The man was black with oil – clinging to a raft.'

Merkel hauled himself erect, thrust a hand in his trouser-pocket and exhaustively scratched his crotch. His chief engineer appeared, a man universally envied for his ability to whistle on two fingers. Merkel's Chief could produce a whole range of sounds – wolf-whistles, raiding-party signals, throbbing melodies.

'It's no fun any more!' Kortmann bellowed abruptly into a lull in the general hubbub. Beaky-nosed 'Big Chief' Kortmann, the flouter of orders and saviour of German seamen, had been on the C-in-C's black list ever since the affair of the Bismarck tanker when he had prejudiced the fighting efficiency of his submarine and failed in his operational role for reasons of maudlin emotionalism. Kortmann, after all, was an old-time captain who subscribed to the antiquated motto: 'A sailor's first duty is to those in peril.'

Bad luck had played its part too, of course. After all, why need a British destroyer have cruised up while Kortmann was refuelling from a tanker? The tanker was really destined for the *Bismarck*, but the *Bismarck* was past refuelling – she had already gone to the bottom with 25,000 men on board, so the top brass decided to let her suckle a few submarines instead. And just as Kortmann was nibbling at the tit, it happened: the Brits shot the tanker away from under his nose. Fifty members of the tanker's crew in the drink, and Kortmann too soft-hearted to let them swim for it.

He was still proud of his catch: fifty extra bodies in a VII-C U-boat which could barely accommodate her own crew. Where he stowed them all was his own secret, but he probably used the sardine technique – head to tail and take it in turns to breathe.

Inebriation was beginning to efface the boundaries between the old salts and the young Turks. Everyone talked at once. I could hear Böhler arguing: 'But we've been given absolutely clear instructions, Otto – firm orders . . .'

'Clear instructions, firm orders,' mimicked Thomsen maliciously. 'Don't make me laugh. They couldn't make them any vaguer if they tried. It's all part of the system, leaving things vague.'

Saemisch stuck his carrot-head into the circle. 'Why beat your brains out?' he said in a blurred voice. 'We aren't paid to think.'

Böhler rounded on him earnestly. 'Look, it's like this. You can't achieve complete operational efficiency under conditions of total war unless . . .'

'Christ!' exclaimed Thomsen. 'You're in the wrong job – you ought to be working for Goebbels.'

'No, let me quote you an example. One of our fleet auxiliaries picked up a Brit who'd been in the drink three times. Well, what are we supposed to be doing – fighting a war or demolishing enemy property? What's the point of sinking freighters when their crews get fished out and sail with the next convoy? They earn enough, God knows!'

They were off now. Böhler had supplied the cue for a burning but prohibited topic of conversation: whether to destroy the enemy himself or only his ships, sink merchantmen or drown their crews as well.

'It works both ways,' Saemisch persisted, but Trumann heatedly intervened.

'Talk a bit of sense,' he commanded. 'The C-in-C's orders are: seek and destroy the enemy by all available means – tough, bold, resolute, firm-jawed, tight-arsed and all the rest of it. He didn't say anything about machine-gunning men in the drink – or did he?'

'No, of course he didn't. He simply pointed out that crew-losses would hit the British where it hurts.'

Trumann looked sardonic. 'Well?'

'Well,' Thomsen continued obediently in a voice of protest fuelled with cognac, 'everyone can read what he likes into that. Smart idea, I call it.'

Trumann came to the point. 'I know someone who solves these problems in his own way and can still boast that he hasn't killed a man in cold blood. He shoots up lifeboats instead. If weather conditions are right the survivors don't last long in any case. The conventions are observed and the C-in-C can feel that his point has been taken.'

Everyone knew who he meant but nobody looked in Flossmann's direction.

My mind turned to the things I proposed to take with me. Only the barest essentials. My new sweater was a must, also some Cologne. Razor-blades I could do without . . .

'It's illogical, the whole thing,' Thomsen was saying. 'As long as someone's got two planks between him and the water you can mow him down. Stick him in the drink and your heart bleeds for the poor bugger. Crazy, isn't it?'

Trumann chimed in again. 'If you want to know the real truth of the matter . . .'

'Well?'

'See someone adrift and you imagine he might be you, that's what it is. You can't identify with a whole ship, but an individual, sure. The picture changes at once.'

The new roll-neck which Simone had knitted me was a murderous great thing. Ear-high collar, cable-stitch, nice and long – no bum-freezer. We might be going north. Denmark Strait or all the way up: the Murmansk run. It was awful, not knowing.

'But as survivors they're defenceless,' Saemisch was saying

in a righteously indignant tone.

'Put another record on! Same old argument as before.'

They began again from the beginning. Thomsen was getting more and more muddled.

'Oh, shit!' he muttered resignedly, and slumped back in his chair.

I had an urge to get up and leave in time to pack my gear properly. Anything rather than inhale more liquor fumes. Better keep a vestige of a clear head. Last night ashore. One or two books, spare roll of film, wide-angle lens, pompom hat. Black pompom hat and white roll-neck. Must look a real joke.

'Is this a piss-up or a cardinals' conclave?' Dirty Doc trumpeted above the music, which had started again. 'Drop the fucking subject!'

As if the pianist and the band weren't creating enough din, someone switched on the radiogram and turned up the volume. '*Where zat tiger, where zat tiger?*' blared a voice of preternatural power.

A lanky fair-haired lieutenant flung off his jacket, vaulted on to the table and did a belly-dance.

'You ought to be on the stage!' – 'Terrific!' – 'Hold me back, someone, I'm beginning to fancy him!'

Our Chief, who had been quietly meditating at the table, went berserk. He climbed the decorative trellis-work above the stage, miming a chimpanzee, plucked out artificial vine-leaves in time to the music. The framework gave a lurch, sagged away from the wall, and finally crashed to the platform with the Chief still on board.

The pianist started to bang out a march with his head lolling backwards at an angle. A group formed round him.

'*Onwards, ever onwards,*
Though the heavens pour with piss.
Send us back to Dullsville
'*Cause it can't be worse than this.*'

'That's what I like to hear,' growled the Captain. 'Earthy, virile, Teutonic . . .'

Trumann stared at his glass, then leapt to his feet and yelled 'Skol!' He poured the contents into his mouth from a height of at least six inches, sending a wide river of beer down his reefer.

'Bloody hell!' Trumann mumbled when he saw the mess. Clémentine bustled up with a cloth. The zip at the back of her skirt had burst down one seam. The hollows of her knees stood out cheesy-white against the black material as she bent over Trumann.

'*Cochon!*' she whispered into his ear, mopping him dry. Her plump breasts hung so close to his face that he could have sunk his teeth in them. She exuded maternal solicitude.

'A real orgy!' crowed Meinig, who was reputed to be the flotilla's only virgin.

'All we need now is some girls.'

Merkel's first and second lieutenants vanished as if in response to a codeword, exchanging conspiratorial winks as they disappeared through the swing doors. I thought they had left long before.

'Nerves,' the Captain muttered. 'They need it the way troops need a tot before they go over the top.'

With half an ear I heard chanting from the next table:

> *Our butcher-boy was feeling sharp,*
> *The randy little oaf.*
> *He nipped on to the marble slab*
> *And fucked a minced veal loaf . . .*

Same old story: the Führer's knights in shining armour, noble custodians of the nation's future . . . A few rounds of cognac and their spotless mail shed some of its lustre.

'Very cultural,' observed the Captain, reaching for his glass. 'These sodding armchairs – once you're in them you can't get up.'

Baldy Keller was shaking his head stubbornly. 'This is it, you mark my words. I'll never make it. This time it's curtains.'

'Of course you'll make it,' Trumann told him soothingly.

'A case of cognac I don't come back – wanna bet?'

'Who am I supposed to pay if you don't?' Trumann demanded. 'An angel with a fucking harp?'

Baldy blinked at him uncomprehendingly.

'Look,' Trumann said, spelling it out, 'if you make it you've lost – that's plain enough, isn't it? Okay, so you buy me a case of cognac. If you don't make it, you've won . . .'

'Sright.'

'Then I hand over the cognac.'

'Right again.'

'The question is, who to?'

'Who to? Me, of course!'

'But you're dead.'

'Dead? How do you figure that?'

The table was a wilderness of decapitated champagne bottles, ashtrays awash with beer and cigarette-ends, tins of pickled herrings and shattered glasses. Trumann had been pleasurably eyeing this display during his exchange with Keller. Taking advantage of a lull in the sing-song, he raised his right hand

and bellowed: 'Stand by!'

'The tablecloth trick!' said our Chief.

Deliberately, Trumann started to roll one end of the table-cloth into a sausage – it took him a full minute because the material eluded his fingers more than once. Then with his free hand, he gave a signal to the pianist, who promptly – as though the act had been rehearsed – produced a roll of thunder on the bass keys. With the intense concentration of a weight-lifter, Trumann adopted a firm stance and fastened both hands on the rolled tablecloth. He stared down at his clenched fists for another thirty seconds, gave a sudden primeval yell, and, with a mighty sweep of the arms, yanked the cloth halfway off the table. Bottles and plates cascaded to the floor with a medley of crashes, tinkles and thuds.

'Shit and derision!' swore Trumann, and collapsed into a chair where Dirty Doc pulled three or four splinters from his palms. Blood spattered the table as he raised a hand and wearily wiped his face.

The Captain gave a grunt of distaste.

'Squeamish?' roared Trumann. He hadn't been slumped in his chair for more than five minutes when he bounded to his feet again and pulled a crumpled scrap of newsprint from his pocket.

'Unless you've got a better idea, gentlemen, allow me to read you some golden words . . .'

I recognized the cutting in his hand. It was the last will and testament of Lieutenant-Commander Mönkeberg, officially killed in action but really the victim of a mundane accident. He broke his neck at a quiet spot in the Atlantic because fine weather had tempted him to take a quick dip. Just as he was diving from the bridge the submarine gave an unexpected roll and he hit his head on a ballast tank. Every German news-paper had carried his ringing message to posterity.

Trumann held the slip of paper at arm's length. '. . . Each for the other and all for Germany . . . and so I urge you, comrades . . . unswerving loyalty and utter commitment . . . dramatic struggle of historic dimensions . . . nameless heroes . . . unique grandeur . . . standing alone and unafraid . . . time of trial and self-sacrifice . . . the supreme ordeal . . . coming generations . . . worthy of our immortal heritage . . .'

'No stopping him now,' said the Captain. 'I know him when he gets like this.'

Someone else had sat down at the piano and was playing jazz, but Trumann didn't care. His voice cracked with emotion. 'We brothers-in-arms . . . standard-bearers of the future . . .

a shining example to those we leave behind . . . a courage stronger than destiny itself . . . cool acceptance of the odds, infinite daring, love and loyalty as boundless as the seas we sail . . .' He broke into a shrill cackle of laughter. 'And so he found his last resting-place in the depths of the Atlantic . . . ready and eager to make the ultimate sacrifice for our beloved German people, our glorious, God-given Führer and supreme commander – Heil! Heil! Heil!'

One or two revellers joined in. Böhler subjected Trumann to a governessy glare, rose to his full height and stalked off.

Trumann relapsed into giggles. Head lowered, he stared round the room with a long skein of spittle hanging from his lower lip.

'All the thoroughbreds have pissed off – all the *crème de la crème*. Nothing but proletarian scum left – the dregs of Doenitz's private navy, that's us! Anyone who leaves now gets shot!'

'You! Leave my tits alone!' screeched Monique. The surgeon-commander had apparently taken one liberty too many.

'Pardon me while I slink back into my foreskin,' drawled Dirty Doc, and his party roared with laughter.

Trumann fell backwards into a chair and clapped his eyelids shut. The Captain must be wrong after all, I thought. Trumann was passing out under our very noses. I was wrong. A moment later he jumped up, fumbled in his jacket pocket and produced an automatic pistol.

The lieutenant beside him had enough presence of mind to knock his arm down. A bullet tore into the parquet just in front of the Captain's right toecap, but he only shook his head. 'Anything's preferable to that racket on the piano.'

The pistol was confiscated and Trumann subsided again, pouting.

Monique, who registered the shot after a ten-second delay, emerged from behind the bar and hopped nimbly on to the platform where she started moaning into the microphone.

Out of the corner of my eye I saw Trumann rise in slow motion and stand swaying with a crafty smirk on his face. Then, while everyone was clapping, he groped his way between the tables and all of a sudden, pulled a second pistol from his waistband.

'Right!' he yelled, the veins in his neck distended with exertion. 'Everyone hit the deck!'

This time there was no one near enough to deflect his aim.

The Captain stretched his legs and slid off his chair. Three or four of the party took cover behind the piano. I sank to the floor in an attitude of prayer. Utter silence descended.

One shot smote the air like a whiplash, then another, then another. The Captain counted aloud. Monique, cowering beneath a table, punctuated the fusillade with spine-chilling shrieks.

'That's it!' called the Captain. Trumann had emptied his magazine.

I peered over the edge of the table. Plaster was still trickling from the pock-marks in the wall. The Captain was first on his feet. He studied the damage with his head on one side.

'Not bad for a man with his hands cut to ribbons – well up to rodeo standard.'

Trumann, who had already pocketed his gun, grinned from ear to ear.

He stared blissfully at his handiwork, almost delirious with self-satisfaction.

'Madame,' appeared, upraised hands conveying horror and mouth emitting high falsetto screams reminiscent of a tram rounding a bend.

As soon as the Captain saw her he slid to the floor again. Someone shouted 'Dive dive dive!'

Considering the noise, it was miraculous that we hadn't received an earlier visitation from the over-rigged old galleon who functioned as manageress of the Bar Royal. Madame affected the Spanish look: kiss-curls gummed to her temples with spit and a gleaming tortoiseshell comb in her hair, black velvet slippers on feet like slabs of fish and pudgy fingers laden with huge imitation stones, quivering rolls of fat tautly encased in satin. The monstrous old woman enjoyed the particular favour of the garrison commander.

Her voice, which usually sounded like frying bacon, was now raised in a stream of French and German expletives. '*Kaputt, kaputt,*' I distinguished among other lamentations.

'She's got a point,' said the Captain.

Thomsen put a bottle of cognac to his lips and sucked like a calf at the udder.

It was Merkel who saved the situation. He laboriously climbed a chair and started to sing, conducting his own performance with broad, sweeping gestures.

Delightedly we all joined in.

Madame's cries only occasionally penetrated our choral singing. She wrung her hands with melodramatic fervour and then with a last shrill squawk, scuttled off.

'Jesus, what a mess,' said the Captain.

I suddenly remembered my body-belt – lovely warm angora.

Mustn't leave that behind.

Dirty Doc pulled Monique on to his lap. With his right arm spanning her backside, he used his disengaged hand to fondle her left breast like someone guessing the weight of a cake. The pneumatic hostess in her tight little dress uttered a screech and broke away, only to dissolve into giggles as she lurched against the radiogram and sent the needle skidding across the grooves with a dull but resonant fart.

The surgeon-commander banged the table with his fist until the bottles danced, puce with suppressed laughter. Someone flung both arms round his neck from behind, but not in affection. Dirty Doc's tie had been neatly severed just below the knot. The lieutenant with the scissors proceeded to snip off Saemisch's tie, then Thomsen's. Monique was so consumed with mirth that she fell over backwards on to the band plat-form with her legs in the air, revealing that all she wore under her skirt was a minuscule pair of black panties little bigger than a G-string. Quick as a flash, someone seized a soda-siphon and directed a sharp jet between Monique's thighs making her squeal like a dozen piglets caught by the tail. Merkel, noticing that most of his tie was missing, picked up a half-empty bottle of cognac. The tie-snipper caught it full in the solar plexus and jack-knifed.

'Good shooting, sir,' the Captain commended him. 'Bang on target.'

A section of ornamental trellis-work sailed through the air. We all ducked except the Captain, who started to recite an obscene epic.

'Drink makes you im-po-tent!' burbled Thomsen. He could barely stand by now.

'Feel like a nightcap at the Majestic?' the Captain asked me.

'No thanks, turning in. Must get a couple of hours' kip.'

Thomsen grabbed our elbows. 'Same here. I'll tag along — gotta heavy day tomorrow. Jussa minute, though, muss have a quick pee first.'

The white moonlight beyond the swing doors smote me like a fist. I was unprepared for its shimmering, glittering intensity. The coastal strip was a blue-white ribbon, an icy conflagration. Road, buildings — everything was steeped in the same cold fire.

Surely that couldn't be the moon! It was round and white as a Camembert cheese, a luminous Camembert easily bright enough to read by. From shoreline to horizon, the whole vast expanse of the bay resembled a single sheet of crumpled silver foil with a million metallic facets. The horizon stood out silver against a sky of black velvet.

I screwed up my eyes. The island offshore floated in the glittering flood like a carp's back. The funnel of the sunken troopship, the stumps of mast – all razor-sharp. I leant against the concrete parapet. A sensation like pumice stone beneath my palms – enough to set your teeth on edge. The geraniums in their boxes, each bud clearly discernible. Mustard gas was supposed to smell like geraniums.

Cast shadows, the soughing of surf on the shore. My head was filled with undulating billows. The shimmering silver lamé of the moonlit sea bore me up and down, up and down. A dog threw back its head and the moon barked.

Where was Thomsen, the new Knight of the Iron Cross? Where the hell had he got to? There was nothing for it. Back into the Bar Royal. You could have cut the air with a knife – sedimentary air, like a stale layer-cake.

'Where's Thomsen?'

I kicked open the wash-room door, carefully avoiding the smeary brass handles.

There he lay, flat out on his right side in a porridge-like mass of vomit. Thomsen, sprawled in the turbid yellow broth, was emitting sounds. Straining my ears, I made out: 'Victory or death! Victory or death! Victory or death . . .'

I was on the verge of puking myself.

'Come on, you, get up!' I said between clenched teeth, and grabbed him by the collar.

'Meant – meant to get it out of my system tonight,' Thomsen mumbled. He lapsed into halting English. 'Now-I-am-no-longer-in-a-condition-to-fuck.'

The Captain appeared. Seizing Thomsen by his wrists and ankles, we half-carried, half-hauled him to the wash-room door. His face streamed with what he had been lying in, and the whole of the right side of his uniform was soaked.

'Bear a hand,' said the Captain.

I had to let go of Thomsen and dash back into the wash-room. In a single mighty surge, the entire contents of my stomach splattered on to the tiled floor. I bent double, retching convulsively. With tears in my eyes, I propped myself against the wall on splayed fingers. My left cuff had ridden up and I could see the dial of my wristwatch. Two a.m. Shit! Simone was waiting for me and the car would be there at 0630.

DEPARTURE

There were two routes to the harbour. The Captain chose the slightly slower one, which took us along the coast.

With smarting eyes I registered the things that sped past us. Anti-aircraft batteries, their chequered camouflage merging with the grey light of dawn. Notice-boards identifying various military establishments: bold black lettering and mysterious geometrical emblems. A belt of furze-bushes. A few grazing cows. A squat village. Two ponderous horses being led by the halter. Late-flowering roses in deserted gardens. The blotchy grey of house walls.

I had to blink repeatedly because my eyes still smarted with tobacco-smoke and lack of sleep. The first bomb craters. Gutted houses heralding the harbour. Heaps of twisted metal. Rusty petrol-cans. A car dump. Sunflowers bent and desiccated by the wind. Grey shreds of washing. Groups of Frenchmen in Basque berets. Columns of army trucks. The road descended towards the river. Dense fog still enveloped the low ground.

A tired nag clip-clopping through the murk in front of a cart with two wheels the height of a man. A house with glazed roof-tiles. A veranda, once glassed in but now a pathetic jumble of wrought-iron ribs and broken panes. In a doorway, a man in a blue apron with a soggy cigarette-butt gummed to his lower lip.

The clank of buffers. Sidings. The shattered railway station. Everything grey – grey in countless gradations from dirty plaster-white to yellowish sooty black. I could feel grit between my teeth.

French dockyard mateys with black, crudely stitched shoulder-bags. Amazing that they worked on, considering the number of air raids.

A half-submerged vessel flecked with red lead. Probably an old herring-boat which had been earmarked for conversion to patrol duties. Big-bottomed women in ragged dungarees, holding their riveting hammers like sub-machine-guns. The stilt-legged cranes still stood despite the incessant raids: their iron filigree offered no resistance to bomb-blast.

We had to walk the last few metres to the bunker. Our car could not penetrate the maze of railway lines, some of them bent upwards at a crazy angle. Four heavily swaddled figures proceeded in Indian file through the gloom: the Old Man first, stooping as he walked, his eyes on the ground ahead. A red muffler projected above the stiff collar of his leather jacket, almost to the rim of his soiled white cap. He carried a bulging canvas bag in the crook of his left arm. His waddling gait was made still more graceless by the clumsy sea-boots with their cork soles.

I followed two paces to the rear of him with the Chief at my heels. The Chief's progress was frisky and erratic. Rails which the Captain crossed with measured tread he cleared with quick, springy little leaps. He wasn't wearing leathers like us, just grey-green overalls: a dungareed fitter with an officer's cap on his head. He carried his bag neatly by the handle.

In the rear came the second lieutenant, the shortest of us all. From his murmured remarks to the Chief I gathered that he was afraid the boat would be unable to sail on time because of fog. I couldn't detect a breath of wind in the coagulated murk.

We crossed a moonscape of fog-filled bomb craters like bowls of gruel.

The second lieutenant was also carrying a canvas bag under his arm. This had to hold all the belongings a man needed on patrol: a big bottle of Cologne, woollen underwear, a body-belt, knitted gloves and a few shirts. I was wearing my new sweater. Oilskins, leathers, and escape gear would be awaiting me on board. 'Black shirts are best,' the quartermaster had knowledgeably asserted. Black shirts didn't show the dirt.

The first lieutenant and second engineer were already on board with all hands, preparing the U-boat for sea.

The sky above the west harbour was still thick with shadow, but above the roads in the east, beyond the dark silhouettes of freighters lying at anchor, a pale glow had already climbed as far as the zenith. The vague half-light invested everything with a strange ambivalence. The skeletal cranes sprouted above the square roofs of the warehouses; the tar-paper roofs seemed to bristle with ships' masts wreathed in white waste-steam and oily black fumes.

The plaster on the windowless side of a half-demolished building had been consumed by leprosy and was falling away in scales. The word BYRRH, painted in massive white letters on a muddy red background, sprawled across the seat of the infection.

Overnight, hoar-frost had settled like mildew on the ubiquitous heaps of rubble left by recent air raids. Our route meandered between these mounds. Splintered facia-boards above empty windows were the only reminder of the shops and bars that had once bordered the streets. 'Café de Commerce' was reduced to a single syllable: 'Comme . . .' The Café de la Paix had entirely vanished into a bomb crater. The girders of a gutted workshop had subsided inwards to form a gigantic iron spider.

A convoy of trucks ground towards us laden with sand for the construction of the bunker lock. Their slipstream whipped empty cement bags into the air and flailed them against the Captain's legs. For a while, cement dust robbed us of breath and settled on our boots like flour. We passed two or three shattered cars with army number-plates and wheels pointing at the sky, then more charred beams and a couple of roofs which had been blown off bodily and lay among the twisted rails like tents.

'Another bloody shambles,' growled the Captain. The Chief, scenting a communication of importance, hurriedly caught up.

The Captain came to a halt, clamped the canvas bag between his knees and groped his leather jacket. He brought out a battered pipe and a clumsy old lighter. While we stood around, huddled against the cold, he methodically lit up and set off again, trailing a whitish plume of smoke like a steam-tug. Now and again he half-turned to us without breaking step, his face twisted in a wry grimace. His eyes were completely hidden in the shadow cast by the peak of his cap.

Without removing the pipe, he addressed the Chief in a hoarse voice. 'What about the search periscope? Have they cured that blurring?'

'Yes, sir. A couple of lenses had become detached from the mastic. Probably during that air attack.'

'And the faulty steering gear?'

'All in order. There was a break in the motor-room conduit, that's why we were getting an intermittent contact. We've replaced the cable.'

We made our way along a muddy lane deeply rutted by truck tyres. Our route was flanked by a dense entanglement of barbed wire. Sentries with turned-up collars and invisible faces stood outside a guard-house.

The air was filled with a sudden metallic clangour. Then the din ceased abruptly and the swelling crescendo of a siren sliced the cold damp air, reeking of tar, oil and putrid fish. We were in dockyard country.

A huge shaft yawned on our left. Long strings of tipping wagons disappeared into its milky mouth and rattled along unseen beneath the ground.

'They're supposed to be building additional pens all over the place,' said the Captain.

We were now walking along the quay. The stale water under its mantle of fog teemed with such a dense array of vessels, that the eye could not distinguish their individual shapes: battered, salt-encrusted trawlers which now served as patrol-boats, bizarre-looking lighters and oil barges, harbour defence boats – the 'flea flotilla', as we called the plebeian mass of shabby, worn-out work and supply boats which were a feature of any dockyard.

The Chief jabbed a forefinger into the mist. 'See that building over there? There's a car on the fifth floor.'

'Where?'

'Just above the far end of the warehouse – the one with the busted roof.'

'Good God! How did it get there?'

'It was the last raid on the pens that did it, day before yesterday. They dropped some really big ones. I actually saw the car take off and land – plumb on its wheels!'

'Must have been quite a sight.'

'You should have seen the French take off too. There one moment, gone the next.'

'What French?'

'The anglers, of course – the quayside's alive with them. There are always some squatting by the entrance to No. 1 Pen.'

'Probably employed by the Brits to keep tabs on arrivals and departures.'

'They aren't keeping tabs on anything, not now. They didn't budge when the siren went, just stayed put. Twenty or thirty of them. A block-buster landed smack on top of them.'

'The bunker caught one too.'

'Yes, a direct hit, but it didn't penetrate. Seven metres of ferro-concrete . . .'

Steel plates yielded under our tread and sprang back into place with a hollow clang. A locomotive emitted a strident shriek of pain. Above and beyond the Captain's stooping, straightening figure there gradually materialized an all-commanding concrete façade whose lateral extremities were lost in the fog. We were heading for a smooth wall devoid of cornices, doors and window embrasures. It resembled one side of a huge plinth designed to support a tower so tall that its summit would soar far above the clouds. The lip of the seven-metre-thick roof projected slightly, its immense weight seeming to ram the whole structure even deeper into the ground.

We had to skirt the concrete mass, picking our way over lengths of track, stacked timber and pipes as thick as a human thigh. Eventually, set in one of the narrower sides, we found an entrance protected by heavily armoured gates.

A furious clatter of riveting hammers assailed us from the dark interior. The devil's tattoo ebbed for brief moments, only to resume almost at once and become condensed into a single deafening roar.

Semi-darkness reigned inside the bunker, broken by pale shafts of light from the entrances to the outer basin. The U-boats lay moored in their pens, two by two. The bunker had twelve pens, some of them constructed as dry docks. Each pen was separated from its neighbours by massive concrete partitions, and the entrances could be shielded by lowering massive steel shutters.

Dust, fumes, the stench of oil. Oxyacetylene burners snarled, air lines hissed and cutting torches gave sporadic firework displays.

We trudged in single file along the broad concrete ramp which traversed the entire bunker at right angles to the pens. We had to keep our eyes skinned – bulky objects lay strewn everywhere. Tangled cables caught at our ankles and wagon-loads of machine parts barred our advance. Trucks nestled close to the wagons. In them, special cradles supported torpedoes or dismantled 88s and anti-aircraft guns, also unidentifiable pieces of equipment. Pipes, tackle, wires and piles of camouflage nets lay everywhere.

On our left, warm yellow light issued from the windows of the various workshops: pattern shops, smithies, machine shops, torpedo, gun and periscope workshops.

The Captain turned, his face bluish in the flickering glare of of a welding torch.

'Chief,' he shouted, 'you think we've cured that singing noise in the starboard propeller at Slow One?'

'Yes, the new one's dead true. That blade on the old screw was more bent than it looked.'

'And the planes? They were pretty noisy too.'

'Yes, there was a lot of rust on the gearing when we dismantled them. They're all right now.'

In the pens on our right lay damaged submarines. Mutilated vessels streaked with oxydization and gangrenous patches of red lead. There was a smell of rust, paint, oil, stale acid, burnt rubber, sea-water and – as everywhere – rotting fish.

In the depths of a dry dock lay a U-boat with her belly gaping like a disembowelled whale's. A whole gang of dockyard mateys were at work on her – Lilliputian insects swarming over a lifeless carcass. Large sections of the outer skin were being excised with cutting torches, and the maltreated torso shone jaggedly in the glare. From the belly of the boat, like intestines, spewed great bunches of compressed air line and electric cables. The steel cylinder of the pressure hull had been laid open along the full length of the fore-casing, also over the engine-room. Yellow light streamed from the boat's interior. I could peer deep into her entrails and see the massive outlines of the diesel engines, the bewildering maze of pipes and cables. As I watched, the hook of a crane glided down to collect another load. It looked as if the boat was to be completely gutted.

'Severely counter-attacked,' was the Chief's laconic explanation.

'I wonder they made it at all, in a wreck like that.'

The Captain headed for a flight of concrete steps which led down into the dry dock. The steps were coated with oil and the guard rails festooned with rubber-sheathed cables.

The sudden glare of a welding torch wrested a section of ballast tank from the gloom. More torches flared up farther aft until the whole hull was bathed in fitful radiance. These were not the lithe, familiar outlines of a surface ship. The foreplanes jutted from her flat sides like fins and her hull ballooned amidships. Plump excrescences bulged on either side of the belly: the main ballast tanks, welded to the boat like saddle-bags. Everything was convex and rounded about this deep-sea creature with its specially designed anatomy. Even the ribs were all-enclosing rings of steel.

A circular steel door on one side of the bow began to move. The disc swung slowly back, revealing an orifice which expanded into the sinister mouth of a bow torpedo tube.

The bow-cap closed again.

'Looks worse than it is!' bellowed the Captain. 'Pressure hull still pretty good – she'll be all right.'

I felt a nudge at my elbow. The Chief was standing beside me, head tilted, gazing up at the rounded belly of the boat.

'Impressive, eh?'

A sentry stared down at us with his sub-machine-gun slung over one shoulder.

We made our way farther aft, scrambling over chocks. The basic, elongated steel cylinder shape of the submarine showed up clearly. This steel cigar-tube housed the propulsion units, batteries and crew's living quarters. Together with its contents, it weighed rather less than the water it displaced and was just light enough to float on the surface. Fine adjustments to its weight were obtained by varying the amount of water in trimming and compensating tanks. It could thus be made neutrally buoyant – the dived condition. A further system of main ballast tanks, mostly outside the pressure hull, enabled the submarine to be raised in the water for positive buoyancy on the surface. The fuel tanks were also situated outside the pressure hull, oil being replaced with sea-water as it was used by the engines. This was a VII-C boat, like ours. I dredged my memory: length 67.1 metres, beam 6.2 metres, displacement 769 cubic metres on the surface and 871 cubic metres dived – not much difference because little of the boat projected above the water. Draught when surfaced, 4.8 metres – a standard figure only, because draught on the surface could be varied, centimetre by centimetre, according to the amount of water in the main ballast tanks. A draught of 4.8 metres on the surface corresponded to a displacement of 600 tons.

In addition to our own type, there was Type II, of 250 tons, and Type IX-C, which had a displacement of 1,000 tons on the surface and 1,232 tons dived. The VII-C was designed for combat duties in the Atlantic. She could dive quickly and possessed great manœuvrability. Her surface range was 7900 miles at a speed of 10 knots, 6500 miles at 12 knots. Dived, the range was only 80 miles at 4 knots. Maximum speeds: 17.3 knots on the surface and 7.6 knots submerged.

The Chief was yelling in my ear. 'This one got clobbered aft, too – rammed by a sinking freighter.'

Here and there, Jupiter lamps stood on tripods. Dented plates were being planished by a bevy of dockyard mateys. Nothing serious. The plates belonged to the outer casing, which flooded freely when the submarine dived and did not have to withstand pressure at depth.

Only a section of the submarine's true cylindrical shape, the pressure hull, could be seen amidships. Forward and aft, the pressure hull was enclosed by a thin outer skin which disguised the inflated deep-sea fish as a surface vessel when it came up for air. At intervals down either side, the casing was pierced by holes and slits which enabled water to infiltrate between pressure hull and outer skin when the submarine dived. Otherwise, water-pressure would have buckled the thin casing like cardboard.

On the underside of one of the main ballast tanks I spotted the flooding flaps which remained open when the boat was on the surface. The main ballast tanks supported it like waterwings. As soon as air was allowed to escape through the

39

vents on top of these tanks, water poured in through the flooding flaps. Buoyancy decreased and the boat dived.

My eyes wandered over the gutted hull. I noted the bulge of a fuel tank, the round aperture of the cooling-water inlet for the diesels, the location of the quick-dive or Q tanks. Like the trimming tanks, these were pressure-resistant.

The Captain had already moved farther aft. He raised his right arm and pointed upwards. The submarine's screws were completely encased by timber scaffolding.

He turned to the Chief with a look of enquiry.

'Propeller shafts – new lignum vitae bush,' shouted the Chief. 'Too much noise, probably – invitation to counter-attacks.'

Immediately above the screws was the bow-cap of the stern tube. Halfway up the lateral excrescences, afterplanes sprouted like abbreviated aircraft wings.

I was almost knocked over by a man daubed from head to foot with paint. He carried a brush mounted on an outsize broomstick. While I was waiting for the Captain he began to paint the belly of the boat from beneath. The dark-grey patch grew as I watched.

When we reached No. 6 Pen, which was flooded, the Captain made another detour and headed for a submarine secured alongside the right-hand wall. 'Kramer's boat,' the Chief shouted in my ear. 'The one that caught a direct hit from the air.'

Kramer's story was still fresh in my mind. He'd just surfaced when he saw a plane. The bomb doors opened, the bomb plopped out and headed straight for him – so close that he ducked. It crashed into the bridge casing, but slightly off centre and sideways on. 'No explosion – it just disintegrated.'

The Captain inspected the conning-tower from forward and aft, the grotesque curlicue of metal which the bomb had shaved off the sheet-metal casing of the bridge, the pierced breakwater. An amorphous, muffled figure – one of the sentries – came up and saluted.

The Chief said: 'By rights, Kramer should have been playing a harp for the past week.'

The basin of No. 8 Pen was also flooded. The still surface had the dark sheen of gun-metal.

'Ours,' said the Chief.

U-A was scarcely distinguishable from the gloomy water, but her lines stood out better against the pale concrete wall above the low wharf. The casing was a bare metre clear of the oily surface. All the hatches were still open. I surveyed the full length of the submarine as if to imprint it on my mind for all time: the wooden planking which extended in one long forward sweep, flat and without sheer, to the bow; the conning-tower and cumbersome-looking anti-aircraft arma-ment, the slightly inclined stern, the steel cable and green china insulators of the jumping-wire which ran down forward and aft of the conning-tower. A picture of perfect simplicity: a VII-C U-boat, seaworthy as no other vessel afloat.

I spotted a wry grin on the Captain's face. He looked like a racehorse owner before the off.

The boat was fully provisioned and equipped, tanks full of fuel and water, but she did not emit the vibrant hum of a ship about to sail. The diesels were not running, although the wire-handling party were already standing by in their heavy gloves.

'They're giving us a send-off in the lock,' the Captain said. 'Usual damned nonsense!'

The crew were mustered on the casing abaft the conning-tower. Just a mere fifty men – eighteen-, nineteen- and twenty-year-olds. Only the petty officers and chief petty officers were a year or two older.

I couldn't make out their faces in the gloom and failed to register any of their crisply enunciated names when the roll was called.

The casing was slippery with the sea-mist that drifted in from the outer basin. The grey-white foggy light was so dazzling that it dissolved the outlines of the exit gates.

The first lieutenant saluted. 'All hands on board except Control-room Hand Bäcker. Crew at harbour stations. Secured for sea.'

'Main engines, motors and steering gear ready, sir,' added the Chief. 'Air on the whistle.'

'Very good.' The Captain raised his voice. 'Eyes front! Close up and stand at ease!'

He waited for the shuffle of feet to die away.

'I expect you heard that Bäcker was killed. Air raid on Magdeburg. Bloody shame – Bäcker was a good man.' A pause. 'Well, we didn't have much luck last time out.'

A longer pause. The Captain gave a scowl of disgust.

'Fair enough, not our fault. Just the same, make sure we do better this time. Keep on your toes, that's all.'

A grin stole over one or two faces.

'Never wastes words, does he?' murmured the Chief.

Warm vapour streamed from the open galley hatch aft. The chef's face appeared. I handed him my belongings.

Silently, the attack periscope slid upwards. The cyclopean eye turned in all directions, rose to maximum height atop its gleaming silver antenna, then sank again and vanished from sight. I climbed the conning-tower. The paint, which was still tacky, left smears on my palms. The forehatch had already been secured. The galley hatch clanged shut. The only remaining access to the interior was through the conning-tower, with its upper and lower hatches, or 'lids'.

Confusion still reigned inside the boat. It was impossible to get anywhere without squeezing and shoving. Spare hammocks crammed with loaves of bread hung from the deckheads. Crates, sacks and canned food littered the passages. I wondered where the surplus stores could possibly be stowed. Every last nook and cranny seemed to be occupied.

The builders of the VII-C had been as sparing with storage compartments – normally spacious in surface ships – as they had with washing facilities. They had simply installed their engines in the big steel cigar and taken it for granted that, however neatly the maze of pipes, the massive power plants, numerous auxiliary motors and weapons systems were dovetailed into the space available, there would still be enough room for the crew and their gear.

U-A had embarked 14 torpedoes. Five were in the tubes, two in stowages in the casing and the rest beneath the deck of the fore-ends, or bow compartment. We also carried 120 rounds for the 88 millimetre and a large quantity of anti-aircraft ammunition.

The quartermaster and the coxswain, the two senior ratings, had their hands full. The coxswain's duties on board were those of a sea-going sergeant-major. Behrmann by name, he was a formidable-looking fellow who topped most of the others by a head. I already knew him by ear : 'You cheeky sod, you! I'll have your guts for garters!'

Half an hour to sailing time. That left me a few minutes to look round the engine- and motor-rooms – an old love of mine, the engine-rooms of ships secured for sea. First, however, I perched on the flooding panel in the control-room, surrounded by pipes, valves, handwheels, gauges, auxiliary machinery and convoluted tangles of green and red leads. In the semi-darkness I made out the rudder indicators, one electrical and one mechanical. Above the hydroplane operating position with its push-button controls for depth-keeping I could just distinguish the inclinometers, coarse and fine. The Papenberg, a depth indicator situated between the dials of the conventional depth-gauges with their rotating needles, resembled a large thermometer. It showed the boat's depth to the nearest ten centimetres and was an invaluable aid to accurate depth-keeping when the periscopes were in use.

The control-room had watertight bulkheads forward and aft — dished bulkheads whose semi-spherical shape made them more pressure-resistant than the flat variety. They divided the pressure hull into three main compartments, not that this offered much protection in the Atlantic because, with even one compartment flooded, the boat would sink far below maximum escape depth. The designers had probably been thinking of shallow waters like the Baltic.

The engine-room, my ultimate goal, lay beyond the galley.

I clambered aft over the crates and sacks in the petty officers' mess, where I was to bunk, and on through the galley, which had still to be squared off.

Our engine-room did not bear comparison with that of a big ship. Ours was no lofty cavern extending the full depth of the vessel in a multi-storeyed succession of gleaming walkways and stairways. Here there was only a narrow tube into which the two massive diesels and all their ancillary machinery had to fit like crouching beasts. Every last niche in the confusion of pipes that surrounded them was pressed into use: circulation pump, lubrication pump, oil separator, starting air bottles, fuel pump, and, dotted among them, a multiplicity of gauges, thermometers, torque meters and rev counters.

The two diesels, each of which had six cylinders, developed 2800 h.p. between them.

With the bulkhead doors shut, the intercom system provided the sole link with the control-room. In action, the narrow walkway between the engines was a particularly undesirable spot to be because most of the hull valves — the weakest points in the pressure hull — were at engine-room level. If a depth-charge cracked the hull anywhere, the engine-room was likely to be the first compartment flooded.

The two engine-room artificers were hard at work. Johann was quiet, pallid, hollow-cheeked and stoop-shouldered with a calm gaze and fatalistic manner, fair-haired, almost beardless. The other, Franz, was equally bent and pallid, but dark, keen-eyed, and bearded. He looked surly. Having originally assumed that they addressed each other by their Christian names, I now knew that Johann and Franz were surnames. Their first names were August and Karl.

Still farther aft was the motor-room. The electric motors were powered by batteries which were in their turn charged by the diesels. Their combined output was 750 h.p. Everything about the motor-room was clean, cold and hidden from view, as in a generating station.

The casing of the motors, which propelled the submarine under water, did not project far above the gleaming silver floor-plates. On either side were switchboards with black dials and a throng of ammeters, voltmeters and rheostats. The electric motors functioned without external air. They were DC motors which drove the tail shafts and screws direct. When the diesels were running on the surface, they revolved in unison and served as generators for re-charging the batteries. At the after end of the motor-room was the rear door of the stern torpedo tube, flanked by the two compressors which made HP air for blowing the main ballast tanks.

I threaded my way back to the control-room and climbed to the bridge.

Drawn out of the bunker stern first by her motors, the U-boat slid into a mother-of-pearl radiance which turned the damp casing to shimmering glass. Our siren gave a muffled hoot, then another. A tug responded with an even more muted signal.

The Captain was giving the motor and steering orders himself. He leant far out over the bridge rail so as to survey the full length of the boat while conning us through the cramped basin.

'Stop port. Slow ahead starboard. Hard-a-port!'

The submarine nosed cautiously through the fog, metre by metre. It was still cold.

The tip of the bow swung across a row of vessels moored cheek by jowl. They were little tubs – harbour defence boats, a patrol-boat among them.

The water of the harbour stank ever more strongly of oil, garbage and seaweed.

Isolated masts reared above the swathes of fog, then a forest of derricks. The black filigree-work of the cranes made them look like drilling rigs in an oil-field.

Workmen streaming across a swing-bridge into the dockyard were concealed from the neck downwards by its rusty brown parapet: a procession of severed heads.

In the east, a reddish glow gradually mingled with the milky haze that swam above the pale-grey warehouses. A large block of buildings swung slowly aside, and all at once, through the ribs of a crane, I saw the crisply outlined ball of the sun – but only for a moment. Then it was obscured by greasy smoke from a tug which was towing some black, heavy-laden sand and coal barges.

I shivered in the moist breeze and held my breath to avoid

drawing too much of the stinking air into my lungs. A knot of figures had assembled at the lock-side: dockyard workmen in oil-stained overalls, some ratings, a few officers from the flotilla. I recognized Gregor, who hadn't been with us the night before, Kortmann, and the Siamese twins Kupsch and Stackmann. Trumann was there too, of course, showing no signs of his alcoholic debauch. Behind him I saw Baldy Keller and Bechtel, the depth-charge collector, also Kramer of the unexploded bomb. Even the line-shooter, Erler, was there, surrounded by a covey of girls hugging bouquets. Thomsen was missing.

'Look at the talent,' said a rating beside me, who was coiling down the heaving line to which the headrope had been secured.

'Stupid twats,' said another.

'See the third one from the left – the nurse with the big bubs? I've laid her.'

'You and who else?'

'Word of honour.'

The water on the port quarter suddenly boiled. Foam surged round the boat. No. 1 main ballast tank was blown until it held nothing but air. A moment later the surface swirled at several points along the sides as one main ballast after another was blown to full buoyancy. Our free-board increased perceptibly.

A gunner on the wharf shouted 'Good hunting!' and spread his arms like an angler bragging about his catch. One of our men stuck his tongue out. Two or three nudged each other or grinned. Lined up on the casing like chorus-girls, they mimed their delight at the prospect of departure. The send-off party on the wharf entered into the spirit of the charade. How we envy you! Off you go to pit your strength against the foe and win medals while we poor sods have to kick our heels in this godforsaken country with a bunch of godforsaken French tarts!

I settled myself in the stiff grey leathers and thrust my hands deep into the pockets of my felt-lined jacket, which reached to my knees. I stamped my feet on the gratings, insulated against the cold iron by heavy cork-soled sea-boots.

The Captain glanced at me and grinned. 'Raring to go, eh?'

The bandsmen on the wharf stared down at us, blank-faced under their steel helmets. The jack-booted bandmaster raised his baton and there was a sudden reverberant crash of the opening bars.

The Captain, with an air of total unconcern, applied himself to a fat cigar. On the wharf, Trumann had also lit up and the two men exchanged casual cigar-laden salutes.

'Where's Merkel?' the Captain called, when the music died. 'Isn't he coming out with us?'

Trumann shrugged. 'Not secured yet.'

'Ought to be ashamed of himself.'

The Captain squinted at the sky, then wreathed himself in smoke with a vigorous pull at his cigar.

'Let go all wires!'

Then, 'Slow ahead port, slow astern starboard. Stop both. Midships!'

U-A detached herself from the wharf, a dark ferry on an oily black Styx with a complement of leather-clad figures crowding the anti-aircraft platform abaft the bridge, Silently, as though by magnetism, the electric motors drew her away from the wall.

Little bunches of flowers landed on the bridge. The look-outs stuck them in the wind-deflectors.

The dark strip of water between the grey steel of the sub-marine and the oil-streaked side of the wharf widened steadily. There was a stir among the onlookers as someone forged his way through their ranks. Thomsen! He raised both arms, the new decoration twinkling at his throat, and called across the brackish water: 'Ahoy U-A! Good hunting!'

The Captain, still with the cigar between his fingers, returned the salutation as nonchalantly as only he knew how.

Thomsen's figure dwindled. The U-boat nosed slowly through the fog-enshrouded outer basin. Our bow was pointing at the open sea.

Little by little, the curtain of fog lifted. The sun climbed higher up the black iron girders of a crane. Its potent crimson permeated the whole of the eastern sky. The edges of the clouds became tinged with red foam, and even the sea-gulls took on a reflected splendour. With folded wings they swooped down through the pink luminescence, almost to the water, only to soar skywards at the last moment, screaming harshly.

Now the veils of fog evaporated altogether and the oily water, too, was engulfed in a red glow. Quite close to us, a floating crane belched a huge cloud of steam which the sun at once daubed red and orange. Even the BYRRH hoarding paled beside it.

The sky turned yellow-green, the clouds a dull dove-grey. The sun climbed higher and gained strength.

A green wreck buoy slid past. To starboard, the roofs of sea-side villas congealed into a red blur and slowly disappeared behind a forest of bright yellow derricks.

I suddenly became aware of a high, strangled whine followed by a harsh bubbling sound. The casing began to tremble, the bubbling became more throaty and acquired a steady rhythm: our diesels had started up. It was as though the submarine had only now shaken off her dockyard inertia.

I rested my palms on the cold iron of the bridge casing and felt the animate throb of the main engines.

The sea was running across the harbour mouth. Short, choppy waves exploded on our ballast tanks.

We passed a freighter camouflaged in grey, green and black. 'Six thousand tons, or thereabouts,' said the Captain. No bow-waves: she was lying at anchor.

Our route took us so close inshore that I could make out each individual fishing-rod on its stand. Some soldiers waved to us.

We were travelling at a jog-trot.

'Diving stations,' ordered the Captain.

The bollards to which the wires had been attached were re-tracted, the boathooks secured, the wires and fenders stowed beneath the gratings. Seamen tightened every clip on the hatches with wrenches, took down the ensign staff, cleared away the machine-guns and laid out ready-use ammunition.

The coxswain saw to it that every operation was carried out smoothly – unnecessary noise was a submariner's anathema. The first lieutenant double-checked, then reported to the Captain: 'Ready to dive, sir. Hands at diving stations.'

We increased speed. Foam bubbled up through the gratings and spray pattered against the conning-tower.

The rocky coastline fell away, its indentations still bathed in shadow. The anti-aircraft emplacements were so well camouflaged that I could hardly detect them with binoculars.

Two patrol-boats, converted trawlers, steamed up to escort us. They were joined a little later by a barrage-breaker, a large camouflaged vessel crammed with barrels and other buoyant material for protection against mines. Her deck bristled with anti-aircraft guns.

'What a job!' said the quartermaster. 'They stand on tram-polines so they don't bust any bones when a mine goes up. In and out, same old routine day after day. Sooner them than me.'

U-A ploughed steadily along in the barrage-breaker's wide, swirling wake.

'Complicated channel, this – all kinds of wrecks around. See those mastheads over there? That was an Allied troopship, sunk by Stukas. Took a bomb straight down the funnel – still visible at low water.[5]

We had no port of destination. Our immediate objective was a grid position defined by two letters in mid-Atlantic.

The C-in-C's operations division had divided every sea area into a mosaic of such squares. This facilitated wireless communications but made it more difficult for me, being used to conventional co-ordinates, to spot our position on the chart at a glance.

Our escort left us at 1100. The patrol-boats quickly fell astern. The barrage-breaker peeled off in a wide arc, leaving a dark spreading stain of smoke against the sky. A final exchange of semaphore messages passed between us.

The quartermaster turned to face the front with a single resolute movement, raised his binoculars and propped his elbows on the bridge casing.

'Well, Kriechbaum,' said the Captain, 'here we go again.' He disappeared down the conning-tower.

One of the look-outs plucked the flowers from the wind-deflectors and tossed them overboard. They were quickly swallowed by our seething wake.

I craned over the bridge rail to get a good view of the submarine from stem to stern.

A long swell rose to meet us. The bow dipped again and again, cleaving the waves like a ploughshare. Each new thrust flung the water high and sent showers of spray hissing over the bridge. I licked my lips and could taste Atlantic salt.

A few strato-cumulus clouds hung in the blue vault of the sky like blobs of whipped egg-white. The bow lifted, streaming with moisture, then rammed the waves once more, and for minutes the whole forepart of the boat ran with foam. The sun awoke a full spectrum of colours in the spray, and miniature rainbows arched above the fore-casing.

The sea, bottle-green no longer, was an intense dark blue. Thin white streaks of foam threaded its expanse with the irregularity of veins in marble. A puff-ball of cloud momentarily obscured the sun, turning the water to blue-black ink.

Astern, a broad band of whey. As it fanned out, our wash collided with the swell and plaited it into long white manes which stretched for as far as the eye could see.

Bracing my feet against the periscope standard, I craned even farther out of the bridge and lay back with my arms round the jumping-wire. Sea-gulls swooped over the boat on geniculated wings, staring fixedly at us.

The noise of the engines varied from moment to moment.

It dwindled when the outboard exhausts were awash and swelled when they cleared and the diesel fumes could escape without hindrance.

The Captain reappeared. He raised his binoculars and peered through them with narrowed eyes.

Ahead, a cloud like a ball of grey wool hovered close above the sea. The Captain scrutinized it keenly, flexing his knees to the rhythm of the boat so expertly that he needed no support.

He increased speed and ordered a zigzag course. The submarine heeled with every change of direction.

'Watch out for torpedo-tracks – tricky part of the world.' Then turning to me: 'The gentlemen of the opposition have a habit of lying in wait for us here. They know our sailing times backwards. It's a piece of cake, with all their informants – dockyard mateys, charwomen, prostitutes . . .'

He continued to cast wary glances at the sky, shifting impatiently from foot to foot with his brow furrowed like a wash-board and his nose wrinkled. 'We could be jumped by the RAF any minute – they're getting more and more cheeky these days.'

The clouds gradually jostled closer until barely a patch of blue sky showed through. I became physically aware of the tension that now reigned on the bridge.

'Tricky part of the world,' the Captain repeated. 'Better go below. The fewer bodies on the bridge the better, if there's trouble.'

That was directed at me. I took the hint.

My bunk was in the petty officers' quarters, one of the least comfortable places on board, mainly because it suffered from the most through traffic. Anyone bound for the galley, engine-room or motor-room had to negotiate it. Whenever the watches changed, six men squeezed through at a time. The messmen, too, had to shuttle back and forth with brimming fannies and mess-tins. The compartment was really nothing more than a narrow corridor with four bunks on either side. Plumb in the centre was a fixed table with flaps which could be folded down like the wings of a naval aeroplane. There was so little room round it that the POs had to sit down to meals on the lower bunks with their heads bowed. Meals were inevitably rudely interrupted whenever someone from the engine-room had to go to the control-room or vice versa.

Admittedly, the POs' meal-times were arranged so that the messmen serving the forward compartments did not have to commute between them and the galley, but there were constant interruptions all the same. It was my good fortune that I did not have to eat in the POs' mess as well as sleep there. A place would be laid for me in the wardroom.

Some of the bunks were used by two POs alternately. I was lucky enough to have a bunk to myself.

The POs of the watch below were still busy arranging their lockers. Two stokers passed through on their way aft, causing an instant traffic jam. My aluminium bunk-rail, which also served as a ladder, was folded down and added to the bottle-neck.

My bunk was still littered with canned food, a bundle of sheepskin waistcoats and some loaves of bread. A rating appeared with oilskins, leathers and an escape pack – wonderful new heavy stuff, all of it. The padded leather jacket hadn't a crease.

The escape gear was packed in a brown canvas bag with a zip fastener. Also brand-new. 'Pure show,' remarked the control-room PO. 'Designed for the Baltic.'

'Come in handy against diesel fumes, though,' said a tall dark-haired fellow with bushy eyebrows – Frenssen, one of the stoker POs. All the same, the escape gear did have some value as a life-jacket. I turned the knob slightly, and the small steel cylinder at once released oxygen.

I stowed the bag at the foot of my bunk. All I had to accommodate my gear was a tiny locker, not even big enough to house the barest essentials, so I tucked my writing materials and camera between the raised edge of my mattress and the plywood partition. That left no more room for me than there would have been in an average-sized coffin. I decided to take a quick look round before lunch and went forward through the control-room.

Apart from the POs in their cramped mess, all members of the crew including the captain and officers were accommodated in the forepart of the boat. The captain's living quarters were immediately forward of the control-room. The wireless office and hydrophone booth were opposite it on the other side of the passage. A green curtain concealed his bunk, a few lockers on the bulkhead and a diminutive desk, though writing-surface would have been a better description. That was all – even a U-boat commander had to make the best of a bad job. There were no enclosed cabins flanking a central passage-way, as on most surface ships.

The 'settee' in the wardroom on which the Captain and chief engineer took their meals was really the Chief's bunk. The collapsible bunk above it, which was folded up by day like a couchette, belonged to the second lieutenant. The first lieutenant and second engineer had their bunks on the opposite side – a privileged position because they remained permanently in place – and could therefore stretch out any time they happened to be off watch.

The adjacent CPOs' mess, separated from the wardroom by more lockers, housed the quartermaster, Kriechbaum, the two engine-room artificers, Johann and Franz, and the coxswain, Behrmann. Beneath the deck was No. 1 battery. Together with No. 2 battery, which was under the POs' mess, this powered our motors when we dived.

The bow compartment or fore-ends was separated from the CPOs' mess by a light bulkhead. Despite its cave-like appearance, the fore-ends was more of a 'room' than any other. Strictly speaking, it was a combined workshop and stowage for spare torpedoes, but it also housed more men than any other part of the submarine. In them slept the seamen, commonly referred to as 'their lordships', also the torpedo-men, telegraphists and stokers.

The stokers had one bunk between two because they were watch and watch, six hours about. The others, who were in three watches, had two bunks between them. No man had a bunk to himself. When someone went on watch his fug was inherited by the man he relieved. There were not enough bunks to go round, even so, and four hammocks hung from the deckhead.

Members of the watch below seldom remained in peace. Everyone had to turn out at mealtimes. The upper bunks were folded up and the lower bunks cleared to provide seating accommodation for their lordships. When routines had to be carried out or checks run on the torpedoes in the four bow tubes, the compartment became a machine-shop. The bunks were taken down and the hammocks stowed away.

Reloads for the forward torpedo tubes were housed beneath the raised wooden decking. Cramped conditions persisted for as long as these torpedoes remained there, so each one fired meant more elbow-room for the men in the fore-ends. They also enjoyed at least one advantage over everyone else in that there was no through traffic.

At present, the fore-ends looked as if it had sustained a direct hit. Leathers, escape packs, sweaters, sacks of potatoes, teapots, buckets, cordage, loaves of bread . . . It was inconceivable that everything would be squared off to make room for twenty-one junior ratings and the torpedo gunner's mate, the only officer who bunked at his place of work rather than in the POs' mess.

I entered just as the coxswain was chivvying two ratings forward. 'Look lively there! Stow that crate of lettuces between the tubes. Lettuces . . . You'd think we were a bloody greengrocer's!'

He showed off the cramped quarters as if they were a special attraction – a proud personal achievement. 'It's all a question of robbing Peter to pay Paul,' he explained. 'Take the heads: we've got two of them, but one has to act as stowage. That means more room for food and less room for shit. It doesn't add up.'

I and the second lieutenant ate our lunch on folding chairs in the wardroom passage. The Captain and the Chief shared the 'settee', while the second engineer and first lieutenant faced one another at either end of the table.

The Captain was wearing a shapeless pull-over of indefinable hue. He had exchanged his field-grey shirt for a red-checked monstrosity whose collar protruded from the V-neck. While the steward was serving he sat back in his corner, arms folded, and gravely studied the deckhead as though its plywood panelling held some peculiar interest for him.

The second engineer, a lieutenant, was new on board and scheduled to relieve the Chief after this patrol. He was a blond North German with broad, rather rough-hewn features, though I could see little more than his profile while the meal lasted. He looked straight ahead and kept his mouth firmly shut.

The Chief sat opposite me, a slim and gaunt-faced man who looked even thinner alongside the Captain. I saw an aquiline nose which clearly revealed its underlying bone structure, dark hair combed straight back, a high forehead emphasized by a receding hair-line, very dark eyes, prominent cheek- and temporal bones, full curving lips and a firm jaw. The men called him Don Antonio, because after every patrol he cultivated his pointed black beard, before resolving to desecrate it with a razor.

The Chief had been with U-A from the start. He was the second most important man on board and an absolute ruler in matters technical. His realm was completely divorced from that of the watch-keeping officers and his action station in the control-room.

'Good value, the Chief,' was the Captain's verdict. 'Keeps a perfect depth when he has to. Does it by instinct. The new man'll never hold a candle to him – hasn't got the feel. Knowing your stuff isn't everything. You have to sense the boat's reactions and react yourself before anything happens. Experience plus instinct. Either you've got it or you haven't.'

Watching him as he sat there beside the Captain, with his slender mobile hands, dreamy eyes and smooth expanse of long dark hair, I could visualize the Chief as anything but what he was: a croupier or crap-shooter, a violinist or matinée idol of the silent era. From his build, he might even have been a dancer. He wore light plimsolls instead of sea-boots and a sort of track-suit in place of regulation submariner's gear. He was a champion negotiator of bulkhead doors. I had seen the control-room PO stare after him that morning, wagging his head in admiration. 'Squirms through the boat like a fucking eel . . .'

I knew from the Captain that, for all his racehorse tension, the Chief was an imperturbable man. Seldom seen in the flotilla during refit, he spent all day on board and supervised every detail in person. 'You can't put a light bulb into this boat without the Chief breathing down your neck. He'd sooner die than trust a dockyard matey.'

The second lieutenant was known by the men as 'Short-arse' or 'Babyface' because of his small stature and youthful appearance. Like the Captain and the Chief, he was no stranger to me.

The second lieutenant was just as conscientious as the Chief. His face, which wore an alert and faintly sly expression, quickly broke into dimples when he smiled.

The first lieutenant had only one patrol to his credit. I nardly ever saw him in the mess while U-A was refitting. The Captain's manner towards him and the second engineer was constrained, alternating between deliberate reserve and exaggerated affability.

In contrast to the second lieutenant, our Number One was a pale, lanky, colourless young man with the impassive face of a sheep. He offset his lack of self-confidence by acting with excessive sped and zeal. I soon summed him up as someone who, being devoid of native wit, performed his duties by the book. His ears, which were peculiarly underdeveloped, had almost non-existent lobes, and his nostrils were thin slits. Altogether, his face made an unfinished impression. He also had a strangely disagreeable habit of casting quick sidelong glances without moving his head. When the Captain ventured a joke, his usual response was an acid smirk.

'Things must be in a pretty bad way if we have to put to sea with schoolboys and overgrown members of the Hitler Youth,' the Captain had muttered to himself in the Bar Royal. I took him to indicate the first lieutenant.

'Pass your mugs,' ordered the Captain, and poured tea for everyone. There was no room on the table, so I had to clamp the teapot between my thighs and eat my lunch over the top. It was almost too hot to endure.

The Captain sipped his tea with obvious enjoyment. He huddled still farther into his corner and drew up his knees until he could prop them against the table-edge. Then he looked at us in turn, nodding gently like a father content with his offspring.

A malicious glint came into his eyes and his mouth widened as the second lieutenant was ousted from his seat for the umpteenth time. I had to follow suit, of course, complete with teapot, because the chef wanted to pass through the ward-room on his way forward.

The chef was a sturdy little runt of a man with a neck as wide as his head. He gave me a trustful grin which split his face ear to ear. I had a suspicion that his only motive for appearing at this particular moment was to collect a pat on the back for the meal.

'Remind me to tell you a story about him sometime,' the Captain said, chewing, when he had disappeared.

The intercom crackled. 'First watch, patrol routine.'

The first lieutenant stood up and ceremoniously prepared himself for the bridge. The Captain watched in interested silence as he pulled on his bulky cork-soled sea-boots, wound a scarf round his neck with extreme care, and, finally, muffled himself in his thickly lined leather jacket. He took his leave with military punctilio.

The quartermaster, whose watch it had been, came to report a minute later. His face was reddened by the elements. 'Wind nor'-west, veering, sir. Visibility good, barometer 1003.'

Then he forced us to our feet again because he wanted to get changed in the CPOs' mess.

Kriechbaum had also been with U-A since she commissioned. He had never served on a surface ship, only on a series of submarines that went back to the small internally tanked boats of years ago.

The quartermaster would never have made an actor. His facial muscles had a perceptible lack of elasticity which tended to give him a rigid, mask-like air, but his dark eyes, which were deep-set and screened by bushy eyebrows, brimmed with animation. Nothing escaped him. 'Eyes in the back of his bleeding head,' said a junior rating with admiration.

The Captain turned to me and lowered his voice so that he could not be heard next door. 'A dab hand at dead reckoning,

Kriechbaum. There've been times when we haven't seen the sun or stars for days – weeks, even – but he always plots our position to a whisker. I sometimes wonder how he manages it. Plenty to do on board. In charge of the third watch, quite apart from all the navigational crap.'

Close on the quartermaster's heels came the coxswain, Behrmann, thick-set and glowing with apple-cheeked health. He was followed, as though to demonstrate the contrast between seamen and engine-room personnel, by Johann, the pallid ERA. 'Christ Crucified,' the Old Man told me out of the corner of his mouth. 'A real expert – married to his engines and hardly ever sees the light of day. A typical denizen of the deep.'

After five minutes, three members of the new watch squeezed aft through the wardroom. I didn't care by this time, having quickly snaffled the first lieutenant's place when he got up.

'That was Ario,' said the Chief. 'The last one was – can't remember his name – anyway, Bäcker's replacement. They've already christened him the Vicar – he's got religious mania.'

It wasn't long before the men coming off watch filtered forward from the control-room. The Chief sat back and gave me a running commentary. 'That was Stoker Bachmann, otherwise known as Gigolo. Stoker . . . It still makes me laugh. There's nothing to stoke any more, but who cares? He's an electrician. Next, Turbo, the other control-room hand. Sound lad.'

A tall fair-haired man squeezed past in the opposite direction. 'Hacker, torpedo gunner's mate. Senior rating, fore-ends. The only PO who bunks there.'

'Worth his weight in gold,' said the Captain. 'He once dismantled a dud torpedo from the casing stowage and repaired it with quite a sea running – down below, of course. Our last fish, and we used it to sink a ten-thousand-tonner. Hacker's ship, strictly speaking. Won't be long before he gets his German Cross – he's earned it.'

The next man to traverse the wardroom was short and had very dark hair, neatly combed back. He grinned at the Chief with slit-eyed amiability. His forearms were tattooed. Fleetingly, I identified a sailor embracing a girl against a crimson sunset.

'That was Dunlop, torpedo-man. He's responsible for entertainment on board. The squeeze-box in the hydrophone booth belongs to him.'

ERA Franz was the last to appear. The Chief stared sombrely

after him. 'Flaps too easily. Johann – the other ERA – he's the better of the two.'

Lunch over, I made my way aft from the wardroom to the POs' mess.

The coxswain was a past master at stowing things away. He had distributed our stores so evenly and securely throughout the boat that her trim had not suffered and – as he proudly assured me – current necessities would come to hand before long-term requirements. No one but Behrmann himself knew where such vast quantities of provisions had vanished to. Only the cured sausages, sides of bacon and loaves of bread were immediately visible. Our store of sausages hung from the control-room deckhead, as though in a curing-room, and the fresh bread occupied nettings next to the hydrophone booth and wireless office. Anyone who passed the wireless office had to duck beneath a dangling mass of loaves.

I climbed through the after bulkhead. My bunk was now empty save for a neat array of gear on the blanket. My canvas bag of belongings lay at the foot. I was at liberty to draw the green curtain and exclude the outside world. Wooden panelling on one side, green curtain on the other, white paint overhead. Activity aboard was reduced to a blur of voices and sounds.

That afternoon I went on the bridge. The second lieutenant had just gone on watch. The sea was dark-green, or black in the vicinity of the boat. The air was moist and the sky completely overcast.

I stood beside the second lieutenant for some time before he addressed me from under his binoculars. 'They fired a salvo of four at us just about here. Last patrol but one. We saw one fish go by ahead and another astern. Gave me quite a turn . . .'

Small choppy waves danced on the low swell. Peaceful though the water looked, an enemy periscope could have lurked in the shadow of any one of these short waves.

'Have to keep our eyes skinned here,' the second lieutenant said again.

The Captain emerged from the conning-tower. He growled an oath at the weather. 'On your toes, for God's sake! This isn't my favourite spot.'

He gave a sudden snarl at the starboard after look-out, who was pea-green.

'They ought to drape you over a washing-line! Keep it

down, can't you? Like it or lump it, you've got to find your sea-legs some time.'

He scheduled a trim dive for 1600. After her long refit the submarine was to dive and be trimmed so that no excessive blowing or flooding would be required in an emergency. It was also necessary to check the watertightness of all hull valves and openings.

The exercise was heralded by the order 'Clear the bridge!' The anti-aircraft ammunition vanished down the conning-tower. The bridge emptied except for the officer of the watch and the three look-outs.

Orders, reports, bell-signals. The main engines were stopped and clutched out, the electric motors run at full speed. As the engines stopped, so the large outboard exhaust and air induction valves were shut. The engine-room informed the control-room that it was ready to dive. The fore-ends also reported a state of readiness. The look-outs had already gone below. Looking up the conning-tower, I saw the officer of the watch hurriedly spinning the handwheel that clamped the upper lid against its seating.

'Check main vents,' called the Chief. The men at the ballast-tank vent levers reported in quick succession: 'Five!' – 'Three port and starboard!' – 'One-' – 'All main vents clear!'

'Dive dive dive! Open all main vents!' came the order from above. 'Twenty metres.'

The control-room hands opened the main vent levers. The air that had given the boat her buoyancy escaped from the main ballast tanks with a thunderous roar. The planesmen put the foreplanes hard-a-dive and the afterplanes at 10 degrees of dive. The boat became noticeably bow-down, the needle of the depth-gauge crept slowly round the numerals on its dial. A last wave buffeted the conning-tower, and then, quite suddenly, the sounds of the sea died: an oppressive hush – not a wave-beat, no engine vibration. The bridge had dipped below the surface.

I did my best to note every detail. There might come a time when I should have to make the right move.

The Chief was still giving orders. 'Foreplanes ten degrees of rise, afterplanes fifteen degrees of rise.' The bow-down angle decreased. Deflected by the elevated hydroplanes, the waterstream from our screws gradually tilted the bow upwards. This emptied the ballast tanks of their last lingering air bubbles, which might have created unwanted buoyancy.

'Boat trimmed, sir,' the Chief reported to the Captain.

'Very good. Shut main vents.'

The vents on top of the main ballasts were shut from the control-room by means of handwheels.

'Thirty metres,' ordered the Captain. He was lolling back against the chart-table on his elbows.

The Chief was standing behind the two planesmen, where he could keep an eye on the hydroplane indicators, depth-gauges, inclinometers, tank gauges and sea-water temperature gauge.

The needle of the depth-gauge revolved: 15 metres, 20, 25. The gentle hum of the electric motors seemed to come from very far away. Somewhere, water dripped into the bilge with a thin, forlorn sound. A wary expression appeared on the Chief's face. He detached himself from the chart-stowage and started to search among the pipes on the port side with a torch. The dripping stopped of its own accord.

A vibration like a cold shudder ran through the boat.

The Captain seemed quite uninterested in what was going on. But for the sporadic flick of an eyelid in this direction or that, he might have been day-dreaming.

The needle of the gauge was approaching the 30-metre mark. It slowed and stopped. The submarine's compensating and trimming tanks had swallowed enough water to keep her suspended like an airship, but she was not yet horizontal. We had an appreciably bow-up angle.

The Chief re-trimmed. 'Pump 100 litres forward!' Turbo, the control-room hand, spun a handwheel behind the periscope.

The Chief gave more plane orders. U-A now rose without the need to blow any tanks. Very slowly, the depth-gauge needle crept back across its dial. The required depth was maintained simply by inclining our hydroplanes to the water-stream – dynamically.

The planesmen received an occasional adjustment from the Chief. Eventually the Captain broke his silence. 'Periscope depth.' He straightened up with a jerk and climbed ponderously into the conning-tower.

'Foreplanes up twenty, afterplanes down five,' ordered the Chief.

The column of water in the Papenberg slowly descended. The Chief leant sideways and raised his head. 'Periscope depth!' he called up the conning-tower.

Every rise or fall of the water in the Papenberg betokened a change in the submarine's depth. The planesmen's job was to counteract any tendency to rise or fall by adjusting the hydroplanes in good time. If they were too slow, either the periscope protruded too far and might betray our position to the enemy during an attack, or it would dip below the surface and blind us at the crucial moment.

The Chief's eyes, like those of the planesmen, were glued to the Papenberg. The column of water was almost stationary. Absolute silence reigned, broken only by an occasional hum as the Captain extended or retracted the periscope.

'Look-outs stand by. On oilskins,' came the Captain's voice. The look-outs tied sou'westers under their chins and pulled on oilskin jackets, then assembled beneath the lower hatch.

'Stand by to surface!'

Aft, the stokers primed their engines for prompt starting.

'Surface!' came the order from above.

The Chief put the foreplanes hard-a-rise and the afterplanes up five. Then he ordered 'Blow all main ballast!'

Compressed air forced water from the ballast tanks with a hollow rumble.

'Equalize pressure,' said the Captain.

I felt a sudden constriction in my ears as the excess pressure dwindled. Cool air streamed into the submarine from overhead: the upper lid was open. The fans were switched on and began to suck mighty draughts of sea-air into the boat's interior.

A series of engine orders followed.

'Stand by port engine.'

'Port engine ready.'

'Stop port motor. In port engine clutch.'

'Slow ahead port.'

The Q tanks were reflooded. Then the Captain ordered: 'Blow to full buoyancy with diesel.'

The engine exhausts began to expel water from the main ballast tanks. From the bridge, the Captain looked for the exhaust-bubbles along the sides which would tell him that each main ballast tank was fully blown. A few minutes later he called down: 'All main ballast tanks blown. Fall out from diving stations. Patrol routine.'

U-A had risen farther out of the water and become a surface vessel once more.

The Chief stood up and stretched each limb in turn. 'Well?' he said, eyeing me quizzically.

I replied with a submissive nod and sank on to a sack of potatoes beside the chart-stowage. The Chief took a handful of prunes from the communal crate that stood next to the chart-table and held them out. 'Here, fortify yourself. Quite a lot to absorb, first time out on a VII-C.'

'Bound to have some more fun and games today,' he continued in a low voice when the Captain had come below and vanished into his cubby-hole. 'Toning up, the Old Man calls it. He doesn't miss a trick – watches every last man. He only has to catch someone fumbling and we're in for one exercise after another.'

The chart was sandwiched between the tabletop and a thick sheet of celluloid. It still showed a strip of coastline. The inland areas were blank and uninhabited-looking: no roads, no towns – a map for sailors. Dry land held no significance for us except as a vehicle for the odd fix point, light and radio beacon, but every shoal and sand-bank in the estuaries was carefully marked.

Although our mean course was 300 degrees, I heard a series of steering orders. We couldn't yet afford to steer a straight course for fear of British submarines.

In the control-room, a stoker off watch was chatting to Turbo, the control-room hand, who had preserved a reddish beard from his time ashore and looked like a sugar-beet.

'Wonder where we're off to this time.'

'Iceland, from the look of it.'

'No, south's my bet. A long patrol down south. Look at all the stuff we've taken aboard.'

'Doesn't mean a thing. North or south, who cares? You can't get off and dip your wick either way.'

Turbo had done several patrols in U-A. With the blasé air of an old pro, he smirked through his hairy undergrowth and slapped the other man indulgently on the back. 'Cape Hatteras by moonlight, Iceland in the fog – join the Navy and see the world, that's us.'

Before supper the Captain ordered a deep dive to test the hull valves and glands at greater depths.

VII-C U-boats were tested to a depth of 90 metres. However, since the effect of depth-charges diminished the deeper they exploded, they often found it necessary to go far deeper. Nobody knew for sure what the pressure hull would withstand. Knowledge of the precise depth at which a submarine collapsed could only stem from one last lethal experience.

The morning's series of diving orders was repeated, but instead of levelling off at 30 metres we went steadily deeper. A deathly hush descended on the control-room.

There was a sudden high-pitched whistle, awesome and ear-splitting. I intercepted one or two apprehensive glances, but the Captain made no move to halt our downward progress.

The depth-gauge registered 150 metres.

More whistling, mingled with a dull scraping sound.

'Idyllic,' muttered the Chief. He had sucked in his cheeks and was plying the Captain with eloquent glances.

'She's got to be able to take it,' the Captain said tersely. It dawned on me that we were scuffling our shoes on the sea-bed.

'Just testing our nerves,' whispered the Chief.

The din persisted.

The Chief scowled. 'The pressure hull can take it, but the screws and rudder . . .' The Captain behaved as if he hadn't heard.

Mercifully the whining and scraping stopped. The Chief's face was grey.

The Captain winked at me. 'Things sound five times as loud under water,' he said consolingly. 'Hell of a row, but it doesn't mean much.'

The Chief sucked air into his lungs like a drowning man. The Captain favoured him with an interested stare before addressing the control-room at large. 'Right, that's it for today. Thirty metres.'

Ten minutes later the litany of orders for surfacing ran its course. The needle of the depth-gauge revolved anti-clockwise.

The Captain and the bridge watch-keepers went on deck. I followed them up and stationed myself abaft the bridge in the 'conservatory'. There was plenty of room round the quadruple 20mm, anti-aircraft guns. I looked down through the conservatory rail. Although we were only travelling at cruising speed, the water seethed and swirled violently. Myriads of white bubbles danced along, skeins of foam ravelled and unravelled themselves in quick succession. I felt as if I were alone on an iron raft. The wind jostled me, the metal deck vibrated beneath my feet. Ever-changing patterns scurried past. I had to wrench my eyes away for fear of becoming mesmerized.

Suddenly, from behind me, I heard the Captain's deep, drawling voice. 'Pretty, isn't it?'

He performed his usual soft-shoe shuffle, like a dancing bear – 'limbering up', he termed it.

I screwed up my eyes as the setting sun broke through a gap in the clouds.

'A pleasure cruise in wartime – what more could a man want?' He glanced over his shoulder and back again. 'They don't come any tougher than a VII-C – or with longer legs.'

We both stared aft at the wake.

The Captain gave a wry chuckle. 'Classic symbol of impermanence, a ship's wake. Here one minute, gone the next.'

I couldn't bring myself to look at him. 'Hot air' would have been his verdict on such a profundity if someone else had uttered it, but he actually pursued his line of thought a stage further. 'Good old mother earth is a bit more considerate. At least she strings us along.'

I made a noncommittal noise, but he was off again. 'It's true. She lets us think we've immortalized ourselves on her surface with monuments and inscriptions. They take a little longer to obliterate, that's all – a few thousand years, at most.'

My toes curled with embarrassment. 'Sad, isn't it?' was all I could thing of to say.

'Depends how ambitious you are,' he said, and grinned full in my face.

My first night on board. I tried to make myself heavy inside, wipe every thought from my mind. Sleep surged over me and swept me along, but before I could nestle properly into its depths I was cast up on the shore. Was I asleep or awake? Oppressive heat, the stench of oil, fine vibrations penetrating my mattress. The excitements of the last few hours helped to banish sleep again and again.

The engines pounded all night. Every change of watch disturbed me. Every time the bulkhead door swung open or clanged shut, I was back with a jerk from the frontiers of sleep.

Waking in U-A was very different from waking aboard a conventional ship. Instead of the scuttles which blessed one with a view of the foaming brine, windowless compartments hideously lit by naked bulbs.

I was heavy-headed, leaden-skulled with engine fumes. The blare of radio music had already been twanging my nerves for half an hour.

Below me I could see two bent backs but no room for my foot as it groped for a foothold. If I wanted to leave my bunk now I should have to step between half-empty plates and lumps of white bread sodden with coffee. The whole table was a sticky mess. The sight of the pallid scrambled eggs made my gorge rise.

A stench of oil drifted in from the engine-room.

'For Chrissake, man, shut that door!'

I should have quit my bunk earlier. I couldn't very well trudge through their breakfast, so I lay back and listened.

'Shift your fat butt, can't you? I can hardly breathe.'

'This fucking scrambled egg! I can't take the powdered stuff – it's like something out of a nappy.'

'What do you expect us to do, turn the control-room into a henhouse?'

I was tickled by the idea of poultry perched on the flooding panel. At once, I could see deck-plates smeared with greenish-white droppings and hear the birds' idiotic cackling above the roar of the engines. Chickens had always revolted me as a child and still did. The chromosome-smell of broody hens' feathers, the pale yellow skin, the floppy combs . . .

'Sure, and keep ducks in the bilge – miniature ones. We could feed them on maggots.'

'Do you mind! I'm trying to eat.'

'What's wrong with maggots? Think how the ducks'd enjoy tucking in every morning. Lovely fresh grub like that . . .'

I choked back an urge to vomit.

For a while I heard nothing but chomping and lip-smacking. Then came a reverberant belch which ended on a strangled note as though something solid had tried to sneak out with it.

'Jesus fucking Christ!'

'Yes, belt up, you crude bastard. You're spoiling my appetite.'

The loudspeakers were flooding the boat with sound. *'Underneath the lamplight, by the barrack gate . . .'*

The loudspeakers could be turned down low but never switched off entirely because they were also used to transmit orders. That left us at the mercy of the PO telegraphist who was operating the turntable in his cubby-hole. He seemed to have a thing about Lilli Marlene – this was her second time around in half an hour.

I shuddered at the thought that it was really only 4 or 5 a.m. To save conversion in W/T messages, we kept German Summer Time. What was more, we had already travelled far enough west of the zero meridian for the sun to be more than an hour behind ship's time. Not that it really mattered when we made the day begin: the bowels of U-A were artificially lit day and night, and the alternation of watch on, watch off, occurred at intervals that were independent of daylight.

It was time to emerge from the womb. I said 'Excuse me' and insinuated my foot between the men on the bunk below me.

'All good things come from above,' I heard PO Electrician Pilgrim say.

While I was looking for my shoes, which I had wedged between two pipes for safety's sake, I conducted a morning conversation with Isenberg, the control-room PO, who was sitting beside me on a folding stool.

'Well, how does it look?'

'So so, Lieutenant.'

'Barometer?'

'Rising.'

Carefully, I picked some blanket fluff out of my stubble. The comb I drew across my scalp came away black. My hair had separated the solids from the oil fumes like a filter.

I rummaged in my locker for some soap and a flannel. I should have preferred to perform my morning ablutions in the heads, but a quick glance through the forward bulkhead showed that this was impossible: the red light was on. I confined myself to rubbing the sleep out of my eyes and pocketed the soap and toothbrush for later use.

The red light was a brainwave of the Chief's. It came on as soon as the bolt was engaged from within – one of those minor but welcome pieces of improvisation which mitigated the hardships of daily life. No longer did anyone have to work his way along the narrow passage from one end of the boat to the other, gnawed by doubt and uncertainty, only to find himself confronted by a bolted door.

The Chief returned from a morning visit to the engine-room, his oily hands inadequately wiped on a hank of cotton waste. The first lieutenant was nowhere to be seen, likewise the second engineer. The Captain was probably having a wash and the second lieutenant was on watch.

The chef had been woken at 0600. In addition to some thin yellow scrambled egg, which reached the table cold, there was bread, butter and black coffee, known as 'nigger's sweat'. My stomach firmly rebelled against the last. The churning and rumbling in my guts redoubled in intensity. I peered to see if the heads were vacant at last.

'Not hungry?' enquired the Chief.

'It's the look of the stuff, more than anything.'

'Try cleaning your teeth – it might help,' the Chief said, masticating vigorously. The Captain emerged from his quarters. There were spots of toothpaste on his cheeks and his beard was dark with moisture. He said 'Morning, you unwashed lot', squeezed into his corner and stared at nothing in particular.

Nobody spoke.

We were in the thick of the morning traffic. Not a minute went by but someone had to pass the wardroom on his way forward or aft. Thanks to my location on a folding chair in the passage, this kept me bobbing up and down like a yo-yo. The exercise did nothing to ease the turmoil in my guts. I mentally cursed whoever was taking so long in the heads.

No problem would have arisen if it weren't for the morning rush-hour, if demand were evenly spread. It was the same at midnight when the bridge and engine-room watches were relieved simultaneously. Last night in the control-room I had seen the tail-enders doubled up as though someone had kicked them in the stomach.

The heads door opened at last. It was the first lieutenant! I grabbed my things with lightning speed and almost wrenched the door out of his hand. The little fresh-water tap above the basin, which at best never yielded more than a trickle, wasn't working. I turned on the salt-water tap and worked up a thin lather with the sea-water soap but couldn't face using it for teeth-cleaning purposes. I returned to the wardroom to find its occupants still sitting round the table in silence, taking their cue from the Captain.

'*Boom*,' the loudspeaker demanded in a marshmallow voice, '*why does my heart go boom . . .*'

The Chief gave an audible sigh and rolled his eyes like a fifth-rate comedian.

I rinsed a good swig of coffee round my mouth till it went frothy, forced the brown juice through my teeth from behind, sent it gurgling into the gap left by a missing molar, swilled it from the right cheek-pouch to the left until all sputum crusts and oil deposits had been washed away, and swallowed the resulting beverage, phlegm and all. My breathing improved. A vigorous snort, a discreet hawk, a quick gulp, and the whole lot disappeared down my throat. My nasal and laryngeal passages were clear. Even the 'nigger's sweat' tasted better now. The Chief had a point.

After breakfast the Captain settled down with ill-disguised reluctance to write up his patrol report, having ordered officers' instructions for an hour later. The Chief vanished aft and the first lieutenant busied himself with some paper-work.

Passing through the control-room on my way aft, I saw the round orifice of the upper hatch, still filled with nocturnal blackness. The air that came from above was cold and damp. Although I didn't feel the slightest inclination to go on deck,

I braced myself and set one foot on the aluminium ladder.

I came level with the helmsman, who was sitting hunched over his dimly glowing disc in the conning-tower.

'Man on the bridge?'

'Affirmative,' came the second lieutenant's voice.

I poked my head over the hatch coaming and bade him good morning.

It was some time before my eyes grew accustomed to the darkness and I could make out the horizon. A few pale stars still twinkled high overhead. Fingers of red light crept slowly up the eastern sky and the horizon became more distinct. Very gradually the water paled too.

I shivered.

The quartermaster came up on the bridge. He looked round silently, cleared his nose, and called for the sextant.

'Stop-watch ready?' he shouted down the hatch in a hoarse voice.

'Yes,' came the muffled response.

Kriechbaum aimed his instrument at Saturn and applied his right eye to the eyepiece. He stood there for a while with his head tilted and his face screwed up. Then he lowered the sextant, simultaneously adjusting the micrometer screw: he brought Saturn down from the sky and on to the horizon.

'Stand by – Saturn – now!' he called below.

Down in the control-room, a stop-watch clicked. The quartermaster had difficulty reading off the figures in the dawn light. 'Twenty-two degrees thirty-five minutes,' he reported.

The combination of time and altitude would yield a position line on which the submarine must lie. A position line did not pinpoint a ship's position, however. For that, a second fix was required.

Kriechbaum aimed his sextant anew.

'Stand by – Jupiter – now!'

A pause, then: 'Forty-two degrees twenty-seven minutes.'

He carefully handed down the sextant and climbed through the hatch. I followed him below. He pulled off his jacket and bent over the chart-table. The quartermaster had no spacious chart-house like the navigating officer of a big ship. He had to make do with the tiny table in the control-room, fixed to the port side amid a jumble of switches, pipes and valves. Above it was a locker for the sextant and star-globe, and beside it a shelf containing nautical tables and navigation manuals, altitude-azimuth tables, tide tables, sailing directions, light lists, weather manuals and monthly charts.

Kriechbaum took a pencil and scribbled some calculations.

He was on intimate terms with sines and cosines, tangents, haversines and their respective logarithms.

'Quite consoling, really,' I said, just to puncture the silence. 'I mean, the fact that we still make use of the stars.'

'I don't follow you.'

'I only mean, with all the technological perfection on board, it seems odd to determine our position with a sextant . . .'

'Can you think of a better way, Lieutenant?'

I subsided, realizing that my remarks were out of place. Perhaps it was too early in the day.

The quartermaster raised the celluloid sheet covering the chart. It was a uniform blue-grey. No fringe of coast, no shallows – just a dense mosaic of squares, letters and figures.

With the dividers between his teeth, Kriechbaum murmured: 'There we are. Bit of a set – all of fifteen miles.' He clicked his tongue and drew a pencil-line between our last position and the new fix, then tapped a neighbouring square on the chart with his knuckle.

'Had quite a party there. It was nearly "Off caps".'

Evidently, the quartermaster was anxious to show that he could, after all, be inveigled into a little small-talk. He took his dividers and jabbed the spot where the 'party' had occurred.

The control-room PO came across and stared over his shoulder.

'On our fourth patrol, it was – a real swine. Force 10 a lot of the time, and they were after us from the start. Counterattacks all day long. We almost lost count . . .'

Kriechbaum kept his eyes fixed on the dividers-points as if traces of the engagement might still be visible. Then he drew a deep breath, shut the dividers and laid them brusquely aside.

'No joke, I can tell you.'

I knew better than to expect any more. So did Isenberg, who stopped eavesdropping. Kriechbaum carefully laid the sextant to rest in its case. The dividers had left a tiny hole in the chart.

The quartermaster's sou'wester, rubber jacket and binoculars were hanging on a hook. He took them down and prepared to go on watch.

Rather than obstruct the morning traffic, which was still heavy, I decided to pay another visit to the bridge.

The clouds were sharply outlined now – marquetry shapes let into a dove-grey sky. One of them drifted across the sun, and its shadow destroyed the sea's greenish-white luminescence. The cloud was so big that its lower edge seemed to dip below the skyline, but there were rents in it through which the sun fired oblique shafts of light at the sea. One of them headed straight for the boat, and for a while we were caught in the beam of a celestial searchlight.

'Aircraft on the port beam!'

PO Dorian's yell jolted me like an electric shock. In the second it took me to reach the upper lid, I glimpsed a dark speck against a grey background of cloud. The clip of the lower lid caught my shins, almost making me cry out with pain. As I dropped through I distinctly caught sight of the leather sheath with which the protruding iron handles should have been protected.

Landing heavily, I leapt aside too late. The next man was already on his way. One of his boots slammed into my neck. I heard Dorian hit the deck-plates with a thud.

'Bloody close!' he gasped, chest heaving.

The Captain was already standing beneath the conning-tower with his mouth open, staring up.

'Dive dive dive!' the second lieutenant shouted down. The main vents were opened. Water cascaded from the lower lid as the dripping figure of the second lieutenant dropped through.

The needle of the depth-gauge turned slowly, as though overcoming stiff resistance. The submarine seemed glued to the surface.

'All hands forward!' bellowed the Chief.

Men rushed forward through the control-room in a blundering, crouching cavalcade. The bow went down and the boat tilted until I was forced to hang on to preserve my footing.

The second lieutenant reported breathlessly to the Captain: 'It was coming from the port beam, sir, through a gap in the clouds. Couldn't identify the type.'

I saw in my mind's eye the black speck and grey background, then a close-up of bomb-doors opening.

My breathing faltered. The Captain's eyes never left the depth-gauge. His face was impassive, almost indifferent. Water dripped into the bilge, tip-tap, tip-tap. The motors hummed gently.

A chest-constricting minute of expectancy. Finally, a cautious breath.

Nothing?

'First watch, patrol routine,' ordered the Chief. The men worked their way back against the angle, hand over hand like mountaineers.

'Both planes to rise.'

I straightened, breathing deeply. A sharp pain shot through my leg. I didn't realize until then how hard I had hit the clip.

'Very good,' said the Captain. 'Thirty metres.'

'Bloody hell,' muttered Kriechbaum.

The Captain was standing in the middle of the control-room, hands in pockets. He had pushed his cap to the back of his head.

'They've pinpointed us now. Let's hope they don't bring a whole armada down on us.' He turned to the Chief. 'We'd better stay deep for the time being.' Then, to me: 'I told you yesterday – they know exactly when we leave harbour. Now we'll suffer for it.'

The second aircraft alarm came some hours later, during the quartermaster's watch. He shouted 'Alarm aircraft, starboard!' and again I glimpsed a speck in the grey, a hand's breadth above the skyline. The next instant I was sliding down the metal ladder with my hands and feet curled round the uprights.

Kriechbaum yelled from above: 'Dive dive dive!'

I saw him hanging from the handwheel of the upper lid, feet scrabbling for a hold. At last the hatch was secured.

'Five!' – 'Three port and starboard!' – 'One!' The control-room hands swung the vent levers open. Water gurgled angrily into the main ballast tanks. 'Aircraft on the starboard bow, distance three thousand metres,' Kriechbaum reported. 'Not coming straight towards.'

More breath-retention.

'Going down well,' reported the Chief, and soon afterwards: 'Blow Q!' The quick-dive tanks were blown with HP air. Holding five tons, they were kept flooded on the surface and gave the submarine that extra weight which helped her to overcome surface tension quickly when diving. Now she was too heavy by the same five tons. HP air was released with an explosive roar and water escaped outboard, rumbling fiercely.

Still no bombs.

Only thirty seconds could have passed since we dipped below the surface, but the swirl that formed at the point of diving remained visible for about five minutes – an aiming-mark for depth-charges . . .

Still nothing.

The Captain expelled a deep breath. Kriechbaum discreetly followed suit. The control-room PO caught my eye and gave an infinitesimal nod.

At 80 metres the Chief gave some gentle plane orders. U-A took a slight bow-up angle and levelled off.

'Boat trimmed,' he reported. 'Shut main vents.'

'Very good,' said the Captain.

We stood around in silence for a good five minutes. Eventually the Captain ordered periscope depth. Both sets of planes were put hard-a-rise and the motors ordered half-ahead.

Then something which surprised me: the Chief gave a flooding order although the submarine was supposed to be rising. It was only a matter of 50 litres, but the order seemed illogical. I had to think hard before I remembered: the hull expanded as pressure decreased nearer the surface. The boat's increased volume increased her buoyancy, so she had to be made heavier to offset this and prevent her rising too quickly. If a submarine was to be held at a required depth she had to be trimmed with precision, her weight equalling that of the water she displaced.

The Captain scratched his head. 'Maybe they didn't spot us after all.'

The third aircraft alarm came several hours later. This time it was the first lieutenant who yelled 'Dive dive dive!' He dropped to the control-room deck, chest heaving. 'Came straight out of the sun . . .'

The bow didn't tilt fast enough for the Captain's taste. 'All hands forward!'

Another sliding, slithering stampede through the control-room – anything for a rapid descent.

The Chief employed an additional trick to accelerate the bow-down angle. He didn't vent the after main ballast tank until U-A had already tilted with the aid of the hydroplanes, all of which were set hard-a-dive. In other words, he had momentarily used its buoyancy to help point the boat downwards.

'Every time a winner,' muttered the first lieutenant, when a reassuring interval had elapsed.

'Don't speak too soon,' the Captain said reprovingly.

The Chief wagged his head. 'They're getting above themselves these days. No manners.'

'We'll stay down for a while,' said the Captain. 'Can't all be as lucky as Kramer.'

We retired to the wardroom. 'Good for Number One,' said the Captain – loud enough for it to be heard in the control-room. The first lieutenant had earned this tribute by spotting the aircraft in good time. Not easy, when some crafty aviator flew at you out of the sun. Nine times out of ten it was sea-gulls. They glided towards the boat on stiffly spread wings, just above the skyline, and you found yourself yelling before the truth dawned. Deception could be complete, too, especially when the glittering surface seared your eyeballs like molten glass.

'Always turn to windward, with aircraft,' the Captain said. 'Number One did the right thing. The plane gets excess wind on its inclined wings. That deflects it outwards – not much, but every metre counts.'

'To windward. I'll make a note of that.'

'Can't help taking my hat off to the flyers they're sending out these days.'

The Captain chewed his lower lip and nodded a couple of times, eyes narrowed. 'Stuck up there miles from anywhere, but they still go for us like bats out of hell. What's to stop them dropping their eggs in the drink and emptying their belts into thin air – who's going to see?'

He continued to sing the praises of the RAF. 'Those bomber pilots who raid the base – they're no slouches either. How many was it we brought down last time?'

'Eight,' I said. 'One of them almost landed on our roof at La Baule – right among the fir-trees. I'll never eat brains on toast again.'

'Why's that?'

'There were three men still inside. The cockpit was com-pletely ripped open. They'd brought their sandwiches along. Snow-white bread with roast beef and lettuce in the middle. The pilot's brains were draped over one of them. I wanted to salvage some papers – anything – but the plane was already burning. Then the ammunition started to go off and I had to run for it.'

I picked up a seamanship manual and tried to read. After a while, I heard the Captain's voice again. 'The pilot who got the *Gneisenau* must have been quite a lad. No sandwiches, just a pocketful of French letters . . .'

I laid the book aside.

'Maybe he planned to celebrate by dipping his wick in the Rue de la Paix,' said the Chief. 'Practical folk, the Canadians.'

The Captain grinned. 'He was unlucky. All the same, what a performance! He glided down in spirals. Nobody spotted him at first – no AA barrage, not a single shot. Found the right angle and dropped his fish – a real circus act. Pity the poor bugger didn't make it. They say he hit the water like a stone. Well, gentlemen, let's see what the form is . . .'

I followed him and the Chief into the control-room.

The Chief reported: 'Ready to surface, sir.'

'Surface,' ordered the Captain, and climbed the ladder.

I heard the quartermaster muttering to himself. 'Let's hope the bloody flyers leave us in peace for a while.'

The control-room, half an hour before midnight. A gentle hum from the fans. The engines were sucking a stream of fresh air through the open conning-tower. The few lights were dimmed so that no tell-tale glow would betray us to an alert night-flyer. The boat seemed infinitely spacious in the gloom. All that could be seen in the uncertain pools of shadow was a line of phosphorescent green pointers designed to lead us to the conning-tower hatch in an emergency, if every light failed. These were a fairly recent innovation dating from Kallmann's disastrous collision with a Norwegian freighter in autumn 1940. His submarine, a small vessel with no watertight bulkheads, was rammed just abaft the control-room and ripped open so effectively that she sank in seconds. Only those on the bridge escaped. When the U-boat was raised – Kallmann had to be present – some of the crew were found jammed together in the control-room, but not beneath the hatch. They were on the other side of the periscope well – in quite the wrong place.

Phosphorescent pointers wouldn't do us much good in mid-Atlantic. If the boat foundered here she would hit bottom a couple of thousand metres below. The green arrows could phosphoresce down there as much as they liked.

The control-room looked immense. At one end, where the forward door stood open, a light punched a neat round hole in the gloom. The light came from the lamp in the wireless office and the bulb burning in the passage to the wardroom. Two men perched on the chart-stowage, were silhouetted against the glow. They were peeling potatoes. Barely visible, the duty control-room hand lolled against his desk and entered the contents of the trimming tanks in the control-room log. Bilge-water hissed and gurgled as it slopped to and fro beneath the deck-plates. The sound of the engines came muffled, as though by a filter, from beyond the two closed bulkhead doors abaft the POs' mess. The control-room was filled with a swelling, dying roar from the waves that brushed our sides.

I climbed through the forward bulkhead. The PO tele-graphist on watch was hunched over a book with his hands cupping the earphones of his head-set and his elbows propped on the flaps which supported the wireless sets each side of him. The green curtain opposite the W/T office was drawn, but light showed through the cracks. The Captain was probably at his usual pastime of writing letters which couldn't be posted until we returned to base.

The wardroom, too, looked much larger than it did at meal-times. The Chief was asleep on the bunk behind the table. Dangling from a short chain above his face, his watch swung irregularly back and forth.

Behind the curtain of the lower bunk on the port side, the first lieutenant wallowed in his remaining minutes of slumber. The fore-ends door clanged open. The Chief grunted, rolled over with his face to the lockers, and snored on. A tousle-haired man tottered aft into the wardroom and gave a bleary salute. He blinked irresolutely for a few seconds then drew the curtain of the first lieutenant's bunk. 'Twenty minutes to your watch, Lieutenant.'

The first lieutenant's face emerged from the shadowy depths of the bunk, stupefied with sleep. He laboriously extended a leg, shoved it over the aluminium leeboard and swung his body after it. Rather than irritate him by watching, I went farther forward.

The fore-ends was dimly lit by two low-powered bulbs. A heavy, acrid smell came to meet me : human sweat, oil, bilge-water, the effluvium of wet clothing.

Here in the bow, the pitching was at its most noticeable. Two mummified figures were suspended in hammocks slung abaft the torpedo-tube rear doors. I heard irate voices. 'Anti-social, that's what it is, turning us out in the middle of the fucking night . . .'

Two men appeared from the hammocks and another from one of the port-side bunks.

'Bloody hell!' That was Ario's voice.

The boat was rolling so heavily that they only donned their sea-boots after several vain attempts.

'Bit lumpy, isn't it?' said one of them. 'We'll get our feet wet again.' They fought their way into bulky sweaters and wound towels round their necks so that no water would penetrate the collars of the rubberized jackets that awaited them in the control-room.

The men of the old watch, who clambered stiffly below, were streaming with water. The quartermaster had his collar turned up and his sou'wester pulled down low. The faces of the others were scarlet with driven spray. Hanging their binoculars, they peeled off their wet jackets as silently as the new watch had donned their dry ones, but with awkward, ungainly movements. Then they helped each other to pull off their rubber leggings. The junior hand of the watch loaded himself with the entire bundle of wet oilskin trousers, jackets and sou'westers and toted it aft. The best place for drying was between the motors and on either side of the stern tube.

Hurriedly, the men just off watch gulped hot coffee, cleaned their binoculars and stowed them away.

'Well,' enquired Kriechbaum, 'still feeling chirpy?'

PO Wichmann went aft, the quartermaster and the two look-outs forward.

A sudden commotion in the control-room: the new engine-room watch was mustering. I recognized Stoker Ario and Electrician Zörner.

In the POs' mess, Wichmann had made himself comfortable and was chewing noisily.

I climbed into my bunk. I could hear the waves groping along the side, close to my head. An abrasive roar which swelled and ebbed, sometimes rising to a sharp hiss.

The door to the galley opened and Kleinschmidt and Rademacher appeared, hurling abuse.

'Leave some for us, fatso. You ought to see yourself — always stuffing your guts!'

'Get stuffed yourself.'

Peering round the edge of my curtain, I could see Wichmann uninhibitedly scratching his crotch. He even rose slightly for ease of access.

'Leave yourself alone, mate,' jeered Rademacher. 'There's nothing to screw round here.'

Wichmann turned on him. 'Belt up or I'll ram it down your throat.'

This exchange appeared to stir some chord of memory in Kleinschmidt. He sniggered so obtrusively that all eyes turned in his direction.

'Puts me in mind of something I saw in a Paris bistro,' he said. 'I was sitting there minding my own business, and opposite me was a nigger with a tart who kept fumbling around under the table. You know how they are in Paris — free and easy.'

Rademacher gave a nod of expert confirmation.

'All at once the nigger starts panting and rolling his eyes. Right, I say to myself, let's have a look. I pushed my chair back just in time to see the bugger come – all over my bleeding shoes!'

'You're joking!' said Wichmann.

'What did you do?' Rademacher wanted to know.

'Do? I picked up my bowl of onion soup and emptied it over the nigger's dong. You should have heard him holler! They took off like greased lightning, the pair of them.'

Rademacher was still marvelling. 'Jesus, the things you hear about . . .'

Wichmann, who seemed to have digested the story at last, leant back and wagged his head.

'The French are a filthy lot, when all's said and done.'

A snort of protest came from the midshipman's bunk, but the three table companions took no notice.

It was a good fifteen minutes before silence finally descended on the POs' mess.

The new control-room hand showed little promise and had already earned several reprimands from the control-room PO.

Most of the men were against him because he devoted his spare time to black-bound tracts instead of skylarking with the rest of the fore-ends comedians. He seemed to have completely isolated himself by his holier-than-thou manner, and his occasional essays in self-ingratiation were greeted with rebuffs such as 'Piss off, Vicar!' or 'Go find another bum to suck.'

Ario appeared to have a particular aversion for the new man.

'Him and his bloody airs! Muck in and toe the line, that's what he needs to do.'

Once, when I was down in the fore-ends, I learned from Ario that TGM Hacker's brother was in prison. He was twenty-two, only a year older than Hacker. Apparently, he had avenged himself on a troublesome neighbour by ringing five of his fruit-trees.

Ario put it this way: 'Circumcise a tree like that, and it's a goner.'

I raised by eyebrows. 'Surely they don't send you to prison for that?'

'These days they do. It's called "imperilling the dietary freedom of the German people" – sabotage, in a manner of speaking.'

Ordinary Seaman Schwalle, who had been listening to Ario's account, blurted out: 'Christ, he's done all right for himself.'

'How do you mean?'

'Well, nothing can happen to him in there, can it? I mean, he's fire-proof.'

Ario groped for a retort. 'Some attitude to take!'

Schwalle was unruffled. Calmly he took a big swig of fruit-juice from a china skull.

Crazy of the man to bring such a bulky thing aboard, I thought.

The ship's log described our first two days as follows:

Saturday	0800.	Sailed.
	1630.	Trim dive.
	1800.	Deep-diving trial.
Sunday	0746.	Aircraft alarm. Dived deep to evade.
	1055.	Aircraft alarm.
	1544.	Aircraft alarm.
	1605.	Set course for patrol area.

'You've still got eyes like an albino rabbit,' the Chief taunted me next day, our third at sea.

'Not surprising. The last few days have been pretty hectic.'

'More so for some than others. I gather you went to that binge at the Café Pompadour. The night before Thomsen got his gong, wasn't it?'

'That's right. You missed something. The way he sailed through that plate glass window . . .'

'Who did?'

'Scholle,' I said. 'You know who I mean – the naval architect who thinks he's so indispensable to the war effort. He started by waltzing in and buying drinks all round. The lads were still being fairly civil to him at that stage. Herr Scholle must have had a couple beforehand – he was obviously feeling his oats. There was no holding him.'

I could see the portly figure teetering to and fro, the hamster-like cheeks with beer froth round the mouth. 'Fantastic,' he chortled, 'simply fantastic, these magnificent successes of yours! Sterling chaps, chips off the old block. Yessir!' I could see the circle of contemptuous faces but Scholle was engrossed in his own rhetoric. 'Stiffen our backs, bring perfidious Albion to her knees – yessir! The boys in blue can rely on us – last drop of blood for the Fatherland – brothers-in-arms . . .'

'It was a bad case of verbal diarrhœa,' I told the Chief. 'Quotations from every propaganda article you ever read:

bloody but unbowed, stiff upper lip, shoulders to the wheel, etcetera. He obviously included himself – himself first and foremost. Good old Tieck had been simmering away for quite a while. He's an easy-going chap but when Scholle slapped him on the back and yelled, "Go to it!" and then capped it all by belching and saying "After all, what's a few depth-charges between friends?" Tieck finally blew his top. He went purple with rage and couldn't get a word out, but the others were on their feet in two seconds' flat. Table, chairs – everything went flying. They grabbed Scholle by the arms and legs and half-dragged him the length of the bar. I think they meant to kick him down the steps, but someone had a better idea. Maybe it was the sight of him suspended by his wrists and ankles like an overstuffed hammock. They got him parallel to the big glass window, still struggling and kicking. Then it was "One, two, three . . ." – and away he went. He sailed through the window and landed outside in the street. You should have heard the crash!'

I could still hear it myself, then the tinkle as a few slivers of the big pane belatedly followed Scholle on to the pavement. Somebody said 'That's that,' and the show was over. Without a word, the four men turned about and marched back to the table, where they dusted their hands off like labourers completing a dirty job.

They were just reaching for their glasses when someone gave a shout and pointed to the door. A bloodstained face loomed through the haze of tobacco-smoke.

'He's lost his Himmler specs!' said a voice.

The quartet staggered to their feet. Drunk as they were, they reached the door in a flash and dragged the naval architect, who was crawling along on his hands and knees, back across the threshold. He clung to the door-post, but one of them prised his hands free and slammed the door. 'That'll teach him, the stupid cunt!'

'What about the law?' enquired the Chief.

'The shore patrol turned up an hour later, when the ratings had the place to themselves. There was quite a punch-up. One of the shore patrol got a bullet in the thigh.'

'Pity he didn't get something else shot off,' said the Chief.

I knew why the Chief had such a thing about shore patrols and military police in general. It dated from a scene at a Paris station, when he was returning from leave. He and a lieutenant from U-Y had settled themselves comfortably in a first-class compartment and were dozing in the midday heat. The Chief had undone the bottom button of his jacket, the better

to lounge with legs extended. Then the door slid open. I re-called the Chief's account of it one night at the Bar Royal:
'I opened my eyes and saw this figure standing there, field-grey uniform, sweating face, piss-pot helmet, boots and spurs, riding-breeches – naturally – and a gun across his paunch – full war-paint, so to speak. His two side-kicks were staring through the corridor windows like dumb oxen. "Your travel warrant, Lieutenant," he said, "and kindly adjust your clothing. You're not on board ship here, you know." '

According to the Chief, he not only failed to secure the offending button but stood up and undid the rest. Then he chucked his papers at the guardian of military discipline and ostentatiously stuck his hands in his pockets.

'It was a treat to watch. He almost went pop. Bellowed at me like a bull: "I'll report you for this! I'll report you for this!" '

'Ah,' I said, 'so that's why they're thinking of replacing you – that's why they've assigned you an understudy. Flotilla Staff must have said to themselves: better axe that man. The Führer wouldn't approve of his example to the lower deck.'

I remembered how the Chief's mouth dropped open in surprise. Then he beamed like an illuminated Christmas tree. I had evidently struck the right note.

Monday night in the wardroom. I caught sight of the clock: 2000. I could hardly believe that it was only our third day at sea. Dry land seemed light-years away.

'Brushing up your mental arithmetic?' asked the Captain.

'Not exactly, sir. I was thinking about Thomsen.'

'Ah, that uniform . . . I hope he's chucked it away.'

TUESDAY, 4TH DAY AT SEA. The Chief seemed to be at a loose end for once. I seized the opportunity to extract some tech-nical tips. I only had to say 'It all sounds terribly complicated', and he was off.

'Complicated? You can say that again – a damn sight more complicated than it is in surface ships. They operate on the wash-tub principle. They've got a water-line corresponding to each loaded weight and degree of positive buoyancy. If they take on more weight, the tub sinks a bit on the load-line, but that's all. No cause for concern – at the worst, a case for the marine inspectors. With us, excess weight means a whole host of remedial measures . . .' The Chief paused and gave a couple of nervous blinks. I was afraid he might dry up altogether. I concentrated on his lips, but he kept me waiting.

I had always found it hard to comprehend the phenomenon of buoyancy – the fact that water could 'carry' things. Boats were a source of wonder to me as a child. Not wooden rowing-boats so much as steel-hulled ships – steel shells that could float on water! Then, one day beside the Elbe, I saw some concrete barges with sides as thick as air-raid shelters. It seemed incredible that such huge hunks of concrete not only floated but carried cargo.

A pontifical note crept into the Chief's voice. 'The basic difference is this: a normal ship derives buoyancy from the water displaced by her hull, whereas we get ours from the air in our tanks. We're kept on the surface by water-wings, so to speak – release the air, and we sink.'

He waited for me to nod intelligently.

'We have to watch our weight like a middle-aged woman. We don't have time to mess around in an emergency. Everything has to go like clockwork. That's why the boat must be trimmed for the dived condition in advance, both as to bodily weight and longitudinal and transverse balance – in other words, trimmed while she's still on the surface. That means balancing her by adjusting the amount of water in the trimming and compensating tanks so that, when we dive in an emergency, we only have to destroy the buoyancy of our main ballast tanks. Once the boat's submerged, she must be neutrally buoyant.'

He paused again. 'Are you with me?'

'All the way.'

'At the required depth, therefore, the boat's weight must equal that of the water she displaces. Being in a state of unstable equilibrium, she'll readily react to the waterstream over her control surfaces – that is, she can be manœuvred in any direction at very slow speeds, just by using the rudders and hydroplanes. She mustn't tend to rise or fall of her own accord, but her weight changes every day – food and water consumed, fuel used, and so on. The stupid thing is, the weight of the water she displaces can vary too, because the density of sea-water is nowhere near constant. In other words, nothing but variable factors at every turn. There's no end to the list. You get so you hardly dare cough.'

The Chief took a breather. He fetched a bottle of apple-juice from his locker, prised off the top with a hinge, and put it to his mouth.

He was off again almost before he'd wiped his lips. 'Most of our troubles stem from this variation in sea-water density. Everything would be plain sailing if we always dived in pure fresh water. We'd only have to increase the volume of water in our compensating and trimming tanks to match the consumption of food, oil and drinking-water – no sweat. Trouble is, salt-water conditions are downright perverse – no other way to describe them. In other words, there's sea-water and sea-water. That's why our buoyancy varies from one day to the next – from hour to hour, for that matter.'

He paused again for effect, glancing sideways to check my reaction.

'The density of sea-water is affected by all kinds of factors. Depth comes into it. So do temperature, time of year, currents, even vegetation or plankton. A slight increase in plankton and we have to blow. Then there's the sun.'

'The sun?' I looked duly surprised.

'Yes, sunlight causes evaporation and raises salt content near the surface, and increased salt content means greater density.'

'But the difference can only be minimal, surely?'

He knit his brows and pondered for a while. 'A change in the density of sea-water – let's say one thousandth part, or about 10 grammes per cubic metre, to keep it really minimal – means that the boat's weight must also be adjusted by one-thousandth to offset it. That's logical, isn't it? Fair enough. Assume the boat weighs 750 tons. One-thousandth of that is 750 kilograms, but a change of 750 kilos would mean we'd gravely miscalculated the contents of our compensating and trimming tanks. To keep the boat more or less neutrally buoyant we have to adjust her weight to within 5 kilos. I say "more or less" because it's impossible, in practice, to trim with such accuracy that she remains in perfect equilibrium without the aid of screws and planes. Overfill the tanks by half a litre – even a thimbleful – and the boat will sink; a thimbleful too little, and she'll rise. That's why we have to take daily hydrometer readings to check the specific gravity – and hence the density – of the water round us.'

The Chief savoured the dying echoes of his lecture with a hint of self-satisfaction, like a latter-day Newton.

The Captain, who must have been eavesdropping for some time, passed us on his way forward. 'Can I have that in writing, Professor?' he asked, before climbing through the bulkhead.

It was enough to stop the Chief in his tracks. He sounded quite plaintive when he next spoke. 'The Old Man isn't interested in anything except a perfect trim – not a litre too much, not a litre too little . . .'

He mimed exhaustion, but I could tell he was groping for a punch-line.

'Ah, well,' he said eventually. 'We certainly go to sea with a lot of physics.'

'And chemistry.'

'Yes, and chemistry,' he agreed. 'However, when things get really chemical in a submarine, they get psychological as well. And that means we're three-quarters of the way up the creek.

He rose abruptly. I hadn't a chance to ask him what he meant.

The Captain looked amused at lunch. Nobody knew what had brightened his day. He even adopted a bantering tone I hadn't heard him use before. The first lieutenant was the last to appear.

'Well, Number One?' the Captain enquired smugly.

'No problems, sir.'

The Captain amiably waved him into the corner seat. Bewildered by so much cordiality, the first lieutenant glanced covertly at each of us in turn. I could guess what was in store: I had seen the Captain slip a note into the control-room PO's hand as I passed through on my way to the wardroom.

The alarm bell sounded only a few minutes later. The first lieutenant squeezed out of his corner with difficulty as the flooding-flap operating-rods began to revolve on the deckhead above us. Crockery slithered across the table.

'Hold tight!' shouted the Captain.

The first lieutenant shot him a venomous look, but it was pointless. He had to make for the control-room anyway.

'Nimble as a stoat!' the Captain called after him.

The clamour from the control-room confirmed that we were in for something other than an exercise alarm. It sounded more like a damage-control drill.

Everything on the table slid forward. There was much tinkling and crashing. My feet grated on fragments of glass and china.

Our bow-down angle steadily increased.

A look of enquiry from the second lieutenant achieved nothing. The Captain behaved as if he had no connection with the turmoil.

Someone in the control-room shouted: 'Leak behind the forward depth-gauge!'

Instead of jumping up, the Captain favoured his second lieutenant with a broad grin until Babyface realized that the alarm was simulated.

The Captain took a malicious delight in the curses and babble of voices issuing from the control-room. He rose and trudged uphill to the seat of the disturbance with the deliberate tread of a mountain guide.

There was a general cacophony of rattles and crashes, then the heavy thud of something bulky falling over. U-A tried to stand on her head.

The first lieutenant had gone goggle-eyed.

We assembled the remains of the crockery in the forward corner of the 'settee'. The table was besmirched with food. Unfair of the Old Man to choose mealtime, considering our limited supplies of crockery. But then, any tradition was worth breaking in the interests of super-efficiency . . .

As for him, he leant against a bulkhead making snide remarks such as 'Practice makes perfect,' and 'The Brits won't wait for you to finish lunch either.'

Thank God! We gradually returned to the horizontal. The Captain had mercy on us and ordered the boat to 60 metres. The steward appeared and silently began to restore order.

After a quarter of an hour the Chief returned, sweating and out of breath. The Captain, with extreme courtesy, poured him a mug of tea.

'That went pretty well, Chief.'

The Chief's response was a sidelong glare.

'Temper, temper,' said the Captain.

The Chief leant back and inspected his hands. They were daubed with oil. The Captain stared at them disapprovingly.

'But Chief, what's our fastidious Number One going to think if you come to table like that?'

The first lieutenant went puce. The Chief stuck his hands in his trouser pockets and said: 'Is that better? I've already eaten.'

'You'll waste away if you aren't careful. Come on, gentlemen – eat, drink and be merry.' The Captain chewed away with bulging cheeks. Then, in the same caustic tone: 'Tell me, Chief, weren't you going to do a minor repair job on the port engine? This is a perfect opportunity. Maybe you'd like to carry out a bit of maintenance on the starboard engine as well, while you're at it – we'll be staying down long enough. And all for your sweet sake . . .'

The Chief grinned round the table and rubbed his hands. 'Nice to be back at sea again, isn't it? All that boozing at base . . . You get sick of it in the long run.'

The Captain's mood since our departure had varied between exuberance and quiet satisfaction. He had even returned from leave early. The boat could happily have refitted without him, but no – he insisted on being there.

To the men, their commanding officer's sacrifice of a whole week's leave could only mean that his home life wasn't a bed of roses.

It seemed that no one knew much about the Old Man's private life. My only impressions of it were based on a few grudging reminiscences and cynical asides. He sometimes thumbed a bundle of letters, all of them written in green ink in a large, commanding hand. Their author was an airman's widow whose father was something big at the Ministry of Justice. The Captain had casually alluded to a piano with candlesticks – red candles – and her 'gorgeous evening dresses' Peevishly he also let slip some fragmentary information about his last leave. He had been expected to wear his Knight's Cross 'the whole damned time' and do escort duty on shopping trips 'That way, they stick a bit more meat on the scales There was something on every night, too. One do after another – enough to drive you round the bend. They also wanted me to lecture some schoolchildren. "Count me out," i told them.'

Another confession : 'All we want to do on leave is change our clothes, stew in a bath for hours and let everything go hang No papers, no radio, just switch off and stretch out. But oh no! There it is, neatly pressed and laid out on the bed : number ones complete with dirk-belt. White shirt, black silk tie, black lisle socks, aiguillettes, and on top of it all your gong, carefully cleaned with an old toothbrush and dangling from its lovely clean ribbon. Jesus wept!'

Work in the engine-room ceased an hour later. The Captain's voice, rendered metallic by the intercom, rang through every compartment : 'Stand by to surface!'

The bridge watch mustered beneath the lower hatch.

'Surface!'

The watch went on the bridge. The rocking motion gave way to forward thrust and the slap of the waves yielded to a sibilant hiss. When the tanks were fully blown, the Captain ordered : 'Dismiss from diving stations.'

A stoker climbed into the conning-tower. He lit a cigarette, squatted down like an Arab on the helmsman's left, and abandoned himself to the pleasure of the moment. Even before he had finished, the next in line for a cigarette was agitating from below.

Afternoon. The submarine had been on the surface for two hours, 'half-ahead both', for a change, but without load because the batteries were fully charged. At this engine speed we made 14 or 15 knots – no more than an energetic cyclist.

ALARM! The clangour of the bell seemed to paralyse my heart and lungs.

A man rushed out of the heads with his trousers at half-mast.

The engines stopped and the boat tilted. It seemed an age before the Chief levelled her off. It was only then that I realized the alarm was genuine.

We stayed down a mere fifteen minutes. Then the waves resumed their hissing along our steel sides.

The Chief sighed. 'I reckon that's enough for one day.'

'Baah,' said the Captain.

Back in the POs' mess, Zeitler gave a groan. 'The Old Man and the Brits make a perfect team. Never a dull moment.'

FIRST SLOG

WEDNESDAY, 5TH DAY AT SEA. I was half-wakened by a continuous bleeping from the wireless office. Then the galley door clanged open. A babble of voices filled the compartment. PO Electrician Pilgrim bellowed: 'Hey, steward! What's this cunt-slime doing on the table? Mop it up sharpish!'

I glanced round my curtain. PO Wichmann, who was peering at a blob of jam on the table, laughed raucously. 'Looks as if the lady was flying pennant Z.'

Pilgrim and Wichmann had one topic of conversation only, but there were times when their vocabulary and allusions defeated me.

'Snow White and Red Rose,' said Wichmann. His eyes were wide-set They also protruded slightly, giving his face a frog-like appearance. To keep his dark hair smoothly slicked back, he used stick-brilliantine, squeezed methodically between the teeth of a comb and distributed over his head with loving care He was fond of picturing the sort of life he aspired to – theatres, nightclubs, high society – and preened himself on a brief spell of secondary education. For all his conceit, he was reputed to be a good seaman and had been the first to sight a number of convoys.

Pilgrim, a short, pale man with a pointed beard, was a Thuringian like his fellow-PO electrician Rademacher, but more talkative.

He and Wichmann were now swopping comments on the ratings' brothel.

'She's always moaning about something, that girl. Don't touch me there, *chéri*! Ah no, not that, *chéri*! Don't come in my hair, *chéri*! Too bloody finicky, that's her trouble.'

'She's not a bad lay, all the same.'

'Got a man-sized arse on her, I'll say that.'

Pilgrim had tangled with his father while on leave. He went on to explain why.

'It got to be too much of a good thing,' I heard him grumble. 'I'd just screwed the bit from the news-stand on a bench in the municipal gardens, but I didn't slip my Frenchy off till I reached our front door. The old man started on at me as soon as I walked in – how much I owed him and all that crap – so I slapped my load on the table and said: "Here, have your expenses back." That floored him! Then I grabbed my bag and pissed off – it was the only thing to do.'

I crawled out of my bunk.

My tongue clove to my soft palate like a strip of biltong, no matter how hard I cleared my throat. With no water handy, I was obliged to dress with the gluten still coating my mouth and nasal passages. The mucus welled up inside.

The steward reported that my breakfast was ready. I clamped my lips together and added. I found a scrap of newspaper and spat the mucus out into it. My throat tautened with nausea.

At last I could head for the control-room and call, in a reasonably unconstricted voice: 'Man on the bridge?'

'Come on up,' the second lieutenant called back.

I stuffed the newspaper into the pocket of my leather trousers and shinned up the ladder.

'Morning, Number Two.' Overboard with the newspaper, mouth wide to catch the salt breeze, and off to the conservatory. Wind direction checked, flies unbuttoned, and – *quelle joie!* – bladder voided with infinite relief.

At last I could spare a glance for the sea and sky.

Leaning over the rail, I became engrossed in the water, roaring and hissing along the side below me making bubbles and swathes of foam. Astern, our route was marked by a long track a few metres wide. The waves were flattened as though a steamroller had subdued their spasmodic dance.

'Tell me,' I asked the second lieutenant, 'what's pennant Z?'

The answer came back pat, like something out of a training manual: 'Pennant Z is the signal for General Chase. Colour: red.'

'Dirty beasts!' I blurted out.

The second lieutenant stared at me with his mouth open.

'Thanks,' I said, and disappeared through the upper hatch.

Inside the conning-tower, the helmsman had little to do. The same figure on the compass card swung to and fro beneath the lubber's line: 250 degrees. We were steering a steady course.

By the quartermaster's reckoning, it would take us another ten days at cruising speed to reach our patrol area. We could be there sooner if we ran the engines at full speed, but cruising speed had been chosen in the interests of economy. Our fuel must be conserved for the chase.

I sat down to breakfast. The Captain was nowhere to be seen.

The alarm bell shrilled, making me jump. Bloody planes! We seemed to be diving every two minutes.

Then I caught sight of the Captain through the bulkhead door. He was standing in the control-room with a stopwatch in his hand.

Thank God, an exercise alarm. The Old Man was checking the time it took to dive.

I stepped aside to avoid the sudden stampede. The submarine was already bow-down. I tried to keep the plates on the table but two or three slid off and smashed.

I couldn't help recalling all the pitfalls that could beset an exercise alarm. On Kerschbaumer's boat someone had inadvertently failed to open the cocks to the depth-gauges. Kerschbaumer had ordered the boat to 80 metres. She duly dived, but because the gauge needle didn't budge Kerschbaumer thought she was still on the surface and kept flooding. By the time the error became apparent the boat was at 200 metres — more than twice her permitted depth.

The next exercise alarm came while we were assembled for lunch. The Chief swept a tureenful of soup off the table, straight into the second lieutenant's lap.

The Captain still seemed dissatisfied, even after this second run-through. Not a word of praise passed his lips.

The third alarm occurred at 1600 on the dot. The Chief had

just settled down with a thriller.

This time it was the teacups that slid off and smashed.

'Much more of this,' someone muttered ruefully, 'and we'll be eating out of slop-pails.'

'That's it,' the Captain said at last.

I went to the control-room and resumed my attempt to master the intricacies of submarine technology. An altercation between Frenssen and Wichmann – the eternal wrangle between deck and engine-room – was nipped in the bud by the appearance of the quartermaster. Wichmann called Frenssen's diesels 'fart-machines', whereupon Frenssen brandished his oily fists under Wichmann's nose.

Peace descended, and I could once more concentrate on our tank lay-out. Main ballast tanks kept the submarine on the surface when filled with air – three of them, two outside the pressure hull and one inside. The internal tank had sufficient capacity to keep her afloat if the external tanks were damaged. Flooding flaps were located on the underside of the main ballast tanks and vents on top. Both had to be open when diving, the air escaping through the vents while water entered through the flooding flaps. In addition to main ballast tanks, the submarine had internal fuel tanks which were filled with fuel when she left base and could provide additional buoyancy when the fuel had been expended. Depending on whether these tanks were filled with fuel or air, the submarine was said to be in trim condition A or B.

The trimming tanks were used to adjust the boat's position when dived. If bow-down or bow-up, she could be restored to the horizontal – technically, trim position zero – by pumping water from one trimming tank to the other. Trimming tanks were vital to any submarine. They were her balancing-pole, because she had an equal tendency to 'pitch' or 'list' under water. Under water, she was exceptionally sensitive to shifts in weight and hard to hold on an even keel. She could easily take a 40-degree angle, bow-up or bow-down. The trimming tanks were neatly situated at the boat's extremities. Seen from the control-room, they thus lay at either end of a long-armed lever.

A dived boat would take a bow-down angle if 50 kilos of potatoes were humped from the control-room to the fore-ends. To achieve a balance, 25 litres of water had to be pumped aft – only half the weight of the potatoes because the water was taken from the trimming tank at the other end of the boat. This simultaneously lightened the fore-ends by half the said weight.

I drummed the rule-of-thumb into my head: compensating tanks were used to adjust a submarine's bodily weight, trimming tanks to keep her longitudinally horizontal under water.

I climbed into my bunk soon after supper, dog-tired.

The POs whose quarters I shared had long ceased to be inhibited by my presence. They blithely devoted themselves to Subject No. 1, whether or not I was in my bunk. It appeared that I only had to draw my curtain to vanish from the face of the earth. I felt like a zoologist studying animals long inured to observation by man.

The day having begun with Pilgrim and Wichmann, Frenssen and Zeitler rounded it off. Their store of obscene stories seemed inexhaustible. I yearned to know if they were all based on personal experience. Were Frenssen and Zeitler really the hardened brothel-frequenters they affected to be?

PO Zeitler, a North German, had a pale boyish face and sparse beard which went incongruously with his cynical talk and heavyweight's build. He was reputed to be an excellent seaman and belonged to the first watch. Unless I was much mistaken, the Captain rated him more highly than the first lieutenant.

Stoker PO Frenssen was a stocky young man who exuded self-assurance at all times. His manner was modelled on the callous, cynical desperado of the third-rate Western. He must have practised his air of hard-bitten menace in front of a mirror. Ario and Sablonski, the stokers of his watch, had to mind their step with him, although he was a mere twenty-two years old. He bunked immediately below me.

Voices drifted through the half-drawn curtain of my bunk.

'This place stinks like a sewer.'

'You can't expect it to smell like cunt.'

Grunts and yawns.

'What was she like, then?'

'Hot stuff, take my word for it.'

A ruminative silence followed.

'What's your trouble? Narked because you only got your finger up?'

'Bollocks! I can do more with my big toe than you ever did with your prick, any day.'

'Oh sure, that's the way they do it in your part of the country – with their toes.'

Sounds of breathing, another resonant yawn. Then a nose-clearing snort.

'Any road, fucking's out for the present. They're getting it from somebody else now – all of them, and that includes yours.'

'Who says? You ought to get yourself transferred to the staff, with a brain like yours. They need bright lads like you to stick pins in maps.'

'And you should've stuck a cork in it to keep the opposition out. Pity they don't make chastity-belts any more.'

Plates clattered and boots scraped. My curtain bellied inwards as someone squeezed between the table and the starboard bunks. Then I heard voices again.

'Bit of rest can't hurt after a leave like that. One air raid after another. Choked, I was. This is a fucking rest-cure in comparison.'

'Don't speak too soon, mate.'

'Couldn't even have a quiet poke any more, not even in the shed. Her parents have got an allotment with a wooden shack in the middle. Couch, ice-box, the lot. And then, just when you're halfway up, the fucking sirens go off and she gets the jitters. I tell you, mate, all the fun's gone out of it . . .'

THURSDAY, 6TH DAY AT SEA. I was on the bridge with the Captain even before breakfast.

The sky was hung with clouds of turquoise batik, linked by delicate little threads. Showing through them was a reddish glow which slowly began to overwhelm the turquoise of the clouds, climbing behind them until it streamed through every rift. Then, slowly, the flash and glitter waned as though the light had spent its energy. The colours in the sky faded: the sun had risen above the clouds.

'Nice day,' said the Captain.

The watches were changing. I thought I saw some new faces.

'Don't know that one.'

The Captain shrugged. 'Well, fifty's plenty. I've even failed to recognize my own men sometimes. Back at base, when they come on watch clean-shaven, I feel as if I'd taken a kindergarten to sea. Thank God the newsreel camera-men concentrate on incoming boats with bearded crews – if only to spare the enemy's feelings.'

He paused for a moment before he went on: 'The British would be ashamed to see who was giving them hell – nursery-school toddlers officered by a few bright lads from the Hitler Youth. It's the Children's Crusade all over again – makes me feel as old as Methuselah.'

I'd never seen the Captain in a mood like this before. He generally preserved the dour silence of a brooding and phlegmatic introvert. Yet there he was, cruising along merrily – missing on the occasional cylinder, as usual, but covering plenty of ground at a time.

Everything on board had found a permanent home. No more crates to obstruct the traffic and we no longer went round bent double. Life aboard had taken on a regular rhythm, blissful after the chaos and confusion of the first few days.

I still felt, even so, as if I were insulated from reality. I seemed to be living in a faintly trance-like state. The bewilderment and consternation aroused in me by the jungle of pipes, gauges, power units and valves had ebbed a little. Handwheels, levers, valves and lines had fallen into a comprehensible pattern, and I had developed a sort of respect for the functional world of machinery that surrounded me. For all that, there were many things which I could only accept with wonder, as a believer accepts miracles.

The Chief went out of his way to blind me with science.

'You can hang the boat on her periscope,' he said casually, watching me out of the corner of his eye to see if I would bite.

'Hang the boat on her periscope?' I sounded surprised and favoured him with the expected look of enquiry.

'That's right,' he said. 'If I stop the motors under water the boat will rise or fall. I can't trim her accurately enough to eliminate all tendency to sink or float. That's why screws and planes are needed to keep a constant depth.'

I nodded to indicate the familiarity and plausibility of what he had just said. He raised his eyebrows and looked me full in the face.

'However, if the sea's calm enough and the boat's well trimmed, we can maintain periscope depth even with our motors stopped. It's like this. If the boat has a tendency to sink with her periscope extended, her underwater volume increases because that part of the periscope which projected above the surface has sunk below it. On the other hand, if the boat's volume increases, so does her buoyancy – logical?'

He extracted another nod from me before continuing his exposition.

'The increase in buoyancy eliminates the boat's previous tendency to sink and causes her to rise. That's logical too. So she rises, her periscope projects further, and her underwater volume decreases until she develops a tendency to sink. And so it goes on, up and down, up and down, until the boat gradually hangs on her periscope.'

'Subtle stuff!'

It was obvious from the Chief's manner that there was more to come. He allowed me a brief respite. 'For instance, if you dunk a model submarine in a bucket of water . . .' I raised my hands in surrender and he had mercy on me. Instead of lecturing on, he took a few generous swigs from my bottle of apple-juice.

The second engineer was still something of an enigma to me. The Captain enjoyed baiting him. I couldn't make out whether his failure to rise to these verbal challenges should be put down to cussedness or slow wits. He remained stolidly impassive, even when the Old Man treated him with jovial solicitude. I concluded that he was devoid of imagination – the typical product of an officer training system designed to turn out brainless, heel-clicking robots with a dog-like devotion to the Führer.

I knew only the barest details of his private life – little more than appeared on his next-of-kin card – but then, the other officers were almost as much of a closed book.

The Chief was the only one who had volunteered something of his personal circumstances. His wife was expecting a baby. His mother was dead, but he had visited his father during his last leave. 'Not a howling success,' was how he described the occasion. 'I took him a load of canned stuff but he wouldn't touch it – depriving the boys at the front and all that crap. In the morning he stalked up and down beside my bed. Not a word, just silent reproaches. The room I had to sleep in was a nightmare. Sistine angels over the bed and a hunk of birch-bark with postcards gummed to it. Pathetic, really, living alone like that. Soup three times a day and a hot drink last thing at night. He drapes his clothes over four chairs, night after night, and reverses the procedure every morning. He designed a wash-basin once – that's what keeps him going, the sheer creative pride of a wash-basin designer. These days he bends wire into salad-strainers and barters them for things to eat. He makes his own butter substitute out of yeast. Frightful stuff. "Very palatable," he calls it. "Must pass the recipe on to my lady-friends. Spread a little joy, that's my motto." It is, too – he's always saying it. Always trying to prove he's the opposite of what he looks. He carries a battered photo around in his wallet. Him and some bird having it off on a sofa.

"Running season 1926" – that's what's written on it. People are funny . . .'

Talking of mottoes, every sheet of the wardroom calendar was adorned with a different pearl of wisdom. The Captain made the first lieutenant read out each daily offering.

'To love or not; by this we stand or fall. Milton.'

'Come again?' the Chief asked pointedly, and the Captain sat up with a jerk.

The first lieutenant blinked, as he always did when something embarrassed him. I choked on a spoonful of scrambled egg and spat it into the passage. 'To love or not,' the first lieutenant gabbled hurriedly, 'by this we stand or fall.'

'Let's have a look,' the Captain demanded, mock incredulity in his voice.

'At this hour of the morning?' The Chief simulated revulsion. 'I always said the English had one-track minds.'

The first lieutenant flushed scarlet.

The calendar sheet circulated from hand to hand.

Later, it reached the POs' mess. I was still wondering how it had got there when Frenssen started reminiscing about a spell in hospital.

'I used to wake up every morning with a stand on me like the Eiffel Tower. Well, there was this nurse who brought round the piss-bottles bright and early. Man, did she have a neat way of calming you down! Lovely backhand, she had . . .'

'They ought to have upped your soda ration,' said Dorian, grinning round his bunk curtain. His tousled red hair and the freckles round his nostrils made him look like a cheeky urchin.

Soda . . . The word took me straight back to my stint in the Labour Service, where a young man's libido was deemed unconducive to hard work. At first we thought they mixed herbs with our tea, but then we found it was soda. We used to call the stuff 'eunuch powder' or 'droopoline'.

Back at the breakfast table, the Captain nodded at the departing figure of a man who had just passed through on his way from the fore-ends.

'That one's Benjamin. They call him Manchu.'

A full minute went by before he condescended to explain why. 'No connection with China. It's that beard and moustache of his. I once remarked to someone that they made him look like Adolf Menjou. My French pronunciation can't be up to much, because they got it wrong. He's been known as Manchu ever since. Etymologist's nightmare, eh?'

Katter, the chef, grinned broadly as he ducked through

the bulkhead. The small black forage-cap on his head looked as if it had been put there for a joke. His neck was so short and thick that it almost merged with his skull. Muscles bulged on his bare forearms.

'We had to spring him from gaol three times by teleprinter,' the Captain said. 'Now his leave is stopped for the duration. We can't afford to let him cross the German border.'

Fancy that, I thought. Our friendly chef with the persistent grin! So that's what the Old Man had been going to tell me . . .

'The thing is, he behaves as if I were a cross between God and Adolf Hitler. "Better tell that to the Captain," he says. "Better ask the Captain about that." A truly devoted soul, Katter. He's a sort of one-man dog – sinks his fangs in any outsider who comes too close.'

I recalled a member of Kallmann's crew whose failure to fulfil the requirements of military etiquette had saved his life. He had been charged with insubordination and was safely locked up in the guardroom when his boat sailed. It sank a week later.

'Unfortunately,' the Captain went on, 'it's dawned on Katter that he doesn't run much of a risk by opening his mouth too wide. The boat needs him. There aren't many chefs of his calibre on the books, not these days. Can't be many with the Iron Cross First Class, either.'

It was my turn to keep the ball rolling. 'How did he get it?'

'A depth-charge lifted the galley hatch. He reacted like lightning – cleared the clip that had fouled the seating with water pouring in all over him. If he hadn't – if he'd lost his head – the boat would have taken too much water for us to hold her. Watertight doors wouldn't have been much use. If one compartment fills – well, I don't have to tell you what that means . . .'

In the fore-ends. The new control-room hand discreetly enquired what the Captain was like. Someone condescended to enlighten him.

'The Old Man? He's a funny cuss. Beats me why, but he's as happy as a dog with two tails every time we go out. Oy-oy, I always say to myself – something wrong there. Seems he's engaged to one of these Nazi bits. Nobody knows much about her except that she's an airman's widow. First the Luftwaffe, now the Navy – maybe she's trying them all for size. One thing's certain; she doesn't keep the Old Man well supplied. Must be the stuck-up type – you can tell from her picture.

Great long streak of piss, she is. The Old Man deserves something better.'

Schwalle chimed in. 'They say the Nazi bits aren't bad.'

'How come?'

'Well, they get taught all kinds of things at these State
marriage schools. For instance, they have to stuff a piece of
chalk up their arse and write "Otto-Otto-Otto" on the blackboard – keeps them supple . . .'

Many times a day, while passing the open door of the wireless
office, I would catch a glimpse of Herrmann, the PO telegraphist, who sat crouched between the tabletops that carried
his radio sets like a spider in a web. He was almost invariably
reading a book with his head-set pushed back so that only
one ear-phone nuzzled his ear. This enabled him to pick up
incoming Morse signals and hear orders from inside the boat
at the same time.

Like the quartermaster, Herrmann had been with U-A since
she commissioned. He bunked opposite me in the POs' mess.
His father, so I learned from the Captain, had been an officer
in a cruiser which went down with all hands in 1917.

'The youngster had a decent education before he joined
the service. Started off in 1935 as a telegraphist in the cruiser
Köln, then PO telegraphist in a torpedo-boat, then submarine
school. He served with me during the Norway campaign –
earned his Iron Cross First Class a couple of times over. Next
time it'll be the German Cross in Gold.'

Herrmann was a quiet young man with a face of exceptional
pallor. He had the Chief's knack of gliding smoothly through
the boat as though nothing could hamper his progress. There
was an unremitting tension about him, a wary and alert air
which reminded me of a caged beast. He kept himself to himself and did not mix with the other POs. He and the midshipman, Ullmann, preferred to read rather than play cards.

Bending over Herrmann's shoulder, I could hear the thin
insect-like chirping of Morse in his head-set.

There was a sudden flicker of animation in Herrmann's
face. A minute later he straightened up and handed the
second lieutenant a sheet of paper inscribed with a meaning-
less series of letters. The second lieutenant took the signal and
briskly set about decoding it. He had it in clear a few minutes
later.

'C-in-C U-boats from U-W. 2 MVM – KAJB 2163 – sunk –
convoy 070 – 11 – counter-attacked 7 hours – now pursuing.'

A typical signal embodying the story of an attack in a

navy nutshell: two medium-sized merchant ships sank, seven hours' worth of depth-charges, pursuit resumed in the teeth of enemy opposition.

The second lieutenant entered it in the radio log and passed it to the Captain to read. The Captain initialled the signal and handed it back. The first lieutenant also read and initialled it. Finally, the second lieutenant returned the log to Herrmann, whose arm emerged from the wireless office like a tentacle.

'Two more MVMs – not bad,' said the Captain. 'U-W is Bischof's boat. They'll be pinning another medal on him soon.'

Not a word about the seven-hour counter-attack. The signal might never have mentioned it.

Only minutes later, Herrmann again handed the radio log out of his cubby-hole. A re-transmission from C-in-C U-boats to a submarine in the far north. She was to proceed at full speed to a new patrol area, evidently in the path of a suspected convoy. Like a puppet on invisible strings, the U-boat would move by remote control, thousands of miles from headquarters, to a different part of the Atlantic. She would take up the chase without a sight or sniff of the enemy. On the big wall-map in the C-in-C's operations room, someone must have shifted one of the little red flags which marked the position of every German submarine.

We took advantage of our peaceful underwater progress during the daily trim dives to check the torpedoes.

The fore-ends transformed itself into a machine-shop. The hammocks were stowed and the bunks hinged up. The men, who had stripped off their shirts, were securing blocks and tackle to the loading rails. The rear door of the first tube swung open and the first of the fish, glinting dully under its thick layer of grease, was retracted slightly with a horizontal tackle. Hoisting-rings were used to support its weight. At an order from the torpedo gunner's mate, everyone hauled like a tug-o'-war team. Slowly, it slid out of its tube and dangled from the loading rail, where its ton-and-a-half of steel and explosive could be easily moved in any direction.

Each man had his own job to perform. One checked the propulsion unit, another made sure that all bearings and shafts moved freely. HP air-lines were attached and the torpedo's air-vessels topped up with compressed air, rudder and hydro-plane gear tested and lubrication points tended. Finally, it was coaxed back into its tube.

The second was submitted to the same treatment. The men seemed to have got into their stride. Ario directed their labours with a stream of obscene allusions. 'Whip it out quick, there's others in the queue besides you! Stick it in, she's panting for it!'

The last rear door was finally shut and clipped. Bunks were folded down and the compartment gradually reassumed its familiar lived-in appearance.

Ario scowled. 'About time we got rid of the buggers . . .'

Unlike the rounds for our 88mm. gun, the highly sensitive torpedoes demanded regular attention. They were not shells, but small vessels crammed with mechanisms of the utmost intricacy. Apart from the rudders common to all vessels, they had hydroplanes. They were, in effect, precision-engineered midget submarines weighing one-and-a-half tons. All we did was to eject them from the tubes by impulsion. After that they proceeded under their own power – electricity or compressed air – and steered a pre-determined course.

Four of our 14 torpedoes were in the bow tubes and one in the stern tube. Two were fitted with contact pistols and three with influence pistols. Contact pistols detonated the explosive charge on impact, blowing a hole in the target's side. The more intricate and sensitive influence pistols, with their magnetic firing system, detonated the torpedo as it passed beneath a ship at the appropriate depth. This meant that the pressure-wave struck the vessel at its structurally weakest point.

The days passed in a steady alternation of watch on, watch off – the cycle common to ships the world over. Stokers and electricians stood six-hour watches and seamen three watches of four hours, each followed by eight hours of relaxation.

The first watch was taken by the first lieutenant, the second by the second lieutenant and the third by the quartermaster.

It was the first watch that worried the Captain – I could tell. The Old Man was unimpressed by his second-in-command's zealous mien and suspected that he might crack in an emergency. It was fortunate that Zeitler belonged to his watch. Zeitler became a changed man on the bridge. With the binoculars glued to his eyes, he concentrated wholeheartedly on his sector and seemed to forget his sexual fantasies altogether.

I had been detailed to stand in for Jens, a member of the second watch who was confined to his bunk with a high fever. In other words, I was sentenced to the bridge between 0400 and 0800 ship's time.

It was 0300 when I woke – half an hour earlier than I need

have done. Silence reigned in the darkened control-room.

The second lieutenant swore softly as he strove to pull on his damp sea-boots. He asked the control-room PO about weather conditions.

'Not much spray, sir,' I heard Isenberg reply. 'Bit parky, though.' That meant my woollen muffler and thick sweater, possibly a Balaclava under my sou'wester as well. Having plenty of time in hand, I perched on the chart-table and did some homework.

My eyes had grown accustomed to the dim light. I let them wander from one installation and item of equipment to another, silently mouthing each name as though stock-taking: the twin rev counters; the adjustable lamp over the chart-table, the chart-stowage, that monstrous metal chest whose capacity – a good two cubic metres – was such that it could hold charts of every sea area to which the C-in-C might, in his wisdom, dispatch us; the echo-sounder, so far unused; the evaporation plant for drinking water; the control-room desk.

Among the jumble of handwheels and levers, I picked out the switch that disengaged the hydroplanes. In the port after corner was an abundance of handwheels set one above the other. This 'Christmas-tree', which almost entirely filled the cramped space between pressure hull and periscope shaft, was made up of flooding distribution valves and high- and low-pressure air distributors.

There was one valve here for each ballast tank and each half ballast tank. The valve-wheels above the Christmas-tree belonged to the HP air-line blowing system for the trimming tanks. All lines leading from the high-pressure air-bottles converged on this distribution panel for the compressed air which expelled water from our tanks.

The low-pressure lines were fed from the HP line via a reducing valve. Below me was a serpentine maze of pipes with numerous projecting valve-wheels: the flooding and pumping distributors. Close beside them were the telemotor pump and air-loaded accumulator for the periscope. The gauge-glasses near by evidently belonged to the compensating tanks.

Farther aft, distributed among the pipes on the shell of the pressure hull, and barely visible in the gloom, were grey steel boxes pierced to reveal numerous dials: the torpedo firing system; selector switches for the attack and air-to-surface search periscopes, for individual torpedo tubes, for single shots and spread salvoes, for stern and bow firing; compass and echo-sounder. Situated on the forward bulkhead was the emergency steering gear. The main steering position was in the conning-tower, but if this could not be manned because the conning-tower was damaged or flooded, the submarine could be steered from the control-room.

My mental inventory was cut short by the appearance of two fellow-sufferers, Dorian and the midshipman.

'Nice and cold up top,' the PO said eventually. 'It's a bastard, second watch.' He raised his voice: 'Five minutes to go.'

At that moment the second lieutenant stepped through the forward bulkhead doorway, so heavily muffled that only a firing-slit of face was visible between collar and sou'wester.

He flexed his knees a couple of times and led the way up the ladder. It was an unwritten rule to give the outgoing watch five minutes' grace.

I was assigned the starboard after sector. My eyes soon adjusted themselves to the darkness. The sky was a trace lighter than the inky sea, so the horizon showed up as a faint line. Our binoculars misted over quickly in the damp air.

'Pass up the shammies,' the second lieutenant called below, but it wasn't long before the leathers became saturated and started to blur. Soon, my eyes were smarting and I had to shut them for seconds at a time. Nobody spoke. The vibration of the engines and the hiss and roar of the waves rapidly merged into a peaceful cocoon of sound, broken only by an occasional dull boom as someone's knee struck the bridge casing.

The port after look-out gave a loud yawn. The second lieutenant swung round. 'Watch it!' he said reprovingly. 'Keep your eyes open.'

My neck started to itch, but I was swaddled like a mummy and denied a privilege which any baboon could have exercised. In any case, the second lieutenant got restless if anyone so much as undid a button.

All I knew about our Number Two was that he came from a Hamburg suburb, had been destined for a university career but abandoned it in favour of banking. Then he volunteered for the navy. Blessed with a happy temperament, he was well regarded by everyone – a young man who performed his duties to the letter with casual self-assurance and a total absence of fuss. Although his approach differed radically from that of the first lieutenant, he was the only person on board whose relations with him were anywhere near cordial.

Our wake glowed phosphorescently. The night sky was a black cloth embroidered with diamonds. Every star stood out clearly. The moon was full but lustreless. Its light was pale, bleached and slightly greenish. Visibility over the water was very poor.

Some clouds drifted across the moon. I could barely distinguish sea from sky. What were those shadows on the horizon? Should I report them or wait and see? Shadows, common-or-garden clouds? They seemed to come and go. I narrowed my eyes and stared until they watered, until I was positive: nothing, no shadows at all.

I sniffed hard to clear my nose of moisture. Many a look-out had smelt out a convoy in pitch darkness – caught a faint whiff of funnel smoke or oil fuel seeping from a damaged freighter.

'Black as a witch's tit,' fumed the second lieutenant. 'We could be run down and never know what hit us.'

It was no use looking for lights. The British were careful not to show any. Even the glow of a cigarette could spell their undoing.

The Zeiss binoculars seemed to weigh a ton. My arms gradually flagged and my biceps started to ache. The same procedure, endlessly repeated: let the binoculars dangle from their thong for a moment, stretch one's arms – fling them out as if they were only loosely attached to one's body – then up with the heavy glasses once more, brow-ridges nestling against the rubber cups round the eye-pieces, fingertips supporting the instrument to insulate it from the vibration of the hull. Comb the sky and sea, scour the horizon millimetre by millimetre. Then lower the binoculars and survey the entire sector, sky included. Finally, resume one's snail-speed scanning of the horizon from left to right.

The minutes dragged by. I felt more and more tempted to let my eyelids droop and surrender to the motion of the boat, enjoy her gentle rise and fall, allow myself to be lulled to sleep.

I suppressed an urge to ask the second lieutenant what time it was. In the east, a trace of pinkish light had appeared. A range of blue-black clouds hovered close above the skyline. It was some time before the light behind them crept higher and turned their edges to flame. The forepart of the submarine became discernible as a dark mass.

More time passed. The sky grew light enough for me to distinguish the individual slats on the fore-casing. Gradually the faces of my three companions took shape. They looked grey with fatigue.

Someone came on deck to relieve himself. He turned to

leeward and made water through the conservatory rail. I heard it splash on the casing like a fountain and smelt the tang of urine.

Again a voice from below: 'Man on the bridge?' A succession of dim figures emerged one by one for a breath of air and a leak. I could now smell cigarette smoke and hear scraps of conversation.

'Jesus, that's better. Another couple of minutes and I'd have had to tie a knot in it.'

A little while later the second lieutenant made a routine report. The Captain had appeared on the bridge. He must have materialized very quietly. I caught a glimpse of his face lit by the red glow of a cigarette, then called myself to order: no outside interests, no distractions, no eyes for anything beyond my allotted sector. My sole task was to peer and peer again.

'Tubes 1 to 4, open bow-caps!'

So the Old Man was going to hold another fire-control exercise. Without turning my head, I could hear the first lieutenant calling out director angles. Then came the report from below: 'Bow-caps 1 to 4 open.' The first lieutenant continued to utter his monotonous incantations. Not another word from the Captain.

The horizon grew more and more distinct. A red conflagration was blazing in the fissure between the sea and the purple bank of cloud. The sun climbed higher. Fiery serpents of light were already undulating across the sea. I spared only a brief glance for the sun and the colour of the sky because the lighting might have been designed for enemy aircraft. It was strong enough for them to have distinguished the U-boat by her foaming wake but too dim for us to spot them quickly against the sky.

Confounded sea-gulls! They were harder on the nerves than anything. God knew how many dives they had been responsible for. I thanked my lucky stars that I hadn't been given the up-sun sector.

The first lieutenant continued to churn out orders. 'Tubes 1 to 4 ready. Stand by to fire tubes 1 to 4, safety range four-zero-zero, interval eighty seconds. Bearing?'

'Bearing zero-nine-zero,' came a voice from below.

The sea awoke completely now. Short waves sparkled in the light of day. Our fore-casing glistened. The sky turned orange, yellow and pale green in quick succession. The bluish haze from our exhausts seemed to merge with some pink tulle clouds far astern. When my neighbour turned to face me, I saw that the sunlight had tinged his cheeks with carmine.

All at once I caught sight of some black dots in the waves. They came and went, came and went. The port after look-out had also spotted them.

'Dolphins!'

They approached like rogue torpedoes, alternately cleaving the water and breaking surface. One of the herd must have spotted us, because they all bore down on the submarine as though at a given signal. Before long there were dozens of them on either beam. A flash of pale-green belly, and then the perpendicular dorsal fins knifed through the water like a ship's bow. Effortlessly keeping pace with us, the creatures did not swim so much as cavort in a series of graceful leaps and bounds. It was a conscious effort to ignore them and concentrate on my sector.

Short gusts of wind pecked at the swell. The sky gradually clouded over until the light appeared to filter down through an immense sheet of opalescent glass. Our faces were soon streaming with spray and the submarine's movements became more pronounced.

The dolphins abruptly took their leave.

Coming off watch, I felt as if my eyes had slid from their sockets and were hanging on stalks. It was agony to move my stiff limbs as I peeled off my wet oilskins and wearily turned in.

The POs' mess was too warm. Within minutes, sweat beaded my forehead. I threw off the blankets. Light fell on my face through a crack between the curtain and partition. A thin drizzle of music came from the loudspeakers, which were turned down low. From outboard came an incessant hiss and roar as the sea groped and fumbled its way down the full length of the boat. Sometimes it yielded to a slithering, rasping sound, sometimes to moans interspersed with slaps and blows. The pounding on our hull could be muffled as a slack drum-skin one moment and metallic as a tin can the next. The voices in the control-room sounded infinitely remote.

Another hour before the third watch came below. For the thousandth time, I stared at the grained surface of the plywood panelling beside my bunk.

Then I sat up with a jerk as the alarm bell sounded.

I was out of my bunk and staggering about before my brain started to function. The quartermaster was on watch — what could have happened?

I started to pull on my boots, still reeling. The POs' mess

came alive with hurried movement. A stoker's face loomed through the blue haze drifting from the galley. With studied indifference, he called: 'What's up?'

Nobody knew. The submarine was still on an even keel. I wondered what it meant. Our horizontal position seemed incongruous after the alarm bell.

'Belay alarm, belay alarm!' quacked the intercom. Eventually, the word came from the control-room: it was a false alarm.

'What? How come?'

'The helmsman pushed the button by mistake.'

'Bloody hell!'

'Which stupid sod was it?'

'Benjamin.'

A moment of speechlessness, then general fury.

'Chuck the bugger overboard.'

'Well, fuck me!'

'As the actress said to the bishop.'

'Who asked you to shove your oar in?'

A chorus this time 'As the actress said to the bishop!'

The coxswain was beside himself with rage. He didn't say a word, but his eyes rained fire and brimstone. Lucky for the helmsman that he was esconced in the conning-tower. Even the Chief looked as if he'd like to flay the man alive.

The POs were still giving vent to their indignation when I climbed back into my bunk.

'Careless son-of-a-bitch. You wait till I get my hands on him!'

'Leave some for me.'

A fart rang out. Peering past the curtain, I saw Dorian fanning his buttocks. He gave a mock bow. 'And now, for my next number ...'

'Put a sock in it!' someone protested.

The response was inevitable. 'As the bishop said to the actress!'

Nobody talked politics in the wardroom, but even in private conversation the Captain promptly put paid to any serious discussion with a sardonic curl of the lip. Enquiries into the purpose and prospects of the war were completely taboo. However, I had little doubt that these questions – and not his personal problems – were what preoccupied the Captain during his day-long spells of brooding silence.

He wore protective camouflage. Only occasionally did he lift his visor and venture an ambiguous remark which fleetingly disclosed his real attitude.

His aversion to Nazi propaganda became particularly apparent when he was angry – and news broadcasts almost always enraged him. 'Bleeding the enemy of cargo space, they call it – wiping out enemy tonnage. Tonnage! They're talking about good, seaworthy ships. Their lousy propaganda makes us sound like executioners, shipwreckers, butchers . . .'

He seldom showed any interest in cargoes, which tended to be more precious to the enemy than the ships that carried them. Ships were the love of the Old Man's life. They were animate beings possessed of mechanical hearts which pounded with a regular beat. To have to destroy them struck him as an abomination.

I often wondered how he coped with the inescapable dichotomy inside himself. He seemed to have reduced all his problems to a common denominator – destroy lest ye be destroyed, bow to the inevitable – but he showed no inclination to clothe his sentiments in long words.

I was sometimes tempted to coax him out of his shell by suggesting that he might simply be deluding himself like the rest – albeit more subtly than most – by asking if it didn't require plenty of self-deception to live with the belief that all doubts could be cloaked in the concept of duty. It was no use, though. The Old Man neatly side-stepped me every time. All I did was discover more about his aversion and allergies.

The first lieutenant and second engineer were a constant source of irritation to him. He bristled at the pedantic rigidity with which the first lieutenant handled his knife and fork like surgical instruments. Every tinned sardine was subjected to a thorough post mortem. Having excised the backbone with extreme care, he doggedly proceeded to remove every last shred and sliver of skin while the Captain watched the autopsy, goggle-eyed and purse-mouthed.

Second only to the tinned sardine as a favourite object for dissection was a species of peasant sausage with an extremely thin skin which refused to be parted from its contents. The first lieutenant only succeeded in detaching tiny fragments of skin because its dry and wrinkled texture endowed it with great adhesive powers. Everyone else devoured these sausages skin and all. Not so the first lieutenant. After vainly hacking and probing with knife and fork for what seemed like an eternity, he ended by cutting away so much of the sausage that little remained. The Captain could contain himself no longer.

'Pity we don't keep a dog on board.'

But even that was too subtle for the first lieutenant. He glanced up without expression and stubbornly continued to sculpt away at his sausage.

The second engineer was as little to the Captain's taste, because of his vulgar grin and bombastic manner.

'How's your understudy, Chief?' I overheard him ask. 'No great shakes, eh?' The Chief merely shrugged and wagged his head to and fro. It was a gesture borrowed from the Old Man himself.

'Come on, Chief, let's hear the worst.'

'Hard to tell,' the Chief replied evasively. 'He's what you might call a Nordic type.'

'A pretty slow Nordic type, I'd say.' The Captain chuckled. 'Just the man to step into your shoes – perfect chief engineer material.' He ruminated for a while. 'All that puzzles me is how we're going to dump him.'

At that moment the second engineer appeared. I studied him closely: square-headed and blue-eyed – the ideal model for an illustrated training manual. His brilliantined sluggishness was the exact opposite of our feline Chief.

Because he found so little response in the wardroom, the second engineer spent most of his time with the chief petty officers. The Captain disliked such territorial violations and eyed him askance when he vanished into the CPOs' mess. Insensitive as he was, the second engineer did not notice and blithely joined the CPOs' table whenever space permitted. Small wonder that the atmosphere in the wardroom seldom relaxed when the first lieutenant and second engineer were present.

Conversation remained strictly noncommittal and thorny topics were avoided, but the Captain's self-control occasionally snapped – as at breakfast one day.

'Our lords and masters in Berlin seem to be busy dreaming up new names to call Mr Churchill. What are his latest official titles, the old pirate? Ah yes, I remember. Drunkard, sot, paralytic . . . I must say, he's giving us plenty of trouble for a drink-sodden paralytic.'

The first lieutenant was sitting bolt upright with a look of mulish incomprehension on his face. The Chief had adopted his usual pose – both hands clasping his left knee – and was gazing at a spot between two plates as though it might yield a revelation at any moment.

Silence fell, but the Captain was undeterred.

'Churchill isn't on his knees yet, not by a long chalk. I wouldn't care to guess how many of his ships are getting through – getting through at this moment, while we sit around twiddling our thumbs . . '

A sudden fit of bonhomie seemed to overwhelm him.

'What about some music? Perhaps our ex-Hitler Youth leader would be good enough to put a record on.'

Although nobody looked at the first lieutenant, he flushed and jumped up. The Captain's voice boomed after him: 'Let's have "Tipperary", if you've no objection.'

The first lieutenant returned as the introductory bars blared through the boat. The Captain gave a sarcastic grin. 'I trust the record doesn't offend your ideological sensibilities, Number One?' He turned to the rest of us with his forefinger portentously raised. 'His master's voice – but not ours!'.

I was sitting on the deck in the fore-ends with my knees drawn up and my back against the bulkhead. Seating accommodation was limited in the fore-ends, with all the torpedoes stowed below.

'The cruelty to animals people ought to pay us a visit – then there'd be some fireworks. If cats or dogs had to doss down here . . .'

'They did away with pit-ponies. Nobody cares a fuck about us lot.'

The fore-ends was a free-speech forum. No agonized inhibitions of the sort that reigned in the wardroom. The chief spokesmen were always the same: Ario, Turbo, Dunlop and Manchu. Some of the less articulate brethren steered clear of their quick-fire exchanges. Leaving the others to bicker and brag, they crept into their bunks like nocturnal animals.

'A tart pissed on my back once,' came a voice from one of the hammocks. 'Some sensation, I can tell you.'

'Bet you haven't had a bath since . . .'

'Sensation?' scoffed Ario. 'That's kids' stuff. We had a type on my last boat who said there was nothing to beat a cork with a nail in it and a violin string on the end. All you do is stick the cork up your arse and get somebody to play a tune.'

'Bit complicated, isn't it?'

'Maybe,' Ario insisted, 'but it doesn't half tickle you up.'

Fragments of conversation drifted to my ears from elsewhere in the compartment. 'She still doesn't know who got her in the family way.'

'Why not?'

'Why not? Jesus wept, how dumb can you get? Stick your bum against a circular saw and tell us which tooth nicked you first!'

Uproarious laughter.

I saw ERA Johann on the bridge for the first time. The daylight made him look twice as haggard as he did in the artificial light of the engine-room. Although he had only just come on deck he was already shivering like a hospital case.

'Parky enough for you, Johann?' I asked. Instead of replying, he stared grimly over the bridge rail. It was clear that the sight of the sea made him uneasy. I had never seen him look so peevish. His gaze registered quiet satisfaction when it rested on pipes and gauges. The gleaming silver floor-plates of the engine-room were his proper basis of existence, the aroma of oil was balm to his lungs, but this here – this spectacle of Nature in the raw – ugh! His air of revulsion conveyed that while seascapes might be all right for primitive forms of life like seamen, they meant nothing to specialists, intimate with highly complex machinery.

Thoroughly disgruntled, he gave a shudder of chill distaste and disappeared below.

The second lieutenant chuckled. 'He's gone to tell his engines about the naughty sea. Trogs are a funny lot. Fresh air chokes them, daylight gives them pink-eye and sea-water is their equivalent of hydrochloric acid.'

'That doesn't apply to the Chief,' I said.

The second lieutenant was seldom stuck for a quick rejoinder. 'Oh him – he's plain perverted.'

In my book, visits to the bridge were an unalloyed delight. Taking full advantage of the rule that allowed two men on the bridge plus the look-outs, I sampled the fresh air as often as I could. A sense of freedom overcame me as soon as I poked my head out of the upper hatch. Goodbye to the mechanical chicken-coop with its steel walls, fumes, stench and humidity, and up into the light and pure air.

First search the sky for weather signs, then glance quickly round the horizon. Breathing deeply with my head back, I could look far into infinity through windows in the clouds. The sky was a vast kaleidoscope which threw up new images with every passing hour.

Now, for instance, the sky overhead was an intense blue. Every hole in the swiftly moving blanket of cloud was filled with ultramarine. Rents appeared in the blanket as it neared the horizon. There the blue was thinner, as though the colour had been diluted with bleach. Ahead of us, a little patch of red still hung above the horizon with a single violet cloud floating at its centre.

Before long, something miraculous happened astern. Halfway to the zenith, a moist and spreading pool of steel-blue light mingled with the flood of ochre that rose from beyond the horizon. The marginal areas at first took on a dirty greenish tone, but this was gradually swamped by a faintly luminous Veronese blue in which only a trace of green persisted.

At noon precisely, the sky was flooded with a cool silvery grey wash. The cloud-castles had disappeared. Only a handful of silky cirrus clouds remained to spread their veils before the sun and spin its light into shimmering strands of silver. A gentle pastoral took shape, composed of pale and delicate tones like those inside an oyster-shell.

By afternoon, another transformation had taken place to starboard. Yellow and orange streaks were glowing behind dark-blue clouds. Their colour was rich and heavy, almost oily. The dusky clouds welled from them like smoke from a bush-fire. It was an African sky. My mind's eye supplied table mountains, acacia-trees, gnus and antelopes.

Far away to port, beside a range of clouds resembling unwashed fleece, a rainbow had climbed into the sky. A second and paler rainbow arched above it. Hovering in the centre of the semi-circle was a dark ball like a shell-burst.

Late that afternoon the celestial stage underwent a complete scene-change. The metamorphosis was not achieved with a few drop-curtains and lighting effects alone. Instead, a grandiose cortège of clouds formed up and rapidly invaded the whole sky. Then, as if the interplay of shapes were not dramatic enough, the sun tore a rent in the clouds and transfixed them with slanting spears of flame.

I returned to the bridge after supper. The day was wearily dissolving into night. The only vestige of its light was an occasional dab of crimson on the clouds which floated in the western sky like a row of abacus beads. Soon, only one tuft of vapour continued to reflect the dying radiance. The glow of the setting sun lingered above the horizon for a while, then paled and died there too. Day was done. Night had already scaled the eastern sky, cloaking the water in violet shadows. The sounds of the sea grew louder. Waves soughed beneath our hull like the exhalations of a sleeping giant.

I was regularly wakened when the engine-room watch changed

at midnight. Both watches, the old and new, had to pass through the POs' mess. For a while, both bulkhead doors between it and the engine-room stood open. The muffled pounding swelled to a roar and my bunk curtain flapped as the diesels quaffed huge draughts of air. A member of the outgoing watch squeezed past the table, which had not been folded down, and brushed my curtain completely aside. It would be quite a time before peace descended once more.

I clung to sleep, keeping my eyes closed and trying to ignore the voices round me. Then someone switched the light on beside my bunk and I abandoned hope. The off-watch POs removed their oil-stained jackets and trousers, took a few swigs from their bottles of apple-juice, and climbed into their bunks, chatting in subdued voices.

The bulkhead door opened with a crash. It was Wichmann. He slammed the door shut and switched on all the lights. Although I knew from past experience what would happen next, a perverse curiosity impelled me to watch yet again.

Wichmann had stationed himself in front of the mirror on the bulkhead and was squinting at his reflection. Before combing the hair forward over his face, he ran his thumb-nail over the teeth of his comb, three or four times in each direction. Several attempts were needed to get his parting in the right place. I could see, as he drew back slightly, that his face was irradiated with a sort of religious fervour. He surveyed his image, tilting his head this way and that. Next, he went to his locker and rummaged about in it before returning with a tin of brilliantine. Painstakingly he clogged the tines of his comb with goo and passed it through his hair, again and again, until he obtained a finish sleek enough to reflect individual light bulbs.

Satisfied at last, Wichmann put his beauty aids away, removed his jacket, pulled off his shoes without untying the laces, and rolled into his bunk. He left the lights blazing. Five minutes later, when I climbed down to get at the switch, I glanced into his bunk and saw that tossing and turning had already destroyed the short-lived splendour of his appearance

FRIDAY, 14TH DAY AT SEA. I met the Captain in the control-room. He seemed conversational. I kicked off by asking why so many men still volunteered for U-boat duty in spite of the casualty figures.

The usual minute's reflection. Then, hesitantly :

'You won't get far by pumping the lads themselves. Of course, U-boat Command does have a certain glamour. *Crème de la crème*, Doenitz's private navy, and so on. Propaganda comes into it, naturally . . .'

A longer pause. The Captain stared hard at the deck-plates before continuing. 'Maybe they can't visualize what's in store for them. School, Labour Service, call-up, basic training . . . They've never seen anything or been anywhere – never experienced anything. No imagination, most of them.'

He half-turned to me with a faint grin. 'It can't be much of a thrill, clumping around in jack-boots. We're better off here, God knows. No foot-slogging, no blistered heels. Regular meals, proper bunks, central heating and plenty of invigorating sea-air. Natty uniforms and lots of lovely medal ribbons for going ashore in . . . No, if you ask me, better a U-boat any day than square-bashing or getting your head blown off in a ditch. Everything's relative, after all.'

The Captain's cynical grin went as he picked up his former thread again.

'Maybe it's only possible to run this show with youngsters because they're still – well, under-exposed, in a manner of speaking. Mind you, it's nearly always the senior ranks who survive when the chips are down – men with wives and kids back home. We once picked up some survivors from a destroyer – one of ours. It was only about two hours after she sank. Summer-time, too, so the water wasn't that cold, but most of the younger seamen were already limp in their life-jackets. They'd simply given up, let their heads sag, and drowned, although there was only a moderate sea running. It was the older ones who'd put up a fight. One of the badly wounded must have been forty-plus. He came through in spite of losing a bucket of blood, but the eighteen-year-olds in perfect physical condition – they didn't.'

The Chief wandered up, cocked an eyebrow at the Captain's ruminative tone of voice and began to leaf through the control-room log.

'Actually, we ought to be able to make do with far fewer bodies. I often dream of a submarine crewed by two or three men. Insufficient mastery of technical problems – that's the real reason why we have to carry so many. Most of them are stop-gaps. They plug the deficiencies which the designers have left in the boat's machinery. Men who turn handwheels or throw switches aren't sailors in the true sense. You know the C-in-C's recruiting poster – "Locate, attack, destroy!" It gives me the pip. Who does the attacking in a U-boat? Only the captain. Nobody else gets a peek at the enemy.'

He paused, but there was no need to prompt him. The

Captain was proceeding under his own power today.

'Bloody shame, old Doenitz throwing in his lot with the windbags. We swore by him at first,' he said quietly.

I'd known for some time where the shoe pinched. The Captain's admiration for the C-in-C had been dimmed by his last official communiqué.

'We used to think of him as a sort of naval Moltke, but now it's "Each for the other and all for the Fatherland" – "The Führer's eyes are on you" – the Führer, the Führer, the Führer . . . It's enough to turn your stomach.'

The bitterness in his voice was unmistakable. He tried to camouflage it with a sigh. 'Oh well, that's life.'

The Chief stared straight ahead and played deaf.

'Why so many volunteers?' the Captain said, coming full circle. 'Comradeship, togetherness, team spirit – they have an emotive appeal. And so does the idea of belonging to an élite. You only have to watch the boys on leave, strutting around with the U-boat combat badge on their number ones. Seems to have an effect on the ladies, too . . .'

The intercom crackled. 'Second watch, patrol routine!' This time the summons applied to me. I was to keep one watch as a stoker.

The Chief had given me some cotton-wool for my ears. 'Six hours in an engine-room is plenty when you aren't used to it.'

The suction from the engines held the bulkhead door so tight that I had to exert all my strength to open it. At once, the noise of the diesels smote me like a slap in the face. The hurried clatter of valve tappets and rocker arms provided a percussion accompaniment to the steady flow of sound made by the explosions in the cylinders and the deep bass roar which came, I assumed, from the supercharger.

Johann, the ERA whose watch it was, took no immediate notice of me. He was keeping an eye on the rev counter. The needle oscillated sharply. Sometimes it jumped a few degrees and gave a nervous tremor because our screws encountered varying resistance in the turbulent sea. Even without the rev counter, I should have been more aware in the stern than in the control-room of how the waves first held the boat back, then released her and imparted a forward thrust. The screws laboured hard at first, but they turned all the quicker once we had struggled clear.

Johann checked the oil and cooling-water pressure in turn. Then, with the averted gaze of a diagnostician, he felt the oil-pressure lead which branched off beneath the forced lubrication pump, to gauge its temperature. Finally he mounted a gleaming step that ran along the side of the engine and felt the pulsating rocker arms, all with very slow, precise and deliberate movements.

In a shout, Johann told me what I had to do: make sure that nothing ran hot, feel the cooling-water pipes, check the rocker arms as he had just done, and, when he gave the signal, de-coke the exhaust flaps.

He retired to the control position and wiped his hands on a hank of multi-coloured cotton waste. Then he produced a bottle of juice from the box beside his little desk. His Adam's apple jerked as he took several vigorous swallows.

The pulsating joints were dripping with oil. I felt them leap under my hand, one after another. Every joint was uniformly warm and the detonations in the cylinders succeeded one another smoothly.

Fifteen minutes later Johann opened the door to the galley and turned a handwheel on the deckhead. 'Closing the outboard induction valve,' he yelled in explanation. 'Now the engine'll draw air from inside the boat. Nice draught!'

Another hour passed. Johann left his control position and walked down the aisle between the engines. Moving along the diesel that was running, he opened one test-cock after another. A jet of flame spurted from each. Johann gave a satisfied nod. I couldn't help thinking how illogical it seemed that smoking should be forbidden below deck when this firework display was permitted.

Balancing like a tightrope-walker, Johann returned to his control position. He wiped a couple of spots of oil from a polished surface as he passed and mopped his hands again on the ball of cotton waste. After a while he reached up and adjusted the flow of fuel by opening a water-pressure valve. Then he glanced at the electric telethermometer which registered the temperature of every cylinder and exhaust manifold. Using a pencil-stub so short that he could only hold it with his fingertips, he made various entries in the engine-room log: estimated oil-consumption, temperatures, fluctuations in pressure.

The helmsman who had just been relieved shot through the bulkhead door like a cork and squeezed past me with his arms full of wet oilskins. He tottered farther aft, steadying himself by the engine hand-rails, to the motor-room, where he draped the wet garments round the stern tube to dry.

The stoker PO was sitting on a low tool-box in front of the port engine control position, engrossed in a dog-eared paperback. His engine was stopped, so he had nothing to do, but he had to remain at his post. The port engine might be called on at any moment.

Repeatedly I teetered back and forth along the polished step flanking the starboard engine. The gauges were registering normal pressure.

Johann signed to me to sit in the bulkhead doorway to the motor-room. Brown bags containing escape gear hung from the switchboards close beside it. The sight of them was an invitation to brood on the distance between me and the control-room. It was a long way to the conning-tower hatches. Not that it would matter how far you were from the conning-tower if the boat got clobbered 100 metres down, but the sensation of being cooped up in the stern could be nerve-racking. Besides, a submarine could just as easily meet her end on the surface – by ramming, for example. Look-outs and control-room hands might survive such things, stokers – under normal circumstances – never did.

A bell shrilled above the noise of the engine and a red light went on. I started violently. The stoker PO had jumped to his feet. Johann made a reassuring gesture, and I got the message: it was a call to start the port engine. I had to open the port engine exhaust flaps. The stoker PO clutched in. Compressed air hissed into the cylinders. Johann had already opened the fuel lever. Valves snapped open, the first cylinder fired, tappet rods sprang to life and the port engine awoke from its slumbers. In a moment it was firing on all cylinders, its thunder blending with that of the starboard engine.

Another spell of inactivity. The gauges showed that both engines were supplied with all they needed: fuel, air, lubricating oil and cooling-water.

Three hours of the watch had gone: half-time.

The air in the engine-room rapidly became warmer and heavier, now that the port engine was running as well.

At 1000 the chef brought us a can of sweetened lemon-juice. I drank greedily, straight from the dipper.

Johann raised his thumbs and jerked them at the deckhead. It was time to de-coke the exhaust flaps. Not a job to neglect, because exhaust flaps sealed off the diesel exhaust pipes for diving. They had to be absolutely watertight, or sea-water would penetrate the engines. But incomplete combustion built up deposits which could destroy a watertight seal when the boat dived. At the beginning of the war, U-boats had actually filled and sunk because these deposits prevented the flaps from shutting properly. Now the flaps had to be decoked every four hours.

Another red light, and the engine-room telegraph jumped to half-ahead. Johann moved the fuel-control lever upwards to reduce the flow of oil to the cylinder pumps. The starboard engine dropped its revolutions and the cylinders began to fire less evenly. Then he moved the lever to zero. The engine stopped altogether. Armed with a ratchet-spanner, I exerted all my strength to turn the disc of the exhaust flap back and forth and dislodge the carbon deposits. Back and forth, back and forth, until Johann put a stop to my labours.

Bathed in sweat and panting hard, I stood and watched the starboard engine spring to life again. Shortly afterwards the port engine was stopped and the same procedure began again. Straining at the spanner, I used up what little strength I had left. Rivers of sweat ran down my face.

The two engines had not been running for long when a tense expression came over the ERA's face. He froze, listening to the throb of the diesels, then picked up a torch and an adjustable spanner and squeezed past me. Near the after bulkhead he raised a floor-plate, shone the torch downwards and beckoned to me. A wild confusion of pipes, filters, valves and cocks met my eyes: the systems that controlled water and oil circulation, also fuel supply.

Now I could see it too: a fine jet of water spurting from one of the pipes. Johann gave me a meaningful glance and wriggled between them. Bending over like a contortionist, he managed to reach the fault with his spanner. A minute later he handed up some nuts and bolts and removed a section of packing. He shouted something to me but had to raise his head from the jumble of pipes before I understood. All at once there was plenty to do. The repair proved awkward. A big patch of sweat appeared on the back of Johann's shirt. Eventually, smeared with oil, he extricated himself from the maze and winked at me. The fault was cured, but how had he spotted it in the first place? I could only conclude that, where engines were concerned, he had a sixth sense.

The new watch appeared five minutes before noon. Another swallow of lemonade, a final scrub-up with cotton waste, and I exchanged our Nibelungs' cave for the fresh air of the control-room.

In the POs' mess, Wichmann and Kleinschmidt were conversing from their bunks.

'Beats me sometimes how the womenfolk stand it. I mean, no meat injection for months on end.'

Wichmann was engaged. He evidently brooded about the temptations to which his fiancée might be exposed.

Never one to tread delicately, Kleinschmidt twisted the knife. 'Don't talk to me about women. You only have to say "take a seat" and they're down on their backs with their legs open. I tell you, mate, I could have screwed a dozen a day, this last leave.'

'Fancy yourself, don't you?' was all Wichmann could find to say.

'Why, don't you believe me?' Withering sarcasm. 'Mind you, I'm not saying it applies to your little darling. I bet she keeps hers stuffed with broken glass.'

Kleinschmidt was cut short by a sudden spate of through traffic. He waited for it to subside. 'Let's see, where was I?'

'Belt up,' Wichmann said tersely, and the miracle happened: Kleinschmidt lapsed into offended silence.

SATURDAY, 15TH DAY AT SEA. Two weeks out of St Nazaire. The waves were short today, a confusion of crests devoid of any regularity. The submarine rode them unevenly, her movements made still more erratic by a diminishing swell which rose and fell at wide intervals beneath the choppy surface.

We had sighted nothing for days except a barrel, a few crates and, on one occasion, hundreds of champagne corks – a phenomenon for which the Captain could find neither rhyme nor reason. 'Can't have been a booze-up. Just corks and no bottles – doesn't make sense.'

I stood watch with the quartermaster. My biceps were in better condition than they had been, but my arm and shoulder muscles ached from the weight of the binoculars. I had to rest them with increasing frequency after the first hour. Kriechbaum could keep his glasses poised indefinitely, as though his arms were locked at right angles.

'When you come down to it,' he began abruptly, 'we lead a double life.'

I didn't know what he was driving at. Kriechbaum was anything but articulate. 'I mean – half aboard and half ashore.' He started to say something more but evidently failed to find the right words.

We continued to scan our sectors. 'It's true,' he said at length. 'Out here we're – well, completely self-contained – no mail, no phone calls – nothing. Just the same, there's a sort of – well, link between us and home.'

'Yes?'

'Take worrying, for instance. You can't help wondering

how things are going back home. It's even worse for them — they don't know where we are.'

Another pause. 'When we go to sea – we're as good as dead. If something really happens to a boat, months can go by before the official announcement.'

The quartermaster fell silent, then blurted out: 'If a man's married, he's only half a man. Out here, I mean.'

Light dawned at last. He was talking about himself. In replying, I treated it as a generalization.

'I wouldn't know, Kriechbaum. Does a wedding-ring make that much difference? Tell me, how long has the Chief been married?'

'Eighteen months or so.'

He began to talk freely, relieved that his own problems were no longer under discussion. 'She gave him an ultimatum: "You can't expect me to ruin my life for you" and so on. Not that she looks the type to sit around moping while we're at sea. Hard luck on the Chief. Now she's pregnant again, into the bargain.'

When Kriechbaum resumed after a lengthy pause, his hesitancy had returned. We were obviously back to square one. 'You carry a lot of ballast around with you in this life, like it or not. It's best to forget about home altogether.'

Conversation lapsed. We went on scouring the horizon.

Ahead of us, two points on the port bow, a fog-bank hugged the horizon like a bank of dirty green wool. The quartermaster scanned it repeatedly. Fog-banks held special perils.

A good ten minutes went by before he picked up the thread again. 'Maybe you're right, Lieutenant. Maybe it's best to forget everything for the duration.'

My thoughts turned to Midshipman Ullmann, who had worries of his own. Ullmann's snub nose and freckles made him look fourteen, an impression heightened by his faint air of boyish cunning. I had seen him once at base, going ashore in his number ones. The over-sized peaked cap might have been purchased by a thrifty mother for her growing son.

Ullmann was universally popular. Stocky rather than short, he looked physically tough. He also looked older, seen close to. The lines round his mouth were more than laugh-lines.

One day when I was alone with him in the POs' mess, Ullmann's manner became odd. He fidgeted with the cutlery, pushed things to and fro, laid a knife parallel with a fork and glanced up, trying to catch my eye. Eventually he came to the point.

'Do you know the florist's next to the Café Pierrot?'

'Sure, and the two girls who run it. Pretty little things, both of them. Jeannette and – what's the other one called?'

'Françoise,' Ullmann said. 'I'm engaged to her – off the record, of course.'

Involuntarily I clicked my tongue. Our little midshipman – engaged to a French girl . . .

'She seems very nice,' I said.

He perched on his bunk with his head in his hands and looked helpless, as though the confession had sapped his strength.

Little by little it came out: Françoise was pregnant. Ullmann wasn't so naïve as to be unaware of what might happen. We were the enemy, and collaborators received summary punishment. The midshipman knew how active the Maquis were. I gathered that his girl realized it even better than he did.

'She doesn't want to go through with it,' he said, but so hesitantly that I prompted him.

'No?'

'Not if we come back.'

I had a sudden memory of U-A gliding out of the bunker. The Captain had glanced round the basin and turned to me. 'Friend of yours?' he growled, nodding in the direction of an empty building on the right of the lock. I saw a girl waving from a second-floor window.

'Not that I'm aware of,' I said. 'I thought the whole area was off-limits to civilians.'

'So it damn well is.'

Ullmann was still waiting for some comment. I said: 'When we left harbour, was that your – what's her name – Françoise waving goodbye?'

'Yes. I told her it wasn't on.'

'But there are sentries all over the place.'

'I know, but she insisted. She came on her bicycle,' he added, as though that explained everything.

'Mm,' I said. Embarrassment had robbed me of ideas. 'Look, Ullmann, don't worry – everything'll turn out fine, I'm sure it will.'

'Yes,' was all he said.

Up with the glasses again, wishing they were half the weight. Beside me, Kriechbaum waxed bitter. 'I wish a few of our armchair warriors could see this – miles of open sea and not a sniff of the enemy. I can guess how they think it goes: cruise around for a day or two, and along comes a nice fat convoy – scores of ships laden to the gunwales. Into the attack, let fly with everything you've got, shrug off a couple

of depth-charges, and head for home. Victory pennants fluttering from the periscope, grins all round and a brass band on
the wharf.'

Throughout this speech, Kriechbaum's eyes never left his
sector. Now he lowered his binoculars and glanced at me
with wry amusement. The glasses were scarcely poised again
when he added a postscript.

'They ought to make a film of the real thing. Close-ups of
bugger-all. A few clouds, a couple of sea-gulls. Mouldy bread,
grubby necks, rotting lemons, torn shirts and sweaty blankets
– not to mention our miserable bloody faces.'

SUNDAY, 16TH DAY AT SEA. The Chief seemed to be in a good
mood, probably because he'd carried out an unusually complicated repair that morning.

'Haven't heard tell of Trumann for quite a while,' the
Captain said. 'He must have sailed days ago.'

Nothing from Trumann. Nothing from Kortmann or Merkel
either. We'd picked up some relayed signals to Kallmann and
Saemisch asking for position reports, also reports from Flechsig
and Bechtel.

'It's a lousy month,' grumbled the Captain. 'The others don't
seem to be having any more joy than we are.'

Another hour and ten minutes to kill before supper. Seventy
minutes, four thousand two hundred seconds.

PO Telegraphist Hinrich came in with a signal addressed
to us direct. The Chief took the strip of paper and fetched
the cipher machine from its locker.

As though by chance, Kriechbaum appeared. He hovered,
watching the Chief out of the corner of his eye, but the Chief
made a great show of concentration and gave nothing away.
Eventually, with a wink at Kriechbaum, he handed the decoded signal to the Captain.

It was simply a request for a position report.

The Captain disappeared into the control-room with Kriechbaum. Before long, the telegraphist would be tapping out a
reply.

SECOND SLOG

I went on the bridge as often as I could. The sky was a different colour each morning. There were skies of vitriol and pistachio green, skies astringent green as lime-juice held to the light, or dull as the greenish froth from a boiled-over saucepan of spinach, or ice-cold as a cobalt green shading to Naples yellow.

The vault of heaven had many yellows to offer. A frequent morning shade was pale chrome yellow, whereas the evening skies were a rich colour like brass. Sometimes the whole sky became enveloped in yellow flame. The clouds, too, could turn a dirty sulphurous shade of yellow.

For sheer splendour, the red skies were unsurpassed. Morning and evening alike, the atmosphere was flooded with intense red light. The reds seemed to be the richest and most varied shades of all, ranging from a faint pink flush to delicate opaline rose, from hazy mallow-red to harsh hydrant-red. Between these lay mother-of-pearl red, geranium-red and scarlet, and between red and yellow lay infinite gradations of orange.

Violet infernos in the sky were rarer than red. The diffuse and fugitive violets, which swiftly dulled to grey, were reminiscent of worn taffeta, but the blackish, turbid blue-violets looked malign and menacing. There were also evenings steeped in purple-violets so gaudy that no painter would have dared to reproduce them.

The grey skies were infinitely varied in tone. They could be warm or chill, mingled with umber, dark ochre or burnt sienna. Velasquez grey, dove-grey, totally inexpressive grey like concrete or steel.

Apart from grey, the sky was mostly blue. A splendid deep blue above a turbulent sea, whipped high by angry gusts of wind: a cobalt blue infinity bare of storm clouds. Sometimes the blue was as rich as indigo dissolved in water or greenish cerulean blue, rare and exquisite.

The colours of the sea were as variable as those of the sky — crepuscular grey, black and bottle-green, violet and white — and ever-changing in texture: silky, matt, ribbed, ruffled, splintered, choppy, corrugated, undulant . . .

U-A was still freighted with fourteen torpedoes and 120

rounds for the 88mm. Test firings had made minor inroads into the anti-aircraft ammunition, and a sizeable quantity of our 114 tons of oil had been used. We were also lighter by a considerable proportion of our supplies.

So far, we were a dud investment on the part of Germany's Supreme Commander. We had failed to inflict the slightest damage on the enemy. We had merely stood watches, eaten and digested, inhaled bad smells and produced some of our own.

We hadn't fired a single torpedo. Misses would at least have made more room in the fore-ends, but every fish was still in residence, lovingly tended, carefully greased and regularly maintained.

As the sky darkened, so the rags of water that fluttered from the jumping-wire at every dip of the bow turned as grey as laundry washed in wartime soap.

We were bludgeoning our way into a head sea. The submarine pitched like a rocking-horse, up and down, up and down. The strain of peering through binoculars became a torment. The grey light seemed to press upon my eyelids through a gauze filter. The grey soup contained nothing solid to look at, and fine spindrift made the grey still more opaque.

If only something would happen! I longed for a brief spurt at full power – anything that would make U-A cleave the waves instead of lurching into them at this soul-destroying jog-trot.

As the oldest inhabitant of the fore-ends, Electrician Hagen enjoyed universal respect – and his manner conveyed that he knew it. The upswept ends of his moustache almost brushed his eyebrows, and his forehead was hidden by a thick quiff of hair. His black beard was dense and powerful because he retained it ashore. Hagen's favourite interpolation – 'I don't mean to boast, but . . .' – had become a fore-ends catch-phrase. He had seven patrols to his credit, six of them in another U-boat.

'Tcha!' said Hagen, and everyone stopped talking.

Hagen savoured our expectancy to the full. He ceremoniously wiped his palms on his hirsute chest and tilted the tea-pot, then sipped with serene enjoyment.

Gigolo was the first to crack. 'Come on, Hagen, don't be bashful. Speak, Lord, for thy servant heareth.'

'I was just thinking,' Hagen began.

'Not that he means to boast, but . . .' came a voice from

one of the bunks.

Hagen turned and shot the speaker a look of histrionic scorn. 'This lousy weather puts me in mind of the time they nearly got us in the Bristol Channel. A dozen escorts up top and not much water under the keel. Not a hope of getting away dived. Whoomphas all day long . . .'

He took a mouthful of tea and swilled it noisily between his teeth a couple of times before swallowing it.

'Plenty of malfunctions – earths all over the place and the box dropping through the bottom. The Brits were just hanging around, waiting for us to come up. Then it'd have been off to Canada with the next batch of lumberjacks.'

'Optimist,' said someone.

Hagen ignored him. 'Come the second night, we took the bit between our teeth – surfaced like a fucking cork and high-tailed it out of there trimmed down to a whisker. Next day we got a destroyer. Almost bumped into her in the fog – had to shoot it out at spitting distance.'

Hagen lapsed into profound meditation. Gigolo again played the midwife : 'All right, mate, let's have it.'

'We got her at point-blank range.' Hagen clarified the position with two matches. 'Here's the enemy destroyer and here's us.' He arranged them head-on. 'I don't mean to boast, but I spotted her first.'

'There he goes again!' came the voice from the bunk. 'What did I tell you?'

Hagen cut the story short. Wordlessly he illustrated the attack by shifting the matches about. 'She went down in seconds.'

He picked up the match representing the British destroyer and snapped it across the middle. Then he rose and mashed it with his boot for good measure. Everyone could see the full and implacable extent of his wrath. Gigolo said : 'Encore!'

'Manchu' Benjamin declared himself overcome with emotion. He looked Hagen full in the eye and simultaneously tried to purloin a slice of bread which the electrician had just buttered. Hagen alertly rapped his knuckles.

'Hands off, little man.'

Manchu was wholly unabashed. 'My mistake,' he quipped, 'as the hedgehog said to the lavatory-brush.'

Turbo too had a contribution to make. He had cut a cigar and a plum out of an illustrated magazine and glued them together to form an obscene montage. This he proudly handed round.

'Filthy bugger,' said Hagen.

It was three days and three nights since the wireless office had picked up anything except relayed position reports from other U-boats. No news of any sinkings. 'Worst month ever,' was the Captain's comment. 'Absolutely rock-bottom.'

The waves seethed and effervesced. Repeated gusts plucked masses of water into the air, whipping the surface into a grey-white expanse. Whenever our bow struggled free of a wave, water streamed from either flank like an icing-sugar fringe.

The Captain was so broody at breakfast that he forgot to chew. It wasn't until the steward came to clear away that he surfaced with a start and hurriedly operated his lower jaw for two minutes before relapsing into meditation.

Listlessly, he pushed his plate away and returned to the present. He glanced at us amiably enough and opened his mouth to say something. Not a word emerged. Finally, he took refuge in a few official pronouncements: 'Trim dive 0900. Midshipman's instruction 1000. Maintain course until midday.' Same old thing . . .

The first lieutenant did nothing to improve the Captain's mood. His expression, always faintly censorious and often disdainful, was enough to fray the strongest nerves. Above all, the Captain was irritated by his ill-disguised political convictions. Staring after him as he left to go on watch the day before, the Old Man had commented on his apparent hatred of the enemy. 'Must be his training, I suppose. Oh well, at least he takes a line and sticks to it.'

I would have given a lot for half-an-hour's walk. My thigh muscles were flaccid with lying, standing and sitting. I craved hard manual labour – tree-felling, for instance. A scent of resin invaded my nostrils at the very thought.

The telegraphist had received a signal. We strove hard to look casual, though each of us was hoping for a word that would bring our pleasure-cruise to an end. The Captain stared scornfully at the cipher machine, took the slip of paper and read it, lips mutely spelling out the message, then disappeared through the bulkhead without a word.

We exchanged meaningful glances.

Gnawed by curiosity, I went to the control-room. He was there, bent over the chart. I waited in vain for some hint of what the signal contained. The Captain was holding it in his left hand and using the dividers with his right.

'Could be,' I heard him utter. 'Not entirely out of the question.'

Uncertainty proved too much for the first lieutenant, who asked to see the strip of paper. It read: 'C-in-C from U-M. Convoy Square XY, mean course 060, zigzagging, speed 8 knots.' A glance at the chart showed me that Square XY was within reach of us.

The quartermaster cleared his throat and casually asked the Captain for a new course. From his manner, the signal might have contained the latest wholesale potato prices.

The Captain showed equally little emotion. All he said was: 'Better hang on a bit.'

Nothing happened for a while. The Chief explored a hollow tooth with his tongue and Kriechbaum inspected his finger-nails while the Captain drew intercepting courses at various speeds.

I took a handful of prunes from the crate and chewed them vigorously, doing my best to detach every last shred of flesh from the stones. The control-room hand had nailed an empty milk-can to the wooden bulkhead panelling. It was half-full of stones. Mine were the cleanest by far.

U-M. That was the boat commanded by Martens, who had been the Captain's first lieutenant and was now serving with the 6th Flotilla at Brest.

Further signals informed us that three U-boats had received orders to take up the chase, then four, then five.

Ours wasn't among them.

Hours trickled by, and still we received no signal addressed to U-A. The Captain sat huddled in the corner of his bunk and busied himself with an assortment of coloured folders containing pamphlets of every description, confidential and secret instructions, tactical rules, flotilla orders and other directives. In view of his well-known aversion to official bumf in all its forms, he could only have been masking an excitement like ours.

At 1700 another signal came in. The Captain raised his eyebrows. His whole face seemed to blossom. A signal addressed to us! He read it, and gloom descended once more. Almost absently, he shoved the slip across to me. It was a request for a weather report.

The quartermaster drafted one and gave it to the Captain to sign. 'Barometer 1005 rising, air temperature 5 degrees, sea 7 degrees, wind north-west 6, sea and swell 5-6, four-eighths cloud, cirro-stratus, visibility 7 miles, position KM.'

To avoid being infected by the Captain's black mood, I fled

the control-room and went up on the bridge. The gauzy cirrus clouds had thickened and were gradually obscuring the shreds of blue that remained. The sky would soon be dressed in grey once more. The light cooled. Dark clouds had gathered on the horizon, their lower edges merging imperceptibly with the grey of the sky beyond. They only stood out clearly against the whitish grey above them. As I stood there with both hands thrust deep into the pockets of my leather jacket, offsetting the boat's movements with my knee-joints, the clouds swelled like slowly inflated balloons. On the starboard bow, the wind tore a gash in the overcast and almost as swiftly closed it again. The clouds formed a gigantic phalanx and started to overrun the entire sky. Next, as if to compound the chaos of these multitudinous displacements and intersections, the sun appeared through a rift. Its slanting fasces of fire embellished the throng of tumid shapes with a dramatic interplay of light and shade. A bright patch flared up on the sea, too, broad on the starboard beam. The solar spotlight wandered over an arched and swollen curtain of vapour, setting it ablaze and accentuating the darkness beyond. Then it scurried to and fro as if forbidden to linger and uncertain which cloud to bedeck with its aureole.

The second lieutenant was unimpressed by celestial transformation scenes. 'Bloody RAF clouds!' he grumbled. To him, the magnificent spectacle smacked of guile and deceit. Again and again he raised his binoculars to scan the cloud-castles, which had now climbed almost to the zenith.

I went below to fetch my camera. Evening was upon us when I returned. The sky was sprinkled with iridescent colours – saturated with them. Suddenly abandoned by the sunlight, the clouds resumed their own grey uniform. The full moon, pallid as a spectre, hovered above the horizon. It was 1800.

Conversation languished after supper as hopes of another signal receded. The Captain was restive. Every fifteen minutes he disappeared into the control-room and busied himself at the chart-table. Five pairs of eyes homed on his lips whenever he returned, but in vain. He said nothing.

Eventually the Chief tried to coax him out of his peevish silence. 'About time we heard something more from Martens, isn't it?'

The Captain gave no sign of having heard. The Chief picked up a book. Very well, if conversation was out, I might as well pretend to read too.

The second lieutenant and the second engineer were leafing through old magazines. The first lieutenant devoted himself to some official-looking files.

I was just squeezing past the wireless office on my way to fetch a book from my locker when I saw the telegraphist hurriedly writing in the glow from his little desk-lamp.

I halted in my tracks. Back to the wardroom, where the second lieutenant quickly decoded. A look of rueful surprise. Something was wrong.

The Captain took the decoded message. He read it aloud to us.

'C-in-C from U-M. Surprised by destroyer in rainstorm. Counter-attacked 4 hours. Contact lost. Now pursuing Square BK.'

His voice trailed off into silence. He stood staring at the signal for a good minute, drew in a lungful of air, stared again, and finally expelled the air with rounded cheeks, slumping into his corner of the settee as he did so. Not a word, not a profanity. Nothing.

Later that evening we were leaning against the conservatory rail abaft the bridge.

'That's the crazy part,' the Captain said. 'You get the feeling you're swanning round the Atlantic all on your own, but you can bet there are hundreds of ships at sea this very minute – some of them not far away, probably, except that they're beyond the horizon.' Bitterly, he added: 'The curvature of the earth – the Almighty must have invented it specially for the Brits' benefit. What are we expected to see at this height? We couldn't be much lower if we were sitting in a duck-punt. It's bloody ridiculous that they haven't thought of something.'

'Like aeroplanes?' I said hesitantly.

'Oh sure, aeroplanes – you mean those things the British use. Where are our naval reconnaissance aircraft, that's what I'd like to know? The Reich Forester-in-Chief talks plenty, but it's all wind and piss.'

The Chief appeared, just in time to spare Goering a further tongue-lashing.

'Thought I'd grab a breath of air.'

'Getting a bit crowded up here,' I said, and went below.

A glance at the chart. No change: the pencil-line marking our course zigzagged to and fro like a carpenter's rule.

The Captain followed me down. He perched on the chart-stowage and sat in silence before resuming. 'We may be lucky, even so. If they deploy enough boats, there's always a chance that one of them will make contact.'

Next morning I read the signal that had come in during

the night: 'C-in-C from U-M. Search negative Square BK.'

The next day was our worst since leaving base. We eschewed conversation and shunned each other like lepers. I spent most of the time on the wardroom settee. The Chief failed to emerge from the engine-room for lunch and the second engineer followed his example. We three, the first and second lieutenants and I, didn't venture to address the Captain, who stared absently into space and scarcely touched his plateful of thick soup.

Silence also reigned next door in the CPOs' mess.

PO Telegraphist Herrmann refrained from putting a record on the turntable, and even the steward went around with the downcast gaze of one serving baked meats to a funeral party.

Finally the Captain's lips moved. 'The bloody British have stopped making mistakes, that's all.'

The atmosphere in the fore-ends was equally lugubrious. Ario whiled away the time by baiting the Vicar.

'Know your trouble, Reverend? Your head's full of crap and you've forgotten to pull the chain.'

'Forgotten?' sneered Dunlop. 'Too fucking lazy to, you mean.'

No retort from the new control-room hand, who looked from one to the other and rolled his eyes at the deckhead in search of divine aid.

'And you can take that look off your face for a start!' fumed Ario. The Vicar promptly switched his gaze to the deck. His ears had gone bright red.

'Makes me downright randy to watch him,' Ario informed the company at large. 'All this blushing and bridling . . . I'm surprised the quacks passed him – I bet his balls haven't dropped yet.'

The Vicar gulped but said nothing.

I entered the POs' mess in time to hear Zeitler remark, knowledgeably: 'First thing in the morning? Nothing to beat it!' No prizes for guessing what. Wichmann and Frenssen were an attentive audience.

'I had to deliver a letter for my Chief once, in Hamburg – that was when I was still in minesweepers. Well, I knocked, and the door was opened by this little blonde piece – she couldn't have been above sixteen. Madam was out shopping, she said, but she wouldn't be long. I nipped inside – they had a sort of hall with a couch in it. I was up her in two minutes flat – no mucking. We'd just finished when the front door opened, but not too wide because of the safety-chain. By the grace of God, you couldn't see the couch through the crack The dolly stuffed her panties under a cushion and I got my flap buttoned just in time to shake stink-fingers with the Chief's old woman. Zeitler's the name, pleased to meet you and all that. It wasn't till I got outside and went to the gents for a leak that I noticed I still had my gear on. That's to say, I didn't notice soon enough. It looked like a yellow cucumber by the finish. The bloke beside me almost bust a gut laughing – I made a proper mess of myself . . .'

The first lieutenant's daily shaving routine was a favourite topic of discussion in the fore-ends.

'He gums up the whole fucking works. Who does he think he is, hogging the heads like that?'

'The Old Man ought to tear him off a strip.'

'One shit-house for the whole crew, and we can't get near the place. Fucking bathing belle!'

Electrician Hagen extracted some photographs from his wallet. One of them showed a middle-aged man lying dead in his coffin. 'My father,' he explained. It sounded like a formal introduction. 'Cut off in his prime, you might say. That's how I'd like to go myself.'

Not daring to look him in the eye, I mumbled: 'Nice picture.'

Hagen seemed satisfied.

I remembered what the Captain had said a few days before. 'With most of the men, their emotional lives are a complete mystery. Who knows how their minds work? Sometimes you hear something and it knocks you sideways – like the story of Frenssen's girl-friend. Frenssen met her two leaves ago. When she received no mail from him she consulted a fortune-teller – they still exist, apparently. Seems Frenssen hadn't made it clear that post offices are few and far between in mid-Atlantic. Anyway, after a lot of palaver, the fortune-teller babbled something like: "Water – I see nothing but water." '

The Old Man mimicked the voices of the clairvoyante and the girl-friend in turn:

' "What, no submarine?" – "No, just water." The girl, who fancied her chances as the future Frau Frenssen, gave a screech: "Oh my God, he must be dead!" – but the fortune-teller clammed up tight. Know the girl's next reaction? She fired off a salvo of letters to Flotilla – wrote to me as well. I had the rest of the story from Frenssen himself. He never got beyond Paris this last leave. Once bitten!'

I was alone in the wardroom except for the Captain. The latest batch of re-transmissions from Kernével included a signal addressed to Bachmann – the third request for a position report in four days.

The Captain wagged his head. 'Not a peep. I reckon he must have had it. They shouldn't have sent him out, the state he was in.'

The old, old subject. When was a U-boat commander ripe for transfer to a shore job? Why didn't some medicine-man ensure that no U-boat sailed with a commander who was verging on total collapse?

Bachmann's Number One was Ziemer. Hard to imagine him dead. I could see Ziemer lying in the sun with the waitress from the officers' mess, busily absorbing an anatomy lesson in French. He used her as a live model. First he grabbed her breasts and said: 'Les tits.' The girl corrected him. 'Les seins.' Then he shoved his hand between her legs. 'Le pussy.' – 'Mais non, le vagin.'

The first lieutenant's voice came to us from next door: instruction in security procedures. The Captain mused in silence for a while. 'All this security lark – it's exaggerated. The British got their hands on an undamaged U-boat ages ago.'

'Really?'

'Yes, Ramlow's boat surrendered in open sea south of Iceland. Code books, ciphers, keys – the Brits got them all at one fell swoop.'

'I'd like to have seen the C-in-C's face.'

'Yes, especially when you think that Ramlow may even have been an undercover agent! You can't trust your own right hand any longer. Heaven knows how he talked his officers round . . .'

At long last, a day that promised fair. I could tell from the first whiff of fresh air in the control-room.

I stood motionless on the bridge, hands deep in the slanting pockets of my leather jacket, knees flexing to the gentle movement of the boat. The lofty vault of the morning sky slowly filled with blue. As soon as the wind had swept it clean, the sun's cyclopean orb peered over the horizon.

I went below and looked at the chart. The line that snaked erratically back and forth across the network of grid squares was punctuated by four-figure times. The pencil-lines between them corresponded to the distance covered every four hours, so their varying length was an indication of our speed during any one period.

The quartermaster appeared at my elbow.

'Not much to show for our efforts, Lieutenant. A few scrawls on a chart, and even they aren't permanent. I have to erase them after the patrol because charts are wanted for re-use. All we ever keep is a tracing.'

I continued to stare at the chart because Kriechbaum showed every sign of pursuing his low-keyed monologue. Instead he asked, after a pause: 'Anything wrong?'

'No, why?'

'I just wondered, the way you were looking.'

Two or three minutes passed. Then he muttered to himself: 'Maybe it's a good thing we don't get any mail. The Navy likes a man to keep his mind on the job.'

Kriechbaum was the last person to indulge in personal confessions. I hadn't suspected that he would ever come out of his shell. It dawned on me how solitary the quartermaster was. His qualifications far exceeded those of the first lieutenant, yet he was only a CPO. That meant he was separated from the officers by an invisible barrier which could not be pierced from his side of the wall. Although his functions lent him special status – he was the Captain's right-hand man in all things navigational – this only accentuated his isolation, notably from his fellow-CPOs but also from the petty officers and men, from whom he had in any case to remain somewhat aloof.

Caught in the no-man's-land between sleep and wakefulness, I listened to the waves hissing along our hull. Unable to sleep, I finally rolled out of my bunk, pulled on my sea-boots and leather jacket, and climbed through the bulkhead into the control-room. It was dimly lit by the small lamp over the control-room PO's desk. The watch-keeping control-room hand was seated on the chart-stowage, peeling potatoes. It was Turbo of the red beard.

'Man on the bridge?' I called up. The quartermaster's face appeared in the hatch opening.

'Affirmative.'

The helmsman was hunched over his illuminated compass-card in the conning-tower.

I groped my way aft between the periscope standards and bridge casing to the anti-aircraft platform. The starboard after look-out made room for me.

The horizon was clearly discernible in spite of the darkness. So were the clouds that sailed across the sky. At one point, almost exactly on the starboard beam, the gloom was beginning to pale. The pale patch spread like a corrosive spot of acid, tincturing the water beneath. For a time the clouds congealed again, but suddenly they parted to reveal the up-turned sickle of the moon. The curve of the full disc stood out cloudy-grey against the blue darkness. A myriad specks of light danced on the short waves. The foam that eddied along our sides shone white. The wake struck sparks and the fore-casing shone brightly, its damp surface throwing back the moonlight. The clouds that passed across the crescent were momentarily charged with silver.

The moon became shrouded in tattered shreds of vapour, but it soon re-emerged to anoint the sea with rivulets of light. After a time, thick clouds blew up from the west like heavy galleons. They blotted out the stars in their path and covered the moon. At once the sea turned to ink. The slits in the gratings were visible no longer. Our stern became a dark mass tilting ponderously from side to side.

The sea rose and fell. The dark wind struck chill on my face and drove the warmth from my body. Here and there, pale flecks showed up in the gloom and combers broke like rows of bared teeth.

The darkness had opened a gulf between me and the quarter-master. We might have been miles apart. I had an urge to stretch out my hand and touch the motionless figure beside me. Then I heard his disembodied voice: 'Wish the moon would make up its mind.' A few murmured words followed, but I failed to catch them because his head was turned.

More clouds had gathered over the moon. The darkness became still more dense. Every now and then, greenish foam swirled phosphorescently along the casing and picked out the lines of our hull. Sometimes I seemed to see shadows even darker than the night. Peering into the gloom with wide and smarting eyes, I only succeeded in conjuring up an illustration from a child's book of sea stories. It came back to me, vivid in every detail: the gigantic bow of a liner knifing into a small sailing-boat, bow-wave thrusting aside a tangle of broken masts and splintered planks, a few shreds of canvas and two figures with their arms raised in mortal terror. And below, engraved in cursive, the caption *Run down!*

The submarine's bow plunged and reared. The phosphorescence grew stronger, illuminating our wake as well. A momentary glimmer of light showed through the open hatch. Someone in the conning-tower must have lit a cigarette.

There was a sudden cold white flash in the sky ahead of us. The edges of the clouds were clearly etched against the darkness. A second shaft of lightning threaded its way silently through the overcast. For seconds on end, a nervous flicker ran along the horizon.

'Odd,' Kriechbaum said. 'Looks like an intermittent contact.'

My mind went back to that night in the approaches to the Bristol Channel. I was standing with my back clamped to the bridge casing when the searchlights began to grope their way through the darkness. As though hovering in a mist, the first white apparition showed up: a trawler with her nets out. The slanting shafts of light picked up another and another, and another – a whole fleet. Tracers from the machine-guns took only seconds to register on their first target. It was less like war than shooting fish in a barrel. Then the 88s opened up, their crews cursing because not a single shell found the sitting targets. It seemed an eternity before the wooden boats went down. What had begun as a surprise attack ended in laborious butchery. Straightforward extermination, not a naval engagement. I'd pictured my first experience of war quite differently. Poor bloody trawlermen. A sudden glare of searchlights followed by the chatter of machine-guns and scream of shells. Not a body to be seen when we ran in close. Had they all jumped overboard? Had someone picked them up? We never found out.

Only one more day at cruising speed to our new patrol area. A signal came in. We waited tensely to know its contents.

The signal was addressed to Flechsig and instructed him to adjust his position 70 miles westwards. Apparently, a convoy was expected to pass there. The quartermaster showed me the spot on a small-scale chart. It was near the American coast, many days' cruising from our own position. A little while later we copied a signal to a submarine near Iceland – Böhler's – and a third signal to one operating near Gibraltar. This was U-J, commanded by Kortmann, who had blotted his copybook by picking up the crew of the *Bismarck*'s fuel tanker.

One U-boat reported that she was unable to dive. Meinig, the flotilla virgin. A U-boat that couldn't dive was halfway to the bottom.

'Bloody hell,' said the Captain. 'They can't even give him

fighter cover – out of range. We'll have to cross our fingers.'

He bent down and tapped the underside of the table three times. 'Let's hope he makes it. It would have to be Meinig.'

None of us spoke. The Captain's lips moved silently. He was probably estimating how long it would take Meinig's boat to reach St Nazaire at cruising speed.

A shiver ran down my back. What would they do if some Sunderlands turned up? Or destroyers? A U-boat was hopelessly inferior to her enemies on the surface. Not enough horse-power to outrun them, no armour-plating, undergunned, more vulnerable than most ships afloat. A single hit on the pressure hull was enough to clinch matters.

The Chief could only click his tongue. It was obvious how closely he identified himself with his opposite number on Meinig's boat. He had gone quite pale.

'Who's Meinig's chief engineer,' asked the Captain, 'Schulze II or Schulze III?'

'Schulze II, sir. A classmate of mine.'

We all stared at the wardroom table for inspiration. My chest felt tight. I also knew someone from Meinig's boat: Habermann, the young Balt who had accompanied me to Gotenhafen on that frightful training course. Midwinter, twenty-five below and an east wind.

The Captain was the first to say something. He tried to change the subject but, strictly speaking, stayed with it.

'A proper submarine, that's what we need. These aren't submarines in the true sense, they're mobile diving bells.'

Silence. I raised my eyebrows and he went on, pausing every other sentence. 'After all, the reserves of power in our batteries are only sufficient for brief periscope attacks or limited periods of evasive action. When you come down to it, we're entirely reliant on access to the surface. We don't have enough amps for more than 80 miles dived, even at economical speed. Run the motors at a maximum submerged speed of nine knots and the batteries pack up inside two hours. Not much, is it? What's more, the batteries represent a vast amount of dead weight. Their lead plates weigh more than all the boat's machinery put together. My idea of a real submarine is a vessel that can travel under water for an indefinite period, in other words, without engines that need air and produce exhaust gases. It wouldn't be as vulnerable, either, because it wouldn't require all the gadgets and installations necessary for surface travel: exhaust flaps, air induction valves – all those openings in the pressure hull. What we need is some form of propulsion that's independent of the atmosphere. Baah!'

We had barely reached our new patrol area when a signal came in. Together with various other U-boats, we were to form a reconnaissance patrol. Our patrol-line lay some distance farther west. It would take us two days at cruising speed to get there.

'They've code-named the group "Werewolf",' the Captain said sarcastically. 'Very imaginative! The C-in-C must have appointed a sort of court poet to dream these names up. Werewolf! Puss-in-Boots would have done just as well, but no – never pass up an opportunity to bang the drum . . .'

Even 'theatre of operations' was too high-flown for the Captain's taste. If he had had his way, current naval jargon would have had its fangs drawn. He sometimes pondered for hours until he found words of suitable banality to inscribe in his patrol report.

I re-read what I had noted in my blue excercise book.

Sunday, Day 16. Convoy reported heading east. Are steering 090 to intercept probable route.

Monday, Day 17. New patrol-line received. Farther south. In other words, the dragnet has been shifted southwards. Only five boats – some dragnet! Either the mesh is too big or the net's too small. Speed 8 knots. Let's hope we've got our fixes right. Let's also hope Flotilla Staff appreciate how unfavourable weather conditions are in our area.

Visibility too poor for surface action. The Old Man: 'Could bump into anything, in this lot.'

Tuesday, Day 18. New patrol-line, course 170, speed 6 knots.

Wednesday, Day 19. Another sweep. Slight swell, very misty, surface action still impossible. The weather must have joined the Allies.

Thursday, Day 20. Wireless silence except for sighting reports. More than five boats now massed in our area. The enemy mustn't get wind of us. Search courses have yielded nothing. Medium swell. Light wind from the north-west. Strato-cumulus, but layer of mist clinging to water. Still no sign of convoy.

FRIDAY, 21ST DAY AT SEA. We were allotted yet another patrol-line.

Captain's comment: 'God knows where they've got to!'

Always the same picture. The Old Man, hunched over the chart on his elbows. Deep in thought, he occasionally reached for the dividers and checked a position.

'They could be dodging north because the nights are long. Start looking in the north and they promptly swing south in a wide arc. They steer a crazy course when they have to — time seems to mean nothing to them these days. Bigger patrol areas, that's the answer.' He suddenly raised his voice. 'What price our heroes of the air, Herr Goering?'

As if he'd made enough noise, he relapsed into a murmur. 'Anyway, their navigation's always to cock. Twenty or thirty miles mean bugger-all to the Luftwaffe.'

Carefully, he applied the parallel ruler to the chart, bending low over the table. He tried it in various positions and finally enlisted the aid of the dividers.

The performance continued until he thrust the dividers at a spot in the uniform blue. 'That's where our patrol-line ought to be. That's where they'll pass, or my name's Winston Churchill.'

I could see nothing but two little puncture-marks in the network of grid squares — no other directional aids at all. It was none the less clear that vivid images were taking shape in the Captain's head: plumes of smoke beyond the horizon, thin and diffused, barely visible. Perhaps he could see deck-houses, liner superstructures, derricks, ships with big hatches, vessels whose superstructure towered aft: tankers.

'It's a godforsaken business,' he snorted, 'this interminable swanning around.'

At last, with an effort, he heaved himself up off the chart-table. He stared irresolutely at the chart for a while before tossing the ruler on to it with a sigh. His hands twitched in a gesture of resignation. Then he abruptly turned to go forward, ducked through the bulkhead doorway, and disappeared into his cubby-hole.

SUNDAY, 23RD DAY AT SEA. The wind had freshened, turning the sea into a vast expanse of combers. The waves were not very high, but every one broke. As a result, the sea looked grizzled and ancient.

The sky was still opaque, a uniform grey blanket suspended close above our heads. To starboard, a voluminous curtain of rain began to fall from the overcast. The wall of rain was slate-grey with a trace of violet. Moisture drifted from it in every direction, like mist. The Captain sent below for his oilskins and sou'wester. He swore under his breath.

And then the curtain engulfed us. Tongues of rain scourged the sea. The waves cowered under their impact, flattened and robbed of any lustre. Our plunging bow continued to rip them apart and send up foaming geysers. Torrents of rain and salvoes of spray met and mingled on our faces. The deluge seemed to descend on us from some gargantuan bucket.

The white-veined glassy green of the waves vanished. Not a glimmer, not a hint of colour. Nothing but uniform, soul-destroying grey.

The look-outs stood like monoliths defying a primeval flood. Binoculars were useless – they would have blurred in seconds. Not a trace of light anywhere. It was as though the rain meant to drown us on our feet.

The ferocious violence of the downpour did not lessen until evening. Night had fallen before the rain entirely ceased.

MONDAY, 24TH DAY AT SEA. In the control-room. The Captain was talking half to himself and half to me. 'Strange how quickly any new weapon or technique loses its edge. The advantage seldom lasts more than a few months. As soon as we devised the pack system the British re-vamped their escort system. It worked, too – Prien, Schepke and Kretschmer were all lost in action against a single convoy. Then we bring out acoustic torpedoes with homing warheads, and straight away the British start towing these damned foxers on long steel wires – they attract torpedoes because they make more noise than a ship's screws. Action and reaction – it's always the same. There's nothing like blood-lust for stimulating the spirit of invention . . .'

We had been sailing into limbo for over three weeks. The days limped monotonously by. They crept above the eastern skyline, spread their threadbare quilt of grey, and subsided in the west.

We were ploughing northwards through the high swell in accordance with the convoy's putative line of advance. The engine-room telegraph stood at 'Slow ahead'. The throb of the engines was thin and irregular. Our bow-wave rolled aside in a weary and lacklustre fashion. We were literally creeping through the water. Fuel economy was the watchword, but our reserves were dwindling minute by minute, even at economical speed.

U-A's last patrol had been a wash-out. Without firing a single torpedo, she returned to base after a tedious and protracted outing. The second lieutenant, who was alone in trying to make a joke of it, swore that U-A's reputation had scared the British away.

It took us half a day to reach the northern end of our patrol area. The helmsman called up through the open conning-tower hatch: 'Time to alter course!'

'Hard-a-port. Steer one-eight-zero,' ordered the officer of the watch.

Slowly the bow swung halfway round the horizon. Our wake described a hairpin bend, and the sun, filtered to a white patch by superimposed layers of cloud, crawled to the other side of the boat.

'Course one-eight-zero, sir,' came the helmsman's voice from below.

The compass card showed 180. Before, it had shown 360. Nothing else had changed.

There was little to be seen from the bridge. The sea had dozed off too, its only sign of life a few wavelets on a diminishing swell. The air was still and the clouds hung motionless like captive balloons.

For all the weariness in my bones, I found it impossible to resist watching the minute-hand creep round the dial on the galley bulkhead. At last I drifted into a twilight state.

Abruptly, my thin shroud of sleep was rent by the alarm bell.

The deck tilted.

Dishevelled from his bunk, the Chief was perched behind the two planesmen. The Captain stood motionless at his shoulder. The quartermaster, who had given the alarm, was clinging to the ladder, still panting from the effort of securing the upper lid.

'Afterplanes to rise,' the Chief ordered. 'Foreplanes up ten, afterplanes up fifteen – keep that depth.'

Kriechbaum finally put me in the picture. 'There was a shadow on the starboard beam – a sharp one.'

The hydrophone was manned. The operator's inclined head jutted into the passage. His eyes were unseeing as he slowly searched the water for sounds. 'Propeller noise zero-seven-zero, sir – going away,' he reported. Then, after a while: 'Propellers growing fainter, still going away.'

'Very good,' the Captain said impassively, and gave a slight shrug. 'Steer one-eight-zero.' He disappeared through the forward bulkhead. From the look of it, we were staying deep for the time being.

'Thank God for a bit of peace and quiet.'

'Must have been travelling fast and unescorted. Not a chance, on a night as dark as this.'

I was asleep before my head hit the bolster.

'C-in-C from U-X. Enemy convoy in sight.'

'C-in-C from U-X. Convoy sighted Square XW, course 160, speed 10 knots.'

'C-in-C from U-W. Enemy zigzagging, mean course 050, speed 9 knots.'

'C-in-C from U-K. Convoy proceeding in several columns with flank protection. Course 020, speed 9 knots.'

Relayed signals obliged us to take note of everything that happened in the theatre of operations, but none of the reported convoys was within range. They had all been sighted in the North Atlantic. Our present position was too far south.

The captain sucked at his cold pipe.

'The people at Kernével scrape together all they can find in the way of intelligence, and still nothing goes right. Maybe our agents are asleep — certainly, our aerial reconnaissance is non-existent. What's more, our cipher experts seem to be incapable of cracking an enemy code.'

A pause. 'But the Brits . . . They seem to know everything: our times of sailing, our losses, the name of every ship's captain — every last detail.'

The gurgle from his pipe suggested that the entire bowl was awash with saliva.

'There've been times when it looked as if they'd broken our code. We'd set up a patrol-line at ninety degrees to a reported route, only to find that the fattest convoys had jinked their way right round our reception committee. The Brits may even be able to plot our position when we send squash signals — perhaps the few groups in a daily position report are enough to work on. They must have dreamed up another little surprise for us, I reckon.'

Seaman Merker informed me in pure Saxonian dialect where he came from: Kötzschenbroda. No one had ever heard of it.

'Isn't that where the dogs wag their pricks instead of their tails?' enquired Seaman Dufte.

'And fart instead of barking?' someone chimed in.

'Must be a grand place,' Dufte improvised. 'Is it true they bring up the afterbirths and chuck their babies on the dung-heap?'

Merker was still floundering. Dufte followed up. 'You mean

to say it's the done thing in Kötzschenbroda?'

Understanding dawned in Merker's eyes.

'What are you getting at?'

'Nothing, mate, nothing at all,' Dufte said soothingly. 'Nothing, my old afterbirth,' he added in an undertone.

The others laughed.

Merker looked suspicious. 'Watchit, Dufte, or I'll part your hair with my boot.'

'If things go on like this we'll be at sea for Christmas,' Zeitler said.

Rademacher shrugged. 'So what? We've got a Christmas-tree on board.'

'Pull the other one.'

'Cross my heart. It's an artificial one – folds up like a brolly. I've seen the cardboard box. Ask the coxswain if you don't believe me.'

'That's the Navy for you,' Ullmann said. To my surprise, the midshipman proceeded to unload some Yuletide experiences. 'We always had casualties at Christmas in my last flotilla. New Year's, too. Last year it was a seaman PO. He pulled his little stunt about midnight on Christmas Eve. Russian roulette. Put the gun to his head and pulled the trigger while we all stood there with our mouths open. He'd removed the magazine first, naturally, but he'd forgotten to check if there was one up the spout. Blew the back of his head off – you never saw such a mess.'

The PO's blunder struck a chord of memory in Hinrich. 'I knew someone who blew his face off. New Year's Eve, it was. I was still serving on a patrol-ship at the time. We'd all had a skinful. Dead on midnight, one of the POs came on deck holding a thunderflash – the old-fashioned type with a fuse you had to light. He leant against the rail, held his fag to the fuse and blew on it. The trouble was, he got his hands mixed up – chucked his fag into the drink and held the thunderflash under his nose. Made a proper hash of himself, I can tell you.'

I didn't wait to hear any more. The POs' mess-table was suddenly encircled by hard-bitten dogs of war who acted as if they had been reared on raw meat.

Midshipman's instruction in the wardroom. We could hear the first lieutenant lecturing. '. . . fell in action against a convoy.'

The Captain glanced up irritably.

'Fell? Damn silly way of putting it. What did he do, trip?

I've seen plenty of photographs of fallen heroes. Falling didn't improve their looks, believe me. Why not come straight out with it and say the poor bugger drowned? I see red when I read the stuff they write about us. Makes us sound like a bunch of sadists who get their kicks from watching ships go down.'

He hauled himself erect and headed for his bunk. A moment later he returned with a newspaper cutting. 'Here's what I mean – I kept it for you, specially. "*Well, Number One, that's that. Another 5000 g.r.t. to our credit, but it's my wife's birthday tomorrow – pity we can't bag another to mark the occasion.*" The first lieutenant gave a sympathetic grin and the Captain stretched out on his hard bunk to catch up on some much-needed sleep. Only an hour later, he felt a hand on his shoulder. "*Birthday ship, sir!*" The Captain was on his feet in a flash. Everything went like clockwork. "*Tubes 1 and 2 ready for firing!*" Both torpedoes found their mark. "*6000 tons at least,*" said the Captain. "*Pleased with your birthday present, sir?*" asked the Number One. "*Delighted,*" replied the Captain, and his first lieutenant's face lit up.*"

The Old Man glowered. 'And that's what they're feeding them back home. It's puke-making. Teutonic caricatures versus British incompetents – that's the official picture.'

Sour expressions wherever I looked. Apathetic faces stamped with disgust, irritation and resentment.

It was hard to imagine the existence of dry land, cosy homes, front parlours, soft lights, warm stoves.

Everyone had gathered round the wardroom table for the daily lemon-squeezing session, a self-imposed chore which had gradually assumed ritual character. Our minds were haunted by visions of the ravages of Vitamin C deficiency. I pictured a circle of scurvy-ridden scarecrows, painfully mumbling hard crusts between toothless gums.

Each of us had evolved his own way of ingesting the juice. The Chief began by cutting his lemon in half. As leisurely as if he meant to spend the entire evening at it, he mashed the juice-cells with a knife-handle, stuck a lump of sugar in each hemisphere, and sucked the juice through the sugar with a noisy disregard for table manners.

The second lieutenant had hit upon a peculiarly outlandish method. He squeezed his lemon into a glass and stirred in some sugar and condensed milk. The milk immediately separated, endowing the whole mixture with a frightful appearance. The Captain shuddered every time, but the second lieutenant persevered. He proudly christened his concoction 'Submarine Special'. 'Jealous?' he enquired at large, and slowly poured it down his throat with an appreciative roll of the eye.

The second engineer was the only one who took no trouble at all. He persisted in the crude but effective practice of sinking his healthy teeth into a bisected lemon and devouring it complete with pith and peel.

The Captain watched him with marked distaste. He found the junior engineer's uncouth manners quite as antipathetic as his primitive turns of phrase.

The second engineer was a constant source of amazement to me. At first I had put him down as pig-headed. I now realized that he was, quite simply, a man with a hide like a rhinoceros. He gave an impression of imperturbability, equanimity and strength of character when all the time he was merely obtuse and thick-skinned. Slow-witted and slow-moving, heaven alone knew why he had opted for engineering or how such a snail-like intellect had threaded its way through the various courses and examinations.

Our lemons kept us fully occupied for several minutes. As soon as the mound of sucked and squeezed halves was complete, the steward came and swept them into his bucket. Then he mopped up the vitamin-rich residue with a sour-smelling swab.

The shipboard day had now dwindled to roughly six hours. Our grey matter took a vacation. We vegetated like pensioners on a park bench.

U-A boasted a library, housed in a locker on the Captain's partition, but its contents were far less in demand than the thrillers which littered the fore-ends. Their covers were gruesomely illustrated and bore titles such as *The Man in Black*, *Shots in the Dark*, *Vengeance is Mine* or *The Guiltless Bullet*. Most of them had passed through so many hands that their covers were in tatters and their grimy pages barely held together by the staples. Seaman Schwalle, the current record-holder, was reputed to have devoured twenty such volumes last patrol. His present score was eighteen.

THURSDAY, 27TH DAY AT SEA. A signal addressed to Werewolf from C-in-C U-boats: we were to take up a new patrol-line at 7 knots by 0700 on the 20th. It meant a change of course, nothing more.

A voice came on the wireless. 'Outnumbered but undismayed, our gallant soldiers continue to . . .'

'Switch it off!' the Chief snapped, so loudly that I jumped.

The Captain turned to me with a wry expression. 'Sounds as if the Brits are really going to town. Run your eye over the last few signals: "Dived to avoid aircraft" – "diverted" – "contact lost" – "dived to avoid destroyers" – "counterattacked". Always the same story. The boot seems to be on the other foot these days. I wouldn't like to be in the C-in-C's shoes. Adolf will chew his balls off if he doesn't produce something for the special communiqué basket soon.'

'He could always invent something,' I said.

The Captain looked up. 'You really believe he'd . . .'

'Believe? That sounds like church.'

But the Captain wouldn't be provoked.

Frenssen, who had just come off watch, accosted Isenberg in the control-room. 'Hey, where are we these days?'

'Off the coast of Iceland.'

'You don't say! And I thought we were on the Yankees' doorstep.'

I could only wag my head. Typical of someone from the engine-room, whose denizens seldom gave a thought to where their boat was operating. It was the same in every submarine. Stokers coddled and pampered their diesels and power units without caring if it was day or night. They shunned the fresh air and regarded seamen with puzzled incomprehension.

Our happy band of seafarers was riven with caste divisions. Whenever seamen displayed an arrogant contempt for 'trogs', stokers responded with an exaggerated display of pride in their expert qualifications.

Even in the cramped confines of the POs' mess, the caste spirit prevailed as it did in all ships. The two main castes were deck and engine-room personnel. Below deck, the underworld caste subdivided itself into electricians and stokers. There was also the control-room caste, the torpedo-man caste and the exclusive little coterie of telegraphists and hydrophone operators.

It turned out that the coxswain's hidden reserves included some canned knuckle of pork and a few tins of sauerkraut. The Captain had summarily ordained a feast. 'About bloody time!' was his sole form of justification.

The Old Man's face shone like a birthday boy's when midday arrived and the steward came bearing our gala meal. Standing, he sniffed the aroma that rose from the gobbets of pork as, round and bulbous, they jostled each other on an outsize aluminium dish. Garnished with slices of onion and pickled cucumber, the massive portions reposed on a befitting bed of boiled sauerkraut.

'I could use a beer with this,' remarked the Captain, as if he weren't fully aware that U-A carried only one bottle of beer per man for consumption after a successful attack. However, the Captain seemed to have the bit between his teeth. 'No time like the present. Very good, half-a-bottle of beer each – one bottle between two.'

The news travelled swiftly to the fore-ends and was greeted with a bellow of approval.

The Chief took the wardroom's allocation of three bottles and whipped off the caps with a locker hinge. Even before we had our glasses at the ready, white froth welled from the bottlenecks like foam from an extinguisher.

The Captain raised his glass. 'Cheers, and let's hope we start earning our pay.'

The Chief drained his beer at a gulp and lingered with his head tilted to catch the ultimate drop. For good measure, he licked the froth off the inside of the rim and swallowed it with much smacking of lips. He groaned with sheer delight.

When the cemetery of bones had been cleared away, the steward reappeared. I couldn't believe my eyes. He was carrying a huge chocolate-coated cake.

The Captain summoned the chef and berated him for his extravagance. Katter looked crestfallen and pleaded that the eggs had to be used up or they would have gone bad.

'How many did you make?'

'Eight cakes, sir. Three slices per man.'

'When?'

'Last night, sir.'

Something in the Captain's face told Katter that he was at liberty to smirk.

Peace and contentment followed our orgy. The Captain folded his arms and grinned amiably at us. The Chief settled himself in his corner of the settee, a laborious procedure. He took as long as a dog to find the right position. Just as he succeeded, the word came from above: 'Chief on the bridge.'

He rose, grumbling. It was his own fault: he insisted on being notified whenever there was something of interest to be seen. Only the day before he had been furious because nobody had called him when three whales surfaced quite close by and gave the U-boat temporary escort, spouting mightily.

I followed him up the ladder and put my head over the hatch coaming just in time to hear him say resentfully: 'What the hell's up?' The second lieutenant responded in an unctuous voice. 'Terribly sorry, Chief, I thought I saw a seagull. False alarm.'

I could tell the look-outs were grinning, even from behind. 'I say, I hope I didn't interrupt your lunch.'

The Chief scowled. 'Just you wait!'

He went and sat in the control-room, brooding on revenge.

The Captain saved him the trouble. There was a practice alarm during the second lieutenant's watch. The hatch was awash before he could secure it properly. The result was a shower bath. The Chief eyed his dripping figure happily as it descended the ladder to the control-room. Suddenly the second lieutenant grabbed his head and felt it all over.

The Captain looked solicitous. 'What's the trouble, Number Two?'

The second lieutenant drew a deep breath and bit on an imaginary lemon. 'My cap, sir,' he stammered. 'I took it off and hung it on the master sight.'

'I see.' The Captain assumed an obsequious head waiter's tone. 'Perhaps your excellency would like us to surface, steer a reciprocal course and carry out a square search?'

The second lieutenant subsided, hopelessly beaten.

A fly was flitting aimlessly to and fro beneath the chart-table lamp. Its presence mystified me. Flies were no trans-Atlantic sailors, and the fly season had ended by the time we left St Nazaire – it was too late in the year, too cool even by French standards. The only remaining possibility was that it had come aboard in the guise of an egg, perhaps accompanied by thousands of fellow-eggs which had undergone less successful development. It might even have entered our steel cigar as a maggot and grown up in the bilge, menaced by the coxswain's ingrained mania for cleanliness. That it had survived at all was a miracle. Everything on board was hermetically sealed – not a crumb of cheese lay around for the taking. I wondered how it had managed.

We knew far too little about our neighbours in general. There we were, all very much in the same boat, and I had been wholly unaware of the fly's existence. I knew nothing whatever about the emotional life of the common house-fly. The fruit-fly I at least knew by its Latin name. *Drosophila melanogaster* was all the rage at school. We kept an appropriate number of short- and long-winged fruit-flies in separate breeding jars and fed them on mashed banana. Our biology master mated carefully selected specimens in a third jar, but the results of their copulation never tallied because we always insinuated a few outsiders. He stood there in front of the class, trying to fiddle his statistics, until we all shouted 'Cheat!'

The fly's eye under a microscope – a marvel of the first order. You had to catch flies from ahead because they couldn't take off backwards, QED. This one wouldn't be caught, though – it was under my personal ægis. It might even produce young, and its young might produce young of their own. Generation upon generation of shipboard flies, and me their patron – and I didn't even like the creatures particularly.

Plump bluebottles settled in the corners of Swoboda's eyes almost as soon as we fished him out of the Bisensee. He had stiffened into a peculiar crouching position with his knees drawn up. The scent of acacia hung in the summer heat of Mecklenburg. Swoboda's rigor did not relax until evening, when we managed to straighten him out. That was when I discovered pea-sized clutches of flies' eggs in the corner of each eye.

I hoped that our fly cherished no such designs on me. 'If so, old pal, you've got another think coming. Hard luck!'

My private thought escaped in the form of a muttered remark. The Captain glanced curiously at me.

The first lieutenant was conducting midshipman's instruction. An isolated phrase penetrated the clatter of plates made by the steward : '. . . break the enemy stranglehold . . .'

The Captain rolled his eyes at the deckhead and winced. 'At it again, Number One? I thought you'd disposed of perfidious Albion long ago.'

The quartermaster had sighted an object on the starboard bow. The Captain went on the bridge as he was, in his sweater and drill slacks. I stopped to grab a rubber jacket from the hook. Luckily, I was already wearing my leather trousers and cork-soled boots.

The flotsam was easily visible with the naked eye. After watching it through his binoculars for two minutes, the Captain gave a steering order which headed us straight for it. The object rapidly increased in size and became a small boat.

'No need for us all to have nightmares,' the Captain murmured, and sent the look-outs below.

It proved to be an unnecessary precaution. The lifeboat was empty.

He stopped both engines and turned to the quartermaster. 'Take her in a bit closer, Kriechbaum. See if you can get the name.'

'Stel – la Mar – is,' the quartermaster said slowly. The look-outs were recalled to the bridge. 'Make a note in the log,' the Captain said, and issued new steering and engine orders.

A couple of minutes later we were back on course. I followed the Captain below. The sight of a lifeboat slopping about in the grey-green sea must have jogged his memory. 'I remember one occasion when a boatload of survivors headed straight for us. Ironical, really.'

All right, I said to myself, let's hear how ironical.

But he dried up. One day, I thought, the Old Man would drive me mad with his five-minute pauses for effect. It was all I could do not to shake him.

But for once, this wasn't one of his usual feats of stage direction. From the look of him, he simply didn't know how to begin. Fair enough, I could wait. Time was a plentiful commodity.

At last, when the hiss and roar of the waves had me nearly mesmerized, he started to speak. 'We sank a freighter one time. Our third patrol, it was. The torpedo caught her pretty far forward and ripped away the bow. She went down by the head at once – dipped like a submarine. There one minute, gone the next – almost incredible. Hardly any survivors.'

After a while, he added: 'Funny, considering it wasn't much of a shot, but that's life.'

'So they never made the boats . . .'

'No, that lot didn't.'

I refused to gratify him by probing further. He snorted twice, then rubbed his nose with the back of his right hand. 'It doesn't pay to get too cynical . . .'

My move. I signified expectancy with a turn of the head, nothing more, but he stared obstinately into space as if he hadn't noticed. I waited until he'd squeezed the interlude dry before asking, casually: 'How do you mean, cynical?'

He chewed on his pipe-stem. 'That lifeboat put me in mind of something that happened to me once. Some British survivors rowed over and thanked me, although I'd just sunk their ship. Quite effusive, they were.'

I couldn't feign indifference any longer. 'How was that?'

A few more sucks at the old pipe. '*Western Star*, the ship was called. Handsome tub, all of ten thousand tons. Unescorted. We were lucky to get her at all – pure accident that we happened to be in the right place at the right time. We fired a salvo of four, but only one fish caught her. Remarkably little effect. She settled slightly and lost speed. Then we scored another hit with the stern tube. She was still a long way from sinking. I saw her crew abandon ship, then I surfaced. 'They'd lowered two boats. Both of them headed straight for us. When they were within hailing distance, one of the men stood up and thanked us several times for being such perfect gentlemen. It took me a while to catch on. They thought we'd held off to let them get clear. The fact was, we didn't have anything left up the spout. They weren't to know we'd missed with three torpedoes. The lads worked like Trojans, but reloading takes time. And they thought we'd postponed the *coup-de grâce* for their benefit . . .'

A quick glance at the Captain disclosed that he was grinning. He went on to impart a freshly minted moral. 'See what I mean? You can sometimes do the right thing by accident.'

We received a signal assigning us to a new patrol area. We were not to head for a specific point, but – just for a change – plod along in a prescribed direction at a prescribed speed. This would, at a predetermined hour, bring us to a spot where Operations deemed it necessary to plug a gap in our ranks. Once there, we were to stand on and off in the accustomed manner: half a day northwards at economical speed, half a day southwards at ditto.

I was in the control-room when the Captain came below. His sweater had acquired some damp patches. There were drops clinging to his cheeks and the peak of his cap.

'The bloody wind's getting up,' he informed Kriechbaum, and vanished through the forward bulkhead.

I could feel U-A labouring. The sausages strung from the deckhead were soon swinging back and forth like pendulums. Bilge-water sloshed from side to side with increasing momentum.

Morale had hit a new low. Leaden silence reigned for hours on end.

The Chief took a paperback from the shelf and pretended to read. I stared at him for five minutes, then advised him with all the scorn I could muster to turn over a page sometimes. 'Not that there's much difference between one page and another. Crap's crap, whichever way you look at it.'

He gave me a withering look. 'Culture vulture!'

'Thanks,' I said. 'All the same, I wish you'd turn over. You'll go blind.'

He shrugged resignedly and turned a page.

'See?' I said. 'It's quite easy when you try.'

Instead of flying off the handle, he demonstrated how neatly he could turn pages. He leafed through the paperback as if he were looking for a specific passage. I gave him my undivided attention. He kept it up for a good five minutes, then slammed the book down on the settee like a winning card, right between him and the Captain.

The Captain glared at him indignantly and said 'Hey!'

The second lieutenant came in from the control-room, dressed for the bridge; he was due on watch in a few minutes. I knew what he was after: new recognition-signal cartridges. They were kept in the locker behind the Chief's back.

I jumped up to make way for him. What was it today? Three stars, four, five? Blue, baby-pink? Where would we be if some trigger-happy member of the same league cruised up and mistook us for Britishers?

The second lieutenant stood there awkwardly, waiting for the Chief to get up too.

There was nothing for it. The Chief rose with extreme reluctance. The Captain followed his every movement like an entranced witness of some unique occurrence.

The show ended and we returned to our tedium. The first lieutenant had a better idea. He opened his locker and extracted the typewriter. The Captain braced his hands against the wardroom table, murder in his eyes.

The first lieutenant tapped away with two stiff forefingers, like the desk sergeant in a police station.

'Sounds like a ticket-punch,' said the Chief.

To my surprise, the Captain had a sudden fit of optimism. 'Something'll turn up soon, you mark my words. The Almighty can't afford to desert us – we owe him too many back payments. Or don't you believe in the Almighty, Chief?'

'Of course, sir,' the Chief replied, nodding vigorously. 'Of course I believe there's a Great Submariner in the Sky.'

'You're a sinful soul, Chief,' grumbled the Captain, but the Chief was unrepentant. He gleefully recounted how he had once received a visitation from Our Lady. 'She materialized just above the jumping-wire, all pale pink with a hint of lilac. Transparent, too – quite an eyeful. She pointed to the sky and puffed out her cheeks.'

'She probably wanted to join the Luftwaffe,' the Captain suggested. 'Goering could use another gas-bag.'

'No,' the Chief said drily, 'that wasn't it. We'd just surfaced and I'd forgotten to blow out with diesel.'

The Captain struggled to retain his composure. 'You'd better inform the Vatican. Only twenty-five years to wait and you could be sanctified.'

We all agreed that the Chief would make a lovely saint. 'Noble and devout,' said the Captain, 'and even more like an El Greco than he is now – a real credit to the Catholic Church.'

Kriechbaum was tidying his locker as I passed through the CPOs' mess. I perched on the table and leafed through a seamanship manual. The quartermaster pulled some photographs from a battered wallet and presented them for inspection. Some extremely underexposed snapshots of children – three small muffled figures astride a toboggan in descending order of magnitude. A diffident smile flitted over Kriechbaum's face. His eyes hung on my lips.

'Strapping youngsters.'

'Yes, three boys.'

It seemed to strike him that tender emotions were out of place in a steel cave dripping with condensation. Almost guiltily, he took the photos back.

FRIDAY, 28TH DAY AT SEA. The sea had become like yellowish-grey broth. The horizon gradually dissolved. Within an hour, tongues of fog were flickering round the hull.

'Visibility nil!' the quartermaster called down. The Captain ordered us to dive and stay deep.

With the boat at 50 metres, we made ourselves comfortable in the control-room. Legs up, boots propped against the chart-stowage. The Captain sucked and champed at his pipe-stem pensively. An occasional nod conveyed that he was engrossed in memories.

I flicked through the log and read the entries covering our time in harbour. According to the record, U-A had been at the base for nearly a month, about as long as we had been at sea.

'Dreaming of *la belle France*?' the Captain asked abruptly. Very well, I too could use that hackneyed phrase to summon up visions more delectable than the maze of pipes in a U-boat's control-room. For instance, a forest of masts seen through grey nets with green glass floats enmeshed in their borders. The blue-painted boats of the tunny-fishermen, who went to sea no longer because fuel was unobtainable and their trade too risky. The fishing village across the bay, at evening. Open fires, voluminous-skirted old women seated in the firelight mending nets. Sunset over the salt-pans: a sky of violet-tinted silver, the sun's red disc close above the horizon, almost bereft of radiance, the air already cool and damp. Here and there, gleaming in the grey-green dusk, a mound of off-white salt. In the distance, stone windmills of such perfect rotundity that they might have been turned on a lathe. Squat white villages with black window-eyes, every house a domino. A peasant, still at work in his field with a hoe, stoops, half-straightens and stoops once more: a picture by Millet. A rattle of cartwheels close at hand, then a voice from behind the furze-bushes: a man talking to his horse. Innumerable spiders have spun threads across the track. The horse's brow is adorned with a veil of grey gossamer. The rutted mud is hard as stone. Cows, too, have left their hoof-prints in it: a multitude of small craters. Crickets fill the air with their chirping.

A disembodied voice from the conning-tower: 'Tell the Captain – first light.'

'Man on the bridge?' The words issued hoarsely from my throat.

The second lieutenant's crumpled face turned to greet me. He looked even more diminutive than usual, only just tall enough to peer over the rail of the bridge casing.

'The wind's getting up,' he said happily. 'Third watch'll be fun.' As if to confirm it, a wave raced up from astern and lapped round the bridge. The water gurgled away through the drain-holes.

Towards midday the motion of the sea increased. We were bombarded with spray. It was pointless wiping our binoculars, which got soaked every two minutes. The shammies used for polishing the lenses became clogged with salty moisture and left smears all over them. The best way of keeping them clear, at least until the next inundation, was to lick them.

SATURDAY, 29TH DAY AT SEA. I stood the forenoon watch with Kriechbaum. Grey curtains of cloud surrounded us. I shivered in the cold damp air. Fierce gusts scythed through my sweater and chilled me to the bone. The sea was rougher. The waves were making spindrift. The wind bowed the taut string of the jumping-wire, paused and started afresh like a fiddler trying out a new violin.

The grey overcast was a shade thinner in the east than the west. I could even discern a pale patch with streaks and veins traversing it. For a while the patch grew bigger, the veins and streaks more transparent. It looked as if a piece of cloth were being drawn across a lamp. The whole sky was travelling eastwards in a solid mass.

I noticed that the quartermaster's glasses sometimes strayed into my sector. Evidently he didn't quite trust me to remain alert.

I scanned the starboard forward sector, centimetre by centimetre. Reaching its right-hand extremity, I lowered the glasses and allowed my smarting eyes to sweep the sky. Then I made a general survey of the entire sector, raised the glasses, and very slowly, hairline by hairline, swept the horizon once more.

After an hour, eyestrain brought on a dull ache inside my skull, just above eyebrow-level. As for my eyes themselves, they felt as if they were seeping out of their sockets and into the binoculars. Tears repeatedly blurred my vision. I wiped them away with the back of my leather gauntlet.

'On your toes, everyone,' Kriechbaum exhorted. He turned to me. 'They're almost smokeless,' he said, meaning the enemy destroyers. 'What's more, they generally post mast-head look-outs. Rumour has it they feed them on carrots.'

The horizon remained as empty on our thirtieth day at sea as it had for the preceding month. An east wind sprang up, bringing colder air with it. The look-outs muffled themselves in extra clothing. Below, the electric heaters were turned on.

A signal came in. The Captain signed the slip of paper and handed it to me.

'Werewolf from C-in-C. Take up patrol-line between points G and D by 0800 on 25th. 10-miles intervals, course 230, speed 8 knots.'

He unrolled the big general operations chart and tapped our position with a pencil. 'Here's where we are now, and that's where we're headed.' The pencil swooped far to the south. 'It'll take us a good three days. Seems the present scheme has been dropped. This is something quite new, whatever it is. We'll be down on a level with Lisbon.'

'And out of the cold, thank God.' The Chief gave a theatrical shudder to demonstrate the extent of his suffering.

Voices drifted through the half-open door of the fore-ends bulkhead, lethargically raised in song.

> *Ten thousand miles from Hamburg,*
> *A lonely sailor lad*
> *Lies dreaming of the Reeperbahn*
> *And all the girls he's had . . .'*

They never progressed beyond the first verse, repeating it

over and over again like a gramophone needle stuck in a groove. The singing grew more and more sluggish with every repetition. I went forward. Only two dim lights were burning in the fore-ends. The bulging hammocks swung to and fro.

The chef appeared, fuming. 'Know what? Five bloody great cans of sardines have leaked into the sugar.' He was beside himself. 'Bleeding mess! We might as well chuck the whole lot away.'

'I'd keep it,' Ario said. 'You never know, you might want to sweeten some fish sometime.'

An arm groped its way over the side of one of the upper bunks, followed by a tousled head. It was Gigolo, brandishing a paperback. 'Listen to what it says here,' he broke in. 'It's unlucky for a whaler to wash. No harpooner ever gets a whale unless he stinks to high heaven.'

'There you are!' said a voice from one of the hammocks. 'I knew we'd be out of luck, with a couple of soap-and-water fanatics like Schwalle and the Number One aboard.'

Everyone promptly fell on the topic of hygiene and its vices. It only intensified my own craving for a bath.

Back in the wardroom, perched on the Chief's bunk, I joined the second lieutenant in an orgy of self-torment. We vied with each other in designing epicurean bathrooms.

For the tub itself, I suggested green marble from the quarries of Carrara. Not to be outdone, the second lieutenant proposed alabaster 'white as a virgin's bum'. The Chief, naturally, wanted everything in chrome-nickel steel – 'with needle-point showers that sting you up one moment and stroke you the next . . .'

From the chromium-plated showers he proceeded, almost as a matter of course, to Circassian bath-attendants, female. 'All plump and sexy, garlanded with fresh watercress, and so on.'

'Down, boy!' I said. 'I always thought there was more in your veins than lubricating oil.'

He cocked his head and expelled a long stream of air through his nose. 'Engineer officers are a sexy lot, didn't you know? It must be the sight of all that machinery pounding away.'

We headed south-south-west at cruising speed for three days without seeing a sign of the enemy, only some driftwood and a few empty drums.

Once more we relapsed into the dogged back-and-forth of a reconnaissance patrol. C-in-C U-boats tried everything, busily trawling his net to and fro, but its coverage was inadequate.

The eternal sameness had long ago destroyed our sense of time. I could hardly remember how long the patrol had lasted. Weeks, months, or had U-A been slogging round the Atlantic for half a year? The frontier between day and night became increasingly blurred.

Our stock of anecdotes was long since exhausted. We fell back on vapid witticisms, clichés and catch-phrases which made no demands on the intellect.

Like an epidemic disease, the entire boat had become infected with the adjective 'stupendiferous'. Nobody knew where the crass expression had originated, but it was suddenly applied to everything not actively repellent. A new and universal unit of measurement was also rife, namely 'sliver'. 'More coffee? Thanks, just a sliver.' 'Sorry, I'm due on watch in a sliver.' The Chief even asked me if I wouldn't mind shifting a sliver to one side.

He reached for a tattered puzzle-page. 'Hey,' he said after a while, 'when does forty-five minus forty-five equal forty-five?' I knew it was pointless to try and go on reading – he'd only repeat the question. The Chief couldn't bear other people to be occupied when he was at a loose end. I allowed my gaze to roam over the plywood panelling on the opposite bulkhead. I knew every line in the grain, every pipe and rivet in the deckhead, the Andalusian pin-up on the partition, the little raffia dog with insane glass eyes which served us as a mascot. Dangling from the wardroom safe, as usual, was the Chief's old-fashioned fob-watch and chain, complete with a small winding-key. Dust had settled on the framed photograph of U-A's launching ceremony. The curtain over the second lieutenant's bunk swung back and forth. The third curtain ring from the left was missing.

I could have drawn every detail from memory.

'Nary a ship but plenty of shit,' I heard Gigolo poeticizing in the control-room.

He was right about the boom in dirt. Its origin was a mystery. Water all round us, yet the daily clean-ship revealed sedimentary deposits beneath coconut matting and duckboards.

I watched the ship's fly promenade across the face of the Andalusian belle on the locker partition. It halted just below her left nostril, then leisurely progressed to the girl's peach-like cheek. Here it stayed put, simulating a beauty-spot. From time to time it raised its hind legs and rubbed them together.

I slid lower in my seat and lolled there like a badly filled sack of flour, knees wedged against the wardroom table for support.

Even the fly had run out of ideas. Adhering to the pin-up and dozing seemed to be the limit of its ambitions.

The steward came to lay the table for supper. He disturbed my fly in the process. Pity.

The Captain was in the control-room, muttering to himself over the chart. He laid aside the parallel ruler and pencil with schoolmasterly precision and climbed into the conning-tower.

I stayed behind in the control-room, leant against the chart-stowage and tried to read. Before long the Captain clumped down the ladder again.

'The pace is killing me,' he said with a scowl. He strode tigerishly up and down the control-room three or four times, then sat down beside me on the chart-stowage and sucked at his unlit pipe. I lowered my book because I sensed that he wanted to talk. We stared ahead of us in silence.

I waited for him to kick off. He felt in his pocket and extracted a crumpled letter written in green ink. 'Here,' he said, tapping it a couple of times with his knuckles, 'I just came across this. My God, but they've got a queer picture of the way we live.' Green ink, I knew, was the trademark of his lady-friend, the airman's widow.

The Captain shook his head vigorously, lower lip protruding. 'Enough said,' he snapped with sudden asperity, and gestured as though to wipe his remark off an imaginary blackboard.

All right, I thought, not if you don't want to.

Although an improvement in the weather enabled us to leave the upper lid open, the POs' mess stank abominably of mouldy bread, rotting lemons, putrescent sausages, the greasy exhalations of the engine-room, wet oilskins, rubber boots, rank sweat and cheesy genitalia.

The bulkhead door swung open and a miasma of diesel fumes entered with the outgoing engine-room watch. Oaths and imprecations, a slamming of locker doors. Frenssen suddenly broke into quasi-drunken song. The words were obscene, as usual.

'Christ, could I use a beer?'

'Lovely and cool, with a nice white head on it. Line up half-a-dozen and sink them one after the other. Glug-glug!'

'Belt up, you're giving me a thirst.'

'I wouldn't mind a Calvados – or a gin, come to that. Christ, they used to mix some fantastic gin drinks on the old *Caribia*

'– White Ladies, Collinses. Can't remember them all, but you didn't know what hit you.'

'I said belt up!'

A fluttering sound, followed by a thwack and more imprecations. One of the three POs must have hurled a paperback. I turned over and thought about drink. I'd never deliberately set out to get drunk. Now would be the time to try, if only we weren't a floating home for teetotallers. Not a drop of alcohol on board, apart from the half-bottle of beer per man that remained after our knuckle-of-pork extravagance. There was a bottle of brandy, but the Captain kept that in his locker for medicinal purposes.

The engines were running slowly to conserve fuel. They sounded jerky. You could almost distinguish the separate strokes: induction, compression, power, exhaust. Most of the time we ran on one diesel only. The other rested until its turn came to be clutched in and fed with precious oil from the ready-use tank.

The Chief was worried about his engines. All this slow-speed running was bad for them – bad for him too. The agonized throb of the diesels gave him a twinge in the kidneys.

It was small consolation to know that, farther north, other U-boats were shuttling to and fro in a similar torpor.

The chart looked like a bad joke: a convoluted maze of lines without any obvious rhyme or reason.

The bow-wave had dwindled to a sluggish ripple. Driftwood crept by at a snail's pace, as though to underline our weary progress through the water.

'We might as well draw fires and drop anchor,' the second lieutenant said, with the air of one who has uttered a profundity.

The men were dejected. Melancholy faces on every side, as if to return without a victory pennant would be the height of ignominy, a disgrace beyond atonement.

The atmosphere in the POs' mess had become touchier. People were quicker to take umbrage and retorted more sharply. Some of them slunk about as though life had dealt them an insult from which they would never recover.

The Captain made no secret of his black mood. He bawled out the helmsman for signing his name in the sea, although the combination of slow speed and lurching waves made it genuinely hard to steer a perfect course.

'Lousy waste of time!' groaned the Chief.

The Captain wagged his head. 'Not entirely. The mere fact

that their ships are forced to travel in convoy is enough to hit the British where it hurts. Laden ships sometimes have to hang around for ages. Ports are geared for continuous operation, not sudden spurts of activity.'

He paused and pricked his ears. The tap of a typewriter came from the wardroom.

'Oh God,' he snorted, 'someone chuck the bloody thing overboard!'

The Chief cleared his throat. 'Beg leave to ask, sir, but is that an order?'

At least the Captain was grinning again.

The sky looked like curdled milk. Not a hint of movement. The water had become a monochrome expanse of blackish green.

Big ships could at least offer an occasional splash of colour: funnel markings, load-lines, ventilator cowls. With us, everything was grey; grey, unrelieved by any nuance.

We ourselves toned admirably with our surroundings. Our skins had taken on a pale and cheesy shade of grey. Even the coxswain, whose cheeks shone like apples when we sailed, looked as if he had suffered a long illness. He was still in good voice, though. 'You there,' I heard him bellow, 'shut your trap and give your arse a chance!'

We were all ripe for the psychiatrist's couch, especially the first lieutenant with his pedantic behaviour, his nose-wrinkling, his faint but oh-so-condescending smile.

The Chief, too, showed signs of nervous tension. The tic at the outer extremity of his left eyelid, his grimacing, cheek-and lip-chewing, aimless mouth-pursing and, worst of all, his habit of starting violently at the slightest sound.

Then there was the Captain's noise fetishism: the beard-scratching, the pipe-sucking, the bubbling hiss like fat frying in his pipe-bowl, the sniffing and snorting and grunting. Sometimes, too, he forced spit through a gap in his teeth with a gurgling noise.

Johann was growing more and more Christlike. When he pushed back his pale-yellow forelock and exposed his high forehead, he need only have let his eyelids droop to resemble a perfect sudarium.

It was unfair to examine people too closely. Some of the men looked absolutely wretched. They recalled press photographs of miners rescued after weeks below ground. Little wonder, considering that we lived in a species of subterranean gallery, stooped and bowed like miners, permanently exposed to artificial light. The bridge was our pithead, the conning-tower our shaft. Galleries ran fore and aft from the control-room to the faces where the torpedo-men worked. Their torches deputized for safety-lamps.

Our midshipman worried me most of all. My first impression of him had been one of schoolboy cunning. The artful look had gone now. Once or twice I saw him darkly brooding in his bunk.

We learned by radio that Kupsch's U-boat had sunk an unescorted refrigerator ship of 9000 tons.

'He must have been dead lucky,' said the Captain. 'You can't do that sort of thing without a spot of luck, not these days. It's hopeless unless you happen to be ahead of the target. Then you hang on till she passes across your tubes. Unescorted means fast. No use steaming up from astern — she'll shake you off. I've tried it often enough, but all I ever did was waste fuel. We couldn't outpace a fast unescorted merchantman by more than a couple of knots, even at maximum revs. She'd only have to zig once in the right direction and we'd have missed our chance for good.'

WEDNESDAY, 33RD DAY AT SEA. We received an Intelligence report at 0800. 'Convoy expected in Square GF, proceeding west.'

Bent over the chart-table, the Captain gave a sceptical grunt. 'Not perfect, but still . . . With a little luck we might just make it.' New course, more revs. No other changes.

'About time we downed a couple,' said the second lieutenant, and promptly looked embarrassed, realizing that the remark sounded too brisk and brash to suit our present exasperated mood.

Midday. I went up top with the first lieutenant, whose watch had just begun. The air was soupy and inert. The sea had cowered away from the diffused light and was wearing a grey skin, smooth apart from the odd bulge and wrinkle. It was a monotonous and soul-destroying sight.

But at evening, during the second lieutenant's watch, colour entered the picture. The flat and isolated banks of cloud on the horizon began to glow like a forge fire. Quickly the whole sky turned red, mantling the sea with splendour. The submarine ploughed steadily through the crimson haze, engines puttering. The entire hull glowed until the fore-casing resembled a red-hot ingot. The look-outs' faces were also steeped in flame. The whole scene could have been reproduced in red and black: the sea, the sky, the hull and the faces under the sou'westers.

Sky and sea continued to blaze for a quarter of an hour. Then the clouds lost their carmine glow and swiftly dulled to a dark sulphurous grey. They looked like mountains of ash with a core of faintly glowing embers.

All at once, immediately ahead of us, a glimmer appeared in the grey wall. Unseen bellows fanned it into new life, but within minutes the blaze had subsided again. It glowed for a while, like the mouth of a smelting-furnace, and finally died altogether. The sun had dipped below the horizon.

A pink flush still lingered on the face of the sky, high above the cloud-banks. Almost imperceptibly it turned thin and streaky and was replaced by a saffron-yellow which slowly became tinged with green and sank to the horizon.

The sea reflected this poisonous green infusion. It lay as though paralysed under a yellow-green film.

The Captain came on the bridge. He sniffed and glanced at the sky. 'Hm,' he said sourly. 'Very pretty, but I don't like the look of it.'

The second lieutenant tore a sheet off the wardroom calendar. The word THURSDAY appeared.

At breakfast, the submarine was rolling so heavily that the steward had to fit the fiddles. These divided the table into neat rectangles, small pens in which to corral our cups and plates.

The Captain announced that we were heading into a low that was moving eastwards from the Newfoundland Banks — the product of a collision between the Gulf Stream's warm-air masses and the cold-air masses of the Labrador Current.

'The wind backed nor'-nor'-east during the night,' he said. 'It won't stay there, though. I wouldn't mind betting we're in for some violent shifts during the next few hours.'

It was all the steward could do to carry the full plates down the passage. Not having a hand free, he steadied himself with his elbows.

The Captain squeezed into his corner and wedged himself in with care. At the same moment, the wardroom teetered from one side to the other. Then we rose and fell, corkscrewing.

'Heeling nicely,' said the second engineer.

'Rolling,' amended the first lieutenant.

The second engineer's jaw dropped. Encouraged by his apparent eagerness to learn, the first lieutenant lectured on.

'Heeling defines a position – an angle of inclination from the vertical. Rolling is a frequentative term.'

'*Quod erat demonstrandum*,' snarled the Chief. 'What it is to be a *real* sailor!'

Whenever he wasn't on the bridge, the Captain spent much of his time in hermit-like seclusion behind his green curtain or astride the periscope saddle in the conning-tower. The sporadic hum of the periscope motor betrayed that he was playing merry-go-rounds out of sheer boredom. The men, who hadn't heard his voice for days, might have been forgiven for imagining that U-A was captainless.

Inactivity was also taking its toll of the Chief, who had lost much of his élan. The green shadows round his eyes made him look like a theatrical demon, but they were genuine. Little was seen of him, when he wasn't actually busy with his engines, except the top of his head. The Chief had been smitten with a mania for reading. He only looked up at mealtimes or when directly addressed by the Captain.

Minor irritations apart, the mute empathy that existed between him and the Captain remained intact. It seemed that seven joint patrols had long ago dissipated any tensions that might otherwise have alienated them.

We were now almost 3000 miles from base. Although the U-boat's radius of action was roughly 7000 miles, traipsing back and forth had left us little fuel to play with. Distant convoys were almost beyond reach of our slender reserves, which would scarcely allow the long spells at full power that were essential during anti-convoy operations.

The first lieutenant unnerved the Chief by opening and closing lockers, rattling keys and poring over files. Nobody knew what he was assimilating from his motley collection of folders.

'Learning brothel regulations by heart,' the Chief conjectured, when the first lieutenant vanished in the direction of the control-room. He had left one of the folders open on the wardroom table. I couldn't resist the temptation to flick through it. '*Notes on Man Management in Submarines*', I read in scarlet ink on the title page. Enthralled, I turned over.

I. Special features of life in a submarine:
For long periods, life on board is monotonous. Weeks of failure must be taken for granted. Add to this the possibility of counter-attack, and the result is a 'war of nerves'

which weighs principally on the U-boat commander.

More red lettering: *'The morale of the crew depends:'* Then, itemized in blue fountain-pen ink:

(a) on their discipline;

(b) on their commander's degree of success. (A crew will always have more regard for a successful captain, irrespective of his real competence, than for an unsuccessful one. On the other hand, it is the unsuccessful captain who stands in greatest need of high crew morale.)

(c) on the efficient administration of daily life aboard;

(d) on the good example and impeccable conduct of their officers;

(e) on spiritual leadership in the true sense, coupled with an exemplary concern for the men's welfare.

Red ink: *'Discipline'*. Then back to blue:

It is the captain's duty to ensure that, in his vessel; the spirit prevailing among the better members of the crew predominates while the views of the dregs count for little. His attitude may be compared to that of a gardener who cultivates healthy plants and eradicates weeds.

Another headline in red: *'Excerpts from a lecture by Lt-Com. L.'*

I am well aware that wives can undermine their husbands' morale. They can also strengthen it, however, and I have often noticed that married men seem to return from leave with their spirits better refreshed and fortified than most. Married POs must be told what is expected of a sailor's wife. It has been my pleasure to invite most of my crew members' wives to coffee, make their acquaintance and impress on them that the Navy expects them to preserve a courageous attitude. I venture to believe that this has helped to stiffen a few upper lips. I have also asked my wife to write the occasional letter and keep in touch.

An appeal must be made to the men's determination to keep in good physical trim and take minor problems in their stride. If two ratings are in line for the Iron Cross First Class and only one can be awarded it, I recommend the one who remains with us and soldiers on, rather than the one who is fortunate enough to be on the verge of promotion and a transfer elsewhere. The Iron Cross is not a welfare institution, after all. It is a reward for valour in the face of the enemy, and one which must be earned anew, even after its bestowal.

My eyes were on stalks by this time. So this was the first lieutenant's approved reading! I didn't have far to go to discover another vein of pure gold:

On long patrols, young ratings tend to break a lot of crockery. Admonishment seldom does much good, as messing is difficult in heavy seas. I now hold crockery inspection once a week. If breakages are excessive, the messman has to eat out of a can for three days. Banning smoking is an even severer punishment, and a three-day ban on card-playing can work wonders.

Then came a mimeographed sheet:

It is a point of honour, and one to which I attach due importance, that etiquette should be observed on board – more strictly in harbour than at sea, of course, where it must suffice for a compartment to be called to attention when the captain makes his first appearance of the day, for the senior rating present to report what is in progress there, and – naturally – for the watch-keeping officer on the bridge to make his routine report. While refitting, at least one muster should be held every day. I set particular store by a smart turn-out for Colours. There should be periodic locker inspections at sea, also constant supervision of general neatness . . .

I was further titillated by the heading 'Festivals and Festivities'.

During Advent, every compartment was lit with electric Advent candles mounted on fir-wreaths made of twisted hand-towels and lavatory paper painted green. Christmas baking continued for a fortnight, and all hands were allowed a taste, just as they would have been at home. An improvised Christmas-tree was rigged up in the festively adorned fore-ends on Christmas Eve. A tropical Santa Claus, clad only in a sheet, presented every member of the crew with some sweets and an inscribed book.

FIRST ATTACK

The telegraphist handed a signal out of the wireless office. His habitual expression was a contented grin. It did not change now.

All self-importance, the first lieutenant deposited the cipher machine on the wardroom table and neatly laid the telegraphist's slip beside it. He turned his head this way and that like a hen seeking a grain of corn, checked the setting, and finally began to peck at the keys.

The Chief assumed a look of ineffable boredom. The second lieutenant, who was off watch, didn't even bother to glance up. I also mimed indifference.

With a hint of haste which belied his apparent disdain for the whole proceedings, the Captain tore the strip of paper out of the machine almost before the first lieutenant had decoded the last group. He read it, sucking in his cheeks, then rose without a word and went to the control-room. I watched him through the bulkhead doorway as he carefully adjusted the lamp above the chart-table.

Meaningful looks passed between me and the Chief.

'On ne sait jamais,' he said.

I curbed my impatience for a full two minutes before sidling into the control-room. The quartermaster had been summoned from the bridge.

The Captain's shoulders loomed over the chart. He was holding the signal in one hand and a pair of dividers in the other. The chart claimed his full attention.

'Could be worse,' he murmured at length. He pushed the signal across to me. I read: 'C-in-C from U-R. Convoy sighted 0810, Square BM, proceeding north, Delayed by aircraft. Enemy now out of sight.'

The Captain indicated Square BM with his dividers. It was not far from our present position.

'At a rough estimate, we should be able to get there in twenty-four hours if we flog the engines.'

Everything depended on whether U-R re-established contact, because only then would Operations send us in pursuit of the convoy.

'All right, maintain course and speed for the time being.'

The next few hours were devoted to conjecture. 'Looks as

if it's heading for America,' I heard Kriechbaum say. 'On the other hand, it could be a Gibraltar convoy – hard to tell, yet.'

'U-R is Bertold,' said the Captain. 'One of the best – knows his stuff. Bertold won't be shaken off that easily . . . They were scheduled to sail a week after us. Periscope trouble.'

He gestured to me to join him on the chart-stowage. Anticipation and excitement had raised his spirits. 'Bloody aeroplanes,' he said. 'Added to that, their destroyers have been operating in packs recently, and God help anyone who gets put down by them . . . You hardly ever saw a flyer in this area, once upon a time. Those were the days. You only had to watch the sea – what's more, you had a pretty fair idea of what to expect.'

The control-room hand, who was busy at his little desk making entries in the diving log, paused to listen.

'Nowadays, they do all they can to keep us at arm's length. They stopped using their destroyers for immediate convoy protection long ago. The latest technique is to send them dashing around at top speed quite a distance from their precious charges, so as to fend us off or keep us deep. As for their advanced support group, that steams along ahead of the convoy . . . I tell you, times are hard. They've even converted some of their larger freighters into auxiliary aircraft carriers. Small carriers and destroyers make a perfect combination, as long as they co-ordinate their tactics. The aircraft spot us and alert the destroyers, and the destroyers clobber us until the convoy's so far ahead we don't have a snowball's chance of finding it again. All we do is bust a gut and burn fuel.'

I had seldom seen the Old Man so relaxed or talkative. 'We ought to have gone all out from the start,' he said, 'before the Brits woke up and got themselves organized. We only had fifty-seven U-boats at the outset, and only thirty-five of those were fit for the Atlantic. Naturally, that wasn't enough to blockade the approaches – hardly the stranglehold our bosses are always boasting about. Then there was the submarine versus battleship argument. Our predecessors in the Imperial Navy never suffered from the same qualms. They insisted on their big fat capital ships, whether they were any use or not. A conservative bunch, that's what we are.'

Later, while I was stretching my legs in the control-room, we received another re-transmission. 'C-in-C from U-R. 0920, dived to avoid aircraft, one hour. Enemy convoy again sighted Square BK. Exact line of advance uncertain.'

'I told you Bertold wouldn't let them slip through his fingers ! How about it, Quartermaster ? They seem to be steering a parallel course, don't they?'

This time the Captain was busy at the chart-table for no longer than two minutes. He straightened with a jerk. 'Steer 270. Full ahead both.'

The orders were echoed. The engine-room telegraph rang A violent shudder ran through the boat and the rhythmical beat of the engines swelled to a solid roar which drowned all other noises. The Old Man was going hell for leather without waiting for a signal from Kernével.

The thunder rose in pitch, then fell to a muffled roar as though it had been throttled. The throttled note signified that our bow had buried itself in a large wave, the high singing note that we were racing into a trough.

Everywhere, men were at work, checking the lines and pipes they had so often checked before. They did so unbidden and unobtrusively – unofficially, as it were.

'Man on the bridge?' I called.

'Affirmative!'

My first sight was of our wake, a dense white train of seething water which extended almost to the limit of my vision, where it became unravelled into separate strands and was swallowed by the bottle-green sea. On either side of the white train were pale-green tracks the colour of Venetian glass backed by sunlight. Bluish diesel fumes eddied over the gratings.

I turned forward. Instantly a whiplash of spray caught me in the face. I should have remembered the engines were propelling us into a head sea at full power.

Water dripped from my nose.

'Congratulations,' said the second lieutenant.

With narrowed eyes, I peered at the fore-casing from the shelter of the bridge. We were speeding along at such a pace that the bow flung curtains of spray into the air and sent broad bands of foam hissing along the U-boat's flanks.

The Captain had his hands thrust deep into the pockets of his leather trousers. The once-white and picturesquely battered cap with its tarnished braid was pulled down low. He screwed up his eyes as he scanned the sea and sky. 'Watch it, lads,' he exhorted the look-outs, 'we can't afford to be jumped at this stage.'

Lunch-time came and went, but it was afternoon before he left the bridge to study developments on the chart. I followed him through the hatch.

Below the quartermaster was still hard at work on his calculations.

'Hm,' said the Captain to Kriechbaum. 'Shaping nicely, wouldn't you say?'

A new pencilled cross on the chart marked the enemy's last reported position. We could now read his course and speed from our own chart. Another pencilled cross: the intersection of his estimated course with ours. Our thoughts returned to it again and again, with the inexorability of a compass needle swinging north.

Hour after hour went by. Fuel sped through the pipes.

The second lieutenant ducked through the bulkhead, holding another signal.

The Captain took it with undisguised eagerness. He even deigned to read it aloud.

'C-in-C to U-A. Intercept convoy reported by U-R, utmost speed.' He paused. 'Officer of the watch: steer three-four-zero and await further orders.' The helmsman's voice echoed his words from the conning-tower.

'It's working – it's really working.'

The Captain pointed to our own position and the enemy's. 'We should intercept tomorrow morning, about 0600.'

Enquiring faces appeared in the bulkhead doorway. To their astonishment, the men saw our commander stomping unsteadily round the control-room like a dancing bear. He picked up the intercom microphone and broadcast to all compartments.

'Do you hear there? We're now operating against a convoy sighted by U-R. We expect to intercept any time from 0600 onwards.' The loudspeakers gave a concluding crackle. 'That's all.'

Raucous singing drifted through the half-open door to the fore-ends.

> 'Natasha from Odessa
> Can squeeze like a compressor.
> Her eyes are like the Black Sea
> And so's her great big jacksy.'

The Captain put his head back and leant against the fore-planes emergency handwheel with his elbows between the spokes. He detached one arm, removed the pipe from his mouth and made a sweeping gesture. 'Fantastic contraption, a boat like this. Some people disapprove of machinery. They say it blunts a man's intelligence, kills his initiative and so on . . .'

He fell to musing. Minutes passed before he picked up the thread again. 'To my mind, submarines take a lot of beating. Not that I'm fanatical about them – God forbid.'

He sighed deeply and gave a couple of self-derisive snorts

before continuing. The pipe-laden fist remained poised in mid-air for a while. Before lowering it, he pushed his cap to the back of his head. Curly fair hair escaped from under the peak, giving him a slightly rakish look. 'I love the diesels when they're running flat out, though there are people who can't abide the sound.' He wagged his head as though he couldn't marvel enough at their aversion. 'Other people can't stand the smell of petrol. My girl detests the smell of leather – it's funny.'

He suddenly compressed his lips like a boy caught telling tales out of school.

I couldn't think of any suitable comment, so we both stared at the deck-plates. Then the Chief appeared and asked if the port engine could be stopped for fifteen minutes. The reason: crankshaft running hot.

Abruptly the Captain grimaced as if he had bitten into a lemon. 'All right, Chief, if there's really no alternative.'

The Chief hurried aft. A few moments later the thunder of the engines diminished. The Captain chewed his lower lip. His face didn't brighten until he was handed another signal. 'C-in-C from U-R. Enemy last sighted Square BA.'

The second watch mustered in the control-room. Safety-belts were no longer required. When the minute-hand of the clock approached twelve, the four men went up top. The helmsman made his change-over report:

'Course three-four-zero, starboard engine full ahead, port engine stopped.'

The old watch came below. The men's faces were the colour of boiled lobster. The quartermaster, who was last down the ladder, came to attention. 'Reporting off watch, sir. Slight build-up of cloud from the north-west. Wind nor'-west to west, veering. Coming over green at times, on account of speed.'

As though to confirm his statement, a douche of sea-water cascaded through the hatch.

'Thanks.' The Captain nodded. The four men saluted, then shook themselves like dogs. Their oilskins spattered the deck. One of them ventured a muttered question.

'How far to go?'

'Quite a way,' replied one of the control-room hands.

The steward came through. He seemed to be feeling his oats, judging by the way he bustled along like a wine waiter. The only surprise was that he hadn't draped a napkin over his arm.

After the steward came the chef, bound for the fore-ends,

wearing the assiduous smile of a publican who welcomes his customers and enquires their pleasure.

'Bunch of school-kids,' growled the Captain, blind to his leading role in the charade. He was sitting in his corner, beaming at all and sundry like a contented paterfamilias.

It was as though an iron band had snapped – as though we could all breathe freely again. No more patrolling, no more standing on and off in the same area : at last. clear instructions to head straight for the enemy at full power. The only one who took no delight in the roar of the engines and the hiss of the waves was the Chief. 'It's playing hell with my fuel reserves,' he grumbled, but even his voice was tinged with satisfaction when he reported the port engine back in service.

The Captain nodded. 'Fine, Chief – I could hear it. Now take a breather. You'll have plenty to do later on.'

Visiting the fore-ends, I could sense the prevailing mood of elation as soon as I opened the bulkhead door. The chef followed me in with a big can of fruit-juice and was besieged by a mob of thirsty ratings.

Little Benjamin gulped the contents of his mug and sighed happily. 'Let's hope we're in for a bit of action at last.'

'I'm in no hurry,' Schwalle said coolly.

'Speaking for myself, I'm fed to the back teeth with all this farting around.'

'My hero!' sneered a voice from the gloom near the bow tubes.

'Never mind, lad. Don't let them get you down – you've got the right idea.'

'Christ,' said the same anonymous voice, 'you must have been at the lime-juice again.'

Nothing was heard for a while but the hiss and slap of the waves and, in the intervals between them, a slumbrous murmur of radio music. Conversation suddenly reverted to the convoy.

'If the Old Man's going to do anything,' a torpedo-man said earnestly, 'he'd better do it tonight.'

'Why's that?' asked the Vicar.

'Because tomorrow's Sunday, you heathen,' Benjamin snarled in his ear. 'You know what it says in the Bible : keep the Sabbath and fuck not thy sister.'

I felt I was surrounded by actors. Our amateur submarine company was presenting a play about sang-froid and heroism, but the players were only talking to exorcise their fear.

The sea grew rougher during the night. I sensed it distinctly through layers of sleep.

I went on the bridge shortly after 5 a.m. It was the second lieutenant's watch. The Captain was also on the bridge. First light. U-A was buffeting her way through the dark waves. Spray drifted from their crests like smoke and filled the intervening troughs. Everyone was on the alert. If the convoy had tacked overnight, we might cut across its course at any moment.

A milky disc of sun appeared astern, but the sky ahead was still barred by black walls of cloud. Very slowly, they detached themselves from the horizon like unwanted scenery being hoisted on a grid-iron. The poor light persisted.

'Bloody thick weather,' grumbled the second lieutenant.

Within minutes another bank of cloud crept towards us, close above the sea. It draped itself into a sombre curtain. Right ahead, the curtain began to fray at the edges. The frayed ends were as black as the cloud itself. They hung so low that they brushed the water and blotted out the skyline.

Another cloud started to jettison its cargo of rain, fine on the port bow. Before long, the trailing fringes of both clouds merged.

Isolated drops were already falling on our sou'westers and oilskin jackets with the insistent tap of a bird's beak. The wall of rain expanded still farther. Larger and larger portions of the skyline became shrouded in gloom. The submarine seemed to be enmeshed in a dark net. It closed behind us, obliterating the last of the horizon.

Tensely we scanned the walls of grey vapour for a sign of the enemy. Any one of them could conceal a destroyer, any one of the clouds racing overhead might suddenly reveal a low-flying aircraft.

Spray swept over the bridge casing. I licked the salt off my lips. My sou'wester was a roof. The rain drummed fiercely on it. I could feel the crisp impact of the drops on my scalp. The brim shed them close before my eyes like a leaking gutter, a mere trickle compared to the torrents that coursed down the creases in our glistening oilskins. We stood there with the immobility of rocks in a cloudburst.

Bubbles and wrinkles appeared on the waves. Their foaming crests had vanished and their flanks were as lustreless as corrugated shale. I could clearly see them being steam-rollered by the rain, slate-grey except where our bow whipped them into a lather of dirty froth. Not a sign of the sun. The whole sky was cloaked in the same dismal shade of grey.

It was 0700 by now, an hour past our estimated time of interception.

I heard Dorian cursing to himself. 'Sodding weather! It's enough to give you the pip.' The second lieutenant rounded on him. 'Save your breath and keep looking!'

In spite of the hand-towel wound round my neck like a scarf, the water had seeped as far as my navel.

The control-room PO stared expectantly at me when I went below. I could only muster a sigh and a shrug. Then I got changed completely and carried my wet things to the motor-room.

'Wind north-west 5, sea and swell 4-5, sky overcast, visibility poor,' ran the entry in the log. U-A was rolling with increasing severity.

The latest report from the boat in contact was three hours old: 'Enemy now steering 110, open formation. Approximately 30 ships in 4 columns.' No news since then. The engines were still pounding away. I could hear the sea firing salvo after salvo at the conning-tower.

The watch was relieved at 0800.

Isenberg, the control-room PO, buttonholed Dorian and asked how things looked up top.

'It's stopped raining – now it's bloody well pissing down.'

'Come on, mate, give us a straight answer. How are we doing?'

'Getting nowhere fast. Can't see a bloody thing up there.'

Ario muttered something in Turbo's ear. I caught something about 'forty days and forty bleeding nights . . .'

Sudden fury overwhelmed the Captain. 'Damn the weather! It's always the same, just when we don't want it. We could miss them by a couple of miles in this soup.' Then, in a more subdued tone: 'If only Bertold would make another sign of life.' But, eagerly as we waited, no more signals came in.

We were stymied without another report from the contact boat because our calculations were shaky enough as it was. Bertold could hardly have had a fix in the past forty-eight hours. The sky must be as overcast in his area as in ours, so his reported position was putative. However accurate his quartermaster's dead reckoning, he could only guess the effect of wind and sea.

Kernével remained silent. Had Bertold been forced to dive? Had he been jumped by a destroyer?

No sighting reports could be expected from the other U-boats sent to attack the convoy, all of which were farther away than us. The fact that nothing had been heard from them was quite in order, but the contact boat was another matter.

The Captain shook his head. 'Bertold must be suffering from the same trouble as us.'

The engines continued to throb. There was little for the Chief to do. 'Our colleagues must be having a bumpy ride,' he said.

It took me a while to realize that his sympathy was directed at the crews of the enemy ships. 'The destroyer people are the ones I pity, thrashing about in those tin cans of theirs.'

Seeing my look of surprise, he said: 'Well, you can't help feeling sorry for them. Our own destroyers never put out if there's a breath of wind in the offing.'

The control-room was bursting at the seams with anyone who had the least excuse for being there. Apart from the Captain, the quartermaster and the control-room PO and his two hands, I noticed the first lieutenant, the second engineer and PO Dorian.

'We might as well give up,' Dorian said, but so softly that only I heard him. Everyone else seemed to have been struck dumb.

The Captain raised his head. 'Right – stand by to dive.'

I knew what he had in mind: the hydrophone. The sound of the enemy's screws and engines would carry farther under water than our eyes could see through the murk.

The usual sequence of commands followed.

I watched the depth-gauge. The needle began to rotate. Within seconds, the waves ceased their onslaught on the hull.

The Captain ordered us to 30 metres and squatted in the passage beside the hydrophone booth. Lit from below, the face of the hydrophone operator looked quite expressionless. His eyes were vacant. With his head-set on, he combed the multitude of underwater sounds for a sign of the enemy.

'Anything?' the Captain asked again and again. After a while, tense and impatient, he said: 'Nothing at all?'

He listened himself for a moment or two, then passed the head-set to me. I could hear nothing but the dull roar of a conch held to the ear.

An hour passed, and still we stayed deep. Still nothing to be heard. 'It's the luck of the draw,' the Chief murmured. He ran his fingers nervously through his hair.

The Captain was just about to get up and give orders for surfacing when he caught sight of the operator's face. The man's eyes were shut and his mouth had tightened in a grimace of something like pain. He turned the wheel of his apparatus very slowly clockwise, then anti-clockwise. The amplitude narrowed to a couple of centimetres: he had isolated something at last. Subduing the excitement in his voice with an effort, he reported: 'Propeller noises bearing zero-six-zero, sir – very faint.'

The Captain rose with a jerk. He borrowed one of the earphones and listened intently.

Suddenly the hydrophone operator gave an almost imperceptible start. The Captain bit his lip.

'Depth-charges. They're pasting someone. Bearing?'

'Zero-seven-zero – drawing aft. Still very faint,' replied the operator.

The Captain ducked through the bulkhead into the control-room. Briskly he ordered: 'Steer zero-five-zero. Stand by to surface.' Then, to the quartermaster: 'Make a note for the log, Kriechbaum: "In spite of weather, decided to close convoy on the surface." '

Conditions had deteriorated still further. The submarine rolled heavily. Water showered down the conning-tower, but the upper lid had to be kept open because the enemy might surprise us at any moment.

The screws raced, the engines gave their last ounce of power. The Captain never budged from the bridge. Standing motionless, he turned his head slowly back and forth, scanning the sea from under the lowered brim of his glistening sou'wester.

After a quarter of an hour I went below to study developments on the chart-table. Kriechbaum was hard at it, as usual. Without looking up, he said: 'Here we are and here's the estimated position of the convoy. Of course, they may have zigged again by now.'

It embarrassed me to feel like an aimless loiterer. My hand was already on the ladder when I changed my mind. I must look jumpy, shinning up and down every two minutes.

I retired to the wardroom and toyed with a book until the steward came to lay the plates and mugs for lunch. The Captain didn't appear.

We had scarcely settled ourselves round the table – the Chief, the junior engineer and I – when there was a shout from the control-room. The Chief cocked his head, listening. It was a report from the bridge.

'Masthead on the port bow!'

I was halfway to the control-room before I knew what had

happened. I raced up the ladder ahead of the Chief, forgetting to grab an oilskin jacket from the hook. Rain and spray soaked my sweater within seconds.

I heard the Captain's voice. 'Hard-a-starboard. Steer one-eight-zero.'

A look-out handed me his binoculars unasked. I followed the direction of the Captain's gaze. A grey swathe of rain filled the lenses, dismal and unrelieved. I held my breath and forced myself to remain calm, searched the left-hand extremity of the downpour, then traversed it very slowly from left to right. A hairline swam into my field of vision and vanished. An optical illusion? Had I only imagined it? I took a deep breath, flexed my knees and balanced the glasses on my fingertips. The U-boat rolled under me. I failed to get my bearings immediately and had to take another cue from the Captain. There it was again!

It trembled and danced in the lenses. A mast, no doubt about it, but a mast without an accompanying plume of smoke. Just a single hairline of a mast? Strain my eyes as I would, nothing showed but this pig's bristle which seemed to climb above the skyline as I watched.

Every merchantman trailed a plume of smoke which betrayed her presence long before her masts showed above the horizon. Ergo, this was no merchantman.

I swore under my breath. The damned thing had disappeared – no, there it was again. It should be visible with the naked eye by now. I lowered the glasses and looked. Sure enough, there it was.

The Captain was gnawing his lower lip. He raised the binoculars again. 'Blasted destroyer!' The words escaped from his lips in an angry hiss.

A minute went by. I kept my eyes glued to the pig's bristle and felt my throat throb with mounting excitement.

All doubt had vanished. The mast was growing steadily taller, so the destroyer must be heading our way. There was no possibility of evasion on the surface, not with our engines.

'They must have spotted us – damn and blast!' The Captain hardly raised his voice as he gave the alarm.

I reached the upper lid in a single bound. My boots hit the deck-plates with a metallic thud. The Captain gave the order to open all main vents even before he had fully secured the upper lid.

'Periscope depth,' he called down to the control-room. The Chief restored trim. The needle of the depth-gauge halted, then travelled slowly back across the dial. Dufte stood panting beside me in his wet oilskins. Zeitler and Böckstiegel, the two planesmen, were seated at their push-button controls, intently watching the water-level in the Papenberg. The first lieutenant inclined his head and let the rainwater drip off the brim of his sou'wester.

Nobody spoke. The only sound was a gentle electric hum which seemed to come from behind padded doors.

The silence was eventually broken by the Captain's voice. 'Depth?'

'Twenty metres,' reported the Chief.

'Periscope depth.'

The water in the Papenberg slowly sank. The submarine rose until the periscope broke surface.

We were not levelled off yet, so the Chief pumped aft from the forward trimming tank. U-A gradually returned to the horizontal but did not lie still. The waves nudged her in all directions, heaving, pulling, shoving. Periscope observation would be difficult.

I was listening for the Captain's voice when the hydrophone operator reported propeller noises on the starboard beam.

I passed the report to the conning-tower.

'Very good,' replied the Captain. Then, just as drily: 'Action stations.'

The hydrophone operator was leaning out of his cubby-hole into the passage. His unseeing eyes were dilated, his face mask-like. Apart from the Captain, he was the only man aboard whose senses extended to the world outside our steel shell: the Captain could see the enemy, the hydrophone operator could hear him. The rest of us were blind and deaf. 'Propeller noises increasing,' he reported. 'Drawing slowly aft.'

The Captain's voice was muted. 'Flood tubes 1 to 4.'

I thought so. The Old Man planned to take on the destroyer – he had his sights on a red pennant. He needed a destroyer to complete his collection, I knew it as soon as I heard him order us to periscope depth.

Another order from the conning-tower: 'Captain to control-room – Chief, accurate depth, please.'

A tall order, in this sea. The muscles in the Chief's lean face tautened and relaxed spasmodically as though his jaws were busy with chewing-gum. Woe to him if the boat rose too far, if she broke surface and betrayed us to the enemy . . .

The Captain was sitting astride his saddle in the cramped space between the periscope shaft and the conning-tower casing, head clamped to the rubber eye-pieces and splayed thighs gripping the massive shaft. His feet rested on the pedals which enabled him to rotate the shaft swiftly and silently through 360 degrees, saddle and all. His right hand gripped the lever which extended and retracted it.

The periscope motor hummed. He had slightly withdrawn the periscope head, so as to keep it as close to the surface as possible.

The Chief was standing motionless behind the two look-outs operating the hydroplanes. His eyes, too, were fixed on the Papenberg. The column of water slowly rose and fell, each rise and fall corresponding to the height of the waves on the surface.

Subdued murmurs. The hum of the periscope motor sounded as if it had been passed through a fine filter. It started, stopped, started again. The Captain was extending the look-stick for seconds at a time, then letting the sea wash over it. The destroyer must be quite close now.

'Flood No. 5 tube,' came a whisper from above.

The order was quietly passed to the stern torpedo compartment. We were in action.

I sat down on the sill of the bulkhead door. A whispered report from aft: 'No. 5 tube ready, bow-cap shut.'

Every tube was now flooded. All that remained was to open the bow-caps and send our fish on their way with a blast of compressed air.

I suddenly became aware that I still had a wad of bread in my mouth – pulpy bread mingled with shreds of salami. It tasted sourish.

The Old Man was crazy to think of attacking a destroyer in this sea. On the other hand, the sea had its good side. The streak of foam which might have betrayed our periscope would be hard to distinguish in the spindrift.

If we fired, the Chief would have to flood at once to compensate for the weight of the torpedoes, otherwise the submarine would break surface. A torpedo weighed 1500 kilos, so that meant roughly 1500 litres per torpedo. Multiplied by four or five, that was a lot of water.

No word from the Captain.

It was extremely difficult to hit a destroyer, with its shallow draught and high degree of manoeuvrability. Once hit, however, it vanished like a puff of thistledown. An explosion, a geyser of water and fragmented steel, and finis – nothing remained.

The Captain's steady voice came from above. 'Open bow-caps, tubes 1 and 2. Enemy speed fifteen. Angle on the bow, four-zero left. Range one thousand.'

The second lieutenant set the values on the calculator. The fore-ends reported bow-caps open. The first lieutenant passed the word, quietly but distinctly: 'Tubes 1 and 2 ready, sir.'

With his hand on the firing-lever, the Captain waited for the enemy to cross the hairline.

I longed to see.

Silence lent wings to my imagination. Baneful pictures took shape: a British destroyer bearing down on us at point-blank range. A ship's bow with its creaming bow-wave loomed over us like a bird of prey about to ram. Dilated eyes, a rending of metal, jagged steel plates, a torrent of green water pouring into our torn hull.

The Captain's voice rang out, sharp as a whiplash. 'Flood Q. Sixty metres. Shut all bow-caps.'

The Chief, a fraction of a second later: 'Planes hard-a-dive, full ahead both. All hands forward!'

A babble of voices. I flung myself to one side, feet scrabbling the deck-plates. The first man dived through the after bulkhead, tripped, regained his footing and hurried on forward past the wireless office at a crouching run.

I caught a series of wide-eyed enquiring looks as more men passed me, slipping and stumbling. Two bottles of fruit-juice rolled down the passage from the PO's mess and smashed against the control-room bulkhead.

All hydroplanes were still hard-a-dive. The submarine was already at a steep bow-down angle, but still the men kept coming. They slid through the tilted control-room like skiers. One of them swore sibilantly as he fell headlong.

Only the engine-room watch remained aft now. I lost my footing but managed to grab the shaft of the search periscope just in time. The sausages seemed to be almost parallel with the deckhead. I heard the Captain's voice superimposed on a slither and thud of boots: 'Any time now.' It sounded quite casual, like a passing remark.

He climbed slowly down the ladder with the exaggerated deliberation of someone demonstrating a drill movement, ascended the incline and propped one buttock on the chart-stowage. His right hand encircled a pipe for support.

The Chief brought us slowly up by the head and ordered all hands back to diving stations. The men who had hurried forward worked their way aft again, hand over hand.

Using the sausages as a rough-and-ready inclinometer, I estimated that we were still thirty degrees bow-down.

RRABUMM! RRUMM! RRUM!

I was jolted by three resounding blows like axe-strokes.

Half-stunned, I heard a muffled roar. Icy fingers clutched my heart. What was the roaring sound? Then I realized: water was rushing back into the submarine cavities created by the explosions.

Two more colossal thuds.

The control-room PO had retracted his head like a tortoise. The new control-room hand, the Vicar, swayed and clung to the chart-table.

Another detonation, louder than the rest.

The lights went out, leaving us in Stygian gloom.

'Secondary lighting's failed!' I heard someone shout.

The Chief's orders seemed to come from far away. Cones of torch-light drilled yellowish holes in the darkness. A voice demanded fuses. The captains of stations made their reports by voice-pipe: 'Fore-ends well.' – 'Motor-room well.' – 'Engine-room well.'

'No leaks reported, sir,' said the quartermaster. His voice sounded quite as unemotional as the Captain's.

A moment later the deck-plates danced to the impact of two double detonations.

'Blow Q.' The pump started up with an incisive noise. As soon as the sound of the detonations had died away, it was stopped again to prevent the enemy's hydrophone from getting a bearing.

'Bring up the bow,' the Chief ordered his planesmen. Then, to the Captain: 'Boat trimmed, sir.'

'There'll be more to come,' the Captain said. 'They actually spotted the periscope, damn them. Almost incredible, in a sea like that.'

He looked round without a trace of dismay. I even detected a note of mockery in his voice. 'Psychological warfare, gentlemen, that's all.'

Nothing happened for the next ten minutes. Then a violent detonation shook the hull. More thuds followed in quick succession. The U-boat quaked and groaned.

'Fifteen,' counted the quartermaster, 'sixteen, seventeen. Eighteen, nineteen.'

The Chief was staring at the needle of the depth-gauge, which jumped a line or two at every concussion. His eyes were wide and looked even darker than usual. The Captain's eyes were shut in concentration: own course, enemy course, avoiding course. His reactions had to be instantaneous. Alone of us all, he was fighting a battle. Our lives depended on the accuracy of his decisions.

'Hard-a-port.'

'Hard-a-port, sir.'

'Steer north.'

The Captain was engaged in continuous mental arithmetic. The basic factors affecting his calculations changed with every report he received.

He must gauge his avoiding course from the destroyer's propeller noises and line of approach. Divorced from any immediate sensory perception, he had to control the submarine like a pilot flying blind and base his decisions on indirect information.

I saw in my mind's eye, grey-black canisters leave the throwers, sail ponderously through the air and plop into the water. I saw them drift down, trailing pearls of air, and explode in the blackness: magnesium-white balls of flame, fiery suns beneath the sea.

Water transmitted blast far better than air. Shock-waves could rip a submarine apart at the seams as they ran through her. A depth-charge could destroy a boat anywhere within its range. The light depth-charges dropped by aircraft weighed 60 kilos, destroyer depth-charges 200. At a depth of 100 metres, their lethal range was 80-100 metres.

Peace returned for a while. I strained my ears to the limit: no sound of propellers, no splash of depth-charges, just the gentle hum of our electric motors. A breathless hush. Gradually the Captain seemed to remember our presence. He glanced round without shifting his position.

'I could see them on the bridge, standing there staring at us. There was a man in the crow's-nest. A corvette.' He leant forward and called softly to the hydrophone operator. 'See if she's going away.' A minute later, still leaning over, he asked: 'Well, any fainter?'

Herrmann, the operator, replied at once. 'Range pretty constant, sir.'

The pressure hull itself could take plenty of punishment. The openings – each with its accursed hull wave – were our Achilles' heel: main ballast tank vents and floods, pump suctions and discharges, engine induction valves and exhaust flaps, cooling-water pipes, stern glands for propeller shafts, rudders and hydroplane glands – and probably a lot of other things I didn't know about.

The most dangerous depth-charges were those which exploded obliquely beneath the keel, where flanges and hull openings were at their most numerous. The lethal range decreased at greater depths because the water-pressure that menaced our seams had the additional effect of reducing a depth-charge's destructive potential to 40 or 50 metres.

There was an abrupt rattle as though someone had tossed a handful of gravel at the hull.

'Asdic!' a voice muttered from the after regions of the control-room. My mind's eye transposed the spiteful-sounding word into neon-lit capitals: ASDIC.

A second handful of gravel, then a third.

A shiver ran down my spine. *Anti-submarine Detection Investigation Committee* – a bureaucratic euphemism for death. It was the detector-impulses striking our hull that produced this grasshopper sound, which acquired the intensity of a siren in the stillness. The impulses were roughly ten seconds apart.

I wanted to shout 'Switch off!' The chirping grated on my nerves. We froze, hardly daring to breathe, although Asdic would find us even if we turned to stone. Silent routine was useless against Asdic, as was drifting with motors stopped. Normal listening devices were crude in comparison. Asdic did not pick up sounds, it reacted to mass. Depth had lost its power to shield us.

Nervous tension gripped me. My hands were trembling. I thanked my lucky stars that I was seated in the bulkhead doorway, not standing. Cautiously I tried out some static physical movements: swallowing, blinking, biting, jaw-clenching, forcing saliva through gaps in my teeth.

The hydrophone operator murmured: 'Getting louder.'

The Captain detached himself from the periscope shaft and walked over to me on tiptoe. 'Bearing?'

'Bearing steady at two-six-zero, sir.'

Four explosions in quick succession. Before the roar and gurgle of their aftermath had died away the Captain said in an undertone: 'She was handsomely painted. An oldish ship with a heavily raked fore-castle, but otherwise flush-decked.'

I was jolted by another explosion. The deck-plates rattled.

'Twenty-seven, twenty-eight,' counted the quartermaster, emulating the Captain's studiously offhand tone.

A bucket rolled across the deck.

'Quiet, blast it!'

This time it sounded as if someone had put the gravel in a tin can and shaken it to and fro, once in each direction. The Asdic was overlaid by a brisk, intermittent chirping of a different kind: the throb of the corvette's propellers. They were clearly audible. I froze again as though the slightest movement, the smallest sound, would bring the propeller-beats nearer. Not a blink, not a flicker of the eye, not a breath, not a change of expression, not a goosepimple.

Another five depth-charges for the quartermaster's tally. My face remained a frozen mask. The Captain raised his head. Articulating the words clearly, he dropped them into the dying echoes of the last explosion: 'Easy, everyone. It could be a lot worse.'

The calm in his voice was good to hear. It settled on my jangling nerves like balm.

Then we lurched under a single shattering blow which sounded like a gigantic club thrashing a sheet of iron. Two or three men staggered.

Wisps of blue smoke hung in the air. And again: BRUMM! BRUMM! RRABUMM!

'Thirty-five, thirty-six, thirty-seven.' This time the words came in a whisper.

The Captain said firmly: 'Never mind the noise—a few bangs never hurt anyone.' Then he reinterred himself in his course calculations. A deathly silence fell. After a while he murmured: 'How does she bear now?'

'Two-six-zero, sir, growing louder.'

The Captain's head lifted. He had reached a decision. 'Hard-a-starboard,' he ordered, then: 'Hydrophone operator, we're turning to starboard.'

An adjustable spanner had to be passed aft. I grabbed it hurriedly and handed it on. It would have been bliss to do something—anything. Spin a handwheel, pull a lever, operate a pump . . .

Herrmann was leaning far out into the passage. His eyes were open but unseeing. He was now our sole link with the outside world. His fixed and vacant stare gave him the appearance of a medium.

'Propellers bearing two-three-zero, two-two-five, growing louder.'

'Turn out all unnecessary lights,' ordered the Captain. 'God knows how much longer we'll need the box.'

Herrmann again: 'Now bearing two-one-zero, closing fast—probably attacking.' Excitement marred his phraseology.

Seconds dragged by. Nothing. Nobody moved.

'Let's hope they don't call up their friends.' The Captain had put into words what was already preying on my mind: the sweepers, the hunter-killers, the weight of sheer numbers . . .

The skipper who had put us down was no novice, and we were defenceless in spite of the five torpedoes in our tubes. We couldn't surface. We couldn't pounce from a place of concealment and hurl ourselves at the enemy. We even lacked the grim determination that comes from the mere feel of a weapon in the hand. We couldn't yell defiance. We could only cower away, dive deeper. How deep were we, anyway? The needle of the depth-gauge stood at 140 metres. Maximum recommended diving depth: 90.

Ten minutes of inactivity, then another handful of gravel hit us. I could tell from Herrmann's face that more depth-charges were on the way. He slipped his ear-phones off and silently counted the seconds between entry and detonation.

The first charge was so well placed that it jarred my spine. I saw the quartermaster's mouth open and shut but heard nothing. I thought I'd gone deaf until the Captain spoke. He ordered an increase in speed. Then, raising his voice above the pandemonium: 'Steady as you go. We're doing all right, lads. Keep up the good work and –'

He broke off in mid-sentence. Silence had fallen again, a tingling silence as taut as a bow-string. The only sound was an occasional slap and gurgle from the bilge.

'Bring the bow up a bit.' The Chief's whispered order sounded over-loud in the stillness. We were back at Slow One. Bilge-water slopped aft. I wondered why there was so much of it.

'Thirty-eight to forty-one,' reported the quartermaster.

To my ears, still ringing with the thunder of exploding depth-charges, the ensuing silence seemed like a vast acoustic abyss, black-lined and bottomless.

Just to spoil its agonizing quality, the Captain muttered: 'Hard to tell if they're still in contact.' The next moment, more detonations rocked the depths. It was a straight answer.

My ears had lost their power to discriminate. I couldn't tell whether the charges were exploding right or left, above or below us. The Captain had no such difficulty. Moreover, he was probably the only man apart from Herrmann who knew our position relative to that of our tormentor – unless Kriechbaum was also following the picture. My own sense of direction had gone. I only saw that the needle of the depth-gauge was creeping slowly round the dial: we were going still deeper.

The Chief was craning over the planesmen's shoulders. The lamplight silhouetted his face against the darkness beyond, moulding every feature into planes of light and shade like the face of an actor lit by footlights. His hand looked waxen. There was a dark smudge on one cheek. His eyelids were tightly compressed as though the light dazzled him.

The planesmen sat motionless in front of their push-buttons. Our hydroplanes were power-operated. U-A had every modern convenience. Except, of course, a gadget for observing the enemy below periscope depth.

A respite? I tried to settle myself more firmly. The corvette would not keep us waiting long. She was only making another sweep, confident that her thrice-accursed Asdic would keep us on the hook. Above us, all available men must now be on the bridge, scanning the choppy sea for a sign of our presence. They would see nothing but zebra-markings on the bottle-green surface, white-and-green marbled paper with a few traces of black. The shimmer of escaping oil would be more to their taste . . .

Still no move from the hydrophone operator. No new contacts. The Captain raised his head abruptly. 'Wonder if we'll catch it again . . .'

He leaned forward and addressed Herrmann. 'Check if she's going away.' Impatiently, he added: 'Well, any change?'

'Constant, sir,' Herrmann replied. After a while: 'Growing louder.'

'Bearing?'

'Bearing steady at two-two-zero, sir.'

At once the Captain went hard-a-starboard. We were doubling back on our tracks.

Both motors were ordered slow ahead.

Drops of condensation punctured the almost tangible silence at regular intervals: Plink, plonk – tip, tap – plip, plop.

A new series of concussions made the deck-plates dance and rattle. 'Forty-seven, forty-eight,' Kriechbaum counted. 'Forty-nine, fifty, fifty-one.'

I glanced at my wrist-watch: 1430. When had we dived? It must have been shortly after midday, so we had been under counter-attack for two hours.

My watch had a red second-hand. I focused my attention on it and set myself to measure the interval between one detonation and the next. Two minutes thirty seconds passed: another jolt. Thirty seconds: the next. Twenty seconds: the next.

I was glad to have something to concentrate on. Nothing existed for me save the rotating red hand. The fingers of my right hand tightened round my left wrist as though to sharpen my concentration. It would pass – it had to.

Forty-four seconds: another hard, dry detonation. I could distinctly feel my lips, which had been forming silent syllables, freeze in an oval which bared my teeth. I put out a hand to steady myself and lost sight of the watch dial.

The Captain ordered us deeper by another twenty metres.

Two hundred metres now. An angry creaking sound ran through the submarine's hull. The new control-room hand showed the whites of his eyes.

'Death-watch beetle,' whispered the Captain.

Very funny. It was the wooden panelling which produced these violent groans and creaks. The U-boat's internal structure was responding to the forces at work on her hull. Two hundred metres: a nice round figure. Each square centimetre of steel skin was now withstanding a weight of 20 kilos – 200 tons to every square metre, yet our plates were only two centimetres thick.

The creaking grew louder.

'Not my favourite tune,' murmured the Chief.

The strain on our steel shell tormented me as though my own frame were being compressed. My scalp twitched as another pistol-shot rang out. The insane pressure was making our plates as vulnerable as an eggshell.

A double detonation, then another, barely weaker than the first. Our pursuers seemed to be trawling for us with a net of even finer mesh.

Another rattle of deck-plates, followed by the inevitable after-roar.

Silence for a few heartbeats. Then came two shattering blows which extinguished the lights again and sent glass tinkling to the deck.

A cone of torch light roamed over the bulkheads and came to rest on the dial of the main depth-gauge. I turned cold at what I saw: the needles of both gauges had gone. The gauge-glass between the two planesmen had cracked and was sending a jet of water clear across the control-room.

'Depth-gauge leaking,' I heard someone report in a tremulous voice.

'All right,' the Captain growled, 'no need to make a song and dance about it.'

The blank dials looked like eyes glazed in death. We could no longer tell whether the boat was rising or falling.

My scalp crawled. Our instruments had forsaken us. Without them we were incapable of sensing our position in the water.

The control-room hand was groping among some pipes by torch-light, apparently in search of a cock which would stem the jet. He was soaked before he reached it. Although the jet dwindled and died, he continued to grope around on the deck. All at once he straightened with something held gingerly between his thumb and forefinger like a precious gem. Very carefully he took the pointer and replaced it on the square boss of the small gauge which registered extreme depths. I felt as if our lives depended on whether this thin strip of metal stirred or not.

The man withdrew his hand. The needle quivered and began to move. The Captain gave a nod of silent commendation.

The gauge now stood at 190 metres.

'Propellers bearing two-three-zero, two-two-zero,' reported Herrmann. 'Growing louder.'

The Captain removed his cap and put it on the chart-stowage. His hair was damp and matted with sweat. He drew a deep breath, almost a sigh of resignation, as though he couldn't trust himself to speak.

'Propellers bearing two-one-zero, growing louder. Attacking again.'

The Captain ordered full speed ahead and U-A gave a slight lurch forward. He leant back against the shiny, oily shaft of the search periscope and stared at the deckhead.

Long-forgotten images took shape in my mind. I saw the pasteboard discs of two ice-cream machines at an annual fair, endlessly counter-rotating until the red and white spirals filled my head to bursting point. Then I recognized them as the trails of two depth-charges, fiery comets which seared everything in their path.

Another report from the hydrophone operator startled me. I stared at his mouth but the words failed to penetrate my brain.

More waiting with bated breath. My nerves seemed to be lying exposed on top of my skin. The least noise jarred them like a dentist's probe. I was possessed by one thought only: they were overhead – right overhead. I forgot to breathe until lack of oxygen forced me to fill my lungs slowly and carefully with air. My closed eyelids were imprinted with pictures of depth-charges trailing perpendicular streamers of sparkling bubbles, then exploding into white fire-balls. Rainbow colours sprouted from the molten cores in a dazzling display of fire-works, until the whole of the sea's interior glowed like a blast furnace.

The spell was broken by the control-room PO, who informed the Chief by whisper and gesture that an oil save-all can was overflowing in one corner of the control-room. That oil should be overflowing was – at this moment – a matter of supreme unimportance, but it clearly offended Isenberg's sense of propriety.

A nod from the Chief conveyed permission to do something about it. The end of the discharge pipe was immersed in the save-all, so it had to be tilted for withdrawal. More oil flowed on to the deck and formed a repulsive black puddle.

The quartermaster wagged his head in disgust. Isenberg withdrew the brimming can as gingerly as a safe-breaker negotiating an electronic burglar system.

'Propeller noises drawing aft,' reported Herrmann. Two more depth-charges exploded almost simultaneously, but the detonations were fainter and more muffled than their predecessors.

'Miles away,' said the Captain.

RRUMM, RRABUMM!

Still more muffled. The Captain reached for his cap. 'Dummy runs. They might as well go home and practise.'

Isenberg had already substituted some new glass tubes for the broken gauge-glasses, as though he realized that the sight of their shattered remains was bad for morale.

I stood up. My legs were stiff and numb. I extended a bloodless foot and felt as if I had stepped into a void. Grabbing the table for support, I looked down at the chart.

There was the pencil-line representing U-A's route, and there was the pencilled cross which marked our last fix. The line ended abruptly. I resolved to make a note of the grid reference if we got out alive.

Herrmann made a sweep through the full 360 degrees.

'Well?' asked the Captain, looking bored. His left cheek bulged as he rammed his tongue against it from the inside.

'Going away,' Herrmann replied.

The Captain looked round with an air of satisfaction. He even grinned. 'Well, that seems to be that.'

He stretched and shook himself. 'Quite instructive, really. In line for a red pennant one minute, clobbered the next.' He ducked stiffly through the bulkhead and vanished into his cubby-hole, calling for a piece of paper.

I wondered what he was drafting – something pithy for his patrol report or a signal to base. If I knew anything about him, it would be a handful of bone-dry words like 'Surprised by corvette in rainstorm. Counter-attacked three hours.'

Five minutes later he reappeared in the control-room. He exchanged a glance with the Chief, ordered us to periscope depth and climbed leisurely into the conning-tower.

The Chief gave a series of plane orders.

'Depth?' came the Captain's voice from above.

'Forty metres,' the Chief reported, then: 'Twenty metres, fifteen metres – periscope depth.'

I heard the periscope motor hum, stop, hum again. A minute went by. No word from above. We waited in vain for a sign of life.

'Something must be up . . .' murmured the control-room PO.

At last the Captain spoke. 'Take her down quick! Fifty metres – all hands forward.'

I repeated the order and the hydrophone operator passed it on. The words travelled aft like a multiple echo. Men began to hurry forward through the control-room, grim-faced once more.

'Bloody hell,' muttered the Chief. The needle of the depth-gauge resumed its slow progress.

The Captain's sea-boots appeared. He clambered slowly down the ladder. All eyes were fixed on his face, but he only gave a derisive grin. 'Slow ahead both. Steer zero-six-zero. The corvette's lying a thousand metres away. Stopped, by the look of her. The crafty sods were planning to jump us.' He bent over the chart. After a while he turned to me. 'Cunning bastards – you can't be too careful. We may as well dawdle west for a bit.'

'When's dusk?' he asked the quartermaster.

'1830, sir.'

'Good. We'll stay deep for the time being.'

The immediate danger seemed to have passed, judging by his normal tone of voice. He drew a deep breath and arched his chest, nodding at each of us in turn.

'After the fray,' he said, with a demonstrative glance at the mess of buckets, broken glass and trampled oilskins.

I was reminded of drawings by Dix: dead horses lying on their backs, bellies gaping like derelict hulks, all four legs stiffly extended skywards; uniformed corpses embedded in the mud of the trenches, teeth bared in mute frenzy. Although we had just escaped annihilation by a hairsbreadth, there was no sign of convoluted entrails, charred limbs or butcher's meat bleeding through canvas stretchers. A few splinters of glass, some broken gauges, a split can of condensed milk and two shattered pictures in the passage – these were the only traces of our battle. The steward appeared, wrinkled his nose at the mess and started to clean up. I noticed to my regret that the C-in-C's photograph was intact.

The engine- and motor-rooms had been less fortunate. The Chief reeled off a list of technicalities.

The Captain nodded patiently. 'Do your best, Chief. It wouldn't surprise me if they needed us before long.' Then, to me: 'Time we ate something. I'm famished.' He pulled off his cap and hung it on top of some oilskins.

The second lieutenant's face twisted in a wry grin. 'That scrambled egg must be cold by now.'

'Hey, Chef,' the Captain called aft, 'dish up some more scrambled egg.'

I felt dazed. Were we really hob-nobbing round the table as usual, or was it a delusion? My ears still rang with the thunder of depth-charges. I found it hard to grasp that we had run the gauntlet unscathed. I sat in silence and shook my head to clear it of hallucinations.

Less than an hour after the last depth-charge, the PO tele-graphist put a record on the turntable. Marlene Dietrich's voice came purring through the loudspeakers. '*Put your cash away, you can pay another day . . .*' It was a record from the Old Man's private collection.

It was 1900 when the Captain's preliminary order for sur-facing came over the intercom. The Chief ducked through the bulkhead and gave instructions to the planesmen. The look-outs climbed into their oilskins and mustered below the hatch, fumbling with their binoculars.

'Sixty metres, fifty metres – coming up fast,' reported the Chief. When the depth-gauge showed thirty, the Captain levelled off and ordered a hydrophone sweep. Nobody breathed a word. I didn't breathe at all. The operator detected nothing.

The Captain climbed the ladder. When the boat reached periscope depth I could tell from the click of switches that he was taking a look round.

We waited tensely. Still nothing.

'Surface !'

HP air hissed into the main ballast tanks. The Captain re-tracted the periscope, which came to rest with a click. Only then did he remove his head from the rubber eyepieces.

'Upper lid clear,' the Chief called up. 'Equalize pressure !'

The first lieutenant spun the handwheel and the upper lid sprang open with a champagne-cork pop which showed that pressure-equalization had been incomplete. Fresh air streamed into the boat. It was chill and damp. I sucked it in greedily through my mouth, receiving the cold draught like a benison, pumping my lungs full and savouring the salt on my tongue.

The boat was pitching.

Loud orders from the bridge: 'Stand by to blow to full buoyancy. Engine-room will remain at diving stations.'

The Chief gave an approving nod. The Captain was wary, reluctant to take unnecessary risks.

In the disc of dark sky framed by the hatch coaming, a few scattered stars twinkled like tiny lanterns stirred by the wind.

'Stand by port engine.'

'Port engine ready, sir.'

The submarine rocked. The round eye of the upper lid swung to and fro across the glittering backcloth.

'Slow ahead port.'

A tremor ran through the hull as the engine started.

The Captain summoned the look-outs and the quartermaster to the bridge.

'Must get a signal off,' I heard.

The quartermaster reappeared. Peering over his shoulder, I couldn't repress a grin because the text he jotted down matched my forecast almost word for word. Puzzled by my amusement, he raised his eyebrows.

'Short and sweet,' I said, but that foxed him too. I saw him shake his head as he made for the wireless office.

'Man on the bridge?' I called up.

'Come on,' the Captain called back, and I climbed the ladder.

The clouds had parted in front of the moon, a supine crescent floating in its own reflected splendour. The sea shone and glittered where the moonlight struck it. Soon the curtains of cloud drew together again. The only light now came from a sprinkling of stars and the sea itself. Foam phosphoresced at our stern with a magical green glow. Waves sizzled over the fore-casing like water spilt on a hot stove. The sharp hiss was underlaid by a dull roar. Sometimes a largish wave would rear up and strike our side with the muffled boom of a Chinese gong.

I had the impression that we were less water-borne than suspended on a thin crust between twin abysses, one above and one beneath: a thousand storeys of darkness above us, a thousand storeys of darkness below. My thoughts strayed, confused and without focus. We were saved – voyagers to Orcus who had returned.

The Captain spoke, close to my ear. 'Lucky for us this pond is three-dimensional, when you come to think of it.'

Breakfast at the wardroom table.

Fragments of conversation drifted from the CPOs' mess. I listened to them with half an ear. ERA Johann seemed to be reminiscing about his last home leave.

'We managed to get hold of a stove in the end. Talk about wangling! Nothing to be had anywhere, not even with a U-boat badge on your jacket. Prams are unobtainable. I said to Gertrud: do we really need a pram these days? After all, the niggers tote their babies around on their backs . . . She's coming to the boil nicely, Gertrud is. Six months gone. I wonder if we'll be moved in by the time she has it . . . As long as it's got four walls and a roof, that's what I always say. They had eight raids in one week.'

'It can't last for ever,' someone said consolingly. It sounded like the coxswain.

'You could paint the table white and build a little box round the gas meter. The lads at the dockyard would knock one up for a couple of beers – you could take it back with you next leave. A little box like that wouldn't be much trouble.'

The coxswain chuckled. 'I'd get the armourers to knock you up a pram too, while you're at it.'

'Oh sure, thanks for the tip – we could use a bullet-proof pram.'

Just before 0900 next day we entered an area littered with flotsam from some ship that must have been sunk in convoy. Planks black with fuel oil rose on our bow-wave and swung sluggishly aside. Then we saw a rubber dinghy. There was a man in it, sitting as he might have sat in a rocking-chair, with his legs over the inflated side and his feet almost trailing in the water. His forearms were raised in the attitude of a news-paper-reader. As we drew nearer, I saw that both hands were missing. All that remained of them was a pair of blackish stumps. His face was a charred black mask with two rows of bared teeth, as if he had pulled a black stocking over his head.

'Dead,' said the quartermaster.

He could have saved himself the trouble.

The dinghy and its lifeless passenger swam quickly past. Our wake left them bobbing rhythmically. The man, com-fortably ensconced with his invisible newspaper, seemed to enjoy the motion.

Nobody spoke. Eventually, Kriechbaum said: 'That was a merchant seaman. I wonder where he got the rubber dinghy – freighters usually carry rafts. The dinghy looked like an RN job.'

His professional observation broke the spell. The Captain seized upon the subject with alacrity and spent several minutes discussing the likelihood that British freighters had long been carrying naval personnel. 'After all, who's going to man the guns?'

The flotsam persisted. The sunk merchantman had left a wide swathe of débris: crates, oil drums, splintered lifeboats, charred and shattered rafts, buoys, whole sections of bridge superstructure. We passed three or four men floating dead in their life-jackets, heads awash, then a whole string of corpses drifting face down, most of them without life-jackets and many badly mutilated.

The quartermaster spotted the human flotsam too late for us to avoid it.

Chill-voiced, the Captain ordered an increase in speed. We bulled our way through the maimed and tattered remains. The bow-wave swept everything aside like a snow-plough. The Captain stared ahead and the quartermaster watched his sector.

I saw the starboard after look-out gulp as we passed a body spread-eagled over a baulk of timber.

'There's a buoy!' said the Captain. His voice grated like a rusty hinge.

He gave two or three steering orders in quick succession. Our bow swung slowly towards the red-and-white buoy, only visible for moments at a time.

The Captain turned to Kriechbaum and said, far too loudly: 'I'll take her on the port side. Get the coxswain.'

I focused my gaze on the bobbing speck of colour. It quickly grew larger.

Behrmann reported breathlessly to the bridge, then climbed down the ladder on the outside of the conning-tower. He was armed with a small grappling iron.

Although everyone knew what he had in mind, the Captain said: 'Right, let's see what the tub was called.'

The quartermaster craned over the bridge rail so as to command the full length of the boat. 'Slow ahead port, full ahead starboard,' he called down. 'Hard-a-port.'

The helmsman echoed his orders from inside the conning-tower. Every now and then the buoy disappeared into a trough, making it hard for us to keep track of it.

Kriechbaum stopped the port engine and ordered slow ahead starboard. Not for the first time, I was struck by U-A's lack of manœuvrability. She was long in relation to her beam and her screws were too close together.

The buoy seemed to have vanished. It should have been almost on the port beam. A moment of uncertainty, then it reappeared.

Slowly we bore down on it. Kriechbaum ordered course adjustments. He seemed satisfied with our progress.

The coxswain was holding the grappling iron in one hand and a line coiled lasso-fashion in the other. Clinging to the jumping-wire for support, he edged stiffly forward over the slippery gratings. By now, the buoy was level with our bow. Exasperatingly, the name appeared to be on the far side — unless it had been obliterated by the elements.

The buoy drifted slowly past at a distance of three metres — an ideal lie. The coxswain took aim, cast the grappling iron, and missed. Before he had hauled it in again, the buoy was abreast the conning-tower. He raced aft and had another shot from the after-casing, but he jerked the line too soon — the iron splashed into the sea. He stared up at us, almost sheepishly.

'Round again, please,' the Captain said frostily. I strained to keep the buoy in sight while we turned full circle.

This time Kriechbaum took us in so close that the coxswain could have got a hand to the buoy. He preferred to rely on the grappling iron, which at last found its mark.

'Gulf Stream!' he bellowed to the bridge.

Lunch in the wardroom. The Captain looked pensive. 'Let's hope our morning's work doesn't rile anyone.'

The Chief raised his eyebrows enquiringly. Even the first lieutenant looked up, but the Old Man took his time. It was a minute before he haltingly disclosed what was running through his mind. 'That freighter — say the U-boat commander that sank her didn't get her name. Say he erred on the generous side and estimated her tonnage at 15,000 g.r.t. Along comes U-A and reports seeing wreckage from the Gulf Stream, which turns out to be a 10,000-tonner . . .'

He paused to make sure we were with him. 'Well, I mean — it could be embarrassing, couldn't it?'

I stared at the linoleum tabletop and silently asked myself what he was on about. First that gruesome paper-chase and now these trivialities.

I looked up. He had leant back and was stroking his beard with the knuckles of his right hand. A tremor crossed his face as I watched. Of course. The Old Man's hard-bitten perform-ance was a way of inoculating us against emotion. He was as impressionable as any of us. He over-acted, surmised, conjectured, solely to banish our nightmare visions.

But the image of the dead seaman refused to be banished. It lingered, swamping my other recollection of the scene. From a distance he had looked as if he might paddle leisurely away at any moment, head slightly tilted for a better view of the sky. Those charred wrists . . . Someone must have hauled him into the dinghy – he could never have made it without hands. It was an abiding mystery.

Not a survivor to be seen, I reflected. Another vessel must have picked them up. Seamen who lost their ship in convoy stood a chance, but the others – the ones who travelled without escort?

The Captain had retired to the control-room and bent over the chart-table. He ordered both engines ahead two-thirds. Then he straightened up, squared his shoulders, and stretched elaborately, clearing his throat for a full minute before uttering a syllable. It was like an engine starting up from cold.

'I'll eat my hat if we aren't right in the convoy's path. God knows how many signals we missed while we were deep. Let's hope we hear something from U-R – or any other boat in contact.' Inconsequently, he added: 'Depth-charges are the most inaccurate weapon there is.'

The Chief, who had also been listening, looked puzzled. The Captain nodded with a trace of smugness. Everyone in the control-room had heard him. He had succeeded in drawing the moral from our recent counter-attack: depth-charges always missed. Our survival proved it.

Bertold was repeatedly called upon to report his position, course and speed. We waited as tensely as Kernével to hear that he had replied.

The Old Man hurrumphed, chewing on a few strands of beard.

THE STORM

FRIDAY, 42ND DAY AT SEA. The north-west wind grew stronger. The quartermaster explained its behaviour as follows: 'Looks as if we're south of a family of cyclones which is being forced towards Europe between the trade winds and the polar high.'

'Strange habits they have, the Cyclopes and their families,' I said.

'Who said anything about Cyclopes?'

'The Cyclops is a one-eyed wind.' Kriechbaum eyed me suspiciously.

I felt it was time for another breath of fresh air. The sea was a dark shade of blue-green. I tried to define its colour. Onyx was near the mark.

In the distance, the sea looked almost black beneath a low canopy of massed cloud. The only sign of turmoil was in the west, where more and more clouds spilled over the skyline and swelled. I watched them invade the sky. First, scouts were dispatched by the dark legions encamped close above the western horizon – small parties which worked their way to the zenith and established a bridgehead there. They were followed by the whole dark horde. Slowly ascending, it was caught and deflected by the wind, but beneath and beyond it a new army marched over the horizon, seemingly drawn from some inexhaustible reservoir. The procession was never-ending.

Seaman Böckstiegel, a nineteen-year-old giant, reported to PO Telegraphist Herrmann, who doubled as sick-berth attendant, with what he described as a rash in the armpits.

'Rash?' Herrmann said derisively. 'Crabs, more like. Drop your pants.' He gave a sudden snort. 'Good God, you've got a whole colony down there. Lucky they haven't swallowed you whole.'

Herrmann reported to the first lieutenant, who ordered an inspection for the watch below at 1900 and another at 2030 for the current watch-keepers.

The Captain was asleep and did not hear the news until an hour later. He glowered at his Number One like a bull mesmerized by the cape. 'God give me strength,' he said through gritted teeth; 'that's all we needed.'

There was much banter in the POs' mess. 'Who brought them on board, that's what I'd like to know?' – 'Kit inspection? Well, it makes a change.' – 'Suits me, my balls haven't had an airing since we sailed.'

So now we had crab-lice on board as well as a ship's fly. U-A was becoming a Noah's Ark for lower forms of life.

The first line-up yielded five more cases of infestation. Before long the submarine was pervaded by a cloying aroma of paraffin.

The wind came at us like jets of air from a nozzle. The sea became increasingly agitated. The waves began to look malign, rearing and subsiding with sporadic menace. Again and again, foam washed over the fore-casing and gushed up through the gratings. The wind sliced through it and fired needle-sharp volleys of spray into the faces of the forward look-outs.

In the control-room, everything gradually became filmed with moisture. The ladder felt cold and wet.

It was impossible to remain on deck without oilskins and a sou'wester. The stylus on the barograph had drawn a descending flight of steps like the Wilhelmshöhe Falls. If the line continued its fall unchecked it would soon reach the lower edge of the paper.

The Captain was obviously worried about the weather. 'Depressions like this can travel at a hell of a lick,' he explained. 'Lots of turbulence, alterations between subtropical and polar air, wide areas of disturbance – wind conditions can go absolutely haywire.'

The Chief grinned at me. 'The Captain's an amateur meteorologist, didn't you know?'

The Old Man pored over the chart with Kriechbaum at his elbow.

'These North Atlantic fronts are quite something,' he said. 'The cold air will be at the rear of the depression. It'll probably bring squalls – better visibility too, with luck. We could always turn north, but we'd only be heading deeper into the centre, and skirting it to the south is out for tactical reasons.' He sighed. 'Well, Kriechbaum, I suppose there's nothing for it. We'll just have to plug on and hope for the best. Pity the sea's on the port beam.'

'Yes, sir,' the quartermaster replied. 'It's going to get a lot more lumpy before it's finished.'

The steward, heavily laden, squeezed through the narrow alley between my bunk and the mess table. I followed him to the wardroom.

We had to fit the fiddles for lunch, and even then it was a feat of dexterity to keep the soup out of our laps.

At one point during the meal, the Chief turned to his junior and asked casually: 'What's that in your lashes and eyebrows? Better show it to the quack some time.'

He didn't pursue the subject until the second engineer and the two watch-keeping officers had left the table. Then, just as casually: 'First time I ever saw them up there, I must say.'

'Saw what?' asked the Captain.

'What my side-kick has nesting round his eyes – crabs, of course.'

'You're joking!'

'No, seriously, you can't get them any worse than that. It's the tertiary stage, so to speak.'

The Captain inhaled a vast quantity of air and stared at the Chief thunderstruck.

'With all due deference to your medical knowledge, Chief, does that mean your successor-designate has been . . .'

'Come, come, sir. No need to suspect the worst.'

A cynical smirk settled on the Chief's face. The Captain slowly wagged his head as though testing the mobility of his cervical vertebrae. At last he said : 'Well, well, fancy that. All that puzzles me is, what's his next move?'

The Chief's smirk broadened. 'Ah, there you have me.'

Peace descended on the boat, accentuating the hum of the ventilation fans. The only disturbance was an occasional snatch of song and hubbub of voices when someone opened the door to the fore-ends. I got up and made my way forward.

'High jinks in the chain locker,' Kriechbaum told me with an indulgent nod as I passed through the CPOs' mess. The light in the fore-ends was even feebler than usual.

'What's going on?' I enquired.

'Fun and games,' Ario replied mournfully. The watch below were sitting cross-legged on the decking, shoulder to shoulder. Their oil-stained drill jackets and striped sweaters made them look like a chorus from the brigands' scene in *Carmen*, dressed in the scrapings of the props basket.

The boat suddenly heeled. Leather jackets and oilskins swung sideways and we had to grab the lifelines on the bunks for support. Violent curses sounded from the depths of the compartment. Peering between heads and hammocks, I saw a naked figure staggering about in the gloom.

'It's Schwalle,' Benjamin explained, 'washing his lily-white body. He does it all the time, Lieutenant. We reckon he fancies himself.'

Lugubrious singing came from two forward bunks and one of the hammocks. Benjamin produced a mouth-organ, drew it across his lips a couple of times and finally settled on a tune.

> 'Along the Hamburg-Bremen line
> A love-sick maiden crept,
> And when the train from Flensburg came
> She laid her down and wept.
> The driver saw her lying there
> And braked with trembling hand.
> The loco failed to stop in time
> — Her head rolled in the sand.'

The others came in on cue:

> 'Who begrudges the miser his money
> or the King of Morocco his crown?
> There isn't a finer sensation
> than screwing the best tart in town!'

'More tea, Tiny?' Benjamin asked Zörner, the diminutive electrician.

'Thanks.'

Benjamin tilted the massive pot. Nothing happened. He went on tilting, and suddenly the spout emitted a thick jet of tea. Bread, sausage and tinned sardines were inundated.

'Jesus,' Fackler said, 'only ten minutes to go. Fuck this for a life – you've hardly parked your arse when it's time to shift it again. A bloody mockery, that's what it is.' He left the circle, still swearing.

Schwalle also buckled on his belt and started to go aft. 'I'm off,' he said as he disappeared through the bulkhead.

'Give the coxswain my love!' Böckstiegel called after him.

The Chief was still lounging in the wardroom. Eyeing me expectantly, he said: 'What does a glazier do when he's got no glass?'

I rolled my eyes in despair.

'He drinks out of the bottle, of course!'

I shook my head wearily.

Spray showered the deck of the control-room with a noise like squally rain. Sometimes a huge fist smote the submarine's bottom with a hollow boom. There was a sudden rumble beneath the deck-plates, so loud that it made me flinch. The Captain grinned. 'Walruses,' he said, 'scratching their backs on the keel.'

Again the dull rumble. The Chief stood up. Steadying himself carefully, he lifted a deck-plate and beckoned me over. 'Look, there's one now.'

I peered through the crack and, by the light of a torch, saw a small trolley suspended on two rails. It was occupied by the crouching figure of a man.

'He's checking the acid content of the batteries.'

'Some job, in this sea.'

'You can say that again.'

I picked up a book, but it quickly dawned on me that I was far too tired and shaken up to absorb the printed word. A bender would have been the thing, an honest-to-God session with the bottle and then out like a light – anything rather than this irksome inactivity. Beck's Beer, Pilsner Urquell,

Munich Löwenbräu, Martell, Hennessy, three star, five star . . .

A sweetish taste came into my mouth. Instantly I saw glasses of cheap green liqueur and, by contrast, hot toddies the colour of red ink. Heaven alone knew where the two girls had procured the muck, but it would have been fine for gumming paper bags. Friedrich was a cheeky young devil, picking them up in the café like that: 'Mm, you smell divine, sweethearts! Where do you live?'

'If it moves, fuck it,' was Friedrich's shore-going motto. His only qualification: 'But not before you've had a skinful.'

God, what a crazy night! Two mettlesome fillies, one blonde, one red-headed, bangs in front and shoulder-length sausages behind . . .

'On leave, are you?' – 'I've always had a soft spot for the boys in blue.' – 'What's that medal you're wearing? Really? This calls for a celebration.'

Two minutes and we were well away. The blonde advanced her pelvis and clamped her legs round my thigh.

'Dancing's forbidden,' somebody complained. 'Not at our place it isn't, so stick that in your pipe! Hey, Ida nip off and call a taxi.'

Nudges and giggles.

A display cabinet stuffed with fair-ground dolls in little pleated skirts, arranged in order of size like organ-pipes. Between the two aspidistras, fully a dozen garden gnomes of the smallest available make, interspersed with glossy varnished angels in wood. Plaster deer with tinsel-dusted backs, a red-tinted bulb in the standard lamp, sofa cushions karate-chopped in the middle to make the corners stand up like rabbits' ears. Circular cushions too, crocheted in every colour of the rainbow, and nestling among them three or four teddy-bears, one of them actually pink. On the wall, fairies performing a round-dance. It all came back to me in full colour: the lace mats under the liqueur glasses, and beneath them a marquetry tray depicting St Mark's in Venice. The huge doll who spread her pink celluloid legs on top of the display cabinet looked like another souvenir from Venice.

The sofa was patterned in dark-red vine-leaves, the curtaining in outsize hydrangeas, the carpet in rose-red flowers of fanciful design. There were black velvet silhouettes of churches, grouse and windmills. Mercifully, the red bulb concealed most of the horrors – even the glasses of sticky green rot-gut turned almost black in the dusty pink glow.

'What are you trying to do?' Friedrich demanded. 'Poison us?' He took a swig and shuddered.

'I hope you don't think, just because we invited you back
. . .' the redhead began tartly. Friedrich cut her short. 'It
never crossed my mind, darling.' A few soprano squeaks.
'Hey, hands off! What do you think you're doing?' Friedrich
again: 'Only what comes naturally.'

Later. The redhead, who had made herself comfy on the
carpet with Friedrich, started to punctuate his flow of small-
talk with moans. 'We're respectable married women, you
know – my hubby's a sergeant!'

All at once, the other – the blonde, who lay sprawled beside
me on the sofa with her blouse unbuttoned – flung her arms
round my neck.

Afterwards the blonde berated the redhead for starting it
all.

'You must be mad! I only gave in when you two started
rolling around on the couch.'

'Loves you?' Friedrich began to intone in a sort of sing-
song. "Course I loves you – fucks you, don't I?'

He was brought up short by a sudden slap in the face, but
the redhead didn't know our Friedrich. Much squirming and
wriggling was followed by several resounding smacks on her
backside.

The bottle of rot-gut fell over and the glasses got smashed.

'Stop it, the pair of you!' screamed the blonde. 'You're
crazy! What'll the neighbours say?'

I suddenly realized that the Chief had fixed me with an
intent side-long stare. 'Ruminative,' he said mockingly, 'yes,
that's it: our ruminative ship's poet.'

I spun round, bared my teeth and snarled like a beast of
prey. The Chief liked that. His grin persisted for a long time.

The Captain's patrol report entry for Friday read: 'Wind
north-west 6-7, sea 5. Search courses.'

SATURDAY, 43RD DAY AT SEA. I kept the forenoon watch with
the quartermaster.

Overnight the wind had rent the diminishing swell into
white-jawed crests and hurrying green troughs. Fortunately
we now had the sea right ahead instead of on the port beam.
I did not know what had prompted our overnight change of
course.

Volleys of spray stung my face. The water infiltrated the
collar of my oilskins and trickled down my chest and back,
making me shiver.

The wind was changeable. Its direction varied, as did the

force of the individual gusts.

Superimposed on the almost unbroken grey of the sky were darker clouds like mounds of soiled cotton-wool. The universal and dispiriting drabness was unrelieved by any friendlier shade, unless one counted the white veins on the flanks of the steel-grey combers and the soiled white froth on their crests. A pallid glow indicated where the sun should have been.

Midway through the watch, the sky ahead of us solidified into a wall faced with blackish-grey stucco, which extended from the horizon almost to the zenith. All at once, the wall came alive. Tentacles of vapour reached out and embraced the sky, swiftly extinguishing the last faint glimmer of diffused sunlight. The air grew steadily heavier, leaden with pressure. The howling of the wind ceased, but the lull only accentuated the venomous hiss of the waves.

And then the storm hit us. It leapt from the looming black wall with a sudden ferocity that stripped the waves of their grey-green skin.

The seas, which grew steeper minute by minute, advanced on us like a pack of ravening wolves. The sky was an unbroken mouse-grey layer, seemingly motionless except where a few darker patches in its otherwise uniform expanse betrayed that the entire overcast was in violent motion.

Some waves reared higher than the rest, as if terrified by the lowering sky, but the storm seized hold of them and swept their twitching crests away.

The song of the jumping-wire became shriller. It screeched, howled and ululated in every imaginable note and pitch of intensity. Whenever the bow plunged and the wire dipped, its strident voice momentarily ceased, only to resume as soon as we emerged from the pale-green swirl and flurry. The watery pennants that flew from the jumping-wire were ripped and shredded by the wind like old rags – whisked away in a trice.

Bracing my back against the periscope standard, I craned high enough above the bridge casing to command the entire forepart of the submarine.

At once wind bludgeoned my head. It was no longer air in motion – not an ethereal element but a solid corporeal substance which gagged me when I opened my mouth.

At last a storm worthy of the name tempest! I could have yelled with exhilaration. Screwing up my eyes, I took snapshots of the waves in action, pictures of a world in the throes of creation.

Showers of spray lashed my face and forced me to take cover behind the bridge casing. My eyelids had started to swell and my feet were awash in their sea-boots. My gauntlets were equally useless. I had long since handed them below, soaked through. My knuckles were whiter than I had ever seen them – washerwoman's knuckles.

The sheet-metal bathtub in which we cowered like beaten boxers was open at the after end. It had no right to be called a bridge. Our vantage-point had nothing in common with the enclosed bridge of a surface ship, which was dry, warm, and a sure defence against the buffetings of the sea.

U-A's bridge was little more than a shield or parapet. It was open aft, and offered no rear protection whatsoever, yet waves could descend on us from astern as well.

I spent most of the watch knee-deep in a swirling flood which plucked and sucked at my legs like a mountain torrent in spate. No sooner had the water gushed aft and out through the drain-holes than there was another shout of 'Hold tight!' from Kriechbaum and the next salvo hit the bridge. I ducked away like a boxer on the ropes, chin tucked well in, but the crafty sea abandoned its straight lefts for a full-blooded uppercut.

To keep my feet, I jammed myself between the master sight and the bridge casing. It was a question of hanging on, snatching lungfuls of air and weighing heavy. However robust they might look, safety-belts were not to be relied on alone.

I stole a look aft. Beyond the rail and the mounting of the anti-aircraft armament, none of the after-casing could be seen. It was thickly blanketed in seething foam. The exhaust flaps were invisible. So were the air induction valves. The engines had to take their air from inside the submarine.

The blanket of foam over the after-casing thinned rapidly until the stern reared and tore its last remaining shreds asunder. White beards of water streamed from both flanks of the hull. The exhaust flaps lifted clear. Oily blue diesel fumes welled up and were whisked away by the gale before they could expand.

Only seconds passed before a new wave slammed into the conning-tower with a muffled thud and leapt high like a breaker meeting a reef. Two walls of dazzling foam converged abaft the conning-tower, collided with a roar and rocketed skywards. The after-casing vanished beneath another maelstrom. Then the hull surged upwards through the swirling flood, lifted the effervescent masses of water complete with their topping of greyish-white lather, and tremulously shook off the last lingering traces. For a few moments, the entire stern was visible. Then the waves swung their foaming fists and buried it yet again. The cycle was endless and unvaried: wallow and break free, swoop and soar, plunge and rear.

My limbs were numb when I went below. I peeled off my rubber jacket with a groan. Everything beneath it was sopping wet. Beside me, Dorian cursed and swore. 'Whoever designed this gear ought to have his head examined – it soaks up water like a sponge.'

'Better complain to the C-in-C,' Isenberg needled him. 'They say he welcomes suggestions from the men on the spot.'

The Captain's comment on the sea was 'Quite rough'. He was sitting at the wardroom table leafing through some blue and green folders.

I toyed with the notion that U-boat Command had forgotten us. What then? How far could we travel at our most economical speed? U-A's range might be unrivalled, but how long would our supplies hold out? Of course, it should be possible to grow mushrooms on board. Our twilit dungeon was an ideal environment for fungi – the mould on the bread proved that. Or watercress. Watercress was reputed to grow in artificial light. The coxswain could surely find room for some – in the passage, for instance. I pictured us ducking a little lower to avoid hanging gardens of watercress mounted on gimbals.

Finally, we could grow sea-weed. Algae were rich in Vitamin C. There might even be a variety which would thrive below the deck-plates, fertilized by the grease in the bilge.

SUNDAY, 44TH DAY AT SEA. 'Crusty rolls,' the Chief said at breakfast, 'spread with lashings of yellow salt butter, oozy because they're still warm inside – fresh from the baker's oven. Washed down with a cup of hot chocolate. Not sweet – the bitter kind, preferably – but good and hot. Set me up for the day, that would.'

He rolled his eyes in rapture and ostentatiously wafted the imaginary fragrance to his nostrils.

'Very amusing,' the Captain said. 'Now imitate someone eating scrambled egg at the Navy's expense.'

The Chief retched and gagged and jerked his Adam's apple violently up and down.

The Captain was tickled. Not so the first lieutenant, who displayed a wooden devotion to duty, even at mealtimes, by consuming his rations neatly and completely. The Chief's act must have been too much for him, because he pushed his plate aside with an air of martyrdom.

'Clear away!' the Captain called aft, and the steward appeared with his evil-smelling swab. The first lieutenant's nose twitched fastidiously.

Breakfast over, I retired to the PO's mess to put in some sleep if I could. 'Plenty more weather where this came from,' was the Captain's parting shot as I staggered aft through the control-room.

The submarine pitched yet again and the control-room door swung back on its seating with such a crash that it jolted me awake. Pilgrim greeted Isenberg's entrance with a mock bow : 'The french windows opened, and in walked the Count.' Isenberg gave a rueful grin, laboriously peeled off his wet oilskins and squeezed in behind the table.

I wondered what the control-room PO was doing in oilskins – he hadn't come from the bridge. Then I heard water drumming fiercely on the control-room deck and knew the answer.

'Here,' Frenssen protested, 'no need to take up so much room – stow your clobber somewhere else, can't you?'

A clatter of eating irons.

'Christ, I feel queasy.'

'Can I have yours, then?'

'Like hell you can! Sling that loaf across.'

However hard I strove, and however many positions I tried, I couldn't wedge myself into the bunk firmly enough to prevent myself from rolling or slipping. The pitching I could have got used to, if its rhythm had remained more or less regular, but I was driven to despair by the hammer-blows on the fore-casing and the brutal jolt as the bow bit water. There were menacing and unfamiliar noises as well : the thump of waves hitting the conning-tower and a whole gamut of novel acoustic effects which ranged from rasping and buzzing, scraping and rubbing, to a persistent but irregular drumming overhead with a nerve-racking succession of banshee wails and whistles. My response was one of torpid resignation.

Night brought no respite. The storm must have been speeding along at a good sixty miles an hour.

Ptchumm! The submarine tilted forward at an ever steeper angle. Our gear canted away from the bulkhead at forty-five degrees. My curtain slid open of its own accord, my legs became weightless and my head dug deep into the bolster.

Then a corkscrew movement as U-A sideslipped rather than stand on her head. The hull gave a malarial shiver. Metal beat a fierce tattoo on metal.

At last the POs' mess returned to the horizontal. I drew my curtain. Why bother? The next comber must be on its way.

Half-asleep, I heard Dorian come in. 'You stokers have got it cushy. You ought to try a spell up top – the wind's enough to ram your teeth down your throat.'

MONDAY, 45TH DAY AT SEA. I hadn't been on the bridge for two days. It was time to go up for an airing, but I quailed. My only reward would be lashes from a watery cat-o'-nine-tails, limbs frozen stiff, numb fingers, eyes on fire.

Sound arguments for staying put in the wardroom. At least it was dry.

A book had slid to the deck. I felt an urge to pick it up. A voice told me to move but I refused to listen. My nerves had the tension of overtaxed elastic. I switched off and let my last spark of initiative die. It wouldn't hurt to let the book lie there.

The Chief returned from a visit to his engines, noticed the book and stooped to retrieve it. So there!

He jammed himself into his bunk, knees drawn up, and produced a newspaper from under his bolster. Not a word. He just sat morosely, giving off a scent of diesel oil.

Fifteen minutes later the midshipman came to fetch some new R/S cartridges. The Chief's powers of perception had suffered. He didn't hear. Ullmann had to repeat his request in a louder voice. At last the Chief looked up with a scowl. R/S cartridges were a serious matter. God knew if we should ever need them, but the daily change-over was a hallowed routine.

Eventually the Chief stood up and opened the locker. He couldn't have looked more disgusted if someone had held a bowl of excrement under his nose. The newspaper slid off his bunk and landed in a puddle of goo from our last meal. Ullmann disappeared with his cartridges, looking harassed. The Chief swore silently and retired to his lair. This time he drew his knees up even higher, like a barricade between him and the world.

Ullmann was back within five minutes. Of course, he had to replace the old flares. No liberties could be taken with R/S cartridges – they mustn't be left lying around. I waited for the Chief to fly off the handle. Instead he rose quite briskly, tucked the newspaper under his arm and vanished aft. Two hours later I found him in the motor-room, perched on a crate of prunes with his back against the stern tube. Heedless of the reek of oil, he was re-reading his newspaper for the tenth time.

After supper, an inner voice reminded me that I hadn't been on the bridge all day. I silenced it by arguing that the light had almost gone.

For diversion's sake, I visited the fore-ends. My nostrils were assailed by the smell of bilge-water, stale food, sweat-soaked clothing and rotting lemons. Two dim bulbs emitted a subdued and brothel-like glow.

I made out Schwalle with a large aluminium bowl clamped between his knees. A ladle protruded from it. All around lay a wilderness of bread, sausage, gherkins and open sardine cans. The hammocks overhead bulged with the weight of two sleeping figures. The upper bunks to right and left were also occupied.

The motion was even wilder here in the bow. Every few minutes the fore-ends tilted and corkscrewed so violently that Schwalle had to pick up the bowl to prevent it from slopping.

Dunlop, the torpedo-man, emerged from the gloom on all fours with a pair of red and green electric light bulbs, which he proposed to exchange for the white ones. The effect enraptured him.

'Very sexy,' said an approving vioce from one of the hammocks.

The submarine gave a sudden lurch. Schwalle's knees lost their grip on the bowl, which anointed a loaf with soup. We heeled to a crazy angle, then soared into the air. A bucket wedged against the bulkhead toppled over and voided its cargo of mouldy crusts and squeezed-out lemon peel. A gurgle of bilge-water. Our bow hit the next wave with a crash and the whole compartment shivered. Bilge-water rushed forward again.

'Fucking hell,' Schwalle said.

Benjamin rolled across the boards, cursing, then clawed himself erect and sat cross-legged like a Buddha with his arm hooked round the rung of a bunk leeboard. He jostled Ario as he did so.

'That's right,' Ario said, 'spread yourself.'

'Pardon me for breathing, I'm sure.'

Now it was Ario's turn to hang on. He flung an arm round the life-line secured to a lower bunk. Reaching for the loaf of bread, which was green with mould, he hugged it to his

sweat-soaked singlet and used a clasp-knife to carve off un-
wieldy hunks. The sound portions were the size of an average
plum. His biceps went spherical with exertion.

The boat heeled again. More jangling and clattering. A fanny
was rolling to and fro between the bow-tube mountings, but
nobody made a move to secure it. A towel hanging from one
of the leeboards on the port side canted slowly outwards and
remained at an oblique angle for some seconds, as though
stiff with starch.

The towel slowly reassumed a less nightmarish position,
then plastered itself against the leeboard. U-A had rolled to
port.

'Shit and derision!' groaned Dunlop, who had wedged a
bucket between the frames up forward and was trying to
wash up. The whole compartment reeked of dishcloth. The
dirty water which had moments earlier been in his bucket
now crept across the decking towards the seated figures. Ario
started to rise, but the water came to a halt and receded. It
looked like a triumph of mind over matter.

Having wiped a glistening forehead on the back of his hand,
Ario struggled to his feet and leant against a bunk, still embracing the life-line. He peeled off his jacket. Black hair
welled from the holes in his singlet like the stuffing from a
torn mattress. His whole body was soaked with sweat. Breathing hard, he resumed his seat and announced that, storm or
no storm, he was going to cram his belly so full we could
crack fleas on it with a thumbnail. The earnestness of his
intention was soon apparent. Taking the not entirely mildewed
remnants of a hunk of bread, he carefully heaped it with
layers of butter, sausage, cheese and sardines.

'Just like the Tower of Babel,' Gigolo said admiringly. Ario,
mindful of his prestige, calmly topped the confection with a
thick layer of mustard. His jaws opened and engulfed it. The
nard dry bread required noisy and extensive mastication.

'Beats the tinned stuff any day,' he said in a muffled voice,
and washed the thick pulp down with orange-coloured tea.

Every mouth shone with grease, reminding me of cannibals
round a cauldron. The eaters' legs were enmeshed like those
of commuters in a crowded compartment. Every now and
then, Ario testified to his enjoyment with a belch. A bottle
of apple-juice circulated.

One or two men got ready to go on watch and disappeared
aft. Some minutes later the bulkhead door opened and a red-
haired stoker named Markus came in. His blue-and-white
striped jersey made him look like a nineteenth-century

wrestler. He reeled drunkenly to and fro before slumping into a gap between the others. Chewing, he announced that FC Hertha had lost. 'It came over the radio a while back. They really got clobbered. Five nil – three nil at half-time. That puts them out of the semi-final.'

'You're having us on!'

'I wouldn't joke about a thing like that.'

FC Hertha had lost. At once the storm that was battering us dwindled into insignificance.

The news kindled a fierce debate. 'FC Hertha, for God's sake!' – 'Not even a consolation goal – it's enough to make you weep . . .'

'Serves them right. Hertha always were too big for their boots.'

A quarter of an hour later, when the topic had been squeezed dry, Ario confided to the circle that Benjamin cherished ideas of marriage. A wild shout greeted this announcement. Little Manchu was bombarded from all sides.

'Him, get spliced?' – 'You must be crazy – they'd do better to put you in the monkey-house and pair you off with a chimpanzee.' – 'Poor cow, she must be hard up for it.'

Benjamin's feelings were so stung that it took all of Ario's powers of persuasion to appease him. In the end he was sufficiently pacified to go to his locker and bring out a dog-eared wallet containing a whole series of photographs of the lady in question. Gigolo snatched them eagerly, passing a suitable comment on each: 'Boy, what a chassis! – Oh Mummy, you never told me it would be like this! – Some day my prince will come! – Lay me down and do it again!' At last he turned to Benjamin in mock amazement and said: 'You mean to tell me you've actually laid that tired old bag?' But Benjamin wasn't listening – he was desperately trying to regain possession of his treasures. The teapot went over, adding to the mess. The decking became a chaos of soggy bread, sliced sausage, sardine-tins, kicking legs and groping hands. The uproar did not subside until quelled by an angry roar from the bunk of TGM Hacker, 'president' of the fore-ends.

Although he had recovered all his photos, Benjamin was still hopping mad – or rather, acted like it. I got the impression that he was secretly revelling in the fuss.

Noises of eating predominated for the next five minutes, then Schwalle emerged into the subdued red glow and started to rummage in his locker. A number of bottles came to light.

'Looking for something?' Fackler enquired from his bunk.

'My face cream.'

Cue for universal and unrestrained hilarity. 'Isn't he lovely!' – 'Don't forget to pluck your eyebrows, darling!' – 'Lay off, Schwalle, you're giving me ideas!'

Schwalle rounded on them angrily. 'Filthy sods! You don't know the meaning of the word hygiene.'

'All right, keep your hair on!' – 'Opened your bowels today, have you?' – 'Six weeks' dirt and a layer of grease on top – very hygienic, I must say!' – 'Hark who's talking! Smears that stuff all over his face and lets his cock rot away to Gorgonzola!'

Another bellow from TGM Hacker: 'Jesus Christ Almighty! Are you going to pipe down or aren't you – yes or no?'

'No,' Ario said, but too softly for the senior rating to hear it in his bunk.

TUESDAY, 46TH DAY AT SEA. A further deterioration in the weather. The submarine plummeted with such suddenness that my stomach gave an involuntary heave. For a full half-minute, the hull shuddered violently in every rivet. It seemed that the bow would never lift, so deeply was it embedded in the unseen wave. U-A rolled from right to left – I could distinctly feel her seeking a lateral escape route – and then at last the bow rose and the screws stopped straining. It was like the cessation of an embrace.

I tried to keep my breakfast down. I even tried to write, but the wardroom careered downhill so fast that my gorge rose repeatedly. We clung to the table with all our might because experience foretold that every descent would end in an abrupt lurch. This time things went smoothly. The screws raced once more.

Lunch consisted of bread and sausage. Hot meals had been stricken from the agenda. The chef could no longer keep his pans on the stove. It was a miracle that he managed to keep us supplied with hot tea or coffee, not to mention a mid-watch snack. Katter was certainly doing his indefatigable best.

The Captain went up top after lunch. He put on a thick sweater under his oilskins. Instead of a sou'wester he wore a head-hugging rubber hood which only exposed his eyes, nose and mouth.

He was back inside five minutes, streaming with water and swearing inarticulately. Still muttering, he struggled out of his glistening oilskins, pulled the sweater over his head and showed me a big black ring of moisture that had blossomed on his shirt during his brief spell above. He sat down on the chart-stowage, breathing hard. One of the control-room hands pulled off his boots. Water gushed from the shanks and disappeared into the bilge.

Just as he was wringing out his socks like floor-cloths, water cascaded through the conning-tower, hissed back and forth on the deck-plates and also found a home in the bilge.

'Pump out,' the Captain ordered. He skated barefoot across the wet deck, climbed through the bulkhead and hung his wet clothes to dry near the electric heater in the wireless office.

He imparted the fruits of his observations to the quartermaster, who had just squeezed past him: 'Wind's backing.' No surprises so far. Our storm was behaving precisely as expected.

Kriechbaum said: 'Are we to maintain this course?'

'We've got to – while we can. We're all right for the present.'

As though to prove him wrong, we heeled sharply. The bulky accordion case flew out of the wireless office and crashed against the partition on the opposite side of the passage.

We rolled the other way. The case hurled itself at the wireless office bulkhead, burst open and disgorged its contents. The Chief peered down the passage, half-curious and half-concerned. 'That won't improve it,' he said drily.

The control-room hand appeared at a crawl rather than a run and gathered up the squeeze-box, together with the battered remains of its case.

Swaying, the Captain made his way to the wardroom and squeezed behind the table. He shuffled to and fro with his eyes shut, almost as if it was a mental effort to recall where he customarily disposed his limbs. After trying various positions, he finally achieved sufficient stability to avoid dislodgement when next we rolled.

The three of us bent over our books. After a while the Captain looked up. 'Here, read this – it's topical.' He prodded the passage with his forefinger.

The caprice of the winds, like the wilfulness of men, is fraught with the disastrous consequences of self-indulgence. Long anger, the sense of his uncontrolled power, spoils the frank and generous nature of the West Wind. It is as if his heart were corrupted by a malevolent and brooding rancour. He devastates his own kingdom in the wantonness of his force. South-west is the quarter of the heavens where he presents his rage in terrific squalls and overwhelms his realm with an inexhaustible welter of clouds. He strews the seeds of anxiety upon the decks of scudding ships, makes the foam-stripped ocean look old, and sprinkles with grey hairs the heads of shipmasters in the homeward-bound ships running for the Channel. The Westerly Wind asserting his sway from the south-west quarter is often like a monarch gone mad, driving forth with wild imprecations the most faithful of his courtiers to shipwreck, disaster, and death . . . I turned to the title page. It was Joseph Conrad's *Mirror of the Sea*.

WEDNESDAY, 47TH DAY AT SEA. How to look on the bright side, by the Old Man : 'A gale a day keeps the flyers away.'

I hardly slept during the night. My bunk tried to eject me in spite of the leeboard – or plaster me against the plywood panelling. Now I felt as if I hadn't slept for a week.

The storm showed no sign of abating. I spent the day in a leaden stupor. The whole crew sank steadily deeper into a slough of apathy.

THURSDAY, 48TH DAY AT SEA. The Captain read out the concluding words of his latest entry in the ship's log : 'Wind south-south-west 9-10, sea 9. Misty. Barometer 981. Severe squalls.'

'Misty' . . . The usual understatement. 'Turkish bath' would have been nearer the truth. Up top, it seemed that the four elements were being reduced to three by the fusion of air and water. The storm had increased, just as the Captain predicted.

I took my oilskins from their hook, knotted the usual terry-towel round my neck and fetched my rubber boots from the wireless office, where I had left them to dry in front of the bowl-fire. I was going on watch with the quartermaster. When my first boot was half on, the deck fell away from under me. I rolled around in the passage like an upturned beetle. As soon as I found my feet I was up-ended by another lurch. Already out of breath, I managed to haul myself erect by the flooding panel.

The boots were still wet inside. My groping foot refused to slip down the shank. Standing was hopeless, so I tried sitting. Success at last. The Captain's curtain slid back when we next pitched. He was drafting his patrol report. I saw him chew his pencil, probably because he had written one word too many. The Old Man always behaved like someone composing an overseas telegram whose every word would cost a fortune.

Boots on. Now for my oilskin leggings, also damp inside. An archaic term, oilskin – they were really made of rubberized material. I performed a number of contortions before I got them as far as my knees. Now to hoist my backside and pull them up. The diabolical things fought me all the way, and I was sweating profusely by the time I succeeded.

Next, my oilskin jacket. It was tight under the arms because of my two sweaters. November and northern latitudes made watch-keeping a cold business. Without looking at the chart, I guessed we must be slogging along in the Sixties – not too far from Iceland, probably – when we ought really to be on a level with Lisbon.

Finally, my sou'wester. The interior was soaking. My scalp flinched at its clammy embrace. The strings were knotted and the knot so swollen with moisture that it resisted my fingers.

The Captain abandoned his telegraphic composition and stood up. He stretched, caught sight of me and grinned sarcastically. 'It's a hard life at sea, eh?' Then 'Whoops!' as another violent plunge threatened to send him flying.

I negotiated the bulkhead with comparative elegance, but once in the control-room I was caught by a roll. I failed to grab the edge of the chart-table, lost my balance and fell hard against the blowing panel. The Captain started to sing 'The Daring Young Man on the Flying Trapeze.' A bit before my time. Now the control-room lurched to port. I staggered against the domed cowl of the gyro compass before grabbing hold of the conning-tower ladder. The Captain claimed to have seen a Cuban rumba which was kid's stuff beside my own performance. He paid mocking tribute to my balletic skill.

His own footwork could not be faulted. Whenever his equilibrium was in peril, a swift sidelong glance assured him of a suitable landing-place. Skilfully exploiting the motion of the boat, he came to rest with dignity. His usual practice on such occasions was to gaze round serenely as though his sole intention had been to perch at that particular spot.

A dripping figure descended the ladder. It was the second lieutenant. Breathlessly he announced that a large fish had just leapt right over the boat. 'We had a steep sea so high on the port beam it was like a wall. The fish shot straight out of it and over the gun – never seen anything like it.'

I buckled on my broad safety-belt with its heavy carbine swivel and started up the ladder. The conning-tower was in darkness except for the helmsman's dim instrument lights. A gurgling sound came from the bridge overhead. I waited a few seconds for the gurgling to subside, then flung open the heavy hatch-cover as fast as I could, scrambled out and slammed it shut. The next moment, I and the others were forced to cower behind the bridge casing as another wave struck. A solid mass of water barged me in the back. More water swirled round my legs. Before it could topple me, I clipped the swivel-hook to the master sight and wedged myself between the periscope standards and the bridge casing.

At last I could afford a glance over the bridge rail. My heart almost stood still at the sight. The sea had gone, and in its place was a heaving mountainscape from whose towering peaks the wind plucked blizzards of spindrift. The universal whiteness was threaded with dark fissures – black bands which darted hither and thither, forming kaleidoscopic patterns. All that remained of the sky was a flat grey dish that almost touched the grey-white wilderness of water.

The air was a mist of salt and spray, a ritual mist which reddened the eyes, numbed the hands and swiftly drained the limbs of body-warmth.

The bulbous belly of our starboard main ballast tank rolled sluggishly out of the eddying foam. The wave that had lifted us began to subside. U-A heeled farther and farther to port and lingered at an extreme angle for seconds, falling fast.

A succession of fluted billows bore leisurely down. From time to time there came one whose foaming crest reared monstrously above its neighbours. The wall of water would start to hollow out ahead of us, slowly at first, then more and more rapidly until it collapsed and crashed on to the fore-casing like a steam-hammer.

'Eyes down!' bellowed Kriechbaum. The wave geysered up the conning-tower and broke over us. A swinging blow between the shoulders, then water swirled up waist-high from below. The bridge quaked and trembled, a violent shudder ran through the hull. At last the fore-casing lifted above the foam. Kriechbaum was shouting something. 'Watch it – wave like that – wash you clean out of the bridge.'

For a few seconds, U-A raced into a trough. Mountainous white combers hemmed us in. Then we lifted again. The submarine was gliding up a huge incline, higher and higher, until we hung on the foaming lip and could survey the storm-riven sea like look-outs in an observation post. It was not the dark-green Atlantic that met our gaze, but the surface of some planet in the making.

Watches had been cut in half. Two solid hours of crouching

and peering were enough for anyone. It was a relief to find, when the time came, that I could still move my limbs sufficiently to go below. Nobody could have endured a four-hour watch in these conditions.

I was so exhausted when I reached the control-room that I could happily have slumped to the deck in my wet gear. Sights and sounds penetrated my consciousness through a thick fog. Every blink of my inflamed eyelids was agony.

Undressing was impossible without lengthy pauses for recuperation. I had to grit my teeth to repress the groans. Then came the worst part – the gymnastic ascent of my bunk. No sleeping-car ladder for me. It was a question of reaching with the right foot and pushing off with the left. My eyes were watering by the time I made it.

A week of storm already, and still no end in sight. It seemed incredible that our bodies could withstand such martyrdom. No rheumatism, no sciatica, no lumbago, no scurvy, no squitters, no gastritis, no serious complaints of any kind. To all appearances we were fit as fiddles, tough as rawhide.

FRIDAY, 49TH DAY AT SEA. A day of torpid dozing and arduous attempts to read. I lay in my bunk, listening to the water pattering down from above. The upper lid was shut but not secured, so a cataract descended whenever the bridge was awash.

The quartermaster came aft. He mentioned in passing that a member of his watch had succumbed. 'He's just sitting there on the deck, puking his guts up.'

One of the stokers had initiated a new vogue. Already, three other members of the crew were going about with improvised 'puke-tins' strung round their necks like gas masks.

I found it impossible to maintain the same position for longer than five minutes at a time. Gripping one rung of the leeboard with my left hand, I doubled up so that my back was jammed against the panelling. It wasn't long before the metallic chill of the hull seared my back through the thin plywood and the aluminium rung turned to ice in my hand.

The galley door opened. The pressure on my eardrums promptly increased and every noise became shallower. The outboard induction valves had shut off in the heavy sea, so the engines were drawing their air from inboard. Excess pressure, vacuum effect, eardrums in, eardrums out – who could sleep through that alternation? I rolled face-down and draped my left arm over the leeboard for support.

The bunk which had seemed so narrow on first acquaintance had become too wide. Whatever my position, I couldn't find a decent purchase. Finally, I hit on the idea of wedging the bolster between my body and the leeboard. It wouldn't fit broad side on, only edgeways. I now lay jammed between the panelling and the bolster like a knife in a knife-rack – a poor substitute for comfort, but better than nothing.

I pictured myself as a posed figure in an anatomical atlas, muscles picked out in red and numbered. My anatomy course had finally paid off – at least I could give each twinge a name. Under normal circumstances I carried the fibrous parcels of meat around with no emotion save an occasional touch of pleasure at the way they contracted and relaxed – a semi-autonomous and serviceable set of equipment, well designed and smooth of operation. Now, the system had seized up. It jibbed, protested, fired off warning signals : here a stab, there a nagging ache. Many sections of my muscular apparatus were making their presence felt for the first time ever – the platysma, for example, which I needed for head movements, or the psoas which helped me flex my hip-joint. My biceps gave little trouble – they were in training. It was my pectorals which started the rot. I must have been lying at an unnatural angle, or they wouldn't have hurt so much.

SATURDAY, 50TH DAY AT SEA. Jottings in my blue notebook : 'Futile, tossing about like this in mid-Atlantic. Not a sniff of the enemy. We might be the only vessel at sea. Bilge-water and the smell of vomit. Our midshipman finds the weather quite acceptable. He talks like an old Cape Horner.'

SUNDAY, 51ST DAY AT SEA. The daily trim dive, usually considered tedious, had become a boon. We longed for the chance to stretch out, breathe deep, stand erect without the need to crouch or cling.

'Stand by to dive!' heralded the happy ritual. The Chief stationed himself behind the two planesmen. He had to raise his voice on the last word to make himself heard above the roar of the water gushing into the main ballast tanks. At 15 metres he blew Q. The fury of the sea gave way to the hiss of compressed air and simultaneous thunder of water being expelled from the quick-dive tanks.

The needle of the depth-gauge came to rest at 35 metres. The U-boat lay almost level, but her movements were still sufficient to roll a pencil back and forth across the chart-table. The Chief gave the order to shut all main vents. 'Forty-five metres,' said the Captain, but U-A remained in motion even at that depth. He adopted his customary position, back propped against the periscope. 'Fifty metres.' A pause, then: '*Voilà* – peace at last.'

The joy of it! No more torture for an hour at least. Not a moment to be lost – into my bunk in double-quick time.

My head still buzzed and roared as if I had strapped two large seashells to my ears. The reverberations inside my skull abated, but only by degrees.

God, how I ached . . . I lay limp with my arms at my sides and my palms flat against the mattress. Raising my head a little, I could watch the steady rise and fall of my rib-cage. My eyes smarted even though I hadn't been on the bridge. I chewed my lips and tasted salt. My whole body must be coated with it, steeped in brine like salt pork or cured spare-ribs. Oh, for some sauerkraut-bedded *Kasseler Rippchen* flavoured with bay-leaves, pepper-corns and plenty of garlic! Strange how one's appetite returned as soon as the motion of the boat ceased. It must have been ages since my last proper meal.

My bunk was heaven. I'd never realized what a glorious sensation lying flat could be. I made myself flat as a board and felt the mattress with every square centimetre of my buttocks, shoulder-blades, inner arms, palms, calves, heels. I flexed the toes of my right foot, then my left, stretched each of my legs in turn. My frame expanded – I grew longer and longer.

The steward came in to tell me that lunch was served.

'Already?'

I was informed that the Captain had advanced the meal by an hour so we could stow it away in peace.

At once, digestive misgivings assailed me. Eating in peace was fine, but how to cope with a full stomach when the jouncing started again? I shuddered at the thought of our return to the surface.

The Captain seemed to have no worries. He devoured huge lumps of hogshead brawn thickly daubed with mustard and accompanied by gherkins, pickled onions and canned bread. The first lieutenant, operating on his brawn with surgical precision, severed a piece of skin adorned with a few white bristles and daintily pushed it to the edge of his plate.

'Stubble trouble, Number One?' enquired the Captain, munching heartily. 'All we need now is a glass of beer and some French fried.'

Instead of beer, the steward brought tea. The second lieutenant was about to clamp the pot between his knees when the needlessness of the precaution dawned on him. He smote his brow theatrically.

The Captain prolonged our dive by twenty minutes 'in honour of the Sabbath'.

The inmates of the POs' mess devoted their underwater respite to the usual topic. Frenssen recounted how his leave train had been halted at Strasbourg by an air raid. Predictably, he sought out the nearest brothel.

'She said she had a speciality but she wouldn't tell me what. I followed her upstairs. She stripped off and lay down. I was just going to ram it in and see what the big surprise was, when she said: "You want an old-fashioned fuck, dearie? My God, how crude can you get?" Next thing, she whipped out an eye – a glass one, naturally – and pointed to the hole. "There you are," she said, "get stuck into that."'

For two solid seconds I heard nothing but heavy breathing. Then tumult erupted. 'Of all the filthy-minded buggers . . .' – 'Pull the other one, it's got bells on!' – 'Pardon me while I throw up!' – 'They ought to castrate you, Frenssen!'

When the uproar subsided, the stoker PO said equably: 'All the same, it's quite an idea.'

My throat tightened with nausea. How could anyone actually *invent* such monstrous obscenities?

I was still in my bunk when we surfaced. My whole body sensed the first gentle stirrings. The POs' mess started to corkscrew, the first wave smote us like a gigantic paw, and the St Vitus's dance began all over again.

Curses from Isenberg in the control-room. Water rained down incessantly through the conning-tower.

I ducked through the bulkhead. Seeing me, he started again. 'Bloody mess! We'll be needing brollies, next.'

MONDAY, 52ND DAY AT SEA. The quack was in demand. A few minor injuries. Bruises, nipped fingers, a blackened nail, blood blisters – nothing serious. One man fell out of his bunk, another cracked a rib on a handwheel in the control-room, another ran headlong into the echo-sounder. The cut looked nasty.

'Great,' said the Captain. 'Let's hope the quack can cope with it or I'll have to dig out my darning needle.'

I prepared to go on deck with second lieutenant's watch at 1600. One of the look-outs had been incapacitated by seasickness. I was standing in for him.

I was soaked even before I pushed open the upper lid. As

212

fast as I could, I wedged myself between the periscope standard and the bridge casing and clipped on the spring-hook of my safety-belt. That done, I hauled myself erect and peered over the casing.

Again the sight took my breath away. The waves had turned cannibal – they were falling on their neighbours' backs and devouring them.

U-A was hovering at the summit of an immense wave – riding pick-a-back on a gargantuan whale. For some seconds I could look out across the primeval seascape like someone in the gondola of a Ferris wheel. Then the U-boat began to teeter. Her bow swung this way and that, as though uncertain of its destination, and the Ferris wheel became a roller-coaster.

Before we could climb out of the trough, a second vast wave descended on us. Tons of water crashed on to the casing with a thunderous roar, bludgeoned us to our knees, engulfed us and swirled round our huddled bodies. It seemed an eternity before we struggled clear. The full extent of the fore-casing was visible for moments only, then the next blow fell.

My neck began to smart. The collar of my oilskin jacket chafed my skin. The sea-water burnt like acid, making it hurt still more.

I had a cut on the palm of my left hand. It would never heal as long as sea-water got to it. I cursed it, likewise the wind, which transformed showers of spray into grape-shot and made us cower behind the casing for protection.

The second lieutenant turned his raw red face and grinned. His voice came to me through the pandemonium: 'How'd you like to go for a swim in that lot?'

The hiss of the waves was as sharp as a tiger's snarl, but he managed to make himself heard above it. 'With a suitcase in each hand!'

Another assault on the conning-tower. Water buffeted our bent backs, but the second lieutenant had already straightened up and was peering ahead. 'Water, water, everywhere,' he bellowed, 'and not a decent drop of beer in sight!'

I felt disinclined to out-shout the sea, so I merely tapped my forehead when he happened to be looking my way.

We were only visible for seconds at a time. We averted our faces, hunched our shoulders, presented the tops of our heads to the sea. I scanned my sector through narrowed lids, then ducked and clinched. Even so, I was stung by thin strands of spray. There was no defence against them. Better a full-blooded deluge than these sharp and spiteful lashes across the face, which seared like flame.

We greeted the end of our two-hour watch like reprieved prisoners. For all his bounce, the second lieutenant would have been quite as unequal to a four-hour stint as the rest of us.

Night was a ghastly prospect. I winced at the thought of interminable hours spent on a bucking, swooping, sideslipping mattress.

WEDNESDAY, 54TH DAY AT SEA. A week and a half since the storm began. Ten days of slow torture. The Captain and I were sitting on the chart-stowage. A string of curses filtered down from the bridge. The Captain rose, grasped the ladder to the conning-tower and – with his head tilted upwards at a safe distance from the periodic shower-baths, asked what the devil was the matter.

'Wheel's hard-a-starboard, sir, boat's turning to port,' the helmsman called back. 'I can't hold her.'

'Keep your hair on.' The Captain continued to stare up through the lower lid for a few minutes. Then he bent over the chart-table. It wasn't long before he summoned the quarter-master. I only caught a word or two: '. . . no point. We're virtually marking time.'

The Captain pondered for a while, then reached for the intercom microphone. 'Stand by to dive!' The control-room PO, who was draped against the flooding panel like an exhausted fly, sprang to life with a sigh of relief. The Chief stepped through the bulkhead and issued some preliminary orders. Water cascaded through the hatch as the look-outs scrambled down in their gleaming oilskins. Two of them went to man the hydroplanes.

'Flood all main ballast!'

Air escaped from our tanks with a dull rumble. The bow tilted rapidly. Bilge-water rushed forward with a bubbling hiss. A wave smashed into the conning-tower, but the next sounded muffled and its successors met no further resistance. A final roar and gurgle, then silence. We stood around stiffly, bemused by the sudden absence of noise.

The first lieutenant's lips were bloodless. His eyes were sunken and his cheek-bones encrusted with salt. Still panting, he tugged the soggy hand-towel from his neck.

The depth-gauge showed 40 metres, but the needle crept on to 50, 60. This time our quest for repose took us still deeper. The Chief did not level off until we had passed the 65-metre mark. Bilge-water swished aft, then back again. Gradually it settled. The liquid gurgle ceased. An empty can which had been rolling across the deck-plates came to rest.

'Boat trimmed, sir,' the Chief reported.

The first lieutenant sank on to the chart-stowage and hugged his bleached white hands between his knees, too exhausted to remove his wet things at once.

Sixty-five metres of water overhead.

We were as safe from the bludgeoning of the waves as soldiers in dead ground from rifle-fire – shielded from the sea by the sea itself.

The Captain grinned at me. 'Try letting go,' he said. I suddenly realized that I was still clinging to a pipe.

The steward came to lay for supper. He was just fitting the fiddles when the first lieutenant snapped 'No need for those, man!' and helped himself to food with more than usual alacrity.

The loaf that confronted us had been almost entirely spoiled by the dampness on board. The green fur which daily sprouted from the brown crusts was daily wiped away with the steward's malodorous swab, but it was little use. The interior was threaded with green mould reminiscent of Gorgonzola. Yellow deposits had appeared, too, that looked like sulphur.

'Nothing wrong with mould,' the Chief declared, 'it's healthy. After all, the French call it *pourriture noble* – noble decay. In our job, we ought to be thankful for anything that grows.'

We all applied ourselves with equal patience to the intricate fretwork operation whereby semi-edible nuggets were excised from the thick slices. Entire loaves could be whittled away to lumps smaller than a child's fist.

The Captain's derisive name for the occupation was 'hobby time'. The second lieutenant, who claimed to enjoy it, cut irregular stars out of grey slices of bread with ostentatious diligence. While so doing, he told us of mariners who had survived for months on a diet of biscuit-dust, weevils and rat-shit. He might have sampled it himself, to judge by the detail with which he embellished his account.

'Oh sure,' the Chief cut in, 'I know. That was the time you sailed the Pacific under Magellan because he wanted to name a strait after himself, vain old bleeder. I get the picture – must have been a tough trip.'

After lunch I went to the fore-ends. A babble of voices hit me before I was halfway through the CPOs' mess. 'Twenty-four! Clubs takes it!' Fists thumped the deck. They were playing skat.

Dunlop entered with the patched-up accordion case held reverently in front of him like a child's coffin.

'Come on, Dunlop, give us a tune!'

The torpedo-man surveyed the circle with a patronizing air and loftily announced that half a dozen of his basses were sticking because of the damp.

'So what? Who cares about a few buttons?'

Yielding to universal entreaty, Dunlop settled himself on a lower bunk and inflated the bellows. Stoker Fackler called for a song.

> *The women of the desert*
> *Have tits two metres long,*
> *So tie them in a sheepshank*
> *Before you do them wrong . . .*

Raucous voices drowned the melody. The skat-players lost interest and turned in their cards. After limping unevenly along for a while, the song clicked into gear.

Later, Dunlop assumed a high falsetto and warbled:

> *There once was a mother,*
> *The greedy old bitch,*
> *Who auctioned her daughter*
> *For what she would fetch.*
> *And the bastard who bought her was me, was me,*
> *And the bastard who bought her was me!'*

Overhead, heaving billows and foaming crests; here below, men sitting with their knees drawn up, singing. I had an urge to pinch their cheeks and assure myself that they were flesh and blood.

THURSDAY, 55TH DAY AT SEA. Dead beat, whacked, all in. No lessening of the storm. Deliverance finally came when, towards evening, the Captain ordered us deep because of failing light.

Peace descended. Dorian sat beside the control-room bulkhead, dismantling a pair of binoculars which had some water between the lenses.

The wireless office was deserted. The telegraphist sat next door in the hydrophone booth. He had his head-set on and was idly turning the wheel of his listening gear.

In the wardroom, the first lieutenant was predictably busy with his multi-coloured set of folders. He had produced an office punch from somewhere. We seemed to have a whole range of office equipment on board. There was even a mechanical pencil-sharpener. At least we were spared a solo on the typewriter.

The Chief was studying some photos. The second engineer

appeared to be in the engine-room. The Captain was dozing.

Out of the blue, the Chief said: 'I bet it's snowed already, back home.'

'Snowed?'

The Captain opened his eyes. 'No reason why not – it's late November. Odd thing is, I haven't seen any snow for years.'

The Chief passed his photos round. Snow scenes, figures like black specks in a solid expanse of white. One snap showed the Chief and a girl-friend. Behind, a slope furrowed with ski-tracks. Left, an intrusive stretch of fencing. The snow round the posts had melted.

Looking at the picture, I remembered a village in the Erzgebirge just before Christmas – the cosy warmth of the low-ceilinged rooms, the variety of knives and cutters with which busy hands carved soft pinewood into new figures for the many-storeyed rotating pyramid or the mechanical Christmas mountain. Wood-smoke and stove-warmth flowed over me, also the scent of paint and glue, the schnapps-fumes from the big loving-cup in the centre of the table, the churchy smell of the smoke-candles that sent blue clouds billowing from the mouths of figurines in black leather aprons or miner's costume. And, outside, snow and cold of a razor-edged crispness that scorched the nose when one breathed. The polyphonous jingle of horse-drawn sleighs, carriage-lamps shining white on the plumes of steam from horses' nostrils, window after window adorned with illuminated angels propped between pillows of moss . . .

'Yes,' the Captain said. 'Real snow again – I'd like that.'

The Chief advanced the time of our evening meal. 'No reason why Number Two shouldn't eat his supper in peace.'

The second lieutenant had barely washed down his last mouthful when the intercom crackled.

'Stand by to surface!'

At once my muscles tensed.

FRIDAY, 56TH DAY AT SEA. We did not surface until just after breakfast. The swell became noticeable 40 metres down. Then the lurching and swaying quickly increased until, all too soon, the first breakers smashed against the conning-tower. So much water came from above that the bilge filled fast. There was no posture or position which enabled me to relax. Each of my muscles ached independently and the bones in my buttocks ached fiercely too.

The waves must have changed direction yet again. Although U-A had maintained course under water, she now yawed and rolled to port with even greater severity. We sometimes lay right over at an extreme angle and stayed there for an alarming length of time.

The quartermaster reported that the wind had veered and was now coming from the west-south-west. That explained it.

'Beam sea,' the Captain observed. 'We won't be able to keep this up for long.'

But at lunch, while we were painfully clinging to the table, he dispensed words of consolation: the sea was on the beam, true, but the wind would soon back. That would solve all our problems.

I decided to remain in the wardroom after lunch. A book was sliding back and forth on the deck in front of the second lieutenant's locker. I reached for it and flicked through the pages at random. Isolated words caught my eye: cross-jack yard, inner jib, main topmast staysail, spanker boom, main topgallants . . . handsome, well-rounded words.

The roar of the waves along our steel sides swelled repeatedly to a savage furioso.

All at once the U-boat rolled to port with such violence that I was tipped out of my seat. The book-shelves voided their entire contents, and anything left between the fiddles on the wardroom table tumbled off. The Captain leant back like a tobogganer braking with his heels. The Chief had slid to the deck. We froze in our respective positions as though posing for a time-exposure photograph. U-A held her extreme angle. It was too much – she'd never make it. My mouth went dry.

But, after what seemed minutes, the wardroom returned to the horizontal. Pent-up breath issued from the Chief's lips with a noise like a steam whistle. The Captain regained his seat in slow motion and said: 'Boy, oh boy!'

Muffled cursing from the fore-ends.

All stability had gone. The next moment we rolled to starboard. The roar of the waves attained a new pitch. I wondered how the look-outs were faring.

I pretended to read, but my brain reeled. She's got to be able to take it, the Captain had said. More sea-worthy than any other vessel afloat. Ballast keel half-a-metre wide, half-a-metre deep, filled with iron bars – a long-armed lever with a pivot at the boat's centre. All her weight low down. No superstructure except a light conning-tower, centre of gravity well below the centre of buoyancy. No other ship could have withstood such treatment.

'What's that?' the Captain asked, nodding at my book.

'Something about sailing-ships.'

'Humph,' he said scornfully. 'Force 10 aboard a sailing-ship – you ought to try it some time. This is nothing to speak of.'

'Thanks for telling me,' I said.

'Securing the upper lid, that's our only concession to a real storm, but in sailing-ships! Sails reefed right in, storm lashings on the yards, hatches battened down – plenty of work for all hands, I can tell you. After that, nothing to do but sit in the poop and trust to the Almighty. Nothing to eat, either, but you're still expected to climb into the shrouds, unbend torn canvas, splice parted sheets, make up new sails – and that's another back-breaking job. Then there's the eternal manning of the braces with each shift of the wind . . .'

Taking advantage of a lurch to port, I got up and tottered to the control-room for a look at the roll.

The lateral inclinometer was a simple pendulum mounted on a scale. The pendulum stood at 50, so we were now heeling 50 degrees to starboard. It remained on the 50-degree mark as though nailed down. Instead of righting herself, U-A lingered at the same extreme angle. I could only conclude that a second wave had descended before she could extricate herself from the first. The pendulum swung still farther – to 60 degrees. For a moment, it even touched 65.

The Captain had followed me in. 'Looks impressive,' he said over my shoulder. 'You have to knock a bit off, though. Momentum makes it swing too far.' His tone suggested that, to make a real impression on him, U-A would have to float keel-upwards.

The men on watch in the control-room were wearing oil-skins. The bilge had to be emptied at ever-decreasing intervals. The pump seemed to be working continuously.

The quartermaster appeared, supporting himself with both hands like a man with a broken ankle.

The Captain turned to him. 'Well?'

'I estimate 15 miles to leeway since 2400 last night, sir, but it's only a rough guess.'

'Why not have the courage of your convictions, Kriechbaum? You're bound to be right.' For my benefit, the Captain added in an undertone: 'Hates committing himself, but he's nearly always spot-on. It's the same every time.'

A signal had been relayed to us. The wireless log was handed to the Captain. Looking over his shoulder, I read: 'C-in-C U-boats from U-T. Regret unable reach designated patrol area by designated time owing to weather.'

'We might as well copy and substitute our own call sign,'

said the Captain. He rose and tottered forward, skilfully exploiting another violent roll. A minute later he returned with a chart which he spread out on the stowage.

'Here's U-T – pretty well on our route – and here are we.' I could see that the two points were several hundred miles apart. The Captain looked gloomy. 'If they're talking about the same low, God help us. It seems to be an immensely widespread complex with no tendency to move fast.'

He methodically folded the chart and hitched up the sleeve of his sweater to glance at his watch. 'Supper soon,' he said.

I could hardly believe my eyes when supper-time came. The Captain was wearing oilskins. He was so heavily muffled as to be almost unrecognizable. Everyone stared at him curiously.

'On oilskins,' he said, grinning at us between his upturned collar and the brim of his sou'wester. 'On account of the soup,' he explained. 'Well, gentlemen, not feeling peckish this evening? I'd hate to disappoint the chef. A real triumph, soup in this weather.'

A second or two of dazed inertia elapsed before we tottered like obedient children to the control-room, where the oilskins hung. Contortions and gyrations as we struggled into our wet things.

We finally installed ourselves round the table like a gang of fancy-dress pirates. The Captain's face shone with glee.

There was a sudden commotion in the passage. We turned to see the steward measure his length with the soup tureen held high. Not a drop spilt.

'Never seen him beaten yet,' the Captain said calmly. The Chief gave an admiring nod.

'Fancy going straight into a routine like that. Personally I'd need a couple of dry runs.'

Soup, which contained potatoes, meat and tinned carrots, was distributed by the Number Two. Even though I was steadying him by the belt under his oilskins, his second ladleful missed the plate.

'Damn and blast!'

A moment later the Chief tipped his plate too far and appreciably enlarged the puddle of soup on the table. Pale chunks of potato slopped to and fro in the dark-brown broth between the fiddles. The next time we rolled, only the potato remained. The soup itself had flowed into the laps of the Chief and the Captain.

A muffled thud cut short the second lieutenant's chuckles. The Captain stopped grinning and looked wary. The Chief had just jumped up to make way for him when a voice from the control-room reported that the chart-stowage had fallen over.

Looking through the bulkhead, I saw four men straining every muscle to restore the heavy iron chest to its proper place.

The Captain shook his head in astonishment. 'Incredible. That stowage hasn't budged an inch since we commissioned.'

'They'd never believe it back home either,' the Chief said. 'People don't have a clue what it's like out here. We ought to try playing submariners next time we're home on leave. I can see us now, unshaven, unwashed, no clean underwear, going to bed in our boots and leathers, bracing our knees against the dining-table, pouring tea into our laps . . .'

He hurriedly spooned up some soup and continued the theme. 'And when the phone rings, we'll yell "Alarm!", knock over a chair or two and head for the door like greased lightning.'

SATURDAY, 57TH DAY AT SEA. The gusts had been succeeded by a steady gale which ceaselessly assailed us head on. The atmosphere became a single and uninterrupted flow of movement, the earth and its burden of Atlantic water counterrotated beneath a racing sky.

The line on the barograph fell steeply.

'All I'd like to know,' the Captain said, 'is how the Brits manage to keep their tubs together in this lot. They can't heave to, surely – not a whole great convoy of them.' He shrugged. 'Got to hand it to their destroyer people. They must be having real fun.'

I could remember destroyer-trips at Force 5. That had been bad enough. At 6, our destroyers did not leave Brest. Unlike them, British destroyers could not pick their weather. They had to perform escort duties in any gale, this one included.

In the afternoon I muffled myself up like a character from *Moby Dick* and went up top. I waited just below the upper lid for a torrent of water to subside, flung up the hatch and scrambled out. Then I kicked it shut and secured my safety-belt in one quick movement.

The sloping back of a huge leviathan loomed ahead of us. It grew and grew, lost its convexity and became a wall. The wall hollowed and went glassy as it bore down. Our bow sliced into it. 'No point . . .' The second lieutenant had got no further when it smashed against the conning-tower. U-A heeled under the impact.

'No point any more,' the second lieutenant concluded after

a minute's interruption.

I was aware that outsize waves had been known to pluck whole watches from the bridge unbeknown to anyone below deck. Murderous seas of this kind could evolve without warning. No belt was proof against their prodigious strength.

I tried to imagine how it would be, struggling in a suit of waterlogged oilskins as the U-boat ploughed on, growing smaller and smaller, visible for moments between the crests, then gone for good. I pictured the face of the first man to discover that the bridge was deserted . . .

We were making little way. More speed would have been dangerous in these conditions. Experience showed that a submarine travelling too fast could maintain the angle at which she slid down a mountainous wave, ram the next one like a dowel and plummet to 30 or 40 metres, drowning her lookouts. A boat could even founder because too much water penetrated her air induction valves.

Fortunately the Chief was a careful man. He would be in the control-room at this moment, ready to act fast in an emergency. Even so, I couldn't help wondering periodically if our buoyancy was sufficient to keep us afloat in this raging sea – if we wouldn't take in too much water despite the closed hatch, and if the control-room would pump out in good time.

The second lieutenant turned his reddened face in my direction.

Suddenly he shouted: 'Watch your front!'

I just had time to register the way his mouth hung open. I saw the green monster rear fine on the port bow, saw its white paw poised above us. And then, with thunderous force, it crashed on to the fore-casing. The boat yawed under the blow. Eyes down! A foaming flood boiled up over the steel parapet and swirled about us. The bridge was submerged. No more deck underfoot.

But the same wave resurrected us. The bow reared right out of the water and hovered in a void until the wave dropped us like an abandoned plaything. Water streamed aft and out through the drain-holes. Frothing eddies tore at our legs.

I had the impression that huge hands were shaking us, shaking us maracca-like in a fierce and frantic rhythm, flinging us aside and grabbing us anew, over and over again.

The second lieutenant swore inaudibly. When the next wave had slid beneath us, he opened the upper lid and shouted below: 'Tell the Captain, visibility badly obscured by breaking waves. Permission to steer three-zero-zero?'

For a moment, music could be heard through the hatch opening. Then a disembodied voice called: 'Approved.'

'Steer three-zero-zero,' the second lieutenant instructed the helmsman. Slowly the bow crept round until the waves were coming at us fine on the quarter. They lifted the stern-post high, surged madly along until they came abreast the conning-tower, then burst asunder. The bow curtsied deeply, buried itself in the departing flood, broke free and plunged into the trough between two mountainous waves. The water round the submarine was a seething white expanse invaded by an endless succession of green billows.

My face burned when I drew my sleeve across it. I could only speculate on the number of lashes it had received. The one surprise was that my eyes hadn't swollen shut. Every blink was an ordeal – my lids seemed twice their normal thickness.

I nodded silently at the second lieutenant, waited for the latest flood to ebb, and disappeared through the hatch.

I felt infinitely depressed. The patrol had become a test of human endurance, an experiment conducted to ascertain the limits of our capacity for suffering.

The telegraphist picked up a number of SOS calls.

'Busted hatch covers and holds taking water, that'll be their trouble,' the Captain said. 'Waves like this must be battering their lifeboats to matchwood.' He went on to describe the variety of damage a storm could inflict on a normal ship. 'If the steering engine packs up or a screw goes, there's nothing to do but pray.'

The roar of the breakers, patter of falling water and hiss of the bilge provided a musical accompaniment to the muffled but reverberant thump of our bow ramming the waves.

I could only marvel that this incessant rearing and plunging hadn't started every seam in the hull. The only casualties to date were some items of crockery and a few bottles of apple-juice, but the element which seemed powerless to harm U-A was gradually bringing her crew to its knees. Machinery was durable – only human beings were ill-equipped to withstand such punishment.

I ducked into the control-room. The quartermaster was making an entry in the log. I read what he had written. 'Barometer 998, falling, air temperature 3 degrees, sea 4, wind south-east 9, gusting to 11. Sea very rough, east to south-east.'

The Captain tottered in, grumbling. 'This must be the lousiest month on record. No fanfares this November – they can put their trumpets away. If it keeps up much longer, we might as well draw fires.'

Our lack of success was readily apparent from the scanty wireless traffic. Requests for position reports, routine signals, dummy signals – nothing more.

I remembered a passage in which Conrad described how the bark *Judea*, bound for Bangkok, ran into an Atlantic storm which demolished her piecemeal : bulwarks, stanchions, boats, ventilators, and upperworks complete with galley and crew's quarters. All hands, from the master down to the ship's boy, manned the pumps day and night.

The recollection of it consoled me. The sea could not drown us – no ship was more durable than ours.

MONDAY, 59TH DAY AT SEA. I mustered enough will-power to record the following in my notebook :

'Proper meals impossible. Futile, the whole thing. Dived just before 1400. Ecstasy! We stayed deep. More and more minor ailments – ugly boils, rashes and so on. Ichthyol ointment for everything.'

TUESDAY, 60TH DAY AT SEA. The Captain's jottings for the previous day :

1300.	Almost stationary with revs for 12 knots.
1355.	Dived – weather.
2000.	Surfaced. Sea very rough. Operational capacity limited.
2200.	Dived – weather.
0130.	Surfaced. Sea very rough. Visibility poor.
0215.	Hove to.

WEDNESDAY, 61ST DAY AT SEA. The wind had backed again to the south-east. Its strength had increased to Force 11. '*Very rough sea from east and south-east. Glass falling rapidly,*' wrote the Captain.

In the control-room, Kriechbaum was propped against the chart-table with his legs planted wide apart. When I went to look over his shoulder, he glanced round with a surly expression. 'Ten days without a fix,' he growled, 'in this crazy sea and wind. We could be anywhere.'

He sniffed noisily, and jabbed his pencil at some paper covered with columns of figures. 'These here are all guesswork. If I simply went on dead-reckoning like this, God knows where we'd end up. What I've done is try and work out how many miles the boat would be set by wind and sea in so-and-so many hours, assuming – for the sake of argument – that we're going slow ahead at 30 degrees to the sea . . .'

A waterfall cascaded through the hatch and drowned his voice. I hitched my backside on to the chart-stowage and lifted my feet just in time. The water sizzled across the deck-plates, then receded to port.

Kriechbaum splashed around in it in his heavy sea-boots like a naughty child. He may only have been stomping the frustration out of his system.

THURSDAY, 62ND DAY AT SEA. With the coming of dawn, Kriechbaum decided to try his luck once more. Visibility had actually improved a little. Odd stars were discernible through rents in the overcast and the horizon was a semi-distinct line broken by the humps and bulges of the waves.

But as soon as he aimed his sextant and called out the name of a star, spray showered the bridge and made the instrument unusable. He had to hand it below and await its return from the control-room, duly wiped and polished. After a quarter of an hour he gave up. 'An inaccurate fix is as bad as none at all,' he fumed as he disappeared through the hatch. There might be another chance at dusk.

The sea appeared to be lessening. Just before 1100, during the second lieutenant's watch, a call came for the quarter-master. It seemed the sun was making brief appearances. I transmitted the message to the CPOs' mess.

'Chance of a sun shot!'

No reply. The quartermaster must be asleep. I got up, staggered next door and shook him by the shoulder. 'Chance of a sun shot.'

Kriechbaum shot bolt upright. 'Seriously?'

'Of course.'

Still bleary-eyed, he disappeared into the control-room. A moment or two later I saw him climb the ladder.

FRIDAY, 63RD DAY AT SEA. 'It's a dog's life,' was the Chief's verdict at breakfast.

'You know, sir,' I said to the Captain, 'our search technique reminds me of a method used by Italian fishermen. They lower big square nets into the water, wait a while, and then haul them in over rollers. The hope is that some fish will be dozy enough to stay put while they're at it.'

The Chief shook his head reprovingly. 'That sounds suspiciously like criticism of our leaders.'

'Typical defeatist talk,' declared the Captain, and the Chief added: 'Brains at the top, that's what's needed. They ought to sack the whole of Operations and put you on the staff instead – then we'd get some results.'

'And transfer you to the Maritime Museum,' I just managed to get in before he retired to the control-room.

SATURDAY, 64TH DAY AT SEA. It was early – 0640 – when the bridge reported a vessel on the port quarter. Wind 8-9, sea 8, visibility very poor. It was a miracle the look-outs had been so quick to spot anything in the uniform grey murk. The ship was definitely unescorted and zigzagging sharply.

We were in luck. U-A was well placed in relation to the dark-grey shadow that loomed sporadically above a foaming crest, only to vanish like magic for minutes on end.

The Captain stroked his jaw. 'She probably thinks she's faster than she is – can't be doing more than fourteen knots in this. She'd have to make a big zig in the wrong direction to lose us. Let's run in a bit closer – we can't be seen against the clouds.'

Ten minutes later we dived.

'Stand by to fire tubes 1 and 3, single shots.'

I wondered how the Captain proposed to attack in this sea. Stake everything on a single throw of the dice?

The Captain called out the firing values himself. His voice was entirely without excitement. 'Enemy speed fourteen knots. Bearing one-zero-zero. Range one thousand metres.'

The first lieutenant reported the tubes ready in an equally matter-of-fact tone. All at once the Captain swore roundly and reduced speed, presumably because of periscope vibration.

The periscope motor hummed repeatedly. The Captain was doing his best to keep the target under observation in spite of the heavy sea. I guessed that the look-stick would be higher out of the water than usual. The risk was slight. Who on board the freighter was likely to suspect that the surrounding turmoil concealed a U-boat about to attack? Text-books and experience taught that submarines were rendered almost non-operational by weather conditions of this severity.

The Captain called down: 'Must be ten thousand tons at least. She's got a murderous-looking gun up front. Damn these squalls!' There was a pause. 'This is getting us nowhere,' he said suddenly. 'Stand by to surface.'

The Chief reacted like lightning. The first heavy wave hit us fair and square and sent me reeling across the control-room, but I managed to cling to the chart-table.

The Captain allowed me up on the bridge.

All round us, dark-grey curtains of rain hung low over the heaving sea. There was no sign of the freighter. The rain-squalls had swallowed her up.

'Watch it!' warned the Captain as a bottle-green wave rolled down on us. When it had spent itself, he shouted in my face: 'They can't have spotted us!' I couldn't tell if it was a statement or a pious hope.

We followed the general direction of our last sighting, which brought us head on to the sea. I endured the spray for ten minutes. Then I went below, accompanied by a deluge. The Chief was having to pump out every few minutes. 'Pointless,' he said after a while. 'We've lost her.'

Braving the shower-baths from above, I peered obliquely up the conning-tower. The helmsman was little Benjamin – a good man, but he had his work cut out to maintain course. Even without seeing the onset of the waves, I could feel them repeatedly thrust the bow aside. The upper lid was closed, so the only way of communicating between bridge and control-room was by voice-pipe.

The Captain ordered us down for a listening-watch. Evidently, we could hear farther than we could see.

The look-outs came below lobster-faced and streaming with water.

We went to 40 metres. Dead silence reigned except for the sound of bilge-water slopping around in the swell which still rocked us, even at that depth. Everyone watched the hydro-phone operator, apart from the two look-outs who were manning the planes. Turn the wheel as he might, he could pick up nothing. The captain altered course to 060.

After half an hour he took us up again. Wondering if he had thrown in his hand, I went up top with the quartermaster's watch. The Captain stayed below.

The waves presented a spectacle normally reserved for ship-wrecked sailors. The U-boat rode so low and was so continu-ously awash with foam that we might have been drifting through the maelstrom on a raft.

'Bone-shakers!' yelled Kriechbaum. 'Watch yourself. I knew someone – ' He got no further because a wave started to break ahead of us. I huddled sideways against the bridge casing and tucked my chin in. The inevitable blow caught me between the shoulder-blades and a welter of foam plucked at my legs.

Kriechbaum hardly waited for the water to subside before continuing, 'Broke three ribs – belt snapped – carried aft –

landed plumb on top of the Oerlikon – lucky for him!'

When the boat had taken another three combers, he turned and pulled the plug from the voice-pipe. 'Tell the Captain, visibility zero.'

The Captain saw sense. Down for another hydrophone sweep: still no joy.

Was it worth peeling off my wet things? The planesmen had even kept their sou'westers on. Another fifteen minutes proved them right. The Captain ordered us up again.

'Only one chance left,' he said. 'They may sacrifice their lead by making a big zig or altering their mean course.'

He sat there for a good half-hour, brows knit and eyelids drooping. Then he jumped up with a suddenness which made me start. He must have heard some sound from the bridge, because he reached the hatch even before Kriechbaum reported another sighting.

A second alarm. We dived.

The Captain was back in the conning-tower with his eyes glued to the periscope. I held my breath. Subdued cursing drifted down through the lower lid. The sea was too rough to focus on anything for longer than a few seconds.

'There she is!'

Three or four minutes passed. Suddenly: 'Hard-a-dive! Sixty metres.' We stared at each other. The control-room PO looked flabbergasted.

Why the sudden rush?

It was the Captain who dispelled our uncertainty. Climbing down, he announced: 'You wouldn't credit it, but we were spotted. The tub headed straight for us – came in to ram. Cheeky bugger! I wouldn't have thought it possible.'

He struggled in vain for self-control. Furiously he hurled a glove at the deck. 'This weather! Of all the lousy, rotten, godforsaken luck . . .'

Breathless with vituperation, he slumped on to the chart-stowage and relapsed into inertia.

I loitered, feeling slightly embarrassed. My one hope was that we wouldn't re-surface and become a plaything of the waves.

I had developed a deep-seated dread of incessant muscular tension, of acoustic torture, of the sea's unending thunder.

'Up the bloody spout,' I heard Dorian mutter.

SUNDAY, 65TH DAY AT SEA. We stayed deep. The men were probably offering up secret prayers for poor visibility because poor visibility meant diving and diving meant repose.

We had turned into emaciated old men, half-starved Robinson Crusoes. There was enough to eat, but none of us felt inclined to load his belly.

The engine-room hands were worst affected. They never saw daylight at all. It was a fortnight since anyone had set foot in the conservatory. Although the Captain had permitted smoking in the conning-tower, it was almost impossible to light up. The down-draught was too strong because the engines had to draw most of their air from inboard.

Even Frenssen was monosyllabic, and 'skylarking in the chain locker' was a thing of the past.

Only the hydrophone booth and hydroplane controls were manned. The control-room PO and his two hands kept watch, as did the electricians. Up in the conning-tower, the helmsman was hard put to it to avoid dozing off like the rest of us.

Somewhere, a motor hummed – I was long past bothering to work out which. We were making 5 knots. Much less than a cyclist, but more than we should have made on the surface.

Our lack of success weighed heavily on the Captain, who became moodier every day. Never the most sociable or gregarious of men, he now bordered on the unapproachable. His air of dejection conveyed that the failure of U-boat Command was his personal responsibility.

U-A seemed to grow steadily damper. Mildew had now attacked my spare shirts in large blackish-green patches. The leather of my sports shoes was coated with a similar green film. Our bunks smelt mouldy too. They appeared to be decaying from within. My sea-boots turned grey-green with mildew and salt if I left them unworn for a single day.

MONDAY, 66TH DAY AT SEA. Unless I was much mistaken, the storm had eased a little overnight.

'Quite normal,' the Captain said at breakfast. 'No cause for rejoicing. We may even be on the edge of quite a calm zone – depends if we hit the centre of the depression or not. You can bet your life it'll start again on the other side.'

Although the sea was as steep, the look-outs were not exposed to a continuous barrage of spray. They could even risk an occasional look through their binoculars.

We travelled with the upper lid open. Water occasionally swirled round the bridge well and spattered the control-room, but not in greater quantities than the bilge-pumps could cope with at fifteen-minute intervals. The piercing howl of the jumping-wire had diminished.

The sea looked as if it were being agitated by vast eruptive forces – hundreds upon hundreds of volcanoes which had come to life far below, causing masses of water to heave and rear.

The steep swell was such that the men below noticed little difference from the day before. For them, the news that the storm had abated remained an abstraction. The submarine plunged and shuddered as violently as ever.

TUESDAY, 67TH DAY AT SEA. No more need to look around for handholds when traversing the control-room. We could even eat without fiddles, also without clamping the dishes laboriously between our knees. There was a proper meal : salt pork with potatoes and brussels sprouts. I could feel my appetite returning as I ate.

The POs' mess succumbed to a frightful bout of farting. Wichmann, who acquitted himself with particular virtuosity, ripped off a series of staccato reports followed by a muffled peal of thunder.

The others seemed torn between outrage and admiration. Only Kleinschmidt showed any real annoyance. 'Stuff a cork in it, you dirty bugger!'

Sleep was out in that stench, so I rolled off my bunk. The disc of sky in the upper lid was only a shade lighter than the black rim of the hatch itself. I waited in the control-room for ten minutes, lolling against the quartermaster's desk, before going up top.

'Man on the bridge?'

'Affirmative.' It was the second lieutenant's voice. The dim control-room had accustomed my eyes to the darkness. I identified the look-outs at once.

I leant against the bridge casing. 'Boom, shboom!' Our sides rang like a muted gong as the sea smote them time and time again. Occasionally, when a wave broke over the fore-casing, the jumping-wire emitted a low singing note.

The reflection of a single star flitted to and fro on the beam. Craning over the bridge rail, I could see the whole of the fore-casing. The water bubbling along our sides gave off a greenish glow. The lines of the hull stood out clearly against the darkness.

'Damned phosphorescence,' grumbled the second lieutenant.

'Bloody dark,' Dorian muttered to himself. He turned imperiously to the after look-outs. 'Eyes peeled, you two!'

Returning to the control-room just before 2300, I saw two

of the hands grating boiled potatoes.

'What's that in aid of?' The answer came from behind me, in the Captain's voice. 'Potato-cakes, for want of a better name. Come on, bear a hand.'

We repaired to the galley, where he got out some lard and a frying pan. Excited as a schoolboy, he tipped the grated potato into the pan. Hot fat spurted on to my trousers. Carefully, the Captain watched the dough gradually harden and turn brown at the edges. 'Won't be long now, you see!' His nostrils flared as he sniffed the mounting aroma. The big moment came. A quick flip, and the potato-cake flew into the air, turned a somersault and landed neatly in the pan, flat and golden-brown.

We each took a piece of the first completed pancake and held it between our teeth, lips retracted, until it was slightly less than red-hot. 'Just the job, eh?' mumbled the Captain. Katter was roused from his bunk and instructed to open some tins of apple purée.

The pile of potato-cakes slowly assumed respectable proportions. It was nearly midnight – time for the engine-room watch to be relieved. The bulkhead door opened to reveal the oil-stained figure of Gigolo. He stared at us curiously and tried to squeeze past. 'Halt!' called the Captain. Gigolo froze. 'Eyes shut, mouth open – that's an order!'

Stuffing a segment of pancake into the stoker's mouth, the Captain anointed it with apple purée. Gigolo's chin got a dollop as well.

'Right, carry on. Next!'

The procedure was repeated six times. The new watch received similar treatment. Our stock of pancakes ran out in no time. We worked with a will.

'The next batch goes to the seamen.'

It was 1 a.m. when the Captain straightened up and ran a sleeve over his sweaty face. He shoved the last pancake towards me. 'Go on, dig in.'

WEDNESDAY, 68TH DAY AT SEA. An afternoon spell on the bridge. The sea's appearance had altogether changed. Gone were the roaming mountain chains with long slopes and precipices. Instead, the whole of the watery landscape was afflicted with irregular spasms of movement. U-A performed a sort of dervish dance. She lurched and swayed, unable to find a steady rhythm. The bow swung to and fro, but many of its blows fell on air.

We were sentenced to a new punishment: it had turned

cold again. Icy gusts of wind cut into my face like knives.

THURSDAY, 69TH DAY AT SEA. Wind west-north-west, barometer falling. I cherished an insane hope that it would rain
oil. Nothing seemed more desirable than a sea-smoothing
downpour of oil.

The Captain appeared for supper looking glum. Prolonged
silence. Then, between his teeth: 'Four weeks of it. Not bad
going.'

We had been tossed and shaken, lashed and thrashed for a
whole month.

The Captain brought his fist down hard on the tabletop.
He drew a deep breath, held it for half a minute, and expelled
it with an equine flutter of the lips. Then he shut his eyes
and put his head on one side: an allegory of fatalism. We
sat there feeling uncomfortable.

Kriechbaum reported a clearer skyline. The north-west wind
must have blown away the low cloud and restored our vision.

FRIDAY, 70TH DAY AT SEA. The sea was a huge green quilt,
viciously slashed until the white kapok stuffing flowed from
a myriad rents. The Captain did everything possible to miti-
gate the effects of our drubbing. He blew the Q tanks, but it
was no use. The beam seas were intolerable. There was
nothing for it in the end but to alter course.

With smarting eyes I scanned the craters, ridges and cre-
vasses around us, but there was nothing – no dark specks to
be seen. Aircraft were far from our thoughts. What flyer
could survive a storm like this or even see us in the turmoil? Our wake, the telltale train of white lace, had disappeared.

Again we plunged into a trough, and again a billow towered
on our quarter. The second lieutenant stared at it but didn't
duck – instead, he seemed to freeze.

'I saw something . . .' I heard him yell, and then the next
wave struck the conning-tower. I tucked my chin in, held
my breath and hung on tight as another swirling flood tried
to wrench my feet from under me. Then I straightened up
and scanned the raging sea, trough by trough.

Nothing.

'I saw something!' the second lieutenant yelled again. 'Broad
on the port quarter. There's something out there – eat my
hat!'

'You!' he snapped at the port after look-out. 'Didn't you see
it?'

Another express lift bore us upwards. I stood shoulder to shoulder with the second lieutenant, matching the direction of his gaze. There! Suddenly, among the scudding clouds of spindrift, I saw a dark shape tossed high. The next moment it disappeared.

A cask? If so, how far away?.

The second lieutenant removed the plug from the voice-pipe and called for binoculars. I crouched beside him, as he shielded the lenses with his hand. We waited tensely for the flotsam to reappear. There was nothing to be seen but a confusion of white-streaked hills. We were in a deep trough.

I screwed up my eyes as we started to climb again, narrowing them to slits.

'Damn, damn, damn!' The second lieutenant raised his glasses with an abrupt jerk. I stared in the same direction. Suddenly he yelled: 'There!' This time I saw it too. He was right – no doubt about it. There it was again! A dark shape. It rose, hovered for a second or two, and sank from view.

The second lieutenant lowered his binoculars. 'That was a . . .'

'A what?' I shouted back.

His jaws moved as if he were masticating the words before uttering them. Then he looked straight at me and blurted out: 'That was a submarine!'

A submarine – that bobbing cask a submarine? He couldn't be serious.

'Recognition signal, sir?' called the PO of the watch.

'No, not yet – hang on – not a hundred per cent certain.' The second lieutenant bent over the voice-pipe again. 'Pass up a shammy, quick!'

He crouched behind the bridge casing, tense as a harpooner stalking a whale, and waited for us to rise. I filled my lungs to bursting-point and stared over the seething cauldron as though holding my breath was an aid to better vision.

Nothing.

The second lieutenant handed me his glasses. I wedged myself like a climber in a chimney and searched the sea on our port beam.

'Damn and blast!' I could see nothing but a disc of grey-white water.

'There!' bellowed the second lieutenant, and flung up his right arm. Hurriedly, I handed back the glasses. He peered hard, then darted to the voice-pipe. 'Bridge to Captain, submarine on the port quarter!'

A huge wave bore us up. I took the binoculars and scanned

the watery waste for two or three seconds. Then I found it. The second lieutenant was right beyond a shadow of a doubt — it was a submarine's conning-tower. A moment later it vanished like a ghost.

The upper lid opened as soon as the next wave ebbed. The Captain climbed out and asked for a rough bearing.

'You're right!' he growled beneath his binoculars. A sudden note of urgency came into his voice. 'They aren't diving — surely they aren't diving? Get me the lamp, and hurry!'

For some seconds, our three pairs of straining eyes saw nothing. The Captain gnawed his lip. Then a speck appeared in the grey-green expanse — the bobbing cask was still there.

The Captain headed for it. I wondered what he planned to do, why he hadn't fired a recognition signal — why they hadn't fired one. Hadn't they spotted us?

Heavy showers of sprindrift and spray were raining against our backs. I stood as tall as I could and looked aft. A whole alpine chain was advancing on us from astern, snow-capped and menacing. I had a momentary fear that the first huge wave would break over us instead of bearing us up, but it hissed beneath the hull and went on to obscure our forward vision like a massive house-high rampart. Simultaneously, our view astern was blocked by the next wave in the series.

Suddenly, the conning-tower of the other boat materialized among the foaming crests. It bobbed up like a cork, then dipped and vanished for a full minute.

The second lieutenant shouted something. No words, just a blur of sound. The Captain lifted the upper lid and bellowed: 'What about that lamp?'

The signal lamp was handed up. The Captain wedged himself between the periscope standard and the bridge casing and raised it in both hands. I braced myself against his thighs to give him more stability and height. I heard the click of the shutter: dot – dot – dash. It stopped. I sneaked a look at the sea. The other submarine seemed to have been swallowed up. There was nothing to be seen but a watery grey waste.

I heard the Captain swear loudly.

All of a sudden, a flash pierced the murk: dot – dash – dash. Nothing more for a while, then more flashes in the hurly-burly.

'It's Thomsen!' shouted the Captain.

I clung to his left thigh with all my might, with the second lieutenant clinging to his right. Our own lamp started to flicker. I couldn't see what the Captain was making because my head was bowed, but I could hear him dictating to himself in a loud voice: 'Maintain – course – and – speed – will – close – you.'

A mountain of water, more immense than any we had seen before, bore down on us from astern. Smoking white spindrift swirled from the crest of the gigantic comber like powdered snow from a cornice. The Captain lowered his lamp and slid quickly off our shoulders.

My heart missed a beat. The hiss and roar of the four-storeyed colossus drowned the noise of every other wave in sight. We cowered against the forward screen of the bridge. The second lieutenant shielded his face with his forearm, like a boxer on the ropes.

We stared at the huge wave as it approached with a sort of sinister deliberation, heavy as molten lead, made sluggish by its own unimaginable volume. Spume glinted angrily on its back. It drew closer, rearing ever higher above the grey-green turmoil. Suddenly the wind dropped. Around us, smaller waves leapt erratically in a random dance. It dawned on me that the monster had erected a barrier between us and the gale: we were in its lee.

'Eyes down – hold tight!' the Captain bellowed at the top of his voice.

I cowered still lower and tensed every muscle so as to brace myself between the casing and the master sight. My pulses raced. It was too much. If this one broke, God help us! The boat would never take it. We would never take it – our bones would snap like twigs.

There was a vicious hiss as of red-hot sheet steel doused by a thousand heartbeats. Then I felt our stern lift. Higher and higher we rose, hanging bow-down on the watery mountainside, until we were higher than we had ever been. Fear relaxed its stranglehold on my throat, but the upper extremity of the crest broke none the less. Tons of water bludgeoned the conning-tower and made the whole hull tremble violently. I heard a savage gurgle, and a maelstrom of water shot into the foaming well of the bridge.

I filled my lungs and clamped my lips tightly together. Everything was blotted out by a sheet of green glass. I made myself as heavy as I could, willing my legs to withstand the almost solid surge of water. For a moment I thought we were going to be drowned on our feet – the whole bridge was full to overflowing.

Then the conning-tower tilted. I surfaced and snatched a

lungful of air, only to feel my chest tighten with a new fear. The bridge lay farther and farther over, as though threatening to tip us out.

Could a submarine turn turtle? Was our ballast keel equal to such forces?

The foaming vortex plucked at my oilskins. My legs felt as if they were enmeshed. I sucked in another breath and lifted each foot in turn. At last I raised my head. U-A's stern was pointing at the sky. I abandoned my crouching posture and peered over the bridge rail. Our fore-casing was deeply embedded in a greenish-white swirl of foam. I caught sight of the second lieutenant's gaping mouth. He seemed to be shouting at the top of his voice, but no sound came.

Water was trickling down the Captain's face and streaming from the gutter of his sou'wester brim. The wind had flayed his cheeks red. His eyes were motionless, fixed on something ahead of us. I followed the line of his gaze.

The other U-boat was now on our port bow. All of a sudden, her entire length became visible. The wave that had passed beneath us was now lifting her skywards. A few moments more, and her bow, too, was buried in a welter of foam. It looked as if Thomsen and his crew had lost half their hull. Then a column of spray shot vertically up their conning-tower, like breakers hitting a rock, and they vanished completely in a cloud of grey water-smoke.

The second lieutenant shouted something that sounded like 'Poor devils!' Poor devils? Was he crazy? Had he forgotten that we had just been tossed and shaken with the same abandon?

We continued to swing. The angle between our bow and the direction of the sea narrowed until we were head-on to the waves.

'Perfect!' bellowed the second lieutenant, then: 'Ouch! Let's hope they aren't picking daisies over there.'

I was also afraid that the others would be unable to maintain course in such a sea. Our turning circle quickly brought us closer. Before long, the waves sliced apart by the bow of the other boat were impinging on the cross seas churned up by our own. Ragged fountains of water flew high into the air – dozens of geysers, small, large, immense . . .

Then we were lifted again. Another mighty wave had arisen and taken us on its back like a whale of monstrous dimensions. A black steel Zeppelin, we soared into the sky with our fore-casing wholly exposed.

I had a rooftop view of the other boat's bridge. Wasn't the

Captain pushing his luck? If the wave sent us crashing down on them . . .

No orders came. I could actually recognize the five figures braced against the starboard bridge screen, Thomsen in the centre. They were all staring up at us with their mouths gaping like Aunt Sallies – like fledgelings awaiting their mother's return.

So that was how we looked. That was how the pilot of a low-flying aircraft would have seen us: a cask with five men lashed to it, a dot in a patch of foam, a white-fleshed fruit with a black kernel. The illusion persisted until the waves drained to reveal the long steel cigar beneath.

We started to side-slip off the whale's back, ever faster, ever deeper.

Still nothing from the Captain. I caught a glimpse of his face. He was grinning. The Old Man could ride a tiger and still grin.

Then he yelled: 'Eyes down!'

Into a quick crouch and hang on tight, knees jammed against the casing, back against the periscope standard, muscles tensed, abdominal wall taut. A wall of water, bottle-green and heraldically plumed, rose ahead of us like Hiroshige's *Wave*.

The top of the wall went hollow and loomed over us. I averted my head, took a last quick gulp of air and doubled up, hugging my camera to my chest. The hammer fell. I held my breath and counted, suppressed an urge to retch and went on counting until the floor drained away.

Our dreaded side-slip proved illusory. I marvelled. The Old Man, in his wisdom and presumption, had known how the leviathan would behave. He could feel what went on beneath us, sense the movements of such a sea-monster in advance.

Now it was the other boat's turn to teeter on the crest of a mountainous wave. Higher and higher she rose, as though poised on a giant fist. Peering through the viewfinder, I could see the light glint dully on her exposed ballast tanks. She hung there long enough for me to take four or five pictures – an eternity – then plummeted into the next trough. A ragged white crest leapt high between the two submarines, blotting out the others as if they had never been there. I saw nothing for the next half-minute but seething grey-white waves, heaving mountains of dirty snow. They looked twice as huge with a submarine in their grasp.

Strange to think that, down in the bowels of the other boat during this savage fandango, stokers were tending their engines, the telegraphist was hunched over his wireless, the men in the fore-ends were wedged in their bunks, reading or trying to sleep, lights were burning and human beings in occupation . . .

I caught myself mumbling a reproof – I was as guilty as the second lieutenant of forgetting that we were aboard a sister-ship in the same sea. There was no difference between their men's lot and ours.

The Captain called for signalling flags. Signalling flags? The Old Man must have gone round the bend at last – no one could semaphore in this.

Holding the flags like a pair of relay batons, he swiftly unclipped his belt as we breasted the next wave and jammed himself high up between the casing and periscope standard. With the leisurely movements of a lake-steamer skipper, he unfurled the flags and made our call sign. Then: 'A . . n . . y . . l . . u . . c . . k ?'

Incredibly, someone over there raised his arms in the 'Under-stood' signal. A pause, and then, as we continued to swoop and soar, he spelt out: 'T . . e . . n . . t . . h . . o . . u . . s . . a . . n . . d . . t . . o . . n . . s.'

Like deaf-mutes imprisoned in the passing cars of a cable railway, we signalled to each other through the flying spray. For some moments, the two boats hung level. When we rose again, the Captain made another series of letters: 'G . . o . . o . . d . . h . . u . . n . . t . . i . . n . . g . . y . . o . . u . . j . . a . . m . . m . . y . . b . . a . . s . . t . . a . . r . . d . . s.'

Flags had appeared on the other bridge by this time. In unison, we spelt out the message that was flapped in our direction. 'R . . e . . c . . i . . p . . r . . o . . c . . a . . t . . e .'

Suddenly the wave dropped us. We raced into a spume-filled valley, heeling hard to starboard.

High above, the bow of the other U-boat protruded many metres clear of the abyss and hovered in this unbelievable position for another eternity – long enough for us to see both starboard bow-caps, each individual flooding flap and the entire underwater shape. Then the overhanging bow dropped like a guillotine blade. It clove the sea with a force that would have severed steel. The hull followed it in like a wedge, splitting the wave asunder. Huge glass-green shavings of water curled aside on either flank before the bow buried itself in a welter of foam which swirled up and over the bridge. Nothing could be seen in the frothing turmoil but a few dark dots: the heads of the look-outs and an arm brandishing a red flag.

I saw the second lieutenant glance uneasily at the Captain,

then found myself looking into the ecstatic face of the Chief, who must have been on the bridge for a quite a while.

With one arm round the periscope, I raised myself for a better look. The other boat had receded into the troughs astern of us. I saw the black cask tossed high. It bobbed, dipped, and dwindled to a dancing cork. Two minutes later it was gone.

The Captain ordered us back on course. I waited for a wave to subside, opened the upper lid and scrambled down the narrow shaft.

The helmsman leant aside but the boat rolled to starboard and he caught a douche from above.

'What's up, Lieutenant?'

'We passed another boat – Thomsen's. Spitting distance.'

Someone on the bridge kicked the hatch cover shut. Pale faces swam in the gloom like turnip-ghosts. We were back down the mine. It occurred to me that not even the helmsman had witnessed our encounter.

I untied the strings of my sou'wester and struggled out of my oilskin jacket. The control-room PO was all ears. I had to throw him a few crumbs – it was the least I could do. 'The Captain's handling was a dream,' I said, 'precision work, honestly.'

Excitement seemed to have galvanized me. I stripped off my wet things much faster than of late. Beside me, the Chief was methodically towelling himself down.

We reassembled in the wardroom ten minutes later. Although my pulses were still racing, I did my best to seem nonchalant.

'Wasn't it a bit unconventional, sir?'

'What?' the Captain asked.

'Well, that exchange of compliments.'

'In what way?'

'Shouldn't we have fired a recognition signal?'

'Good God,' he said. 'I knew that conning-tower straight away. They'd have shit a brick if we'd sent up a flare. They'd have had to fire one back, and who knows if they had one handy, in this weather? We might have caught them on the hop.'

'I'll remember that, sir, next time somebody turfs me out of my seat to get at the flares.'

'No griping,' said the Captain. 'Needs must – regulations.'

Ten minutes later he reverted to my objection. 'Anyway, no need to worry about British submarines in this weather. What would they be doing – looking for a German convoy?'

SATURDAY, 71ST DAY AT SEA. The excitement had worn off. The curtain had fallen. We were jammed round the wardroom table, chewing. Those off watch relapsed into their former lethargy.

The Captain said nothing till the meal was over. Then: 'They were quick off the mark.'

By 'they' he meant Thomsen and his crew. He was clearly surprised to see Thomsen in our area. 'After all, he didn't get back till just before we sailed – plenty of damage, too.'

'Yessir,' he continued. 'The C-in-C's in a hurry these days.'

Shorter refits, quicker processing. No more hanging about. The patient had to vacate his bed and get back on his feet in double-quick time.

A good fifteen minutes went by before the Captain started again. 'Something wrong there. We can't have more than a dozen U-boats in the Atlantic. A dozen boats strung out between Greenland and the Azores, yet we nearly ran each other down. Something wrong there,' he repeated. 'Ah well, not my worry.'

Maybe not, but it didn't prevent him from brooding day and night about the obvious dilemma: too large a patrol area, too few U-boats, no air support.

'It's time they worked something out.'

Supper. The canned bread was diabolical – I simply couldn't swallow it. The Captain was also having trouble. He shifted a wad from cheek to cheek before finally gulping it down. Our brush with the other boat had given him something else to chew on. 'Thomsen probably has the adjoining patrol-line,' he remarked hesitantly. A minute later he called the quartermaster.

'Our position is right, I suppose – more or less?'

'You said it, sir – more or less. We haven't taken a fix for a week, and the wind's changed a few times since then.'

'Very good, Kriechbaum. Thanks.'

He turned to us. 'You see? Add two discrepancies together and you get a brace of U-boats tripping over each other with a monumental gap north and south of them. The British could sail through with a whole armada, and we'd be none the wiser. Things look different on a wall map in Kernével than they do in the bosom of the deep.'

When I woke on the third morning after our encounter, it

240

was apparent that the storm had lessened.

I climbed into my oilskins as fast as I could and went on the bridge. It was not quite light.

The horizon had been scoured clean. Waves still broke on the long swell, but only here and there. Although they hoisted and lowered us almost as far as on previous days, their motion had become smoother. The boat was no longer shaken and jolted.

The north-west wind blew steadily, seldom deviating more than an uneasy point or two from its general direction. The air struck chill.

The sun was about to rise. A reddish glow in the east and like gleaming lances, its first rays soared above the horizon. Orange hems stitched themselves on to robes of cloud still dark with night.

Our fore-casing glinted in the incipient sunlight. Dawn violently accentuated the chiaroscuro of the towering billows. The ocean became an immense woodcut, all light and shade.

Towards midday the wind dropped to almost nothing. Its strident voice yielded to a subdued hiss and roar. My ears still rang with the savage song of the storm. Bemused by the unaccustomed stillness, I felt as if a film had suddenly lost its sound-track. The waves, a restless white-manned herd, still pranced gravely towards us.

I found it almost inconceivable, watching their swift progress, that they were not really advancing – that the sea's whole surface was not in rapid forward motion. I had to enlist the image of a cornfield undulating in the wind before I could grasp that these huge masses of water were as static as wheat-stalks.

'Seldom seen such a big swell,' the quartermaster said. 'Must stretch a thousand miles or more.'

Next morning the ocean appeared to be stirring beneath a layer of molten lead. The sky lay becalmed – a motionless pool of curdled milk.

'Always the wrong way round,' Kriechbaum said resentfully. 'We could have done with these conditions a bit earlier, God knows!'

Later, down in the control-room, he jabbed his dividers at a pencilled cross on the chart. 'Here we are now, and here was our position this time yesterday.' The corners of his mouth twitched ruefully. 'We've been slogging back and forth across the same little patch.' He went to the chart-stowage, produced the general operations chart and indicated a grid square south-west of Iceland. 'There, that corresponds to the sheet on the table.'

His divider-points traced our route to date. 'We started off with a long run to westwards. Then came the bad weather. We swung north, then a big zig south, then west again, then another swing north. A few zigzags, then west for the third time. And that's where we are now – bogged down.'

I stared at the sheet as if it might yield some clue to our future. So that was the sole result of all our laborious slogging: a pencil-line snaking crazily across a printed grid.

Kernével relayed a signal from Flossmann in the Denmark Strait: he had sunk an unescorted ship with a salvo of three.

'He'll make flag rank yet,' said the Captain. It sounded more like disgust than envy.

He vented his bitterness in an outburst of fury. 'They can't leave us swanning around here, simply on the off-chance! We'll never get anywhere at this rate . . .'

Morale on board was at rock bottom. The men had exhausted their reserves of good-natured phlegm. The coxswain seemed to cope best of all. His voice had lost none of its barrack-square volume. Every morning, while lesser mortals were still tongue-tied, Behrmann vituperated as of yore because clean-ship had not been carried out to his satisfaction. Once the Captain was on the bridge, he flew off the handle as though his tirades entitled him to extra rations.

For variety's sake, I rearranged my tiny locker. Everything was spoiled – every shirt spotted with mould, a leather belt stained green with mildew, underwear reeking of damp. The only miracle was that we ourselves had not decayed or dissolved into mucus.

With some, the process seemed to have begun. Electrician Zörner's face was disfigured by crimson boils with yellow cores. They looked peculiarly repulsive against his cheesy complexion, although the seamen fared worst of all because regular immersion in sea-water prevented their cuts and boils from healing.

The storm was spent. The bridge had again become a place of recreation.

Nothing marred the sweep of the horizon, an immaculate line which marked the perfect seal between sea and sky.

I pictured our surroundings as a big disc surmounted by a dome of opalescent glass. Wherever we moved, the dome moved too, mathematically centred on our dark-green disc of sea. Only sixteen nautical miles separated us from the disc's perimeter, so its diameter measured thirty-two miles — a pinhead in the vastness of the Atlantic.

CONTACT

The day's first signal was a relay from Kernével asking Thomsen to report his position.

'How far away is he now?' I asked the Captain.

'He hasn't reported yet,' he said. 'This is the third time of asking.'

At once I was haunted by a mental image of depth-charges bursting like cauliflowers of white flame.

No, I said to myself, they must have a good reason for keeping quiet. Situations did arise in which even the shortest signal could betray a U-boat's presence.

At breakfast next morning I asked, as casually as I could: 'Anything from Thomsen?'

'No.' The Captain continued to chew, staring dourly ahead. Flooded aerial duct, I told myself, atmospheric disturbance.

The PO telegraphist came in with the radio log. The Captain took it, a shade too eagerly. He read the latest signal, initialled it and shut the folder with a snap. I passed it back to Herrmann. The Captain said nothing.

There had very recently been cases in which U-boats damaged by aircraft were unable to send out a distress call.

'He should have reported days ago,' the Captain said, 'of his own accord.'

The following day nobody mentioned Thomsen at all. The subject was taboo, though anyone could tell what the Captain thought.

Towards midday, just as lunch was about to be served, the control-room passed a report from the bridge: 'Tell the Captain, smoke bearing one-four-zero.'

The Captain jumped up as if he had been shot. We hurried after him into the control-room. I grabbed a pair of binoculars in passing and shinned up the ladder close at his heels.

'Well, where is it?'

The quartermaster pointed. 'There, sir, on the port beam,

beneath the right-hand edge of that big cumulus. Very faint.'

I could detect nothing in the direction indicated, however hard I looked. Kriechbaum was unlikely to have made a mistake, but the sector in question was thickly hung with a rich assortment of grey and mallow-coloured clouds. The Captain peered through his glasses. The skyline danced violently in my own lenses as they edged along it. Nothing to be seen. I strained my eyes to the utmost. They were already watering.

At last I discovered a thin streak, fractionally darker than its pinkish background. The same shape was repeated close beside it – a trifle fainter and more blurred, but unmistakable for all that. And there, suddenly, I saw a whole cluster of them. The Captain lowered his binoculars.

'A convoy, no doubt about it. Ship's head?'

'Two-five-zero, sir.'

Not a moment's hesitation. 'Steer two-three-zero.'

'Two-three-zero, sir.'

'Half-ahead both.'

The Captain turned to Kriechbaum, whose eyes were still glued to his glasses. 'They seem to be steering a southerly course, Quartermaster.' Kriechbaum continued to peer. 'My guess too, sir.'

'I'll bring them ahead and see how the bearing grows.'

No excited outbursts, no fever of the chase. The faces round me were impassive – all except Wichmann's. His excitement was plain to see. Wichmann had been the first to spot the plumes of smoke.

'Third watch,' he muttered smugly beneath his binoculars, 'I said it'd be the third watch . . .' Realizing that the Captain had overheard him, he flushed and fell silent.

The little plumes told us nothing about the convoy's course. South was only a conjecture. The ships could be drawing towards us or going away.

Another steering order. I kept my binoculars on our quarry as the boat turned slowly beneath me.

'Midships.'

Inside the conning-tower, the helmsman put his wheel amidships.

The boat continued to swing.

'Ship's head?' asked the Captain.

'One-seven-zero!' came the answer from below.

'Steer one-six-five.'

We turned, more slowly now, until the scattering of masts lay right ahead. The Captain screwed up his eyes and warily scanned the thick grey overcast. He tilted his head back and turned an almost full circle. Aircraft were the last thing we wanted.

Lunch was announced.

'No time for that,' the Captain growled. 'Bring it up here.'

The food was placed on small fold-down seats let into the bridge casing. It stayed there. Nobody touched a crumb.

The Captain asked Kriechbaum the time of moonset. Evidently he intended to wait until nightfall before attacking. There was nothing for us to do until then but keep watch and maintain contact so that other U-boats could be deployed against the convoy.

Little by little, the plumes of smoke climbed higher above the horizon and shifted to starboard.

'Drawing right,' said Kriechbaum.

'Outward bound,' the Captain agreed. 'They must be in ballast. Pity – inward bound would be better.'

'Twelve mastheads visible so far, sir,' reported the second lieutenant.

'That'll do for starters.' The Captain called below : 'Helmsman, ship's head now?'

'One-six-five, sir.'

The Captain thought aloud in a mutter : 'Convoy bearing green two-zero, i.e. true bearing one-eight-five. Range? Medium-sized ships, so roughly sixteen miles.'

Our wake frothed like fizzy lemonade. Small white clouds in the sky looked like unaimed shrapnel-bursts. U-A ploughed on through the grey sea with a slaver of foam at her jaws.

'They're close enough. This one won't slip through our fingers,' the Captain said. 'Other things being equal,' he qualified swiftly. Then, to the helmsman : 'Starboard wheel. Steer two-five-five.'

Slowly the wisps of smoke swung left until they were back on our port bow. U-A was now on a course roughly parallel with the convoy's estimated line of advance.

The Captain lowered his binoculars for seconds at a time only. Now and then he murmured to himself. I caught the odd phrase : 'Never made to order . . . heading the wrong way . . .'

In other words, he would have preferred a fully laden convoy bound for England, not only for the cargo but also because the pursuit would have taken us nearer home. He was worried by the prospect of heavy fuel consumption at full speed. Any U-boat commander preferred a chase which took him closer to base.

'Fuel . . .' I heard the quartermaster say. He usually shunned

the word like an obscenity. The Captain frowned and exchanged a few whispered remarks with him. Finally the Chief
was consulted, wearing his most sombre expression.

'I want the whole position thoroughly double-checked,' I
heard the Captain tell him, and he vanished below with the
agility of an acrobat.

It must have been roughly half an hour later when the
Captain ordered both engines full ahead, his intention being
to gain a position on the convoy's bow before nightfall.

The note of the engines rose in pitch. The bow-wave curved
higher.

The Chief appeared like a jack-in-the-box, driven on deck
by concern for his fuel reserves. 'They're pretty low, sir,' he
said lugubriously. 'We can't afford more than three hours at
these revs.'

About a thumb's breadth above the horizon, the frayed
balls of smoke gradually merged to form a greasy ochre-brown
bank of haze. The mastheads beneath it resembled slowly-
growing stubble.

The Captain lowered his binoculars before turning to the
first lieutenant. 'Don't let those mastheads grow any higher
than they are now, Number One. Not on any account.' Then
he disappeared through the upper lid. Not quite as nimbly as
the Chief, I thought, and followed him below.

Down in the control-room, Kriechbaum had transferred
our changes of course to a large sheet of graph paper. He
was just entering a new enemy bearing and range.

'Let's have a look,' said the Captain. 'I see, that's where
they are. Seems to be shaping nicely.' He turned to me. 'The
convoy's exact course will become apparent from the range
and bearing plot we build up over the next few hours.' A
note of eagerness came into his voice. 'Kriechbaum, get out
the big one and let's see where they've come from.' Bending
over the chart, he launched into a muttered monologue. 'Must
have come from the North Channel . . . Which would make
their mean course what, exactly? Soon see . . .' He laid his
parallel ruler between the convoy's position and the North
Channel and rolled it down to the compass rose. 'Roughly
two-five-zero.' He thought for a moment. 'They can't have
held that course all the way. They must have stood off far
to the north to avoid suspected U-boat concentrations. Well,
it hasn't done them much good. C'est la vie . . .'

The steady roar of the engines filled U-A from end to end.
Its effect on us was that of a life-giving elixir. We all held
our heads higher and moved with greater resilience. My pulse

246

seemed to beat more strongly.

The Captain was a changed man. His manner was relaxed, almost gay, and the corners of his mouth curled in an occasional smile. The engines were running full ahead, and already the world looked rosier. After a while he said: 'Anyway, we can't close them before nightfall – they may have a few surprises up their sleeve.'

Nightfall . . . That was hours away.

I retired to the POs' mess to stock up on sleep. Zeitler and Kleinschmidt were ensconced at the table. Subject No. 1 had regained its normal appeal.

'Don't tell me you never screwed a married woman,' Kleinschmidt was saying. 'They're the randiest of the lot. After all, what are they supposed to do, pack it in just when they've got used to it? Fair's fair, mate! You don't act like a virgin yourself, so why expect her to? It isn't logical, being jealous when you spend every run ashore in the nearest knocking-shop.'

'Get stuffed! Just because your bit does it with the milk-man, it doesn't mean they all do.'

'You don't know you're born, mate. They get the taste, I tell you – it's habit-forming.' The conviction in Zeitler's voice would have graced a missionary preaching to the heathens. Suddenly he turned aggressive. 'There's none so blind as can't see – and if you can't see that, you're a stupid cunt.'

Wichmann, who had appeared in the meantime, joined the discussion. 'Married women?' he mused. 'You can keep them. I went upstairs with one once, and just as we'd got down to it her nipper started crying next door. Happened twice in a row, it did. If you can keep your mind on your work with that going on, you're a better man than I am.'

I endured the conversation for another fifteen minutes before deciding to see how things looked in the engine-room. The bulkhead door refused to open. I had to exert my full strength before I overcame the suction created by the racing engines. The noise was like a box on the ears. I opened my mouth and eyes, both. The gauge needles trembled feverishly across their dials. Oil fumes filled the compartment.

Johann was the watch-keeping ERA, Frenssen the stoker PO. Johann grinned when he saw me. His recent air of lethargy had gone. Pride shone in his eyes: his engines were showing their paces.

He wiped his oil-blackened hands on a mottled ball of cotton waste. It was a miracle the noise hadn't deafened him, but to his ears the infernal din probably sounded like the rustle of spring. He put his mouth close to my ear and shouted at the top of his lungs: 'What gives?'

'Con – voy – in – sight!' I bellowed back, straight into his ear. 'Wait – ing – till – nightfall!' Johann blinked twice, nodded, and returned to his gauges. It took me a few seconds to grasp that the men in the stern had no idea why we were going full ahead. The bridge was far away. To those who trod the floor-plates, the world ended beyond the engine-room bulkhead. Their only links with the upper world were the engine-room telegraphs and intercom system. Unless the Captain chose to broadcast the reason for a change of speed, nobody down here knew what was brewing.

Whenever I set foot inside the engine-room, I was overwhelmed by the mighty surge of sound. It dazed me. I had a sudden, haunting vision of a big ship's engine-room with its thickly lagged pipes and vulnerable boilers, its gears, its high- and low-pressure turbines. No bulkheads. A ship's engine-room filled quicker than any other compartment if she took a torpedo, and a ship with a flooded engine-room was doomed.

Tormenting images flitted through my head. A hit midships and the nightmare reaction: boilers spewing high-pressure steam, pipes bursting, the ship robbed of her motive power, the silvery glint of a ladder just wide enough to accommodate one man, and suddenly a dozen hands clawing at it in a mad upward scramble through darkness and the hiss of escaping steam.

What a job, I reflected. Three metres below the water-line and aware that, from one moment to the next and with no warning whatsoever, a torpedo could rip through the ship's side. How often, while in convoy, must a man's eyes stray to the thin plates that separated him from the flood – how often must he covertly prospect the quickest route aloft, his mouth already sour with the foretaste of panic, his ears already filled with the harsh rending of metal, the thunder of high explosive and the sea's roaring inrush. Never a moment's sense of security or freedom from fear, just an endless wait for the klaxon to sound, a month-long dying of many deaths.

It was even worse for a tanker crew. A single hit amidships could transform their ship into a blazing inferno from stem to stern. When the pent-up gases exploded, the result was a mighty eruption of fire and smoke. Petrol tankers flared up like giant torches.

I was wrested from my horrific day-dreams by a slight change of expression on Johann's face. A look of wary concentration settled on his features, lingered for a minute and dissolved: all was well. The door to the motor-room stood open. The compartment was filled with oil-laden hot-house warmth. The motors were turning in unison with the diesels, but without load. A staccato beat indicated that the air compressors were working. PO Electrician Rademacher was engaged in checking the temperature of the shaft bearings. Electrician Zörner was seated on a heap of oilskins, reading. He was too engrossed to notice me peering over his shoulder.

The Baron took Maria in his arms and bent her lissom body backwards so that the light glinted on the dark ringlets that framed her face. He was met by a gaze of the same fierce defiance as that which he felt his own eyes burn into her, as though each of them yearned to know that their passion was reciprocated to the utmost – to the point of ultimate ruin; reciprocated at the expense of a return to that obscurity from which they had both emerged into the tinselled glamour of a life fraught with danger and soured by the frustration of their fleeting moments together . . .

'They must be using a damned complicated zigzag system,' the Captain said when I returned to the bridge. 'Incredible how they manage it. They don't just steer a mean course with a few routine zigzags thrown in – not them. To stop us cottoning on too fast, they build in all kinds of variations. It's a quartermaster's nightmare. Poor old Kriechbaum! He's got his hands full – enemy's estimated course, own course, collision course. It can't be easy, juggling with so many balls at once.' It took me a moment to realize that the last sentence referred to the British commodore, not Kriechbaum. 'Once upon a time they used to alter course at regular intervals, so we soon got the general picture. Since then, they've learned how to make life harder for us. Must be quite an interesting job, master-minding a convoy like that, herding an assortment of pregnant cows all the way across the Atlantic, always on the *qui vive* . . .'

U-A was the boat in contact now – now it was our turn to keep watch without being diverted or forced to dive. We had to be as stubborn as our ship's fly, which promptly returned to its former place after each ineffectual swipe. The fly: a symbol of pertinacity – a genuine heraldic beast. Why hadn't it ever been used as such? U-boat commanders adorned their conning-towers with wild boar and snorting bulls, but none of them had ever hit on the fly. A great big fly on the conning-tower – I ought to suggest it to the Old Man, but not now. With his hands deep in his trouser-pockets, he was currently performing a clumsy bear-dance round the open hatch. One of the look-outs stole a puzzled glance at him. The Captain bit his head off.

'Eyes front, man!'

I'd never seen him like this. Every now and then he banged the bridge casing with his fist. 'Quartermaster,' he shouted, 'time to make a signal. I'll take a quick bearing first, so we can send them a reliable mean course.'

The binocular sight was brought to the bridge. The Captain fitted it on the compass repeater, took a bearing on the plumes of smoke and read off the degrees. 'Captain to quartermaster,' he called below. 'True bearing one-five-five degrees, range fourteen miles.'

A minute later Kriechbaum reported that the convoy's course was 240 degrees.

'Just as we thought,' the Captain said to himself. He gave a satisfied nod and called below again. 'How about speed – can you tell yet?'

Kriechbaum's face appeared in the hatch opening. 'Between seven-point-five and eight-point-five knots, sir.'

Another minute, and he handed up a draft signal to C-in-C U-boats. The Captain read it through, signed it with a stub of pencil and passed it below.

The Chief came on deck, wearing his most pensive expression. He looked up at the Captain like a beaten dog. Whatever he had meant to say, the Captain got there first.

'Ah, there you are, Chief. What's the matter, come to collect our fares, or are you really worried about something?'

'Nothing wrong with the engines, sir. It's getting back that worries me.'

'Stop belly-aching, Chief. Everything's fine.' The Captain waited until he had gone below before doing some rough calculations with Kriechbaum's assistance. 'When did you say it gets dark?'

'About 1900, sir, but the moon doesn't set till 0600.'

'Then we won't need to press on at full power much longer. We're good for a preliminary attack. After that, we'll have to fall back on the Chief's hidden reserves. Engineers are all the same – born hoarders.'

The clouds of smoke now looked like captive balloons

arrayed along the horizon on short cables. I counted fifteen.

In a studiously casual voice, the Captain said: 'We'd better have a look at the opposition. Take her in a bit closer, Number One. Come tonight, it may be useful to know the sort of escorts we're dealing with.'

The first lieutenant promptly altered course 20 degrees to port. The coxswain, who was watching the starboard forward sector, muttered: 'About time we took a crack at something . . .'

The Captain cut him short. 'Anything can happen between now and nightfall.'

Pessimism, but I was sure he felt secretly confident. The old superstition: don't count your chickens.

It emerged from the C-in-C's signals that five U-boats had been deployed against the convoy. Five – quite a pack. We concluded from Flechsig's position report that he would join us during the night. His boat lay farther west.

I bumped into the Chief in the control-room. His air of composure didn't conceal the fact that he was on tenterhooks. I eyed him with a silent but ostentatious grin until he furiously demanded to know what I found so amusing.

'Now, now,' said the Captain, appearing from nowhere.

The Chief frowned. 'Let's hope the exhaust pipes hold out. There's a minor leak in the port engine manifold gasket.' He started fidgeting and vanished aft without a word. Five minutes later he was back.

'Well, how goes it?' I asked.

'So-so,' came the reply.

The Captain, who was busy at the chart-table, didn't appear to be listening.

The telegraphist came in to have his log signed: another two hours had gone.

'Just our newsletter,' said the Captain. 'A signal for Merkel. Nothing special – only a request for a position report.'

It was a source of universal amazement that Merkel still survived at all. I remembered his Number One's account of the high-spot of their last patrol – an encounter with a tanker in very heavy seas: 'The target had bad luck – she altered course at the wrong moment and ran right across our bow. The sea was so rough we couldn't hold her in the periscope. We had to close the range in case she spotted the tracks and jinked. The Old Man ordered a single from No. 3. We heard the fish go up, then another explosion. The Chief did his best to hold us at periscope depth but we lost sight of her. It was minutes before the Old Man got a decent look, and by that time the tanker was on top of us – she'd turned a full circle! Not a hope of avoiding her. She rammed us at fifteen metres. Both periscopes were a write-off but the hull held up by a miracle. Another couple of centimetres and we'd have had it. Surfacing was out – the impact had completely jammed the upper lid. Not a nice feeling, travelling blind with the conning-tower hermetically sealed. We eventually got out through the after hatch and prised open the upper lid with a hammer and crow-bar. Couldn't risk going deep after that . . .'

Nobody had ventured to enquire how Merkel had felt about covering the two thousand miles back to St Nazaire with a smashed conning-tower and no look-sticks. Merkel had always been prematurely grey.

Going to the POs' mess to get my camera ready, I found its occupants engaged in loud conversation. Despite the convoy's proximity, they were back on Subject No. 1.

'I used to have a bird who always put a kettle on the gas before she stripped off . . .'

'I don't blame her, not with your slice of Gorgonzola waving around. Give you a wash and brush-up, did she?'

'Bollocks, that was for after – she always had a quick sloosh. Practical little thing, she was – never forgot to light the gas first. Not exactly romantic, mind you.'

'Dead necessary, though.' Wichmann turned to the others. 'You should have seen his last bird. Vintage eighteen-seventy. You'd have had to piss away the cobwebs first . . .'

Zeitler emitted a belch which started at the pit of his stomach and lingered in the air like thunder.

'Staying-power!' Pilgrim said admiringly.

I fled to the fore-ends. Five or six members of the watch below were sprawled or seated on the wooden decking with their knees drawn up. The hammocks overhead deputized for swaying branches. All they needed was a camp fire.

I was bombarded with eager questions.

'Everything seems to be going according to plan.'

Gigolo was stirring his mug of tea with a greasy knife. 'We won't be eating off the deck this time tomorrow,' he announced loudly. 'The fish'll be gone. Then we can put the table up.'

'Don't forget the damask tablecloth and the gold-rimmed cups,' Ario added. 'Not to mention the family silver.' He gave a sudden scowl. 'Hey, you, belt up! I can't take any more of your goddam gibbering.'

He picked up a swab and flung it at the Vicar's hammock. 'Missed,' said Gigolo, but Ario was well away.

'All right, show a leg! Stop mumbling – get down on your knees and pray a bit louder. Maybe he'll cook up something special for us, your old man with the white beard. Maybe he'll haul you out of the drink and leave the rest of us to swim for it.'

'Leave him be,' said Hacker.

'Bloody mumbo-jumbo,' Ario grumbled. 'He's driving me round the bend.'

Hacker assumed a more authoritative tone. 'Just pipe down, that's all!'

Nothing more was heard from the Vicar's hammock.

Nerves drove me back to the POs' mess. By now, Zeitler was leading the debate.

'We had a pud-puller like that in minesweepers.'

'If that's a dig at me,' Frenssen said, 'you can get stuffed.'

'Balls! Who said anything about you?'

'If the cap fits, wear it,' Pilgrim inserted gleefully.

I looked round the mess. Rademacher had drawn the curtain over his bunk. Zeitler seemed to have followed Frenssen's example and taken umbrage, but Pilgrim had another contribution to make. 'I knew someone once,' he said, 'had a sort of rubber contraption he used to pull on. Neat little gadget, it was – hair round it and all.'

'Rubber?' sneered Frenssen. 'Rubber wouldn't do much for me, mate.'

'Why, got a better idea?'

'Rubber's a dead loss. I'd sooner buy myself a pound of pig's liver and cut a slit in it. I mean, if you can't get hold of the real thing at least get something like it.'

A respectful silence fell. Pilgrim said admiringly, 'Brains!' and tapped his forehead. 'Oh Mummy,' he went on in a piping falsetto, 'they're putting nasty ideas into my head!'

The galley door swung back. The door to the engine-room beyond was already open. Further conversation was drowned by the diesels. 'Ten minutes to go!' I heard someone shout. A hubbub of cursing, bustling and stamping signified that the new engine-room watch was preparing to take over. It must be 1800.

Back on the bridge again. The light would soon begin to fade. Dark clouds were already marshalled beneath a grey sky.

The thunder of engines was drowned by the inrush of air into the induction pipes on either side of the bridge.

'I wouldn't like to be in command of that lot if we attack in a pack,' the Captain said loudly under his binoculars. 'They can't travel faster than the slowest ship in the convoy. No speed, no manœuvrability. Some of those skippers are bound to be knuckle-headed. Just imagine trying to impose a pre-arranged zigzag system on men who are used to steering a straight course with precious little regard for the rule of the road . . .'

He paused. 'All the same, anyone who sails in one of their petrol-tankers must have nerves of steel – or no nerves at all. Creeping along for weeks on a lakeful of high octane? No thanks!'

He peered mutely through his binoculars for a good while.

'Tough customers,' he growled at length, 'no denying that. I heard of one who was fished out of the drink four times – three ships sunk under him and he went back for more. That takes some doing . . . Of course, they're handsomely paid. Patriotism plus hard cash – maybe that's the best formula for breeding heroes.' Drily, he added: 'Hard liquor can do it too, sometimes.'

The W/T mast had been raised. We were now transmitting bearing signals for the U-boats in the vicinity. Squash signals were also being sent at hourly intervals for the flag-stickers at Kernével – specific groups of letters from which they could deduce all they needed to know: convoy position, course, speed, number of ships, escort system, own stocks of fuel, weather conditions. Our own changes of course enabled them to form a picture of the convoy's movements. We were not permitted to attack before other boats had been summoned.

The mood on board had changed. It was unusually quiet in the various compartments. The elation seemed to have worn off. Most of the men had turned in and were trying to snatch a wink of sleep in the few hours that remained before we attacked.

All control-room installations had been cleared away long ago, all systems checked and double-checked. Nothing re-mained for the control-room POs and hands to do. The PO on watch was doing a crossword puzzle. He asked me for a French city beginning with 'L'.

'Lyon.'

'Just the job. Thanks, Lieutenant.'

The Chief appeared from aft. 'How's it shaping?' he asked.

'Well, as far as I know.'

The Chief seemed to have no pressing problems apart from his worries about fuel. Having done some ferreting around, he perched on the chart-stowage and chatted a while.

'Maybe I was wrong – maybe all that hard graft is going to pay off. These are lousy times. It was *veni, vidi, vici* in the old days – you could straddle their routes and wait till a convoy came along. Nowadays they play hard to get. You can't blame them.'

1900. The night firing sight lay ready in the control-room. Three men were busy checking the torpedo firing system. With half an ear, I heard someone bless the fact that things were starting to hum.

Back to the bridge again. It was now 1930. All the officers were up top except the second engineer. The Chief was seated on the master sight pedestal like a hunter in his hide. We were steering 180. In the west, the sky had split into horizontal blood-red streaks like a striped awning. The sun had sunk below the clouds. The streaks slowly dimmed to a pale silky green until the red glow lingered only on a few clouds whose frayed edges almost brushed the skyline. Suffused and dappled with pink, they floated along like a rare species of goldfish. Their scales suddenly flared up. They gleamed and sparkled, then paled again. The fish became mottled with dirty fingermarks.

Night climbed the eastern sky. Little by little, the heavens were invaded by the darkness we awaited so eagerly.

'Quartermaster, note this: "1930, nightfall. Convoy proceeding in echelon, four columns clearly visible. Intention, night attack." Well, there's something for the war diary.'

The Captain gave an engine order and the thunder of the diesels waned. Their beat became a reminder of our tedious wanderings in past weeks. The white mane of the bow-wave collapsed, transformed once more into two pale-green ridges.

We were far enough ahead of the convoy. Our task now, despite the quickly fading light, was to spot any alteration of course in good time and keep the convoy within striking distance.

The sky was already hung with the chalky white disc of the moon, which slowly grew brighter.

'Could be quite a while yet,' the Captain said. The words were hardly out of his mouth when the starboard after lookout reported an object astern. Our binoculars all swung in the same direction. My first sweep disclosed nothing. The Captain was muttering: 'Damn, damn, damn!'

I glanced at him to check the direction of his gaze. Then I picked up the horizon and scanned it slowly from left to right. The line between sea and sky was only just visible. Suddenly, there it was – a narrow shape scarcely darker than the sky beyond. No smoke, so the odds were in favour of an escort vessel. A corvette, a destroyer? A hunter-killer doing its evening rounds in the hope of sweeping the area clean before nightfall?

Had they already spotted us? Possibly, with a keen pair of eyes in the crow's-nest. They had us right ahead of them and were facing the lighter horizon.

I wondered why the Captain didn't act. He was still standing there, slightly crouched like a harpooner. Without lowering his glasses, he ordered both engines full ahead.

No steering order, no diving order.

The superchargers roared and the boat gave a lurch. I quailed. The seething whiteness of our wake was bound to attract attention. The hull was camouflaged grey, but this white streamer and the cloud of blue exhaust-fumes . . . The engines were belching as much exhaust gas as a defective farm tractor. The dense plume completely blotted out the horizon stern, mast-head and all. I couldn't tell if we were losing or gaining. Lack of vision gave me an ostrich-like sense of security.

The noise of the engines was infernal. We were really eating into the Chief's fuel reserves now. I noticed that he had gone below. The Captain kept his binoculars trained aft. We had not altered course by a single degree. The quartermaster was also peering aft.

'Slow ahead both!' Our wake subsided and the blue haze lifted. Tensely, the Captain and the quartermaster searched the horizon. I did the same, millimetre by millimetre. There was nothing to be seen.

'Hm,' said the Captain. Kriechbaum didn't speak. He continued to balance the glasses on his extended thumbs and middle-fingers. At last he said: 'Nothing, sir.'

'Did you note the time when we sighted her?'

'Yes, sir. 1952.'

The Captain stepped over to the hatch and called below: 'Make a note: 1952, escort vessel sighted – got that? Withdrew on surface at full speed. Escort failed to spot us because well screened by exhaust fumes – are you with me? – because well screened by exhaust fumes . . .'

I caught on at last. The diesel fumes had been intentional

– an improvised smoke-screen.

My heart was still thumping.

'Quite a performance, eh?' the Captain said. Then a new shock ran through me: a rocket climbed above the horizon. It hung there for a while, then fell back, describing an umbrella-handle curve, and was extinguished.

The Captain was the first to lower his glasses. 'What was that in aid of?'

'They're altering course,' said Kriechbaum.

'Perhaps,' the Captain growled. 'They could be calling up some support, though. Keep your eyes skinned, everyone – we don't want them breathing down our necks at this stage.' He paused. 'A rocket . . . They must be out of their minds.'

The quartermaster called below: 'Make a note: signal rocket over convoy. Add the time.'

'Strange,' the Captain growled again. He glanced at the moon. 'Let's hope we get shot of that before long.' I stood beside him, also looking up. The moon resembled a human head – round face, bald pate. 'Like a podgy old regular in a French brothel,' was the second lieutenant's simile.

'Mastheads growing higher,' Kriechbaum reported.

The convoy must have zigged towards us.

'Sheer off again,' ordered the Captain.

The moon acquired a rainbow-coloured corona.

'Hope to God they leave us in peace,' the Captain muttered. Aloud, he asked for a report on our fuel reserves.

From the swiftness with which he appeared, the Chief might have had one foot on the ladder. 'We ran a thorough check at 1800, sir. So far, operating at full speed has used up 5.25 cubic metres. We've got virtually nothing in hand.'

'There's always the coxswain's store of cooking oil,' jibed the Captain. 'If the worst comes to the worst we'll have to sail her home.'

I perched on a wooden seat beside the Oerlikon platform. It was wet with spray. Below me, white strands of foam wove themselves into ever-changing designs. Our wake shattered the reflection of the moon. A thousand tiny splinters formed and re-formed like the contents of a shaken kaleidoscope. The sea looked transparent, lit from within by small green dots. U-A's hull stood out sharp against the phosphorescent flicker of plankton. The uprights of the conservatory rail threw crisp shadows across the gratings. Combined with the linear shadows between the separate planks, they formed a sharply drawn pattern of rhomboids. The pattern shifted as I watched. The shadow of the rail glided across my boots: we were edging closer to the convoy.

All at once the sky was transfixed by a fan-shaped pencil of pale-green rays.

'Aurora borealis,' I heard the Captain say. 'That's all we needed . . .'

The rays developed into a curtain of glittering glass rods like the pendants on an old lamp at home. Pale-green radiance surged through the glass curtain in waves. Shafts of light leapt above the skyline, died, flared up, half-subsided and flared up once more, growing longer each time. The water around us scintillated as if a myriad fireflies were dancing just below the surface. Our wake became a glittering train.

'Very pretty,' said the Captain. 'Hardly what the doctor ordered, though.'

From the brief remarks that passed between him and Kriechbaum, I gathered that he was contemplating an attack on the convoy's centre from ahead. Kriechbaum wagged his head uneasily. The Captain seemed equally dubious.

'Perhaps not,' he said eventually, and turned to take another look at the moon. An almost circular hole punched into the sable tent of sky, it shed a chalky but unusually powerful light. A handful of clouds drifted on the horizon like grey ice-floes. As soon as the moonlight struck them they glowed, in places with sapphirine splendour.

The sea became a vast sheet of crumpled silver paper which winked and sparkled and multiplied the moon's white light a thousandfold. The water seemed like a motionless, scintillating plain. My thoughts turned suddenly to our last night ashore at the Bar Royal. Thomsen . . . No time for that, not now.

We defied the moonlight to draw closer, the Captain relying on our dark background and a lack of alertness among the look-outs in the escorted ships. U-A lay low in the water and her bow-wave was negligible at this speed. If we had presented our narrow silhouette to the enemy, we should have been almost invisible. Unfortunately we were not in a position to do this. Our present course and speed kept us parallel to the convoy and slightly ahead.

Why no more escorts? Had we already encountered everything the British could offer so large a convoy in the way of flank protection – were we already between the convoy and its outer ring of defences?

The Captain would know what to do – this wasn't his first convoy. He was familiar with the enemy's habits. On one occasion he had actually watched the progress of a counter-attack on U-A by a destroyer captain who assumed her to be deep-dived in a position which she had long vacated. He cut the motors, hung the boat on her periscope, and watched the destroyer fire pattern after pattern of depth-charges. He was even said to have given a running commentary for the benefit of the crew.

No running commentary now. 'Definitely four columns' was his only remark in the next fifteen minutes.

We had been dawdling for a considerable time; presumably our sprint from the escort had taken us too far ahead of the convoy. Kernével must have summoned a number of U-boats which had yet to arrive. Our only task for the moment was to maintain contact and transmit bearing signals.

'How about taking her in a bit closer?'

The question was meant for Kriechbaum.

The quartermaster merely grunted, keeping his glasses trained on the convoy. The Captain seemed to construe this as an affirmative. He gave a steering order which pointed our bow obliquely at the convoy's line of advance.

'Action stations.' The Captain's voice sounded ill-oiled. He had to cough to clear his vocal chords. A succession of shouted readiness reports came from below : 'Chief Engineer, engine-room at action stations!' – 'Chief Engineer, control-room at action stations!' Then the Chief : 'Machinery spaces and control-room at action stations, sir!' Even then the shouting was not over : 'First Lieutenant, torpedo armament at action stations!' Finally, the unmistakably Hitler Youthful voice of the Number One : 'Torpedo armament at action stations, sir!'

The night sight was handed up. The first lieutenant fitted it on to the master sight – gingerly, as if he were handling a crate of eggs.

From the convoy's point of view, we were up moon. I couldn't understand why the Captain had remained on this side of the convoy instead of going down moon. Presumably, he was putting himself in the enemy's shoes. Why should a U-boat choose to operate on the moon side, where the sea shone brighter than in broad daylight?

In other words, he was gambling on the likelihood that flank protection would be weaker on the moon side. He must be right, too, or the enemy would have spotted us long before.

I could picture the disposition of the convoy and its escorts with the clarity of an aerial photograph : an elongated rectangle deployed in four columns, the precious tankers stationed centrally. An advance-guard of two corvettes racing back and forth in a wide arc, their task to stop any U-boat diving to attack the freighters from ahead. More corvettes or destroyers scurrying to and fro as flank protection – down moon, of course. Then, at an appreciable distance from the herd, the stern escorts or hunter-killers, support vessels not deployed for the convoy's immediate protection because U-boats seldom indulged in a stern chase. Their job was to take over the U-boats put down by the escorting corvettes and deal with them while the convoy ploughed on.

2000. It occurred to me that I might need a second night film for my camera. I had hardly reached the control-room when a medley of voices came from above. Hurriedly I regained the bridge. 'Ship coming up,' the Captain said. 'There she is, drawing in from the outside.'

I caught my breath. The freighters were to port of us, but the Captain was facing aft. I followed the direction of his gaze, and there it was: a thin shape jutting above the sky-line.

What now? Dive, give up – call it a day?

'Full ahead both.' The Captain's voice was flat and unemotional. Was he going to try the same trick twice?

'Port ten '

Obviously not. A minute passed before he made his intention clear. 'We're going to close the convoy.'

I had just re-trained my glasses on the freighters when Kriechbaum said, in a tone that could have been fractionally more matter-of-fact: 'Mast-heads growing higher, sir.'

From one minute to the next, we had been impaled on the horns of a dilemma. Either we must dive to escape the rapidly approaching destroyer, or we should find ourselves far too close to the convoy.

Our wake streamed out behind us like a train. A plume of exhausts fumes billowed above it, screening us from view. Perhaps it would work a second time – I certainly couldn't see the shadowy destroyer through the haze.

I swung my glasses yet again. The convoy was right ahead of us.

'Damnation!' rasped the Captain.

'Vessel seems to be dropping back,' Kriechbaum reported. Minutes of suspense dragged by before he broke the spell. 'Range increasing.'

The Captain had not been watching the destroyer. His whole attention was focused on the dark shapes immediately ahead.

'Ship's head?'

'Zero-five-zero, sir.'

'Starboard fifteen. Steer one-four-zero.'

My nerves were still jangling.

'They're pretty well spread out . . .' the Captain mused. Only then did he revert to the destroyer. 'Lucky we didn't dive. That was close.' Abruptly, he said: 'Well, Kriechbaum, what do you think?'

The quartermaster withdrew his eyes from the binoculars but kept his elbows propped on the bridge rail. 'Better than evens, sir. It ought to work.'

'Bound to.'

Peculiar dialogue, I thought. I could only conclude that it was a form of mutual encouragement.

I glanced quickly into the conning-tower. The covers had been removed from the deflection calculator, firing-interval calculator and torpedo firing switches. The dials emitted a bluish glow.

'Time?' the Captain called below.

'2010, sir.'

It was incredible to me that we should be allowed to manoeuvre so close to the convoy unchallenged, as if we belonged to it.

'I don't like the look of that one over there,' the Captain murmured to Kriechbaum.

Turning in the same direction, I picked up the shape in my binoculars. It was at a narrow angle. Closing or going away – inclination 30 degrees or 150? I couldn't tell, but it certainly wasn't a freighter. The Captain was already turning away again.

The first lieutenant fiddled nervously with the master sight, peered through the eyepieces, then straightened up and stared over the bridge casing in the direction of the convoy. The Captain, sensing his uneasiness, enquired with a hint of mockery: 'Having trouble with your eyesight, Number One?'

Again and again he turned to glance at the moon. 'Pity we can't shoot the bloody thing down . . .' he said bitterly.

I pinned my hopes on the thick banks of cloud which lay heaped on the horizon and were slowly ascending – but so slowly that it would be an appreciable time before they reached the moon.

'They're zigging to starboard!' said the Captain. Kriechbaum echoed him a moment later.

Sure enough, the shapes had grown narrower.

The Captain altered course 40 degrees to starboard.

'Surely they aren't going to bugger us about at this stage?'

I was standing so close to the master sight that I could hear the first lieutenant breathing. It worried me that I had lost sight of the paler shadow.

'Time?'

'2028, sir.'

SECOND ATTACK

The moon had become still whiter and more glacial. The sky surrounding its sharply defined disc was clear, but a cloud was advancing from the horizon like the vanguard of a whole army.

I had eyes for this cloud alone. It progressed satisfactorily for a while, then slowed until its ascent almost ceased. Worse still, it grew threadbare and began to break up. Finally it dissolved until nothing remained.

The quartermaster swore sibilantly.

Then another cloud showed signs of detaching itself from the horizon. It was denser and plumper than the first. The wind nudged it slightly aside, just as we wished. Nobody swore now, as though swearing might offend it.

I looked away from the cloud and back to the horizon. Picking out one particular freighter in my binoculars, I could clearly distinguish her forecastle, bridge superstructure and deck-houses aft.

The Captain was telling the first lieutenant his intentions. 'I plan to approach and fire immediately. After firing, I'll turn to port at once. If that cloud behaves itself, we'll go in straight away.'

The first lieutenant passed the requisite orders to the calculator, which was operated by one man in the conning-tower and duplicated by another in the control-room.

'Clear tubes 1 to 4 for surface firing.'

All four bow torpedo tubes were flooded.

The fore-ends reported by voice-pipe: 'Tubes 1 to 4 ready for surface firing.'

'Calculators follow master sight,' ordered the first lieutenant. 'Bridge firing.'

The words of command flowed smoothly from his lips. His homework was paying off. At least he could learn by rote.

The PO manning the calculator in the conning-tower confirmed each order as it was carried out.

The Captain behaved as if the conversation had nothing at all to do with him. Only the tautness of his stance betrayed how intently he was listening.

First lieutenant to conning-tower PO: 'Angle on the bow three-zero left – range three thousand metres – torpedo speed three-zero – depth three metres – follow for bearing.'

The first lieutenant did not have to worry about the correct angle of lead. That was worked out by the calculator, which was now directly linked with the gyro compass and the master sight on the bridge, and fed the necessary information direct to the torpedoes. Their course mechanism followed automatically because every alteration of course and bearing was transmitted to them in the form of a course correction. All the first lieutenant had to do was keep the target in the illuminated cross-wires of the binoculars mounted on the master sight.

He bent over the sight. 'Stand by to check bearing – now!'

'It's now or never,' muttered the Captain. He took another look at the moon. The second cloud had come to a full stop, like a barrage balloon which had reached its predetermined height. It hovered three thumbs'-breadth below the moon and refused to budge.

'Bloody thing!' The quartermaster shook his fist at the sky – an emotional outburst which surprised me, coming from a man as impassive as Kriechbaum. But I had no time to savour my surprise. The Captain swung round sharply and rapped out a series of orders: 'Full ahead both. Hard-a-port. Attacking. Open bow-caps.'

The orders were echoed in a hoarse shout from below. U-A's bow was already beginning to traverse the skyline in search of her shadowy prey.

'Midships – meet her – steer zero-nine-zero!' We were now racing straight for the dark shapes, which loomed larger moment by moment.

Our bow sliced the sea's silver skin like a ploughshare, flinging aside luminous sods of liquid. The bow-wave rose and sparkled with a myriad points of light and the fore-casing reared higher in the water. Spray showered the bridge. The engines awoke sympathetic tremors in the casing.

'Target identification,' said the Captain.

The first lieutenant bent over his sight.

'We'll take the two that are overlapping. See the ones I mean – three, left of the single freighter? Double shot on the larger, single shots for the others. On the double shot, take the leading edge of the bridge and just before the mainmast.'

I was standing close behind the Captain. His slightly lowered head jutted at the target ships. The pulse in my throat beat hard. My thoughts whirled. The thunder of the racing engines, the shadows ahead, the silvery sea, the moon, the headlong dash across the surface . . . We were a submarine, not a surface ship!

The first lieutenant kept the target in his binocular sight. Head down, he passed bearings in a crisp and businesslike voice. His right hand was already gripping the firing-lever.

'Lock on tubes 1 and 2 – bearing zero-six-five – follow for bearing.'

'Bearing?'

'Bearing zero-seven-zero . . . zero-eight-zero.'

The Captain's voice: 'Tubes 1 and 2, fire when ready.'

Seconds later the first lieutenant reported: 'Tubes 1 and 2 fired.'

I strained all my senses but could detect nothing – no report, no jolt. U-A sped on, even closer to the freighters.

They hadn't spotted us!

'Lock on tube 3.'

'Tube 3 fired.'

'Port ten,' ordered the Captain.

Again the bow swung questingly across the line of ships.

'Lock on tube 4,' I heard the first lieutenant say. He waited for the next target to centre itself. 'Tube 4 . . . fired!'

Just at that moment I sighted a long shadow close to the target ship – slightly paler than the rest, probably camouflaged grey.

'Hard-a-port. Lock on stern tube!' That was the Captain's voice. U-A heeled ponderously as she turned. The shadowy procession swung to starboard.

The quartermaster called: 'Vessel turning towards!'

Our stern was pointing at the pale shape, but it narrowed as I watched. I could even discern a white fringe of bow-wave.

'Fire 5! Hard-a-starboard!' yelled the Captain. U-A had scarcely begun to turn when an orange shaft of lightning rent the gloom, followed almost instantly by another. A huge fist flailed me to my knees. There was a sharp hiss which seemed to transfix me like cold steel.

'The buggers are shooting – ALARM!' bellowed the Captain.

I leapt for the hatch and dropped through. Sea-boots trampled my shoulders. I sprang aside and cowered against the chart-table, bent double with pain. Somebody rolled across the deck in front of me.

'Dive dive dive!' the Captain shouted, and a moment later: 'Hard-a-port!' A cataract of sea-water preceded him down the ladder. High speed helped to increase our bow-down angle, but he still ordered all hands forward.

'That was damned good,' he gasped as he hit the deck-plates.

Rather laboriously, I gathered that this was a tribute to the British gunners. Men stampeded through the control-room, some showing the whites of their eyes. Everything started to slide. The leather jackets and binoculars hanging on either side of the forward door stood well away from the bulkhead.

The needle of the depth-gauge rotated rapidly until the Chief levelled us off. The jackets and glasses slowly nestled against the bulkhead: we were horizontal again.

I tried to catch the Captain's eye but failed. My reaction to the enemy's marksmanship was less professional than his. It suddenly occurred to me that our torpedoes were still running.

'That was a destroyer,' the Captain said. 'I thought as much.' He sounded breathless. I could see his chest rise and fall.

He surveyed us as though to assure himself that we were all present. 'Won't be long now,' he said in an undertone.

The destroyer – the rapidly closing range! The Captain must have known all the time that the paler shadow was no freighter. British destroyers wore grey paint, like our own.

A destroyer racing straight at our diving position. No, it wouldn't be long now.

'Ninety metres – easy,' said the Captain.

The Chief repeated his order in a subdued voice. He had perched behind the planesmen and was intently watching the depth-gauge.

Someone whispered: 'Now we're for it!'

I tried to weigh heavy, make myself small, retire into an invulnerable carapace.

The torpedoes! Had they all missed? Was it possible? Four bow shots – one double and two singles – followed by the stern shot as we turned away. No doubt the fish from No. 5 had been imprecisely aimed, but what of the others? Why no bangs?

The Chief's head inclined still closer to the round eye of the main depth-gauge. Sweat beaded his forehead like drops of dew. I could see individual drops combining to leave moist snail-tracks down his face. He drew the back of his right hand nervously across his brow.

Snail-tracks . . . We were barely moving ourselves. They would be overhead any time now. What was wrong? Why no bangs?

We all stood hunched and silent – lemurs clad in leather. The depth-gauge needle pivoted another ten subdivisions.

I tried to think clearly. How long since we dived? The destroyer's speed? Misses – all misses. Bloody torpedoes! The usual trouble – sabotage. What else could it be? Five defective torpedoes, and the Brits would be tearing the arse out of us any moment. The Old Man must have been crazy. That was more like a torpedo-boat attack. Heads down and charge, flat out across the surface. How their eyes must have popped! First he acted so calmly, and then that . . . How many metres range was it? How many seconds for a destroyer to reach us at maximum revs? Those muddled steering orders! The Old Man had dived under full helm – most unusual. What did it mean? Then I caught on: the enemy had seen us dive to starboard. It was a bluff on the Old Man's part. I hoped his opposite number wasn't equally crafty.

The Captain had propped one thigh on the chart-table. All I could see of him was his bent back and, above the turned-up collar of his sheepskin waistcoat, a dirty white cap.

The quartermaster's eyes were almost shut. The slits between his lids might have been scribed in wood with a keen-edged graving tool. His lips were indrawn and clamped between his teeth. One hand gripped the search periscope for support. Only two paces away, the control-room PO's face was a pale blurred patch in the gloom.

The silence was broken by a muffled, muted sound like a blow on a slack drumskin.

'That was a hit,' the Captain said softly. He raised his head. I could see his face now: narrowed eyes, mouth set in a mirth-less grin of concentration.

A second muffled thud.

'So was that.' Drily he added: 'Damned long running-time.'

The second lieutenant had straightened up. He clenched both fists and bared his gritted teeth like an orang-outang. His urge to shout was unmistakable, but he only gulped. The grimace lingered on his face for some seconds.

The needle of the depth-gauge continued its slow progress round the dial.

Another drumbeat.

'Number three,' someone muttered.

Was that all – just three muffled detonations? I shut my eyes tight. Every nerve in my body seemed centred on my auditory canals. Nothing more?

Then came the sound of a sheet being ripped down the middle while another was rapidly shredded. A fierce grating of metal, and we were suddenly engulfed by sounds of rending, rasping, snapping and breaking.

I had held my breath for so long that I found myself gasping for air. What did it mean?

The Captain raised his head again.

'Two going down – two, wouldn't you say, Quartermaster?'

That noise – were those the bulkheads giving way?

'They won't sail again.' The syllables were toneless, breathed rather than spoken.

Nobody moved. Nobody uttered a yell of triumph. The control-room PO stood near me in his customary position, motionless, one hand on the ladder, head facing the depth-gauges. The two planesmen sat encased in stiff folds of rubber. The needle of the pale depth-gauge eye was stationary. With a start, I noticed that the planesmen were still wearing their shiny wet sou'westers.

'They took long enough. I'd written them off.'

The Captain's voice was its usual bearlike growl. The cracking, snapping, groaning and rending continued unabated.

'Well, they've had it . . .'

A sudden fearful blow sent me reeling. There was a tinkle of broken glass.

I hauled myself erect by the nearest pipe, automatically took two unsteady paces forward, barged into someone, and subsided on to the door coaming.

We were off again. It was time to pay for our fun. I clamped my left shoulder fiercely against the metal frame and gripped the pipe that ran beneath my thighs. My old haunt. The paintwork felt smooth under my thumbs in contrast to the brittle, crumbly rust on the underside of the pipe. My hands tightened like a pair of clamps. I stared intently at the knuckles of my right hand, then my left, as though staring would reinforce their grip.

And the next?

Tortoiselike, I warily raised my head – ready to retract it at a moment's notice. All I could hear was someone clearing his nose.

My gaze was magnetically drawn by the Old Man's cap. He moved aside a little. Now I could see the red-and-white scales flanking the gauge-glass. They reminded me of harlequins' swords or the outsize lollipops on wooden sticks which Parisian confectioners stuck in glasses, like flowers, or the lighthouse on our port beam when we left St Nazaire. That was also painted red and white.

The coaming bucked like an unbroken horse. A deafening explosion almost rent my eardrums. Blow after blow rained on our hull as though someone had sown the depths with slabs of gun-cotton and was detonating them in quick succession.

A multi-charge pattern.

Good shooting. That was the second approach. They weren't stupid – our bluff hadn't worked.

Evything inside me seemed to shrivel.

The sea around us roared and gurgled. We rocked to and fro in the unseen turbulence until water stopped rushing back into the cavities made by the exploding depth-charges. The gurgling ceased, but we could still hear the muffled rending and snapping of metal.

The Captain chuckled insanely. 'They're going down all right. We won't have to finish them off. Pity we can't watch the buggers sink, that's all.'

I blinked in surprise, but he had already reverted to his habitually unemotional tone. 'Two down, one to go.'

I suddenly heard the voice of the hydrophone operator. My powers of perception must have been partly suspended. Herrmann had undoubtedly been giving a running commentary.

'Propellers bearing three-three-zero, closing fast.'

The Captain kept his eyes glued to the operator's lips. 'Well, any change?'

Herrmann hesitated before replying. At length he reported: 'Propellers drawing astern.'

The Captain promptly ordered more speed. The mists at last cleared from my brain. I could follow what was going on and share in the general hope that the destroyer would cross our course well astern, as the Captain seemed to intend.

We still had no idea which way the destroyer would turn in readiness for a fresh attempt to overrun us. The Captain must have been betting on port, because he ordered us to starboard.

ERA Franz came through the control-room. His face was chalky white. Beads of sweat glistened on his forehead, fat as glycerine. Although there was no sea running, he steadied himself with each hand in turn. He called loudly for some fuses for the gyro compass.

The Captain rounded on him angrily. 'Keep your voice down!'

We were shaken by four depth-charges in quick succession

– almost a single concussion – but the underwater eddies failed to reach us.

'Astern, miles astern,' scoffed the Captain. 'They'll have to do better than that.'

Raising one leg, he propped it on the chart-stowage and started to unbutton his sheepskin waistcoat. The Old Man was making himself comfortable. He thrust his hands into the pockets of his leather trousers and turned to Kriechbaum.

Another single detonation, not close but remarkably prolonged. The bubbling roar seemed to last for ever. In the midst of the muffled tumult, the Captain said: 'They're spitting in the wrong place.'

The destroyer seemed to have lost her bearings – the next two explosions were equally distant – but we were still harassed by the acoustic effect of every depth-charge. The enemy must know how demoralizing depth-charges could be, even those that exploded well off target.

'Quartermaster, take a note . . .'

'Yessir.'

'Twenty-two-forty, closed to attack – it was twenty-two-forty, wasn't it? Convoy proceeding in four columns, closer than originally thought. Destroyers clearly visible ahead and up moon . . .'

Clearly visible – destroyers clearly visible ahead and up moon? That meant there must have been more than one. My mouth went dry. The Captain hadn't said a word about that. On the contrary, he had acted as if there were no escorts on our attacking side.

'Clearly visible – got that? Approached on starboard bow of second column – are you with me?'

'Yes, sir . . . Starboard bow of second column.'

'Moon extremely bright . . .'

'You can say that again,' murmured the second lieutenant, too low for the Captain to hear.

'. . . extremely bright but insufficient for an attack from dived.'

I had to get up to make way for some left-overs from the 'all hands forward' order. They tiptoed past me, balancing like tightrope-walkers.

The Captain took us deeper. He then maintained the same depth and course for about five minutes. Not until the hydrophone operator reported a new approach did he take us still deeper. He was now gambling that the enemy had failed to spot his second hydroplane manœuvre and would set their charges to explode at the depth we had maintained long enough for the destroyer's detector-gear to register.

The next reports from the hydrophone booth made it clear that the destroyer was on our track.

Despite the urgency in Herrmann's voice, the Captain issued no new steering orders. I knew why. He was deferring any course alteration until the last moment so that the destroyer would be unable to respond to our avoiding manœuvre. A destroyer could turn much faster than a submarine. On the other hand, a destroyer travelling at high speed suffered from an inability to change direction fast. Her relatively shallow draught gave her little purchase on the water.

'Pretty good shooting,' the Captain said. 'A bit too shallow, that's all . . .' He shrugged. 'Hard-a-starboard. Full ahead port.'

All the auxiliary machinery had been switched off long ago : wireless transformer, ventilation fans – even the gyro compass. I hardly dared breathe.

They ought to have got us on their first approach, being so close to our diving position, but the Captain had been too clever for them. First he presented narrow silhouette to narrow silhouette, then he turned away to starboard and dived, then he swung hard-a-port. Standard penalty-taker's technique : aim at one side of the net and shoot at the other.

The Captain gave me a nod. 'We haven't shaken him off yet. Tough customer – knows his stuff.'

I managed a noncommittal grunt.

'They're bound to be feeling a bit narked,' he added.

We went deeper still : 150 metres. To judge by Herrmann's reports, the destroyer had us on a leash. It was only a matter of time before she increased speed and launched another counter-attack.

The Captain increased speed himself. Risky, because the faster our motors ran the more noise they made. I felt that their hum must be audible for miles, but supposed that the Captain was making a determined attempt to get out of range of the enemy's Asdics.

'Propeller noises getting louder,' the hydrophone operator reported in an undertone.

At a whispered order from the Captain, we reduced speed again. So that was no good – our bid to escape had failed. They were still with us. They refused to be shaken off. They would rather let their charges plod on unescorted than abandon that rare treat, a located U-boat.

The hull was struck with a giant sledge-hammer. Almost simultaneously, the Captain issued shouted orders to pump out the bilge and increase speed. As soon as the din outside waned he stopped pumping and ordered the motors slow ahead. 'Thirteen, fourteen,' said Kriechbaum, and made two more chalk marks on his board. The last explosion must have been a double one. Before that, four.

Another three or four blows, so violent that the deck-plates rattled. I could feel them jolt my diaphragm. Gingerly, I turned my head in time to see Kriechbaum make another four chalk-marks.

The Captain hadn't budged a millimetre. He kept one eye on the depth-gauge and one ear cocked for the latest news from the hydrophone booth.

'I don't think they like us.'

That was the midshipman. Having said his piece, Ullmann went scarlet and stared at the deck. The words must have slipped out. Everyone had heard him. The quartermaster was grinning. The Captain turned his head. I detected a momentary flicker of amusement on his face.

Gravel! Their Asdic had located us. I felt as if we were suddenly illuminated from all sides, exposed to a thousand eyes.

'Bastards!' Isenberg muttered, half to himself. I too felt momentarily overcome with hatred, but of what or whom? Who was the enemy? That shadow, that narrow silhouette a shade paler than the merchantmen – that was all I had managed to see of our adversary. We were blind – we could no longer see, only hear, so why no news from our listener-in-chief? The Captain blinked impatiently. Nothing? Still nothing?

Every ear turneth unto Thee, O Lord, for Thou wilt bestow great joy upon all them that harken to Thy word – something like that. The Vicar would know. I could barely recognize him in the dim lighting.

Herrmann raised his eyebrows, a sign that our ears would soon be well catered for.

They have ears, and hear not: *Psalms*, cxv. Eardrum, ear wax, earlobe. What else? Oh yes, earwig.

I was all ears – I was one enormous ear. My auditory canals were knotted with nerves.

A flea in the ear, little pitchers have long ears, in one ear and out the other, turn a deaf ear – ah, if only I could!

I wondered how things looked up top.

A murderous glare. All searchlights on and the sky thick with parachute flares to ensure that the arch-enemy didn't sneak away. All barrels fully depressed and ready to vomit death if they drove us to the surface.

The hydrophone operator reported: 'Propeller noises bearing zero-two-zero, getting louder.' A moment's hesitation. 'Running in to attack.'

Two swingeing blows, this time with a battle-axe. Again the savage roar and gurgle, and then – while the tumult was still at its height – another two blows.

I had opened my mouth to protect my eardrums. A relic of my gunnery instruction. I had opened my mouth often enough in the past because the detonation would have been intolerable otherwise. Now, I was on the receiving end.

There was no escape, no point in flinging myself to the deck. Dig in? A hollow mockery. All I had underfoot was an iron deck-plate adorned with cunt-patterns, as Zeitler called the thousands of tiny non-slip rhomboids. It was all I could do to choke back claustrophobia and the urge to run wildly in any direction. I mentally nailed my boots to the deck and prayed for leaden soles like the colourful little tumbler-dolls that bobbed up again and again, no matter how often one knocked them down.

All in all, I was lucky. I couldn't be up-ended either. The bulkhead doorway that enclosed my cowering form was as good a place as any, under the circumstances

I relaxed my grip on the pipe. Apparently we could take a breather, unwind our taut sinews, waggle our jaws, loosen our limbs, slacken our stomach muscles, let the blood course freely. Only now did I realize how painful my tensed position had been.

We were entirely governed by the enemy. They could even dictate our physical posture: we drew in our heads and flinched as we waited for the next depth-charge, straightened up and relaxed when it had gone off. Even the Captain took care to reserve his derisive chuckles for the gurgling aftermath of each counter-attack.

The hydrophone operator half-opened his mouth. My lungs froze in mid-breath. What was it? If only I knew the exact location of the last pattern, the range at which it had exploded, the distance we had covered since diving. It seemed as though the chase had taken us nowhere since our first fruitless bid to escape. Turn to starboard, turn to port, rise and dive, rise and dive – we might have been riding a slow switchback. That was it: we had gained no ground at all. The enemy had spotted each of our attempts to sneak off at a tangent.

Herrmann closed his mouth and opened it again. He looked like a carp in an aquarium. Now he reported a new approach.

'In contact,' he called a moment later. He could have saved himself the trouble. The pink-pink was audible to everyone on board, from the fore-ends to the motor-room.

We were locked in the enemy's supersonic beam. The men on the surface would now be turning steel handwheels and combing their three-dimensional environs with beamed impulses. Chirp-chirp, pink-pink . . .

Asdic, I recalled, could only be used at speeds of up to thirteen knots or thereabouts. Fast approaches rendered a destroyer blind. At high speed, Asdic suffered appreciably from the interference caused by a ship's engine noise and the turbulence from her screws. Luckily for us, because we could take advantage of this fact to make a minor change of position at the last moment. The enemy skipper naturally realized that we would not sit still when we heard him approach. On the other hand, his Asdic operators could not tell him which way we had dodged. For that, he had to rely on his imagination – or gambler's instinct.

Lucky for us, too, that the enemy's patent gadget couldn't tell him our precise depth. Here, Nature came to our aid. Water, to quote the Chief, was not just water: it formed layers and contained sediment. The salt content and physical characteristics of the various layers were dissimilar. Asdic impulses were interrupted by them – in fact Asdic detection became inaccurate if a U-boat suddenly left a warm layer and entered a cold one. Accuracy was also impaired by layers rich in plankton, and Asdic operators could not make reliable adjustments to their picture of a U-boat's position because they were ignorant of the depth at which these deceptive layers occurred.

Herrmann busily worked his wheel.

'Bearing?' the Captain hissed in the direction of the hydrophone booth.

'Propellers bearing three-five-zero, sir.'

Before long, we could all hear them with the naked ear.

'Ritchipitchipitchipitchi . . .' That was no high-speed approach. The destroyer was maintaining a speed precisely compatible with accurate detection. Her Asdic impulses bounced off us like hail.

Another pass. Four or five detonations. Close. I saw, projected on my eyelids, jets of flame, huge balls of St Elmo's fire, the glitter of chrysoprase, sparks cascading round dark-red incandescent cores, the pale glare of naphtha flames, whirling Chinese fire-wheels, dazzling white excrescences, pencils of amethyst light transfixing the darkness, bronze fountains sprouting fire in every colour of the rainbow.

'Dummy run,' whispered the Captain.

His description, not mine.

A huge hand buffeted the U-boat and lifted her. I felt our sudden upsurge in my knee-joints. The needle of the depth-gauge jumped. There was another tinkle of glass and the lights failed. An eternity of cramped heartbeats. Then the emergency lighting came on.

The Captain was gnawing his lower lip. He had to decide whether to match the depth of the last pattern or move nearer the surface.

He settled for a combination of full helm and hard-a-dive. We performed another switchback turn and descent. Where best to hide? Above, below, right, left? The last pattern sounded as if it had exploded on the port bow, but above or below us?

We were off again. Herrmann continued to report the enemy's movements.

The next blow caught me full on the third dorsal vertebra. It was followed almost instantly by two forearm smashes on the neck and the back of the skull.

Smoke was seeping from the steering position. Fire, on top of all our other troubles. Some leads must be smouldering – a short, probably.

Take it easy. Nothing could happen to this sardine-can – *I* was aboard: *I* was immortal. With me aboard, U-A was immune.

No mistake, the switchboard was on fire. Follow instructions: *Keep Calm. Fight Fire From Below.* Immune, my brain repeated – immune, immune, immune!

The control-room PO leapt at the fire. Flames and smoke almost hid him from view. Two or three men went to his assistance. I noticed that the boat had taken a bow-down angle, gradually increasing. 'Main line fractured!' I heard someone call, but that couldn't be the whole story. Why didn't the Chief pump aft? What were trimming tanks for, if not to level us off?

In spite of the destroyer's nearness, the Captain ordered full ahead. We had taken too much water. We couldn't hold the boat statically. We needed the power of the screws and their waterstream on the hydroplanes to bring the bow up fast. The Old Man would never have risked the noise under normal circumstances, because at these revs we might as well be wearing a cow-bell. Sink or increase speed – that was the choice.

Our motors, screws and pumps must be clearly audible on the surface. The Brits could have switched off their Asdic and saved amps.

Apart from his intricate course calculations, the Captain was now beset by a persistent depth-keeping problem. Our condition had become unstable. The rule-book no longer applied.

Everything was wet, filmed with condensation.

'Port stern gland leaking!' someone called from aft. Another voice from forward: '. . . valve leaking!' I didn't listen closely. I was past racking my brains over which valve it could be.

Four thuds in quick succession, then an insane gurgle and roar as the black flood poured back into the caverns blown by the depth-charges.

'Thirty-three – four – five . . . Thirty-six,' Kriechbaum counted loudly. They were close.

The gauge showed 120 metres.

We went down another 40 and swung to port.

The next explosion rattled my teeth. I could hear someone snuffling. It sounded like the Vicar. Surely he wasn't going to break down and weep?

'Good timing,' the Captain interpolated drily at the height of the pattern that followed.

I tensed my stomach muscles as though they had to shield my vital organs against the unimaginable pressure on our hull. Minutes passed before I dared detach my left hand from the pipe beneath me. It rose of its own accord. The knuckles slid across my forehead on a slipway of chill perspiration. I noticed that my whole back was equally wet and cold.

The Captain's face looked hazy.

Of course, the smoke from the steering position! Although the smouldering had ceased, smoke still hung in the air. The sour smell made me heave. I felt a dull pressure inside my skull. Holding my breath only aggravated it.

Not long now. The destroyer would soon have completed her regaining circle. That much of a respite the bastards had to grant us whether they liked it or not.

More Asdic. Another two or three brisk showers of gravel. A cold hand stole under my collar and wandered down my back. I shivered.

The pressure in my head became intolerable. What now? Why no action? Every whisper had died. Drops of condensed water plipped and plopped at one-second intervals. Mutely I counted them. When I got to twenty-two, the hammer struck.

It doubled me up and slammed my head on to my chest.

Was I deaf? I saw the deck-plates dance, but it was seconds before I heard their metallic rattle, mingled with a creaking, groaning sound. That was the pressure hull. U-A rocked and lurched convulsively in the raging eddies. Men staggered into each other. The turbulence seemed never-ending.

Another double concussion. The submarine groaned aloud. More jangling and clattering.

The Brits were being thrifty now. No more big patterns. Instead, two depth-charges at a time, probably with varied depth settings. I still hadn't dared to relax when the hammer hit us again with enormous force.

Quite close to me, someone was breathing fast. Saliva rattled in his throat. The stertorous gasps gave way to groans, almost as if he had been wounded. I was puzzled for a moment, then dismissed the idea. Drown we might, but shrapnel couldn't touch us.

The Captain would have to think of something new. No hope of sneaking away – the Asdic impulses had us by the throat. They must have some first-class operators up there, men who didn't bluff easily. How much time left? How long did they take to complete their turn and come in for another attack?

Lucky for us the enemy had to fire their charges at speed. If the swine could creep up on us with their Asdic pinking and dump the things over the side when they were immediately overhead, the cat-and-mouse game would have been over long ago. Fortunately they had to approach at some speed to avoid cracking their own hull when the depth-charges exploded.

What was the Captain up to? He had knit his brows. I could gauge the intensity of his thoughts from the way his forehead was working. Would he again manage, at the very last moment, to steer us away in the right direction, at the right speed, at the right depth? It was time for him to open his mouth and give an order. Or had he resigned, thrown up the sponge?

A vast sheet of canvas was suddenly ripped down the centre. The Captain's hoarse voice rose above the din. 'Pump out! Hard-a-port! Full ahead both!'

U-A lurched forward. The pumps were inaudible in the general tumult. Men staggered and clung to pipes. The Captain sat well braced against the chart-table. Kriechbaum gripped his desk.

With a sudden flash of inspiration, I understood the gamble

the Captain had just taken. Asdic notwithstanding, he had doggedly maintained course. A new trick – a variation served up for the first time. It was obvious. The destroyer captain was no novice either. He didn't dash blindly for the spot where we had last been located. We knew when he was making his approach. We also knew that he knew he could not keep us pin-pointed at high speed, that we would try to evade his line of approach and change depth. But whether we jinked to port or starboard, up or down, was a matter for him of guesswork. So, just for a change, the Old Man had dispensed with evasion and simply maintained course and speed. Bluff and double bluff.

'Time?' asked the Captain.

Kriechbaum checked. '0330, sir.'

'Really?' The word emerged in a bass drawl. Even the Captain seemed to think the show had lasted long enough.

'Surprising,' he murmured. 'I suppose they want to make quite sure.'

Nothing happened for a while. The Captain took us deeper, then deeper still.

'Time?'

'0345, sir.'

Unless my senses were playing tricks, even the gyro compass had been switched off. The submarine was hushed except for the rhythmical dripping of condensed water.

Had we done it? Fifteen minutes at Slow One. The stillness was broken by the grisly noises referred to by the Captain as 'death-watch beetle'. The pressure-tightness of our cigar-tube was being brutally tested at extreme depth. U-A's steel skin must be bulging inwards between her frames. All our wooden fittings creaked and groaned.

We were back at 200 metres, more than twice the recommended depth, creeping through the black depths at a speed of two knots with our hull subjected to the immense weight of a column of water two-thirds the height of the Eiffel Tower.

Depth-keeping had become a feat of equilibrium. If the boat dipped now, her tortured frames might yield to external pressure. Every centimetre counted. Was the Captain relying on British ignorance of our maximum diving depth? We ourselves never uttered the magic figure, but employed a euphemism: 'three times r plus sixty'. It sounded like an alchemist's formula. Were the enemy really ignorant of the true value of 'r'? Every German stoker knew what it stood for, so the number of initiates probably exceeded fifty thousand.

No reports from the hydrophone booth. I couldn't believe we had escaped. The bastards were probably lying stopped, biding their time. They knew they were almost on top of us. Our depth was the only factor missing from their calculations. The Chief moved his head uneasily to and fro. Nothing seemed to fray his nerves so much as 'death-watch beetle'.

Two detonations of passable intensity. The gurgling ceased abruptly. Our bilge-pump overlapped it by several seconds. Surely they must have heard the damned thing! Why couldn't we build quieter pumps?

The longer we maintained this depth, the more agonizing my awareness of our vulnerability. We carried no armour-plating. Nothing stood between us and the pressure outside, not to mention the shock-waves from exploding depth-charges, but two centimetres of sheet steel.

'Damned long show,' whispered the Captain. If he made such an admission, we must be up against some pretty stubborn customers.

I tried to picture what was happening on the surface. It wasn't so long since I had been on the side of the hunter. An exact reversal of roles, except that the British had their highly sophisticated Asdic whereas our only aid was the hydrophone: electronics versus acoustics.

Listen – run – in – fire – turn – listen – run – in – fire. Shallow setting, deep setting. Then the *pièce de résistance*: the multi-charge pattern – a salvo of up to a dozen canisters, set to explode simultaneously. There wasn't much to choose between us and the British.

Each of our depth-charges contained four hundredweight of Amatol, so a dozen contained over two tons of high explosive. We held the contact, ran in and fired all throwers together – port, starboard and stern. I could still hear the skipper's voice: 'Not my favourite form of sport . . .'

The inactivity was puzzling. Had they called off the hunt? I was able to relax the tension in my muscles – gingerly, because I mustn't flinch if it started again. A counter-attack: extermination by slow degrees. The thought of another pass made my guts churn with terror. I groped for a memory to occupy my mind.

I was back in the destroyer *Karl Galster*, a sardine-tin crammed with guns and machinery. We made contact off the south-west tip of the British Isles. A sudden shout from the starboard wing of the bridge: 'Torpedo bearing green three-zero!' The voice still lingered in my ears, hoarse but incisive.

I would never forget it, not if I lived to be a hundred.

I could distinctly see the line of bubbles. It seemed an eternity before the pale train of our wake swung aside.

I gulped. Fear gripped me by the throat – a double fear, born of then and now. My thoughts were in chaos. I must take care not to get them mixed. 'Torpedo bearing green three-zero!' – that was on the *Karl Galster*. A terrible few seconds of numbing tension, then the cry of deliverance: 'Torpedo crossing the bow!'

Stick it out, go the distance! How long was it now? I still couldn't bring myself to move. This time I was one of the hunted. Down deep, on board a U-boat with empty tubes, defenceless even if we managed to surface.

The *Karl Galster* could only have missed the torpedo by a metre or two. Full helm and maximum revs until the ship turned parallel to its line of approach. How the hull had vibrated – almost to the point of disintegration. The alarm-bell shrilled a warning to the men in the engine-room. Then the torpedo officer, into the telephone: 'Fire port and starboard!' Breathless expectancy until a double detonation jolted the ship from stem to stern. Nothing to be seen but two white whirl-pools left and right of our fading wake, much as if a pair of rocks had toppled into the water.

Then the order: 'Hard-a-port!' The skipper reduced speed so that the men in the bowels of the destroyer could operate their hydrophones. The same tactics as our enemy's – exactly the same. The destroyer gave a perceptible lurch as her speed increased again, and we raced for the echo.

The pattern was fired at the point of strongest response. Shallow settings, detonations short and sharp. It sounded as if we had struck a cluster of mines. I could still see the big white geysers hanging there majestically for several seconds before they collapsed in a drizzle of fine spray.

Still nothing. I ventured a few long, lung-stretching breaths.

The Captain was staring at the gauges as though his eyes could influence their needles by remote control, but nothing stirred. No Asdic noises either. The hydrophone operator seemed wrapped in pious meditation. I wondered why our pursuers made no move. We couldn't have escaped their electronic net at a meagre two knots.

'Steer two-two-zero,' ordered the Captain.

Another spell of silence.

'Course two-two-zero, sir,' the helmsman reported after an appreciable pause.

The next whispered report – 'Propeller noises bearing zero-two-zero. Growing fainter' – brought a mocking grin to the Captain's face.

I re-transported myself to the bridge of the *Karl Galster*. Cold, uncommunicative faces bathed in moonlight. Not a sign of the enemy, no matter how hard we looked. Just shouted orders, the splash of depth-charges, the thump of underwater explosions. Cross-bearings and more salvoes. White vortexes frayed our pallid plait of wake.

And then, on the dark water, a slick of oil. The searchlight probed it with a thin white finger. We turned and made for it at once. Every gun was trained mercilessly on the oil-slick. 'Fire port! Fire starboard!'

Fish with ruptured air-bladders floated belly-up in the glare of the searchlight – hundreds of them, but no wreckage. Just the patch of oil. The echo had vanished.

There was no time to continue the search. A British cruiser might have turned up at any moment and barred our route home. The skipper had to head for Brest willy-nilly. That was when he said drily: 'Not my favourite form of sport.'

The hydrophone operator's voice suddenly penetrated my consciousness. From what I could gather, the destroyer was turning our way. Another pass after all. They had merely kept us dangling – played cat-and-mouse with us. Our hopes of escape evaporated. We were still on the hook.

Herrmann grimaced, removed his earphones. I started counting, and then they came, one after another. We were pounded and shaken. The whole sea became a single explosive charge.

Again the endless rumble of displaced water, then more propeller noises. Why no intermission? How could the propellers return so soon? It was the placid shuffle of slowly turning screws, not the swift coffee-grinder pounding and malevolent whine that signified maximum revs.

A sinister realization took shape at the back of my mind: these screws could not belong to the ship that had just counter-attacked us. She would take time to complete her regaining circle – she couldn't be coming at us stern-first.

More depth-charges came almost immediately. A foursome fired in quick succession.

The lights went out again. Somebody called for spare fuses. The Chief shone his torch on the depth-gauge. He couldn't afford to lose sight of it for a moment. We were so deep that any further descent might be lethal.

'Bearing?'

'Two-seven-zero, sir.'

'Hard-a-starboard. Steer three-one-zero.'

The Captain was trying to keep end-on to the approaching destroyer, just as he had done on the surface. The aim was to present our bow or stern to the enemy so that his Asdic beam met as little resistance as possible.

'Propeller noises bearing two-zero-zero, sir. Getting louder.'

Again the detector-impulses hit us. I was possessed by a sort of rigor. My skull felt as fragile as glass, subjected to the same extreme pressure that weighed on our steel skin. The least touch might be too much. Amplified heartbeats filled my ears. I shook my head, but the pounding did not diminish.

Terror of hysterical intensity seemed to be destroying my capacity for thought. At the same time, it honed my powers of perception to a fine edge. I could see and feel all that went on round me with preternatural distinctness.

'Range?' asked the Captain. 'What about the second one?' His voice had lost its even tenor.

So I was right. The Captain's shell was cracking. The second noise must have upset his calculations, yet everything depended on his clarity of thought. In place of precision instruments, he had to work with a perceptive system whose centre might – for all I knew – be located at the pit of his stomach.

Sweat was trickling over the washboard corrugations that lined his forehead. He knuckled it away, tilting his cap still farther. Sauerkraut-coloured hair escaped from under the peak. He bared his teeth and brought them sharply together, three times, with a sound like distant castanets.

My left leg was going to sleep. Cautiously I stood up and flexed it. Just as I was poised on one foot, the boat was shaken by a string of frightful detonations. I lost my balance, staggered sideways and landed on my back.

With an effort, I rolled over. My arms straightened in a press-up but I kept my head down, waiting for the next blow to fall.

The cries seemed to come from far away. Only one phrase registered: 'making water'. Was it my imagination, or were we stern-down? First bow-down, now stern-down . . .

'Afterplanes up ten, full ahead both!'

That was the Captain. So I could still hear. Full ahead – in this situation? What about the noise? My God, the boat was still trembling and groaning as if, even at this depth, we were labouring through a steep swell.

I wanted to go limp and hide my head in my arms.

Not a glimmer of light. The thought of drowning in the

dark, of being unable to see the green torrent when it poured into the boat . . .

A torch-beam danced over the bulkheads and found its objective, the depth-gauge. From aft came the sharp singing note of a circular saw eating into wood. Two or three figures came to life with a jerk. Orders were hissed. Another torch-beam caught the Captain's face. It might have been cut out of grey cardboard. Our stern-down angle was still increasing — I could sense it with my whole body. How much longer would he keep the motors running full ahead? The roar of the depth-charges had ebbed long ago. Everyone could hear us now — everyone in the ship above. Or could they? Only if she was lying stopped, perhaps.

'Reports,' I heard the Captain growl, 'let me have some reports.'

Elbow contact with the man on my left told me he was trembling. I couldn't identify him.

Again the temptation to subside on the deck. I held it at bay — just.

A man stumbled. 'Quiet!' snarled the Captain.

I noticed that the motors were no longer running at full speed. Some emergency lighting came on. So it wasn't the Chief's back I had seen — his depth-keeping duties had been taken over by the second engineer. He had probably gone aft. There was something very wrong back there — the malicious whine of the circular saw persisted.

We were moving, though. Not level, but the angle was no steeper. The pressure hull must have held and the motors were still working.

A peculiar rasping noise made me lift my head. It sounded like a wire scuffling the outside of the hull. Sweep wires? Impossible — they wouldn't use sweep wires in mid-Atlantic. It must be something else, perhaps a novel form of detector-impulse.

The rasping ceased, and in its place came the familiar pink-pink of Asdic. They had us! They were making sure we didn't sidle off.

How late was it? I couldn't see the dial clearly, but it looked like 0400.

'Propellers bearing one-four-zero. Getting louder.'

Again the spiteful rattle of detector-impulses on our hull, this time as if someone were shaking a tin can filled with pebbles. It wasn't even loud, but loud enough to send another horrific series of images flickering through my brain. Blood cascaded over the ballast tanks into a red-tinged sea, scraps of white cloth fluttered from imploring hands. Everyone knew what happened when a crippled U-boat came up. The Brits liked to see red – as much red juice as possible. They blazed away with all they had, riddling the conning-tower as the crew clambered on deck, smashing the bridge, mangling anything that moved, holing the main ballast tanks to destroy the grey whale's buoyancy. Then they came to ram. Their bows sliced into the disabled boat with a screech and howl of rending metal. No one could blame them. Here at long last was the enemy for whom they had strained their eyes for days, weeks and months on end, the insidious tormentor who never gave them a moment's peace. Here at last was the author of all their fear and discomfort. Small wonder that their thirst for blood remained unslaked until fifteen or twenty men had been murdered.

The pressure hull continued to creak and groan. Without my noticing, the Captain must have taken us deeper. The Chief's eyes were fixed on the depth-gauge. He glanced quickly at the Captain, but the Captain did not react.

'Bearing?'

'Two-eight-zero . . . Two-five-five – two-four-zero . . . Getting louder.'

'Hard-a-port,' the Captain whispered after a moment's reflection. This time he communicated our course to Herrmann: 'We're turning to port.' His comment to the rest of us: 'The usual.'

Perhaps they had relieved each other. Perhaps the ship overhead was not the one that had originally opened fire. Every escort vessel had its allotted task. The destroyer that fired on us was providing flank protection. She had probably left us to be dealt with by a hunter-killer.

Damn the condensation! Every godforsaken drop sounded like a hammer-blow.

At last the Captain turned his head – not his body, which didn't budge. His head simply rotated on a turntable of sheepskin collar and grinned at us. It looked as if the extremities of his lips had been dragged upwards and outwards with surgical clips – lop-sidedly, so that five millimetres of white canine showed in the left-hand corner of his mouth.

What was the next move? They couldn't have packed up and called it a day.

A day? It must be at least 0400 by now, if not 0430, and we had been in their clutches since 2253.

That second noise . . . An unsolved mystery.

Still no hydrophone reports. Herrmann's lips might have

been sewn shut. His head still protruded from the hydrophone booth, eyes open for once, but his face was vacant like that of a corpse.

The Captain's mocking grin had become a trifle less ominous. The relaxation in his face was like a laying-on of hands: arise and go in peace. Go take a stroll round the snow-white promenade deck. With pleasure – just what we needed to help us unwind, except that nobody had spared a thought for our recreational needs. We had as much scope for exercise as caged tigers.

I had a sudden remembrance of the travelling-cage at Ravenna Marittima, with the big cats pacing thirstily in the full glare of the midday sun or sprawled against the back wall in a dung-strewn patch of shade. Immediately in front of the cage, fishermen had laid out dead tunny-fish on the ground, shining steel-blue projectiles almost as sleek and slim as torpedoes. Plump bluebottles swarmed over them. They went for the eyes first; as with Swoboda, so with tunny-fish. The muffled throb of jungle drums rang out across the sun-baked courtyard, which was deserted save for a lone figure in the far corner. It was this swarthy man in ragged overalls who provided the tomtom accompaniment by thrusting massive blocks of ice down a sort of metal gullet. In its depths, rotating madly, was a spiked roller. It tossed the ice-blocks high, snapped at them, tossed and snapped and chewed them into fragments with a boom and a clang and a roll of drums. This wild tattoo, the dead tunny-fish and the five tigers with lolling tongues in their inferno of a cage – that was all I remembered of Ravenna Marittima.

Very softly the Captain gave a steering order. There was a dull click as the helmsman pressed his button. We were turning.

If only someone would say what this latest interlude meant. They could only be lulling us into a false sense of security.

But why no more contacts? First two noises and now none. Had we managed to sneak away, or couldn't Asdic reach us at this depth?

In the intensified silence, the Captain whispered: 'Paper and pencil ready, please.'

The quartermaster took a few moments to grasp that the request was directed at him.

'Might as well draft a signal,' the Captain murmured.

Kriechbaum was unprepared for this. Clumsily he reached for a pad lying on the chart-table. His fingers closed on the pencil like a blind man's.

'Ready?' said the Captain. '2 MV estimated 8000 and 5000 g.r.t. heard to sink – probable hit on MV estimated 3000 g.r.t. – add position. Go on, get it down.'

The quartermaster bent over his desk.

The second lieutenant turned to stare at me. His mouth was ajar with surprise.

Kriechbaum finished writing and straightened up. His face betrayed nothing. It was as expressionless as ever. Impassivity came easily to Kriechbaum. Nature had endowed him with almost immobile features. His eyes were equally uncommunicative in this light – too deeply embedded in the shadows beneath his eyebrows. 'That's all they'll want to know,' the Captain said in an undertone. Kriechbaum half-extended his arm. I tiptoed over to him and passed the slip of paper to Herrmann. It would be his job to keep the signal ready for transmission when circumstances allowed.

'That last hit –' the Captain was just murmuring to himself, when the depths were shaken by four explosions. He gave a disdainful shrug. 'Ah well,' he sighed, and clicked his tongue a few times.

Herrmann began to read off bearings in a stage whisper. The hydrophone had picked up a definite propeller noise.

Still no Asdic. I titillated myself by imagining that the Brits had switched off to spare our shattered nerves.

The moon – the confounded moon! It was all the fault of the moon . . .

An unexpected visitor would have been amazed to see us standing around like dummies, not saying a word. Loitering with intent to die – that was a fair description. An unexpected visitor . . . 200 metres down? Very funny. I stifled a rising tide of laughter.

'Time?'

'0410, sir,' Kriechbaum said.

The Captain nodded. 'Bit stuffy, isn't it?'

I had no idea what the form was. How long could we go on like this? What was the oxygen situation? Was the Chief already topping up the atmosphere with precious breathing-gas from his bottles?

The quartermaster had produced a stop-watch and was following the hands as intently as if our lives depended on it. Could he really have any idea of the distance we had covered since diving? Transferred to a chart, our avoiding manœuvres would have looked like a tangled skein of wool.

The Captain was restive. No reason why he should trust this specious calm. He couldn't let his thoughts stray like mine – all that mattered to him was the enemy and his tactics.

'Well?' he said in a sarcastic drawl, and raised his eyes theatrically to the deckhead. I half-expected him to add: 'Are you going to be long?'

He even grinned at me with his head cocked. I tried to reply in kind but felt the grin congeal. My cheek-muscles stiffened involuntarily.

'We really clobbered them, eh?' he said softly, settling back against the periscope to savour our attack in retrospect. 'Remarkable, the way those bulkheads gave – you could hear them as plainly as anything. The first one must have gone down bloody fast.'

Death-rattle . . . Where had I last heard the word? Surely in a propaganda broadcast – nobody else would use such flatulent language.

What about 'die' itself? An honest word, but universally eschewed. Nobody ever died in obituary notices. They departed this life, passed away, fell asleep, went to their eternal repose or breathed their last – never died. The simple and unambiguous verb was shunned like a leper.

Silence on board. A touch of hydroplane and an occasional alteration of course, that was all. The gyro compass seemed to have been switched off again.

'Propeller noises closing fast,' Herrmann reported. There was the Asdic! This time it sounded like a child pressing too hard on a slate pencil.

'Getting louder,' Herrmann said.

My eye was caught by the sausages hanging from the deckhead. They were filmed with white. The stench and humidity did them no good, but salami was durable – so was smoked meat. Dead meat, living flesh. My blood still circulated, my hearing worked, my heart beat hard and fast. They had us cold . . .

'Time?'

'0423, sir.'

A whining noise. Where from? Inside the boat, outboard? A definite contact. I could see the destroyer's bow-wave – the white bone in her beak.

The Captain perched on the chart-table and undid some more buttons. He might have been settling down for a dirty-joke session.

I wondered what really became of submarines sunk in mid-ocean. Did they join a grotesque armada of boats that hung in a state of perpetual suspension at a depth where the pressure exactly matched the weight of their crushed hulls, or were they ever more fiercely compressed until they sank thousands of metres and came to rest on the ocean floor? I made a note to ask the Captain some time. The Old Man knew all about pressure and displacement – he would tell me. Rate of descent 40 kilometres per hour – I ought to know it myself.

The Captain was grinning his habitual, slightly lop-sided grin, but the irises lurked warily in the corners of his eyes. He gave a subdued steering order. 'Hard-a-port. Steer two-seven-zero.'

'Propellers one-seven-five, closing fast,' reported Herrmann.

The white bone . . . They were coming at us flat out.

We were still at 200 metres.

A minute's suppressed breathing. Herrmann winced and shifted his head-set. I knew why. He had heard the depth-charges hit the water.

Elasticated seconds. The canisters were drifting down. I stored air, tensed my muscles. A series of shattering blows almost knocked me over.

'Well really!' the Captain said irritably. Somebody shouted: 'Leak in forward depth-gauge line!' – 'Keep your voice down!' he snapped.

The same thing as last time – a weak point. A jet of water shot straight across the control-room, stiff as a ruler, and bisected the Chief's face: in the lower half his mouth, agape with surprise, in the upper his raised eyebrows and the deep lines in his forehead.

A strident whistling and crackling accompanied by unintelligible shouted exchanges. My blood ran cold. I intercepted a terrified glance from the new control-room hand.

'I'll fix it.' That was Isenberg. He reached the leak in a single bound.

Rage surged through me. The bastards! Nothing to do now but wait for them to drown us like rats in our own boat.

The control-room PO was sopping wet. He had closed some valves. The jet dwindled to a drooping finger which spattered the deck-plates.

I noticed that we were again stern-down. Under cover of the next explosions, the Chief trimmed forward. U-A crept back to the horizontal.

The sight of sea-water jetting into the boat under enormous pressure had pierced me like a dagger. A foretaste of disaster, thin as a finger but none the less horrific – worse than the mightiest of waves.

More depth-charges. The sea poured back into their excavations with a sound like the rattling breath of an asthmatic.

More already? It seemed impossible that they could have been fired by the same destroyer.

I might have been wrong, but a few men seemed to have gathered beneath the lower lid. As if there were any point! Purely instinctive, this urge to get near the ladder.

We hadn't reached that stage, not yet. There was nothing abject or resigned about the Captain's lolling figure, but the grin had deserted his face.

Herrmann whispered: 'More propeller noises bearing one-two-zero, sir.'

'That's all we needed.' The Captain made a face. Two of them – suspicion had yielded to certainty. A note of urgency entered his voice. 'How does she bear now – the second one?' He had to feed a new set of factors into his mental computer.

A report from aft: 'Outboard induction valves leaking badly!' The Chief went aft at a glance from the Captain, who took over his depth-keeping duties.

'Foreplanes up ten,' I heard him say quietly.

I suddenly became aware of my bladder. The sight of the leak must have been suggestive, but I didn't know where to relieve myself.

The Chief reappeared. Two or three glands were leaking in the stern. His head jerked to and fro as if he had a nervous tic. A leak, and we couldn't pump out – considerations of noise forbade it. The auxiliary compensating pump must be out of action in any case. A confused murmur of voices. I heard, 'Air-vessel – auxiliary compensating pump – cracked . . .' Why did they have to use so much glass in a submarine, of all places? The gauge-glasses had cracked too.

Again the Captain ordered both motors full ahead. Our high-speed avoiding manoeuvres must be burning up the amps. He was gambling with our reserves. If the box started to fail, or if we ran short of compressed air or oxygen, the boat would have to surface come what may. The Chief had repeatedly blown HP air into the trimming tanks to give us the buoyancy which could no longer be created by pumping alone.

HP air was at a premium now, because present circumstances rendered us incapable of making any more: the compressor could not be used on account of the fiendish noise it made.

And oxygen? How much longer could we go on breathing this all-pervading stench?

The hydrophone operator read off one bearing after another. I heard a renewed patter of Asdic.

Even now there seemed to be some doubt whether we had acquired two pursuers in place of one. The Captain thrust a hand under his cap and scratched. He had probably lost all clear idea of the situation. Hydrophone reports were a poor guide to the enemy's intentions.

Or could they deceive us with noise? It ought to be technically feasible. Our utter dependence on the ears of a single hydrophone operator was ludicrous.

The destroyer seemed to be turning in a wide arc. No mention of a second noise, but this might simply mean that the second ship had stopped engines.

Still nothing. The first lieutenant glanced round uncertainly, a shrivelled face with a pointed nose and white patches encircling the nostrils.

The control-room PO was trying to relieve himself into a can. One-handed, he laboriously extracted his penis from the recesses of his leather trousers.

An unheralded explosion. Isenberg's half-filled can slipped through his fingers and clattered to the deck. Instantly, the control-room stank of pissoir. I was surprised the Captain didn't swear.

That too! I breathed shallowly so as to cheat the steel bands round my chest and avoid inhaling too much of the stench. The atmosphere on board was heavy with the stale reek of overheated engines, the body odour of fifty men, sweat – the cold sweat of fear. I caught an undoubted whiff of ordure. Somebody's sphincter had failed him. Sweat, shit, piss and bilge-water – an intolerable mixture.

I couldn't help thinking of the poor swine in the stern. They couldn't see the Captain and take courage from the sight of him, like us. They were the real prisoners. Nobody warned them when to expect another devil's tattoo. I would have died sooner than maroon myself back there with the silent engines.

Even at this depth, there were action stations and action stations, privileged and underprivileged.

Hacker and his men, sweating it out beside the torpedo tubes in the cavernous fore-ends, were just as ignorant of what went on. No steering or motor orders carried to their place of vigil. They couldn't hear the hydrophone operator's reports. They had no idea which way we were moving – even if we were moving at all. Only their stomachs responded when an explosion lifted the boat or abruptly thrust it downwards. Their ears heard nothing but 'death-watch beetle' when we dived still deeper.

Three more detonations. This time the sledge-hammer slammed into us from below. We shot upwards like an express lift.

At roughly 160 metres down – I seemed to recall – a depth-charge was most lethal when it exploded 35 metres below the hull. How deep were we now? 180 metres.

We had nothing to 'give' underneath, just the engine bed-plates, and they were able to withstand concussion from below least of all.

Another six depth-charges, again so close under the keel that I felt the savage jolt of them in my knee-joints. It was like standing on a see-saw while blocks of concrete were dropped on the other end. The depth-gauge jumped and jumped again, just as our enemy meant it to.

This attack had cost a good dozen depth-charges. The surface must be thick with fish floating on their sides. The enemy could scoop them up in nets – something fresh for the galley.

I forced myself to take deep, regular breaths. After five minutes' deep breathing, another four depth-charges went off, all of them astern. The hydrophone operator reported lower intensity.

I concentrated on how to build a papier-mâché stage set of the whole compartment – a full-size reconstruction, perfect in every detail. It shouldn't be difficult. Simply remove the port side altogether. That was where the audience would sit. No raised stage, everything vis-à-vis. A view of the depth-keeping position with the search periscope shifted upstage to lend depth to the whole scene. I memorized the actors' positions and postures.

First, the Captain with his back against the periscope: four-square and ungainly, ragged sweater, sheepskin waistcoat, U-boat-issue leather trousers grey with salt, salt-stained boots with thick cork soles, a refractory tangle of hair under the peak of the battered old cap with its gilt trimming long tarnished to a sooty green.

The rubber-jacketed planesmen: two motionless monoliths, the heavy drapery of their oilskins seemingly hewn in dark basalt and then polished.

The Chief, seen in semi-profile: olive-green shirt with sleeves rolled up, crumpled denim slacks also olive-green but darker, gym-shoes, Valentinoesque hair combed smoothly back. Lean as a whippet, stiff as a wax doll. Only his jaw-muscles moved. Not a word, just a ripple of jaw-muscles.

The first lieutenant had his back to the audience, and I sensed why: he was reluctant to show his face because he couldn't trust it.

The second lieutenant was too heavily muffled for much of his face to be visible. Although he stood stock-still, his eyes darted incessantly to and fro, as though eager to desert their owner and search for an independent means of escape, leaving him stiff and sightless beside the periscope.

The quartermaster kept his head lowered, apparently in contemplation of his stop-watch.

Few sound-effects: just a gentle hum of motors and the sporadic drip of condensation on deck-plates.

Then a trio of depth-charges, definitely astern.

I didn't even hear the pumps.

The quartermaster seemed to have adopted a new method of scoring. Every fifth chalk-mark was horizontally superimposed on the previous four. This saved space and gave a clearer over-all picture. I wondered how he had managed to count the last few salvoes.

The Captain's lips moved continuously. Own course, enemy course, avoiding course. Every report from the hydrophone booth affected his calculations.

What would he do now – carry straight on? No, this time he tried another turn. Hard-a-port.

I hoped that he had picked the right alternative – that the destroyer captain didn't also plump for port, or starboard if he was steering a reciprocal course. I didn't even know if the destroyer was making her approach from ahead or astern.

The hydrophone operator's bearings became scrambled in my head.

'Depth-charges fired!' Herrmann had again picked up the splash as they hit the surface.

My nails bit hard into my palms.

'Pump out,' the Captain ordered, deliberately stressing each syllable, even though the depth-charges had yet to explode. He seemed totally unperturbed by the noise, which made me cringe.

A flurry of detonations.

'Carpet-bombing,' said the Captain.

If singletons and series don't work, try a carpet.

Unshrinkable.

Vaguely, I wondered why the English word should have popped into my head. At last I saw it machine-embroidered in gold thread on a label inside my swimming-trunks, beneath the words *Pure Wool.*

Carpet-bombing . . . A spool in my brain started to unwind. Hand-knotted, traditional Afghan designs, flying carpets, Haroun al Rashid, oriental cunning . . .

'Don't overdo it,' the Captain jeered. He had increased speed while the uproar was at its height. 'Now they're having to reload,' he said mockingly. 'The more they fire, the fewer they have left.'

A gem of a remark – a proverb worthy of the wardroom calendar. 'The more they fire, the fewer they have left.'

He ordered the boat shallower. Why, was he planning to surface? Would the next order be 'On escape gear?'

Hunter-killers of the Atlantic – it would make a film title. I could see the credits superimposed on a close-up of an egg – an egg with a hair-line crack in it. One crack in our shell was all the enemy needed – the sea would do the rest.

How to kill slugs and snails . . . The big black slimy giants we used to collect in buckets, tip down the lavatory and flush away. Drowned in the cess-pit – very effective. Treading on them was just as repulsive as hacking them to bits. Green pulp spurted sideways under the pressure of one's shoe. My ears were assaulted by a fresh set of sounds. The contralto whine of propellers could be heard throughout the boat. I saw the Vicar tremble all over and cower against the flooding panel. Another man – unidentifiable – sat down on the deck-plates and clasped his knees: a huddled allegory of fear. The others seemed to shrink. They crouched as though crouching were the key to survival.

Only the Captain continued to loll as usual.

Just as I was straining my senses to the limit, a depth-charge jarred my spine. I flinched, clamped my eyelids together, tensed my whole body, did all I could to control my muscles, but too late.

More concussions. My left shoulder struck something so hard that I almost cried aloud.

Another two shattering explosions.

I heard the Captain's voice through a torrent of sound: 'Pump out!' For all our squirming, we were still firmly hooked.

The Chief's eyes roamed sideways. From his expression, he couldn't wait for the next pattern. Perversity of perversities! He *wanted* to pump the bilge, and for that he *needed* the roar and gurgle of depth-charges.

The submarine was past holding unless we pumped frequently. Pump when our surroundings roared and gurgled, stop pumping when the roar and gurgle ceased. Start and stop, start and stop *ad infinitum.*

More waiting.

Nothing yet? I opened my eyes but kept them fixed on the deck.

A wicked combination punch. My teeth rattled in unison with the deck-plates. Confused cries. The whole submarine vibrated – the steel howled like a dog. The lights had failed again. I wondered who had shouted.

'Permission to blow fore trim?' The Chief's voice reached me through layers of cotton-wool.

'Negative!'

His torch flitted across the Captain's face. Mouthless, eyeless. Rending sounds, a sharp creaking, then more shattering blows.

The orgy of noise had only just subsided when there was another chirp of Asdic. It sounded malevolent. A myriad little beaks pecked at our nerve-endings. The enemy could not have devised a more sinister sound – it sapped the morale like a Stuka's siren. I held my breath.

04 and how many minutes? I couldn't see the big hand.

Damage reports. Fragmentary sentences from forward and aft at the same time. What was leaking badly? A stern gland?

The emergency lights came on. I saw, in the semi-darkness, that the control-room was crowded with men. They must have come from aft – I was still in the forward doorway, so no one could have passed me unnoticed. I couldn't recognize anyone. My view was partly obscured by Isenberg and one of his control-room hands. They stood there rigidly. I heard the scrape of boots, hurried breathing, a few muttered curses.

The Captain was watching the depth-gauge. He had noticed nothing, but the quartermaster's head jerked round.

'Engine-room making water,' someone called from aft.

The Captain didn't even look up. 'Propaganda,' he said, slowly and deliberately. 'Pro-pa-gan-da.'

The Chief, who had taken a step towards the engine-room, stopped short and devoted his attention to the gauges instead.

'I'm waiting for a proper damage report!' snarled the Captain. Half-turning, he caught sight of the dim figures crowded together beside the after bulkhead.

An almost imperceptible double-take, then: 'Chief, pass me your torch.'

The men came to life, shrinking back like tigers from their tamer. One of them actually managed to duck through the bulkhead in reverse. His legs back-pedalled. The torch picked out his receding back. He had an escape pack under his arm.

The control-room PO's face was quite close to mine. His eyes were wide. He might have been uttering a silent scream.

The Captain ordered both motors half-ahead.

'Half-ahead both,' a voice confirmed.

A sardonic mutter from the Captain: 'They're wasting their bangs . . .'

Kriechbaum's chalk halted in mid-air. Indecision, not paralysis. He didn't know how many marks to make for the last counter-attack. His book-keeping was in jeopardy – one mistake and the whole sum would be ruined.

At last he blinked like someone shaking off a bad dream and made five resolute strokes, four down and one across.

The next explosions came singly, sharp and incisive but with little reverberation, so the Chief had to stop pumping quickly. Kriechbaum drew a new bundle of sticks. The chalk slipped from his fingers on the last stroke.

Another mighty lurch. Metal shrilled and grated.

If a rivet went now it could pierce my skull like a bullet. The pressure was so great at this depth that a thin jet of water could saw through a man.

The rank smell of fear . . . They had us in the wringer. It was our turn now.

'Zero-six-zero, getting louder.' A pause. 'More propellers bearing two-zero-zero.'

Three or four depth-charges exploded inside my head. The swine were trying to blow our hatches off . . .

Low moans and hysterical sobbing.

The U-boat bucked like an aeroplane in turbulence.

Two men staggered and fell. I saw a mouth open and shut, two faces stiff with terror.

Two more detonations. The depths churned and surged.

A dying roar, then silence. Only the persistent drone of the main motors, the plash of condensation, men breathing.

'Foreplanes up ten,' whispered the Chief.

I winced as the hydroplane motor hummed. Did everything on board have to make such a din?

Was the Captain going to alter course, double back, plough straight on?

Why no word from the hydrophone operator?

If Herrmann had nothing to report it could only mean there were no engines running on the surface. The enemy could hardly have receded too fast for him to spot their departure, so they must be stopped and listening. It wouldn't be the first time, although the silence had never been so prolonged.

The Captain doggedly maintained course and speed.

Five minutes passed. Then Herrmann opened his eyes wide and swung the wheel to and fro. They were coming in for another attack. I focused all my energies on sitting tight. A sharp double concussion.

'We're making water!' someone shouted from aft.

The Captain, taking advantage of the after-roar, shouted angrily at the invisible owner of the voice: 'Be specific, damn you!'

Making water . . . Ridiculous naval jargon! It sounded productive. Make connoted manufacture, yet making water was the most counter-productive thing we could do.

The next explosion seemed to hit me below the belt. It knocked the breath out of me, or I might have yelled. I clenched my teeth until my jaws ached. Somebody screamed in a piercing falsetto. The torch-beam flitted about, searching for the author of the scream. I heard a new sound: chattering teeth, then sniffs and nose-clearing. More than one man must be weeping.

A body cannoned into me, almost knocking me backwards. I felt someone grab hold of my knees. He was crouching on the deck.

Still no light from the emergency lamp over the quarter-master's desk. The darkness was like a shroud beneath which panic could proliferate in secret.

Racking sobs. They came from a figure huddled against the flooding panel. I could guess who it was. Isenberg dealt the man such a thump in the ribs that he squawked.

The Captain spun round as if he had been bitten. 'You,' he hissed in the direction of the flooding panel, 'report to me when this is over.'

Who, Isenberg or his victim?

When the light came on again I saw that the Vicar was weeping silently.

The Captain increased speed.

'Half-ahead both, sir,' confirmed the helmsman.

The propeller noises were more audible than ever – a grinding, whirring sound with a swift rhythmical beat in it. Maximum revolutions . . .

The depth-gauge needle crept a couple of subdivisions. We were slowly descending. The Chief couldn't level us off – blowing would have made too much noise and pumping was out of the question.

'One-nine-zero,' reported the hydrophone operator, 'one-eight-five.'

'Steer zero-six-zero. Let's hope we aren't sending up any

oil,' said the Captain casually. Oil! To the enemy, an oil-slick
was as good as a marker buoy.

The Captain gnawed his lip.

It was dark up top, but the smell of oil carried for miles,
day or night.

'Propeller noises very close,' came a whisper from the hydrophone booth.

'Slow ahead both,' the Captain ordered, just as softly. 'Minimum rudder.'

He removed his cap and placed it beside him on the chart-
table. A token of surrender? Had we at last reached the end
of our rope?

Herrmann leant right out of his cubby-hole as though about
to make a report. The tension on his pale face was overwhelming. Suddenly he removed his head-set. Now I heard it
with my own ears.

A crashing, bursting, bellowing volcano of sound, as if the
sea itself were falling in ruins. The lights went out again.
Utter darkness.

Still with my eyes shut, I heard an unfamiliar voice calling
for damage reports.

We were again noticeably bow-up. By the glow of a torch,
I could see telephone cables and oilskins standing well away
from the bulkhead.

The silence was broken by a report from aft: 'Leak in the
motor-room.' Others followed: 'Fore-ends, all hull openings
checked and tight.' – 'Engine-room, all hull openings checked
and tight.' Emergency lighting at last. The needle of the depth-
gauge continued to revolve at an alarming rate.

'Full ahead both,' ordered the Captain. His calm voice a
sharp contrast to the panic in some of the voices.

The submarine lurched forward.

'Foreplanes hard-a-rise, afterplanes hard-a-dive,' the Chief
ordered, but there was no response from the hydroplane
indicator.

'Afterplanes not answering, sir,' Isenberg reported. He
glanced over his shoulder at the Captain, ashen-faced but
trustful.

'Switch to manual,' the Chief said coolly, as if the whole
thing were an exercise drill.

The planesmen rose and strained at the handwheels with
all their might. God be praised! The white needle of the
hydroplane indicator trembled and began to stir. The hydroplane gear wasn't damaged after all. The fault must have
been electrical only.

The motors hummed like a swarm of bees. It seemed madness but we had no choice. U-A was past holding at minimum speed. The motor-room – our Achilles' heel – was still making water.

'Neither main motor showing full revolutions,' someone called, and earned himself a growled rebuke for raising his voice.

The Captain digested this news in two seconds flat. 'Check both batteries. Check the battery bilges for acid.' Obviously, a few of the cells had fractured and emptied. I wondered what else could possibly go wrong.

My heart missed a beat when the first lieutenant stepped aside and revealed the depth-gauge. The needle was still creeping clockwise. U-A was sinking, even with her motors running at maximum available revolutions.

'Blow No. 3 main ballast,' ordered the Captain.

Seconds later, a sharp hiss.

'Full pressure!'

The Chief had jumped to his feet. His breathing was shallow and irregular, his voice vibrated strangely. 'Trim forward – quick as you can!'

I dared not get up for fear my legs might give way. Trembling muscles and fluttering nerves. I found myself praying for the final blow, the *coup de grâce* – anything which would bring our long ordeal to an end.

We had risen 50 metres. The needle slowed to a halt. The Captain ordered: 'Crack No. 3 main vent.'

A new wave of terror. I knew what the order meant. Air must now be surging towards the surface, there to form a bubble which would clearly mark our position. I muttered my formula: immune, immune . . .

My heart was pounding, my breath came in gasps. I vaguely heard: 'Shut No. 3 main vent.'

Kriechbaum turned to the Captain. I could see him full-face now, carved in pale. He caught sight of me and thrust out his lower lip.

'Hysterical bunch of women,' growled the Captain.

If the motors were swamped – if they shorted – how would we keep the screws turning? Without screws and planes, we were lost.

The Captain called impatiently for damage reports from the engine- and motor-rooms.

I caught fragments only: '. . . plugged with wedges . . . compressor seating fractured . . . making water fast, source unidentified . . .'

I heard a shrill whimpering sound. Several seconds passed before I realized that it was not of enemy origin. It was coming from forward, high-pitched and insistent.

The Captain turned in the direction of the sound, almost shuddering with distaste.

'One-five-zero, sir, getting louder.'

'What about the other one – the first one?'

'Zero-nine-zero . . . zero-eight-zero – range steady.'

God Almighty, they were going the whole hog now – playing pat-ball with Asdic bearings. Our first pursuer was handicapped no longer. He could happily render his own Asdic inoperative by running it at full speed while his partner cruised around and transmitted our position by VHF.

'Conniving bastards!' The Captain grimaced.

For the first time, Herrmann showed signs of nervousness – or did he really have to swing the wheel so violently to detect an increase in relative volume?

If the second skipper was another old fox, and the two of them were experienced doubles players, they could hoodwink us by swopping roles as often as they chose.

Unless I was much mistaken, the Captain was heading for the strongest contact in a tight turn.

Switchback, I thought again – switchback. Up and down, curves on different levels, rising and falling arcs, hairpin bends, sudden swoops and swift ascents.

The submarine lurched under two swingeing hammer-blows. Four or five harsh detonations followed, two of them beneath us. Seconds later a figure appeared in the after doorway. It was ERA Franz, coming apart at the seams with terror.

His parted lips emitted a shrill 'hee-hee-hee' like a poor imitation of a destroyer's screws. The Captain, who had momentarily shut his eyes, spun round. Franz had stepped through the bulkhead and was standing, escape gear in hand, near the periscope shaft. His teeth, bared in an ape-like rictus, gleamed white in his dark beard. More sobs were coming from another part of the control-room.

The Captain stiffened. He sat bolt upright for an instant, then lowered his head and looked Franz full in the face. Several seconds went by.

'Are you mad? Get back to your action station – at once!'

Instead of the regulation 'Yessir!' Franz opened his mouth wide, as if on the verge of a full-blooded yell.

The Captain leapt to his feet: 'For God's sake, man, pull yourself together!' he hissed.

The sobbing ceased.

'Propellers bearing one-two-zero,' Herrmann reported. The Captain gave a confused blink.

Mesmerized by his gaze, Franz began to squirm and writhe. I could see the tension slowly drain out of him.

'Get back to your action station!' And again, in a menacing undertone: 'At once, I said!'

'One-one-zero, getting louder.' The hydrophone operator's voice had regained its priestly, monotonous timbre.

The Captain suddenly threw off his inertia and took two or three steps forward. I stood up to make way for him, wondering where he was off to.

At long last, Franz came to life and said 'Yessir' in a strangled voice. He glanced round quickly, bent low and ducked through the after bulkhead.

The Captain halted in mid-stride and looked back with his head at a strangely contorted angle.

'He's gone, sir,' the Chief stammered.

The Captain withdrew his leg. I was reminded of a film running backwards. Like a dazed boxer whose senses are still incapable of accurate perception, he stalked silently back to his place.

'I was going to shoot him.'

Of course – the pistol in the Captain's cubby-hole!

'Hard-a-starboard – steer two-three-zero,' he said in a normal voice. 'Take her down fifty, Chief.'

'Propellers bearing zero-one-zero,' Herrmann reported.

'Very good.'

Detector-impulses pattered over the hull.

'Disgusting!' hissed the Captain.

Everyone in the control-room knew that he meant Franz, not the Asdic. 'Franz, of all people! Disgraceful!' He gave a shudder of distaste. 'Locked up – I'll have him locked up.'

Herrmann did not raise his voice. 'Propellers closing, sir.'

'Steer two-four-zero. Slow ahead both.'

Having exhausted our repertoire of tricks, we dodged sideways for the umpteenth time.

A sour smell drifted through the forward doorway. Just to sweeten the atmosphere, someone had been sick.

Herrmann screwed up his eyes again. Whenever he made that face I averted my head and tucked it between my shoulders.

A flurry of drumbeats, followed by one huge crashing detonation, and then again – like a mighty rolling echo – the roar and gurgle of tons of displaced water.

The echo was punctuated by five resounding explosions,

very close together. Within seconds, every unsecured object began to roll or slither aft. Even while the charges were exploding, the Chief had increased speed and yelled 'Pump!' Now he stood behind the planesmen, crouching slightly like a cornered animal.

The effervescent roar of surging water persisted. We ploughed through a gurgling, hissing maelstrom with our pumps working flat out.

Before the Chief could stop pumping, another three explosions shook the boat.

'Carry on pumping!' The Chief drew a deep breath and glanced at the Captain. I thought I detected a hint of satisfaction – the man was actually pleased that his pumps could continue to work.

'They must like you, Chief,' the Captain said. 'Very considerate of them.'

It was long past 0400. Our attempts to escape had already gone on for – how many hours? Most of the men in the control-room had sat down, pillowing their heads on their forearms. Nobody bothered to look up. The second lieutenant was staring at something imaginary on the deck.

But, wonder of wonders, the hull still held. We were still mobile, still neutrally buoyant. The motors were running, the screws turning. We were travelling through the depths under our own power. The Chief could hold the boat – he even had her level again.

The quartermaster was hunched over the chart-table. He might have been studying something of interest, except that his head sagged too low. He was holding the dividers in his right hand. The points had embedded themselves in the lineoleum tabletop.

The control-room PO had stuck two fingers in his mouth as though he planned to whistle us a tune.

The second lieutenant was trying to emulate the Captain's sang-froid, but his hands betrayed him. They were tightly closed on the pair of binoculars that still hung from his neck. His knuckles were white with strain.

The Captain turned to the hydrophone operator. Herrmann had his eyes closed and was turning the wheel of his apparatus right and left. He seemed to have isolated the noise he sought, because the wheel's movements decreased until it was almost motionless.

In a subdued voice, he said: 'Propellers going away at one-two-zero.'

'They think they've finished us off,' the Captain said. So

much for one of them, but what of the other?

The Chief had gone aft, leaving the Captain to supervise the planesmen himself.

The whimpering had stopped, but I could still hear sporadic sobbing from forward.

The Chief's hands and forearms were black with oil when he returned. I caught a few snatches of his half-whispered report. 'Stern gland – outboard exhaust – compressor – two studs sheared – secured with wedges – gland still leaking – not badly . . .'

A cardboard container of syrup had been trampled underfoot near the Captain's desk. The accordion case lay open in the repulsive ooze. Not a picture remained hanging on the bulkhead. I cautiously stepped over the C-in-C's upturned countenance.

In the wardroom, books lay scattered among towels and leaking bottles of apple-juice. I thought I might as well make a start on the mess to occupy myself. I stooped, stiff-limbed, and went down on my knees. Incredible – I could still move my hands. I was making myself useful. Careful, though – no noise, no clatter.

When I had been pottering about for ten minutes, the Chief came through. He had greenish smudges under his eyes. Hollow-cheeked, pupils as black as coal. He looked all in.

I passed him a bottle of juice. His whole frame shook as he took it. He slumped on to a stool while he was drinking, but once the bottle left his lips he was up again, teetering slightly like an exhausted fighter coming out for the final round. 'Can't stop . . .' he muttered as he went.

Out of nowhere, three more explosions, but this time they sounded like thwacks on a limp drumskin. 'Nowhere near,' I heard the quartermaster say.

'Two-seven-zero, going away slowly,' reported the hydrophone operator.

To think that, somewhere, terra firma existed. Hills and valleys . . . House-dwellers would still be asleep – at least, they would be in Europe. The bright lights of New York must still be burning, and we were probably nearer America than France after our latest sprint westwards.

The boat was hushed. After a while, Herrmann reported in a whisper: 'Propellers bearing two-six-zero, very faint. Low revs – seems to be going away.'

'Prowling at Slow One,' the Captain said, 'with their ears pinned back. Where's the other one got to? Keep trying.'

I heard the tick of the chronometer and the drip of condensation in the bilge. Herrmann searched again and again, but failed to pick up a second contact.

'Fishy,' the Captain muttered, 'very fishy.'

A ruse – that must be it. Any fool could tell there was something wrong.

The Captain stared blankly into space. He batted his eyelids a couple of times and swallowed, seemingly unable to decide on a course of action.

If only I knew what the game was. I longed to ask what our chances were but my mouth was riveted shut. My head was a volcanic crater, dotted with bursting bubbles.

'No more noises?' asked the Captain.

'No, sir.'

Nearly 0500.

No noises? Incomprehensible. Had they really abandoned the hunt, or were we presumed sunk?

I groped my way back to the control-room. The Captain was holding a whispered conference with the quartermaster. I heard: '. . . surface in twenty minutes.'

I couldn't believe my ears. Were we really out of the wood, or did we *have* to surface because there was no alternative?

The hydrophone operator started to say something, hesitated, and went on turning his wheel. He must have heard a faint noise. The wheel turned almost imperceptibly as he tried to pin-point its source.

The Captain stared at his face. Herrmann moistened his lower lip with the tip of his tongue. 'Propeller bearing two-six-zero, sir. Very faint.'

Abruptly the Captain stepped through the bulkhead and squatted down beside me. Herrmann relinquished one of his earphones and continued to turn the wheel with extreme delicacy while the Captain listened too.

Minutes went by. The Captain's expression was cold and intent. Still tethered to the apparatus by its flex, he gave some steering orders to improve hydrophone reception.

'Stand by to surface.'

His crisp and resolute voice startled me. I wasn't alone – the Chief's eyelids flickered too.

Stand by to surface! Still in hydrophone contact, and we were going up. I gave a mental shrug. The Old Man must know what he was doing.

The Chief propped one leg on the chart-stowage. His right hand rested against the search periscope, and he was leaning forward as if to minimize the distance between his eyes and the creeping needle of the depth-gauge. The arrow was rotating anti-clockwise. Every subdivision it passed brought us one metre nearer the surface. Its slow progress deliberately heightened the suspense.

'Got that signal ready?' asked the Captain.

'Yessir.'

The look-outs had already assembled under the lower hatch in oilskins and sou'westers. They were cleaning their binoculars – rather too industriously. No one spoke.

I breathed easier. My knees had stopped trembling – I could stand unembarrassed by the fear that they might give way, but I still had a separate awareness of every bone and muscle in my aching body. My face felt frozen.

The Captain was taking us up. We would breathe sea-air again. We were alive – the hounds had failed to kill.

No sense of elation. Fear still ran in our veins. All we permitted ourselves was a cautious raising of heads and flexing of knotted shoulder muscles.

The men were exhausted. In spite of the order to surface, both control-room hands were leaning limply against the flooding and blowing panels. As for the control-room PO, now so studiously calm, I could still see the terror in his face.

I found myself yearning for a 100-metre periscope. If only the Captain could take a quick look round from the shelter of our former depth, just to check on the opposition . . . I suddenly became aware that the Chief had given a flooding order. It seemed nonsensical – the Captain had blown and he was flooding. I screwed up my eyes, trying to work it out. The water that had penetrated the hull had been offset by blowing the main ballast tanks and increasing their buoyancy. Fair enough, but what next? I gritted my teeth and wrestled with the enigma. The Chief was no fool, so what was the answer? Then it dawned on me. Of course – the old story! The air in No. 3 main ballast was expanding as we rose. The reduction of water in that tank had to be offset, either by opening the vent or by additional flooding. Venting was out on account of bubbles, so flooding it had to be. The tension in my limbs and jaw-muscles dispersed. I drew a deep breath. Nobody could see the look of satisfaction on my face.

U-A had risen to periscope depth: we were just below the surface now. The Chief maintained a perfect depth – not a trace of excess buoyancy.

The Captain extended the periscope. I heard the motor hum, then stop. There was a gentle click of switches engaging as the Captain rode his roundabout.

The tension in the control-room was almost unendurable. Involuntarily, I held my breath until asphyxia made me gasp like a drowning man. No word came from above.

A bad sign. If the coast were clear the Captain would have said so straight away.

'Quartermaster, make a note.'

Thank God, the Old Man's voice at last.

Kriechbaum reached for his pencil. Back to the old patrol report routine so soon ? Only the Captain would have indulged in literary composition at such a time.

'Periscope observation revealed one destroyer, stopped, true bearing two-seven-zero degrees, range approximately six thousand metres – have you got that ?'

'Yessir.'

'Moon still very bright – got that ?'

'Yessir.'

'Stayed deep. Well, that's it.'

Three or four minutes went by, then the Captain climbed stiffly down. 'They thought they'd spring a surprise on us. Crafty but not crafty enough – it's the same thing every time. Chief, take her down to sixty metres. We'll sheer off a bit and reload in peace and quiet.'

His manner conveyed that all was well again. I almost clutched my head in bewildered delight. 'Quartermaster, add this : Sheered off at Slow One away from destroyer. Destroyer assumed to have lost us. No propeller noises in immediate vicinity.'

'Assumed' was rich ! So he wasn't positive . . .

The Captain's eyes narrowed. Apparently he hadn't finished dictating.

'And Kriechbaum.'

'Sir ?'

'One more thing : Strong glow visible, true bearing two-five-zero degrees. Presumed to be vessel hit by us.' He turned and gave a steering order. 'Alter course to two-five-zero.'

Looking round the control-room, I saw nothing but faces like locked doors. The second lieutenant's dimples had reappeared. The Number One was staring blankly into space. Kriechbaum was bent over the chart-table, writing.

'We'll reload in thirty minutes,' the Captain said, and to me : 'Something to drink would be nice.'

He made no move to leave the control-room, so I hurried off to fetch some apple-juice. Every muscle ached as I stepped through the bulkhead. Hobbling past the hydrophone booth,

I saw Herrmann still turning his wheel with concentration. The sight had lost its terrors.

Half an hour later the Captain gave the order to reload.

The fore-ends was engulfed in hectic activity. Wet gear, sweaters, towels and a mass of other articles lay heaped near the bulkhead. The boards had been taken up.

'Glory be to God on high!' intoned TGM Hacker. 'More room at last,' he added for my benefit. He wiped his sweaty neck with a grubby piece of towelling and urged his coolies on. 'Come on, lads, bear a hand on that tackle.'

'Nothing like Vaseline for an easy ride!' Ario hauled on the chain in time to Hacker's cries of 'Heave!' – punctuating them with exclamations of his own. 'Fuck me – fuck me, you randy sod – ooh, ooh, ooh! – that's it – and again!'

I wondered where he found the breath, toiling as hard as he did. Merker, also hauling grimly on the chain, pretended to be deaf.

With the first torpedo safely in its tube, Merker planted his legs apart and mopped the sweat off his chest, then passed the grimy rag to Ario.

Stimulated by obscene banter, my own imagination took wing. The iron hymen of a ship's side ruptured by the torpedo-phallus, the jagged labia, the freighter-cow rearing as the torpedo pierced her vitals and ejaculated its fiery semen, the ripping and rending, writhing and groaning . . .

The first lieutenant came forward to check the pistols. The men continued to labour doggedly amidst smothered curses and the rhythmical cries of the torpedo gunner's mate.

Returning to the wardroom, I saw the Captain in his usual place on the Chief's bunk. He had stretched his legs. His head was back and his mouth half open. A thread of saliva trickled from the corner of his mouth and meandered into his beard.

Wondering what to do, I cleared my throat of some imaginary phlegm. Awake in a flash, he sat up, and silently gestured to me to sit.

'Well,' he said at length, 'how's it going up forward?'

'One fish loaded. The men are just about finished – whacked, I mean.'

'Hm. Have you been aft yet?'

'No, sir. Too crowded.'

He grunted. 'Bloody awful mess back there. Never mind, the Chief'll cope – he's a marvel.' He turned and called down the passage. 'Steward, something to eat!' Then to me: 'Might as well celebrate while we can. Some bread and butter and a pickled gherkin would be better than nothing.'

Plates and cutlery were brought, and we were soon sitting round a neatly laid table.

Fantastic . . . I found myself mouthing the word in silent disbelief. My eyes took in the smooth clean tabletop, the plates and cups, knives and forks, the familiar and reassuring lamp-light. I watched the Captain stirring his tea with a shiny spoon, the second lieutenant forking up sausage, the first lieutenant bisecting a pickled gherkin lengthwise.

The steward asked if I wanted some tea. 'Tea?' I stammered. 'For me? Yes, please.' A hundred depth-charges still hammered in my head. Every muscle ached with strain and I was suffering from cramp in my right thigh. At each bite, my jaws reminded me how I had clenched them.

'What are you staring at?' the Captain asked me through a mouthful of bread. I hurriedly skewered a slice of sausage. No day-dreaming, chew hard, masticate properly, look around, remember to blink.

'Another gherkin?' asked the Captain.

'Oh – er, yes. Thanks.'

A muffled sound from the passage. Hinrich, who had relieved Herrmann at the hydrophone, seemed to be making his presence felt. A scraping of boots, then he reported: 'Depth-charges bearing two-three-zero, sir. Pretty faint.'

Hinrich's voice sounded much higher than Herrmann's – tenor as opposed to bass.

'Time to take her up,' the Captain said with his mouth full. 'Time?'

'0655, sir,' Kriechbaum called from the control-room.

The Captain rose, still chewing, flushed the contents of his mouth with a swig of tea and clumped down the passage. 'We surface in ten minutes. Make a note, Kriechbaum: 0600, commenced reloading torpedoes. 0655, depth-charges heard, true bearing two-three-zero.'

Then he clumped back and squeezed into his corner again.

The TGM came aft, panting hard. He had to take several deep breaths before he could get a word out. Hacker looked a wreck. The sweat was streaming off him and he could hardly stand. 'All bow tubes reloaded, sir. Stern tube . . .' The Captain cut him short. 'Very good, Hacker. I know you can't manage that for the present.'

Hacker tried to perform a smart about-turn but lost his balance. He just managed to save himself by grabbing the edge of the lockers.

'Solid gold, these lads,' the Captain murmured. 'My God, it feels quite different, having something up the spout again.'

He was itching to attack the destroyer that had harassed us for so long – I could sense it. It would have been typical of him to stake everything on a single throw, but he probably had other plans . . .

He rose abruptly, did up three of the buttons on his sheep-skin waistcoat, settled his cap more firmly on his head, and made for the control-room.

The Chief reported that running repairs had been carried out in the stern. To my ear, 'running repairs' sounded pretty sketchy.

Following the Captain into the control-room, I saw that the look-outs had already reassembled. The second engineer was stationed behind the planesmen. The boat was rising fast.

The Captain climbed silently into the conning-tower. The periscope motor began to hum. Again the click of switches, and again I held my breath until a crisp order from the Captain ended the suspense.

'Surface!'

The release of pressure almost knocked me over. I wanted to gulp and bellow simultaneously. Instead, I just stood there like the rest. My lungs sucked in huge draughts of the cool sea-air that poured down from above. With it came the Captain's voice.

'Half-ahead both engines.'

Aft of us in the engine-room, compressed air hissed into the cylinders. The pistons began to rise and fall. Ignition! A shudder ran through the hull, harsh as the vibration of a tractor. Pumps hummed, fans drove air through the boat. My nerves unwound in the familiar flow of sound like someone relaxing in the bath.

I followed the look-outs on deck. The horizon was wrapped in red.

'That must be the third one!' shouted the Captain.

I could see a black cloud above the glow, darker than the sky. A gigantic worm of smoke was writhing its way to the zenith.

The ship's forecastle and poop reared above the water, plainly visible, but little could be seen of her waist.

An acrid, choking stench of fuel oil came to us on the wind.

'Looks as if her back's broken,' the Captain said. He increased speed and gave some steering orders. Our bow swung towards the conflagration.

As we came nearer, I detected a flicker in the fiery glow. Individual tongues of flame could be seen.

From time to time the smoke was transfixed by yellow

flashes, and balls of fire shot high into the darkness like tracer bullets. Then real rockets, pink and blood-red, ripped through the greasy black fog. Their reflections snaked across the dark water between us and the burning ship.

A single mast stood out black against the reflected glare, poised above the flames like an admonitory finger.

Now the wind bore down on the smoke. It was almost as if the doomed ship wanted to hide her final agony from our eyes. Only the dark mass of the stern could still be distinguished. It must have canted towards us. When the wind brushed the curtain of smoke aside I saw the slanting deck, some remains of superstructure and the stump of what had once been a derrick.

'No need to finish her off.' The Captain's voice sounded throaty. The words terminated in a sort of gurgle rather like drunken laughter.

Three or four minutes passed. Then he took us even closer to the inferno.

Crimson tongues of flame were licking round the stern. Escaping oil had set the sea ablaze.

'Perhaps we'll find out what her name was,' the Captain said.

The hiss and crackle sounded like a brushwood fire, but infinitely fiercer. The sea was yellow with the reflection of the blazing stern and red with burning oil.

Now the whole U-boat was steeped in a crimson glow. The spasmodic glare made every slit in the gratings stand out black and stark. I turned my head. All our faces were bathed in crimson – like grotesque red masks.

An explosion rolled across the water. I strained my ears. Was it my imagination, or had I heard a hoarse cry? Were there still men on board – was that a gesticulating arm? I peered through the binoculars: nothing but flames and smoke. Nonsense – no human voice could have made itself heard above the roar of the flames.

The Captain limited himself to an occasional steering order. He had to keep us head-on. The fire would silhouette us dangerously if he didn't. 'Keep your eyes open,' he called. 'She'll be going down any minute.'

I scarcely heard him. We stayed rooted to the spot, licensed arsonists staring at an inferno of our own making.

A sizeable ship. How many crew, at a conservative guess – twenty, thirty? British ships were no doubt sailing with as few men on board as possible – they might even be keeping watch and watch – but they couldn't manage with fewer than ten deck hands and eight for the engine-room, also wireless operators, officers, stewards . . . I wondered if a destroyer had picked them up, but that would have meant stopping. Could any destroyer risk stopping with U-boats close at hand?

Across the water, lurid red flames leapt into the sky. Streamers of sparks spewed from the still floating stern. Then a distress signal went up. So there was someone on board after all, marooned in that welter of fire and smoke.

'Must have gone off by itself,' the Captain said. 'There can't be anyone left – out of the question.' His voice was level.

I scanned the smoke once more. There! No mistake now – there were figures clustered in the stern. For a brief moment I had them sharply outlined against the glare. Some jumped overboard as I watched, but two or three continued to run aimlessly to and fro. One of them was catapulted into the air. I saw him tumble through the orange glow like a disjointed dummy.

The quartermaster was shouting. 'There's some more!' He pointed at the sea in front of the blazing tanker. I raised my glasses and saw a raft with two men on it.

I kept my binoculars trained on them for a full half-minute. Neither of them stirred. They were dead beyond a doubt.

But over there! Those black hummocks in the water could only be swimmers.

The second lieutenant also trained his glasses on them. 'Watch it!' the Captain stormed. 'For God's sake keep a sharp look out astern.'

Couldn't I, after all, hear cries through the hiss and crackle? One of the swimmers fleetingly raised his arm. The other nine or ten were visible only as bobbing black balls.

I lost sight of them for a moment because the wind veiled them in oily black smoke. Then they reappeared. No doubt about it – they were making for the submarine. Behind them, red tongues of burning oil licked across the water in an ever-widening arc.

I glanced sideways at the Captain.

'Risky,' I heard him mutter, and knew what he meant. We had edged too close. It was getting hot.

He said no more for two or three minutes. He raised his binoculars and lowered them again, struggling to make up his mind. At last, in a voice that was little more than a croak, he stopped both engines and took us astern on the motors.

There would be raised eyebrows below. Reversing in mid-ocean was an unfamiliar experience – uneasy, too. A submarine couldn't crash-dive going astern.

The burning oil spread faster than the men could swim. They had no chance, if only because fire was a consumer of oxygen. Asphyxia, burning and drowning – anyone overtaken by burning oil died of all three simultaneously.

It was a blessing that no screams could be heard above the crackle of flames and muffled thud of minor explosions.

The second lieutenant's red-tinged face was sick with horror.

'Nobody picked them up,' muttered the Captain. 'Can't understand it . . .' I found it equally incomprehensible. All those hours! They must have tried to keep the ship afloat – perhaps she had remained buoyant enough and her boilers sufficiently undamaged to produce a few knots. Perhaps her crew had fought on in the hope of survival. I shuddered at the thought of what they must have been through.

'Now we won't even get her name,' I heard the Captain say. He meant to sound sardonic.

A wave of nausea overcame me. I remembered the man I had helped to retrieve from a huge slick of oil in the harbour after an air raid – how he had stood there on the wharf, groaning and retching convulsively. Burning fuel oil had seared his eyes. It was a mercy when a seaman appeared with a fire-hose. The jet was so powerful that it knocked the poor devil over – rolled him across the cobbles like a black amorphous bundle.

Suddenly the stern reared higher out of the water, as though extruded from below. For a few long seconds it loomed above the burning sea, perpendicular as a cliff. Then, with two or three muffled explosions, it slid beneath the surface.

The sea closed swiftly over the spot, engulfing the ship as if she had never been. There was no more sign of the swimmers.

Below deck, our men would now be hearing the music of the tanker's last dive, the gruesome creaking, snapping and groaning, the exploding boilers and burning bulkheads. How deep was the Atlantic at this point? 5000 metres? 4000 at least – deep enough to cover Mont Blanc.

The Captain ordered a turn away.

'No good hanging around here.'

The look-outs were still standing motionless as ever, binoculars raised.

Ahead of us, the horizon acquired a faint reddish glow of the sort projected on the night sky by a distant metropolis. Suddenly the sky lit up, almost to the zenith.

'Quartermaster,' the Captain said, 'make a note: Glow visible – add time and bearing. Some other boats must still be busy over there . . . Let's see what sort of fireworks they are,' he murmured, and pointed our bow at the flushed horizon.

I couldn't believe it. Hadn't he had enough? Were we doomed to plough on until our tanks ran dry? He must be itching to grab himself a destroyer, get his own back, give the British a dose of their own medicine . . .

The Chief disappeared below.

'Right,' said the Captain, 'time to make that signal. Paper and pencil, Quartermaster. Better start again from scratch – we can really get it off our chests at last.'

I saw his point. No need to worry about betraying our presence if we sent more than a squash signal. The British knew there were U-boats operating in the area – they didn't have to bother their D/F stations any longer.

'Very good. Take this down: "Counter-attacked by destroyer" – massive and continuous counter-attack would be nearer the mark – "considerable damage sustained" – no need to give details, they'll get those from the patrol report. Kernével's only interested in what we've sunk, so let's keep it simple and put first things first. "Five torpedoes fired on convoy from surface, four hits. Passenger steamer 8000 g.r.t. and freighter 5000 g.r.t. definitely heard to sink. Tanker 8000 g.r.t. observed to sink. Counter-attacked 8 hours by 2 destroyers."'

Passenger steamer, the Captain had said. It was bound to have been converted into a troopship. My mind balked at picturing a torpedo-hit on a fully-laden trooper. I recalled the drunken blather in the *Bar Royal*: annihilate the enemy, don't just sink his ships . . .

From below came a report that the telegraphist had picked up some SOS signals from British ships, 'Hm,' was all the Captain said. Nothing more.

At 0730 Kernével relayed a signal from one of our U-boats. The quartermaster read out the gist: 'C-in-C from U-Z. Three sunk and one probable. Counter-attacked four hours. Convoy split into ones and twos. Contact now lost, pursuing southwest.'

I stared at the glow above the horizon, fitfully illuminated by pale flashes. I felt a lingering horror at the havoc our torpedoes had wrought. One pull on the firing-lever . . . I blinked, trying to banish the fatal vision, but it returned unbidden: a spreading sea of flames and, in it, small black figures swimming for their lives.

How must the Captain feel when he visualized the fleet of ships he had destroyed? Or when he thought of the small army of men who had died: scalded, maimed, dismembered, burned, suffocated, crushed, drowned. He had a medium-sized harbourful of ships to his credit – nearly two hundred thousand tons.

More relayed signals from below: Kupsch was in contact with the same convoy and Stackmann had scored hits on a 6000-tonner.

Waves of fatigue washed everything away. No leaning against the bridge casing or master sight, or I should have gone to sleep on my feet. My arms could scarcely raise the binoculars. There was a dull void inside my skull and a churning in my guts to add to the pressure on my bladder. Stiff-legged, I descended the ladder.

ERA Franz was not in the CPOs' mess, even though he must have been off watch. He had stayed out of sight since his crack-up, probably too ashamed to leave the engine-room.

I emerged from the heads to find the second lieutenant waiting outside. He looked like an elderly dwarf, with his creased and crumpled baby-face. Had his stubble grown darker overnight? I stared stupidly at him until I realized his face was so white that the patchy beard looked blacker than usual.

When the second lieutenant reappeared he asked the steward for some coffee.

'Better make it fruit-juice,' I cut in.

The steward paused uncertainly. The second lieutenant, who had slumped into a corner, made no response.

'Fruit-juice,' I decided. 'Some for me too, please.'

A cat-nap would do us both good, so why coffee?

I was just stretching out, experimentally, when the Captain entered.

The steward returned with a can of juice and two mugs.

'Get me some strong coffee and a couple of sandwiches,' the Captain said, 'and make it snappy.'

The steward was back in no time. Katter must have had the sandwiches ready cut.

The Captain chewed, paused, and chewed again, staring into space. The silence became oppressive.

'Another three sunk,' he said. There was no note of triumph in his voice. If anything, he sounded morose and disgruntled.

'Us too, sir, damned nearly,' I blurted out.

'Nonsense,' he said, and continued to stare into space. 'At least we carry a respectable coffin around with us. Just like sea-snails, we are – never without a place to curl up in.'

The banal simile seemed to tickle him. 'Just like sea-snails,' he repeated, nodding to himself and grinning wearily.

So there it was. The enemy: a line of dark shapes on the horizon. The attack: not even a lurch as our torpedoes left the tubes. The counter-attack: a lethal flourish of drums. First the fever of the chase, then the sound of sinking ships, then the hours of nerve-racking torment, and then, when we surfaced, the blazing tanker. Four hits out of five, but no exultation.

The Captain seemed to emerge from a half-trance. He leant forward and called down the passage.

'Time?'

'0750, sir.'

'Quartermaster!'

Kriechbaum appeared promptly from the control-room.

'Any chance of catching them up?'

'I doubt it, sir – unless . . .' The quartermaster hesitated and began afresh: 'Unless they make a drastic alteration in their mean course.'

'Which seems unlikely.'

The Captain followed Kriechbaum into the control-room. I heard snatches of dialogue and the Captain thinking aloud. 'We dived at 2235 – let's say 2300. It's now 0750, so we've lost a good eight hours. Convoy speed? About eight knots. That means we'd take hours to overhaul them. All that fuel . . .'

He still made no move to put us on a reciprocal course.

The Chief appeared in the control-room. He said nothing, but his whole stance was an implied question: 'When do we turn back?'

For all my exhaustion, I couldn't sleep. I felt as if I were full of pep pills. Lingering excitement made me restless. There was no one in the CPOs' mess, but sounds emanated from the fore-ends, where a half-hearted victory celebration seemed to be in progress. I peered into the gloom and saw a circle of figures on the decking, which had now been lowered. Languid singing greeted me:

> 'As I was walking through the wood
> I met a big fat momma.
> I screwed the lady where she stood
> And slipped her half-a-dollar.
>
> Chorus: And the hills rang all night
> With her cries of delight,
> With her c-r-i-e-s of delight!'

All very well for them to warble – they hadn't seen a thing. If they hadn't been told that the rending, splintering sounds were made by water-pressure bursting the sides of sinking ships – our victims – the muffled cacophony below the surface would have meant nothing to them.

It was the quartermaster's watch. The glow had waned but was still clearly visible. The sea had increased. Suddenly Kriechbaum gave a shout and pointed into the darkness ahead. The Captain was on the bridge within seconds of his report.

I saw a life-raft with a knot of men on it.

'Megaphone,' called the Captain. 'Take her in closer.' He craned over the bridge rail and bellowed. 'What's the name of your ship?'

The huddled figures replied promptly, as though alacrity would buy them a helping hand.

'Arthur Allee!'

The Captain grunted. 'Just as well to know.'

One survivor tried to cling to our hull, but we were under way again. For a moment the man hung between us and the raft. Then he let go and fell back into our wake. Teeth – I only caught a glimpse of his teeth, not even the whites of his eyes.

Less than fifteen minutes later, a strange twinkle of lights appeared in the paling darkness – tiny pin-points of light, like glow-worms. As we drew nearer, they turned into little bobbing lamps. More survivors, hanging in their life-jackets. I could clearly see them raise their arms, perhaps to attract our attention. They were probably shouting too, but nothing could be heard of their cries because the wind was against them.

Granite-faced, the Captain reduced speed and gave some steering orders which would keep us at a safe distance from the drifting figures. We were still making enough of a bow-wave to lift two or three of them and leave them wallowing. Were they really waving? I couldn't make up my mind. It might have been a last impotent gesture of defiance at the enemy who had consigned them to the predatory clutches of the deep.

We stood stiff and silent, gnawed by the fearful realization that the figures in the sea might have been us. What would become of them? They had survived our torpedoes, but what were their chances? How cold was the water in December? How long had they already been drifting? It seemed hard to believe, but the convoy's rear support group must have passed the scene of the sinking hours ago.

No movement from the Captain, a sailor unable to assist fellow-sailors in peril because a C-in-C's directive forbade the

rescue of survivors. The only exception: downed airmen.
As a potential source of military intelligence, flyers were
officially considered worth saving.

I could still make out the will-o'-the-wisp flicker of the
little lamps astern. 'Port five,' ordered the Captain. 'Those
were RN personnel. From a corvette, probably.'

The second lieutenant came on deck. 'Looks like a volcanic
eruption,' he muttered, meaning the glow. The lamps had
vanished.

A sudden flash lit the sky. Seconds later an explosion rolled
across the water like distant thunder, then another. The helmsman called: 'Hydrophone operator to bridge – depth-charges
bearing two-six-zero degrees.'

A colourless dawn climbed above the horizon. The glow
gradually paled.

Fatigue descended on me like a leaden blanket. I was back
in the wardroom when the bridge reported a burning ship
ahead of us. It was 0900. Nothing for it but to drag myself
on deck.

'She's been hit,' the Captain said. 'Must be a straggler,
possibly from another convoy. We'd better finish her off, I
suppose.'

He raised his glasses. To Kriechbaum, from between leather-
gauntleted hands: 'We'll draw ahead of her first. She can't
have much way on – five knots, at a guess. Helmsman, port
twenty.' The pall of smoke grew larger and swung to starboard. Masts and superstructure would have been visible by
now, but they were shrouded in smoke.

Five minutes later we dived to periscope depth: 14 metres.

After a while, the Captain started to give a running commentary from the conning-tower. 'She won't get away, not this
one. Now she's zigging – no, hang on, she's zigging back again.
Wait a bit. Two masts, four loading hatches. Nice-looking tub,
must be about eight thousand. Down by the stern. Still burning
aft, but she's been on fire amidships.'

His voice went gravelly. 'Watch it, Chief, she's zigging this
way. Blast!'

The periscope must have dipped for a moment.

The Chief pulled a face. His current job was to keep such
a perfect depth that the Captain would be able to maintain
observation with a minimum of periscope adjustments. He
leant forward, staring at the Papenberg.

A string of steering orders. Suddenly the Captain swore
and ordered the motors full ahead. The submarine gave a

perceptible lurch.

From the periscope, bearings were fed into the deflection calculator in the conning-tower and electrically transmitted to the torpedoes.

The first lieutenant had long ago removed the safety-catch from the firing gear. He was standing in the conning-tower, ready to fire at the Captain's word of command.

'Open bow-caps,' ordered the Captain. 'Stand by No. 1 tube.' Two seconds later: 'Fire No. 1 tube! Lock on No. 2.'

The whole sequence of events flowed over me like a waking dream. I heard a dull explosion followed immediately by a far more violent one.

The Captain's voice seemed to come from a great distance. 'That stopped her. Looks as if she's sinking.'

Yet another ship. Credited to us? The fog in my brain thickened. Knees like jelly – it was all I could do to stand. I swayed and grabbed the chart-table before making my way drunkenly aft.

What had woken me?

Silence reigned in the POs' mess. Half-asleep, I climbed painfully out of my bunk. I reeled rather than walked down the passage and groped my way into the control-room like a blind man. My limbs ached as if they had been stretched on the rack.

There were signs of activity in the control-room. Isenberg and the Vicar were engaged in routine duties. I still couldn't grasp what had happened. Had I keeled over and passed out? I seemed to be screened from my surroundings by a gauze curtain. It was hard to tell if I was awake or still dreaming.

Then my eyes fell on the war diary, which lay open on the desk.

13.12:

0900. Sighted damaged freighter, bearing 190, course 120 degrees, speed 5 knots. Closed to investigate.

1000. Dived to attack. Target altered course towards (zigzag).

1025. Fired one torpedo, range 5000 metres. Observed hit amidships. Secondary explosion, presumed f·e¹ ⸱⸱⸱¹· Fire spread to fuel on surface. Target still under way but settled lower in water. Some crew seen on board. 5 guns aft but unmanned owing to fire. No life-boats visible.

The Old Man hadn't mentioned any guns at the time. I wondered when he had found the opportunity to write all this.

1045. Distant propeller noises bearing 280 degrees. Manoeuvred for further attack.

1052. Fired one torpedo, range 400 metres. Observed hit below mainmast. Target practically stopped, extensive fire on board, ship's side torn open amidships for 50 metres. Withdrew eastwards.

1110-1112. Further explosions from target – possibly ammunition. Ship now stopped.

1140. Propeller noises bearing 270 degrees, turbines. Destroyer suspected but could not be seen through smoke from target.

1155. Surfaced 6000 metres east of freighter. Remained trimmed down. Destroyer sighted close to target.

1157. Dived. Course 090, speed 3 knots.

1210. Surfaced. Destroyer hull down to west of target, going away. Course 090, speed 5 knots, charged batteries. Adjusted course to keep 8-9000 metres eastward of target and watch her sink.

1324-1450. Remained stopped, charged batteries. Fire on target decreasing, still afloat.

1530. Closed for surface attack to deliver *coup de grâce*.

1608. Fired one torpedo, range 500 metres. Observed hit ahead of aft superstructure. Hull appeared completely cut in two amidships, fore and after sections held together by upperworks and catwalks only. Total loss certain. Forecastle awash and listing to port. Sighted 2 empty lifeboats adrift. No further sign of destroyer.

1640. Closed to 50 metres. Machine-gunned bow and stern to vent trapped air pockets.

1952. Target finally sank.

2000. Set course 080 degrees. speed 10 knots. Signalled C-in-C from U-A: 'crippled freighter 8000 g.r.t. now sunk, LPSN 3275. Returning to base.'

2300. Relayed signal received. 'C-inC from U-X: 2 MVL sighted Square MR, mean course due east, 10 knots, contact lost 2100, now pursuing. Wind NW7, sea 5, barometer 1127 rising. Operational capacity still restricted by weather.'

So the freighter had been torpedoed three times. Machine-gunned too – of course, I recalled hearing the chatter. In that case, when had I passed out?

I stared at the page. Even the final paragraph was in the Captain's handwriting. Incredible that he should have found the energy to write up the war diary at that time of night, after the previous thirty-six hours. I could just remember him saying 'Right, let's head straight for home' and altering course to zero-eight-zero. We were steering north of east – that much had sunk in.

The engines sounded more uneven than usual. Strictly economical speed.

Economical speed! If I had understood the Chief aright, it wouldn't matter how carefully he regulated our speed. There wasn't enough fuel to lay us alongside in St Nazaire lock.

The quartermaster had brought out a small-scale chart which showed fringes of terra firma. I was amazed to see how far south we were. The Captain seemed unperturbed by our fuel situation. Did he really believe that the Chief possessed secret reserves which could be tapped in an emergency?

The Captain's cubby-hole was shrouded by its green curtain. He must be asleep. Involuntarily, I rose on tiptoe. My limbs were so stiff and painful I had to steady myself with both hands.

Every bunk in the wardroom was occupied. A full complement, for once. I felt like a sleeping-car attendant doing his rounds.

They were all asleep. That meant the quartermaster was up top. It must be after 0800.

My watch had stopped.

A similar hush prevailed in the CPO's mess. ERA Franz's bunk was unoccupied. Of course – the second engine-room watch came on at 0600.

The Captain had made no further reference to Franz's exhibition. I wondered whether he intended to forget all about it or press for a court martial.

We were a floating dormitory.

I lost myself in a maelstrom of conflicting visions. The dead man lolling in his rubber dinghy, black dots bobbing in a sea of fire, the glow-worms . . .

I hadn't seen many dead bodies before. Swoboda, yes, and two men with broken necks: a wrestler competing in the regional Græco-Roman championships at Oberlungwitz – the crack was audible throughout the hall – and a climber who had lost his footing on the Höfat. The grassy slope was as slippery as ice. When we loaded him on the farm-cart, his head dangled limply like a marionette's. Then there was the schoolmistress who drowned in a liquid manure pit one night, and – when I was only fourteen – the little boy who had been run over by a truck. I could still see him sprawled on the asphalt, strangely contorted in the full glare of the midday sun.

THE DEPOT SHIP

Herrmann stuck his head out of the wireless office.

'Cipher officer!'

Routine signals were handled by the PO telegraphist, who ran them through the decoding machine and entered them in clear in the radio log which was submitted to the Captain every two hours.

Herrmann had already processed this particular signal without making sense of it. Only the first words – 'Officer's Signal!' – were singly encrypted. That meant a job for the cipher officer, alias the second lieutenant.

Tousle-haired, Babyface rolled out of his bunk. He assumed an air of importance and set up the decoding machine on the wardroom table. The Captain gave him the day's setting on soluble paper – a security measure, like the soluble plug connections of the machine itself.

Cipher officer . . . The words carried a suggestion of something mysterious and special, something ultra-secret. All we needed!

The Captain scowled. 'Quick as you can, Number Two.'

The first word to come out was 'Captain'. This obliged the second lieutenant to run the entire signal through the machine, still without making any sense. In other words, the text had been ciphered and re-ciphered three times. The Captain would have to repeat the whole process using a setting known to himself only.

Meaningful glances. Our first triply encrypted signal this patrol – the plot was thickening. The Captain picked up the decoding machine and vanished into his cubby-hole, calling for the first lieutenant. Much rustling of paper. The Captain said nothing when he reappeared five minutes later. Silence in the wardroom.

'Intriguing,' he said at length. Nothing more, though the rest of us were hanging on his words. He didn't speak for another two minutes. Then: 'They've given us a new port of destination.'

His tone was a shade less serene than he meant it to be. From the sound of it, there was something ominous about our new orders.

'Really?' the Chief said casually. Fuel was fuel, wherever it came from.

'Yes, La Spezia.'

The Chief started. 'I beg your pardon, sir?'

'La Spezia, Chief. Is it my accent, or are you going deaf?'

The Captain rose and headed for his cubby-hole again. We heard him rummaging around behind the curtain.

I could see the map of Europe – every spur and re-entrant of its outline. Freehand map-drawing was my forte at school La Spezia, east of Genoa in the armpit of Italy.

I had a hollow sensation at the pit of my stomach. Surprise made me blink. My palms went clammy.

'But,' stammered the second lieutenant, 'but that means . . .'

'The Mediterranean, that's right,' the Chief cut in sharply. His throat contracted a couple of times. 'In other words, we go via Gibraltar.'

'Gibraltar . . .' The second lieutenant stared at me open-mouth.

'Jebel-al-Tarik.'

'Come again?'

'Arabic for Gibraltar: Hill of Tarik.'

Gibraltar, an ape-inhabited rock. Close-up of a she-ape cuddling her young, teeth bared. British Crown Colony. The Pillars of Hercules. Ethnic bridge between Europe and North Africa. Algeciras, olé! The belly-dancers of Tangier. Gibraltar convoys. The Rock, home of half the British fleet. Gib-ral-tar, Gib-ral-tar, Gib-ral-tar . . . There was a crack in the record – the needle jumped the groove again and again.

Hardly the Captain's cup of tea either. He wouldn't be interested in the Mediterranean, let alone a temporary base somewhere in Italy. Führer command, we obey – or, rather, we carry the can. An ideal ship's motto – it ought to be inscribed in poker-work on the lid of a lemon crate and hung up in the control-room.

I could now make sense of the news broadcasts in recent weeks. North Africa: heavy fighting round Tobruk, the British advancing westwards along the coast road. The Mediterranean must be teeming with British freighters and escort vessels. U-boats to clean up – was that the idea?

In my mind's eye I saw a chart of the Strait of Gibraltar, complete with a loathsome jungle of D/F stations, anti-submarine nets, booms, mines and security systems.

Somewhere at the back of my mind a word stuck and refused to budge: *refit*. U-A needed a refit after her hammering. How could the Captain dream of proceeding to La Spezia without one?

Another word: 'Fuel . . .' It drifted in from the control-room, twice. The Captain said it once, then the quartermaster.

Next, I heard: 'Alter course to zero-nine-zero degrees.'

Ninety degrees – due east? Now I was completely foxed. The Captain came back from the control-room and sat down at the table with his face puckered like a boy doing mental arithmetic. The Chief should have come out with the question we were all waiting for – 'Where's the fuel coming from?' – but his mouth remained firmly shut.

The Captain spent the next five minutes scratching his beard. At last he growled: 'We replenish at Vigo.'

Vigo, Vigo, Vigo . . . Another name to conjure with. Vigo . . A Spanish port, surely – or was it in Portugal? One of the two.

The Chief drew in his lips so tightly that unaccustomed dimples appeared in his lean cheeks. 'Mm,' was his only comment.

'Very considerate of the powers that be,' the Captain said drily. 'They think of everything – especially their own little problems. Two hundred and fifty miles – we might even manage it without sails. Well, Chief, what do you say now?'

The calendar showed 14 December, our scheduled date of return. Now they wanted us to go Spanish instead of French. After that, Italian. Very exotic, to be welcomed with castanets instead of a German brass band – anyway, I always did prefer sherry to canned beer.

Spanish chestnuts, Spanish fly – what else was Spanish?

The Captain grinned. 'No need to look like that, Chief, everything's laid on. As much fuel as we can carry – torpedoes and stores as well. All the comforts of a home port, in fact.'

I wondered how he knew – the signal had been pretty brief. The Chief shrugged. 'In that case . . .'

It occurred to me that this patrol was supposed to be the Chief's last – his twelfth. U-A was his second boat. Not many men survived twelve patrols, and now, for good measure, he was being offered a special treat – an excellent chance of dying for his country at the eleventh hour.

I pulled myself to my feet and ducked through the bulkhead.

The crew still had no idea what we were in for. Goodbye to a brass-band reception at St Nazaire. Instead, a Macaroni port and a mint of trouble before we got there – if we ever did. I could imagine the general reaction. The fore-ends had gathered that something was up. Excitement and curiosity hung in the air.

Wherever I went, conversation ceased and enquiring faces turned in my direction, but as long as the Captain made no announcement I was obliged to remain poker-faced.

The Captain still hadn't commented on the order, but his sombre expression spoke volumes. Was there any hope of penetrating the Strait – and, even if we did, what then? Enemy air bases were near and numerous, so aerial surveillance was infinitely tighter than over the Atlantic. It might be almost impossible to operate by day. Given the right light and angle of vision, flyers were said to be able to spot the shadowy form of a U-boat 60 metres down in Mediterranean waters.

The coxswain's broad forehead was furrowed by a scar which slanted from the right eyebrow to the bridge of his nose. Excitement turned it pink. Now it was dark-red.

Kriechbaum, who carried no such reliable pointer to his emotional state, specialized in total stolidity. Having taken over the chart-table from the Captain, he growled at anyone who came too close like a tiger intent on a lump of meat. The consequence was that no one could tell which chart he was plying with his rule and dividers.

Ario passed through the control-room on his way forward. 'Must be an hour since we altered course,' he remarked tentatively.

'Smart lad,' jibed Isenberg. 'You don't miss a trick, do you? They ought to put you out to stud.'

Cruising speed. The men spent a second hour stretched on the rack of their own uneasy curiosity. Still no word from the Captain.

Going to the POs' mess to fetch my writing things, I heard: 'Funny sort of course . . .' – 'Well, maybe the wardroom want to watch the sun go down over Biscay.' – 'If you're thinking of dipping your wick at St Nazaire, you can forget it. I don't know what's going on, but it smells.'

A brooding silence.

Then I heard the familiar crackle of the intercom.

'Do you hear there? We've been given a new port of destination – La Spezia, in the Mediterranean. We'll be replenishing at Vigo. As you probably know, that's in Spain.'

No comment, no embellishments, not a mortal word of explanation – nothing. The Captain said 'That's all' and switched off.

The POs exchanged mute glances. Rademacher stared at the piece of bread in his hand as though a stranger had put it there. It was Frenssen who broke the spell.

'Jesus Christ Almighty!'

An assortment of expletives followed.

Gradually the significance of the order sank in. No return to the base which had become a second home to them all, no berthing with a flourish for the benefit of admiring girl telegraphists and nurses clutching bouquets to their bosoms. Christmas leave? That was out too, probably.

Surprise was succeeded by resentment. 'Of all the . . .' – 'Bloody cheek!' – 'Who'd have thought it!' – 'Stop the bus, someone, I want to get off!'

My eyes strayed to the midshipman. Ullmann was perched on the edge of his bunk, staring blankly into space. His limp hands dangled between his knees and his face had gone very pale.

'The Chief'll love this,' Frenssen said. 'We're almost out of oil and fish, so what's it all about? Spain's neutral.'

Shocked silence still reigned in the fore-ends. The rattle of a fanny between the bow tubes sounded unnaturally loud.

'It's not on,' Ario said at last.

'Who says?' Dunlop retorted. 'Never heard of a depot ship?'

'Sure, but how come we're going to – what's the name again?'

'Vigo.'

'Shit,' said Böckstiegel. 'Shit, shit, shit!'

'They m-must be daft!' Gigolo was stammering with dismay. 'I mean, sending us to the Mediterranean!' From the repugnance with which he uttered the last word, he might have been talking about a cess-pit.

Turbo was concerned. 'But we're expected at St Nazaire. What'll they do with our kit?'

'Forward it to our next-of-kin,' Ario told him soothingly.

'Shurrup!' snapped Gigolo. Even his sense of humour had its limits.

'Christmas in Macaroni-land – who'd have credited it!'

'What's the difference? As long as we get some leave, who cares if we take a train-ride across France or across Italy?'

'Up through Italy,' Hagen amended.

'Oh well,' Ario said in a resigned tone. One could almost hear him thinking what nobody dared to say aloud: 'Let's get there first . . .'

'What's so bad about Gibraltar?' the Vicar enquired discreetly.

A head emerged from one of the hammocks, to be tapped expressively with a forefinger. 'What a world!' said a voice from a lower bunk. 'That twat's alive, and Bismarck had to snuff it.'

'No idea of geography, that's his trouble. What's the matter, mate, weren't you in class when they did Gibraltar? Tight as a virgin's crack, the Strait is. Any U-boat that wants to get through better be smeared with Vaseline.'

Nobody spoke for a while.

'It's been known,' Hagen said eventually.

'What has?'

'Getting stuck on the job. It happened to a mate of mine once. Like a bleeding vice, he said it was.'

'You're joking!'

'Cross my heart.'

'What did he do?'

'Nothing he could do. They had to send for the quack. He gave the girl a jab . . .'

Turbo, ever a stickler for accuracy, was dissatisfied. 'How do you call the quack when you're halfway up?'

Gibraltar had momentarily lost its terrors.

'Use your initiative. Shout, maybe.'

'Oh sure, or wait till gangrene sets in.'

The Captain was in the control-room.

'Join the Navy . . .' I said.

'And see the world – I know, very humorous,' he retorted grumpily. He turned and gave me a quizzical stare, chewing on his cold pipe. We stood there for a few moments like a pair of statues. Then he made a gesture of invitation and I joined him on the chart-stowage.

'They probably call it securing supply routes. Africa's going up in smoke and we're supposed to play firemen. Funny idea, sending U-boats into the Med when we don't have enough in the Atlantic.'

I tried a little sarcasm. 'Pity it isn't high summer. The C-in-C might have timed it better.'

'I doubt if it's the C-in-C's idea. He's always fought tooth and nail to prevent us from being shunted into a siding. We need every operational U-boat we can muster. Why else did they build the VII-C, if it wasn't for the Battle of the Atlantic?'

Until a few hours ago, I thought, U-A was an aristocrat of the deep – a self-contained, self-reliant warship. Now she was merely a strategist's pawn. Her bow had been pointed by remote control towards Spain. Our scheduled return to base, and all that went with it, had come to nothing.

'Hard luck on the poor old Chief,' he began again, more hesitantly. 'It's his wife – she's due to produce any day now. He had it all worked out. Even a long patrol wouldn't have bitched his chances of being on leave at the right time, but he couldn't allow for this latest development. They don't even have a flat any more – bombed, patrol before last. She moved in with her parents at Rendsburg. Now he's worried in case something goes wrong. I don't blame him. His wife isn't a hundred per cent fit – she nearly died the last time. The child never made it.'

The Captain never discussed other people's private lives, it wasn't his style. I wondered why he was being so expansive.

An hour after supper I knew. I was just squeezing past when he glanced up from his patrol report, said 'Just a minute' and beckoned me into his cubby-hole.

'I'm putting you ashore at Vigo – you and the Chief. The Chief's due for a shore job after this patrol. That's official.'

'But . . .'

'Spare me the heroics. I'm still working on a signal. Somehow or other, you and the Chief are going to be piloted across Spain – disguised as gipsies, if necessary.'

'But . . .'

'No buts. Two can manage better than one. I've thought it over. We've got agents there – they'll take care of you.'

My brain reeled. Leave the boat now? All the way across Northern Spain? The Old Man must be off his head . . .

I found the Chief in the control-room. 'The Old Man's putting us ashore, did you know?'

'What?'

'We're getting off at Vigo – the two of us.'

'How come?' The Chief pursed his lips. I could see him putting two and two together. At last he said briskly : 'All I'd like to know is, how's the Old Man going to get by with that knuckle-head – now of all times?'

It took me a moment to grasp that he was referring to his successor.

The midshipman, I thought – if only we could take the midshipman along too.

Next time I passed through the control-room, Kriechbaum was back at the chart-table. He could now, for the first time in ages, employ a straight line to mark our progress across the chart. Everyone was busy, but nobody looked up from his work. We were all coming to terms with our personal disappointment and private misgivings.

By the second day, the shock had subsided. Only four days separated us from our final approach to the Spanish coast. The men had recovered far more quickly than the generally low level of morale might have led one to expect. The conversation I overheard from my bunk followed a well-worn path.

'I was dead lucky last time. An army telephonist, she was. We had the compartment to ourselves, all the way from Savenay to Paris. You should try it sometime – no sweat, just shove it in and let the train do the rest. I nearly popped out when we hit some points . . .'

Two minutes later.

'No, not inside the bloody car – outside. Drape her across the front seat and bang her from behind – that way you can use the suspension. What? That's right, mate, standing up outside . . .'

I peered round the edge of the curtain, straight into Frenssen's face. It was transfigured with the act of recollection. 'It pissed with rain, once. She stayed nice and dry. Me, I got soaked. It ran off the roof all over me. Dead convenient, mind you – I rinsed myself off afterwards.'

'Riding bareback, were you?'

'Why not? She knows when to take care.'

On the third day after the signal, shortly before midday and towards the end of his watch, the quartermaster reported an unidentified object on our starboard bow. I followed the Captain on deck.

The object was still about a thousand metres away. It wasn't a lifeboat – too flat and shapeless. It seemed to be drifting towards us across the almost motionless sea. Above it hovered a strangely agitated cloud, not unlike a swarm of bees. Seagulls? The Captain said nothing, just puffed out his cheeks. He lowered the binoculars. 'Yellow patches – that's a life-raft.'

I focused my own glasses on the raft. It was unoccupied and seemed to have small casks secured to its sides – or were they fenders?

Kriechbaum gave an exclamation. 'There are men clinging to it!'

The Captain altered course. 'No sign of life.' The raft grew bigger, the scream of gulls louder and more strident.

The Captain dismissed the look-outs from the bridge. 'Take over their sectors, Kriechbaum.' He turned to me. 'Adults only, I suspect.'

He gave a steering order and we approached the raft in a sweeping left-hand arc. Our bow-wave caressed the bodies that floated round it. One after another, they started to nod like mechanical shop-window dummies.

Five dead men lashed to a raft. Why not on top of it? Why were they suspended from the ratlines? Had they been seeking protection from the wind?

Cold and fear – how long could a man withstand them? How long could his body-heat resist the icy heart-stopping paralysis? How soon did his hands go dead?

One corpse, which was riding higher than the rest, made an endless succession of stiff obeisances.

'Can't see a name anywhere,' said the Captain.

One of the dead seamen had swollen up and subsided on his back in the water. There was no flesh on his cheek-bones. The gulls had stripped them of everything edible. All that remained on his skull was a small patch of scalp with black hair adhering to it.

They had ceased to be men. They were grisly phantoms, not human beings. Cavities yawned where their eyes should have been. In one case, the collar-bone was exposed. Although the gulls had left no flesh undevoured, the corpses looked slimy. Even the tattered shirts and life-jackets were filmed with greenish jelly.

'A bit too late, I'm afraid.' The Captain gave some engine and steering orders in a hoarse voice. 'Let's get out of here,' I heard him mutter.

The sea-gulls swooped over us, screaming malevolently. I itched to pepper them with shot.

The yellowish blob fell astern and dwindled rapidly. Our exhaust-fumes shrouded and dissolved its outlines.

'Those were merchant seamen.'

The Captain's voice was a welcome distraction.

'They were still wearing those old-fashioned cork life-jackets – you don't find them on warships any more.' After a while he murmured 'Lucky I'm not superstitious,' and gave another steering order. The look-outs were recalled to the bridge.

I couldn't banish the spectacle. Horror still clawed at my entrails. Queasily I went below. The Captain followed less than ten minutes later. He saw me sitting on the chart-stowage and came over.

'It's always the same with gulls. One time, we came across two lifeboats. No survivors – frozen to death, probably – and every one of them had his eyes pecked out.'

How long had they been adrift? I couldn't bring myself to ask.

'You don't get these problems with a petrol-tanker – one hit and up she goes. Crude oil is different, I'm afraid.'

Although the look-outs had seen little before being ordered below, it was clear that the crew had got the wind of our discovery. The men were monosyllabic. The Chief must have noticed something too, because he shot the Captain a look of enquiry, then quickly lowered his eyes.

Nothing was said in the POs' mess either. I was even spared the sick jokes which usually served to disguise their true feelings. One might have thought them peculiarly thick-skinned and insensitive, unmoved by the fate of others. The sudden silence, the irritability that hung in the air, told a different story. I felt sure that many were picturing themselves adrift in a boat or clinging to a raft. Everyone on board knew what little chance there was of being spotted in this area. Everyone knew the fate that awaited such survivors, even if the sea behaved itself. Men who lost their ship in convoy had a better prospect of rescue than most – at least there were other ships around to record their positions. These scarecrows were no survivors from a convoy, though. We should have sighted other flotsam as well, not just a solitary raft.

The Vigo landfall presented problems. It was days since our last proper fix, thanks to a haze which permanently obscured the sun and stars. The quartermaster had done his sums as conscientiously as only he knew how, but not even Kriech-baum could make precise allowances for the effect of wind and sea. It remained to be seen how far we had strayed from our estimated position.

U-A was now escorted by a multitude of gulls. They had black wing-coverts and narrower but longer wings than the usual Atlantic gulls. I was almost stifled by a sudden yearning for dry land. How would it look now? The year was drawing to a close, but our only indication of it had been the gradual dwindling of daylight. This was the time when, as children, we used to build potato-bonfires and fly homemade kites bigger than ourselves.

I was wrong, of course – bonfire time must have been over weeks before. My sense of time was awry, but I could still see milky white smoke writhing maggot-like across the moist earth. The haulms wouldn't burn properly – the fire only glowed red when the wind freshened. We used to bake potatoes in the hot ashes, prodding them impatiently with sticks to check their progress. The black skins puckered and burst. Then, with lips retracted, we sank our teeth in the mealy yellow interior. The taste of smoke enveloped our tongues, the scent of smoke clung to our clothes for days to come. Every pocket bulged with chestnuts, every finger was nicotine-stained from shelling walnuts. The little ivory walnut-brains tasted bitter unless you detached the yellow cortex from every last recess . . .

Even Kriechbaum's tongue was loosened by the proximity of land. I no longer had to stand around, shifting from foot to foot and looking receptive. He spoke without prompting, tracing the course of some pencil-lines on the chart with his dividers.

'The ideas they dream up! Anyway, even if we do make the inner harbour, how do we find the right ship – at night? There's bound to be more than one tub in port.'

It was clear that he considered the whole scheme half-baked. 'Never mind, anything for a change . . .'

The Captain came in and bent over the chart. 'We'd better work out an approach round the islands, Kriechbaum. What's the name of that one in the mouth of the bay?'

'Cies, sir.'

'There should be a light at that point, but they're bound to have doused them all. That won't help.'

'We've got thirty metres of water in the bay.'

'Let's take a closer look at the south entrance.'

0600. The circular orifice of the upper lid swung gently to and fro across a darkened sky, its motion made visible by a scattering of stars. I climbed past the helmsman, who was presiding over his instruments at the forward end of the conning-tower.

'Man on the bridge?'

'Affirmative!'

Grasping the clip of the upper lid I hauled myself into the open air. The wind struck chill on my face. Its moisture-laden breath made me shiver. Involuntarily, I scanned the horizon for land but the dim skyline was unbroken.

'The wind went round to the west an hour ago,' the second lieutenant said.

The darkness was paling in the east. A hint of greenish

light floated above the skyline and crept along it in an ever-widening arc. We glided through the dawn like a ghost-ship. I could barely hear the murmur of the bow-wave. The mist that clung to the surface gradually disintegrated into streaks until the water seemed to be smoking. By degrees, it lifted and the dawn light rolled over us in gentle waves. Roused by the coming day, the dark sea danced and trembled at its touch.

The second lieutenant bent over the hatch. 'Tell the Captain it's dawn.' Then: 'Tell the quartermaster there's a chance of star sights.'

From one minute to the next, the clouds caught fire and the whole of the eastern sky burst into flames. Amethyst light welled above the horizon and dispersed. The celestial conflagration was scattered with clouds like black smoke, their lower edges fringed with violet. Turmoil overhead, radiance all around. We slid through the glow with our casing bathed in fire.

Now the sun thrust its lip over the skyline. The sky turned greenish for a minute or two, then acquired a blue-grey tinge which paled towards the horizon. Though gaining little strength, the sun climbed quickly higher. As it did so, the clouds lost colour and the sea darkened once more. Streaks of white foam threaded its sombre surface like cracks in a tinted mirror.

Today the sea resembled an expanse of foothills in miniature, with smooth round knolls and flowing undulations. They slid beneath the hull, imparting a gentle rise and fall. Folds and furrows appeared in their flanks at every breath of wind. A dozen or more sea-gulls circled the boat on motionless wings. Their plumage alternately dulled and flared into dazzling splendour as they lost or caught the sun. They stretched their necks and stared at us with unblinking eyes.

The mist returned during Kriechbaum's watch. He frowned. Sea-mist and an unfamiliar coastline were a navigator's nightmare. Eager to take a bearing of some kind, the Captain kept us nosing towards the mainland at minimum speed.

The first lieutenant was also on the bridge. We all peered intently into the watery haze ahead of us. Suddenly a portion of the grey murk condensed and gained solidity. A fishing-boat was crossing our bow.

'We could always ask them where we are,' growled the Captain. 'You speak Spanish, don't you, Number One?'

'Some – yes, sir.'

The first lieutenant took a while to realize that the Captain was joking.

A breeze sprang up. The mist gradually thinned until the last white shreds disappeared. A line of cliffs loomed fine on the port bow.

'Olé!' said the Captain. 'Stop both!'

We were far too close inshore.

'Let's hope there aren't any fresh-air fiends up there,' he grumbled. 'Not that it's the weather for a stroll.'

Our bow-wave subsided. The sudden stillness took my breath away. U-A began to rock gently. The Captain's eyes were glued to his binoculars. Kriechbaum, too, scanned the coast with intense care.

'Remind me to buy you a beer, Quartermaster,' the Captain said eventually. 'Looks as if we're just where we ought to be, only a bit too close. Right, let's sneak up to the entrance and study the traffic for a while. Slow ahead both. Steer zero-three-zero.'

The helmsman confirmed his orders.

'What water do we have?'

'Eighty metres,' came the answer from below.

'Continuous soundings, please.'

More veils of mist drifted towards us.

'Not such a bad thing,' the Captain said. 'Look-outs, keep your eyes open for small craft. We don't want to run anything down.'

We had arrived off the coast a good two hours earlier than originally estimated.

The Captain was talking, half to himself and a half to Kriechbaum. 'I reckon our best bet is to slip through the north entrance, dived. We may leave the same way – I don't know yet. It'll mean embarking stores through the night and casting off well before dawn. Quartermaster, I want to lay her alongside the *Weser* by 2200. Seven hours . . . That ought to be time enough, but we'll have to get a move on.'

No lights, no fix-points, no approach buoys . . . However straightforward a harbour, no ship entered or left without the aid of a pilot. No chart, however carefully amended, absolved a captain from carrying one. In our case, regulations didn't apply.

The swathes of mist lifted again.

'All or nothing,' the Captain muttered. 'We'd better lie low till it gets dark.'

I left the bridge.

A minute later we dived and went to periscope depth.

With our motors running at slow speed, we nosed gradually closer to the harbour entrance.

The Captain sat astride the periscope saddle with his cap-peak facing aft like a motor-cyclist.

'What's that noise?' he asked quickly. We strained our ears. A high-pitched monotonous whine accompanied by the thud of a muffled drum.

'Can't place it, sir,' said Kriechbaum.

'Odd. Hydrophone operator, what can you hear?'

'A small diesel, sir.' Herrmann's voice.

'Seems to be a coaster of some kind. There's another, and another – and another. Looks like a whole damned regatta. Whoops! That one's shifting . . . Visibility's closing in again, I can hardly see a thing. We'd better find a tub we can tag on to, when the time comes.'

'Forty metres,' reported the man at the echo-sounder.

'How would it be,' the Captain called down, 'if we just dropped anchor?'

No response from Kriechbaum. It was clear that he didn't take the question seriously.

Anchor? I'd almost forgotten – we toted that around with us like any old freighter. I wondered how often U-A had used hers.

The Captain got the first lieutenant to relieve him at the periscope and climbed stiffly down the ladder. 'We'll kill time and go in at nightfall, one way or another.'

I screwed up my courage. 'What then, sir?'

'We proceed according to plan,' he said drily. The 'P' of plan exploded on his lips like a small bomb – the Old Man's way of deriding officialdom. However, he did condescend to explain.

'We have standing instructions. Kernével sent us an exact rendezvous time by wireless. Our agents in Vigo are making the necessary arrangements – if they haven't already made them.'

'Pretty slick,' the Chief murmured.

'You could call it that.'

'Time to surface, sir,' reported the quartermaster.

The Captain stood up and stretched. 'Well, let's go.'

Blue-grey twilight. Smells from the land were wafted to us on the offshore breeze. I absorbed and explored them, isolating the aromas of rotting fish, fuel oil, rust, burnt rubber and tar. With them came the smell of dust, the scent of earth and leaves.

The engines sprang to life. The Captain had evidently decided to press on regardless.

A scattering of position lights twinkled in the middle distance. Red, green, and a white one higher than the rest – a ship's masthead.

The second lieutenant reported a vessel closing on the port quarter.

Watching it silently through his binoculars, the Captain reduced speed. 'Hm, that one looks promising. She's going in, sure as eggs. We'll let her show us the way. Seems to be another of these coasters – the sturdy sort. She's making lots of smoke – must be burning old socks. Pity it isn't a bit darker . . .'

He had not blown to full buoyancy, so our casing scarcely projected from the water. We were almost unrecognizable as a submarine except from abeam.

The Captain pointed our bow at the approaching vessel's green starboard light. From her angle, we were backed by a strip of coastline which swallowed up the outlines of our conning-tower.

We increased speed. We were right in the coaster's wake now – I could smell the smoke.

'Poof!' exclaimed the Captain. 'Look-outs, keep your eyes peeled. We don't want anyone cutting across our bow. There must be ferries and so on . . .'

His own binoculars constantly swept our line of advance. Suddenly a shadow loomed up to starboard. No time for avoiding action. We glided past so close we could see the pinpoint of light from a man's cigarette. If he had been alert he would have seen us, a bizarre shadow half-veiled in smoke.

Now it was our turn to see shadows – three or four of them in the gloom ahead. It was hard to tell if they were approaching or receding.

'Plenty of traffic,' the Captain muttered under his binoculars. More lights – stern lights – and a distant rumbling sound. 'They seem to be at anchor,' I heard Kriechbaum say.

'You reckon we're in the inner roads already?'

'Looks like it, sir.'

A whole necklace of lights had appeared in the distance, neatly strung across the skyline. It could have been a wharf with ships lying alongside.

More ships lay to starboard. Their exact position was hard to discern. If they had all swung to their anchors it would have been simple, but one presented her stern to us while the ship ahead of her was clearly bow-on. The dark silhouettes were accentuated by the lights in the distance.

'Looks as if they're secured head and stern,' murmured the Captain.

I hadn't an inkling how he proposed to identify our German depot ship.

'Time?'

'2130, sir.'

'Perfect.'

The Captain gave two full-helm steering orders in rapid succession, evidently because the currents were tricky. The helmsman had his work cut out.

I cursed our inability to use the searchlight. Even burglars carried a torch.

There were plenty of ships in harbour, warships among them. One dark shape to starboard of us looked like a gunboat or small destroyer.

We stopped engines and glided in silence for a while. The bow swung to starboard.

'Now to pick out the right tub,' I heard the Captain say.

Motor orders, then steering orders, then more motor orders and a series of rapid steering orders which zigzagged U-A between some tall black shadows.

'We're getting nowhere fast,' the Captain growled.

The second lieutenant gave an exclamation. 'Look, sir, a tram!'

What had he said – a tram? There, a blue flash! He was right. As though in confirmation, the trolley-pole struck another flurry of sparks from the overhead cable.

Ahead of us lay a dark and bulky mass, evidently the overlapping shapes of two or three sizeable ships.

'Someone's flashing,' Kriechbaum reported.

'Where?'

I screwed up my eyes. A tiny glimmer of light appeared momentarily at the centre of a shadow.

The Captain watched in silence. The pinpoint came and went twice.

'That's it,' he said, and expelled a deep breath.

Incredulously I fastened my gaze on the intermittent dot of light. There was no doubt it came from a small torch.

'Not much of a welcome,' I blurted out.

The Captain sniffed. 'They can't afford to advertise our presence.'

U-A edged closer to the dark mass, which gradually separated into three distinct parts: a trio of ships lying stem to stern. The winking light came from the middle one. The intervals between the *Weser* and her neighbours increased as we drew nearer.

The Captain stopped motors and gave a steering order. Suddenly I heard German voices: 'Look lively with those fenders! What's the matter – scared of getting your hands dirty? Come on, let's have another one over here!'

The dark strip of water between our bulbous port ballast tank and the vertical cliff of the ship's side narrowed until it was a neck-cricking effort to look up at the shadowy figures leaning over the rail.

The coxswain was on deck now, chivvying his seamen to and fro with subdued curses. Four or five fenders were smartly lowered from above.

'They seem to know their stuff,' said the Captain.

'Maybe they're in practice – or are we their first customers?'

He didn't reply.

A fiendish din drifted across to us from a ship anchored not far away, which was taking on cargo from some lighters by the glare of arc-lamps. Winches provided a rhythmical piston-stroke obbligato.

The Captain grunted. 'Made to order, that racket.'

The only lighting permitted us was a faint glow from the ports.

Fenders rasped and squealed.

A Jacob's ladder slithered down the side. I climbed it immediately at the Captain's heels, muscles stiff and joints creaking – the conning-tower ladder was child's play in comparison. Hands reached out and hauled me aboard. Somebody gripped my hand. 'Welcome aboard the *Weser*, Captain.'

'No, er – I mean, that's the Captain over there.'

We stood, dazzled, in the entrance to the saloon.

Snow-white tablecloths, bunches of flowers, veneered bulkheads polished like mirrors, daintily gathered curtains over the scuttles, deep pile carpet . . . I moved as in a dream. There were ornamental plants everywhere, not only in tubs on the deck but suspended from the deckhead on brass chains. Some plushy-looking armchairs clustered round a table with a bowl of grapes on it.

A knot of uneasiness gathered at the pit of my stomach. I waited for someone to wave a wand and spirit it all away.

I gazed at the beaming, parsonical face of the strange skipper as if he were a creature from outer space: the white beard, the sun-tanned pate with its monk's fringe of grizzled hair, the immaculate collar and tie.

Another handshake, a voice booming at me from far away.

Surely the Old Man might have found something to wear instead of that everlasting pullover of his! The Captain of the *Weser* could hardly have been expected to know that such ragged attire concealed a U-boat commander. I felt myself blushing, but the two men had at last made contact. Vigorous handshakes, grins, simultaneous words of greeting.

We were shepherded into armchairs. The ship's officers appeared in all their finery. More handshakes, more grins. The Old Man could happily have worn his Knight's Cross for the occasion.

The *Weser*'s skipper positively brimmed with eagerness to please. He was straight out of a picture-book – weather-beaten and twinkling-eyed, with ears like an elephant. The ship's bakery had been working flat out since morning. Pastries, fresh bread – anything our hearts desired. Saliva spurted into my mouth – stop, in the name of pity, stop!

'Christmas cake and fresh rolls too, of course,' he added. 'Fresh sausages, boiled pork – only slaughtered this morning – also beefsteaks. Any kind of fruit, even pineapples. As many oranges as you like. Fresh figs, grapes, almonds . . .'

God in Heaven, we had entered the Promised Land! It was years since I'd seen an orange or a pineapple. As for fresh figs, I'd never sampled one in my life.

The skipper basked in our mute amazement. Then he made a sort of magician's pass over the table. In a minute, stewards entered with copious dishes of sliced sausage and ham.

My eyes watered. The Old Man was just as unnerved. He heaved himself out of his armchair as if the sight of such abundance were unendurable. 'If you'll excuse me,' he stammered, 'I'd better see how things are going.'

'Everything's fine – don't worry – no problems,' he was assured on three sides simultaneously, and the skipper forced him back into his chair.

He sat there looking harassed. 'Number One and the Chief,' he said to me, 'I wonder if you'd mind fetching . . .'

I was already on my feet.

'Number Two and the second engineer are to stay aboard for the time being.'

'All hands can take a bath,' the *Weser*'s captain called after me, 'in two shifts. It's all arranged.'

The Old Man was still wearing a self-conscious grin when I returned to the unaccustomed brilliance of the saloon. He shuffled uneasily in his chair as if he distrusted the peacetime atmosphere.

The skipper asked him how our patrol had gone.

The Old Man fidgeted with embarrassment. 'Well, yes — they really had us by the short hairs this time. You'd be surprised what a VII-C can take.'

He nodded to convey that these crumbs of information were more than sufficient to tell the full story.

A battery of bottles had now been put on the table. Bremen beer, German grain spirit, French cognac, Spanish red wine.

Someone knocked. The door opened to reveal two men in trench-coats. They removed their soft felt hats and glanced swiftly from face to face like policemen in search of a suspect.

'Herr Seewald, representing our naval attaché,' I heard.

His companion appeared to be an agent of some kind. The first lieutenant and the Chief squeezed in after the newcomers. We were quite a crowd now.

My heart pounded. We should soon know if the Chief and I were to go ashore or accompany U-A past Gibraltar.

More armchairs were drawn up. The Old Man leafed through some papers which the taller of the two civilians had handed him with a formal bow. Then he looked straight at the Chief over his reading matter. 'Permission refused, Chief — they won't wear the idea.'

I didn't dare look at the Chief. My thoughts raced: the same went for me. So that was that. Just as well, probably — all to the good.

I forced myself to grin.

The Old Man couldn't leave the boat either — nobody could — and the Old Man would have been sunk without the Chief. Yes, just as well. Was I scared? No, the Old Man would pull it off. But there was another consideration: U-A was ripe for a refit. All that damage, and we'd only been able to carry out running repairs . . .

Vigo was in Spain. For the time being, we were safe in Spain. I glanced at my watch: just before midnight. Slowly, the news sank in. Put a good face on it, I told myself, look on the bright side. It wasn't on — never had been. All the same, would I really be feeling so disappointed if I'd never believed in the Old Man's plan?

Of course not — I'd banked on the idea that Vigo would mean the end of the road for both of us. I hadn't wanted to admit it to myself, that was all.

Not having shown any initial enthusiasm for the Old Man's plan to offload us, I was at liberty to behave as if its rejection were all I'd expected. No sign of regret. Permission refused? Fair enough. But what about the Chief? It must be a bitter pill for him to swallow.

The Old Man had taken the news badly – it was written all over his face. He seemed glad when the two trench-coats presented him with a new topic of conversation, but he still sat there looking like a farmer afflicted with hail. The brace of unctuous, servile, hand-wringing toadies transformed the scene into a crude piece of melodrama. The contrast between our worthy host and the two sly-faced villains was too striking to be true.

But what of our own appearance? I studied the Old Man with a stranger's eye. I was still reasonably presentable in my salt-encrusted trousers and semi-washed sweater, but he looked as if he had been roused from a doss-house in the middle of the night. His beard was as unkempt as his hair. On board, we had all become inured to the sight of his decaying pullover, but here in this brightly lit, glossily panelled saloon even I was aghast at its advanced state of disintegration. On the right, above his ribs, gaped a hole nearly big enough to admit his head. Then there was the crumpled shirt, the battered cap, the tattered trousers . . .

I noticed for the first time how pale, hollow-eyed and emaciated he looked. As for the Chief, he could have played Mephisto without make-up. The last few days had wrought havoc with his appearance. Straight into a thirteenth patrol without shore leave was a lot to expect.

The Old Man was obviously at pains to dissociate himself from the two civilians. He made his pickled-gherkin face, refused proffered cigarettes and barely responded to questions.

I learned that the *Weser* had accepted internment at the outbreak of war and become a sort of floating supply dump, periodically replenished with fuel and torpedoes – all in the strictest secrecy, of course, to avoid violating Spanish neutrality.

I marvelled at the predatory faces of the two trench-coats. The taller: sly and crafty, with merging eyebrows, brillian-tined parting, moustache, sideburns and a habit of shooting his cuffs to display chunky gold links. The other: hairy ears, swarthy complexion, fake bonhomie. They both stank of Gestapo, even if one of them did call himself the naval attaché's representative. For backstage conspirators, they were peculiarly ill-disguised by their physiognomy.

From a few scraps of half-heard conversation I gathered that we were not even to be allowed to send mail. Too risky, diplomatic complications, enemy agents, nothing must leak out . . .

It would mean dire forebodings at home. The patrol had already lasted an abnormal length of time, and God alone knew how much longer it would be before we could get rid of our mail. I could imagine the men's faces when they heard they could hang on to all the letters they had so busily written in the past few days.

And the midshipman – how would he take it? I wished he'd never breathed a word about his affair. Comforting romantic adolescents wasn't my forte.

Through a sort of cotton-wool filter, I heard the civilians engaging in social patter. 'One for the road, Captain!' – 'Here's to the next time, Captain!' – 'Must have been an interesting patrol, Captain . . .'

It didn't surprise me, knowing the Old Man, to hear him answer the implied question with a surly monosyllable. They got just as little response when they asked him point-blank if U-A had scored any successes. He just stared grimly from one to the other, waited for his silence to fluster them, and said 'Yes'.

I could see his mind churning away the whole time. Involuntarily, I glanced at his hands. He was screwing them together hard, as he always did when he felt ill at ease.

At last he gave me a nod.

'Going to stretch our legs,' he told the company.

The abrupt contrast between saloon fug and cold night air took my breath away. I could smell oil fuel. The life-blood was flowing back into our veins. The Old Man headed aft at such a pace that it was an effort to keep up with him. Reaching the stern rail, he swung round and leant against it. Beyond the bow of a lifeboat I could see the lights of Vigo. Two gleaming ropes of pearls ascended in parallel, marking the route of a street which ran uphill.

Alongside the wharf lay a destroyer, illuminated over-all. Not far away, arc-lamps flared on board a freighter. One of her derricks pivoted as I watched.

Looking down, I saw the circular yellow disc of our open forehatch. The galley hatch abaft the conning-tower was also open. I could hear voices. 'Look at all that lovely grub!' – 'Stop drooling and bear a hand – you'll get your share.'

Muffled bathroom ballads issued from the bowels of the *Weser*.

I was strangely excited by the twinkling lights round the street-lamps on shore. They seemed to emit a miasma of copulation. I caught the sultry smell of bed, heavy as azalea-blossom, the warm and milky scent of female skin, cloying talcum powder, the anchovy-sharp effluvium of cunt, eau de Javel, semen.

Fragmentary cries, half-commands and a metallic clatter drifted to our ears.

'Some racket,' the Old Man said.

I sensed that the situation didn't appeal to him. 'That fishing-boat,' he said eventually. 'The crew spotted us – couldn't have failed to. And what about all the men on board this tub – who knows if they're a hundred per cent trustworthy? Anyone could flash a quick signal ashore. Anyway, we'll leave earlier than arranged and make our exit by the same route as before – not the south channel, even if our friends do recommend it. If only we had a bit more water under our keel . . .'

Blue flashes ashore, like the flicker of a short circuit: another tram. The breeze carried its rattle and clang across the water. Car-horns tooted, cargo crashed into the loading freighter's hold. Then silence fell.

'Where the devil do they get the torpedoes?' I asked

'Other U-boats – boats returning to base with a full load. The same goes for fuel. The *Weser* pockets anything surplus to requirements.'

'How has the system worked so far? We aren't the first, I take it.'

'Precisely,' he said. 'Three boats have replenished here to date. Two of them were lost.'

'Where?'

'Hard to say, exactly. For all I know, there may be a British destroyer cruising up and down off the south entrance. I don't fancy this sort of caper – it's like something out of a spy film.'

More singing could be heard, this time from the interior of U-A. Somebody was fitting obscene words to the tune of the '*Internationale*'.

I saw the Old Man grin in the faint glow from a distant arc-lamp. He listened for a while before continuing.

'Security isn't tight enough here. It's dicey, the whole set-up.'

I was overcome by a sudden scalding realization. The Spanish matchboxes on the saloon table were familiar to me.

'The local matches,' I said. 'I've seen them before.'

The Old Man didn't seem to be listening. I tried again. 'Those matchboxes on the table in the saloon – I've seen one like them.'

He shrugged. 'Really, where?'

'At La Baule, on a table in the Café Royal. Merten's Number One was fiddling with it. I particularly remember the label.'

'So Merten was here before us – interesting.'

'The matchbox disappeared. No one owned up.'

'Interesting,' he repeated.

'That's not all,' I said, then stopped.

'Well?'

'Nothing.' It was enough to have alerted him to the possibility that the *Weser's* function might not be as much of a secret as our lords and masters imagined. Matchboxes . . . Perhaps it wasn't really so important, and yet, local Spanish matches in France . . .

My thoughts returned abruptly to the midshipman. I hoped Ullmann wouldn't do anything stupid and decided to check on his whereabouts. Feigning a call of nature, I crossed to U-A and disappeared down the conning-tower.

I bumped into Ullmann as soon as I reached the control-room. He was helping to stow some fresh loaves. The netting which had been slung outside the hydrophone booth when we left St Nazaire was bulging once more.

My toes curled with embarrassment. I didn't know how to start.

'Well, Ullmann,' I said, 'too bad things have turned out like this.'

Clearly my talent for consolation was nil. Ullmann looked absolutely miserable. He must have been brooding for days about the growing distance between us and La Baule. I had an urge to take him by the shoulders and shake him till his teeth rattled. Instead, I stared at the deck-plates and mumbled: 'These things happen, you know – it's the luck of the draw.' He made a snuffling noise. I had a horrible feeling that he would break down and weep. Then ingenuity came to the rescue. 'Tell you what, why not give me your letter? No, better still, write her another. Just a quick line, and keep it cheerful – you know what I mean. Meet you back here in ten minutes, all right?'

The *Weser's* skipper looked a sympathetic soul . . .

The Old Man was still lolling against the rail, pondering. I rejoined him without a word. Before long, a bulky shadow loomed up beside us. It was our host. The Old Man performed one of his soft-shoe shuffles and said: 'Never been to Spain before – not that this counts . . .'

I was thinking about Ullmann. Abstractedly I noticed that the lights of the city had acquired a strange tremor, as if the atmosphere between us and the shore were quivering with heat.

The captain of the *Weser* wasn't a voluble man. He spoke in agreeably measured tones, his deep voice tinged with a North German inflection.

'We've got a Flettner rudder, you know – designed by the man who built the rotor ship. The rotor idea wasn't a success but the rudder was. We can turn on a pinhead. Quite an advantage in a crowded harbour.'

Queer fish, I thought, choosing this moment to lecture us on his steering gear.

A dull booming sound made the Old Man restive. The wind was noticeably fresher.

Our host enquired if the Old Man fancied a bath.

'Thanks, better not.'

A steward came aft to inform us that food was being served in the saloon.

'In that case,' said the Old Man, 'let's make the most of it.' He set off at his fellow captain's heels.

I stole a glance at my wrist-watch: 0230. Time to sneak off and find the midshipman. He palmed his letter into my hand like a pickpocket transferring something to an accomplice.

Meanwhile, the Number One and the Chief had relieved the Number Two and second engineer. It would probably be 0500 before we were secured for sea. For all my yearning to stretch out and sleep, I had to return to the saloon.

The civilians had now gone into a boon companions routine. The Old Man was obliged to grin and bear it when the taller of the two slapped him on the back and blared valedictions into his face.

'The Führer would be proud of you, Captain. Best of luck, and good hunting!'

I almost sank through the deck with embarrassment.

Time passed. Fortunately, we didn't have to negotiate the Jacob's ladder again. Buttonholing the *Weser*'s skipper as he guided us down a companionway, I managed to detach him from the rest of the party by lagging behind. There was no need to say much. He took the letter with little hesitation and promised to get it delivered.

A gangway had been secured between our bridge and a lower deck. Back on board! A kind of affection stirred within me. I rested both palms on the damp metal of the bridge casing. Almost imperceptibly, it began to tremble: our motors had started.

The Captain got us away quickly. The waving figures on the *Weser* were soon lost to view.

The port light of a coaster loomed up suddenly, quite close. The Captain called for a signal lamp. I wondered what he had in mind.

He took the lamp and made 'What ship?' A hand-lamp on the coaster started flashing.

'S-a-n-t-a-C-r-u-z-B-u-e-n-v-i-a-j-e,' the Captain spelt out. Then he made 'G-r-a-c-i-a-s'.

'What it is to be a linguist,' he sighed. 'They'd already seen us – must have done. Maybe they'll think we're a boatload of well-mannered Englishmen, or something. Not bad, eh?'

We were steering one-seven-zero. Almost due south.

Our blood transfusion at Vigo had cheered the men up, judging by the exchanges in the POs' mess.

'All very nice, but they might have organized some talent.'

'You're telling me – I could have done with a quick dip. They say those Spanish tarts are hot stuff.'

'What are you grinning at?'

'I was just thinking how it'd have been if we'd tied up alongside the wrong ship.'

'They were dead flattered, having us pay them a visit. The Old Man in that pullover – never seen anything like it . . .'

The consternation that had sobered the POs after the Gibraltar signal seemed to have vanished. It sounded as if they'd always hankered after a trip to the Mediterranean for variety's sake.

Frenssen laid claim to a brother who had served in the Foreign Legion. He pictured a desert landscape of date-palms and oases, mirages, mud-brick forts and luxuriously appointed brothels with a thousand female inmates. 'Bum-boys too, mind you. Something for everyone.'

Pilgrim changed the subject. 'I knew a bird who was queer for trousers with zips. Couldn't keep her hands to herself, even on the tram. There she'd stand, with her hip up against your flies, zipping and unzipping them like a maniac. She almost cut me off in my prime . . .'

'What did you do about it?' Frenssen asked.

'Do about it? Nothing. You fancy it on a tram – I don't.'

'I could fancy it anywhere.'

'Like a bleeding gorilla, you are. No refinement.'

Wichmann said dreamily: 'There's nothing like a nice quiet afternoon screw. A little music, a couple of drinks – nothing to beat it. You can keep your one-minute stands . . .'

Memories flooded in on me. Languid love-making on rainy afternoons, the doorbell ringing unanswered, half-drawn curtains, the apartment deserted except for the cat and ourselves, two fugitives from the everyday world, suspended in timeless oblivion.

'You've got to use your brains,' Frenssen was saying. 'I had a bit on a hillside once. Hard work, I can tell you, banging away uphill. Then I got the right idea and swung her a hundred and eighty degrees.'

Frenssen illustrated the readjustment with both hands. He might have been shifting furniture.

Zeitler swept some imaginary crocks from the table with a dismissive backhand gesture. All eyes turned in his direction.

He paused for effect and then announced that he favoured the supine position. 'Why? Less sweat for you and more fun for her, jogging up and down on the old chopper. Trot, canter and gallop . . . Just the job!'

Isenberg's contribution was something about his last Christmas leave. 'There was this servants' ball at Swinemünde – I've got relatives there. Freezing cold it was, and blowing half a gale. A mate of mine got hold of one of the skivvies and screwed her up against a tree in the grounds.'

The control-room PO wagged his head ruefully. 'I had to stand there, stamping my feet, until he'd got it out of his system – he was giving me a lift, see. It's a bit hard sometimes, being married . . .'

I expected howls of derision, but none came. Later I overheard a whispered exchange between two bunks.

'Feeling narked?'

'Why should I be? It doesn't matter where they send us, does it?'

'Come on, admit it. Think I can't guess why you're mooching around like a tart in a trance? You won't be getting it this Christmas, mate, but don't worry – your girlfriend won't go short. She's a nice-looking bit. Her pussy won't get cobwebs on it.'

By next day the atmosphere in the POs' mess had turned pensive. Zeitler and Frenssen tried a few bombastic remarks, but to no avail. Bunk-to-bunk repartee ceased, and even Dorian became engrossed in his own thoughts. Everyone had grasped the difficulties that lay ahead.

The Captain waited until lunch to air his ideas on penetrating the Strait of Gibraltar. He did so with his usual patience-sapping hesitancy, just as if he were fitting his thoughts together for the first time—as if he hadn't already spent hours hatching the scheme, re-vamping it, weighing the odds, balancing pros and cons.

'We'll run in under cover of darkness—get as close as we possibly can on the surface. There'll be plenty of stuff to steer clear of.'

Stuff like destroyers and patrol-boats, I supplemented under my breath.

'Then we'll simply dive and drift through.'

I restrained an exclamation and looked knowledgeable. Drift through—of course, it was the latest fashion.

The Captain was staring into space. His silence conveyed that he had exhausted his fund of information.

Drifting . . . Not the most attractive of terms, I reflected. The very sound of it produced a sinking sensation in the pit of my stomach, but who was I to quarrel with a ruling by the Delphic Oracle?

The second lieutenant, whose facial control was less effective than mine, blinked like someone afflicted with a nervous tic. He seemed to be questioning the Captain with his eyelashes.

The Captain merely leant back and studied the deckhead for two or three minutes.

'The thing is, there are two currents in the Strait—a surface current flowing from the Atlantic into the Mediterranean, and a deep counter-current flowing the other way.' He thrust out his lower lip and sat staring at the table. 'A strongish current,' he added. The words were tossed at us like a bone to be chewed on.

Nothing could be simpler: we'd dive and let the surface current carry us through the Strait with no noise and little consumption of fuel or amps. Easy once you knew how!

The rules of the game now required us, too, to look bored. Not a nod, not a batted eyelash, no sign of surprise.

The Captain again thrust out his lower lip and nodded deliberately. The Chief ventured a lop-sided grin.

Seeing it, the Captain sighed and asked, in an unexpectedly official tone: 'Well, Chief, all clear?'

'Yessir.' The Chief nodded vigorously, as though anything less would have been discourteous.

An expectant pause followed. The Captain needed an antagonist, a devil's advocate. The Chief was a willing volunteer. He only stroked his jaw, but it was enough to indicate certain misgivings. Although all eyes bar the Captain's swung in his direction, he merely cocked his head like a blackbird scanning the grass for worms. He had no intention of articulating his doubts – he merely hinted at their existence. That would do for the present. The old pro took his time. He hadn't studied under a master for nothing.

The wardroom applied itself to this pantomime for a good two minutes. Then the Captain seemed to have had enough. 'Well, Chief?'

The Chief gave a few equivocal wags of the head before delivering his punch-line : 'Congratulations, sir. Excellent idea.'

I was filled with admiration. Any doubts I might have harboured about the Chief's nerves had been dispelled.

But the Captain's performance was just as polished. No visible reaction. He simply eyed the Chief askance. The slight lift of his left eyebrow expressed mild concern.

The Chief seemed unaware of the Captain's clinical stare. With a masterly display of equanimity, he clasped one knee and bent an earnest gaze on the deckhead.

Just as tedium was setting in, the steward appeared. Even the walk-on parts in our comedy were played with superb timing.

The soup went round. Silently, we manipulated our spoons and chewed.

I caught sight of the fly. It was promenading over the C-in-C's eloquently parted lips. A pity it couldn't do so in reality, in the middle of a patriotic pep-talk. 'For Führer and – aaargh!' – as it popped in and tickled his uvula . . . Our fly could have got off at Vigo, but it had resisted the temptation to settle in Spain. It hadn't jumped ship – no one had jumped ship. We were all on board, the fly included, even though it was the only living creature that could come and go as it pleased. Not, like us, subject to naval regulations, it was spectacularly loyal, steadfast through thick and thin, well worthy of official commendation.

A lunch-time concert seemed to be in progress in the fore-ends. Muffled singing penetrated the bulkhead door and swelled to a crescendo when it was opened.

> 'Sheikh Abdul, the randy old codger,
> Had a new girl each night of the year,
> And when there were none left to roger
> He pleasured himself with a queer.'

> 'There limped through the burning Sahara
> A poor syphilitic old whore.
> He whipped out his red-hot banana
> And soon she was begging for more . . .'

'Arab week,' commented the Captain. 'Must be because we're heading south.'

Böckstiegel woke me in the middle of the night.

'Lisbon on the port beam, Lieutenant.'

I slipped into my gym-shoes and went up top with only a shirt and trousers on. My eyes took a while to accustom themselves to the darkness. The Captain was on the bridge.

'Over there.'

I could see nothing abeam of us but a faint glow above the skyline.

'Lisbon.' The Captain's voice again.

U-A rolled very slowly from side to side. The engines, which were running at two-thirds, emitted a dull and insistent roar.

I stood there with the wooden duck-boards of the gently rolling bridge beneath me, hands on the moist and vibrant iron of the bridge casing, and stared eastwards. The pale flush barely sufficed to distinguish sea from sky.

I swallowed hard. For some reason, the patch of light and the word 'Lisbon' brought a kind of sob to my throat.

Back in my bunk, I listened to the off-watch POs chatting. 'Lisbon – that's a pretty big place.' – 'Why no black-out, then?' – 'They're neutral, idiot!' – 'No raids, no sirens, no bombs, no rationing – sounds too good to be true.' – 'I can hardly remember what Berlin looked like before the war. All those coloured signs flashing on and off – Jesus!'

Already half-asleep, I heard voices arguing through my curtain.

'Of course it counts as two patrols – stands to reason. We've replenished, after all. France or Spain, what's the difference?'

'Two patrols? You'll be lucky!'

Isenberg rolled over on his stomach with a grunt. 'Save your breath. We're in the Navy, remember? They can bugger us about any way they like.'

Because the Captain seemed to have some time on his hands after breakfast, I prodded him into a lecture.

'This strong current through the Strait, sir – I don't quite follow. Where does all the water come from?'

I had to possess my soul in patience. The Old Man was no cold starter. He began by knitting his brow and putting his head on one side. I watched him come slowly to the boil.

'Mm, yes – well . . . Conditions are a bit unusual in the Mediterranean.'

He paused for the regulation look of enquiry before limping on.

'There are two currents, as you know. One flows out – that's the low-level one – and the other flows in. It happens this way. Relatively little rain falls in the Mediterranean area, but there's plenty of sunshine. Consequently, a lot of water evaporates. Since salt doesn't evaporate, the salt content increases, and the higher the salt content, the heavier the water. That's logical enough, isn't it?'

'As far is it goes, sir, yes.'

He came to a full stop and sucked at his unlit pipe as if the whole problem had been fully elucidated. Not another word escaped him until I made a move to rise.

'The brine sinks and forms a layer at the bottom of the Mediterranean. Its tendency to sink even further causes it to flow out through the Strait and into the Atlantic, where it stabilizes at about one thousand metres – the depth at which it meets water of the same specific gravity. Compensation takes place up top. Less salty water flows in from the Atlantic to replace the volume lost by evaporation.'

'. . . and the low-level outflow.'

'Precisely.'

'And we're going to take advantage of this ingenious arrangement – hitch a ride on the surface current?'

'Unless you can think of a better idea . . .'

The Captain ordered me to join the bridge watch as an additional look-out.

Within half an hour the starboard after look-out yelled: 'Aircraft bearing green seven-zero!'

The second lieutenant spun round and stared.

I was already at the hatch. As I slid down the ladder, I heard the shouted alarm and the clamour of the bell. The Chief popped through the forward control-room bulkhead like a cork.

The second lieutenant's voice came from above: 'Dive dive dive! Open all main vents!'

Vents were opened and red-and-white handwheels spun. Slowly, as if suspended in treacle, the needle of the depth-gauge began to turn.

'All hands forward!' ordered the Chief. Men streamed through the control-room, falling rather than running.

The Captain had perched on the chart-stowage. I could only see his rounded back. He thrust one hand deep in his trouser-pocket and waved the other like an exasperated conductor. 'Nothing,' he said. 'We'll stay deep for the present. Fifty metres, Chief.' And to the second lieutenant: 'Well done, second watch.'

He turned to me. 'That's a fine start. We won't make good time at this rate.'

There was just room for me at the chart-table. I found myself looking at a chart of the Strait. The British stronghold projected from the Spanish mainland like a hangnail. Gibraltar had the only naval dockyard this side of Malta and the only one open to freighters damaged in convoy. The British defences must be formidable.

The Pillars of Hercules: in the north the Rock of Gibraltar; in the south, on the coast of Spanish Morocco, the Jebel Musa near Ceuta. The Strait was only eight miles across at its narrowest point. We should probably have to slink along the southern shore – hug the far wall, as it were.

But was that such a good idea? The British would surely be keeping a careful eye on the far side as well, aware that no German U-boat would graze Europa Point if it could be avoided. The Captain must have a plan, of course. I was curious to see what route he proposed to take.

The second lieutenant materialized beside me and bent over the chart-table.

'Gibraltar, delightful climatic rendezvous, where the mellow beauty of the Mediterranean meets the raw vigour of the Atlantic . . .'

I stared at him.

'That's what it says in the tourist guides, anyway,' he said, toying with the dividers. 'Eight miles wide – room enough.'

'Depth?' I asked.

'980 metres maximum,' he replied. 'More than enough.'

The Chief joined us.

'We attacked a Gibraltar convoy once, a pack of us. The survivors must have been happy to see the Rock. There were twenty of them when they sailed – only eight after we'd done our bit. In this area it was, but a little further west.'

The lights I saw on the chart had exotic names. One of them was called Zem Zem. There was Cape St Vincent, too. I tried to recall what I knew about Nelson's part in the battle.

We surfaced an hour later. The first lieutenant had scarcely gone on watch when the alarm bell jangled a second time.

'Came out of the clouds, sir, pretty high,' Zeitler panted. 'I

349

couldn't identify the type.'

'They must be on to us,' the Captain said. 'We'd better stay down.'

He lingered in the control-room, his uneasiness apparent. He was wearing his most lugubrious expression.

'It's all part of their outer defence network.'

Half an hour went by. Then he climbed into the conning-tower and we surfaced.

Another ten minutes and the bell shrilled again. It gave me the usual jolt.

The Captain demonstrated his composure with sardonic remarks like 'Damned good practice!' and 'Anyone feeling airsick?' – but it was obvious he knew the problems involved. Conditions could not have been worse. Only ripples disturbed the surface after our long spell of bad weather. Aircraft would have little difficulty in spotting us, even without a moon.

Even if the British couldn't close the Strait with anti-submarine nets, they would be patrolling it with everything they had. Probably, too, they had long known what Kernével had in mind – after all, *their* intelligence system worked.

Drifting through the Strait submerged might sound fool-proof, but it was useless against Asdic.

I entered the POs' mess in time to see Isenberg produce an escape pack from the foot of his bunk. He was clearly embarrassed that I had seen him and tossed the thing on to his blanket with an indignant air, as if his hands had alighted on it by chance.

Pilgrim appeared, screening something with his body. I could hardly believe my eyes: the senior PO electrician had also fetched his escape gear. Strange how differently different people reacted. Up in the fore-ends, their lordships behaved as if nothing special were afoot; here, escape gear was *à la mode*.

I decided to see how things looked up top. Just as I stuck my head over the hatch coaming, a trawler emerged briefly from a low bank of mist and disappeared again.

'Too close for comfort. They must have seen us.'

Put another record on, I thought.

The Captain snorted. He said nothing for a while, just brooded. 'Looked like a Spaniard.'

'Let's hope he doesn't have a private line to the British Admiralty,' I muttered to myself.

'Well, it can't be helped.'

The Portuguese coast loomed up. Looking through my

glasses, I saw some reddish cliffs surmounted by a cluster of white houses. My thoughts strayed to the Côte Sauvage near Le Croisic in Brittany, where storm-driven breakers exploded against the black rocks like heavy-calibre shells: dull thuds succeeded by fountains of spray, now here, now there. When the tide was out and the sea calm little yellow beaches slumbered among the cliffs. Moist sand scattered with sea-weed, dry and crepitating; spiky broom festooned all over with wisps of foam when the north-west wind assailed the coast; deeply rutted cart-tracks snowed under with spindrift; thistle-heads silver against the pale sand – sometimes, too, a stranded float lost by a minesweeper; the tall two-wheeled carts with which peasants assembled their mounds of half-dried wrack; and, far out, the lighthouse, striped red and white like our Papenberg . . .

I had another vision of the Spanish matchbox. Without wanting to admit it, I had known all the time. That label, with its gaudy yellow sun and fiery red background – I had seen one like it in the crocodile handbag which Simone always carried as a repository for her 'vie privée'. She rummaged in it, looking for a snapshot to show me, and the box fell out. Why the hurry to retrieve it – why shouldn't I see? No reason. Franke's Number One, who often patronized her parents' café, had given it to her – no, left it behind – no, she had asked him for it, for a friend's little boy. My old misgivings returned. Simone and the Maquis . . . Was she – all asseverations to the contrary – playing a double game? Her eternal pumping: 'Quand est-ce que tu pars? Vers quelle heure?' – 'Why not ask your friends in the Resistance? They know the tide-tables better than we do.' Then the tears, the heart-rending sobs, the sudden outbursts of fury: 'Tu est méchant, méchant, méchant!' Smudged make-up, runny nose – all the accoutrements of misery.

On the other hand, why hadn't she received one of those cute little miniature coffins in the post, like her girl-friends? Why not Simone as well? Her piteous look of entreaty: genuine or false? Her weary and woebegone expression: all sham? Nobody could act that well – or could they?

I saw the low, wide bed, the pretentious pattern of roses on the ceiling, the fringed curtains. I felt Simone's dry and fragrant skin. Simone never sweated. How she loved her firm, dainty body – how she moved, everlastingly self-aware . . .

I sat alone in the middle of the café, not daring to catch her eye, but my gaze followed her as she threaded her way between the tables. She moved with the sinuous grace of a matador. Her passes were governed by the arrangement of the furniture, but she was always devising new variations. Simone evaded chairs as if they were bulls' horns, swinging her hips aside or delicately retracting her tummy. She manipulated the white napkin like a cape. I noticed that she never made contact, never even brushed the corner or back of a chair. There was her laugh, too. She scattered her laughter like glittering coins. Again and again the violet jumper flitted across my field of vision. In vain I tried to keep my eyes on my newspaper and ignore the darting patch of violet. What could have inspired her to wear that subtle combination of violet jumper and grey slacks, a very special violet – neither over-red nor over-blue – out of a picture by Braque? Ah, that little angora jumper!

The café was full of locals back from the beach with a thirst. The waitress had her work cut out. It was fun to watch Simone accost her at the cash-desk between tours of inspection and admonish her – surreptitiously, with the gentle menace of a cat.

Outside, the heat shimmered like burnished copper. I wouldn't brave it, not yet. I was enjoying the coolness of the tiled floor and the chill that seeped through my light linen jacket where my forearms rested on the marble tabletop. It was the heat that stopped me leaving, I told myself, not Simone's proximity. All at once she sat down at my table with a bunch of knitting. Another of her sorceress's jumpers, but yellow this time – a strong and unrelieved lemon-yellow. She held the beginnings of it in her lap and placed the ball of yellow wool beside her. As if the violet and grey weren't enough! She asked if it were a nice colour. Nice? A feast for the eye – the loveliest yellow imaginable. Beneath her, the cool blue-and-white tiled floor; behind her, a section of cupboard painted nut-brown . . .

I could still hear us. 'We must be careful.' – 'Why always careful?' – 'You must take care – we both must.' – 'Who can forbid us?' – 'Silly girl, forbidding is a mild description of what they could do!' – *'Je m'en fiche!'* – 'But I care – I want us to come through this.' – *'Pouf!* Nobody will.' – 'Yes, we both will.'

The time she met me at Savenay station . . . God knew where she got the car from. She wouldn't let me speak because she knew I'd be furious, just drove like a maniac. *'Tu as peur?* Don't worry. If we see a military policeman I shall put my foot down. They always miss, *ces types-là.'*

I heard the morning before we sailed. *Si tu ne* roll over and get up *à l'instant, je te repousse dehors avec le cul – avec le* bottom, *compris?'*

Simone, singeing the hair on my right thigh with a lighted cigarette: 'That smells nice, like a *petit cochon*.' She reached for a fur-trimmed belt, clamped one end between her nose and upper lip, moustachewise, looked in the mirror and doubled up with laughter. Then she plucked fluff from the tasselled quilt and stuffed it in her nose and ears.

A German lesson: 'I stand at your disposal – I am healthy – *je suis d'accord* – I am most happy with it – at it – about it – how do you say? *J'ai envie d'être* seduced. And you, you are a *Scheisskerl!* You are *beschissen, ja?* You are too stupid to be nice. You must caress me – here, at this place. That is no good, *tu ne fais que jouer au piano*. I am charming, no? Which you prefer, my breast or your breast? *C'est drôle*, that hair on your breast. *Drôle de garçon, toi!'* She shook with giggles. 'You become fat – *je t'assure* – you become a fat lump. Now I will sing you something:

> *'Monsieur de Chevreuse ayant déclaré que tous*
> *les cocus devraient être noyés,*
> *Madame de Chevreuse lui a fait demander*
> *s'il était bien sûr de savoir nager!'*

All an act? All sham? La Baule's answer to Mata Hari? And yet the morning of our departure . . .

Simone sitting motionless at the table, shoulders sagging, swimming eyes fixed on me, lips parted to reveal a half-chewed mass of roll, butter and honey.

'Go on, eat up!'

Obediently she began to chew. Tears rolled down her cheeks. One hung from her nose. The tear-drop was cloudy – I particularly noticed. It must have been the salt. 'Eat up like a good girl.' I gripped her by the neck like a rabbit, pushing her hair up with the back of my hand. 'Go on, eat. No need to worry, I promise.'

I was thankful for the thick white cable-stitch sweater. It gave me something to say. 'Lucky you finished that sweater in time – I'm going to need it. It's cold as hell outside.'

Simone played along. She sniffed hard. '*C'est une merveille*, that wool. Only such a little bit left.' She spread her thumb and forefinger to show me. '*Même pas pour quatre sous*. Are you kind to your sweaters in the Navy? *Seras-tu fidèle à ton* sweater – will you be faithful to it?'

She sniffed again, held her breath and laughed through the tears. She was being brave. She knew it wouldn't be a picnic. One couldn't tell her anything, as one might have done a

wife at home, yet she always knew when a U-boat was overdue. Circumstantial evidence? No, there were a hundred legi-
timate ways of finding out. Ratings who were regular patrons
of the café failed to appear. The French cleaning-women in
the billets knew when a crew had gone out and when, on
the basis of past experience, they ought to return. There was
too much talk in general. And yet, and yet . . .

A warm glow surged through me. That was no play-acting,
you suspicious bastard! Nobody could be that good. My
throat contracted.

The old Breton clock said six-thirty, but it was ten minutes
fast. We were in injury time. The driver would be there in ten
minutes. Simone busied herself with my jacket. 'You have a
stain here, *mon petit cochon.*'

She scrubbed at it industriously.

'It isn't a pleasure-steamer, you know.'

I could remember every word. 'I come to the lock with you.'
– 'No you won't. Anyway, it's cordoned off.' – *'Pas de prob-
lème* – I'll borrow a nurse's permit. *Je veux te voir sortir.'* –
'Please don't, it could be awkward. You know when we're
sailing – you can see us from the beach half an hour later.' –
'Yes, but so small. *Comme une allumette.'*

Again that word. Fade in a red-and-yellow box. I focused
my memory, captured an object with the tentacles of recollection : the bridge-table with the brown cigarette-burns on its
pale plume-wood top. Now it was a simple matter to conjure
up the *trompe-l'œil* pattern of the floor-tiles, which looked
like three-dimensional dice or negative geometrical recesses,
depending on which caught your eye first, a white or a black
one . . .

Brakes squealed outside. A moment later the horn blared.
The driver, a coastal artilleryman, wore field-grey.

Simone ran her palms over the new sweater. She made herself small against me, so small that my chin brushed the top
of her head.

'Your boots – why do they have to be so big?'

'They're cork-soled and lined. Besides . . .' My brief hesitation
was banished by her smile and look of childlike enquiry.
'Besides, they have to be roomy enough to slip off easily in
water.' Quickly, I cupped her head in my hands and ran my
fingers through her hair. 'Now don't be angry – you did ask!'
– 'Your suitcase, where did you put your suitcase? You saw
all the things I packed? The little parcel – promise me you
won't open it until you're at sea?' – 'I promise.' – 'And you'll
wear the sweater?' – 'Every day, and at night I'll roll up the

collar and pretend I'm with you.'

All very matter-of-fact, thank God.

'You need hand-towels?' – 'No, there are some on board. And take half the soap out. The Navy provides us with sea-water soap.'

I looked at my watch. The car had been waiting five minutes and we still had to collect the Chief. If only it were over, I thought. Quickly down the garden path, sniffing the turpentiny scent of pine-trees. Open the gate, turn once, slam it shut. *C'est tout. Fini!*

The evening light was sumptuous. Darkness fell quickly. The last of the daylight shimmered on our wake.

The Captain cleared his throat. 'Well, Kriechbaum, how do you think it looks?'

'Promising, sir.' The quartermaster spoke briskly – almost too briskly, perhaps.

Half an hour later the Captain sent me and the look-outs below. He and Kriechbaum had the bridge to themselves, a sure sign that we were nearing the perimeter of the British defence system.

The roar of the engines died. We were proceeding on the surface under electric power only.

'Time?' the Captain called down.

'2030, sir,' the helmsman called back.

I stayed in the control-room. Another half-hour passed. The motors made so little noise that I had only to stand beneath the lower hatch to hear everything the Captain said.

'Good God, they must have half their fleet out. Surely they can't all be off to play roulette in Tangier . . . Keep an eye on that one, Kriechbaum – we can't afford to bump into anyone.'

The Chief joined me and stared up the conning-tower.

'Dicey,' he said.

The Captain had to gauge the course and speed of enemy ships by their position lights alone, present our narrow silhouette to a succession of patrolling vessels and outmanœuvre them. It was devilishly difficult to be certain every time which light belonged to which ship, whether she was lying stopped, closing, or going away.

The helmsman, too, had to be on his toes. He confirmed his orders in a subdued voice. The Captain sounded far less inhibited. If I knew him, he was in his element.

'Very decent of them to show their position lights like that – just what we need. What's your tub doing, Kriechbaum? Is she gaining on us?'

It felt as if we were turning a circle. I told myself to concentrate harder on the Captain's steering orders.

'Damn, that was close!'

The Captain did not speak for a while. Evidently, things
were ticklish. My throat throbbed with excitement.

'That's right, old lad, keep going,' I heard him say at last.
'Quite a crowd of them, all doing their bit for King and
Country. Hey, what's that over there? Starboard wheel!'

I would have given a lot for permission to go on the bridge
at that moment.

'Quartermaster, keep an eye on that one. Tell me at once if
she alters course.'

A sudden order to stop motors. I strained my ears. The
Chief drew a deep breath. What was it this time?

The waves slapped our ballast tanks like wet flannels. The
submarine rocked to and fro. The control-room lights were
dimmed, so all I could see of the Chief's face was a pale blob.

I distinctly heard him shift from foot to foot with excitement.

It was a blessed relief when the Captain finally started the
port motor. Ten minutes at very slow speed, then: 'Well, we
got past that one all right,' I heard from above. The Chief
breathed out.

A renewed hum from the starboard motor. Had we sneaked
through the outer ring? How many cordons did the British
maintain, anyway? 'They can't very well put out defence
booms,' the Captain said. 'Not in this current.' Where were
we? Should I look at the chart? No, not now – no time for that.

'Quite a party, eh, Kriechbaum?'

The Captain's deep, carrying voice retained its normal pitch.
'How goes our friend on the beam?'

I couldn't hear the quartermaster, unfortunately. Tension
must have made him whisper.

The Captain gave another course correction. 'On a bit. We're
not doing badly – they can't be expecting us after all. Make
sure that tub over there stays clear, all right? We dive in ten
minutes.'

'Soon as you like,' muttered the Chief, but he showed no
signs of budging. Did he want to display his self-confidence?
U-A certainly trimmed to perfection. The Chief had spent the
last few hours checking every piece of equipment in his
domain. The control-room PO had never stopped once.

'Come on . . . that's it . . . there we are!'

The Captain might have been coaxing a reluctant child to eat.

'Oh well, better get moving,' the Chief said at last, and disappeared.

A sudden thought struck me: Must have a quick squat. I mightn't get another chance for some time.

The heads were mercifully vacant.

Sitting on the pan, one could be forgiven for thinking oneself in the bowels of a machine. No plywood masked the bewildering maze of pipes, and movement was almost impossible in the cramped cubicle. Just to make matters worse, the coxswain had stowed canned food from the *Weser* in every cranny that wasn't already occupied by swabs and buckets.

While straining, I recalled a story I'd heard from a merchant seaman whose ship had been disabled by a storm. He had been detailed to discharge oil from the latrine pipes in the hope of calming the sea. Because the ship was listing badly, the latrine was almost at water-level. Whenever she heeled, sea-water gushed through the drain-hole. The door became wedged, and the seaman knew that nothing could save him from a watery death if the rolling increased. He was even denied the hope that air would collect against the bulkhead and resist the water-pressure because, unlike U-A's heads, a ship's latrine was well ventilated.

And so, caught like a rat in a trap, the man continued to discharge oil whenever the outlet pipe wasn't spouting sea-water – a lone figure battling to save his ship at a humble and forgotten outpost.

Abruptly, I was gripped by a terrible feeling of claustrophobia. I pictured a battery exploding while we were dived, the door warped and jammed by the force of the explosion, myself hammering desperately at the metal plates.

Film sequences flashed through my head: a car plunging into a river with its doomed passengers, fear-distorted faces framed by the bars of a burning prison, a theatre exit jammed with panic-stricken fugitives.

Easy does it! I simulated composure and hoisted my trousers with studied calm. There, back to normal. Pity I hadn't managed anything, but still . . .

Even so, my arms pumped the pan empty faster than my will intended. A quick wrench at the handle and I was outside. Deep breathing, commence!

Had it been fear or claustrophobia? When had I been genuinely scared in my life? In the air-raid shelter? Not really

— we all knew they'd dig us out in the end. Once, when bombers suddenly swooped over Brest, I ran like a hare. Quite an exhibition, perhaps, but was it the real thing?

In Dieppe, on the minesweeper? We'd just lifted one when the siren went. That crazy tide difference! The quayside was as high as a four-storeyed house. Nowhere to go, so we lay on the muddy floor of the basin and waited for the bombers to unload.

But none of it compared with the fear of those echoing boarding-school corridors on Sundays, when most of the boys had gone home and left the huge building deserted. That was when *they* came after me, knife in hand – that was when fingers curled round my throat from behind and footsteps dogged me along the interminable passages. Shivers ran down my spine and the hair prickled on my neck. I would wake in the middle of the night, sticky between the thighs and convinced I was bleeding to death. Not a glimmer of light anywhere. I lay frozen with terror, paralysed by the conviction that I was doomed if I moved a finger.

GIBRALTAR

Watch-changing time. A crush developed in the control-room because the third watch had mustered to find the second watch loitering below.

The fact that we were still on the surface aroused general surprise. Tongues wagged excitedly.

Zeitler took time off to run a comb through his hair.

'That's right, mate,' someone said in a broad Berlin accent. 'Look your best – they say the Brits like a nice piece of arse.'

Zeitler was undeterred. He drew the comb slowly and carefully through his moistened locks.

Turbo was singing to himself in an undertone:

> 'Hair all round
> And a hole in front.
> What can it be
> But a big fat eyeball?'

I stood beneath the lower hatch with my sou'wester tied under my chin and my right hand on the ladder, looking up.

'Man on the bridge?'

Almost simultaneously, the Captain bellowed 'ALARM!'

The quartermaster slid down the ladder. His sea-boots

crashed to the deck close beside me. From above came a rapidly swelling wave of sound.

I was just opening my mouth to ask about the Captain when a frightful explosion knocked me sideways against the chart-stowage. My eardrums must have held, because I could hear someone shouting 'The Captain, the Captain!' Someone else called out: 'We've been hit!'

Water gushed down the conning-tower. The lights had failed. I felt numb, but terror fluttered deep inside me like a trapped bird.

The submarine was already tilting when the Captain landed in our midst like a sack of potatoes. Groaning with pain, he managed to get out: 'Bomb, just forward of the bridge . . .'

The beam of a torch showed him bent double like a leap-frogger. His hands were clamped to the small of his back, as though his kidneys hurt.

'The gun's gone – it damn nearly blew me overboard!'

Somewhere in the gloom, in the after regions of the control-room, somebody screamed – shrilly, like a woman.

'It was a plane,' the Captain went on, gritting his teeth. 'Right over the top of us.'

I could feel the boat going down fast. A plane, in the middle of the night? Not a shell? A plane? It couldn't have been!

Some secondary lighting came on.

'Blow!' shouted the Captain. 'Blow everything!' Then, in an urgent voice: 'Surface at once. Stand by your escape gear.'

My breathing faltered. Two or three appalled faces appeared in the after doorway.

Bow-down, far too steep an angle. The gun had gone. How could a gun disappear? A plane? Impossible!

'A direct hit, right beside the bridge,' the Captain said in a sort of hiss. His voice gained strength. 'What's the matter with you? When am I going to get some damage reports?'

In response, a medley of voices from aft: 'Engine-room making water!' – 'Motor-room making water!' I picked out the abhorrent phrase four or five times, though the confused shouting was half-drowned by the hiss of compressed air and the rumble of water escaping from our tanks.

The needle of the depth-gauge halted at last, trembled for a moment and slowly crept back round the dial. We were rising.

The Captain was now standing beneath the conning-tower. 'All right, Chief, take her straight up. No periscope look. I'll go up top on my own. Keep everything clear.'

An icy thrill ran through me. My escape gear was in the

POs' mess. I took three unsteady paces to the after bulkhead and squeezed between two men reluctant to budge. My hands groped for the foot of my bunk and closed on something solid. Thank God! I could breathe easier.

The hiss and rumble continued. Chaos reigned in the control-room. Rather than add to it, I found myself a niche beside the forward bulkhead.

'Standards awash – upper lid clear!' The Chief's tone was routine, businesslike. He stared up the conning-tower. The Captain was already opening the upper lid. Orders followed a few seconds later: 'Full ahead both! Hard-a-starboard – steer one-eight-zero!' His voice sounded harsh and strident.

Abandon ship? Swim for it? I cuddled my oxygen bottle and fiddled nervously with the life-jacket fastenings. The engines were making an infernal din. How long could we keep it up? I counted off the seconds in an undertone which no one could have heard above the babble of voices issuing from the after doorway.

One-eight-zero – due south. We were heading straight for the African coast, but why?

Somebody yelled: 'The port engine's packed up!' That crazy racket – could it really be the product of a single engine?

A sudden glare from the conning-tower drew my gaze upwards. Beside me, the Chief also stared up at the dazzling magnesium light.

'Star-shells!' he shouted.

The engine noise was driving me insane. I wanted to plug my ears against the flow of sound. Better still, I opened my mouth like a gunner. The next explosion might erupt at any moment.

I heard myself counting. A new cry of panic from the stern: 'Motor-room bilge rising fast . . .'

I'd never swum wearing escape gear, not even in practice. The patrol ships – how far away were they? Far too dark, nobody would spot us in the water. And the current . . . A lot of power behind it – the Old Man had said so himself. It would scatter us in minutes. If we had to swim for it, we were lost. The surface current flowed out of the Mediterranean – in other words, into the Atlantic. Nobody would find us in the Atlantic. Nonsense, I'd got it all wrong: it would carry us into the Mediterranean. Surface current, undercurrent . . . Keep counting! Sea-gulls, slashing beaks, gelatinous corpses, bare white skulls coated with slime . . .

Three hundred and seventy-nine, three hundred and eighty . . .

'Dive dive dive!'

The main vents snapped open. This time the U-boat was bow-down within seconds.

The Captain descended the ladder. Left foot, right foot – normality itself, unlike his voice. 'Bloody star-shells! It's like the Chinese New Year up there . . .' The tremor vanished. 'I could have read a newspaper.'

What now? Weren't we abandoning ship after all? Nothing could be inferred from the Captain's dimly lit face. Lowered lids, deep creases above the bridge of his nose. He didn't seem to register the reports from aft.

Our bow-down angle pressed me hard against the forward bulkhead. I could feel the paintwork cold and clammy against my palms. Was I wrong, or were we going down faster than usual? All hell broke loose. Men reeled into the control-room, slithering, falling headlong. One of them butted my stomach with his head as he fell. I pulled him to his feet but failed to recognize who it was. Had I missed an 'All hands forward!' in the general hubbub?

The depth-gauge! The needle was still turning, though we were trimmed for 30 metres. It should have slowed down long ago. Staring at it, I became aware of a blue haze. Smoke was drifting forward into the control-room.

The Chief glanced round. For a fraction of a second, consternation showed in his face.

He gave a plane order designed to trim the boat dynamically. The waterstream from the screws should have forced our bow up, but were the motors developing full power? I couldn't hear their familiar hum. Were they running at all?

Everything was drowned by the scuff and slither of boots on deck-plates – whimpering, too. Who could it be? The meagre light made it hard to identify anyone.

'Foreplane jammed!' one of the planesmen called without looking round.

The Chief kept his torch on the depth-gauge. In spite of the smoke, I saw the needle swing rapidly from 50 metres to 60. When it passed 70, the Captain shouted 'Blow!' The sharp hiss of HP air soothed my jangling nerves. Thank God for some buoyancy at last!

But the needle continued to revolve. Of course, nothing abnormal in that. It would go on turning until the downward tendency was reversed. There was bound to be a time-lag.

Now, though – now it simply had to stop. My eyelids gave an involuntary flutter. I wrenched them open, forced myself not to blink and peered intently at the dial. The needle showed no sign of slowing, still less stopping. It passed the 80-metre mark, then the 90.

I stared with every ounce of energy I had, trying by sheer will-power to arrest the thin black strip of metal that rotated so inexorably in the beam from the Chief's torch. No use. It passed the 100-metre mark and crept onwards.

'I can't hold her,' whispered the Chief.

Can't hold her, can't hold her . . . Why not? Insufficient buoyancy to offset the weight of the water we had taken in? Had we simply become too heavy? Was this the end? At what depth would the pressure hull collapse? When would the steel skin bulge inwards between the frames and burst?

The needle brushed past the 120-metre mark, still turning steadily. My eyes flinched away from the dial. I stood up, plastered against the bulkhead. One of the Chief's lessons flashed through my mind: at greater depths, water-pressure reduces a submarine's volume, thereby reducing the volume of the water she displaces. In other words, the greater the compression, the smaller the upthrust of displaced water and the greater the boat's relative weight. No more buoyancy, just the earth's attraction and an accelerating rate of descent . . .

'190,' the Chief reported, '200 – 210 . . .'

And deeper still.

The figure reverberated inside my skull: 210!

I stopped breathing. The noise of rending metal could come any time now – and the green cataract.

Where first?

The whole boat creaked and groaned. There was a sharp crack like a pistol-shot, then a muffled whine which pierced me through and through.

The whine grew shriller until it resembled the scream of a circular saw rotating at full speed.

Another sharp report, more creaks and groans.

'260 and still falling,' called an unfamiliar voice. I found myself toiling up the incline. My feet slipped. I just managed to save myself by the hoisting wire of the search periscope, which cut painfully into my palm.

Steel bands encircled my chest.

The needle was about to pass the 270-metre mark. Another whiplash. Rivet-heads must be snapping. No rivets or welded joints could withstand such pressure.

A voice was intoning: 'Yea, though I walk through the valley of the shadow of death . . .' The Vicar? Figures thronged the control-room, groping and fumbling in the gloom.

A sudden impact knocked my legs from under me. I rolled across the deck and hit a figure in a leather jacket. My hands clutched at a dim face. A many-voiced cry issued from the forward bulkhead. Like an answering echo, other shouts came from the stern. The deck-plates rattled and clanged as they jumped in their beds. There was a prolonged tinkle of glass, like a Christmas-tree falling over. The hull reverberated under another violent shock, and another. A moment later my body was sawn clean across by a strident screech. The boat juddered insanely and was smitten by a series of dull blows, as if we were bumping across a gravel-bed. From outside came the throaty trumpeting of some prehistoric monster, the squeal of a thousand pigs, two more blows on a mighty gong – and then, quite suddenly, the tumult died. All that remained was a high singing note.

'We're there.' The words were clearly articulated but the voice seemed to come from behind a locked door. It belonged to the Captain.

The torch-lit gloom persisted. I wondered why nobody had switched on the emergency lighting. My ears registered a gurgling sound. The bilge? Water from outboard wouldn't have gurgled like that.

I tried to distinguish and locate various sounds: cries, whispers, murmurs, voices edgy with panic.

'Damage reports!' I heard the Captain say. Imperiously, a moment later: 'I must have accurate damage reports!'

Light at last – of a sort. What were all those men doing there? I blinked hard, narrowed my eyes to slits and tried to penetrate the semi-darkness. Shouts and disconnected words impinged on my consciousness. Most of the noise came from aft.

My gaze was drawn alternately by two faces, the Captain's and the Chief's. I caught fragments of damage reports, sometimes a whole sentence, sometimes the odd word. Men hurried aft, wide-eyed with terror. One of them barged into me and almost knocked me down.

A shovelful of sand . . . Who had said that? The Captain, naturally. 'At least there's a shovelful of sand under the keel.'

I struggled to understand what had happened. It was dark up top – not pitch-dark, admittedly, but not flooded with moon-light either. No flyer could have spotted us in that gloom. Bomb a submarine at night? It wasn't a practical proposition. Perhaps it had been a shell after all. Ship's gun, shore battery?

But the Old Man had yelled something about a plane. And what of that crescendo of sound immediately before the explosion?

The Chief scuttled to and fro, barking orders.

And then? 'We're there!' The gravel-bed, the pressure hull . . . We carried as little armour-plating as an addled egg. The crazy squealing, the tram rounding a bend . . . It was obvious: we had run full tilt into the rocky bottom. Full ahead both and bow-down. To think that the boat had survived, when her steel skin was already compressed to the point of collapse. And then that impact, that shock, that collision . . .

Three or four men were still sprawled on the deck. The Captain's dark bulk loomed beneath the conning-tower, one hand on the ladder.

Loud and clear above the confused bellowing of orders, I heard the Vicar's insistent voice:

> 'Wonderful will that day be,
> When, from every sin set free,
> We are led by Jesus' hand
> Into Canaan's Promised Land . . .'

He got no further. A torch flashed, and the control-room PO dealt him a terrible backhanded blow across the mouth. There was a crack as though his front teeth had snapped inwards. Through the haze I could see blood welling from his lips. His eyes were dilated with surprise.

The slightest movement pained me. I must have caught my shoulder on something, also my shins. Whenever I stirred I seemed to be arduously toiling through mud.

A cross section of the Strait took shape in my mind's eye. On the left Gibraltar, on the right the North African coast. Shelving down towards the centre, the sea-bed. Midway between the deepest point and the African coast, our tiny steel cylinder.

The Old Man was a mad dog. Had he hoped, against his better judgement, that the British would be off their guard? Hadn't he realized the extent of their defences? There he stood with his battered cap at a rakish angle, one hand still on the ladder that led nowhere.

The first lieutenant's mouth hung open. His face was a single horrified enquiry.

I wondered where the Chief was. He seemed to have vanished.

'Hydrophone's failed!' That was Herrmann.

The planesmen were still seated at their useless controls.

I became aware, for the first time, of a sharp hissing sound from forward. Were the fore-ends making water too? The pressure hull must have survived, or the game would be up by now.

We had sunk like a stone. God alone knew why U-A hadn't broken her back, bottoming so hard at a crazy depth for which she had never been designed. Her resilience inspired me with a kind of respect. Thin steel but premier quality – superbly processed.

Suddenly everything fell into place. The Old Man had headed our leaking boat for shallower water, hence the southerly course. His brief spurt towards the coast had saved us. Full ahead, neck or nothing. I took my hat off to him. Even a few seconds' hesitation might have put our present resting-place beyond reach.

A party of men were toiling at the handwheels under Isenberg's supervision. The shrill whistle stopped abruptly, but what was that? A peculiar shuffling sound had replaced the strangled, high-pitched whine.

I strained my ears. Propellers – no mistaking them. Propellers, and coming nearer.

Everyone froze in mid-movement as though a wand had been waved. Now they had us. The hounds were converging for the kill.

Head retracted between hunched shoulders, I watched the others out of the corner of my eye. The Captain was gnawing his lower lip. The men aft and forward of us must also have heard. The sound of voices seemed to stop at the flick of a switch.

Ritchipitchipitchipitchi . . .

We were staring down the barrel now, waiting for a finger to squeeze the trigger. No movement, not a batted eyelid. Pillars of salt.

Why didn't the baneful noise recede? It had to fade some time. That was a single screw, too.

Ritchipitchipitchi . . . No change, constant. Always the same high-pitched singsong note which flayed my nerves as if they were exposed to the light of day. The ship was travelling at slow speed, or it wouldn't have sounded as if each blade were striking the water separately. A turbine engine, too, or piston-strokes would have been audible.

But how could they mark time overhead with their screw turning? The evil noise should have dwindled minutes ago.

I couldn't see the Captain's face. It would have meant edging forward, and I didn't dare. No movement, not now. Muscles tensed, breathing suppressed.

365

There – the Captain had just muttered something in a deep bass voice. 'Lap of honour,' I heard; 'they're doing a lap of honour.' I understood. The British were turning as tight a circle as they could, immediately overhead. Full helm and slow ahead on one engine.

So they knew exactly where we were lying. They had our position taped.

The noise neither faded nor swelled. Somebody near me was grinding his teeth. I heard a smothered sigh, then a dull groan.

Lap of honour . . . They were waiting for us to surface. All they needed was some evidence – wreckage, oil, a body or two.

But why no depth-charges?

Condensation dripped musically into the bilge. Nobody moved. The Captain growled something unintelligible. Somebody was whimpering, presumably the Vicar.

The phrase 'lap of honour' seemed to swell inside me until it filled my brain-pan. The cycle races at Chemnitz . . . Legs pumping frantically, heads lowered bull-like in a vain attempt to overtake the black leather pacing-shields. A final effort, then ease off. Pedals turning lazily, arms raised in triumph, an outsize golden wreath draped over one shoulder: the victor's lap of honour! Afterwards, an erruption of fireworks and a long black centipede of spectators shuffling tramwards.

Ritchipitchipitchi . . .

Reports from aft were transmitted to the control-room in a series of whispers. I couldn't distinguish a word. I could only hear the propeller-strokes. They took possession of my entire body, which throbbed in unison with the varying shuffle of the blades.

The Vicar was definitely whimpering. None of us exchanged a glance. We all stared straight ahead at the deck or bulkheads. Somebody said 'Jesus!' The Captain gave a hoarse chuckle.

Ritchipitchipitchi . . . Everything receded into a sort of mist – or was it smoke? Had the smouldering started again? Ear-trumpets sprouted from my head. My nerves vibrated to the rhythm of the propeller's song. Close beside me, the control-room PO muttered a few disjointed words. The effort of trying to decipher them brought me back to earth. My eyes refocused but the bluish haze persisted. Smoke, yes, but where from?

My ear caught the words 'oil escaping'. Oh God, an oil-leak! I saw kaleidoscopic pictures of the surface stained with iridescent multi-coloured streaks, art nouveau curlicues, marbled paper, Iceland moss.

I tried to stifle my fear. The fierce current could be our salvation – it would disperse the iridescent slick and carry it away.

So what? The British were on home ground – they would know all about the currents and allow for them. They weren't born yesterday. Heaven knew how much oil had escaped from our tanks, but – on second thoughts – maybe the more the merrier. It might persuade them that their job was done. I wondered which tank had been fractured.

I saw blackish bubbles in the glare of a destroyer's searchlight. Treacly liquid floated to the surface and deployed into a huge iridescent patch. At its centre, as though oil had escaped from a fault in the sea-bed, a bubbling swirl. More and more fingers of light probed the spot, signal rockets and star-shells exploded. And from all sides, their guns trained on the gusher, ships converged with a white bone of bow-wave in every pair of jaws.

I wanted to run away, break through the encirclement of pipes and machinery, turn my back on our useless collection of valves and power units. At once, I felt a bitter urge to become cynical: Your own fault – you wanted it this way. You were sick of the easy life. You felt like a soupçon of the heroic for a change. 'Face to face with the Inexorable . . .' Rudolf Binding and all that crap! You used to get drunk on his stuff: '. . . where no mother tends us, no woman crosses our path, where reality alone prevails, cruel in its grandeur . . .' Well, here it is, your reality!

But I couldn't sustain the sarcasm for long. Self-pity welled up inside me. 'Jesus,' I muttered, 'Jesus Christ Almighty . . .'

Nobody could have heard, the propeller noise was too loud. My heart seemed to be pounding away just behind my soft palate. My scalp had frozen, my skull threatened to burst.

Wait.

Couldn't I hear a gentle rasping against the hull, or was I already suffering from delusions?

Wait, wait, wait.

Defenceless. I didn't know what it meant before. Not even a hammer to hit with, a spanner to wrench at.

The noise from above remained constant. It was incomprehensible that we hadn't heard their detector impulses. Why no Asdic?

Or didn't they carry it? I had to try and think straight. U-A might be lying in a depression. Was her resting-place such that the hull wouldn't send back an echo? We hadn't bottomed on sand, that much was certain. The screech and squeal had been caused by rocks scouring our keel.

The Captain shook his head. 'Incredible,' he muttered. 'Straight for us out of the darkness.' So he was still preoccupied with the plane.

They couldn't be equipped with Asdic. Absurd – no point. They needed no Asdic to tell them the depth of our refuge. A simple echo-sounder would be quite enough, if not a chart. A few cross-bearings, and our pursuers would be able to read off our depth at their leisure.

When would the blow fall? What did it mean, this waiting? How much longer were the bastards going to toy with us? My stomach contracted. I opened my mouth wide and breathed in, sealed the air into my lungs with compressed lips. Hold it, hold it . . . My jugular throbbed fiercely. No use – now I had to breathe out. The air emerged in tremulous little gusts.

They had no need to use throwers. They could simply roll their depth-charges overboard – casually, like surplus tar-barrels.

Swallow, swallow, swallow until my mouth opened of its own accord and I fought for air like a drowning man. Fire, damn you!

More whispered reports from aft. The Captain seemed unaware of them.

'. . . aerial bomb, percussion fuse – right beside the boat, abreast the gun . . . Almost incredible – so dark, and yet . . .'

A crazy scheme, sending us through the Strait. It was bound to go wrong – any fool could have seen that. And the Old Man had known! He had known all the time, ever since we received the order to break through. He had known it was tantamount to a death sentence – that was his sole motive for trying to unload us at Vigo. He saw little hope of making it, but it hadn't stopped him from arguing otherwise. No problem, we'll simply drift through. Very neat. The only trouble was, that sort of trick had to succeed first time. There weren't any second chances, not here.

What was he muttering now?

'Very nice of them, I'm sure.'

Everyone in the control-room heard. 'Nice of them to keep us company like this.'

Only a handful of sardonic words, but they went home. The men raised their eyes and stirred again. Movement gradually returned to the control-room. Crouched but on tiptoe, two men crept past me on their way aft.

I stared uncomprehendingly at the Captain. He had thrust both hands deep into the pockets of his sheepskin waistcoat. It was plain to see, even in this light, that he had lost none of his nonchalance. He even gave us a condescending shrug.

A tool clattered somewhere. 'Quiet!' he snarled. The bilge gurgled. It must have been doing so for some time, but I hadn't noticed until now. A thought struck me: if we were motionless, how could the bilge be gurgling? I visualized water rising beneath the deck-plates.

The Captain continued to play his U-boat hero's role. 'Keeping us company – what more could we ask?'

The 'ritchipitchi' grew fainter – perceptibly so. Our tormentor seemed to be going away. The Captain turned his head from side to side, to catch the sound as it faded. I was just relaxing when the propeller-noise swelled to its former pitch.

'Intriguing,' murmured the Captain, and inclined his head towards the Chief. All I heard of their whispered conversation was 'Not holding . . . oil-leak . . . yes . . .'

The Captain turned to the quartermaster. 'How long have they been circling?'

'A good ten minutes, sir,' Kriechbaum whispered back.

'Bastards,' said the Captain.

The second engineer was nowhere in sight. He had probably gone aft, to our main source of worry. Another stream of damage reports came from forward. We were lucky to have two engineer officers on board. Two of them in one U-boat was a rare phenomenon. Lucky – we were lucky! We nose-dived and the good Lord threw a shovelful of sand under our keel. On top of that, two engineers. What could be more propitious than that?

The Captain frowned. 'Where's the second engineer?'

'In the motor-room, sir.'

'Get him to check the batteries at once.'

There was a general flurry of activity. I again registered the shrill whistling sound. It *had* to come from the engine-room. We had landed bow-down, but now the boat was noticeably down by the stern. Why didn't the Chief level us off? We should have pumped out by now, under normal circumstances, but the main bilge-pump was out of action. Besides, would it have coped with the immense external pressure? 280 metres – in the language of our enemies, something over 900 feet. No conventional submarine could ever have gone that deep and survived. Our pump was surely not built for such a depth.

I managed to steal a glance through the after bulkhead. For some reason, the POs' mess was swarming with men, but the subdued light made it hard to see anything.

The Captain had his back propped against the shiny silver shaft of the search periscope. One hand clasped his kneecap as if it hurt him.

Suddenly his body went taut. He straightened his back and stood up. His voice was a whisper no longer.

'Well, Chief, how much water have we taken? Which tanks are damaged? Which ones can't be blown? Can we pump out at this depth?'

More questions rained down on the Chief: 'What's wrong with the main bilge-pump? Can you patch it up? If we blow every undamaged tank we've got, will it give us enough buoyancy?'

The Chief worked his shoulders like an athlete loosening up. Then he took two or three aimless steps. The control-room PO also came to life.

I cudgelled my brains. We had three-compartment status. Fine, but how did that help us now? If the Captain sealed off the control-room from the stern – always assuming there was some point in doing so – in other words, if he secured the after bulkhead door, the control-room and fore-ends might stay nice and dry. Great! We could then wait in comfort for the oxygen to run out. That would be the sole advantage.

The main bilge-pump . . . If that was a write-off, we still had compressed air. We could use HP air to expel water from our tanks, but did we have enough left after our fruitless burst on the way down? Without pumps and HP air, we were done for. We needed to be able to pump *and* blow, reduce our weight *and* create buoyancy. But what if the ballast tanks would no longer hold the compressed air – if the precious stuff escaped through fractures or damaged vents and streamed to the surface as soon as we blew? What if it just formed bubbles and imparted no lift at all?

There was an infernal stink. Battery gas – some cells must have cracked. Battery cells were sensitive. First the explosion, then the impact as we bottomed. The batteries were our sole source of power. If the cells had gone . . .

'Hurry up!' I heard the Chief say. 'Look lively!' echoed the coxswain. More whispered reports arrived, mostly from aft. I heard them without taking them in. I became aware of a dog-like panting and scampering, and over it all the throb and thrash of propellers. Turbines without a doubt. Were they systematically breaking our nerve? I had an urge to stop my ears, plug them with my forefingers, but that would have cut me off from what was happening. I could barely see anything in the semi-darkness – it was like being down a mine.

Men stalked through the control-room with grotesque tight-rope-walkers' movements. I backed into the base of the search periscope, oppressed by a sense of superfluity.

The second lieutenant was quite near me, also standing aside. There was plenty for seamen to do aboard a stranded ship, but we were sunk, not stranded. Sunken ships provided no jobs for deck personnel. How could they?

What about the first lieutenant? He must also be somewhere in the control-room. A bit low on intellectual resources – any resources . . . He could say that again!

The rapid breathing in my vicinity came from Isenberg. An unnerving sound, like a beast at bay. I felt a renewed temptation to plug my ears. Deafness might be a blessing after all. See nothing, hear nothing, smell nothing – sink into the ground, except that sheet metal would be hard to sink into. A pity about our precious oil, but who knew if we should ever need it? Face the facts, stop kidding yourself: they had us cold. No sneaking off this time. We were nailed to the spot. The hull still held, true, but our machinery was shot to hell. Face facts, no self-delusion. Done for! Without machinery we were finished. Without buoyancy we should lie here till doomsday. The resurrection of the body from 280 metres down – a special technique known only to U-boat Command.

Silhouetted by the faint light over the hydrophone controls, the Captain's shoulders sagged a little. My own muscles relaxed in imitation. Relief travelled the length and breadth of my back. The rhomboid – that was what had just relaxed: one of the two great shoulder-turning muscles. Once learnt, never forgotten. Anatomy classes at Dresden, with their asinine snipping at cadavers. Cases of gas poisoning were best – they didn't decay as fast as deaths from natural causes. The hall full of skeletons, all mounted to resemble classical sculptures. A collection of vulgar simulacra: the Discus-thrower, the Votary, the Boy with a Thorn . . .

'Funny,' I heard the Captain whisper. So he found it funny that nothing had happened, that the men overhead were still holding off. He half-turned to face me. 'It flew in at an angle, like this, side-slipped a bit, and then straightened out.'

I couldn't follow his gestures in the gloom. The Old Man made my head spin. Nothing seemed to exist for him but the aeroplane. 'There may even have been two bombs – I didn't see, exactly.'

The control-room was wreathed in blue vapour. The stench of gas made breathing unpleasant. In the POs' mess, two men had lifted the cover of No. 2 battery. Looking through the bulkhead door, I could see by the emergency lighting that one of them was armed with a strip of blue litmus-paper. The dipstick in his other hand was thrust into the bilge. He extracted it and moistened the litmus-paper.

The Chief spoke hurriedly. 'Get some lime in there, fast. Then find out how many cells are damaged.'

So there was acid in the battery bilge. A number of cells must have cracked and leaked, and their sulphuric acid had amalgamated with sea-water to produce chlorine gas. Hence the appalling stench.

The Captain had pushed his luck once too often, and this was the pay-off. But what else could he have done? The madmen of Kernével were the ones who had us on their conscience.

Another attack of cynicism. Conscience – what conscience? In Kernével terms, we were just a pair of code letters to be deleted from a list. The dockyard would build another U-boat, personnel reserve would supply another crew.

I looked at the Chief. His shirt was drenched and open to the navel. A tangle of hair hung down over his face and there was a slanting graze across his left cheek.

The second engineer appeared. I deduced from his whispered remarks that water was still rising in the motor-room bilge. Then a few snatches: 'Still making water in the engine-room – lots of it . . . there's a split in the flooding valve under No. 5 tube . . . cooling-water pipes . . . motor bearings . . . air induction pipe fractured.'

The second engineer had to pause for breath.

Boots scuffed the deck-plates.

'Quiet!' the Captain said swiftly. The propellers were still circling.

Some of the leaks were mysterious, it seemed. The second engineer had been unable to trace the source of all the water that had found its way into the hull. The level of the control-room bilge was also rising. Though muffled, the gurgle could be clearly heard.

The Captain said: 'What about that oil-leak? Do you know which tanks are involved?'

The Chief disappeared aft. Returning a few minutes later, he reported breathlessly: 'Oil came out of the vent lead to begin with, then water.'

'Strange,' observed the Captain.

Clearly this was against the rules. I gathered that the vent lead was near the engines. If the tank had been holed, water would have spurted from the vent lead under much greater pressure. The Captain and the Chief pondered this phenomenon. The tank was still half-full, so why the sluggish outflow? In addition to the normal fuel tanks, two of our ballast tanks were filled with oil fuel pumped from the *Weser*.

'It's odd,' the Chief said. 'First a stream of oil, but then the test-cock yielded water.'

'This fuel tank,' asked the Captain; 'where do its openings pass through the pressure hull? Where are the vents and filling lines? It seemed there was still a hope that only the vent lead had gone, not the tank itself.

The Chief and the Captain could only make conjectures because the pipes were inaccessible. It was anyone's guess what the main ballast tanks looked like from outside, after the explosion and our crash-landing.

The Chief went aft again.

I tried to visualize the various tanks. In the saddle-tanks, the oil floated on water. That kept pressure equalized – there were no air-pockets, so they were less vulnerable than the other tanks. Probably, one of the external tanks was holed. It should be possible to ascertain the quantity of oil lost by checking the gauges. The only question was, did the Chief know precisely how much oil there should be in his tanks? Oil-level indicators were imprecise, as were estimates of fuel consumed after hours of running. Only regular dip-checks yielded accurate results.

Soaked to the skin, Isenberg reported that he had located a damaged valve and managed to repair it. This was the probable source of most of the water in the control-room bilge.

I suddenly noticed that the propeller noise had ceased. Was it a ruse? Were they lying to, our friends on the surface? Could we breathe again, or were they trying to trick us? I strained my ears.

'Knocking-off time,' murmured the Captain. Then, musingly: 'He couldn't have seen us – he simply couldn't have.'

The Old Man had lost interest in the lap-of-honour merchant. No noise, no point in worrying. His thoughts had reverted to the aeroplane. 'He couldn't have . . . In that light? Impossible! He turned up far too suddenly.' The Captain's voice became a mumble. 'Pity we can't send a signal . . . nasty business . . . damned important . . .'

I saw what he meant. The others must be warned. There

had long been a buzz that the British were developing a new electronic detection and ranging device compact enough to fit inside a cockpit. We were living proof of the rumour's accuracy. We were the guinea-pigs. If the RAF could now detect U-boats blind – if surface travel was unsafe, even on a dark night – it was caps off for prayers. Vital information, and no chance of passing it on.

There was such a crush in the control-room that I retired to the wardroom. Chaos reigned there too. The table and settee were littered with plans and blue-prints.

The Chief was poring over a circuit diagram. He muttered incessantly as he traced its intricacies with a broken stump of pencil. Then he picked up a paperclip and used that instead. Hands trembling, he scratched lines on the linoleum with an abandon which suggested that the desecration of our wardroom furniture no longer mattered.

The first lieutenant sat beside him cleaning some binoculars. Round the bend, I thought. Seamanship was out for the present – even he should have grasped that. As if good vision counted for anything on the sea-bed. Ludicrous! And the way he looked . . . His normally unlined countenance had acquired two deep monkey-like creases between each nostril and the corners of his mouth. Stubble sprouted from his chin. Our dapper Number One was no more.

Something buzzed round the light. Our fly! Not only had it survived the latest ordeal – it was capable of surviving us all.

What time was it? I was dismayed to find that my watch had gone. A bad omen. I tried to read the dial on the Chief's wrist. Midnight plus a few minutes.

The Captain had come in and was bombarding the Chief with looks of enquiry. 'Running repairs . . . impossible . . .' I heard the Chief murmur.

If not running repairs, what? Send for a gang of dockyard mateys? Ring up the designers of the VII-C?

All the deck-plates had been taken up immediately forward of the wardroom table and in the passage. Two men were at work on No. 1 battery. Cables and tools were being passed to them from the control-room.

'Shit!' said a voice underfoot. 'What a God-awful stench!' it seemed to come from far away.

Pilgrim's head emerged from the inspection hatch. The PO electrician coughed violently, eyes streaming. Being unaware of the Chief's presence in the wardroom, he reported to the control-room direct.

'Tell the Chief: twenty-four cells gone.'

Twenty-four out of how many? Was the loss of twenty-four cells calamitous or supportable?

The Chief hauled himself erect and ordered Pilgrim and his assistant to put on escape gear. Two brown satchels were passed forward from the control-room. I handed them down.

While the electricians were putting their gear on, the Chief squeezed through the inspection hatch in front of our table. A minute or two later he wriggled out again, coughing. He quickly produced a plan of No. 1 battery and spread it on top of the other diagrams. His pencil crossed off one cell after another – twenty-four in all.

'Nowhere near enough battery-straps to go round,' he said, without looking up. I got the point. The defective cells couldn't be simply dismantled and dumped overboard. The Chief planned to by-pass them and create a functioning element out of the cells that remained.

It seemed a nightmare task, working out the shortest and most economical route from one healthy cell to the next. Beads of sweat gathered on the Chief's forehead. He drew lines and crossed them out again, sniffing hard every few seconds to clear his runny nose.

Gigolo negotiated the wardroom carrying a large bucket of sloshy white liquid – the milk of lime which was to stop the formation of chlorine gas by neutralizing the sulphuric acid that had drained from our batteries. I heard him open the door to the heads, home of the sprinkler-pipe that conveyed lime to the battery bilge.

'Hurry up, man – make it snappy!' The Chief rose and bent over the inspection hatch of No. 1 battery. Still holding the diagram, he passed some instructions below in an undertone. Pilgrim didn't answer at first but then a series of strangely muffled grunts and groans emerged from the cavity.

The Captain loudly demanded some bread and butter. Bread and butter – now? The Old Man couldn't possibly be hungry. Bread and butter was code for: 'All is well. Your captain fancies a snack. Anyone who fancies a snack must be all right.'

'Like half?' he asked me.

'No, thanks.'

The Old Man produced the semblance of a grin, sat back and demonstrated how to chew properly. He worked his lower jaw back and forth like a ruminating cow.

Two men sidled past the inspection hatch and caught sight of him eating. The news would travel the length of the boat, just as he meant it to.

Electrician Zörner extricated his diminutive frame from the bilge and removed his nose-clip. Sweat was trickling down his bare chest. He saw the Captain and gaped.

ERA Franz ducked through the bulkhead holding an inspection lamp, presumably in search of the Chief. His arms were smeared to the biceps with sticky black oil. What with Pilgrim's subterranean grunts and Franz's breathless delivery, I didn't catch what passed between them. I only gathered that we were still making water aft. The Chief squeezed through into the control-room with Franz in tow, but two minutes later he was back and paying another visit to the battery bilge.

The Captain pushed his plate aside. End of performance.

The Chief's angry voice issued from the depths. 'Damnation! What's the matter? Hey, Zörner, why no light?'

They seemed to be short-handed below deck. I caught sight of a torch in one corner of the wardroom, reached for it and tried the switch. It worked. I lowered myself through the hatch with the torch stuffed in my waistband. The Chief was swearing again. 'What the hell's up? Am I getting some light or aren't I?'

I appeared on cue – Lucifer the light-bringer in all his glory. The Chief accepted my presence without a word. Very cosy. Just as long as he wasn't deluding himself. If the motors were swamped, all his efforts would be futile – even I knew that much. Strange, his absolute silence. I could see his right leg beside me, inert as the limb of a corpse. It was comforting to hear the rasp of his breath. He instructed me how to hold the torch. I saw him flex his oil-smirched fingers in the beam, clenching and splaying them in turn.

Mutely I implored him to press on, stop his nervous fumbling, do a neat job, take his time. It was now or never.

I had a sudden remote vision of us, as in an oft-seen picture: heroes begrimed with oil and filth, horizontally posed filmminers with contorted faces and beaded brows.

My free hand was in demand now. Here, heave on that. Right, I've got it. Easy, or the spanner'll slip. Balls! Too late, try again.

If only one could move . . . Miners at the face – just the same, except that instead of pick and drill we used spanner, pliers and battery-straps. The air was barely breathable. God help us if the Chief flagged now. The spanner in his jaws made him look like an Indian brave on the warpath. He wormed his way forward a good three metres. I crawled after him, bruising both knees in the process.

I was taken aback by the size of the battery area below the deck-plates. I had always imagined our 'battery' as something far smaller. This was a giant version of a car battery, but how much of it was still serviceable? When a sock had more holes than weave, it lost its identity and went in the rag-bag. Our batteries might be fit for scrap, nothing more. The bastards had made a shambles of the entire boat.

A face peered down. I couldn't identify its owner because it hovered at one-eighty degrees to my own. Strange how hard it was to recognize faces upside down.

Air! Why didn't they pipe some down to us? The steel bands round my chest were squeezing all the strength out of me.

The Chief made a signal. We had to get out from under. Helping hands reached down. I was panting hard, like a dog on a hot day.

'Fine old mess, eh?' someone said. I only heard him dimly, as if my eardrums were under pressure. I couldn't spare the breath for an affirmative. My lungs continued to pump. Luckily, there was room to perch among the plans on the Chief's bunk. A voice called out the time: 02. Not later?

The Chief reported to the Captain that we were short of wire. Less than half of No. 1 battery could be patched with the straps available. Suddenly it seemed that finding some wire was our real problem, not surfacing. The Chief issued a general order: 'Wire needed – any kind!'

The nice shiny torpedoes in our tubes, in the fore-ends and casing stowages, cost RM 25,000 apiece, but all we needed was RM 5's-worth of old wire. We had plenty of shells but no wire. Ironical: masses of ammunition, HE and incendiary both, yet the gun lay even deeper than we did. It marked the spot where our remains would now be lying if the Old Man hadn't sprinted south. Ten rounds of HE for ten metres of wire – quite a business proposition.

The coxswain had vanished into the fore-ends. Heaven alone knew how he expected to produce some wire, but if he didn't – and if the second lieutenant, quartermaster and control-room PO were equally unsuccessful – what then?

I heard 'dismantle electrical circuits' and 'twist them together'. It sounded unpromising. The wire had to be of a certain diameter, so what? Plait several strands together? A fiddly and time-consuming job which might take us all night.

We were noticeably lower by the stern now. The stern tube was reported to be two-thirds awash. If the motor-room became swamped, all the wire in the world wouldn't save us.

What was the date? The calendar had disappeared from the bulkhead – gone, like my watch. We were out of time.

The atmosphere in the wardroom was beginning to get on my nerves. I clambered aft to the control-room, skirting the gaps in the deck. Every joint ached from my recent contortions. I had a dagger-thrust between my shoulder-blades and nagging pains all the way down my back. My rump hurt too.

On the deck-plates close beside the periscope well lay the barograph. Two sides of the glass case were smashed. The stylus had been bent backwards like a hairpin, and the undulating curve inscribed on the drum terminated in a downward stroke and a fat blob of ink. I felt tempted to detach the paper and pocket it. If we ever got out alive, I could frame the sheet and hang it – our doom graphically recorded by that wavering downstroke: the bottom had dropped out of our market.

The Chief had evolved a system of priorities in his battle with disaster: first things first, smother the blaze before the wind got to it, check the mischief that was spreading quickest. Here on board, every installation was necessary and none superfluous, but now, in our present predicament, shades of difference existed between the necessary and the vital.

The Captain and the Chief were holding a whispered conference. ERA Johann appeared from aft. The control-room PO also took part – even ERA Franz was allowed to contribute. Every member of U-A's senior technical team had assembled in the control-room apart from the second engineer, who was in the motor-room. I gathered that work in the stern was proceeding steadily and methodically. Progress had been made. The Chief had delegated his battery problems to the two PO electricians.

The meeting broke up. The control-room emptied except for Isenberg and the Captain, who lolled on the chart-stowage with an easy nonchalance not lost on the ratings who tiptoed past. He sat there with his hands buried in the pockets of his sheepskin waistcoat, radiating confidence in his specialists.

Pilgrim came through and asked permission to join the search for wire in the forepart of the boat.

'Of course,' the Captain said. Wire wanted? Wire we should have, even if we had to reel it out of our fundamental orifices.

At that moment the coxswain appeared in the forward doorway, beaming like a birthday boy. Clutched in his oily hands were a few metres of rusty old wire.

The Captain nodded. 'I told you so. That'll do for a start.'

Behrmann splashed through the water that had risen above

378

the deck-plates in the after half of the control-room and ducked through the bulkhead into the POs' mess, site of No. 2 battery.

'Great!' That was the Chief's voice.

Behrmann padded back again, looking as if he had discovered America. A simple soul, the coxswain. He seemed unaware that it would take more than a few metres of wire to solve our problems.

'Keep up the good work,' the Captain told him. Then he lapsed into silence for a good ten minutes because there was no one to witness his performance.

'Let's hope they don't come looking for us with sweep wires,' he said eventually.

Sweep wires? I thought at once of the Breton mussel-catchers who dragged their trawls along the sandy bottom to dislodge half-embedded mussels. We seemed to be lying on rocks, not sand, in which case sweep wires – if I was thinking of the same thing – would hardly be the tool for the job.

The Chief reappeared. 'How's it going?' asked the Captain.

'So-so. Almost finished, sir. Only three more cells to go.'

The Captain's voice acquired a little more urgency. 'And aft?'

'Could be worse.' Perhaps, I thought, but not much.

I subsided on the wardroom settee and tried, with my eyes closed, to assess our situation. The Captain had blown while we were going down – blown like mad, but to no avail because we'd already taken in so much water that its weight could not be offset by expelling water from the ballast tanks. U-A still had negative buoyancy even with every tank blown. It followed that now, although we were on the bottom, there must be air in our ballast tanks – blowing-air. This air could take us to the surface statically, but only if we managed to reduce the boat's weight. It was like sitting in the basket of a balloon which, though inflated, was pinned down by excess ballast. Ballast must be jettisoned from the basket before the balloon would rise. Yes, but only if our main vents had held. If the vents had also been damaged and weren't water-tight, we could pump as much air as we liked into the main ballast tanks – every ounce in our air-bottles – without producing any effect whatsoever.

True, there was also the dynamic method of rising and diving. Under electric power and with both sets of planes a-rise, a submarine could be raised at an angle, much like an aeroplane. But this wouldn't work in our case. U-A was too heavy, and it was doubtful if our remaining amps would suffice to keep the screws turning for longer than a few minutes. I wondered if the Chief had any idea how much power, at best, our few sound cells would develop.

We were probably dependent on the balloon method. The excess water would have to be expelled – expelled at all costs. Then up. Up and overboard and swim for it.

I could hang my films round my neck. I had a watertight pouch. It would certainly take the ones of our encounter in the storm. They deserved saving – they were unique.

If only it weren't for that damned current in the Strait . . . A shovelful of sand under our keel at the very last moment – nothing short of a miracle!

The Captain was chewing his lower lip. Planning and supervision now rested with the Chief. It was on his decisions that everything hung. God knew how he kept going – he hadn't stopped for an instant.

All the leaks seemed to have been checked apart from a little seepage, a few supporting wounds in our steel skin. But the water already on board? I had no idea of its volume. One litre of water, one kilo of excess weight. My whole body sensed the burden we bore. We were heavy, heavy, immeasurably heavy – nailed to the spot by our own weight.

'I can smell shit,' muttered Isenberg.

Frenssen smirked. 'Why not open a window?'

From the stern came a hiss like escaping steam. It went right through me. What in God's name was it this time? The note changed to that of a needle-sharp jet playing on steel. I itched to take a look.

What did the Captain have in mind? What could be passing through his head as he sat there in the control-room, staring into space? Did he plan to take us up, make another dash for the Moroccan coast and beach us? That must be it, because he wanted to surface before daybreak. If his sole intention were to abandon ship, he wouldn't be interested in completing repairs to the engine-room before first light.

Swimming in the dark would be far too risky. The current would scatter us in two minutes flat, long before the Brits could stop us. Our life-jackets weren't fitted with distress lights like theirs. We didn't even carry red flares – in fact we were wholly unprepared for the present emergency.

Still no word from the Captain. I couldn't very well question him. Two minutes later he came into the wardroom.

'They're bound to give him a gong,' I heard him say. 'Something nice and jingly – the Victoria Cross, maybe.'

I stared at him stupidly.

'Well, he's earned it. It isn't his fault we're still alive and kicking.'

I had a vivid picture of the scene. A Nissen hut on the Rock, a gaggle of flying-suited pilots with champagne-glasses at the ready, gathered to celebrate the sinking of a U-boat. Definitely observed by airborne radar and confirmed by the Royal Navy.

'Shit-scared,' the Captain sounded weary but resigned, as though a bit more damage here or there made no odds.

The stern must look worst of all. I wondered why the bomb should have wrought such havoc in the afterpart of the submarine. The damage to the control-room and No. 1 battery was understandable enough, but I couldn't account for the extensive damage aft. Perhaps there had been two bombs after all. Had the explosion sounded like a double one? I couldn't bring myself to ask.

The Chief came forward to make a comprehensive report. I gathered from his torrent of technicalities that nearly every hull opening had leaked. Part of the electrical system was completely out of action, likewise the fire-control system which depended on it. There was also a possibility that the shaft bearings had suffered. If so, they would run hot when the shafts revolved.

The Chief's report amounted to a full inventory of the damage we had sustained. Not only was the main bilge-pump out of action – so were all the others. The forward trimming tank was no longer watertight. The fundamental bolts of the port engine had held, miraculously enough, but those of the starboard engine had sheared. The compressors had been wrenched off their bases. The forward hydroplanes were almost immovable, doubtless because of our collision with the rocky bottom. The compass system was completely up the spout. Magnetic, gyro – the lot. The log and sounding gear had been torn from their mountings and were probably unserviceable. The wireless equipment had suffered badly. Even the engine-room telegraph was out of commission.

'Is that all, Chief?' The Captain's mouth twitched in a wry grin. 'I can assume, then, that the heads are still in order?'

All at once I heard a new sound, definitely from outboard. A high-pitched rhythmical whine underlaid by a duller beat. They were back! My breathing ceased as though quenched by a stopcock. The Captain had noticed at the same moment. He listened with his mouth open, frowning. The throbbing whine rose in volume. Turbines again. I waited for the patter of Asdic. Everyone, seated, standing or kneeling, froze into immobility. I had some difficulty identifying the shadowy figures round me. The one on the left of the periscope must be the quartermaster – I could recognize the tell-tale lift of his left shoulder. The bent back in front of the hydrophone control position belonged to the Chief. The man on his left must be the second lieutenant. Isenberg was standing under the conning-tower.

My pulse seemed to pound like a steam-hammer. Impossible to escape the impression that it was audible to everyone in the compartment.

My ears had become hydrophones of immense sensitivity. They picked up a whole range of tiny noises, many of which they had failed to register until now – the rustle of leather jackets, the rodent squeak of bootsoles on iron deck-plates. The marine engines overhead were far too loud for my high-frequency sound-detectors.

They were going to finish us off. Sweep wires, Asdic? Perhaps the lap-of-honour merchant hadn't been carrying depth-charges – perhaps this was a relief ship. I tensed every muscle and went rigid – anything rather than betray myself.

What was wrong? The whine of propellers seemed to be fading – surely I wasn't mistaken?

A burning sensation in the lungs. My chest expanded unbidden. I drew one tremulous breath, and already I was gasping for the next one. Another, and another. I charged my lungs with air and held it. The steam-hammer started up again.

I was right, the noises were fading.

'Going away,' murmured the Captain. I subsided at once. The pent-up breath escaped with a sort of sigh, and I treated myself to some proper lungfuls of gas-laden air.

''Ware destroyers,' the Captain said impassively. 'The place is swarming with ships – they must have alerted everything that can float.'

Which, being interpreted, meant that the latest visitation was accidental. A weight fell from my shoulders.

Then the rattle and clatter of tools made me jump. Work had resumed in the stern. It occurred to me, as it had done once before, that there were more men in the control-room than rightfully belonged there. Purely instinctive, this jockeying for a place under the hatch when the enemy was within earshot. All hands were well aware of the depth at which we lay – a depth that didn't, for once, favour seamen over stokers. To men in our position, escape packs were useless –

discounting the extra half-hour of life which their cartridges might give us if the oxygen-bottles ran out.

The thought that the British had written us off, and that our supposed destruction must have been signalled to the Admiralty hours before, inspired me with a blend of horror and derision. I found myself mounting taunts in English: Not yet, you bastards, not yet. Don't count your eggs – or was it chickens?

A wave of nausea overcame me. I swallowed hard, flushing the acid upsurge with my own saliva. Then a dull, throbbing ache made itself felt at the back of my skull and, simultaneously, over the right eyebrow. No wonder. The fog we were inhaling had grown denser. It was scarcely credible that we could continue to subsist on this mixture of a hundred foul smells, Diesel fumes and battery gas. Highly combustible too, no doubt – one spark might set it off.

'Trust the Chief,' I heard someone say. 'He'll dig us out, you mark my words.' It was PO Dorian. I nearly punched him on the nose for tempting providence. All the same, our dunce of a second engineer could never have replaced the Chief. Unthinkable that the Chief might have disembarked at Vigo, as planned . . .

I almost giggled at my own mistake. Think straight, friend. If the Chief wasn't on board this hulk, you wouldn't be either – you were going to sign off à deux, remember? But that would have put paid to every member of the crew, sentenced them to death twice over. As long as you're on board, U-A can't rot on the bottom. The lines in your hand say you're going to live to a ripe old age, so we're bound to survive. Nobody must know you bear a charmed life, that's all. Don't tempt providence, keep mum and look brave. They haven't got us yet, not by a long chalk. We're still breathing – in laboured gasps, perhaps, but breathing none the less.

The mutters and whispers from the control-room had long been the only human sounds to reach me in the wardroom. I had an urge to hear my own voice. I wanted to chat to the second lieutenant, who was sitting beside me on the Chief's bunk. Know what, Number Two? All this silence puts me in mind of the Trappist monks who tried to recruit me on that canoe-trip down the Danube. Me, in a monastery? Semi-starvation and no talking – almost as bad as the Navy. Well this is where my amateur boating has got me: 280 metres down in the Strait of Gibraltar . . .

The second lieutenant's jaw would have dropped if he had

heard my monologue, but not a word emerged. A thick film had formed on my tongue, which felt repulsive, like a wad of putrid meat.

If only we could have sent a signal! No chance at this depth, even with a serviceable transmitter. Nobody at home would learn the nature of our end. The usual letter of condolence from Flotilla to our next-of-kin: 'Missing, presumed killed in action.' Our disappearance would remain a mystery – unless, of course, the British used Radio Calais to divulge how they had sunk us.

Their technique was sophisticated these days. They courted the credulity of those at home with telling little details – names, dates of birth, captains' cap sizes. And Kernével? They would delay the news, as they usually did. After all, we might have cogent reasons for maintaining radio silence. We would soon be asked to report our position. Once, twice, three times – the old routine.

In the nature of things, however, the gentlemen of the staff would quickly conclude that we had failed to penetrate the Strait as instructed. There could never have been much chance of running the gauntlet – they must have known that from the outset. Their crazy boss could gently accustom himself to the idea that he had lost another U-boat. Sunk off Gibraltar, British naval base, ape-inhabited rock, delightful climatic rendezvous – wasn't that how it went? God in heaven, I mustn't crack up now. I concentrated on the bananas that hung from the deckhead, quietly ripening. Two or three pineapples nestled in their midst – magnificent specimens, but the sight of them only bemused me. Below, our ruined batteries; above, a hanging garden.

The Chief reappeared. Suddenly he halted in mid-stride, as if the many simultaneous calls on his nervous system had jammed the whole circuit. His eyelids were half-closed, his sunken cheeks twitched. Had he been brought up short by one particular noise among the multitude that emanated from the stern?

At last he set off again, but not in his characteristically lithe and feline way. His movements were stiff and puppet-like, as though it was an effort to put one foot before the other. Relaxation did not set in until he had taken two or three steps. He groped in the locker containing rolled-up plans, pulled one out and spread it on the table. I helped him by weighting its corners with books. It was a longitudinal section of the boat. The pipes and lines were shown as red veins or black arteries.

I didn't know the object of his quest. Was he re-checking the fuel-tank hull openings, still hoping to discover why water was coming from that vent lead?

Oil had deposited itself deep in the lines of his face. He mopped it with a cloth, but the grime clung like ink to an etching plate.

The Chief's mind had to function like a detective's. Under present circumstances, dash and drive would get us nowhere. Occasionally he murmured arcane formulae and drew cabalistic signs. Then, for minutes on end, he lapsed into total silence, cogitating grimly.

The second engineer joined them, dishevelled and out of breath. He also pored silently over the plans. The sound-track seemed to have failed again.

Everything now hung on the deliberations of our two engineer officers. They were sitting in judgement on our fate. Loath to distract them, I kept absolutely still. The Chief rapped something with a pencil and nodded at his subordinate. The second engineer nodded back. Simultaneously, they straightened up and went aft.

It looked as if the Chief now knew how he proposed to rid us of excess water. I wondered how he planned to cope with the external pressure.

I caught sight of a half-eaten piece of bread on the CPOs' mess table – fresh white bread from the *Weser* lavishly spread with butter. A thick slice of sausage reposed on top. My eyes were drawn and held by the round of bread with the semi-circular bite out of it. Nauseating! Somebody must have been eating when the bomb exploded. Odd that the plate hadn't slid off the table when we nose-dived.

Breathing was becoming more and more difficult. Why didn't the Chief boost our oxygen supply? It was hateful to be so dependent on air. I only had to hold my breath for a short time and my ears began to tick off the seconds. Then I gagged. Nice fresh bread and a boatload of fresh provisions, but what we really needed was air. Our inability to live without it was being brought home to us with a vengeance. How often in the normal course of events did I reflect that I couldn't exist without oxygen, that flabby lobes were endlessly inflating and contracting behind my ribs? Lungs . . . I'd never seen them outside the dissecting-room, except cooked. Stewed lights – a favourite dog-food. Lights and dumplings, sixty pfennigs'-worth of nourishment at the main line station, where they used to keep the dumpling soup hot in sauerkraut pans, complete with an admixture of sawdust from the floor, until the sanitary inspectors closed them down.

'Liquid air', title of a lecture at school. It was like a cabaret turn. The visiting lecturer extracted a sausage from the canister and smashed it with a hammer, dipped a rose in it and crumbled the petals between his fingers.

Two hundred and eighty metres. What was the weight of the column of water that reposed on our hull? I should be able to work it out. I knew the figures – I had memorized them, but my brain was functioning at half capacity. The pressure inside my skull made it impossible to think.

I felt as if my grey cells were a fermenting porridge from which bubbles sluggishly rose and burst. I pined for my missing watch. My sense of time was disrupted – I couldn't guess the length of our sojourn on the sea-bed. My orientation had gone too. Considerable distances appeared to separate me from the objects of my perception. My optical system wasn't working properly – it made things seem further away than they were. I couldn't have touched the second lieutenant's face with my fingertips, even though logic told me he was well within reach.

The Chief returned. I gathered my thoughts and focused them on him. The network of wrinkles in his face had ramified. Brilliant highlights flecked his coal-black pupils and his mouth was a gloomy cavern. In this dim light, his features seemed to have been turned inside out, like a rubber mask. A bas-relief – how did it go? Cameo was raised, intaglio negative, so the Chief's face resembled an intaglio. The furrows in his forehead worked swiftly like the shutters of a flashing beacon: open, shut, open, shut.

In my left trouser-pocket I felt my lucky charm, an oval piece of polished quartz. I opened my hand and ran my fingers over the stone. It turned to human flesh, warm and slightly rounded. Simone's tummy. At once I heard her dulcet chatter: '*Ca c'est mon petit nombril* – how do you call it? Button in the belly? Belly-button. Funny word. *Pour moi c'est ma boîte à ordures – regarde, regarde!*'

She fingered some fluff out of the dainty little recess and held it in front of my nose, giggling.

If Simone could only see me now, two hundred and eighty metres down. Not just somewhere in the Atlantic. I had a permanent address now: Strait of Gibraltar, near Morocco. Here lay our cigar-tube with its cargo of fifty bodies: flesh, bone, blood, marrow, pumping lungs, throbbing pulses, pounding hearts – fifty brains, each with a whole world of memories.

I tried to visualize Simone's changing hairstyles. What was

the latest? Apply my mind as I would, I couldn't recall. No matter, it would come back to me. Better not try so hard. Memories returned of their own accord.

I had a vivid recollection of her violet jumper. The yellow scarf, too, and the mallow-coloured blouse with the intricate design which proved, under close scrutiny, to be a thousand-fold reiteration of *Vive la France*. The golden-orange of her skin . . . Yes, now I remembered her hair. It was the strands on her forehead that fascinated me. They were dishevelled, usually, but smooth as silk. Her hair was curly at the back – sometimes it even fell into Biedermeier-style ringlets. Simone favoured the artfully casual look.

It wasn't fair of her, purloining my Service binoculars for her papa. No doubt he wanted to see if the modern sort were really so superior to the old. He must have been intrigued by the new blue-coated lenses which gave such a bright image at night. And Simone? Just another of her little acts? Monique got a toy coffin. Geneviève and Germaine too, but not Simone.

The Captain came in with the Chief. They bent over a diagram. 'Into the trimming tank by hand . . .' I heard the Chief say, presumably referring to our burden of water. By hand? Was it possible?

Possible or not, they both nodded.

'Then outboard from the tank, using the auxiliary bilge-pump and HP air . . .'

The Chief's voice had a distinct vibrato. Looking at him in profile, I felt alarmed. It was a miracle he could still stand. He had been whacked before the latest trouble began. Any man with a score or more counter-attacks behind him was used up, hence the intention to relieve him. Only one more patrol, and now this . . . Mental strain corrugated his brow and prevented the fat beads of perspiration from rolling off. I saw, when he turned his head, that his whole face was glistening with sweat.

'Noise . . . can't be helped . . . no alternative . . . No. 3 main ballast . . .'

Why the mention of No. 3 main ballast tank? Nothing could have happened to that – it was inside the pressure hull. I tried to remember my lessons. U-A could float on No. 3 alone, but one tank's buoyancy was nowhere near enough to cope with the weight of the water we had absorbed. Therefore the water must be expelled. I had no idea how the Chief proposed to pump water from the control-room, first into the trimming tanks and then outboard, but the Chief was no fool. He never committed himself unless he was sure of his facts.

I gathered that no attempt would be made to lift us off the bottom until all essential repairs had been completed. We could only afford one try.

The Captain was speaking. 'Better level her off first . . .' We were down by the stern, true, pumping water forward was out of the question. In that case, how?

'We'll have to manhandle it from aft to the control-room.' Manhandle it – in buckets? From hand to hand? I stared at the Captain and waited for him to be more specific. 'Organize a baling party . . .' he continued. So he meant it literally.

I joined the human chain that formed into the POs' mess and galley. My place was near the bulkhead. Hoarsely whispered instructions and curses filled the air. Someone passed me a fanny of the sort the steward used for rinsing cutlery. It was half-full. I reached for it and swung it through the bulkhead like a dumb-bell. Isenberg caught it at the end of my swing. I heard him empty it into the control-room bilge abreast the periscope. The splash sounded almost obscene, like a drunk vomiting.

Empty buckets and fannies had to be passed aft for replenishment. Bottlenecks developed, but a series of low-voiced orders from the Chief sorted them out and got the two-way traffic flowing smoothly.

My immediate neighbour was Zeitler, wearing a torn and grubby singlet. Grim determination showed in his face every time he swung me a full bucket. The containers progressed along the chain to an accompaniment of hisses, whispers and grunts. A particularly heavy fanny reached me. Its contents slopped over the rim in spite of my two-handed grip. The dirty liquid soaked my trousers and shoes. My back was wet too, but with sweat. Twice, while passing a bucket to Isenberg, I caught a grin of encouragement from the Old Man. Some compensation, at least.

Occasionally the flow ceased because of a snarl-up in the stern. A few suppressed curses, and the chain regained its rhythm.

The control-room PO was exempt from caution. Being our anchorman, he could empty the buckets as he chose. Glancing aft into the POs' mess, I saw that the deck was wet there too. No. 2 battery was beneath it – didn't that matter? I consoled myself by remembering that the Chief was close at hand. He would keep an eye on things.

Another deluge, right over my stomach this time.

A dull thud, then more curses. The traffic halted again From the sound of it, someone had caught his bucket on the galley bulkhead.

Was I wrong, or had the stern risen a few degrees? The control-room was already ankle-deep.

How late was it? It must be at least 4 a.m. A pity about my watch. The strap had gone – modern rubbish, stuck not stitched – but the watch itself was a good one. Ten years without a repair.

'Mind yourself!' Zeitler hissed. Damn, I wasn't concentrating. I'd stopped bending my arms. Zeitler saved me a lot of trouble if he passed the buckets properly. His job was harder – he had to hump them through the bulkhead, which was why he looked so strained. He needed both hands to lift them over the coaming, I only used my right arm. I was past noticing how I gripped the bucket handles and swung them trapeze-like for the catcher to receive.

'When's first light?' the Captain asked Kriechbaum. The quartermaster leafed through his tables. 'o730, sir.' Not long to go!

It might be even later than 4 a.m. If we didn't make a move soon, our attempt to surface would be shelved. That meant waiting till nightfall. Another whole day in which to yearn for the light of the sun.

A whisper ran down the line. 'Rest – rest – rest!'

If the Captain's plan was to beach us with the aid of our last few amps – granted that we managed to surface at all – he would need the cover of darkness. We weren't at the narrowest part of the Strait, so the distance between our resting-place and the coast was considerable. That reduced our chances still further. Would the few amps that remained in the healthy cells provide sufficient power? What price all our work on the batteries if the shaft bearings were shot? The Chief's misgivings must have some basis in fact.

The men looked horrendous. Yellow faces, eye-sockets framed in blackish green, red-rimmed eyes, encrusted mouths gasping for breath. Frenssen resembled a wood carving, except for the fleshy lips that glowed in his beard like a gaudy recognition signal.

The Chief came forward to report that the motors were out of danger. My sigh of relief ended in a groan – he wanted still more water removed from the stern.

'Very good,' the Captain said in a normal voice. 'Carry on.'

Every muscle in my body rebelled as I took the first bucket Zeitler handed me. It was a supreme effort to recover our old rhythm.

Retching, gagging, chests heaving in the fetid air, we laboured on. One thing was certain: we were slowly but surely levelling off.

The Captain splashed over to the bulkhead and called aft. 'How's it going?'

'Not much more, sir!'

I could have dropped where I stood, straight into the oily soup that covered the deck-plates – I wouldn't have cared. I started counting buckets. Just as I reached fifty, the word was passed: 'Stop baling.'

A silent prayer of thanksgiving. I still had to transfer four or five receptacles from Zeitler to Isenberg, but the control-room PO passed them forward instead of handing them back.

And now, off with my wet gear. The POs' mess was crowded because everyone had the same idea. I grabbed my sweater and even succeeded in finding my leather trousers. Dry clothes – fantastic! Finally, on sea-boots. Frenssen dug his elbow in my ribs and Pilgrim trod on my foot, but at last the job was done. I splashed through the control-room like a mischievous urchin and flopped on to a bunk in the wardroom.

Then I heard 'oxygen'. A new order travelled from mouth to mouth: 'On potash cartridges. All hands off watch, turn in.'

The second lieutenant stared at me in dismay.

An additional injunction: 'If someone goes to sleep, make sure his mouthpiece stays in.'

'Haven't used one in a month of Sundays,' I heard the coxswain mutter next door.

Potash cartridges . . . That clinched it. We were in for a long wait – no glorious sunrise for us, not today. The second lieutenant neither spoke nor dimpled. The order was as little to his taste as mine. I saw by his watch that it was 5 a.m.

I paddled aft again and splashed through the control-room. The atmosphere was glum. Goodbye to all our hopes of surfacing before daybreak. The order to breathe through potash cartridges had banished any prospect of going up until darkness returned. I quailed at the thought of another whole day on the bottom. The engine-room personnel would have plenty of time to put their house in order. No need to hurry, not now.

Nervously I groped around at the head of my bunk and brought out the potash cartridge, a rectangular metal container twice the size of an average cigar-box.

The other inmates of the POs' mess were already screwing in air-pipes and gripping the rubber mouthpieces in their teeth. Zeitler, who was slower than the rest, swore savagely.

Pilgrim and Kleinschmidt already had greyish hoses protruding from their mouths. I put on my nose-clip, noticing as I did so that my hands were trembling. I took a cautious breath of air through the cartridge, almost excited to see what it was like. The air from the nozzle had a frightful rubbery taste, and the mouthpiece valve rattled as I breathed out. Something wrong, from the sound of it. Was I breathing too fiercely? I forced myself to inhale and exhale more evenly, slowly and calmly, hoping that the flavour of rubber would fade.

The container was a nuisance. It weighed at least a kilo and dangled against my stomach like an usherette's tray. The filling was supposed to absorb carbon dioxide we exhaled, or as much of it as would keep the air we breathed from containing more than four per cent. Anything over that was dangerous. We could suffocate on the products of our own exhalation.

How long would the oxygen last? The VII-C's submerged endurance was rated at three days, so our air-bottles ought to contain enough oxygen for three times twenty-four hours – not including the brief reprieve granted by the cylinders that formed part of our escape gear.

If Simone could see me like this, with an elephant's trunk and a box on my belly . . .

I looked at Zeitler, examining him with the care I would have devoted to my own reflection. Matted hair, forehead thickly beaded with sweat, staring eyes with a feverish glint and dark-violet smudges beneath them, nose pinched by the clip, rubber tube protruding from a tangled undergrowth of beard – a figure from some wild masquerade.

Those beards! How long had we been at sea? I tried to work it out. Seven or eight weeks – or was it nine or ten?

Simone again. I saw her smiling, gesticulating, slipping the straps off her shoulders. A blink of the eyelids, and her image vanished.

I decided to take a look at the control-room. Painfully I ducked through the bulkhead. Now I could see Simone projected on the pipes, levers and gauges. I saw a confusion of leads, handwheels and shut-off valves, and, superimposed on them, Simone: breasts, thighs, pubic down, moist half-parted lips. She rolled over on her tummy, reached for her ankles and made a 'swan'. The zebra shadows of the shutter slid across her body as she rocked back and forth. I closed my eyes, and there she was above me. Her full breasts hung down, the big brownish areolae looking as if they had been painted round her rosy nipples.

Simone among the grey-green dune grass, her belly and bosom breaded with moist sand; Simone with her head flung back and her throat extended; Simone, a faceless, jerking body.

Yet another superimposition, this time in close-up : a figure with a tube in its mouth. I started. It was the second lieutenant, staring at me as if he had an announcement to make. Clumsily, he extracted his mouthpiece. Saliva dripped from it. 'To all hands : use of fire-arms banned until further notice,' he said in a nasal voice, and winked. 'Danger of explosion . . .' Of course, battery gas.

He replaced his dummy and winked again before repairing to his bunk. I couldn't retort, so I took a hefty pull at my potash cartridge and rattled the valve at him instead. Indestructible, our Babyface. The British hadn't finished him yet – neither him nor the rest of us. Our eyes still watered when we batted our lids, our joints received automatic lubrication, impulses traversed our brains. The metabolic system was a miracle. The engines and motors had stopped but our bodies toiled on as though nothing had happened. They continued to function as usual, without our having to spare them a thought. I could see one of those multi-coloured portrayals of the human body as a factory-cum-generating station : teams of little men spraying the stomach with acid, processing waste matter, adding secretions . . .

The miracle of life, a nerve-ending source of wonder. Take the sea-snails in their glazed shells – how was it possible for such a shell, which had the hardness of china, to *grow* ? How did tender-fleshed fungi manage to thrust their heads through solid asphalt ? How could leeches suck thick blood through human epidermis ?

I groped my way drunkenly along the locker fronts. My hands identified the Captain's curtain, then some plywood partitioning. I could now reach the wardroom without acrobatics. The decking had been replaced. No. 1 battery probably had some left in it – just enough for a short run on the main motors.

A light was on in the wardroom. If we left this single bulb burning, it ought to last for ever and a day. A 40-watt bulb could surely burn for a week on less current than a single revolution of our screws consumed. Eternal light, 280 metres down . . .

Someone had tidied up, partially at least. The pictures, though glassless, were back on the bulkhead, and the books had been restored to their shelf in some sort of order. The first lieutenant seemed to have turned in, judging by his drawn curtain. The second lieutenant was already installed at the far end of the Chief's bunk with his eyes shut. He would have done better to stretch out on his own bunk instead of lolling there like a sack of potatoes, but he had ensconced himself with a finality which conveyed that he would never stir again.

Surprise almost made me scratch my head. The wardroom had never seemed so peaceful. No through traffic, no changes of watch. Pictures and books, cosy lamplight, handsomely grained wood, black leather settee. No pipes or white ship's paint, not even a square centimetre of our maltreated hull to be seen. Add a silk shade over the bulb, a vase of artificial flowers and a fringed tablecloth, and our front parlour would have been complete.

Admittedly the picture was a trifle marred by the second lieutenant – or, rather his air-pipe. Front parlours and fancy dress didn't mix.

Incredible, the hush. It was as if the crew had abandoned ship and left us to our own devices.

I forced myself to recall that outside lay the blackest and densest darkness imaginable – immense forces against which a thin and battered hull was our sole protection. Nature hadn't equipped us to live at such a depth. We had no gills, no fins, no air-bladders for balance . . .

The second lieutenant's head lolled on his chest. He had managed to exclude his surroundings. Nothing troubled the dreams of our Babyface. What in heaven's name enabled him to sleep at a juncture like this? Resignation, as with most of the crew, or was his personal narcotic the Captain's show of confidence? Blind faith in the Chief's expertise and the efficiency of his damage control team? Or was it simply discipline – sleep has been decreed, ergo sleep?

From time to time he grunted or choked on his own spittle. He didn't wake, just continued to suck noisily like a piglet at the dugs of a sow. He seemed to have abandoned himself to blissful memories of babyhood, fled the present and returned to his mother's breast. I couldn't help envying him as he sucked, snuffled and slumbered in peace.

Weary to the point of collapse, I dozed off for minutes at a time, only to surface again. It must have been after 6 a.m.

Scraps of verse and mnemonic rhymes filtered through my layers of consciousness. Then came soap bubbles emblazoned with shimmering visual memories. I tried to capture some of them, focus on one particular image, grasp a coherent thought. We had put too much faith in machines. We had overtaxed them. Now we had to propitiate them and regain their favour. Hostile machines could kill. It was incredible what a machine could do if it chose. I had only to recall my ancient Fiat at the level crossing in Verona. *'Miràcolo!'* shouted the lorry-drivers who ran to help me because my engine continued to run at high speed even though I'd switched off and removed the ignition key. They ripped out one battery lead, then the other for good measure, but the little car's engine raced on regardless. No petrol-tap – only the very early models were fitted with those. The engine had taken charge. Pre-ignition, I learned later. Too much farting around in the hot sun.

Better to keep mobile than contemplate my navel – better to absorb every occurrence, register every detail, zoom in on every object of interest. No need to move for that, though. For instance, I could focus on the second lieutenant's glinting mouse-teeth. Or his left ear-lobe – properly developed and more shapely than the Number One's. I studied him closely, dissected his head into component parts, took close-ups of his lashes, eyebrows, lips.

All at once the enlarged stills began to stir. I stared with all my might at Babyface's sparse moustache, but the pictorial dance continued. I was unexpectedly revisited by the plump commercial traveller who had given me a lift in his battered Opel. He made a point of repeating his philosophy of life once every fifteen minutes : 'Any woman will! Take my word for it – any woman will. Background doesn't matter. You've got to have the right approach, that's all.'

I wrenched my eyes open and the image faded. What stratum of memory could have regurgitated that obnoxious creature? It was five years ago – over five years. My thoughts had never once returned to our encounter, yet I could still see the tufts of hair sprouting from his nostrils, the massive signet ring on his pudgy finger. His tone of voice came back to me, accurate in every nuance : 'Any woman will . . .'

I made a renewed effort to divert my thoughts, but it was like cranking a dud engine : a few half-hearted splutters, then nothing.

Next I tried to drain my mind completely, but the vacuum

wasn't perfect – fear seeped in from below. How many hours had we lain on the sea-bed? It must have been roughly midnight when we dived – by ship's time, anyway, though ship's time was not only inconsistent with our geographical location but wrong by an extra hour. We were keeping German Summer Time. Did that mean adding or subtracting? I couldn't work it out – defeated even by a simple thing like that. By ship's time it must be at least 0700, far too late for any attempt to surface in the twilight of dawn. We should have to wait the return of darkness.

By now the British galleys must have prepared vast quantities of the eggs and bacon which Englishmen considered an essential start to the day. The thought of food revolted me – I dismissed it hurriedly.

The Captain had only hinted that we might surface before dawn, just to jolly us along. Shrewd of him not to commit himself. Sham optimism? Eyewash! Keeping the men on their toes, that was his only motive.

A whole day down here – perhaps even longer. And all the time with this tube in my mouth. Jesus!

The second lieutenant cleared his throat. I drifted up through layers of sleep and broke surface. My eyelids flapped convulsively.

I rubbed my eyes with knuckled forefingers. Heavy-headed, leaden-brained, pains behind my orbital ridges, fiercer pains at the base of my skull. Blasted elephant's trunk! The second lieutenant was still the only other proboscidean creature in sight.

I longed to know the time. Past midday, for sure. My watch was a good buy. Swiss-made, RM 75. Twice lost but miraculously found each time. I wondered where it could be. No one would have filched it.

Persistent silence. Nothing, however hard I listened. No hum from any auxiliaries, still the same deathly hush. The potash cartridge reposed on my belly like a stone hot-water bottle.

Every now and then, someone with oily hands and arms came through the wardroom. Were we still in trouble aft? Had our position improved while I slept? Was there fresh hope? No point in asking – everyone was so secretive.

In that case, how did I know that the compasses – gyro, magnetic and all – were back in commission? Had I gathered it in my sleep? Hydroplane operation was stiff and restricted, but that had been common knowledge before I dropped off.

What about leaks? The Chief had a plan, but did he still believe in it? It served me right, losing touch. I didn't even know how long I'd been asleep.

At some stage, someone had said something. 'We'll have to take her up as soon as it gets dark.' The Old Man's voice, naturally. It still reverberated inside me: '. . . have to take her up . . . gets dark . . .'

How many hours till nightfall? Nightfall – that should be good enough. Such a shame my watch had disappeared.

Looking around, I discovered that our raffia dog no longer dangled from the deckhead. I couldn't see it under the table, so I slid off the bunk and groped about on my hands and knees. The gloom was populated with sea-boots and cans of food. Damn, broken glass! I came across the Chief's bolster. Towels and gloves too, but not our mascot, the raffia dog. However trashy, he was our lucky charm – he couldn't be allowed to vanish. Bloody mess!

As I was sitting down again, my eye fell on the second lieutenant. The dog was clasped beneath his left arm. He was fast asleep, cuddling it like a doll.

Again the wardroom was cautiously traversed by someone with a wrench in his oily hands. I felt ashamed of my in-activity. My one consolation was that the watch-keeping officers and seamen were just as inactive – that we had been ordered to turn in and keep quiet. In fact, we had the worst of the bargain: lolling, lounging, lying, staring, suffering from delusions. I yearned for something to do.

My mouthpiece bubbled like a juicy pipe. Too much spittle in my mouth. Gums as dry as leather to begin with, now overproduction. My salivary glands were not adapted to this way of life.

Only two out of three U-boats returned from their first patrol – that was the current average. U-A belonged to an élite. She had done plenty of damage in her time. Now it was the enemy's turn.

I lectured myself like a refractory child. Lie down properly – it'll end in tears if you don't!

Lie down, climb into my bunk? How could I, when the Captain must still be at his post and the engineers were working themselves into the ground?

'We've all got to go sometime . . .' The words flitted through my head two or three times, tinged with a Saxon accent. I had a close-up of the lugubrious hearse-driver nodding pro-foundly and staring ahead over his steering-wheel. We were on our way to a village in Mecklenburg to collect Swoboda, who had drowned in the local lake: Swoboda, student harvester, twenty years old and a member of my class at college. Even in the intense summer heat, the Mecklenburg farmers used to feed us daily on fat salt pork and potatoes. Flies took the place of mustard. Swoboda disappeared one evening. I found him next morning among spinach-green pond plants, at a spot where the water was less than two metres deep. He could have breathed by standing on tiptoe.

Swoboda might have been posing for a crouched burial. He looked very pale. I shouted three times as loudly as I meant to when I glimpsed his carroty hair in the midst of that vivid greenery.

The cause of death was drowning, though no one knew why Swoboda should have drowned. He was a fair swimmer.

In our case the cause of death would be unquestionable: oxygen starvation. The occupants of some bunks already looked as if they had expired in their sleep, peaceful and serene, with tubes in their mouths. Those lying supine only needed their hands folded to complete the impression.

Wasn't this ordeal long overdue? Thou art weighed in the balances, and art found wanting, saith the Lord. There shall be weeping and gnashing of teeth, saith the Lord.

There it was again – the fear that welled into my throat from somewhere between my shoulder-blades, lifted my rib-cage and expanded until it filled my whole body. I could even feel it tingling in my penis. Hanged men often had an erection, I knew that – or was there some more physiological reason?

The captain of the *Bismarck* was still thinking of his Führer when the final blow fell. He embodied his sentiments in a signal: '. . . to the last round . . . undying loyalty . . .' or words of a similarly edifying nature. A man to the taste of our Number One.

U-A was ill-equipped for such heroics. At this depth, we could compose exalted signals but not send them. The Führer would have to dispense with a last message from U-A. The air down here was even insufficient for a swan-song rendering of *Deutschland über alles*.

Poor old Marfels! A big mistake, signing on with the *Bismarck* – a bit of a laugh too. Marfels had only needed the battleship badge to complete his collection, so he agitated for a transfer. Now his young widow could feast her eyes on a legacy of jingling junk.

What must it have been like after the torpedo destroyed their steering gear and left them limping around in a circle?

By the time the salvage ships *Castor* and *Pollux* were ordered out from Brest, everything aboard the *Bismarck* had been reduced to scrap and butcher's meat.

Dulce et decorum est pro patria . . .

The Battle of Langemarck! How they had dosed us with that bloody fiasco at college! I remembered having to learn a wadge of Binding for the Langemarck Anniversary and recite it at assembly. How did it go? Think hard, blink a couple of times, and I had it pat:

> Then the incomparable happened: in a night attack – one of countless such – at the end of October 1914, amid an already falling hail of enemy fire and illumined by the savage glow of a battle-cloud which had crytallized into cut red agate, hosts of young men, resolute to the last and guided as though by a single spirit, suddenly sprang from folds in the ground or flat terrain and charged with a rousing song on their lips – followed by others whom they swept along with them, also singing – to their deaths.

I ought to recite it for the first lieutenant some time – he'd appreciate the underlying sentiment.

Not surprising they'd managed to drum so much of it into us – shit stuck.

Dire visions descended. I fled from them to Simone. I silently mouthed her name – once, twice, over and over, but the spell failed. Her image was like a faded snapshot. I stared at the bulkhead facing me.

Charlotte appeared there in her place. Charlotte of the pumpkin tits, the heavy chime of bells which pendulated when she raised herself on hands and knees.

Other pictures forced their way to the surface. Inge, the woman staff auxiliary. A Berlin hotel room allocated by the RTO's office – more of a drawing-room than a bedroom. No lights because the black-out blinds were missing. I groped for Inge. She guided me into her, thighs splayed.

'Don't stop, for God's sake! Go on! Just don't stop. Like that, and that, and that, and that . . .'

Her weepy face. Her wet tongue roaming my neck. Her dribbly mouth. Skeins of spittle, saturated pubic hair. I ran my palm over her slimy, swollen labia. Her body quivered like jelly. The pressure of her thighs. Her Ride of the Valkyries – the rearing, plunging, lurching and drowning, the musk that erupted from her skin.

And that one with the Medusa hair style? The women's

mag secretary. Ten to one she wore falsies. Why else did she never take her clothes off? Nothing would persuade her. Randy as hell, but she never shed a stitch. Always the same preamble: Something to eat — a sandwich, maybe? And the inevitable pair of candles. She lay down in the end. No messing about, as she called it, but she always kept her things on.

An air-raid warning halfway through. I patched the window with cardboard. A true gentleman always shows his appreciation for services rendered.

Disjointed remarks floated up through my consciousness like gas-bubbles. 'You and your one-track mind! Don't you ever think of anything else?' Brigitte, who favoured turbans: 'J'aime beaucoup Rombrang — c'est unique, son style . . .' I took a minute or two to grasp that she meant Rembrandt.

Now the one from Magdeburg, she of the unwashed neck and freckled nose. The brimming ashtray garnished with a used contraceptive. Sluts, these student amateurs — enough to put a fellow off his oats. A plaintive cry: 'What's the matter with you? I'm not lying here all night. Go on, jerk yourself off!' Or, alternately: 'Take it easy, sweetie, you aren't beating a carpet.'

Enter the blonde I picked up in the train — the one I privately christened Big-bubs. I couldn't even remember the name of the one-horse town we scoured for a boarding-house. Suspicious stares, then: 'Sorry, we're full up.' I knew I wouldn't be able to stand it much longer. I could feel a viscous wetness between my legs — natural lubrication. Incredible the way it worked. Nowhere to go, but my system was already functioning. Nothing but open fields behind the houses. Not a bush in sight, no chance of a quick dive into the undergrowth. My toes still curled when I remembered how we tried, again and again: 'Would you by any chance have a room for the night?' We found one almost on the outskirts. Turn the key, strip off, and bingo! For the time being. We still had twenty-four hours.

The roundabout turned swiftly, and I saw the amateur pro with the huge pendant breasts. Her response when asked why she did it for free: 'Helping the war-effort.' Conventional performances left her cold. It was up on your hands and toes and into a lightning series of press-ups — that was the way she liked it best.

I glimpsed a pane of frosted glass, the lowest of three in a white door. A pink blur of face: the banished husband on all fours, convinced of his invisibility. 'Look at him, just look at him – peeping's all he's good for!'

And now the teller of fairy-tales. Squatting on top of me with her knees drawn up, she used to prattle on blithely as if she'd no idea what was happening down below. Never wanted to move, just acted childish and told fairy-tales. Where on earth had I picked her up? Of course, in the train from Munich to Berlin.

That pair of tarts in the shabby Paris hotel-room – them I didn't want to see. Get lost! I tried to fix my thoughts on Simone but instead, saw one of the two perched on a bidet, sluicing her middles in the glare of a naked bulb. Flaccid, cheesy skin. Her partner was no better. She had kept her stockings on, likewise her grubby, stringy brassière. Now, from a battered shopping-bag, with much hectic chatter, she produced the skinned half-carcass of a pitiful little hare. Moist grey shreds of newspaper adhered to it. The neck was half-severed. Rivulets of blood had oozed from the wound and congealed. The tart on the bidet, still working on herself with cupped palms, turned repeatedly between splashes and fired shrill cries of delight at the bluish cadaver in the other's outstretched hand. Enthusiasm over their acquisition reduced her to incoherence and raucous laughter. The girl holding the carcass had a triangle of red pubic hair. Close beside it, plastered to her right thigh, was a fist-sized piece of the damp newspaper in which the hare had been wrapped. Her belly shook with giggles and her flabby breasts wobbled in unison.

Now as then, I felt a wave of nausea. My potash cartridge started to rattle. I had to force myself to breathe evenly. Watch it! Concentrate on breathing, master the technique.

The main problem was to avoid exhaling too vigorously. Nice and easy . . . But no matter how much care I took too much spit gathered. How to cope with my salivary glands? My rate of breathing I could control, but salivary glands were another matter – they determined their own output. I'd never practised controlling them.

If we didn't stir, didn't so much as lift a little finger, our consumption of oxygen would surely dwindle to almost nothing. Lying at full stretch, utterly motionless, not even batting an eyelid, we should be able to survive for far longer than the VII-C's specifications allowed.

The very act of breathing consumed oxygen, so the answer was to breathe shallowly – not inhale more air than the body required for its involuntary functions.

But then, any oxygen we saved by inaction was more than consumed by the men who were slaving over the damaged machinery further aft. They were raiding our reserves, taking the oxygen out of our mouths.

Every now and then, a muffled thud and clatter came from the stern. I winced each time. Water magnified sounds five-fold. The men must be doing their utmost to avoid noise, but how could they work silently with heavy equipment? When I recalled the pandemonium in the bunker, and bore in mind that the Chief's party couldn't afford to drop a wrench for fear of alerting a British destroyer . . .

The first lieutenant returned from a tour of inspection. It was his periodic duty to check that all sleepers had mouth-pieces in. The hair was glued to his forehead with sweat. I could see little of his face except the cheek-bones. His eyes were in shadow.

It was an age since I'd seen the Chief. I didn't covet his job. Too much for any one man.

The Captain padded quietly in. Just before he reached the wardroom table there was another clatter from aft. His face contracted in a sudden spasm of what looked like pain.

He wasn't wearing a potash cartridge. 'Well, how goes it?' he asked. I gave a faint nod in reply. He glanced quickly into the POs' mess and disappeared again.

I could have swooned with exhaustion, but sleep was un-thinkable. Pictures flipped over in my mind like filing-cards. Aunt Bella, the Christian Scientist, the faith-healing hairnet queen. A good business, hers. The hairnets were imported from Hong Kong by the bale, hundredweights at a time. Aunt Bella ordered some fancy envelopes with dainty lettering and see-through windows. Assisted by three industrious girls, she sat there picking hair-nets from the heap and slipping them one by one into pale-violet envelopes – a process which multi-plied their market value by fifty. Aunt Bella employed a dozen or more sales reps. Later, I learned that she did a similar trade in contraceptives, but only at night. I often pictured her sitting, deft and diligent, in front of a mountain of pale-pink contraceptives like sheep's intestines, her nimble fingers de-taching them from the tangle and posting them into little packets. Aunt Bella's name was Faber, Bella Faber. Her son, Kurtchen Faber, looked like a thirty-year-old hamster. It was he who commanded the platoon of reps. Barbers were their best customers. Uncle Erich, Bella's husband, was responsible for the slot-machines installed in seedy public-house urinals: '3 for RM 1.' Uncle Erich had to have a drink with every landlord on his round. Back to his bicycle, one-mark pieces in one shabby saddle-bag, contraceptives in the other, then off to the next port of call. Remove takings, reload machine, have another drink. He couldn't stand the pace, poor old Uncle Erich, who never removed his cycle-clips, even at home. He fell off his bicycle between two vending sites and expired. The police carted him away. They must have been amazed at the quantities of coinage and contraceptives he was carrying.

I suddenly noticed that the second lieutenant's mouthpiece had fallen out. How long ago? Had I drifted off myself? I shook him by the shoulder but only elicited a grunt. It wasn't until I shook him harder that he gave a start and stared into my face aghast. It took him several seconds to get his bearings. Then he groped dazedly for his mouthpiece and began to suck at it – assiduously. He was asleep again in an instant.

How he managed it was a mystery. For a moment I thought he was shamming, but no, he had genuinely dropped off. The only thing missing was a barrage of snores. I couldn't tear my eyes from his wan, sleep-crumpled face. Envy? Or was I gnawed by disappointment that I couldn't communicate with him by look or gesture?

I couldn't endure another moment on the settee. My legs were going to sleep, even if I wasn't. I headed for the control-room.

Repairs were still in progress in the wireless office. The two PO telegraphists had rigged up a powerful light and were working without mouthpieces. They seemed to be having trouble. The place was littered with bits and pieces, but the requisite spares seemed to be lacking. 'Can't be done,' I heard Herrmann say; 'not with the parts we've got on board.'

The emergency lighting in the control-room shed a dismal glow leaving the bulkheads in shadow. Three or four vague figures were working at the forward end, crouched like miners at the face. The Captain was staring silently at the chart, his elbows propped on the chart-table. The flooding panel was festooned with parts that didn't belong to it – probably components from the main bilge-pump. In the background, the beam of a torch flitted over instruments and valves. I could just make out the pale eye of the depth-gauge. The needle still pointed to 280. I stared at it with a sort of disbelief. 280 metres . . . Had any U-boat been so deep before?

It was growing steadily colder. We couldn't be giving off much body-warmth, and heating was out of the question. I wondered how cold it was outside.

Thank God, there was the Chief. His movements had regained some of their old lithe grace. Was he celebrating a victory? The Captain turned to him, grunted, and said 'Well?' There was no trace of satisfaction on the Chief's face, which looked suety in the half-light.

Strain my ears as I could, I only gathered that all leaks had been stopped.

'Anyway, we can't surface before nightfall.'

I couldn't quarrel with the Captain's reasoning. An interjection hovered on my lips: 'Can we even then?' It scared me that the Captain and the Chief might be gambling on a long-shot, not a certainty.

A man had just made his way through the control-room from aft. He must have heard what the Captain said. It wouldn't have surprised me if the Old Man had used the verb 'surface' specially for his benefit, so that he could transmit it to the fore-ends: 'The Old Man just said something about surfacing . . .'

I was still uncertain how much of the Captain's confident manner was play-acting and how much based on conviction. He certainly looked years older when he thought himself safe from observation: face wrinkled, jaw-muscles slack, red-rimmed eyelids swollen and drooping. His whole body conveyed resignation at such moments, but not now. Now he held himself erect, arms folded on his chest, head slightly tilted, motionless as a sculptor's model. I couldn't even tell if he was breathing. He was so rigid and unmoving a spider could have spun its web round him. Except that we hadn't embarked any spiders. There wasn't a spider's web anywhere on board. An enigma, the total absence of spiders. U-A was probably too damp for them, too subject to thermal fluctuations. Only our fly seemed to thrive on such fatiguing extremes.

Without being fully aware of it, I had perched on the coaming of the forward doorway.

The Captain's face loomed over me. Had he said something? I must have looked disconcerted as I scrambled to my feet, because he made soothing noises. Then, with a jerk of the head, he invited me to accompany him aft. 'Might as well see what they're doing back there.'

I extracted the rubber tube, swallowed some excess saliva, drew in a lungful of air through my mouth, and silently followed him.

I noticed for the first time that someone was sitting on the chart-stowage. It was Turbo. He looked broken-backed with his head lolling limply on his chest. A figure approached from the opposite direction – Isenberg, reeling with exhaustion like a drunken man. His left hand was holding some long metal rods and electric cable, his right a large cup-spanner. He proffered the spanner to a man crouching at deck-level. The Captain paused near the deserted hydroplane controls and surveyed the dismal scene. Isenberg, who had yet to notice us, swung round at the splash of my sea-boots. He straightened up and tried to square his shoulders. His mouth opened and shut.

'Well, Isenberg?' said the Captain. The petty officer swallowed but couldn't get a word out.

The Captain went over and laid a hand on his shoulder – only momentarily, but Isenberg blossomed under the fleeting contact. More than that, his face creased in an amiable grin. The Captain gave two or three brisk little nods and stalked off.

I knew that, behind our backs, the control-room PO would now be exchanging glances with his men. The Old Man! Never been beaten yet, not our Old Man!

The deck-plates in the POs' mess had not been replaced, so someone was still at work on No. 2 battery. A face streaked with sweat and oil bobbed up from below. I recognized PO Electrician Pilgrim by his square-cut beard. The Captain and Pilgrim looked at each other for a moment, then Pilgrim grinned all over his grimy face. The Captain drawled 'Well?' on a rising inflection and nodded. Pilgrim eagerly returned the nod. It was clear that he, too, felt fortified in his endeavours.

Our route aft presented problems. Pilgrim hurriedly began to replace a section of decking to give us somewhere to put our feet, but the Captain waved him aside. He squeezed aft with his chest brushing the bunk leeboards and traversed the narrow ledge like a mountaineer. Left with a choice, I accepted Pilgrim's help.

The door to the galley was open. Inside, order had already been restored. 'Trust Katter,' muttered the Captain. 'I'd have taken a bet on it.'

The next door, which led to the engine-room, was also ajar. When the diesels were running and sucking air, it had to be prised open to overcome the partial vacuum. Now, the pulsing heart of our boat was still.

The compartment was faintly lit by inspection lamps. My eyes soon accustomed themselves to the gloom. The walkways had been removed, also the shiny floor-plates. Only now did I realize how far below deck the engines extended. Between their seatings I could make out a clutter of tools, oil-cans, packing and heavy machine parts. It was a ship-breaker's yard, not an engine-room. Everything ran with lubricating oil, viscous black engine-blood. Pools of it had gathered on every horizontal surface. Lumps of cotton waste lay around. The whole dim cavern was a wilderness of grimy rags, oily packing, bent pipes, finger-marked asbestos sheeting, greasy nuts and bolts.

Low voices, a muffled clank of metal on metal.

Still whispering to the Captain, Johann continued to wield an outsize monkey-wrench. I had no idea we carried such heavy tools. The ERA's movements were precise and economical – no nervous fumbling or hands trembling with strain. 'The shores are holding up all right,' I heard.

That brought me up short. Wood, in the midst of all this steel? Then I saw them – lengths of timber about 12 centimetres square, wedged into place like pit-props. Carpentry in a world of steel and iron . . . Where had the wood been stowed? I'd never seen any timber on board.

The source of Johann's serenity was a mystery to me. Had he simply forgotten about our limited supplies of oxygen and the 280 metres of water overhead? The Captain peered here and there. He went on his hands and knees for a closer look at the men toiling below deck like contorted fakirs. Although he hardly said a word, just grunted and produced his usual drawling 'Well?' the oil-stained troglodytes gazed at him with the respect due to a miracle-worker. Their faith in his ability to extricate us seemed boundless.

With slow, deliberate movements the Captain clambered aft over the litter of machine parts.

At the far end of the starboard engine, two or three men were bent over the bed-plates cutting large pieces of packing. 'How does it look?' the Captain asked in an undertone. His voice had a warmth normally reserved for enquiries about a man's wife and family.

The Chief became visible, framed between the Captain's body and the crook of his arm. 'Several frames distorted,' I heard him whisper. 'Considerable displacement throughout this section . . .'

A torch illumined his face. Fatigue had painted greenish semicircles under his eyes, which shone feverishly. The lines in his face had deepened, ageing him ten years overnight.

I could only see the Chief's harshly lit face, not his body. It startled me when the pallid, beard-fringed Holofernes-head spoke again. 'Cooling-water pipes . . . pretty bad state . . . need brazing . . . starboard engine . . . write-off, probably . . .

running repairs out . . . all right otherwise . . . out of true . . . shafts . . .'

I gathered that something could only be straightened with a sledge-hammer. The Captain and the Chief agreed that heavy hammering was out of the question.

Again the voice. 'At least that's all right, thank God . . . it'll do the trick, just about . . . bloody shambles . . . more of a job for a watch-mender . . .'

'Going nicely, Chief,' the Captain growled. 'We'll manage.' He addressed me in a stage whisper. 'Damned good thing our plumbers know their job!'

The sullied motor-room was as disconcerting a sight as the engine-room. Gone was our neat and sterile power station in which steel covers concealed every moving part. Inspection plates had been stripped off and deck-plates removed, exposing the guts of the compartment. It too was littered with grimy cotton waste, baulks of timber, tools, wedges, cables, inspection lamps and wandering leads. Water still brooded below deck. There was something obscene about the spectacle, something which smacked of rape and desecration. PO Electrician Rademacher was lying face down. The veins in his neck bulged as he struggled to tighten some fundamental bolts with a wrench.

Rademacher heard us and started to get up, but the Captain laid a hand on his shoulder and gently restrained him, then nodded and pushed his cap to the back of his head. Rademacher grinned.

I caught sight of a clock. Midday. I must, after all, have dozed off from time to time. A tough clock, to have withstood the explosion. My eye lighted on an empty bottle. Where could I find something to drink? How long was it since our last cup of coffee? I wasn't hungry – hollow inside, yes, but not hungry. Just infernally thirsty.

There was another bottle, a half-full one, but I could hardly rob Rademacher of his apple-juice.

The Captain was standing there, stiff as a ramrod, staring pensively at the rear door of the stern torpedo tube. Eventually, remembering my presence, he swung round and muttered 'Let's go.' I steeled myself for another laborious scramble through the regions of the damned, a second dispensation of comfort to those in need, but this time the Captain didn't linger. A few curt nods and we were back in the galley.

Oranges! Of course, we'd taken on some oranges from the *Weser*. There were two crates of ripe ones in the fore-ends.

December was a prime month for oranges. I felt the spittle gather in my mouth, fighting its way through the film of slime that had formed there. It was tough and gelatinous, too much for my salivary glands to cope with, but an orange might sluice it away.

The CPOs' mess appeared to be empty. The ERAs were aft and the quartermaster had been in the control-room when I last saw him. I wondered vaguely where the coxswain was.

I opened the door to the fore-ends as quietly as I could. The usual dim lighting came from a single weak bulb. It took me a good minute to absorb the scene by its feeble glow. Sleeping men occupied every bunk and hammock. Sprawled across the wooden decking, almost to the bulkhead, was a row of figures huddled together like tramps in search of warmth.

I'd never seen so many men crammed into the fore-ends at once. They comprised the ratings who were technically on watch as well as those who were not – a double complement.

The beam of my torch flitted across the deck. It looked like a battlefield – worse, the aftermath of a gas attack. The men lay there in the semi-darkness as though they had collapsed in agony, as though their gas-masks had proved ineffective against a lethal new product. It was reassuring to hear their stertorous breathing and muffled snores.

I doubted if anyone would notice if the Chief stopped enriching our oxygen. The men would slumber on just as peacefully, expire in their sleep with mouthpieces between their teeth and potash cartridges on their stomachs. An epitaph: They kipped their way to eternity, nodded off for Führer and Fatherland . . .

A bent figure was moving around – Hacker, the torpedo gunner's mate, whose job it was to stay awake and check that no one lost his mouthpiece. He stepped gingerly over the recumbent forms as though looking for one in particular.

I tried a tentative step. There wasn't room to put my foot flat on the deck – I had to insinuate it between two bodies. I sought out crevices and inserted the toe of my boot like a wedge, taking care not to become ensnared by an air-pipe.

I knew the oranges must be stowed right up forward beside the tubes. My groping fingers identified a crate, then the fruit inside. I weighed an orange in my hand. It was fat and heavy. I swallowed hard, unable to wait any longer. There and then, ankle-deep in human limbs, I removed my mouthpiece and bit into the peel. My teeth struck juice at the second bite. Noisily, I sucked the nectar in. Some of it ran from the corners of my mouth and dripped on the sleeping forms at my feet. Ah, the bliss and balm of it! I should have had the idea long ago.

Something stirred against my left foot. Fingers closed on my calf. I recoiled as if an octopus had grabbed me. I couldn't see who was in the faint light. A face reared towards me, a fearsome lemur's mask. The man scared me silly, emerging from the gloom like that. I still couldn't identify him. Schwalle, or was it Dufte? I mumbled 'Damned good, these oranges!' but he didn't answer, just sank back into limbo.

Hacker, still flitting about, came over to me. He removed his mouthpiece. The beam of my torch glistened on the threads of spittle that linked it with his lips. He blinked in the sudden glare.

'Sorry, TGM.'

'I'm looking for the chef,' he whispered.

I pointed to a dark corner near the bulkhead. 'I think I saw him over there.'

Hacker teetered across two supine bodies and bent down. 'Hey, Katter,' he said in a low voice, 'rise and shine. The lads aft could do with something to wet their whistles.'

Nothing in the wardroom had changed. The second lieutenant was still slumped in his corner, asleep. I took a dog-eared paperback from the shelf and forced myself to read. My eyes scanned the lines. They shuttled to and fro, registering every letter, every syllable, but while they did so my thoughts wandered off. Unrelated passages superimposed themselves on the printed text. Missing submarine – what happened to them? Would the armada of U-boats sunk in the Atlantic one day sail home under barnacle- and seaweed-power, or would their crews stay deep for the next ten millennia, pickled in brine? And if means were found to explore the depths and garner their harvest of submarines, what then? What sights would greet the salvage-men when they cut us open?

In fact, we ought to present their eyes with a spectacle of wondrous serenity. Other U-boats must look far worse, with bodies locked together in panic or floating turgidly in the passages. We were an exception to the general rule: we were dry.

Our stores would still be edible. No oxygen, no rust. Besides, U-boats were made of tough, finest-quality material. Our recovery ought to be a commercial proposition, with so many saleable items on board. Only the oranges, pineapples and bananas would have perished.

And we ourselves? To what extent did a cadaver decay without oxygen? What happened to fifty bladders of urine or the rissoles and potato-salad in our intestines when the air ran out? Wouldn't the process of fermentation stop too? Did steel-entombed corpses turn dry and withered like *bacalhau* or like the bishops on display at Piana degli Albanesi, high above Palermo? They lay under glass, resplendent in silk brocade, hideous but durable. There lay the difference, though: their lordships had been gutted, but they still stank like stockfish through their glass cases after a few successive days of rain.

I gulped, clamped my lips round the mouthpiece and read on. But it was no good. I saw U-A recovered after many years, overgrown with dark-green weed and studded with barnacles. The conning-tower is prised open, and out pour clouds of plump black flies. *Battleship Potemkin* shot of a million maggots swarming over the coaming of the upper hatch. The fifty bodies below are encrusted with unimaginable numbers of crab-lice, thick as scurf.

Be reasonable, I told myself. How much air did flies require? How long could lice exist without oxygen? In fact, they should be able to manage on very little and still continue the merry work of reproduction long after the air was insufficient for human needs.

I pulled myself together with a jerk.

I was suddenly amused by the absurdity of my laborious attempts to read. Only the tube in my mouth prevented me from laughing aloud. I put down the paperback and started mumbling to myself. Not for the first time, I was struck by the therapeutic properties of rhyming verse. What about all those jingles we used to recite as children, just to shock our elders? Think hard . . .

> 'He wanted to but couldn't.
> He held it in his hand
> And, filled with desperation dire,
> Across the bedroom ran.
> He tried to but he couldn't—
> The hole was far too tight.
> His collar-stud resisted, though
> He shoved with all his might . . .'

Our first or second night on the bottom? My brain grappled

feebly with the problem.

Whispers approached. The Captain came in, followed by the Chief.

The Chief was delivering a situation report. He seemed to have developed fresh energy, like a boxer who recovers after a near knock-out in the previous round. How he managed it was a mystery. He had been continuously on the go, he and the second engineer and the ERAs. Now he was presenting an interim balance sheet. The compressors had been jammed in place with wooden wedges. The heavy bolts that normally secured them to their mountings had sheared under the force of the explosion. Much depended on the compressors because they produced the HP air used for blowing the ballast tanks. Both periscopes were definitely out of action. Nothing to be done for the present. Too complicated . . .

I noticed that, while making his report, he radiated a faint aura of optimism.

Had our prospects improved? I wasn't listening properly. I only wanted to know if the Chief felt confident that he could expel enough water to lift us off the bottom. Who cared about periscopes? All my desires were reduced to a simple craving for the surface. What happened after we got there was secondary.

Even so, nothing was said about pumping and blowing. What price all our other successes? What price our patched-up instruments and machinery if we never left the sea-bed?

All at once, sounds – sounds from outside, slowly drawing nearer. Ships' propellers, without a doubt.

'Propeller noises all round, sir,' someone reported.

All round. What did it mean? Was an entire convoy churning over our heads? At first the propeller noises sounded like a single deep roar. Then my ears distinguished a palpitating ebb and flow of sound, a multiple, shifting thrash and shuffle which lost its rhythm, merged into a roar again, and became mingled with a sharply sibilant 'ritchipitchi'. The Captain glared at the deckhead like an exasperated ground-floor tenant.

I looked round helplessly. Nothing to do but burrow deeper into my corner. Promptly, every bone and muscle declared its presence. I felt as if I had been stretched on the rack. It must have been a muscular hangover from all that bucket-swinging.

The Captain talked on blithely in his deep bass voice. It unnerved me until I realized that the noise overhead was a licence to speak normally – then the Old Man's familiar growl became a solace.

'Must be rush-hour,' I heard him say. The usual sang-froid, but it didn't deceive me. I'd seen him covertly massaging his back and heard him give the occasional suppressed groan. The Old Man's only concession to the bomb and his tumble down the ladder had been a couple of fifteen-minute breathers on his bunk.

The Chief's reaction to the noise overhead was less felicitous. The words died on his lips and his eyes darted to and fro. No one else spoke.

I longed for the final curtain – for our players to emerge from behind the footlights and don their everyday expressions.

At last the noise receded. The Captain glanced at me and gave a contented nod, almost as if he had switched off the noise for my benefit.

The Chief took a hurried swig of apple-juice and disappeared again. I was about to stifle my inhibitions and ask the Captain point-blank how things stood, but he straightened up with a grunt and strode aft.

I couldn't think of anything better to do than follow in the hope of buttonholing him in the control-room. Not a sign of him – he must have gone further aft. I had an uneasy feeling that something was wrong back there. I should have listened more carefully, wrestled with the fog that threatened to blanket my consciousness.

But the slumbrous vapour grew denser. I decided that it might, after all, be better to turn in. Everyone had to sleep some time – no point in hanging around for the sake of it.

I groped my way to the POs' mess in a sort of trance. The hard part was climbing into my bunk. After a sort of high-kick and agonizing contortions, I managed it in the end.

I undid my collar, loosened my belt, unbuttoned my shirt to the waist, arched my stomach, flattened it, stretched out, emptied my lungs. I lay like a corpse in a coffin, the potash cartridge my funeral wreath. Close above me was the deckhead, with its glossy white cross-members and rows of rivets. Condensation had gathered on the rivet-heads, but not thickly enough to drip. The little hemispheres hung there with Damoclean menace. Looking through the curtain rings I could see the numerous overhead pipes that ran along the passage. In their midst was the grey-painted loudspeaker box. No sound from the intercom. Even its customary hiss and crackle had ceased. Not a bad thing, in the absence of any reason for optimistic announcements. No noise of machinery – not the faintest hum. Not a word spoken nor a throat cleared, even though I wasn't alone in the compartment. I was still unused to the silence. It had a transfixing quality.

My consciousness dissolved. Was it sleep that engulfed me, or a kind of anaesthesia?

It was 1700 when I came to. Ship's time. I craned over and read Isenberg's watch.

I was still in my bunk. The line between sleep and wakefulness grew blurred again. Muffled explosions penetrated my semi-conscious state. Instead of surfacing with a start, I tried to wrap myself more closely in the blankets of oblivion. The dull reverberations filtered through. I listened with my eyes shut. They sounded like the prolonged rumble of a distant thunderstorm. Depth-charges. Dropped for psychological effect, or were the British clobbering another U-boat? It must still be daylight up there. No one could have tried to slip through in daylight, surely, so what? Naval exercises? Perhaps the British were simply keeping their men up to scratch.

I strained my ears, trying to locate the thunder's source. It seemed to come from more than one direction. Probably small units were out on barrier patrols. I leant over my bunk rail and peered into the control-room.

At that moment the hydrophone operator reported propeller noises, several of them on different bearings. I was puzzled – surely the hydrophone was out of action? Then I recalled seeing the Captain with an earphone to his head when I squeezed past him a few hours earlier. So the hydrophone was back in commission. We were again equipped to receive acoustic impulses from the enemy – if present circumstances made that any advantage at all.

The oil-leak! The current must have carried the oil too far for its source to be plotted. Probably – with any luck – it had risen to the surface in one big surge, then ceased. Oil wasn't like cork. It didn't float for ever, thank God. It emulsified and dispersed. Viscosity, wasn't that it? Another word to conjure with. I mouthed the syllables silently, like a magic spell.

'We're obviously in the right spot.' The Captain's voice came from the control-room. Always look on the bright side. The rocks which had nearly ripped us open were a protection from Asdic.

Zeitler gave a sudden groan. 'Bugger that noise! I'll go mad if it doesn't let up.' A violation of orders. Zeitler ought to have had his mouthpiece in. I hoped the Captain hadn't heard him.

Don't move, don't follow suit, I commanded myself. Lie there in dogged silence. Every movement consumed oxygen.

Every blink helped to exhaust our store of air.

Zeitler's left arm hung down from the bunk opposite me. I strained my eyes to read his watch. 1800. Only 6 p.m. Not a good omen, losing my watch. It must have fallen off my wrist, just like that. It might even be ticking away in the bilge somewhere. After all, it was *Waterproof, Shockproof, Antimagnetic, Stainless, Made in Switzerland* . . .

Efficient people, the Swiss. Our Oerlikon was Swiss-made too. No doubt the British carried shell-squirters of the same manufacture. Precision engineering from Switzerland. Lethal weapons exported with complete impartiality.

The nose-clip was hurting me. I removed it for a few moments.

Christ, what a stench! It must be gas from the batteries. No, not only gas. The air stunk of urine and faeces as well – as penetratingly as if someone had voided his bladder and bowels in the middle of the passage. Had one of the sleepers lost control of his sphincter, or was there a latrine bucket somewhere?

Promptly, I felt an acute pressure on my own bladder. I clamped my thighs together. The urge to pee subsided, but the gripes that succeeded it were less easy to contain. I hadn't eaten much – only a slice or two of bread and sausage from the *Weser* – yet the fermentation in my guts was unmistakable. I quailed to think what would happen if everyone in the fore-ends got squitters.

The smell of excrement was insupportable now. No good trying to expel the stuff outboard with compressed air – our sea-going lavatory was unusable at this depth. I replaced the nose-clip and breathed through my rattling mouthpiece. A real boon, the ability to switch from nasal breathing to oral. I wasn't dependent on my nose. I could select the oral route and by-pass my olfactory nerves. The Creator of Heaven and Earth had kneaded his clay with more sage forethought than the builders of U-A had devoted to their design problems.

I could surely stand it a bit longer. Child's play. Lie at full stretch, don't move, relax your stomach muscles, concentrate on something other than excreta.

The brothel in Brest . . . The stench had been just as nauseating. Sweat, scent, semen, urine and lysol – a mongrel aroma of festering lust. No amount of cheap perfume prevailed over eau de Javel and its omnipotent smell of bleach. Nose-clips would have been in order there too.

Rue d'Aboukir! Whenever a battleship was in, the tarts used to stay put between customers. No question of squatting

413

on the bidet, panties on, hello sailor and panties off again. The girls were reduced to flaccid cylinders of flesh in which five dozen assorted pistons pounded up and down, day after day.

I could see the steep little alley, the leprous ruins and charred timbers jutting against the sky. A dead dog lay on the pitted pavement, flattened by a passing car. Nobody had bothered to remove the mess. A swarm of blowflies rose from the half-extruded entrails. Scraps of roofing felt, bizarre sections of brickwork like giant lumps of stratified nougat, upended dustbins, rats in broad daylight. Every other building had been gutted, but even the semi-habitable houses were deserted. Splintered window-frames lay in heaps, like barricades. Only a beaten track led through the rubble and garbage.

Two sailors propped against a wall, *vis à vis*. 'Don't worry, mate, I'll stand you a fuck. You need one – it's coming out of your ears. Come on, it'll curdle if you don't get shot of it soon.'

Raucous shouts, then the resentful, nervous yapping of a dog.

Stiff-cocked, they queued two deep outside the medical post at the bottom of the lane. Everyone had to run the gauntlet. Now and then the corpulent sick-bay PO poked his head out and bellowed: 'Next five! And stick it in quick – I don't want anyone up there longer than five minutes!'

The bluejackets grinned. Each man had one hand in his trouser-pocket and was clutching his genitals. Almost everyone held a cigarette in the other. Nervous puffs of smoke ascended.

Only the medical room boasted white paint. Inside, the greasy walls were a rancid yellow. The air was redolent of semen and sweat. No bar – not even the most rudimentary concealment of function.

The madame on her wooden throne clasped an obscene lap-dog to her bosom, in the crevasse between her gigantic tits. 'Looks like a big fat bum,' someone said. 'I wouldn't half mind tossing myself off into that.'

The old trollop had picked up a few words of German. '*Allons-y, les gars! Keine Zeit – los, los, nix Maschine kaputt!*'

As she spoke, the fingers of her left hand crawled up and down her right forearm like plump maggots. She panted prodigiously, took a quick swallow of beer and dabbed the corners of her mouth with a pudgy finger – delicately, to avoid damaging the paintwork. Above her throne hung a sign bearing a gaudy cockerel and the inscription '*Quand ce coq chantera, crédit on donnera.'*

She tried to sell every customer one of her collection of shop-soiled photographs. Someone jibbed. 'Come off it, Aunty, who needs a demonstration? I'm bloody near there as it is.'

Bed-springs creaked through the mottled wall.

A voice said shrilly: 'All right, dearie, leave your money there.'

She speaks German, I thought.

'Don't look so daft! *Fais vite.* Yes, I'm from Alsace – bet that surprised you, eh? Come on, let's see your money – you think I want the sack? It's cash in advance here, darling. What's the matter, scared you won't get your money's-worth? Never mind, it's worse having to fork afterwards. That's right – and a little something extra for Lilli on top. Haven't you got another fifty? Put it down there and I'll show you a couple of nice pictures.' And from next door: 'Come on in, dearie. My word, you're only a nipper! What's this, a nursery-school outing? I've never seen so many young hopefuls. No, keep your pants on and be quick about it.'

At the foot of the bed, a scuffed piece of lino to protect it from shoes. Removing them was locally regarded as a waste of time.

'There you are, then. That was snappy. Smart lad, now you've got it off your chest.'

I heard her peeing into a chamber-pot behind the screen. Unabashedly.

The pallid thighs, the moist triangle of fuzz, the sickly face smeared with powder, yellow teeth, some black with decay, cognac-laden breath, lips like a crimson wound. A pale and intestinal tangle of used contraceptives nestled in the waste-paper basket beside the bidet.

Ructions in the corridor outside. 'Money back . . . too many beers . . . couldn't make the grade . . .'

Downstairs, someone was arguing with the sick-bay PO.

'If you want your pay-book back, you've got to have a squirt.'

'But Christ, man, I didn't do it bareback.'

'Belt up. Everybody gets one.'

'What's in it for you – a free fuck?'

'Button your lip, sailor!'

'Oh, bollocks to it!'

What an avocation, squirting yellow slime up other men's cocks the whole day long.

'There, that's it. Here's your pay-book. You can't beat a rubber and a squirt, lad – it's like wearing a belt and braces.

The Navy's hot on security, didn't you know?'

The pressure on my bladder had become agonizing. It occurred to me that the coxswain had put some buckets in the control-room with a tin of bleaching powder beside them. I rolled out of my bunk and ducked stiffly through the bulkhead

The light was stronger now. I could see things in greater detail. The push-button hydroplane controls still dangled from their wires. Turbid water was gushing steadily from a hose. I wondered where it was coming from and why nobody turned it off. Bulbs, a tin, two escape packs and some sea-boots were floating in the pool. Glass grated under my splashing feet. At least the gloom had been easier on the eye.

Then I saw the buckets. God, what a relief! My urine foamed as if I had eaten a bar of soap. The churning in my bowels subsided at once, perhaps because the reduction of pressure had made more room for my intestines. Silently I gave thanks. I wouldn't have cared to squat in public.

Where now? The chart-stowage – yes, why not sit on the chart-stowage for a change? The Captain seemed to be in his cubby-hole. Two or three figures were busy tinkering with something at deck-level.

There must have been two bombs. It was the only explana-tion. Otherwise the engines wouldn't have suffered so badly. Johann seemed confident, but I couldn't banish my misgivings. Never mind, we didn't need the main engines to surface. However unserviceable the diesel they were still at work on, we weren't dependent on diesels to take us up.

Even assuming we managed to surface, what use would our remaining diesel be? Did the Captain intend to chug through a ring of British ships on one engine? Repeat the process? Hardly. And the motors? They might be all right, but I couldn't believe that our damaged batteries contained enough power for more than a few revolutions. For all that, even a few revolutions might do the trick once U-A was lighter.

My thoughts veered to and fro. Hope had scarcely taken root when doubts recurred. Even if – what then? At best, a chance to swim for it. But not at night. That would be sheer lunacy. What did the Captain have in mind? We couldn't abandon ship in darkness – no one would ever find us. The Old Man *must* reveal his true intentions. If only I knew what the others thought, but there was no one else around. The Chief and his junior must be aft. Unlike me, they had a job of work to do.

The old trick: concentrate on something definite – a rock in the shifting sands. The more I thought, the more luxuriant my hallucinations. Surrender would mean madness, so I tried to build islands in the maelstrom of unbidden images.

The word 'petunia' flashed through my mind. I mumbled it to myself, three times. An interplay of colours appeared: violet, red, pink, white. The petunia, a relative of deadly night-shade, funnel-shaped with frilly edges, fimbriated. Pilose foliage, vulnerable to frost.

Flowers – a good subject. I tried 'geranium', and immediately – in addition to its scent – I had a tactile sensation: the velvety skin of the spreading blue-green leaves. The salmon-red kind, with drooping stems and glossy foliage. Carmine pelargoniums. They grew as tall as farm-house windows, a waist-high mass of blooms. Lots of rich manure, that was the secret. In winter, stick them in the cellar. Not too much water or they rotted. Nip off the shoots. A special variety: ivy-leaved pelargoniums.

My lips silently moulded another word round the mouth-piece: 'pseudoplatanus'. What rhymed with pseudoplatanus? Anus? Harness? Heinous? What was a pseudoplatanus, any-way? *Acer pseudoplatanus*: a maple pretending to be a plane-tree – a sycamore. Sycamore, sophomore, semaphore . . . I repeated the trisyllables like a mesmeric formula.

'Begonia' bobbed to the surface. I clung to it. Tubers like little brown fists, hard to spot in the soil. You had to force them if you wanted the rich and greasy-looking blooms to open early.

I longed to speak aloud, hear my own voice. The silence was oppressive. No gentle hum or throb of any kind, not even a mechanical whisper. Our pulse had stopped. Inanimate matter on all sides – iron, steel, paint. We were a steel sarco-phagus, a lifeless heap of scrap metal.

I could have ducked the patrol if I'd chosen to, but no, I had to justify my existence by hitching a ride with the Old Man.

And now the Old Man had reached the end of his rope, here in the Strait of Gibraltar.

Whenever I tried to imagine the Rock, an old diorama picture projected itself on my private screen. I saw the craggy shape of Gibraltar silhouetted in turquoise against a raspberry-coloured sky. The ships in the foreground were tubby cogs, not modern destroyers. A whole swarm of them, all painted brown, and each of them fringed with the row of soap-bubbles which indicated that its fourteen-pounders were firing a broadside.

I had to remove my nose-clip again. If anything, the stench was worse. To counter nausea while breathing through my mouth, I indulged in some pleasant olfactory illusions: violets, lilies-of-the-valley, celeriac, chives, mushrooms, parsley, thyme.

In a fit of defiance, I switched to unpleasant smells: cow-parsnip seeds, one of my pet abominations, reminiscent of a tiger's cage. Scalded goose – ugh! The stale smell of wet plucked feathers made my gorge rise, even in retrospect.

And now, a bombardment of smells I couldn't at once identify. Vivid smells, but I had to rack my brains before I placed them. That one, for instance . . . Pungent, sweetish, puzzling. I ran it to earth. Of course! Guinea-pigs – our play-room. I could see every stick of furniture, the aquarium in the window – even the striped shells of the water-snails that adhered to the inside of the glass and kept it clean.

A new smell drifted towards me, unlike any other. I recognized it immediately: moulding sand. I saw the lofty halls of our foundry, where the air was heavy with the smell. Big black heaps of moulding sand lay everywhere, except where the men had carefully swept it from around the sunken moulds. It looked as if precious sarcophagi were being cleared of black soil.

The Chief came in. He flopped down beside me on the chart-stowage, panting. No other movement, just the rise and fall of his chest. He pursed his lips and drew a deep whistling breath, recoiled at the sound and breathed more slowly.

I removed my mouthpiece. 'Fancy a glucose tablet, Chief? I've still got a few.' He came to with a start. 'No thanks. I wouldn't mind a drop of apple-juice, though.'

I rose hurriedly, padded to the wardroom and groped in my locker. The Chief took the bottle with one hand and swallowed greedily. A rivulet of juice trickled over his lower lip to his beard. He didn't bother to mop it.

Should I ask how things stood? Better not. From the look of him, the Chief might snap at any moment.

In the POs' mess, the curtains over the port-side bunks were open. Zeitler, Dorian, Wichmann and the midshipman were stiffly displayed like bodies in a morgue.

The other bunks were empty, so the stokers and electricians must still be aft. I stretched out on the nearest of the lower bunks.

The first lieutenant came through. With an air of official concern, he checked that everyone's mouthpiece was properly in place. As I stared after his retreating figure, I felt the mists of sleep close in.

I woke to find Frenssen at the table. It touched me, the sight of him slumped there with such obvious exhaustion. He wasn't wearing a potash cartridge. Of course not – the engine- and motor-room damage control parties would have been hampered by the cumbersome things. Hearing me roll over, Frenssen slowly turned his head. He stared at me with no sign of recognition. His spine seemed incapable of supporting the weight of his trunk. He was propped against the table, but his arms dangled limply, like those of a puppet. His glassy eyes and gaping mouth dismayed me. God knew how the others were continuing to toil in the foul air if Frenssen's bull-like strength had given out.

I felt drained and enervated. I wanted to say 'Just going to see if I can raise some tea' – or words to that effect – but the mouthpiece gagged me. Frenssen didn't move a millimetre. He looked like a wax dummy. We were all getting good at that sort of performance.

Tea. The pot must be somewhere – in the control-room, perhaps. I seemed to recall having seen it there.

I rolled off the bunk with an effort. Frenssen barely raised his eyes. The control-room deck-plates were still awash, so our main problem remained unsolved. The Chief must be hus- banding his resources for a final effort. He had a plan, after all, but the sight of the dark pool and the splash of my boots sent a new chill of terror through me.

Futile, I mumbled to myself. All that wasted effort! Nothing more could happen to the motors because the boat was levelled off. But so what? Even though the leaks had been checked, we were pinned down by a dead weight of water. If we didn't expel it soon we were finished. The oxygen wouldn't last for ever.

I couldn't see the teapot but I knew where to find some apple-juice. Stiffly I ducked through the bulkhead and shuffled over to the locker. I prised off the cap on a hinge and bore the bottle back to the POs' mess. Frenssen took an age to grasp that it was meant for him. He might have spared me the look of dog-like gratitude – after all, I wasn't the Old Man.

Nothing to do but sit down and daydream again. I saw the house in the bay between La Baule and Le Croisic, deserted since early in the war and hemmed in by a forest of outsize rhododendrons. Every path thick with grass, masonry toppled and overgrown with creeper, mostly bindweed, door-jambs rotting. A house in the Basque style, white-washed, with a big gabled roof of fairly shallow pitch. The half-timbering had once been black. An agreeable chill rose from the red-tiled floor of the hall. Little heaps of fine yellow worm-grass lay on the yawning upstairs floorboards, and the walls still betrayed where pictures used to hang. Huge spiders' webs floated everywhere. The front door was peppered with bullet-holes, cleanly punched on the outside and frayed within. A brooding scent of decay. The sea was hidden by a sand-dune. On it stood two cottages, also deserted. A clandestine radio transmitter had been found in one of them. The grey grass was marred in places by the yellow scars of slit-trenches which were always caving in or filling with sand. Among the rhodo-dendrons, a circular bed of giant hydrangeas. How luxuriantly everything grew there! From the crest of the dune I saw, far out in the shallows, a woman with her skirt hitched up. She was bending low, gathering mussels in a basket. Ebb tide. The sun was only a hand's span above the horizon. Beneath it, the wet sand gleamed like bronze.

The picture went grey and flat. That was it: to defend myself against encirclement by doubt and fear I needed stronger images. I forced myself to visualize breasts, a teeming mass of variously shaped bosoms. Nipples too – plump, erect, luscious as chocolates, elongated, stiff and unyielding as a child's lollipop, brown, pink, cherry-red. Big fat dugs and little hummocks which had to be sucked before the teeth could grip them. The surrounding areolae: large brownish moons, small round discs barely distinguishable from their environs, puckered rings of gooseflesh. I saw a breast with a single hair, centimetres long, at the edge of the buff-coloured moon. A shudder ran down my spine. I quelled it with an inward guffaw. I could recall asking Tiemann why the poor girl didn't pluck it.

'Maybe she's proud of it,' he retorted; 'maybe it's a toupee!' Tiemann was no more. Another victim of the Atlantic.

Now I summoned up navels. Navels indented and navels like shady grottoes, navels flat as blazer-buttons and domed like thimbles. Inge's bell-push and Charlotte's pot-hole. Now whole bellies: taut, flat, or protuberant as in pictures by Cranach. Lucretia bellies, soft, warm, voluminous, white, brown – even black, with a violet sheen round the navel.

Dissect, dismember into components. I once saw dismem-berment carried to extremes in a Paris abattoir. Here a pile of entrails, there heads, there tails. All that remained of twelve long horses' legs were the carefully fleshed bones. They stood neatly arrayed against the wall with their hoofs attached, like boot-trees.

420

Why so bashful – why not cunts as well? My imagination summoned up pink blossoms of flesh, ringlets dark with moisture, wet and tumid labia. Yawning chasms, tightly sealed cracks, half-open carps' mouths. Lobes of flesh that unfurled like Japanese water-flowers, pursed pink apertures with crinkly edges, dark and unfathomable sea-anemones which filled the entire hand. Big swollen cunts, mean little chicken-twats, neatly slitted money-boxes, orifices as tight as a clenched anus, flaccid as blancmange. Cunts juxtaposed, infraposed, superimposed. A whole assortment of cunts – a cunt catalogue. *Variatio delectat.* I seemed to hear a soft sucking sound as of snails detached from a sheet of glass, ducks dabbling in a pond.

Too much! I blinked to efface the vaginal parade.

The word Glückstadt came to my aid. Promptly the bile ran green within me. Those countless indignities! Glückstadt – Lucktown, Happinessville – the very name was a mockery. The same unending sequence: dormitory, communal tent, barrack-room. Boarding-school, Labour Service, Navy. Glückstadt was the worst grind of the lot. *Nomen est omen . . .* Maybe, but not in this case. Fragmentary pictures whirled and collided in a flow and counter-flow of recollection.

I remembered the married recruits in our barrack-room, half-dazed by the pain of separation, the bum-suckers who craved a commission at any price, the nasty piece of work who dislocated his shoulder but still turned out for physical training. I could see him as vividly as if it were yesterday, leaping for the rope one-handed to demonstrate his keenness.

Then there was the Greasy Spoon Café, right in the centre of town – not its real name, of course – where we used to wolf chips by the dishful because camp suppers left us ravenous. Three of us found ourselves on CO's Orders because the proprietor got to hear of our nickname for his sanitary inspector's nightmare. A week's confinement to barracks plus fatigues. The main thing at Glückstadt was to cultivate a deafening word of command. My own star turn: marching a squad into dead ground and allowing them to fall out for a game of cards and a quick drag while I stood guard on the skyline, barking orders like a maniac. That kept everyone happy.

I saw myself in the cutter, almost toppling off the thwart with exhaustion as I flung my last ounce of strength at the oar. I saw the glowing faces of the petty officer instructors whose hobby it was to bully and torment the untrained. I relived the persecution of Flemming – nervous, asthenic little Flemming, who was so hopelessly at the mercy of any sadist in PO's uniform. Dress, undress! On overalls, off overalls! On number ones, off number ones! On sports gear, off sports gear! 'Get a move on, you idle shower of shit!'

Five minutes later, kit inspection.

Flemming never had a hope. He developed the insane look of a cornered rat. That was when the bastards really went to work – when they scented that someone was cracking. Three times round the barrack square, at the double. Once around the barrack square, at the crawl. Hop a hundred metres in full marching order. Twenty press-ups, ditto. Three times round the assault course.

And then the special treatment for all: pull the cutter into the mud at full tilt, then refloat it, but only by oar-power – æons of rhythmical thrashing at the water until the mire beneath the keel had been washed away.

Poor Flemming couldn't take it. One evening he went absent without leave.

They found his mutilated body in the harbour, washed up among old fenders, bottles, driftwood and gobs of oil.

It was murder, pure and simple. Flemming had been systematically hounded to death. He had drowned himself in desperation, even though he could swim. His body was an unlovely sight after its argument with a ship's propeller. They detailed me to attend the enquiry in Hamburg. This is it, I thought – this is where the whole damned sweat-shop goes up in flames. But what happened? Flemming's devoted family, an illustrious clan of Hamburg shipowners, found the notion of suicide embarrassing. The official verdict: accidental death while in the service of his country. For Führer and Fatherland, unswerving devotion to duty . . . Flemming's stricken parents declined to forgo a military funeral so we dutifully blazed away over his hole in the ground. Pre – sent, fire! Three times. No grinning permitted.

And before? How was it before? My mouth twisted wrily as I rembered how I used to roam the dark and deserted streets, draining my cup of freedom to the dregs, desperate at the thought of reporting back.

Later, in France, I had wrenched the automatic out of Obermeier's hand on the beach in front of our requisitioned villa. Anton Obermeier, radio commentator, would-be suicide for reasons of racial purity. All that fuss because of his affair with a Parisian girl who turned out to be half-Jewish. The stupid cunt went berserk. 'To think that I, a National Socialist

. . . My gun – give me my gun!' I damn nearly did him the favour.

I shut my eyes, and at once my thoughts resumed their whirls and gyrations. Words flashed through my head like illuminated ticker-tape. I saw speeding pictures, strings of tinsel, huge glass balls in a hundred shades of bronze, streaks of lightning. My mind's eye erupted in a sea of flames. Oil blazed on the water. Conical as mushrooms, oil-singed water-sprites broke surface and flung up their arms. Gelatinous faces drifted towards me in the flickering greenish-yellow light. Red dots, distress lamps . . .

Again my throat contracted in a violent spasm of nausea. My whole mouth was swollen, bitter as gall. The air-pipe became intolerable – my lips rejected it almost of their own accord. Saliva dribbled on to my shirt in long skeins. I stared at them, fascinated. I needed some juice too.

My wrist-watch was lying on the table! How come? Who had put it there? I caressed it like an unexpected present. The spider's leg of the sweep-hand was still scurrying round the dial. Good craftsmanship. It was just after 8 p.m.

Nearly twenty-four hours on the bottom. The Captain had wanted to try and surface at nightfall. 2000 . . . It must be well and truly dark by now – at this time of year. Why the enquiry about moonset? I wasn't wrong, was I? The Old Man had surely asked Kriechbaum a second time, only a couple of hours back. But the moon was new, so there couldn't be any moonset. So what? The same old quandary: I couldn't ask them now – neither of them.

That would mean another whole night. *Another* night? The specifications must be wrong – the oxygen wouldn't last that long. Anyway, what about the potash cartridges?

Goaded by restlessness, I tottered dazedly to the wardroom. My seat on the Chief's bunk was unoccupied. The second lieutenant had disappeared. I felt as if the day had already lasted a hundred hours.

I didn't know how long I had been dozing in my corner when I woke to see the Captain coming down the passage. He was steadying himself two-handed as though we had run into a heavy sea. Limply he sank down beside me on the Chief's bunk. He didn't appear to notice me at all. His face was grey and sunken, his expression vacant. For a good five minutes he said nothing. Then I heard him murmur: 'Sorry about this . . .'

With one short sentence, the Captain had snuffed my last glimmer of hope. Talons of fear clawed at my heart. He must

423

mean we were finished, done for. A few hours' play-acting with upper lips well stiffened, then curtains. The baling party, the running repairs, the sweat and toil – a charade, the whole thing. I had known it all the time: we were doomed to lie here till Judgement Day.

Even in the water, we might have stood a chance. A quick dive overboard the moment we surfaced. But now – now? A slow descent into coma as the oxygen dwindled?

I removed my mouthpiece, but not from any desire to speak. My hands moved by instinct – intelligent hands. Why bother? they asked themselves. Why the snorkel when there's no hope anyway? A thread of dribble oozed from my mouth, stretched and sank to the deck like the excretion of an invisible spider.

I looked full at the Captain. His face was a lifeless mask. I felt I could strip it off, but then – sure as fate – I should be forced to gaze on the exposed flesh and sinews of an anatomical atlas: spherical bluish-white eyeballs, ramified white veins, delicate blood-vessels and strands of muscle.

Had the Old Man's exertions been too much for him after all? 'Sorry . . .' It couldn't be true – he couldn't have meant it seriously.

He didn't move a millimetre. I couldn't catch his eye because he was staring at the deck.

The vacuum in my head began to alarm me. I mustn't snap now, mustn't miss anything. I had to watch myself and keep an eye on the Old Man as well.

He was at the end of his tether – he must be, or he'd never have said such a thing.

It wasn't a sentence of death, just a sign of resignation. Resignation, nothing more.

Perhaps our luck had turned and he didn't know it yet. What should I do? Assure him that all would be well – that man's extremity was God's opportunity?

I felt a denial surge to my lips. No, never! The Captain's two damning syllables couldn't rob me of my private certainty that we should make it. Nothing could happen to *me*. I was taboo. With me aboard, the whole boat enjoyed immunity.

The Captain had come from aft. What could the Chief have told him? The Chief had been confidence itself when I last saw him. He had a plan – a sensible-sounding plan. The Chief wouldn't have kept his men at it hour after hour for no good reason. He wasn't an actor like the Captain. It couldn't be the end. We should all die one day, but not here, not like this . . .

Doubt flooded back. There was something I knew but hadn't admitted to myself: it was dark up top – had been for hours, and darkness was our licence to surface. We ought to have made the attempt hours ago. All that talk about moonset was a hollow sham.

The Captain still sat motionless, as though every spark of life had fled. Not an eyelid twitched. What was the matter with him? I'd never seen him like this before.

I tried to break the stranglehold. It was just an act, all of it. I gulped, choking back a resurgent tide of terror.

Footsteps.

I stared down the passage. The Chief was standing there, steadying himself with both hands as the Captain had done. I tried to read his expression, but the semi-darkness blurred his features.

Why was he loitering in the shadows? Why didn't he join us at the table? Not, surely, because his shirt was in rags or his arms smeared to the shoulders with oil and grime?

His mouth was open. He probably wanted to deliver a report. Now he was waiting for the Captain to look up. His lips moved. Cautiously he let go of the bulkhead and straightened up, perhaps because a position of attention would lend weight to his words. But the Captain's head still sagged. He probably hadn't noticed that the Chief was a bare two strides away.

I was resisting the urge to nudge him when the Chief cleared his throat. The Captain glanced up quickly. 'Situation report, sir,' the Chief began at once. 'Motor-room making very little water, main motors serviceable. I've pumped the motor-room bilge to the after trimming tanks, and we should be able to blow those. Compass and echo-sounder now serviceable . . .'

The Chief stumbled over his words. His voice was hoarse. All I heard was a reiterated echo: 'Serviceable . . . serviceable . . .'

'Very good, Chief,' the Captain said haltingly. 'Very good. Why not take ten?'

I lurched to my feet to make room for him. 'No, sir, thanks all the same,' he muttered. 'Still one or two problems . . . must sort them out . . .' He took two paces to the rear before essaying a sort of about-face. A breath of wind would have blown his tottering figure to the deck.

The Captain had rested his elbows on the table. Half his lower lip was imprisoned between his teeth in a crooked grimace. I waited for him to speak. At last he released his lip and sighed. 'Good men, that's half the battle. Good men . . .'

He put his palms on the table, bent over them and laboriously pushed himself erect. Then he squeezed out from behind the table, hitched up his trousers in the passage and went aft with the wavering steps of an inebriate.

I sat there stunned, fiddling with the mouthpiece in my lap. What did it mean? I was suddenly afraid that the Chief's appearance had been a dream. Where had the Captain vanished to? He had been there beside me only a moment before. 'Sorry,' came the echo, then: 'Serviceable . . . serviceable . . .' Where had everyone gone? I was about to call out when I heard voices in the control-room. 'Have a shot . . . see how it goes . . .' – 'How much longer do you need?' That was the Captain. A note of urgency: 'We don't have too much time.'

The wheels inside me began to grind once more. What was I sitting around for? I stuck the rubber tube in my mouth with trembling fingers. My legs were shaky too – I could hardly stand. My knees quaked at every step.

The Captain, the Chief and the quartermaster had their heads together in the control-room. They formed a compact group round the chart-table.

Slowing down the action, said a sarcastic voice in my head – spinning the play out, ad-libbing an extra scene. Muffled whispers and conspiratorial poses . . . Very effective.

Then I noticed: no more water in the control-room. It was dry underfoot. Since when? I must have drifted off again. As long as I was awake now . . .

The Captain spoke in an undertone. 'How dark is it, Quartermaster?'

'Dusk was two hours ago, sir.'

The Old Man had obviously regained command of himself and the quartermaster had his answer pat. Kriechbaum's senses were quite unclouded.

The control-room PO was tinkering with something on the flooding panel. I saw him prick his ears. Neither he nor I could hear complete sentences, but the crumbs we gleaned were manna enough. My only surprise was that I didn't swoon with relief and measure my length on the deck.

'Very good,' murmured the Captain, 'we've done all we can.' He glanced at his watch and thought for a moment before announcing, in a level voice: 'We surface in ten minutes.'

We surface, we surface . . . The words seemed to ring out like a mystic challenge. I removed my mouthpiece again. This time the thread of spittle snapped.

Sorry . . . serviceable . . . we surface . . . I fled from the maddening echoes into the wardroom. The second lieutenant was back in his bunk.

'Hey, Number Two!' I didn't recognize my own voice. It was half way between a croak and a sob.

He barely stirred.

I tried again. 'Hello!' It sounded better.

He groped for his tube with both hands and clasped it like a bottle-fed baby. His reluctance to wake was unmistakable. He had no wish to emerge from the womb of sleep – he wanted to preserve his bulwark against reality. I had to take him by the arm and shake him.

'Hey, wake up!'

His eyes opened for a second, but still he refused to wake. He tried to elude me and take refuge in sleep once more. I bent low over his face.

'We surface in ten minutes,' I whispered.

He blinked suspiciously, but at least he removed his mouthpiece.

'What's that?' he mumbled.

'We're going up.'

'Going up?'

'Yes, in ten minutes.'

'Who says?'

'The Old Man . . .'

He didn't jump to his feet. Even his face remained blank. He merely leant back and shut his eyes again. Then a smile dawned. He looked as if someone had arranged a party for him and kept it secret till the last moment.

RETURN

'Stand by to surface!'

The low-voiced order travelled from mouth to mouth like a multiple echo. It was followed by another: 'Number One and Quartermaster, stand by to follow me up.'

In the control-room, Kriechbaum and the first lieutenant swayed in an imaginary swell as they found their oilskins and struggled into the stiff jackets and leggings. They avoided each other's eye, poker-faced as tailor's dummies. Kriechbaum donned his sou'wester very slowly, as if he were performing a drill movement by numbers. He knotted the strings under his chin with pedantic deliberation.

For the first time, I really noticed what I was breathing – a stinking vapour that filled U-A with the solidity of a layer-cake. It was sour and stifling. My lungs had to pump fiercely to filter enough oxygen from the airless mixture.

Would the boat really lift? And, even if she did, what then?

As though in response to my unvoiced question, the Captain said: 'All hands, stand by your escape gear.'

So that was his plan of action – up, overboard, and swim for it. But not now, surely? Not in the darkness, in that tearing current?

My films! I groped my way to the POs' mess. Everything was laid out on my bunk. The films were packed in their watertight container, ready to hang round my neck.

I was less in terror of the darkness and current than of enemy gunfire. If a corvette's searchlight picked us up we should be illuminated like a cabaret turn. Other fingers of light would probe the spot, the sky would become a sinister Christmas-tree hung with star-shells. And then the bark of quick-firing guns . . .

We might be lucky, of course – stranger things had happened. Perhaps they wouldn't spot us immediately, but if we took to the water and they *still* didn't spot us, we might drift anywhere.

Lights on our escape gear . . . *We* didn't have any of those. The British were better kitted out – all equipped to abandon ship. Our masters hadn't provided for the present emergency. We had our escape gear, but that was all.

I made a hash of putting on my escape gear. No experience – never thought I'd need the thing. Frenssen gave me a hand. Tentatively I inserted the mouthpiece. I carefully tried the oxygen cylinder and heard it hiss. The gadget seemed to be working.

I was suddenly surrounded by bustling, whispering figures. My terror subsided. Everyone had his escape gear on and was fiddling with it, feigning intense activity to avoid looking at his neighbours.

The second lieutenant caught my eye, also trying to appear calm. He hid his emotions behind a twisted grin.

We were on the razor's edge now. The Chief would release his HP air, and that would decide whether – by blowing the trimming and main ballast tanks – we could gain enough buoyancy to lift us off the bottom. We still didn't know if the tank tops would hold. We could only afford one attempt.

There wouldn't be a second chance – that much was certain.

'Blow!' the Captain ordered in a clear voice. Isenberg spun his cocks and compressed air hissed into the tanks. Would it force the water out? We stood there stiffly, listening. Any movement?

I made myself loose at the knees and receptive to the slightest tremor.

Nothing. We stayed put, inert as a lump of lead.

I slackened my knees still more.

HP air continued to hiss, water escaped with a rumble.

Still nothing.

All hope abandon, ye who enter the Strait . . . No use, the game was up. My knees started to buckle.

There! Surely the submarine had stirred? Something grated against the hull with a sound not unlike Asdic. A squeal – shrill as a knife on china – pierced me to the marrow. The needle of the depth-gauge trembled.

With a perceptible lurch, U-A lifted off the sea-bed, groaning and rasping against unseen rocks. More squeals and howls, then silence.

Jubilation almost choked me.

I gripped the conning-tower ladder with my left hand and stared hard at the depth-gauge, willing the needle on. I made my gaze mesmeric and it tremulously crept another three or four subdivisions. U-A was afloat, rising like a free balloon.

Thank God, we had left the sea-bed behind. We were lighter than the water we displaced – we had a vestige of buoyancy!

I stared at the depth-gauge over the Captain's shoulder – I and half-a-dozen others. The needle continued to revolve anti-clockwise, gaining speed. There was no movement in the control-room. Not even a whisper broke the silence.

The needle still moved with painful reluctance. I wanted to screw it back by hand, as though that would bring us up faster.

And now? Had it come to a halt – weren't we rising any longer? Impossible! We had positive buoyancy now – we *must* continue to rise.

'Two-fifty metres,' said the Chief, as if we didn't know already.

'Two-ten . . . two hundred . . . one-ninety . . .'

Periscope observation was out, I remembered. Both periscopes were unserviceable, so the Captain wouldn't be able to check if the coast was clear. I quickly dismissed the thought and refocused on the depth-gauge. We continued to rise.

'One-sixty,' murmured the Chief.

The Captain took up his station beneath the hatch as the needle kissed the 130-metre mark.

The minutes expanded like limp elastic.

We were still rigid with tension. I didn't dare shift my weight from one leg to the other. The Captain looked misshapen with an escape pack over his sheepskin waistcoat.

At 60 metres he ordered Isenberg to dim the control-room lights. All that remained was the glow seeping through the bulkhead doors, barely strong enough to reveal the figures round me.

I decided to shift my weight after all – slowly and gingerly, so as not to attract attention.

Herrmann was manning the hydrophone. I knew he must have a lot of contacts by now but would only report if one of them was close. He didn't utter. We seemed to be in luck.

'Twenty metres . . . eighteen . . .'

The column of water in the Papenberg was falling. The Captain climbed stiffly up the ladder.

'Upper lid clear,' reported the Chief.

I gulped. Tears came into my eyes. The blind would see again, the half-asphyxiated breathe God's good air . . .

The boat began to move. She rocked gently to and fro. Then a muffled ptchumm, ptchumm! Waves were breaking against the hull.

Everything went quickly, as usual. The Chief reported 'Surfaced!' and the Captain called down 'Equalize pressure!'

A sharp report. The upper lid had sprung open before pressure was fully equalized. Air descended on us in a solid mass. My lungs pumped it in, then stopped as if the abundance of oxygen were too much for them. I reeled. The pain of breathing forced me to my knees.

I waited for the cruel glare of star-shells. Why no orders from the Captain? Had he seen something?

U-A continued to roll gently from side to side. I heard the liquid impact of small waves on the hull.

At last the Captain's deep voice: 'Stand by to blow to full buoyancy.'

Again my throat tightened with suppressed jubilation.

Still no light through the upper lid.

'Stand by main vents.' Then: 'All hands remain at diving stations.'

Diving stations? A thrill of alarm ran through me. Didn't the surface belong to us yet? Could the next few moments rob us of the boon we had just received?

Never mind. That draught of air was mine, and that, and that. Damp black night air! I expanded my rib-cage and drank in as much as my lungs would hold.

The waves continued to lap our hull. I listened to them reverently. I could have flung my arms round the Chief's neck.

Then, from above: 'Stand by main engine.' I relayed the order more loudly than I need have.

A chain of voices conveyed it to the engine-room. Johann and his men would now be opening our one good diesel's exhaust flaps, starting-air bottles and test-cocks, checking to see if it had taken any water, clutching it in.

Confirmation was passed from the engine-room, and again the Captain's voice came down the hatch: 'Half-ahead port!' The helmsman echoed the order from his post in the conning-tower and I passed it aft.

I heard the snarl of the supercharger. A first shuddering heartbeat ran through the hull.

Pray God we made it! Once more, the Old Man was staking all on a single throw. I still found it hard to grasp that we had reached the surface, that we were alive, breathing the night air, proceeding under power. I wondered if we would head for the coast.

The engine was sucking an ample flow of fresh air into the boat. Every bulkhead door stood open to allow it free passage.

The roar of the diesel transfixed me. I wanted to stop my ears. The din must be audible from Spain to North Africa, but what was the Captain to do? We had no choice – we couldn't walk on tiptoe.

I intercepted a glance of birdlike anxiety from the Vicar.

If I only knew how things looked up top . . . All that came from above was an occasional steering order which conveyed no sort of picture at all.

The Captain summoned Kriechbaum to the bridge. Beside me, the first lieutenant was also staring up the conning-tower. We might have been reflections in a double-sided mirror, he with his right hand on the ladder, I with my left.

Three or four steering orders in quick succession, then a counter-order: 'Belay hard-a-port! Keep her at two-five-zero.'

The helmsman lagged behind. He got his confirmations muddled, but no word of reprimand came from the bridge.

'Well, well, well . . .' was all I heard the Captain say. The last 'well' was a protracted drawl. Hardly an abundance of information, but enough to suggest that it had been a close call.

I gritted my teeth and willed him to do the right thing. But then, he was an old hand at tricking his opponents, cruising along under their noses, presenting a narrow silhouette and hugging a dark background. The Old Man knew his stuff.

The first lieutenant sniffed hard and breathed through his mouth. He might have said something, but he didn't. In the same situation, he would have been at an utter loss. No ship-handling course equipped you for what the Captain was doing now. We had sneaked in on our motors. The problem now was to limp back on one noisy diesel. Our attempt to penetrate the Mediterranean had failed.

Involuntarily I sniffed too. We had all caught a bit of a cold, probably. I propped my left foot on the lowest rung of the ladder, bar-fly fashion. The first lieutenant followed suit with his right.

The quartermaster's voice was indistinct. I could never catch more than half his reports. 'Object on the port . . . Object green three-zero . . . closing . . .'

'Sounds like the Wannsee on a Sunday afternoon,' said a voice behind me. Babyface. Let him play the man of iron to his heart's content – he'd never fool me again. I would always see him slumped in the corner of the settee, cuddling a raffia dog.

He edged nearer. I could tell by his breathing.

The control-room seemed to have become a popular place. It was understandable that the watch below should shun the remoter parts of the submarine. Anyone who could do so invented a pretext for hovering near the lower lid. The gloom was a welcome disguise. In spite of the engine noise I distinctly heard a hiss from the air-bottle of someone's escape gear. And another. At least two men were preparing to abandon ship.

The very thought made my heart pound. There was no chance of going deep if we were spotted.

A bewildering series of steering orders : 'Port helm – starboard – midships – at that – hard-a-starboard!' The Captain was swinging us this way and that.

It seemed incredible that we were still undetected and un-scathed, that the British hadn't put out a general alert and hemmed us in with every available ship. Someone *must* have heard or seen us – they couldn't all be asleep. Or was the noise of our engine a blessing in disguise? Did the men on the patrol-ships take us for a British boat? British submarines had conning-towers of a different shape. Yes, I told myself, but only in profile. There couldn't be much difference between one narrow silhouette and another.

Again the sharp hiss of an air-bottle. If only we needn't take to the water . . .

I slackened the knee-joint of my supporting leg as though it would reduce my bodyweight and lighten ship.

And if another aircraft appeared?

But that was no routine patrol – we'd been spotted and plotted. They were waiting for us. Nothing was scheduled for tonight, so the aircraft would stay put on their strip.

We stood there, the two watch-keeping officers and I, scarcely daring to breathe. I could vividly picture the shadowy forms of distant ships, converging, turning, growing, receding, disappearing.

I longed for another bulletin.

The second lieutenant cleared his throat. 'First things first,' he said huskily. 'I expect we'll head west for a fair stretch.'

The Captain didn't speak for five long minutes. I visualized the chart. Yes, better to make a big detour westwards and avoid the traffic round Cape St Vincent.

If only I could go on the bridge and see, see, SEE!

The sky at least had mercy on me. A few stars peeped through a gap in the clouds and swung to and fro in the mouth of the upper lid. I wondered what their names were. The quartermaster would have known, but he was on deck.

'Port twenty – steer two-seven-zero.'

A minute later the helmsman reported: 'Two-seven-zero, sir.'

I was used to the noise of the engine by now. It had ceased to grate on my nerves.

'Time?' the Captain called down.

The helmsman checked. '2130, sir.'

Roughly an hour since we surfaced. An hour on one engine: how far?

I didn't even know what speed it was running at. With both diesels, I should have known by the pitch, but my powers of discrimination were not attuned to one engine alone. It was running under load because we needed every amp we could store. With luck, our remaining cells would accumulate enough power to get us through the morrow. It was obvious – without a word being said on the subject – that we should have to make ourselves scarce by first light. The Chief would do his best to hold us at periscope depth or thereabouts.

At last a few fragments from the bridge: 'No, Kriechbaum, she's going away – take a bet on it. Keep your eye on that one, though. She could be closing. I don't like the look of her.'

Five minutes later: 'Ship's head?'

'Two-seven-zero, sir.'

'Keep her at that.'

'How many miles can we cover before it gets light?' I asked the first lieutenant.

He sniffed. 'Twenty or thirty.'

'We seem to be doing all right.'

'Yes, looks like it.'

I started violently as somebody gripped my shoulder. It was the Chief.

'How goes it?'

'I'll try that on you some time,' I grumbled. 'Pretty well, all things considered.'

'Pardon me, I'm sure!'

'How about you, Chief?'

'Thanks for asking. *Comme ci, comme ça.*'

'Very illuminating.'

'Just came to snatch a breath of air,' he explained, and vanished into the gloom again.

'Looks like the Macaronis won't be seeing us for Christmas after all,' Isenberg said from somewhere behind me.

Of course, La Spezia. Our orders had entirely slipped my mind. Farewell to the beautiful blue Med. Poor old Rommel would have to manage without us. We were an Atlantic boat, after all. The Italians could handle the Malta convoys.

Were we a singleton, or did U-boat Command plan to expose other boats to the same risks? Even if we managed to disengage to the west, what then? One day at periscope depth was all very well, but after that? We couldn't go deep – anything more than periscope depth would be too much for us. Was our transmitter working? Nobody had said a word about sending off a signal. How many miles to the nearest French harbour – or did the Captain intend to sail our wreck of a U-boat into Vigo and march us back through Spain, this time en bloc?

How would we make it through Biscay if the weather went sour on us? Daytime cruising on the surface was a virtual impossibility. We should be at the mercy of any aircraft that spotted us, and Biscay swarmed with enemy planes. Cruise at night and stay dived by day? The nights were long, true, but would it work?

An order from the bridge: 'Steady – at that.'

The Captain had altered course. He was heading south of west. Ploy and counter-ploy: he thought the British thought

– might think – that any other U-boats trying the same game would take the shortest route possible. If they were coming from the North and Central Atlantic, they wouldn't go below the 36th Parallel. Therefore, we must stay south of the 36th. For the time being.

If I was right, we must be in the vicinity of Cape Spartel – or further west but on a level with it. The quartermaster couldn't do his sums at the moment. Nobody was standing in for him, so he'd find a nasty great gap in his route-chart later on.

I suddenly noticed that both the watch-keeping officers had disappeared. I was tottering with fatigue myself. Fewer steering orders came from the bridge now. We seemed to have slipped through the patrol-lines unscathed.

If the situation had become slightly less precarious, why not screw up my courage?

'Man on the bridge?' I called.

'Come on up.'

I could scarcely move my limbs. I was stiff as a board from long standing. Laboriously I climbed past the helmsman. Wind massaged my face even before I looked over the bridge casing, then forced its way between my parted lips.

'Well?' drawled the Captain.

The question was rhetorical. I peered round. No shadowy forms – nothing. To port, a string of nine or ten twinkling lights. The African coast? It seemed incredible.

I stood on tiptoe and craned over the bridge rail. The fore-casing gleamed faintly. I could see, despite the gloom, that the gratings had been grotesquely ripped and mangled. Only the pivot of the gun remained. I wondered what the leading edge of the bridge looked like – the casing must be badly scarred.

'Quite a sight, eh?' the Captain said.

'I'm sorry?'

'The mess,' he said, gesturing at it. 'Quite a sight.' His voice sank to a murmur. I caught: 'Somebody up there must like us.'

The quartermaster cut in. 'I always thought he rooted for the British, sir – they're the ones with the whisky.'

Feeble jokes. I could hardly believe my ears.

A sense of unreality took possession of me. This wasn't Mother Earth. We were gliding over a leaden film, over the surface of a moon that spun through the universe in cold, dead isolation. No living creature existed here apart from us. I felt as if we had been adrift for a century. Had we really survived? Were we still the same people? Had we only won a reprieve? What did it all mean?

For minutes on end, I didn't know if I was dreaming or waking. What was reality? What illusions had I surrendered to? What hallucinations could be bred by fear? How long had the ordeal lasted? When had I been awake? How had I spent the interminable hours? How had the others endured it all?

My body felt as limp as a convalescent's, but the blood coursed vigorously through me. I could hear the throb of my own heartbeats.

I touched the metal casing and felt it vibrate. Our one engine was really running – that was no illusion. We'd made it.

I noticed that I was clenching and unclenching my hands. It gratified me to see my fingers curl and straighten. They moved when I willed them to. My muscles reacted. I ran a hand over my forehead and brushed away the cold sweat.

The quartermaster looked round but said nothing. I didn't break the silence.

More lights twinkled in the darkness. The Captain gave some steering orders. We swung this way and that, but our mean course remained west. The first requirement was to gain ground and put some distance between us and the Strait.

'How much longer have we got, Kriechbaum?'

'A good hour, sir.'

My one desire was to stand there, rhythmically breathing, listening to my heartbeats, scanning the almost indiscernible skyline, hearing the hiss of the bow-wave. Some spray came over. I gave my lips an exploratory lick: they were salty. I could see, taste, hear, smell the night air, feel the movements of the boat. All my senses were functioning – I was alive.

My bladder announced its presence. The usual custom was to retire to the 'conservatory' abaft the bridge, but I hesitated. It seemed out of place somehow – not the right moment. The Captain mightn't like it. I could hold out for a while.

I tilted my head. A few stars peeped through the ragged, almost motionless overcast. We were travelling through the night, a band of resurrected men whose continued existence was unknown to all. Kernével thought we were sunk and the enemy must have reported to that effect. The British could signal to their heart's content, unlike us. Even if Herrmann patched up our transmitter, we would take good care not to use it. Even the shortest squash signal might betray our position.

'Very good,' murmured the Captain. 'Another hour and

we'll tuck her up.'

He bent over the upper lid. 'Stand by, second watch!' He turned to me. 'Well?'

'I don't get it, sir.'

'Don't get what?'

'The way they're letting us slope off.'

'Nor me,' he said drily. 'Lucky I'm not in charge of them.'

'How do you mean?'

'Don't let up till you see the captain's cap break surface – it's an old rule.'

My jaw dropped. If it had been up to the Old Man, we should by now be thoroughly and irrevocably dead. He would have made a better job of it.

'You ought to turn in,' he said thickly, like one drunk giving good advice to another in the firm belief that his own sobriety is beyond dispute.

'I'm all right,' I said casually, but I asked permission to go below.

The stinking buckets and bleaching powder had disappeared. Back to normal again. Humming fans, everything cleared away. Miraculously, the heads were vacant.

Silence reigned in the POs' mess. Three curtains were drawn. I turned in just as I was, clothes and all. My escape gear I shoved to the foot of the bunk, unstowed. The potash cartridge and breathing-tube got in my way. Where to dispose of them? Overboard, preferably – I never wanted to see the aluminium canister again. What had the others done with theirs? Propped them against the bulkhead. Yes, good idea.

I dreamed I heard explosions. I was a resonating kettledrum, vast and metallic. The drumsticks resembled gigantic flails. Inside me – inside the drum – concentric Catherine wheels counter-rotated, magnesium-white within, pink without. Blood-red showers of sparks flew off them and rained against the rim. The drum was flanked by an avenue of huge and incandescent dahlias. At the far end, wrapped in a white glow, Grünewald's resurrected Christ. Above him, against a background of greenish-gold bronze, a dazzling pink aureole whose rays extended to the zenith. On either side, rockets soared above whirling girandolas and blossoms of fire. The whole ground flashed and coruscated. A rending of metal, a shower of sparks, and the projectiles collided inside me with an appalling crash. The impact was succeeded by a thunderous roar.

'Wha – what's that?' I sat up and jerked the curtain aside.

Another three or four muffled detonations came to my ears.

A man was sitting at the table. He turned to look at me. I blinked to clear my vision and saw that it was Kleinschmidt.

'Someone's getting clobbered.'

'Bloody hell!'

'It can't be meant for us. They've been at it for the last half-hour.'

'What time is it?'

'Eleven-thirty.'

'Come again?'

'Eleven-thirty, Lieutenant. Look, spot-on.'

Kleinschmidt raised his arm in a rotary gesture, inviting me to see for myself.

Then I remembered I was wearing a watch of my own. Crazy, quite crazy. I must be going gaga. The POs' mess was deserted except for me and Kleinschmidt. The curtains of the opposite bunks were drawn. Clobbering someone . . . It must be daylight up top. Eleven-thirty – but not at night, surely? No sense of time, completely haywire.

A new series of explosions. 'Maybe they're trying to scare us,' I said.

I swung my legs over the leeboard and slid to the deck. A visit to the control-room might clear my head.

Isenberg had taken over the job of counting depth-charges while Kriechbaum slept.

'Thirty-three,' he sang out, 'thirty-four, thirty-five, thirty-six – thirty-seven.'

The last two were almost simultaneous.

The first lieutenant was also in the control-room. He leant against the chart-stowage wearing a watchful expression and a drill monkey-jacket. Where had he dug that up? Not the attire one usually associated with our punctilious Number One. What was more, he hadn't shaved. The light from the chart-table drove his eyes deep into their shadowy sockets. A flash of bared teeth would have completed the deathshead illusion.

'Forty, forty-two, forty-four – some going!'

'How far?'

Isenberg shrugged. 'Quite a way.'

'At least fifteen miles,' said the first lieutenant.

'Nice to know,' I said.

The Captain's absence from the control-room disquieted me. And the Chief? In the engine-room, or was he sleeping at last? The planesmen sat in front of their push-buttons with an immobility which suggested that they had dozed off.

A whole string of explosions merged into one long rumble of thunder.

'Miles away,' the Captain growled behind my back. He was only wearing a shirt and slacks. His expression was grimly distasteful. Behind him I could see the quartermaster. The Chief appeared a moment later.

'Damn!' he muttered between each depth-charge, like a petulant child. 'Damn – damn – damn!'

Were they at work on an oil-slick – our oil-slick? The depth-charges could hardly be meant for another U-boat. It was broad daylight, after all.

'They're getting warmer,' said the quartermaster.

All we needed. The steering motor was far too loud – everything on board was too loud.

The Captain flapped his hand dismissively. 'Nonsense,' he murmured.

The thunder ceased abruptly, almost as if the Captain's gesture had cut it short.

'Surplus stock, probably,' he sneered. 'They're getting rid of it – the easy way.'

He turned on his heel.

I glanced at the chart. Amazing – Kriechbaum had neatly darned the hole in our route. It wouldn't have surprised me to learn that the position marked at 0600 was based on an astronomical fix. If I knew the quartermaster, he wouldn't have left the bridge without taking a quick star-sight.

On the chart, everything looked quite straightforward. We had steered far more intricate courses before now than this simple dog-leg. The Papenberg indicated that we were 20 metres down.

Herrmann was on duty in the hydrophone booth. He treated me to an unwaveringly owlish stare.

I almost bade his blank face good morning, then remembered that it was past midday. I mustn't disturb him, anyway. The twin ear-phones of his head-set were standing proxy for four pairs of binoculars, his two ear-drums for four pairs of eyes.

What was it Isenberg had said? 'Hobbling home on crutches – not my idea of fun.' Nor mine. Hobbling home, back from the Beresina on crutches. And the Lord slew them all – man, steed and chariot. Faith, hope and charity, these three, but the greatest of these is hope.

The Captain had drawn his curtain. I stalked past on tip-toe.

The second lieutenant was asleep in the wardroom, but the

Chief's bunk was empty. If the Chief hadn't slept by now he would be ripe for a strait-jacket. Twelve hours ago he had been half-dead with fatigue. His child must be due any day now. Strange times we lived in: the wife in a Flensburg hospital while her husband nursed an ailing engine through the Atlantic, 20 metres down and verging on insanity.

I was still dog-tired. Lacking even the energy to drag myself back to the POs' mess, I slumped into the far corner of the Chief's bunk.

The steward woke me. He seemed to have been trying for some time. I distinctly felt him shake me but drifted off, again and again, on billows of sleep. His mouth approached my ear.

'Lunch-time, Lieutenant.'

I screwed up my eyes as hard as I could, then wrenched them open.

'What?'

'Lunch-time.'

'You mean there's a proper meal?'

'That's right.'

I could hear the Captain talking to the hydrophone operator next door. His voice still sounded furry with drink.

He came in, grunted, and sat down.

Bloodshot eyes, twitching lids, cheesy complexion, hair and beard dark with moisture. He had obviously dunked his head in water.

'Well,' he said at last, 'what's on?'

'Beef rissoles and red cabbage, sir,' replied the steward.

The chef was a marvel. I had been counting on bread and sausage, not a Sunday dinner.

'Hm,' said the Captain. He had leant back and was blinking at the deckhead.

'Where's the Chief?' I asked.

'Where do you think? He finally passed out sitting up between the diesels. They fetched a mattress and laid him out flat. He might as well stay there for the present.'

Three steaming dishes appeared on the table. The Captain's nostrils flared at the scent of the rissoles.

Muffled explosions – three or four of them. Were they still at it?

The Captain pulled a face and chewed his lower lip. After the next two thuds he said: 'Bit premature, aren't they? Anyone would think it was New Year's Eve.'

He shut his eyes, passed a hand over his face and kneaded

it like dough. Then he pressed his eyes deep into their sockets with his forefingers and, finally, combed his beard with the fingers of his right hand.

Some colour appeared in his face, but not for long. Within moments his skin had turned pale again and his eyes looked more bloodshot than ever.

'What about the second engineer?' I asked.

He gave a yawn. The words 'Also in the engine-room' emerged with it. 'One or two minor jobs still to be done,' he added.

He yawned again. This time he leant back and flapped his gaping mouth with the back of his hand, producing a tremolo effect.

'It's been a good introduction for him – the Chief's side-kick, I mean. At least he knows the form.' He stopped yawning and forked up a piece of rissole. It was hot. His pursed lips closed gingerly over it.

'Propellers on a true bearing of zero-nine-zero, sir,' called Hinrich.

The Captain was on his feet and outside the hydrophone booth in a flash. He wedged himself in the passage with his left forearm resting against the partition. 'Louder or fainter?' he asked impatiently.

'Constant, sir. Turbines. Pretty faint still – now they're growing stronger.'

The Captain went into a knees-bend. Hinrich leant towards him as if he meant to confide something in a whisper. He had removed his head-set and twisted the earphones so that he could hold one to his left ear while the Captain held the other to his right. Nothing happened. Neither spoke.

Slowly my eyes returned to the wardroom table. The un-eaten half of my rissole was nesting between a mound of red cabbage and a mound of potato. It looked funny, somehow. I was still holding my knife and fork but I couldn't bring myself to eat.

'Going away.' That was Hinrich's voice. A groan and a creaking of joints told me that the Captain had straightened up.

'They might let us eat in peace,' he said as he squeezed behind the table again.

He had scarcely resumed his seat when Hinrich reported a new contact. 'One-seven-zero degrees, sir.'

'It was nice and quiet a minute ago.' The Captain sounded reproachful. 'Let's wait and see, shall we?'

He took two or three chews. I decided to carry on too,

but cautiously, so as not to clatter my eating irons.

The Captain appeared vexed. 'Cold!' he grumbled, inserting another forkful. He glared resentfully at the remains and pushed the plate away.

It was clear the combination of depth-charges and propeller noises made him uneasy. The British might genuinely be on our track. For all we knew, we were leaking oil. Although the current must by now have carried our first big oil-slick far into the Mediterranean, we might still be blazing a trail.

The first lieutenant had carefully ingested his lunch and arranged his eating irons parallel on the plate. Not only was he conversant with the finer points of etiquette – he had also drummed them into the steward; 'If I cross my knife and fork, it means I want a second helping. Otherwise, not.'

'Clear away,' said the Captain. He hauled himself to his feet and headed for the control-room. Just as he perched on the chart-stowage, another six depth-charges went off. They still sounded like distant thunder.

The POs' mess table was a wilderness. Only three men had eaten, but like pigs. Cold dishes of food stood forlornly amid an array of greasy plates. From the look of it, exhaustion had prevailed over neatness. I wanted to facilitate the climb into my bunk, but it was all my foot could do to find a niche in the repulsive clutter on the table.

Another three depth-charges rumbled above the hornet's hum of the motors. A graveyard hush fell after each group of explosions, and it dawned on me why: there was no steady seepage of music from the loudspeaker. The bomb had at least done us that small service.

Another few hours' sleep would be the thing. The joy of stretching out, of curling and uncurling one's toes . . . In our predicament, the very act of lying flat was bliss. I shuddered to think that, but for the Old Man's obstinacy, we might have been swimming for hours. Our iron-nerved gambler knew the value of a floating home, be it never so dilapidated.

It was 1700 when I woke. Curiously, we were steering 030. The Captain must be edging landwards again. If we maintained our present course we would hit Lisbon.

How long ago was it that I had been summoned to the bridge because Lisbon was on the beam?

Hugging the coast was our best bet, presumably. The Captain planned to beach us if necessary – that must be it, but if I knew him he would do anything rather than throw in his hand. U-A was fully stored and provisioned, after all –

masses of oil in spite of what we had lost through leakage, a full tally of torpedoes and any amount of food. The Old Man wasn't the sort to ditch all that in a hurry.

Cape Finisterre would be our jumping-off point for a dash across Biscay. Would he risk it?

'Stand by to surface!' The order was passed from the control-room. Second watch was on duty. It was now 1800, so another two hours of the watch remained.

A crush developed in the control-room. Once again, we were surfacing blind.

'Standards awash . . . conning-tower clear!'

'Equalize pressure.'

The hatch sprang open. The Captain, who was first on the bridge, almost immediately gave an engine order. The boat trembled, and we were back on diesel again. Course: still 030.

I followed the second lieutenant on deck. We were alone on a dark disc of sea. I could distinguish the horizon with ease. The inky water contrasted clearly with the sky, which was a shade paler.

I drew in as much night air as my lungs would hold. I couldn't get enough of it. My teeth chewed on its black freshness. A shower of spray pattered against my face, seasoning the air with salt.

A pale moustache of foam drooped from our bow. Waves slapped the hull and drew a muffled gong-note from our metal casing.

'We'll soon have Lisbon on the beam again,' the Captain said.

'To starboard this time,' I said, and wished it were the only difference.

I passed through the control-room on my way to supper.

'That new boy of yours looks like a road accident,' Dorian was saying to Isenberg. 'What did you do, fix his teeth for him?' It was true – the Vicar had lost a pair of incisors.

The control-room PO gave a subdued shrug.

'Never mind,' Dorian reassured him, 'the bugger got what was coming to him.'

I saw Isenberg's brow darken. He controlled his irritation with an effort. 'Just drop the subject,' he snapped.

The Chief appeared for supper. I hardly dared glance at him, he looked so drawn and weary.

'It must have been radar,' the Captain said.

Radar – all big ships now had those rotating sprung mattresses on their masts. The *Bismarck* located the *Hood* with radar and blew her sky-high before she could poke a masthead over the horizon. And now the Brits must have succeeded in miniaturizing the bulky installations. Dwarf radar sets so compact that the whole apparatus would fit in a cockpit – and ten to one we hadn't developed an answer to it, not yet.

I wondered when Simone would get to hear. Her people kept their ears to the ground. Her people? I'd have given a lot to know her true relationship with the Maquis. We should have been back long ago. Even discounting the Gibraltar fiasco, no other U-boat had spent as long at sea in the past year.

Not a word was said about Gibraltar. No one made the smallest allusion to it. It was as if our hours on the sea-bed had been declared taboo.

The men were equally reticent, but Gibraltar was written on their faces. Even now, many of them showed naked fear. They all knew we were incapable of diving much below periscope depth. A number of frames were badly strained. The U-boat was as limp as a hammock – little more than a drifting wreck. Everyone was afraid she wouldn't make it through the winter storms of Biscay. Our one asset was the enemy's belief that they had cracked us open. At least they hadn't sent out a search party.

Conversation didn't burgeon in the POs' mess until next day.
'Who says I'll shit myself if we don't get a fighter escort?'
No reply.
'It's a fair haul,' Dorian said casually.
'You can say that again,' Kleinschmidt chimed in. 'All the way across Biscay in this heap – Biscay, mark you!'
'Take it easy.' Frenssen seemed mindful of his reputation for sang-froid. 'It'll be a push-over after this last lot. No need to get lathered up.'
'How many miles to the nearest base?' asked Isenberg.
'What do you mean, nearest?'
'Trust a seaman! You don't honestly think we're going to make St Nazaire, do you? Haven't you been aft yet? We won't get far in this floating junk-yard.'

I drifted, rocking gently, into a whirlpool, rotated swiftly on my own axis and was sucked down deep. Below, everything was silvery – a grotto bathed in lunar silver. Bright bubbles ascended like the effervescence in fizzy lemonade. Get going, I told myself. I kicked off, taking care not to cut my feet, and floated lazily to the surface like a fish. A stream of silvery bubbles followed me up. The surface cracked with a sharp report. I struck out, gasped for air, woke up and felt a hand on my arm.

A shock ran through me. 'What's the matter?'

Turbo, the control-room hand, registered my look of dismay. No diesel pounded, no motors hummed either. The boat was hushed.

'Come on, man, what is it?'

'We're stopped.'

Stopped? Normally, every change of speed penetrated my shell of sleep and was duly recorded. Was it possible that I hadn't noticed the cessation of engine noise?

Waves were lapping against our ballast tanks. The U-boat rocked sedately to and fro.

'You're wanted on the bridge, Lieutenant.'

The senior control-room hand was a considerate soul. Having carved his tidings into manageable morsels, he waited for me to swallow one before feeding me the next. 'The Captain's up top. You're wanted too. We've stopped a ship.'

He gave a corroborative nod and dodged any further questions by retreating smartly.

I repeated the last sentence with dazed incomprehension. Stopped a ship? The Old Man must have flipped his lid at last. What did he plan to do, send her back to St Nazaire with a prize crew aboard?

The peace of it! The curtain opposite was drawn, likewise the one below it. Not a soul in sight. Where was everyone – out stopping ships?

I wasn't in command of my limbs. The boat heeled and I staggered sideways with one foot halfway into a boot. The deck reversed its angle. I was thrown against a bunk leeboard. Bugger! I struggled into my jacket and went forward.

There were two or three men sitting in the control-room. I cocked my head and called: 'Man on the bridge?'

The answer came back at once. 'Affirmative!'

A moist breeze. The sky brimmed with stars. Bulky figures in the gloom: the Captain, the quartermaster, the first lieutenant. I took a quick glance over the bridge casing and started. There, immediately above the jumping-wire, lay a big ship. Broadside on, bow to the left, ablaze with lights from stem to stern. 12,000 tons, if not more. A passenger liner. She was simply lying there, stopped. The dark water was spangled with a myriad darting reflections in white and gold.

The Captain didn't turn round. 'We've been working on her

for the past hour,' he growled.

It was icy cold on deck. My spine prickled. The quarter-master handed me his binoculars. A few moments later the Captain spoke again. 'We stopped her exactly fifty-five minutes ago.'

He had his glasses raised. 'We flashed her a signal,' Kriech-baum started to explain in an undertone, but the Captain broke in: 'We told them we'd sink her if they used their radio. I don't think they have. We also asked for identifica-tion, but the name doesn't tally. *Reina Victoria* – that's what they told us. Number One couldn't find it in the Register. Something rotten in the state of Denmark, if you ask me.'

'But the lights?' I said.

'Can you think of a better ploy than switching your lights on and playing neutral?'

Kriechbaum cleared his throat. 'It's odd,' he said between the hands supporting his binoculars.

'A bit too odd for my taste,' muttered the Captain. 'I wish we knew whether Kernével had a line on her. We've enquired – the signal went off ages ago. No reply yet. Maybe our set's still on the blink.'

So the Captain had radioed after all . . . I cursed the thought. Did we *have* to court detection by bombarding the ether with signals?

The Captain seemed to have divined my reaction. 'Can't afford to make any mistakes,' he said.

I again had the feeling that I'd lost touch with reality, that this huge ship was an illusion to be banished by a wave of the wand. A sigh of relief, laughter, applause, end of per-formance . . .

'We'll sink them if they don't send a boat soon,' the Cap-tain rasped. 'They've known that for the past half-hour.'

The first lieutenant was also peering through his binoculars. He said nothing. Madness, utter madness, lying there with this monstrous great ship looming above our bow. Privateer-ing with a crippled U-boat? The Captain must be round the bend!

'We're monitoring her frequency,' he said. 'Number One, make this in English: Send boat within ten minutes or we open fire. Time, Quartermaster?'

'0320, sir.'

'Tell me when it's 0330.'

I noticed for the first time that PO Telegraphist Hinrich was also on the bridge. He leant over the bridge rail with the heavy signal lamp in his hands and loosed a series of flashes in the liner's direction.

There was no response. The Captain almost danced with fury. 'Jesus Christ Almighty, if that doesn't take the bloody biscuit!'

Hinrich had to repeat his call three times before an answering dot of light winked at us from the tiers of illuminated ports. The first lieutenant started to recite our signal letter by letter. Short stab of light, long stab, short, long . . .

Another eternity elapsed before we got a reply. Perversely the Captain declined to read it himself.

'Well?' he snapped at the first lieutenant.

'They say they're doing their best, sir.'

'Doing their best, doing their best! What's that supposed to mean? First they give us a false name and now this eyewash. Time?'

'0325, sir.'

'Infernal cheek! Giving a false name, lying doggo, taking bugger-all action . . .'

The Captain shifted from foot to foot with his hands thrust deep into the side pockets of his leather jacket and his shoulders hunched. I could clearly see him in semi-profile against the lights on the water. He was staring fixedly at the liner.

Nobody spoke. Nothing could be heard but the splash of the waves against our ballast tanks until he started again, hoarsely. 'What the hell do they mean, doing their best?'

'Anything wrong, sir?' the Chief called from below.

'If that boat isn't here in five minutes,' the Captain said in a choking voice, 'I'm opening fire.'

I could tell he was waiting for a sign of approval from the quartermaster, but none came. Kriechbaum raised his binoculars and lowered them again, otherwise nothing. Another minute dragged by. The Captain turned to face him. He started to raise his glasses, but too late. Now he would have to utter.

'I – er, wouldn't like to say, sir. You never can tell . . .'

'Never can tell what?' the Captain barked.

Kriechbaum hesitated. 'Well, there's something wrong somewhere . . .'

'Precisely,' retorted the Captain. 'They're deliberately wasting time. They're calling up destroyers. Or aircraft.'

It sounded like an attempt of self-conviction. Then came the quartermaster's hesitant voice: '. . . never know, better hang on for a bit . . .'

I stared at the glowing yellow strings of portholes, felt the moist night breeze on my face, swayed to the gentle motion of the boat, ran my fingers over the clammy metal of the bridge rail – delicately, like a blind man. I heard the slap and thump of the waves against our sides, heard their sporadic hiss, sharp as the sizzle of spit on a hot iron. I smelt iodine and damp night air. I also caught a whiff of oil fuel. All my senses were at work, yet I felt semi-conscious and unable to trust my own perceptions.

We surely couldn't play the privateer, not with a bent cigar-tube like ours. Lucky the gun had gone or the Captain might have blazed away, just to put a squib under our friends in the ghost-ship.

'Flood No. 1 tube!'

The Captain's voice sounded cool. He was standing behind and at an angle to me. I could feel his exasperation between my shoulder-blades. This was no attack – it was target practice. The enemy stopped, U-A stopped, minimum range. Our muzzle was virtually touching the bulls-eye.

Two waves broke against the ballast tanks in quick succession. The dull gong-strokes threatened to split my skull. Then silence fell. I could even hear hurried breathing above the murmur of the sea. Not Kriechbaum, surely?

'Right, Quartermaster, I've had enough of this.' The Captain's tone was crisp and incisive. 'Can you see anything?'

'No, sir,' Kriechbaum replied from under his glasses, briskly this time. A momentary pause, then he added at half-volume: 'All the same . . .'

'Well, can you or can't you?'

Kriechbaum's gauntleted hands muffled his diffident reply. 'No, sir. Nothing to be seen.'

'So why get metaphysical?'

The splash of the waves sounded unnaturally loud in the silence that followed.

The Captain seemed to be overcome by a sudden fit of cold anger. 'Very good,' he snapped. 'Stand by No. 1 tube.'

He drew a deep breath. Then, with the lack of emphasis appropriate to a passing remark, he quietly gave the order to fire.

A tremor ran through the boat. The torpedo was on its way.

'No. 1 tube fired,' came the report from below.

The quartermaster lowered his binoculars, the first lieutenant too. We all stood transfixed, staring at the sparkling tiers of ports.

I tried to visualize the effect of our torpedo on such a big ship – a passenger steamer crammed with human beings. They would soon be blown to kingdom come or drowned in their cabins. The fish could hardly miss. The ship was stationary. No aiming off, no sea running. Torpedo setting: two metres below the waterline. Point of aim: precisely amidships, Range: ideal.

I stared at the liner with dilated eyes, picturing a monstrous explosion. I saw the whole ship rear up, saw jagged fragments soar skywards and a giant mushroom of smoke sprout from the white and crimson conflagration.

I held my breath. How long before the hammer-blow fell? The liner's strings of lights began to dance before my straining eyes.

Some words impinged on my consciousness: 'Torpedo not running!'

They came from below – from the hydrophone operator. Not running? But I had distinctly felt the jolt of the torpedo's departure.

'No wonder,' Kriechbaum said with undisguised relief. The hydrophone report betokened a malfunction of some kind. The bomb! That was it, the shock-wave must have been too much for the torpedo's delicate mechanisms to withstand.

Now what? No. 2 tube, No. 3, No. 4?

'Very good,' I heard the Captain say, 'we'd better have a go with No. 5.' His voice sharpened. 'Stand by stern tube.'

The requisite engine and steering orders calmly, as if the whole manœuvre were part of an exercise drill.

No. 5 . . . The Captain obviously didn't trust the rest of the torpedoes in the forward compartment and was pinning his faith on the stern tube.

So he wasn't going to leave well alone. Signs from heaven weren't enough for the Old Man – he needed a dig in the rĩbs. U-A got slowly under way and began to turn. By degrees the illuminated ship swung to starboard. In another two or three minutes she would be right astern and well in line for a torpedo from No. 5.

'There they are!'

I almost jumped. The quartermaster had yelled straight into my right ear.

'Where?' snarled the Captain.

'There, sir – I'm sure I saw a boat.' Kriechbaum pointed into the gloom.

My eyes watered from staring across the dark expanse. I could see it too, now: an object fractionally darker than the surrounding sea.

A moment later we had it astern between us and the lights

of the ship. The dark shape stood out clearly against the dancing reflections. A boat – no doubt about it.

'Are they crazy?' I heard the Captain say. 'Putting out in a cutter, without lights . . .'

I stared blankly at the dark blob. For brief moments, I could see half-a-dozen black excrescences silhouetted against the glow from the ship.

'Coxswain and two men stand by on deck,' the Captain ordered. 'Spotlight on the bridge.'

A medley of voices issued from the conning-tower.

'Get a move on!'

The cable had snagged on something. Kriechbaum reached through the hatch and came up with a portable spotlight.

I seemed to hear the splash of oars.

Suddenly the spotlight picked up the cutter's bow. It reared out of the water with cinematic unreality, then vanished into a trough. Only the head of the man in the stern remained visible. He threw up his forearm to shield himself from the glare.

'Watch it, Coxswain,' shouted the Captain. 'Keep her well clear!'

'Jesus wept!' Another voice in my ear, almost as startling as the quartermaster's unexpected yell. It was the Chief. I hadn't noticed his arrival on the bridge.

The cutter rose again. In addition to the helmsman, I counted six shapeless figures bent over their oars.

The coxswain aimed his boathook at the cutter like a lance.

Confused shouts. The coxswain chivvied his fender-bearers along the casing with a barrage of oaths. An oar splintered. The cutter's helmsman gesticulated wildly with his free hand. He seemed to be responsible for most of the shouting.

'Look out!' bellowed the coxswain. 'Watch it, you clumsy bastards . . .'

The Captain just stood there, silent.

'Bridge!' the coxswain shouted. 'Can you shine that light on the casing? You're blinding them.'

The cutter fell away again until five or six metres of water yawned between us. Two men had risen to their feet, the helmsman and someone I hadn't spotted before. That made eight in all.

Meanwhile the coxswain had received reinforcements. Next time the cutter swooped towards us, the two men leapt for our casing in quick succession. The first stumbled and would have fallen if the coxswain hadn't saved him. The second fell short and landed on one knee, but one of our seamen grabbed him by the scruff of his neck like a rabbit. The first visitor stumbled into a bomb-torn hole in the gratings, the second tripped and fell heavily against the gun pivot. There was an audible thud.

Somebody behind me said: 'I bet that hasn't improved his looks.' The coxswain swore.

The two muffled figures climbed stiffly up the side of the conning-tower. They were wearing old-fashioned kapok life-jackets, hardly an aid to agility.

'*Buenas noches,*' I heard.

The bridge was suddenly crowded. An unintelligible torrent of words descended on us. The shorter of the two men flung his arms about like a marionette.

Little could be seen of either man's face between collar and sou'wester. Their life-jackets had ridden up so high during their recent exertions that the arms of the second man, who was not gesticulating, stuck out like casserole handles.

'Take it easy, gentlemen,' the Captain said in English. 'Downstairs, please.' He flapped his hands soothingly.

'They certainly sound like Spaniards,' the quartermaster said.

Despite their small stature, the two men were so bundled up that they found it hard to squeeze through the hatch.

The light in the control-room was sufficient for a preliminary inspection. One visitor, apparently the captain, was plumpish and wore a small moustache. The other man was half-a-head taller and swarthy-complexioned. They both stared round as though desperately searching for a bolt-hole. I noticed for the first time that the plump one was bleeding from a nasty cut over the eye. Three parallel threads of crimson were trickling down his cheek-bone.

Isenberg muttered: 'Man, are they scared!'

He was stating the obvious. I'd never seen such abject terror. Then I realized what a fearsome sight we must be, with our glittering eyes, gaunt faces and matted beards. A band of savages in a mechanical jungle . . . What was more, we probably stank like the plague. Most of us were still wearing the underclothes which had graced our bodies three months earlier. These two were fresh from rosewood saloons, carpeted passageways and deckheads hung with chandeliers. Shades of the *Weser* . . . Had we surprised them at the dinner-table? Not that, at least. It was the middle of the night.

'Anyone'd think we were going to cut their throats,' Isenberg added softly.

The Captain stared at the gesticulating foreigner as if he were a creature from another planet. Why didn't someone say something? We all stood in a circle round the two twitching puppets, gazing at them in silence. The corpulent captain brandished both arms and continued to fire volley after volley of unintelligible syllables.

I felt a sudden surge of fury. I could have leapt at the jabberer's throat and throttled him, mashed his balls with my knee-cap. I didn't recognize the voice that issued from my own lips. 'You goddamned bastard!' I heard myself snarl. 'Asking for it like that!'

The Captain glanced at me curiously. As for the Spaniard, his response to my outburst was one of sheer terror. I wasn't capable of expressing the reason for my fury, but I knew what it was: the idea that he had nearly made murderers of us – that he had simply failed to react, kept the Captain waiting for an hour, pulled across to us in that toy rowing-boat instead of lowering a launch, not bothered to show a light.

The Spaniard had also been struck dumb. His eyes darted from face to face. *'Gutte Mann, gutte Mann!'* he stammered suddenly. Not knowing the most suitable person to propitiate with this grotesque form of address, he revolved on his own axis, ungainly as a bear in his life-jacket and still clasping his oilskin pouch of ship's papers under one arm. This he now withdrew in order to perform a sort of hands-up. We followed the pouch with our eyes.

The Captain reached for it. His grim silence triggered a fresh barrage of lamentations, but he coldly cut them short. 'The name of your ship?' he asked in English.

'Reina Victoria, Reina Victoria!' squeaked the Spaniard.

All eagerness to please, he rose on tiptoe to point out the name on the papers.

A sudden hush fell. After a while the Captain lowered the papers and looked up. 'Number One, you speak Spanish. Tell this gentleman his ship doesn't exist.'

The first lieutenant, who had been watching the scene with a complete absence of expression, seemed to emerge from a trance. His wet cucumber of a face flushed crimson as he directed some rusty Spanish over the stranger's shoulder. The Spaniard's eyes widened. He looked this way and that, trying to catch the speaker's eye, but his life-jacket bulked too high for him to do so without pivoting his entire body. He now had his back towards me, and that was when I saw it.

Stencilled in small capitals across the bottom of his life-jacket was the name *South Carolina*. I felt a wave of exultation. Now we had him! The Old Man was right after all – an American masquerading as a Spaniard . . .

I coughed to attract the Captain's attention and ran my finger along the hem of the life-jacket. 'Something interesting here, sir. It says *South Carolina*.'

The little man spun round as if a scorpion had stung him and loosed a deluge of words at us.

The Captain stared at him with a puzzled frown. Then he turned to the first lieutenant. 'Well?' he snapped. 'What's all that about?'

'*South Carolina*,' stammered the first lieutenant, 'that's what she used to be called.' The Spaniard, who was hanging on his words, punctuated each one with a vigorous nod. 'They re-named her *Reina Victoria*. She was bought from the Americans five years ago.'

The Captain and the Spaniard stared at each other. The silence was so complete that individual drops of condensation could be heard falling into the bilge.

The quartermaster, who was bending over the chart-table, looked up. 'He's right, sir. 14,000 g.r.t.' His finger pointed to an entry in the Register.

The Captain's eyes roamed from Kriechbaum to the Spaniard and back again.

'Would you mind repeating that?' he said finally, in a voice like a razor.

'She's listed in the supplement, sir,' Kriechbaum said. When the Captain still failed to react, he added in an undertone: 'The first lieutenant may have omitted to look there.'

The Captain clenched his fists and stared fixedly at the first lieutenant, fighting a heroic battle for self-control. At last he said: 'I demand an explanation!'

The first lieutenant turned uncertainly to Kriechbaum. He reached the chart-table in two faltering strides and sagged against it like a wounded man.

A cold shiver seemed to run through the Captain. Before the first lieutenant could say anything, he turned back to the Spaniard with a twisted grin on his face. Noticing the change at once, the Spaniard started gabbling again. '*South Carolina* American ship – *Reina Victoria* Spanish ship . . .' He repeated the formula five or six times. Little by little, the fear ebbed from his face.

'Quartermaster,' said the Captain, 'take a look at these

papers.' Before Kriechbaum could examine them, the Spanish captain was off again: *'Dos mil pasajeros por America del Sur – Buenos Aires!'*

The Captain drew a deep breath and expelled it with a cart-horse flutter of the lips. His whole body seemed to subside. Then he slapped the Spaniard on the back. The eyes of the other man, who must have been the first officer, lit up like a Christmas-tree. His mouth contracted and expanded alternately. Purse and stretch, purse and stretch – undoubtedly a nervous tic. I hadn't noticed it before.

A complete change had come over the Captain. He seemed to have forgotten all about the first lieutenant. A bottle of cognac and three glasses appeared as if by magic. 'Any excuse is better than none,' he said. The Spaniard, who construed this as a toast, refused to be outdone. After treating us to some more gibberish, he raised his glass and uttered a triple cry of *"Eil 'Itler!"*

The first lieutenant had gone as white as a sheet. He stammeringly did his best to translate what the Spaniard was saying. 'The captain thought – he thought we were a British submarine on patrol. That's why he took his time. He didn't hurry till he realized we weren't British. He says the first boat they lowered broke adrift . . .'

The Spaniard nodded like a rocking-horse and repeated *'Si, si!'* innumerable times.

'. . . broke loose and drifted away. He begs your pardon.'

'Beg pardon is rich!' said the Captain. 'He ought to go down on his knees and thank the flyer who buggered our fish. Perhaps you'd like to inform him that it's no fault of yours he isn't playing the harp by now – him and his crew and two thousand passengers. You damn nearly had them on your conscience, if it means anything to you.'

The first lieutenant's mouth dropped open. He was utterly at a loss, unable even to control his jaw-muscles.

A few minutes later the Spanish captain returned to the cutter escorted by his companion. With loud cries and sweeping gestures he offered us a consignment of gramophone records and fruit. Only half an hour and we should have the lot. The latest records! Spanish music! Flamenco! Lovely fresh fruit, any amount of it – enough for the whole crew!

'Piss off, you old twit!' shouted one of the seamen. He spread his legs and pushed the cutter away from our ballast tank like someone practising the splits. The coxswain accelerated the Spaniards' departure with a boathook. Oars splashed into the water. I heard fragments of Spanish, then something that sounded like 'Wiedersehen'.

'Are you crazy?' yelled the coxswain. The cutter soon dwindled to a dark speck.

'Crazy's the word,' fumed Kriechbaum. 'Fancy carrying no lights! Lucky we spotted them in time.'

We all stared after the Spaniards, but the cutter had vanished without a trace. It was as if the inky sea had engulfed them. U-A wallowed heavily from side to side.

The Captain gave some engine and steering orders and went below. Following him down, I witnessed his next encounter with the first lieutenant.

'Are you aware – have you got the wit to realize – what you damn nearly did? What *I* nearly did because my paragon of a Number One can't be relied on to perform a simple little chore like searching the Register properly? I'll tell you something for free: you deserve to be court-martialled.'

If the first lieutenant lived up to his principles, I thought, he'd go and shoot himself. Luckily for him, the only pistol on board was locked in the Captain's cubby-hole.

Hubbub in the POs' mess: 'Kriechbaum smelt a rat straight away.' – 'The Number One didn't half get a bollocking!' – 'Jesus, we'd really have been for the high-jump!' – 'Typical of the Old Man. Shoot first and ask questions afterwards.' – 'Man, were they lucky!' – 'Half-asleep, too. Fancy a big tub like that with no launch!' – 'Boy, oh boy, what a twit!' The last remark was, I rather feared, aimed at the first lieutenant.

Hours later in the control-room, the Captain recapitulated. 'It was a chapter of accidents. If the torpedo hadn't failed, it would have been the *Athenia* all over again . . .'

Two minutes' silence. Still chewing on his pipe-stem, he added: 'Just shows you, doesn't it? Human life hangs by a . . . oh, balls to it!' Obviously, the whole subject gave him qualms. He was trying to justify himself to himself. 'All the same, it looked pretty open and shut. They *did* keep us waiting – we gave them ample time. They behaved like cretins.'

'Yes, on the assumption they'd been stopped by a Brit. We flashed them in English, after all. The idea of a U-boat never occurred to them.'

The Captain sighed. 'That's what comes of showing off your languages.'

'They must have wet themselves when they saw who we were.'

He didn't speak for a full five minutes. Then he said: 'Another thing – we can't measure the output of our transmitter. Perhaps Kernével never received our enquiry. The aerial duct was flooded, apart from anything else. Baah! Damaged equipment and an incompetent Number One – too much of a good thing.'

Not to mention the state of our nerves, I added silently. Only Kriechbaum had emerged from the affair with credit. Cool, cautious and calculating, that was Kriechbaum. He had refused to be browbeaten into backing a superior officer's judgement against his own.

The Captain's fussy pipe-sucking was getting on my nerves. 'By God,' I blurted out, 'just think of the rumpus. We'd really have been in trouble . . .'

'No, we wouldn't,' the Captain said curtly.

I couldn't fathom what he meant. He obviously intended to say more, but the silence became unendurable. At last I said : 'I don't understand.'

'Don't you? No problem – we'd have had to make a clean sweep, that's all. It's a classic situation . . .' He paused before adding in an undertone : 'There wouldn't have been any survivors.'

I froze. What was he saying? My look of bewilderment must have prompted him to continue.

'I mean, it's just the sort of set-up you won't find in the rule book. You're on your own. Senior officer's discretion – that's what they call it.'

He made a circular gesture with his pipe-stem, strenuously searching for the right words. 'They hadn't radioed – they knew we'd have detected it, under normal circumstances. If the torpedo had run true and hit the target, the *Reina Victoria* would have struck a mine, so to speak. What's more, she'd have gone down too fast to use her radio. We couldn't have let it look like the work of a German submarine. No alternative, I'm afraid. Like it or not, you have to wipe the slate clean.'

The Captain was sucking at his pipe again. He raised his eyes from the deck, hauled himself erect and stretched. 'It's all or nothing in this business,' he muttered as he stumped off to the wardroom.

I shuddered at the gruesome significance of his cliché. Instantly, I was haunted by visions of life-boats riddled with machine-gun bullets, arms flung up, waves tinged with red, faces aghast with horrified disbelief. My brain whirled at the remembrance of half-heard conversations in the Bar Royal. Dead men tell no tales, hard luck and all that, but it's them or us . . .

My teeth chattered uncontrollably. What more? What more

had to happen before we plumbed the ultimate depths? A sort of sob travelled the length of my body. I clenched my fists and gritted my teeth, choking it back until the lower half of my face was an aching mask. At that moment the Captain appeared.

'Hey,' he said gently, 'what's the matter?'

'Nothing,' I ground out. 'I'm all right.'

He handed me a mug of apple-juice. I held it in both hands and took a long pull. 'Turn in,' I said. 'Think I'd better turn in.'

'Biscay . . . I hope to God we make it!' Seaman Dufte was almost lynched for uttering these words in the fore-ends. No appeals to the Almighty, no jogging the table on which our house of cards reposed. Who knew what further ailments could afflict our crippled hulk? The Captain must have his reasons for hugging the coast. 'On escape gear!' hung unspoken in the air.

Enemy aircraft were our chief dread. If the RAF spotted us now, we could kiss the girls goodbye – everyone knew that. A crash dive was out of the question. Times had changed. We now prayed for bad weather, but only moderately bad. A real storm could spell our undoing.

Things would seem even blacker tomorrow, when the mainland fell away and the crossing of Biscay began. How did we expect to make it without being sighted from the air? The RAF kept Biscay under close surveillance. And what if the Captain's suspicions were well founded – if British pilots now had a gadget which would render us visible on the darkest of nights?

What was the date today? Today – the word had lost its meaning. It was daytime when we crept along submerged and night-time when we travelled on the surface. At present my watch said 10 o'clock and the motors were humming, so it must be 10 a.m.

What day of the week, though? My brain wrestled with the problem. I felt drugged. At last a word took shape: calendar. The calendar would tell me what day it was. Besides, the chart-stowage was hard on my buttocks. Better go to the wardroom. The wardroom – that was where the calendar hung!

My legs wobbled. I seemed to be walking on stilts. Buck up, I told myself, make an effort.

The hydrophone operator was staring stupidly into space. He looked like a porcupine-fish in an aquarium.

I got to the wardroom and braced my thighs against the

table. Quite a good way of standing, really. Not uncomfortable.

Good God, what did the calendar say? 5 December? And the rest! I started to rip off the sheets one by one. Off with the 9th – that could go into my private scrap-book. A day worth remembering. The barograph strip and the calendar sheet: eloquent souvenirs, cheap at half the price. 11 December. Off with that too. Lots of bangs on the 12th. Another memento. The 19th – we must have been on the sea-bed by then. Or was it the 20th? 21st . . . Behold the 22nd – today. So it was Monday, QED.

Someone behind me said: 'Chrismas Eve, the day after tomorrow.' I swallowed hard. Sentimentality? The usual Christmas emotions? The feast of love, celebrated at sea in a battered U-boat? Anything for a change. After all, we were splendidly equipped for the feast of love. Nothing but the best for our boys in blue! Contingency planning, Navy style: the collapsible Christmas-tree that had come aboard with the rest of our stores . . . Christmas – how would the Captain handle it? But then, the Old Man would have more important things to worry about.

He was planning, provisionally, to head for La Rochelle. Up the Gironde to Bordeaux was another possibility, but Bordeaux, though further south, was no nearer. 400 nautical miles separated us from La Rochelle – a 400-mile beeline across the Bay of Biscay. That meant another 36 hours under the most favourable conditions. Given that we had to remain dived during the day, the sum looked worse than that. We might take as long as three days and nights to cover the distance, allowing for meteorological and mechanical vicissitudes.

The Captain and the quartermaster were bedevilled by other worries still. I only caught snatches of their joint deliberations: 'Getting in there, that's going to be the problem . . . not a clue . . . bloody narrow . . . masses of obstructions . . . shallow approaches . . . risk of mines . . .'

The general mood was subdued. Everyone seemed to tread softly, as if a lurking enemy might pounce at the sound of a careless footfall.

I watched the men who passed through the control-room. They all tried to sneak a glance at the chart. Nobody ventured to ask how many miles it was to base – that would have been a sign of jangling nerves – but the same thought ran through every head: Biscay, graveyard of a thousand ships, notorious for the violence of its storms and the frequency with which our enemies patrolled it from the air . . .

Kriechbaum returned to the chart-table and started scribbling on bits of paper. I took my courage in both hands.

'How long to go?'

Our ace dead-reckoner wagged his head from side to side. His only immediate response was 'Hm . . .' I waited for the inevitable qualifications and provisos, but he was more direct than usual.

'Well, now . . .' I watched him in profile until he eventually gave tongue. 'At least sixty-six hours, according to my calculations. That's to say, sixty-six in all, counting the time we spend dived.'

Some of the men wouldn't look you in the face – their eyes veered aside. One of the stokers flinched convulsively when I addressed him. Dufte had developed a nervous twitch of the left eyelid. In an effort to control it, he screwed up his eye and contorted the left side of his face. Fortunately for his self-esteem, he didn't know how repellent he looked. There weren't any mirrors around.

I was told in the fore-ends that Ario had been plagued by an additional fear while we lay on the sea-bed. His kitbag at St Nazaire contained an assortment of contraceptives, some of esoteric design. He listed them : 'Rubber-studded ones, clit-ticklers, you name it . . .' It was this abundant store which had preyed so heavily on his mind. 'I mean, think of that little lot being forwarded to your next-of-kin! I tell you this much : next time we sail I'm going to blow the fucking things up and stick a pin in them.'

Böckstiegel sought to reassure him. 'No need to worry, mate, Flotilla takes care of that. They weed out all the filthy postcards and French letters – anything that wouldn't appeal to widows and grey-haired mothers. I've seen them at it. The casualty officer's an expert. Before your gear goes into the personal effects bag, it's kosher. Take my word for it.'

Benjamin, who deplored waste, wasn't satisfied. 'What does he do with all the French letters? They're private property, aren't they?'

'He makes a list of them, you idiot – in triplicate. Then he files it.'

'Trust the Navy,' said Schwalle.

The Captain flitted from the engine-room to the fore-ends and back to the control-room, shadowed by the Chief. He was trying to form a detailed picture of U-A's condition, though not every item of damage could be visually checked. The frames, for example, were largely concealed by fixtures and fittings.

'She looks like a write-off to me,' I heard him mutter during one of his tours.

The quartermaster reported us on a level with Cape Ortegal, so the crossing of Biscay was about to begin. The first lieutenant was readmitted to the Captain's councils, possibly from a merciful desire to allay his sense of total annihilation. A precise passage plan was worked out, though its validity depended on certain factors. Foremost among them: the continued health of our diesel.

The Captain had barely subsided on the wardroom settee when a sentence emerged stillborn from his lips. 'Not very seasonal . . .' It wasn't hard to guess where the shoe pinched.

Next, he tried to coax me from my reserve by clearing his throat. What was I supposed to say – that nobody was in the mood for Christmas at sea?

'Oh, balls to it!' he said suddenly. 'We'll postpone the festivities and be damned. No Christmas Eve for us till we're back on dry land. Unless, of course, you've set your heart on reading the lesson?'

'No,' I said. Nothing more humorous occurred to me.

'Well, then.' He sounded pleased. 'We'll just pretend it isn't time yet – for Christmas, I mean.'

Christmas . . . Something had always gone wrong at Christmas-time ever since I was fourteen. Glum Christmases, dramatic Christmases, over-emotional Christmases fraught with tears and visits from the police. And then there were the boozy Christmases . . .

Stem the flood of memories, check the surge of emotion. The Old Man was right. Why wallow in maudlin sentimentality? Simply let the day pass normally. The day? What was I saying? Better not think big – better think in terms of hours. Don't tempt providence, my friend, duck the thought of Christmas altogether. No festivities for us – it was out of the question.

The Captain seemed quite refreshed. One problem less. I was only curious to know how he proposed to announce his postponement with the intercom out of action.

'Better tell the POs,' he said. 'They'll pass the word.'

The solitary engine wasn't running as smoothly. Snags had arisen. Nothing serious, but enough to worry and exasperate the Chief.

He secreted himself in the engine-room for hours on end

— 'cosseting the thing', as Kriechbaum put it, meaning the diesel. Not even Kriechbaum could bring himself to utter the word 'engine', just in case he provoked the gods.

It was even quieter on board, now that the men knew we had left the land behind us. Their nervousness manifested itself in a tendency to jump at innocuous noises. The Chief provided a supreme example of this. Even at the best of times, he reacted to infinitesimal and, by ordinary standards, inaudible sounds from the engine-room with the sensitivity of a dog yapping at the rustle of a biscuit-packet. This time he surpassed himself. While we were sitting together in the wardroom, he leapt to his feet with a suddenness that turned my blood to ice, listened for a moment, wild-eyed, and dashed into the control-room. Pandemonium ensued. I could hear the Chief's voice uncharacteristically raised in anger. He was beside himself with rage.

'Damn it all, man . . . must be crazy . . . since when . . . put the bloody things away . . . be quick about it!'

He returned to his corner, breathing hard and scowling. I didn't like to enquire what the matter was. Ten minutes later I casually asked Isenberg the reason for the uproar.

Apparently the Vicar had been working on some knives with polishing compound. This produced an abrasive whisper which the Chief had failed to identify.

24 December. We were still afloat. We had covered a fair distance. Our germ of hope had put forth a sickly little shoot. The weather was being kind beyond belief. Biscay normally produced some terrible storms in December, but the most we had to contend with was wind force 4-5 and sea 3 — one degree less than the wind as usual. Conditions could hardly have been better. We had almost reached the middle of the Bay, the engine was holding up, and we didn't — touch wood — have a hunter-killer group on our heels.

Reason enough to display a little optimism, but no. Everyone slunk around with long faces. The Captain was monosyllabic too, and the Captain's moods were infectious. He never counted his chickens, so he may simply have been practising what he preached. The trouble was, the men quickly lapsed into dejection without an occasional word of encouragement from him. Melancholia reigned. I decided to revisit the fore-ends after lunch — perhaps spirits would be higher there.

I could hardly eat for fatigue and nervous tension. The Chief didn't touch a thing, and the others spent longer staring at their food than eating it. The steward was left with a collection of half-empty plates to clear away. He didn't like that at all. Half-empty plates were awkward to stack.

The fore-ends looked terrible. I'd never seen such a mess, presumably because the coxswain thought it better to turn a blind eye. Gone were the tinted bulbs and bordello atmosphere. Off-duty ratings lay sprawled on the deck. Apathy and fatalism were rife. The men scarcely exchanged a word.

A few hours later, the whole boat was clean as a new pin. The Captain had torn a strip off the coxswain.

'Can't afford to get sloppy at this stage,' he muttered to me as Behrmann left the wardroom with his tail between his legs.

Good thinking. Cling to ship's routine, no seasonal fuss, keep the tear-ducts closed, dispel any premature thoughts of home. Once let things slide and anything might happen. Frayed nerves plus emotional self-indulgence? Nobody was proof against that combination.

'La Spezia,' the Captain mused; 'we'd just have made it in time.'

Oh God, was he back on the Christmas tack?

I was assailed by memories of last Christmas at the Hotel Majestic, with its Flotilla-organized plethora of food and drink. Long white tables decorated with pine-needles instead of German fir. For each of us, a star-shaped cardboard dish filled with spiced biscuits, Russian bread, candies and a chocolate Santa. A full-throated roar of voices: *'Oh du fröhliche, oh du selige, gnadenbringende Weihnachtszeit!'* Then the Flotilla captain's address. Hearts pulsing in unison with the hearts pulsing at home. Our ever-loving Führer, our traditional German Christmas, our mighty German Reich, and above all – to revert – our noble and illustrious Führer . . . A scraping of chairs: *'Sieg Heil – Heil – Heil!'* Finally, the monumental booze-up. Descent into slushy sentimentality, alcoholic collapse, the hung-over misery of the morning after . . .

Our plans had crystallized. We were going to try for the nearest available base – in other words, not St Nazaire but La Rochelle, now twenty-four hours away.

The Captain rigidly adhered to ship's routine. By rights, brothel regulations should have been read out forty-eight hours before entering port. This was really the first lieutenant's job, but the Captain absolved him – an act of grace, because the wording made it something of an ordeal. In the absence of an intercom system, the second lieutenant was detailed to refresh the crew's memory in relays, compartment by compartment. He did it well. His tone was boyishly earnest, as befitted the reading of a Flotilla Order, but nobody could doubt that he considered the entire rigmarole a joke in poor taste.

The control-room PO was painting victory pennants. He had already finished one bearing the figure '8,500' – a memento of our first plump victim from the flock.

The first lieutenant and the Chief were poring over some paperwork in the wardroom. Dockyard requisitions, fuel consumption figures, torpedo firing reports. It wouldn't have surprised me to hear the clatter of a typewriter.

I stole almost hourly glances at the chart, tempted each time to make some small and furtive addition to the pencil-line that crept towards La Rochelle. Fear relaxed its grip with every mile we put behind us.

Snatches of conversation drifted through the half-open door of the fore-ends bulkhead. The men's spirits seemed to have revived. I even heard someone in the CPOs' mess enquiring who would be signing leave passes. 'Don't know yet,' the coxswain replied. It was incredible. We still had a whole night of uncertainty before us, and someone next door was worrying about shore leave.

What I heard in the POs' mess had lost its power to surprise me.

'Hey, Pilgrim, you've been to La Rochelle. What are the knocking-shops like?'

The PO electrician shrugged. 'How should I know?'

'You're a dead loss,' Frenssen said, scowling. 'Why the hell can't you answer a sensible question?'

Not a trace of pre-Christmas spirit, thank God.

I went on the bridge at about 1 a.m.

'Roughly another two-and-a-half hours to escort rendezvous point,' Kriechbaum reported.

Escort R/V point? Were we already so close to the French coast?

'That means we'll be there nice and early,' the Captain said. 'First thing we'll do is lie low and study the traffic.' He turned to me. 'Well, getting itchy? We aren't in any rush, not now.'

I could only heave a sigh. It all seemed to have happened once before, millennia ago.

The night air was like cold silk. Did I only imagine that it smelt of land? Perhaps we would soon see lights ashore

. . . No, of course not – La Rochelle wasn't Lisbon. Everything was blacked out here. The lighthouses along the French coast had doused their beacons.

'How about turning in for an hour?' the Captain suggested.

'It certainly wouldn't do any harm, sir.'

I asked the quartermaster to wake me when he was relieved and went below shortly after the Captain.

Kriechbaum shook me vigorously by the arm. 'It's nice and calm, Lieutenant. Hardly any wind.'

I was back on the bridge in two minutes.

The skyline was sharp, especially in the paling east. The first lieutenant turned and called down the hatch. 'Tell the Captain: dawn!'

The Captain, who appeared a minute later, conducted a silent survey.

'Well, we'll give it a bit longer,' he said at last, but I could sense his uneasiness. He repeatedly cocked his head and cast wary glances at the sky. In the east, the horizon displayed a margarine-yellow streak as thick as a finger The darkness swiftly melted. Ten minutes later the Captain spoke again.

'That's just about it, I suppose.'

The sea was smooth. We might have been gliding across a pond. The echo-sounder was in use. A steady flow of reports came from below. 'Thirty metres . . . twenty-eight . . .' The depth dwindled to twenty and remained more or less constant.

'Perfect,' said the Captain. 'Just what we need. Very good, Number One, let's take her down. It's getting too light for comfort.'

'Diving stations!' Another full sweep of the dark silky sea and we all climbed leisurely below.

'Try and put her down gently, Chief. Twenty metres should be all right, shouldn't it?'

We settled on the bottom with a bump no harder than that of an aircraft touching down.

'*Tiens, tiens!*' The Captain was evidently feeling the proximity of France. I made a note to ask the quartermaster if we were on good French sand or still in international waters.

But the Captain's exclamation meant something. I became aware of some rasping, scraping sounds. There was a muffled thud like a fist hitting a wooden door. Another blow reverberated dully through the boat and was drowned by a shrill groan. The scuffing and rasping began again.

'Quite a current,' said the Captain.

The Chief nodded. 'Yes, and the bottom isn't as smooth as it might be.'

So the thuds signified the presence of rocks. The current was nudging us across the sea-bed.

'Try and hold her down, Chief.'

'Right, sir.'

I heard water rumble into our trimming tanks. We were putting on weight.

'Good. Let's hope we're pointing the right way.'

Silence on board, broken only by the plip-plop of condensation. The watch below had already turned in. As soon as it was fully light the Captain proposed to go to periscope depth – 14 metres. He gave no indication of what he would do then. Approaching the coast unescorted and without a barrage-breaker would be a ticklish business.

Just as my right leg was poised above the sill of the after bulkhead door, there came another thud.

'Damnation,' snapped the Captain. 'We can't be lying head to tide. We'll have to try and screw her round.'

With half an ear, I heard tanks being blown. Another thump made the hull resound. Then came a hum of motors and some steering orders. All seemed to be well.

Suddenly : 'Propellers bearing three-zero-zero, sir. Growing louder.' The hydrophone operator's voice sounded curiously remote.

The Captain had raised one eyebrow like an actor miming surprise. He stood in the centre of the control-room and listened. The Chief stood behind them, half-obscured. I froze too.

Now the Captain swallowed. I distinctly saw his throat contract.

'Piston engines,' reported the hydrophone operator.

The Captain squatted in the passage outside the hydrophone booth and borrowed the head-set. His rounded back was towards us.

'Submarine diesels,' he murmured. 'Damned if they aren't.'

He handed back the head-set. Hinrich listened for another minute, watched by the Captain.

'Well ?'

'Submarine diesels, sir – definitely.'

'German or British, that's the question . . . Very good, Number One, recognition signal ready. Fire as soon as we surface. Bearing ?'

'Steady at two-seven-zero, sir.'

'Stand by AA gun action. Number One, follow me up right away.' From one moment to the next, the control-room hummed with activity. The ammunition locker was opened.

Firework displays on our own doorstep? Were we really going to blaze away with the Oerlikon?

'Pipped at the post . . .' I heard Frenssen mutter.

Pilgrim rounded on him. 'Shut up, you bloody fool!'

The Captain had his hand on the ladder. 'All clear?'

'Yes, sir.'

'Very good. Surface.'

'Blow all main ballast!'

I was standing immediately under the hatch when the flare-pistol popped. Someone was still climbing the ladder, but I glimpsed two balls of fire, one red, one white, between his flank and the coaming of the upper lid. Christmas decorations – very seasonal. I waited with bated breath.

'Good,' I heard the Captain say. 'Signal acknowledged. Run in closer, Number One. Let's take a look at our friend.'

The Chief peered up the conning-tower.

'Man on the bridge?' I called.

'Come ahead!'

It took me a few moments to spot the other U-boat in the early morning murk. Approaching us bow-on, she might have been mistaken for a drifting cask.

'Pass the lamp up, and hurry!' called the Captain. A minute later: 'Very good, Zeitler, make a few polite introductions.'

The seaman PO had already aimed his lamp at the other boat and was clacking out our call sign.

From across the water, another lamp flashed received-and-understood. Then I heard our own shutter clacking again. The quartermaster read out the reply: 'U-XW Lieutenant Bremer.'

Zeitler stood fast, every muscle tensed for another signal. The Captain rubbed his hands delightedly. 'Fantastic luck! They're bound to be expected. All we have to do is tag along.'

Kriechbaum beamed. A weight had fallen from his shoulders. Piloting us into La Rochelle would have been his responsibility.

'Just a question of waiting for their escort to turn up. Ask them when it's due.'

Zeitler worked the shutter and the reply came back within seconds. They must have had a first-class signaller.

'0800, sir.'

'Now make: "Intend follow you in." They'll be wondering why we aren't expected as well. It must seem odd for us to be knocking on another flotilla's door, especially today.'

The Captain showed no inclination to enlighten them.

The two U-boats had closed during our exchange of signals. We were now within hailing distance. A disembodied megaphone-voice echoed across the water: 'What happened to your gun?'

We stared at each other. The Captain hesitated. Even I took a moment to realize that the others could see us clearly as we could see them, and that there was something odd about our silhouette.

'Bloody silly question,' growled the quartermaster.

The Captain put the megaphone to his mouth and shouted: 'Give you three guesses!' Then he turned to Kriechbaum and said in a normal tone: 'He'd do better to man that flak of his. I don't like this hanging about.'

Kriechbaum took this as a direct summons to ginger up the look-outs. 'Yes, keep your eyes open!'

U-A was suddenly jarred by a muffled but violent explosion. I felt the jolt in my knee-joints. Battery gas, motors, something amiss in the engine-room?

The Captain called down the hatch. 'What's wrong? Hurry up, I'm waiting!'

No word from below. The Captain shot a look of enquiry at Kriechbaum. His voice rose to a bellow. 'I want a damage report – immediately!'

The Chief's head appeared in the open hatch. 'Negative, sir. No damage reported.'

The Captain stared fixedly at him. Had we all gone crazy? A bang like that, and nothing to report?

The lamp across the water started to wink at us. Three mouths spelt out the letters in unison: 'H-a-v-e-s-t-r-u-c-k-m-i-n-e.'

'Take her in closer!'

My blood ran cold. Mines seldom came singly. We could be drifting over a minefield.

I aimed my binoculars at the other U-boat. Nothing to be seen, except that she seemed to have settled a little by the stern. She didn't accord with my mental picture of a mine victim.

U-A's bow swung slowly round. They were signalling again. 'Read it out,' ordered the Captain.

'A-f-t-e-r-e-n-d-s-b-a-d-l-y-h-o-l-e-d-u-n-a-b-l-e-d-i-v-e.'

'One of those blasted magnetic mines, I expect,' the Captain said. 'Probably dropped by a night-flyer.'

Kriechbaum nodded calmly. 'And not the only one, sir, you can bet . . .'

'That settles it. Now we'll damned well have to stay on the surface and give them anti-aircraft protection.'

And drifting through a minefield, I thought.

The quartermaster made no comment. He kept his glasses trained on the other U-boat, betraying no emotion whatever.

'Give them a shout, Kriechbaum. Tell them what we propose to do.'

Kriechbaum raised the megaphone. His message drew a terse 'Thank you!' from our crippled neighbour.

I caught myself balancing on the balls of my feet. We might strike a mine at any moment.

'Quartermaster, make a note: "0615, U-XW struck mine." Tell the telegraphist to try again – maybe he'll have more joy at this range. Make: "U-XW has struck mine. Unable dive. Request escort soonest. Will remain at R/V." '

We could do nothing except wait and watch the sky grow lighter.

'I reckon her shafts must be bent,' the Captain mused. 'If the main engines had bought it the motors would be some use.'

We now had our backs to the east. All the figures round me looked as grey as if they had been smeared with wood-ash.

No engine noise, no movement, no vibrations underfoot. We were drifting like a piece of flotsam. Fear festered inside me as it had done for the past half-hour. The silence was the worst thing. I hardly dared to clear my throat. If only our diesel was running – I longed to hear it again.

Buoys – a whole line of them. Why not tie up? The answer came to me even before I framed the question. U-XW was immobilized. We had to drift wherever she drifted, like a Siamese twin.

'Time?'

'0710, sir.'

I wasn't alone in my fear. We had stopped looking at each other, almost as if ocular contact might trigger an explosion.

I wished I could make myself small, turn into a sea-gull and soar eastwards to safety.

No sign of land. No plumes of smoke yet, either. What were they playing at? Waiting could be agreeable when you knew someone had arranged to collect you, but drifting through a suspected minefield put a different complexion on the matter.

I was suddenly transfixed by a strident yell from the starboard after look-out.

'Aircraft bearing green one-two-zero!'

Our heads jerked round at the twitch of an invisible wire. 'Alarm aircraft! Angle of sight?'

'One-zero, sir. Looks like a Halifax.'

I dashed below for some ammunition and passed it through the hatch. Our Oerlikon had already started to blaze away for all it was worth. Just our luck! With no way on, U-A was a sitting target. Above the hammering of the pom-poms I heard a sudden deafening explosion. Abruptly, silence fell. The din ceased as though someone had lopped it with a knife.

I scrambled to the bridge and looked round. Where were the others? An expanse of smooth, opaline sea met my eye, featureless except for the distant buoys and a cluster of dark objects drifting on our port quarter. I vaguely heard some engine and steering orders.

U-A's bow swung towards the flotsam.

At last the quartermaster said: 'Direct hit, just forward of the bridge.'

A kind of trance descended on me. Every image seemed blurred by a grey filter. I screwed up my eyes and blinked. The other U-boat had vanished. And the aircraft? Had it dropped its bomb and vanished too? Was it possible? One pass, one bomb, one hit?

They'd be back, I told myself – swarms of them. Why no fighter cover? That fat swine Goering and his big mouth! Where were our gallant airmen?

The sea was a burnished expanse against a sky of dirty pastel violet. No motion – not as much as a ripple. The skyline was razor-sharp. Nothing remained to show where the elongated hull had lain – just a dark blemish on the smooth quicksilver surface. No swirl or surge of water, no drone of engines. Silence!

I couldn't understand why no one was shouting. The absence of sound seemed preposterous. That was what created such an overwhelming impression of unreality. Our bow was now pointing at the cluster. Seen through glasses, it disintegrated into components, individual heads suspended in lifejackets. The crew of our Oerlikon continued to stand there like statues – expressionlessly, as though they too had failed to grasp the truth. Their chests rose and fell in the aftermath of exertion, but that was all.

The coxswain had already stationed himself on the forecasing with five seamen, ready to haul the survivors aboard. His bellowed instructions rent the silence like a rip-saw.

To starboard, the sea became tinged with red. Someone was bleeding profusely. I couldn't bring myself to look. Better watch the sky instead – the plane was bound to return. Bombs, mines, shallow water . . . The dice were loaded against us.

Close behind me, someone muttered: 'Poor buggers. Some Christmas!'

A dripping figure appeared on the bridge and blurted out a few words with his hand to his forehead. It was Bremer, the other captain.

His schoolboyish face twitched spasmodically. Still staring straight ahead, as though hypnotized, he started to sob and blubber. He compressed his lips in an attempt to stop the castanet-beat of his lower jaw, but it was no use. His whole body shook and tears coursed down his cheeks in a steady stream.

The Captain eyed him in chill silence. 'Look, Bremer,' he said at last, 'why not go below?'

Bremer vehemently shook his head.

'Fetch some blankets,' the Captain ordered. Then, brusquely, as if yielding to a sudden fit of anger: 'Hurry, damn you! Get some blankets up here!'

He grabbed the first blanket to be passed through the hatch and draped it round Bremer's trembling shoulders. Bremer started to speak. 'Something caught me round the neck – I didn't shake it off till we hit the water. It was like a snake.'

No diving depth, no barrage-breaker, no anti-aircraft protection, a sea as smooth as glass . . . What about the Halifax? Only one bomb on board? A crate that size would surely carry more than one.

Bremer was still babbling. 'I felt it – I could feel it round my throat like a snake.'

The Captain turned and stared at him as if he were seeing him for the first time. A look of indignation settled on his face.

A stranger on the bridge, swathed in a blanket. The pitiful little group on the fore-casing. The silky, pastel-tinted sea. I felt I should have to rupture a membrane before coming to grips with reality.

What was the rescued captain talking about, anyway? Were his nerves completely shot? No one who saw him on our bridge, ashen-faced and humbly resigned to his fate, would have taken him for a U-boat commander.

'Watch yourself!' shouted Turbo, who was heaving blankets through the hatch. Bremer started violently. He was in the way. Besides, the control-room hand could hardly be expected to recognize him because he belonged to another flotilla.

The Captain's voice was hoarse. He had to cough a couple of times to clear the frog in his throat.

'Well,' he said, 'diving's out.'

Not enough depth, too much current. We would simply continue to drift over miles until the enemy returned in force. Still no fighter cover, even though the other U-boat had been expected. Bugger Goering!

Anchoring – what about anchoring? Anything was preferable to drifting over mines. I flexed my knees. The next one could go up at any minute. Part of me pitied the men in the engine-room, whose sole protection against mines was a thin steel shell.

Surely the Captain couldn't put it off any longer. He'd have to choose: either wait for the RAF to return or damn the mines and take us straight in without the help of a barrage-breaker or minesweeper.

His face assumed its habitual look of dour reflection. At last he gave some engine and steering orders. Slowly, our bow swung to face the rising sun. I thought so – straight in.

I was wrong. The engine remained at Slow One, keeping us head to tide. We were treading water.

No day had ever dawned as fair. Whether it was the solemn exaltation of this Christmas morning or the misery on deck that brought tears to my eyes, sobs welled up inside me. I choked them back. I couldn't let go, not yet.

If only the heavens had swathed themselves in fog and gloom, the pathetic spectacle might have been easier to endure. As it was, the opalescent golden radiance that now filled the sky and impregnated the water contrasted so agonizingly with the knot of bedraggled figures on our deck that I could have wept aloud. They stood below us, herded together like sheep. Each man was draped in a blanket of charcoal-coloured wool. The dawn glow made it hard to distinguish individuals. Two men were still wearing their caps. One of them, tall and slender, looked like the Number One. The other was a CPO, probably the coxswain. The stokers must have been trapped – as usual. All the survivors seemed to be barefoot. One of them had rolled up his trouser-legs like a seaside paddler.

Our own coxswain was trying to salvage an empty raft with the help of two ratings. Six or seven bright yellow rubber dinghies were already stacked beside the conning-tower.

The Captain evidently had no intention of housing anyone below deck. Pointless. We couldn't dive anyway, and there was the possibility of mines to consider. The poor devils would be better off where they were.

Our escort had to turn up some time. The Halifax wouldn't leave it at that – the pilot must long ago have reported that a second U-boat was awaiting the same treatment. Bloody Navy! They couldn't have failed to hear the bangs at La Rochelle, so why no action? Or was any U-boat in the approaches fair game? Had they run out of patrol-boats?

Just below the conning-tower, the wounded were being tended by Herrmann, our part-time sick-bay attendant, and two seamen. An older man from the other boat was in a bad way. His hands were burnt and his head looked like a bloody peg-top. Salt water on raw flesh . . . A shiver ran through me.

Herrmann swathed the crimson head in bandages until only the eyes, nose and mouth showed, Tuareg-fashion. Then he lit a cigarette and stuck it between the Tuareg's teeth. The head nodded its thanks. Other survivors had also lit up. Some were sitting on the battered gratings in their wet clothes.

U-XW's Number One and coxswain scanned the sky unceasingly, but their men seemed indifferent to it. Two or three of them went so far as to release the air from their life-jackets for comfort's sake.

The Captain wanted to know how many we had rescued. I started counting. Twenty-three on the fore-casing, four wounded abaft the conning-tower. In other words, the commander and twenty-seven men: little more than half the original crew.

How calm the sea was . . . A sheet of virgin metal foil. I'd never seen a sea so calm. The air was unruffled by a breath of wind.

Then Kriechbaum shouted: 'Object on the port beam!'

As though magnetized, our glasses swung in the same direction. He was right. A tiny black speck showed up against the blue-grey sheen, unidentifiable at this distance. I lowered my binoculars and blinked. Kriechbaum scrambled on to the master sight and leant back, the glasses poised on his fingertips. Bremer stared stupidly to port with his mouth open.

'Well?' the Captain said impatiently. 'Can you see what it is?'

'No, sir, but it must be more or less where she went down, allowing for the current. We drifted a long way while we were picking up survivors.'

'Hm,' said the Captain.

A minute passed. With sudden decision, he increased speed and gave a steering order. We headed for the almost invisible object.

What on earth could have prompted the Old Man to plough through mine-infested waters for the sake of an orange-box or an old oil-drum? Was he cocking a snook at fate? Hadn't he pushed our luck far enough already?

I crouched slightly with my stomach-muscles tensed and my knee-joints loose.

Seconds dragged by. Then Kriechbaum, who had not lowered his binoculars for an instant, said impassively: 'There's someone in the drink. He's still alive.'

'I thought as much,' the Captain said, just as coolly.

Alive? Thirty or forty minutes must have passed since the sinking of Bremer's boat. We had all strained our eyes to no avail Nothing had remained to mar the mirror-smooth surface when our rescue operations were complete.

The Captain ordered a further increase in speed. The sooner we got there the better. Peering through my binoculars as we approached, I saw him too – a man. His head was clearly visible above the bulge of his life-jacket. Now he raised an arm

The survivors on the fore-casing had crowded forward and were clinging to the jumping-wire. Tightly, I hoped. We couldn't afford a man overboard at this stage. My heart pounded. There he was! Our eagle-eyed quartermaster had known at once that he wasn't a piece of driftwood.

I clambered down the rungs to the fore-casing, eager to see the man they were hauling from the water. You ought to fling your arms round the quartermaster's neck, I wanted to shout. It was a chance in a thousand. Kriechbaum had brains as well as eyes. To a man of his expertise, it was obvious. the flotsam hadn't been drifting any old where but precisely over the spot where U-XW went down.

Now they had him. A youth of not more than eighteen. No shoes, shirt and trousers clinging to his body. Water streamed off him. He sagged against the conning-tower but kept his feet.

I gave him a nod of silent encouragement. Not for me to enquire how he had managed to extricate himself from the sunken boat. He must be a stoker or electrician, probably the only man to escape from the afterpart of the submarine. But why the time-lag? An air-pocket? Only he knew the answer to that.

'My God,' I heard myself say, 'you were lucky!'

He drew a deep breath, sniffed and nodded.

The coxswain appeared with some blankets. I'd never have believed Behrmann could be so gentle. He wrapped them round the boy with almost maternal solicitude. Christ, why had he done it? The youngster folded up with a strangled sob. His teeth started to chatter.

'Give us a fag!' the coxswain snapped to one of our seamen. 'Go on, man, light it! Now hand it over.'

Gently, he lowered the boy to the gratings, settled him with his back against the conning-tower and shoved the cigarette into his mouth.

'There you are, lad. Have a drag.'

'Time?'

'0810, sir.'

And the escort had been due at 0800 . . .

My life-jacket was becoming a nuisance.

Lucky for the men on deck that the day was mild and windless Christmas Day, but far from cold. The sun would impart some warmth when it rose. Meanwhile, the survivors needed something on their feet. A mass of surplus clothing had already been toted up the conning-tower by Behrmann's minions, mainly sweaters. I went below to get some footwear.

Dorian to Isenberg, in the control-room: 'See what I mean about sorting the men from the boys? That lieutenant from the other boat – he's round the twist.'

Halfway through the wardroom I came to a full stop. The first lieutenant had put the typewriter on the table and was about to let fly Words failed me. I obtrusively clicked my tongue but he didn't even look up, just punched three or four keys with a pointed forefinger and kept his unblinking sea-gull gaze focused on the typewriter. I felt like picking up the machine and smashing it over his head. Instead, I muttered Bloody fool!' and squeezed past him on my way to the fore-ends, where I shouted at the occupants with unnecessary vehemence.

'Sea-boots wanted! Come on, you, bear a hand!'

What in God's name was he typing? An arrival report? A declaration for Bremer – a neatly prepared statement confirming that we had taken him on board together with half his crew?

One minute to organize a human chain, another to get the boots moving briskly. I followed the last pair up.

'Escort in sight!' Kriechbaum bellowed, and pointed ahead. Plumes of smoke stained the landward horizon.

The Captain grunted. 'Too late, my friends.'

I heard a rapid clicking sound close to my ear. I turned to look. It was Bremer. His teeth were chattering again.

A chill breeze had sprung up. I shivered.

The sun rose at last. It slid swiftly above a thick band of mallow-coloured cloud and floated like a huge orange into the mother-of-pearl bowl of the sky. The sea turned to watered taffeta. The blue silhouette of the approaching barrage-breaker and her superstructure stood out sharply against the orange ball. Clouds hung above the river-mouth, dove-grey and delicate. Only a narrow streak of yellow light separated their flattened lower margins from the skyline. The sky overhead was a mottled pink and the highest clouds seemed to be trimmed with gold.

I stared with smarting eyes at the sun's ascending disc. A voice inside me began to sing the Vicar's pious jingle:

> 'Wonderful will that day be,
> When, from every sin set free,
> We are led by Jesus' hand
> Into Canaan's Promised Land . . .'

The Captain averted his head so that Bremer wouldn't hear. 'Funny how it's worked out. They were only expecting one boat, and that's all they're getting.' He trained his glasses on the barrage-breaker. 'Handsome-looking tub – must be all of eight thousand tons. Only two small derricks. I wonder where they requisitioned her from. Hello, what's this?' He drawled the last three words on a rising inflection.

I saw what he meant. The barrage-breaker was only the first in a whole procession of ships.

'You do us too much honour, gentlemen,' the Captain muttered.

A light winked at us from the leader.

'She's signalling, sir.'

'So I see, Number Two. Get that lamp. Let's see what she wants.'

The light went out, then started flashing again. The Number Two read off the letters aloud: 'W-e-l-c-o-m-e-b-a-c-k.'

'Very original,' the Captain said drily. 'What else?'

'A-n-y-l-u-c-k?'

The Captain addressed himself to Bremer, who was still cowering in the well of the bridge and seemed to have shrunk in comparison with the rest of us, now craning over the rail.

'That's meant for you.'

Bremer looked bewildered.

'Blabbermouths,' said the second lieutenant. 'They'll be

475

wishing us the compliments of the season, next.'

The Captain came to a decision. 'Never mind, we'll pretend they mean us. Go on, make: "Three fat ones." '

The shutter of our signal lamp clacked. Promptly, a reply came back: 'H-e-a-r-t-i-e-s-t-c-o-n-g-r-a-t-u-l-a-t-i-o-n-s.'

The Captain frowned and chewed his lip. 'What do you think, Kriechbaum – should we put them in the picture?'

'No need to complicate the issue, sir. They'll catch on soon enough.'

If they hadn't already done so, I thought. The survivors on our fore-casing should have been easy enough to spot through glasses. Fancy-dress parties weren't usual in the U-boat arm, nor did U-boats customarily return to base with no gun and a neat stack of rubber dinghies on deck. They must have gathered that something had happened and could happen again at any moment. The RAF were bound to return – they wouldn't leave us unscathed.

I tried to reassure myself. We'd soon be safe from mines, at least, and an attacking aircraft would have to contend with a lot more fire-power than the Halifax had encountered earlier on. The barrage-breaker bristled with anti-aircraft guns and the gaggle of approaching escort vessels must have some pea-shooters of their own. My confidence was not, however, shared by the Captain. I'd seldom seen him so uneasy. Again and again he shot grim glances at the sky, which was slowly turning blue.

'They always know when something's wrong,' said the second lieutenant, meaning the flock of gulls which now soared round the boat.

They steeped their plumage in golden light and uttered shrill cries of reproach. Not a wing stirred, but their inquisitive heads swivelled this way and that as they planed above us.

The Captain gave the engine and steering orders himself. I had no ears for them and only half an eye for the approaching ships. What really astounded me was the effrontery with which their funnels belched smoke. Ahead of us, the pastel morning sky was wreathed in a dense pall of vapour. It might almost have been designed to divert an enemy's attention from us and focus it on our escorts.

Chores kept me for the next half-hour. Then, just as we were passing her, I caught sight of a suction dredger on our starboard beam. Her dark-red underwater paintwork could be seen, and her black sides were thick with leprous patches of red lead. Minutes later another dark colossus loomed up, also to starboard. It was one of the bucket dredgers which laboured unceasingly to maintain a channel deep enough for ocean-going ships.

At last I was free to pick up some binoculars and peer ahead. The land was still a thin streak above our bow, but I could already see an array of toy cranes. Individual figures were visible on the barrage-breaker, now immediately ahead of us and making straight for the coast.

We had to wait in the outer basin. Our seamen got their wires ready, carefully threading their way round the wounded.

A message was flashed from the signal station. The quartermaster read it out: 'Enter immediately.' Looking through our glasses, we saw a bridge swing open. The wharf came into view, thronged with figures. No brass band, thank God.

A few gulls screamed loudly in the strange hush that fell as U-A glided between the lichen-covered walls of the lock. The welcoming party threw little bouquets trimmed with Christmas evergreen. Nobody picked them up.

The old resentment of the people on the quay . . . I knew that everyone around me on the bridge felt it too. We were irritable beasts, ready to snap at the first false move.

Whistles shrilled instructions to the wire-handling party. The berthing wires lay ready, neatly coiled down fore and aft. So did our fat basketwork fenders.

Heaving lines snaked through the air, to be caught by soldiers who hauled up the heavy berthing wires attached to them. Sailors on the wharf came to their aid and secured the wires to massive iron bollards. Our screws churned the brackish water. U-A nestled gently against the slime-green wall of the lock.

'Stop engines. All hands muster aft.' The Captain's voice was a hoarse croak.

The people above us could now see our battered casing, the huddled knot of survivors, the wounded sprawled beside the conning-tower. A sea of faces stared down, puzzled and dismayed.

A brow was run out. It sloped steeply from our deck to the wharf – our first link with terra firma.

Aircraft! I sensed them even before my ear registered the hum, almost as if I had inhaled the sound of their approach.

It came from the direction of the sea. All heads turned. The hum became a drone, the drone a deep unbroken roar. Anti-aircraft guns were already baying defiance. Out to sea, the sky was dotted with little white blobs like baby meringues.

A wing flashed in the sunlight. I could see dark specks now, five or six of them – no, seven.

Engines snarled above the rattle of an Oerlikon. Shadows flashed across the warehouses. The crowd dissolved.

The Captain was bellowing at us. 'Come on, out of here! All hands to the bunker!'

Bullets ripped into the quayside, sending up showers of splintered stone. Fighters!

But not after us, I thought – they must be trying to gun down the anti-aircraft fire. It was a concerted attack by fighters and bombers.

Here and there the cobbles erupted into fountains of rubble. Lumps of stone sailed lazily through the air.

Only fifty metres separated me from the bunker's armoured door, which had been slid shut from the inside until only a crack remained. I fell over something and scrambled up again, weak at the knees. My legs were rickety stilts beyond my power to control. I had forgotten how to run.

Shouts, wailing sirens, a sky garnished with white puff-balls, the rattle and whipcrack of MG fire, the hurried bark of medium AA guns, the roar of the heavies – explosive caco-phonies in a variety of rhythms. Clouds of smoke, mushrooms of dust, and among them the grey shapes of aircraft. Ours or theirs? I recognized a twin-boomed Lightning and above it a hornet-swarm of heavy bombers.

Light AA guns yapped, machine-guns chattered, splinters whirred. The drone and whine of aero engines was punctuated by the resounding crump of heavy flak on the outskirts of La Rochelle. The enemy planes were coming in at several different altitudes.

In front of me, a grotesque ballet choreographed by a mad-man and performed on a huge cobbled stage, with the mam-moth structure of the U-boat bunker as a backdrop. Figures hurled themselves to the ground, zigzagged like hares, jack-knifed, leapt in the air, converged, scattered, surged to and fro. One man threw up his arms, pirouetted, and then, with his outflung hands palm upwards, subsided into a profound obeisance.

Another crescendo of sound. Invisible fists smote the backs of my knees. Flat on the cobblestones, I heard a renewed howl of engines. I was plastered to the ground by a wall of air. Plane after plane streaked over me.

A bomber disintegrated in mid air. Fragments of wing spiralled down. The fuselage smashed into the ground beyond the bunker and exploded. I could hardly breathe for dust and smoke. Arms flailing, I reached the armoured door, squeezed through the gap, tripped over something soft, cracked my head on the concrete floor and rolled aside.

Just to stop running, just to lie there in the dust-laden gloom . . .

The rattle of gunfire sounded fainter inside. I ran a hand over my forehead and was unsurprised to find it sticky with blood. The man beside me was moaning and clutching his stomach. As soon as my eyes grew accustomed to the half-light, I recognized him. Grey leathers – someone from the boat: Zeitler. Two hands grabbed me under the armpits and tried to haul me to my feet.

'Thanks, I'm all right.'

I stood there swaying, supported by the man behind me. Gradually, the mist cleared. I could stand unaided.

And then, with a force that almost burst my eardrums, a tremendous explosion rent the air. The whole bunker vibrated like an immense tympanum, the ground rocked underfoot. From the roof above the first pen, half of which was visible from where I stood, huge clods of concrete hurtled down, splashing into the water and beating a tattoo on the U-boat berthed there. All at once, harsh white light streamed through a hole in the bunker roof.

Light!

I craned to look.

The hole was a good three metres across. Iron mesh embedded in lumps of concrete drooped from its lacerated edges. The mesh swayed, divesting itself of more loose concrete. Foaming water continued to leap at the sides of the pen.

Seven metres of ferro-concrete? Impossible! Bunker canopies were supposed to be proof against bombs of any size or weight.

Shouts and orders rang out. The bunker, too, became a confusion of scurrying figures. A lot of steam was escaping from somewhere.

Outside, guns still roared and bombs thundered down with the angry rumble of a tropical storm.

The pall of dust began to settle. My tongue felt furry. The air was too thick to breathe. Shaken by a violent spasm of coughing, I had to lean against the wall with my head pillowed on my forearm.

Air – air at any price. I fought my way back to the armoured door through a crush of bodies, elbowed aside two dockyard mateys who tried to bar my path, and squeezed through the crack. There was nothing to be seen outside but oily black smoke. It looked as if a fuel tank had been hit.

But no, the entire basin was ablaze. Only the cranes reared unscathed from the billowing inferno. Above the sharp crackle of flames I heard the tormented and unremitting wail of a ship's siren.

I looked towards the lock on my right. The sky was clearer there. I could see shattered warehouse roofs, buildings reduced to mounds of rubble. Bent wire and jagged hunks of iron caught at my ankles. I nearly slithered into a smoke-filled crater. An injured man loomed up at my feet, madness in his eyes. Groans and whimpers assailed me on all sides. Many horrors must have been hidden by the dust and smoke.

The boat! What had happened to the boat?

A gust of wind brushed aside the curtain of vapour. I climbed through an entanglement of twisted rails, skirted two dead bodies and hurried past a jumble of red-leaded ironwork. In front of me, a smoking bank of shingle shelved steeply to the water. It could only be the wharf . . . And U-A? I caught sight of a mass of steel jutting from the surface like a monstrous ploughshare. Attached to it was a jumping-wire. The bow of a submarine – ours. Shattered baulks of timber bobbed in the water. Water? It was pure oil, and the black blobs adrift in it were human beings. Those creatures among the bursting bubbles must be men from our boat. Another pall of smoke bore down. I heard shouts behind me. Soldiers and workmen were running my way, strung out in a long line. Two trucks careered between the craters with their horns blaring incessantly.

And then I saw him through the haze, streaming with blood, shirt and sweater in shreds. His eyes, usually narrowed in the way I knew so well, were wide and staring. Almost as one, we sank to our knees on the shattered cobbles and crouched face to face, propped on our hands like a pair of Sumo wrestlers. The Old Man opened his mouth to say something, but all that passed his lips was blood.